Louis William DuBourg

Bishop Louis William Valentine DuBourg

LOUIS WILLIAM DUBOURG

Bishop of Louisiana and the Floridas,
Bishop of Montauban, and
Archbishop of Besançon,

1766–1833

VOLUME TWO
Bishop in Two Worlds, 1818–1833

Annabelle M. Melville

LOYOLA UNIVERSITY PRESS
Chicago

© 1986 Annabelle M. Melville
Printed in the United States of America

Loyola University Press
3441 North Ashland Avenue
Chicago, Illinois 60657

Book design by C. L. Tornatore

Library of Congress Cataloging-in-Publication Data

Melville, Annabelle M. (Annabelle McConnell), 1910–
Louis William DuBourg: Bishop of Louisiana and the
Floridas, Bishop of Montauban, and Archbishop of
Besançon, 1766–1833.

Bibliography: p. 1029
Includes index.
Contents: v. 1. Schoolman, 1766–1818—v.
2. Bishop in two worlds, 1818–1833.
1. DuBourg, Louis William Valentine, 1766–1833.
2. Catholic Church—United States—Bishops—Biography.
3. Catholic Church—France—Bishops—Biography.
I. Title.
BX4705.D8M45   1986   282'.092'4 [B]   86-2934
ISBN 0-8294-0501-1 (Vol. 1)
0-8294-0529-1 (Vol. 2)

CONTENTS

CHAPTER XXII

Harsh Beginnings

The frontier town which DuBourg had chosen for his temporary headquarters was a chameleon changing endlessly from what it had been to what it was becoming. When the United States acquired the Louisiana Territory fifteen years earlier, St. Louis had been a settlement of scarcely more than a thousand people, chiefly trappers who roamed the prairies in summer and came together primarily for reasons of protection and trade. The Spanish government west of the Mississippi had discouraged farming, and fur trading occupied the inhabitants to such an extent that deerskins were the money of St. Louis, as lead was for Ste. Genevieve.[1]

Under freer American institutions, which left so much initiative to pioneers, there was a great rush westward during the "Era of Good Feeling" following the War of 1812. On the eve of DuBourg's arrival, although they all—whites and blacks alike—still tended to speak French, the population of St. Louis had more than trebled, and among the successful businessmen willing to support Catholic institutions, Irish names were increasing.[2]

Few American towns were so well situated for growth.

Midway between the Great Lakes and the Gulf of Mexico, between the Appalachian and the Rocky mountains, occupying one of the finest, healthiest positions that the Mississippi River offered—built as it was on rock foundations above the waters' cresting—and surrounded by vast prairies which could become the granary of the whole nation, St. Louis was destined to change radically during DuBourg's residence there.

As a prospect for missionary activity, it presented every opportunity. DuBourg was of the same mind as Flaget, who had told Archbishop Leonard Neale two years before:

> The place is of the upmost importance for the good of religion, not only on account of the many Catholics that live there now, or of those that will immediately emigrate thither, as soon as they hear that there is a Catholic Bishop, but much more so on account of the many nations of Indians, that have never heard of the Christian faith.[3]

Prospects, however, were one thing, present reality quite another, as DuBourg came quickly to perceive.

When Badin went to St. Louis in 1807 he had found the church properties "pretty decent" for a trading post mission, writing to the Bishop of Baltimore:

> The church has a tolerably good bell, high altar, pulpit and commodious pews. The house for the priest is convenient, but rather out of repair. There is annexed to it a large garden, well-stocked with fruit trees, barn, stable and other out-offices.[4]

After years of no resident pastor, however, conditions had deteriorated to those found by Flaget in 1817, and DuBourg told Didier Petit ruefully, "My cathedral, which looks like a poor stable, is falling in ruins, so that a new church is an absolute necessity."[5] Felix De Andreis, who was assigned it as his pastoral charge, morosely called it "a miserable log cabin, open to every wind."[6] It was unanimously agreed among the clergy that a new church headed the list of priorities; conveniences for themselves must wait. To European friends, who were not likely to see his rectory, Du-

Bourg wrote optimistically, "My house is not magnificent; but it will be comfortable when they have made some necessary repairs. I will have a parlor, a sleeping room, a very nice study, besides a dining room and four rooms for the ecclesiastics, and an immense garden."[7] Before these repairs were possible, however, work on a church must be started, and no one enjoyed plunging into unknown waters more than the new prelate of the Mississippi Valley; no one was ever visited with more rosy dreams of the future.

The day after his installation, while Flaget was still there to exert his benign influence over the congregation, DuBourg held a meeting to discuss a new church, and by January 8 he was already envisioning an edifice 150-by-70 feet in size, much larger than the old log one measuring 60-by-30 feet. In his mind's eye he could see that when it was completed it could have a wing on each side of the nave, running its whole length, 22½ feet wide and 25 feet in height, giving the whole a front of 85 feet. There would be a steeple as high again as the building which would support several large bells expected from France.[8] Its construction would take time, of course, he conceded, "especially in a country where everything is just beginning;" but the project was begun.

To finance his church, DuBourg immediately launched a first subscription, and $6,566 was pledged, although only two-thirds of this amount ever reached the hands of the collectors, Thomas McGuyre and Jeremiah Connor.[9] Those who honored their pledges tended to be the more prosperous Catholics or generous Protestants like Alexander McNair, Thomas Hart Benton, and William Clark, who gave $100 or more. It was the smaller subscribers, whose intentions may have been just as good but whose livelihood was less certain, who failed to keep their pledged word. A second subscription launched some months later brought collector Pierre Leduc only $1,303.36, chiefly from Catholics. Before the cathedral could be finished, the woes brought by the panic of 1819 had reached Missouri and financial depression was no respecter of persons, even those of episcopal character and ambitions.

Ground was broken, nevertheless, in the middle of Lent, and by Easter the foundation had sufficiently progressed that DuBourg could announce the laying of the cornerstone for the following Sunday. With more than usual zest he composed the notice for the *Missouri Gazette,* which had no aversion to local news, unlike the *Gazette de la Louisiane* of New Orleans which, aside from local elections, preferred news from more distant capitals. Subscribers to the former on March 26, 1818, could read:

> Next Sunday, 29 inst. at 4 P.M., will be laid by the Rt. Rev. Bishop DuBourg, with the solemn rites used in the Catholic Church on similar occasions, the first stone of the new Cathedral. The intended grandeur of that fabric, together with the sanctity of the object to which it is destined, cannot fail exciting a lively interest in the breasts of all those who have at heart the growth and embellishment of this infant city, but above all, its moral and religious improvement. A collection is intended to be made by the Bishop among the ladies who may grace the ceremony with their presence, the piety which distinguishes their sex encouraging the hope that they will eagerly seize upon so precious an occasion to evince their zeal for the majesty of divine worship. Gentlemen, it is expected, will also be prompted to a new effort of generosity to supply the deficiency of the funds already subscribed for, and enable the building committee to proceed, without interruption, to the completion of that part, at least, of the whole plan intended to be executed this year.

The cornerstone was hollowed in the form of a chest so that two papers could be preserved within it: one containing the story of the foundation of St. Louis, and the other attesting the ceremony of March 29 signed by DuBourg and the other dignitaries attending. For good measure, a few coins were also enclosed. The rite was carried off with all the bishop's flair, and he was attended by the veteran clergy of the region as well as by De Andreis and Niel, who resided with him. Henry Pratte from Ste. Genevieve, Marie Joseph Dunand from Florissant, Francis Savine and Donatien Olivier from the Illinois country, all participated in the company of many altar boys.[10] St. Louis was learning that the Church was alive and active and that a bishop was in residence.

Until the new church became something more than just a foundation, the old log cabin had to suffice. There were times that winter when the cold was so fierce that Sunday Mass had to be celebrated in a part of DuBourg's small house in order to escape the "icy blasts blowing through the chinks of the ruinous edifice."[11] In spite of these chagrins, DuBourg did everything he could to make his "cathedral" a proper place of worship, using to best advantage the rugs, paintings, and fine altar ornaments he had brought from Europe. He was determined to make his first Holy Week in St. Louis fitting for the sacred rites.

Maunday Thursday in 1818 was distinguished by both the blessing of the holy oils and the ordination of Francis Niel. A repository that would have satisfied Tessier had been prepared and De Andreis found it "a sepulchre which, without any exaggeration, with its magnificent adornment, its countless candlelights and its majestic appearance, would not have been out of place in a Roman church." Dunand and Savine came from their respective stations to augment the clergy, while a "company of musicks with voices and instruments" had been prepared. Once the Blessed Sacrament was placed in the repository, two militiamen, relieved every hour, stood sentry night and day before it; the choir in the evening sang to the accompaniment of a band the *Stabat Mater* and the French hymn *Au Sang qu'un Dieu va repandre*.[12] Music was one of the things sorely lacking in this outpost, and the bishop wrote urgently to Bardstown while his recruits were still there, "Have copied two or three Masses in chant after De Monti, and every other piece of music suitable to the Seminary or the Cathedral. Please do this as quickly as possible."[13] Flaget and David, at least, had something worth copying.

The splendors of Holy Week and the Sunday after Easter were not a harbinger of things to come. Although the walls of the new church were fifteen feet above ground in June, the roof was not in place until late November, and it was clear that the old church would have to serve through another winter. In fact, it was Christmas 1819 before any service could be held in an unfinished building and the actual consecration of the church took place on January 9,

1820. The first cathedral of St. Louis, as it turned out, was never really completed.

History is expected to account for successes and failures; but biographers of individual protagonists are constrained by their sources. It is not much help to read that "whatever the cause of the delay, the work slackened considerably." Was the plan too ambitious at the outset? The two previous churches of St. Louis had been log cabins which had fallen apart;[14] DuBourg wanted a church like those designed by Godefroy—St. Mary's in Baltimore or Flaget's cathedral in Bardstown—and used brick for his in a place where neither materials nor skilled bricklayers were as readily available. Was the cost too high for the victims of the panic of 1819? Or was it the fault of the trustees who controlled the financial affairs of the church and had been accustomed under French or Spanish regimes to having the government support their churches and clergy?

Only the middle nave, consisting of a rather narrow rectangle measuring 135-by-40 feet, was ever erected; the five large arches on either side, originally intended to separate the middle from the side aisles, were filled up with masonry and served as outer walls. Without the protective support of these side aisles and their walls designed to be the outer walls of the whole structure, the emasculated nave suggested a "narrow-shouldered and narrow-chested consumptive body" which could not endure. Before DuBourg died it was already doomed, with his successor complaining to Rome:

> The work was badly done, so that a sidewall 130 feet long is about to collapse. . . . This church cannot survive much longer because it is dangerous to leave it in its present state and because it cannot be repaired for a sum smaller than it would take to erect a new church.[15]

To a man who loved beauty as intensely as DuBourg, it must surely have been galling to have an episcopal cathedral in New Orleans usurped by Sedella, while this half-finished jerry-built brick rectangle was the best he could achieve in St. Louis for himself and the greater glory of God.

A more vain, a more self-centered man might have done things differently. If a handsome church had meant more to him than other things, if he had thirsted after a lasting monument to perpetuate his name, it seems likely he could have had one. His gifts of persuasion were formidable, certainly. But his was the challenge of a region that had *no* episcopal institutions or even traditions. His was an impatience that chafed until everything was at least begun. So he did what he could with the new, as he had done with the old house of God, to beautify the interior with the works of art and ornaments he had gathered in Europe, and to enhance the liturgy with dignity and ceremonial grace.

The first directory of the city of St. Louis, issued the year after DuBourg consecrated his new cathedral, asserted, "The cathedral of St. Louis can boast no rival in the United States for the magnificence, the value and elegance of her sacred vases, ornaments and paintings, and indeed few churches in Europe possess anything superior to it." Meanwhile in the old stone *presbytère* left standing near his cathedral, the collector and furnisher of this munificence rose daily from the buffalo-skin pallet which served as a temporary bed to expedite other establishments necessary to spreading the good news to the burgeoning population of Missouri.

Only two days after laying the cornerstone of the cathedral in March 1818, DuBourg headed for Perryville eighty miles south. This settlement which was inland from the river and twenty-three miles southeast of Ste. Genevieve was popularly known as the Barrens and owed its origins not to the French or Spanish but to Anglo-American colonists from Maryland who moved west to Kentucky, and then to Missouri. Since 1813 the eighty families of the Barrens had been visited four times a year by the Trappist whom they called Father Prior, Marie Joseph Dunand from Florissant. With his urging they had built a small log church, and when Dunand learned that a bishop was to settle in St. Louis, he advised them to buy up the land around their church with the idea of offering it to DuBourg for either a seminary or college to ensure always having Catholic ser-

513

vices in their community. It was this offer, first tendered to Flaget, De Andreis, and Rosati on their trip to Missouri in 1817, which DuBourg was now going to discuss.[16]

The Barrens locale immediately appealed to DuBourg, much as Mount St. Mary's had done a decade ago, and it was further enhanced by the generosity of its inhabitants. Their offer included 600 acres of fertile land not only susceptible of easy cultivation but also far enough from the river to be healthier more seasons of the year. In addition to their willingness to be taxed to raise the money for the land's purchase, the people engaged themselves to share in the work of building the seminary and, most importantly, to raise $7,500—at the rate of $1,500 a year—toward the building of a seminary, the expenses of the church services, and the support of the missionaries. Finally, during the first year they would feed the workmen erecting the buildings. Once these obligations were fulfilled, the Catholics would be free from all further obligations of paying for a priest, since the seminary would always serve them.[17]

DuBourg's thoughts churned as he wrote of these prospects first to Flaget and then to Rosati in Kentucky, telling the latter in a rush: "I wrote by last mail to the Bishop, requesting he would direct my Flemish band of cultivating Brothers to depart immediately under the guidance of their saintly Father Mr. de la Croix. I forgot to mention that Mr. Moranvillé & Brother Medard should come in company with them." Charles de la Croix, whom DuBourg had ordained in Ghent, was the chaplain of the Flemish workmen who had formed a quasi-society pledged to work under the bishop's guidance; Francis Moranvillé and Brother Medard di Lattre had arrived with the first group in 1816 and had some intention of becoming Vincentian lay brothers. Du-Bourg had already learned something of the Mississippi's meanderings and the geography of its west banks, and he directed Rosati, "These two, and other two of yr. choice may take the four horses. The others should come in a Barge or Keel Boat. They must all arrive below the *Barrens;* those who come by water shall have to land at Widow

Fenwick's at Apple Creek—those on horseback may cross at Cape Girardeau."[18]

DuBourg was glad that he had been in Kentucky long enough to observe Flaget's seminary carefully. Building in a wilderness on the edge of the frontier was a century removed from the skills and materials available to tidewater Maryland; yet he was confident a seminary would emerge once his workers reached the Barrens, telling Rosati:

> The good people at the Barrens are anxious to see them arrive, and get their assistance in the building of the Seminary and its dependencies. This is a vast undertaking; a house of sixty by thirty-six, 2-1/2 story, with such a cellar under the whole as there is under the Brick house at St. Thomas, in which we may have halls of 25 by 17 feet, and two cellars of the same dimensions. Those people of the Barrens are the best set I ever knew. They engage to find all my crew in provisions for the first year, nay even for the second, if necessary.[19]

It was like the bishop to believe in late April that they might all be reunited at the Barrens "late in the next fall."

The site chosen for the seminary was a quarter of a mile south of the Barrens's little church, and when De Andreis listened to DuBourg's breathless description of all he planned, the poor vicar general said to Rosati in some bewilderment it seemed "a kind of combination of log-house, frame-house, brick-house and stone-house, having a little of every kind; it was to be plastered and decent inside and outside."[20] DuBourg's seminarians were doomed to live in a variety of other accommodations, however, before they ever entered what came to be St. Mary's of the Barrens; and they were destined to adapt themselves to sundry other occupations before settling down to a regime of study for the sacred ministry.

In the first place the site had to be cleared of forest and undergrowth, a lengthy and backbreaking drudgery. Then the lumber had to be sawed from the felled trees and, if it were to be really serviceable, dried in a kiln. With the number of outbuildings DuBourg anticipated, it seemed obvious they ought to own their own sawmill, an adjunct not readily available. It was not until August that he could announce:

> Here I am become also a Miller! I have made the acquisition of a very valuable water wheel, a mile and a half away from our establishment at the Barrens. I am going to build there a saw mill which will be very important for our construction work. . . . I am receiving from everyone congratulations on this purchase. They assure me it is worth four times the money it cost me. . . . The mill is built on a rock and the water is very abundant, even in the driest seasons.[21]

He hoped this news would cheer up the people left in Kentucky; as for himself, he admitted, "All this exhausts me." It seemed there was no end to the things a bishop had to learn.

Most of the work that summer still had to be done by manpower, and it progressed very slowly. DuBourg had gone down to the Barrens in July, hoping to speed things up; but he realized that no amount of effort could make the seminary ready for occupation that fall. Nevertheless he felt he could no longer leave his recruits in Kentucky, and he notified Rosati from the Barrens on July 29 that he was arranging to lodge them as best he might in Missouri until the seminary could receive them. "I've rented a large house in Ste. Genevieve, where almost all of them can live while waiting," he explained. "Mr. Pratte will take two, and a third will come here with Mr. de la Croix." The house rented for six months would not be available until October 1, so Rosati should calculate the time of arrival with that in mind.[22]

DuBourg was already arranging the nature of their hegira while still in the Barrens, and during his trip back to St. Louis he clarified these plans. From Kaskaskia he advised Rosati:

> Here is what I have thought; try to conform point by point. At the beginning of September send an intelligent person to Louisville to buy a flat boat, as cheap as possible, and at the same time hire a Pilot to leave between the 15 and 20, and

conduct you to a house on the bank opposite the mouth of the Ohio. It is necessary to learn from the Pilot the time it takes to get there, and fix positively the day of departure, by the 20th, if possible. When these two points are irrevocably fixed, send in advance, about the 12th, that is, 7 or 8 days in advance, two of our men on the two horses we have left at St. Thomas, by way of Shawnee Town, and from there to Gill's Ferry, where they will cross to go to the Barrens.[23]

Once it was learned from these advance scouts that the trek was to begin, the rest of the plans could be carried out. Until then, the bishop had things to do in St. Louis.

August was the month to put in motion the third major project DuBourg had set himself that year. On August 21 Philippine Duchesne and her little band of Religious of the Sacred Heart arrived in St. Louis to begin the work of educating Catholic girls in Upper Louisiana. To the bishop it seemed that eons had elapsed since their last meeting in Paris on a May morning in 1817, a meeting she still remembered to the very hour.[24] A great deal had happened to both of them since then.

Because DuBourg wished to have the women accompanied by a priest if it could be arranged, it was not until d'Aviau consented to Bertrand Martial's going that the first volunteers and Madame Duchesne could make concrete plans for their own departure. When Martial notified rue des Postes that he was leaving in mid-February, Philippine told a friend, "It had been arranged that six of us should leave in May, but the earlier sailing of a vessel whose captain is well-known and which is carrying one of the vicars general and other missionaries makes us leave sooner than expected."[25] It meant hasty last-minute preparations in Paris and sailing arrangements in Bordeaux, but as usual—when *Monseigneur de la Louisiane's* interests were at stake—at the port of departure Victoire and Louis DuBourg exerted themselves to the extreme.

Madame Duchesne wrote from Bordeaux on February 18:

I have been to the home of Madame Fournier, Bishop DuBourg's sister. She had rented a lodging for us and also got

517

> us a servant and a person to attend to our meals. . . . She
> has reserved our sleeping quarters on shipboard and is now
> talking about *comforts*, that is things to take with us for the
> sake of the body—mostly food.[26]

Victoire had crossed the ocean six times and knew exactly
what a woman would need for such voyages. The nuns from
Paris found her perhaps a little "too bent on precautions,"
but it was a relief to have all arranged for the trip, to be
accompanied even to the banks of the Garonne by the
bishop's family, and to sail with Bertrand Martial and his
companion Evremond Harrisart who were both entering
DuBourg's diocese. Although they did not know it in February, DuBourg had also requested a papal blessing on their
new venture. Cardinal Litta, still DuBourg's staunch friend,
made sure *le départ des Dames du nouvel institut de l'instruction chrétienne* was known to Cardinal Fontana and
that the Holy Father renewed his blessings on them and the
venerable Bishop of Louisiana. Litta's own view was that
"God seems to be inspiring this voyage to America."[27]

The religious women arrived in New Orleans at the end
of May and again DuBourg, although unable to greet them
there himself, had made sure his relatives and friends acted
his proxy. The Ursulines whose superior was now Mother
Ste. Michel Gensoul welcomed them warmly; Pierre-François accompanied by the French consul called on them
immediately to offer their services; Louis Sibourd welcomed them officially as DuBourg's vicar general. In rue de
Chartres the newcomers heard nothing but the bishop's
praises, and Madame Duchesne reported to Bordeaux,
"Protestants stop preaching on Sundays to hear the holy
Pastor, who preaches in English. They love him as much as
the Catholics do."[28] She obviously had been listening to
DuBourg's Baltimore champion, now Sister Ste. Angela
Johnston. But to her amazement Duchesne learned as well
that Sibourd did not officiate in the cathedral nor receive
any salary from its trustees even though he represented the
bishop in Lower Louisiana. The influence of Sedella was

518

still supreme with the people of the Cabildo, the Presbytère, and St. Louis Cathedral on the Place d'Armes.

Philippine Duchesne was uneasy when no letter arrived from DuBourg himself. In France he had shown such a fatherly interest in her that she had confided in her sister Amelie, "I found myself quite at home with him as if I had known him all my life."[29] She had yet to learn about distances in the United States and particularly about the vicissitudes of correspondence in the Mississippi Valley. He had written of course. As soon as he learned of her arrival in June he replied:

> God be blessed, my very dear daughter, for your arrival, that of your Sisters, and your respectable guide Mr. Martial, the best of my friends, for mitigating or withholding many afflictions. You have come, you say, to find the Cross. Oh! you have chosen the place to find it!. . . . If I were not sure of finding that disposition in you, my dear daughter, I would tremble rather than rejoice at your arrival; but with it let us fear nothing. God will be with us.[30]

She had learned only a few days after her arrival in New Orleans that she might not be living in St. Louis, reporting to her Superior Sophie Barat:

> Three days ago I met a rich man from the North, who told us there is a great demand for both a college for boys and a boarding school for girls. The college is to be located in St. Louis; our school is to be seventeen miles from there at Florissant. . . a village situated in one of the loveliest and most fertile parts of the country.[31]

Whether John Mullamphy who told her this was guessing, or whether DuBourg was compelled to change his plans after Mullamphy's trip downstream began, is a matter for conjecture. By the time the bishop wrote his letter of welcome he had found a place for the nuns at St. Charles on the Missouri River. He consoled Philippine:

> You seem to regret not being near me; but you will not be out of reach there. I have you staying in a house in a little

519

town seven leagues from here where you will find all the little conveniences you could desire, fine garden, orchard & rooms spacious enough to arrange at once 25 boarders. When you are here you will see that in all of Upper Louisiana I could not have found you a situation more suited to beginnings.[32]

He assured her that nothing would be neglected on his part to give her satisfaction. If he ever left her without a priest at St. Charles it would be because there was none to furnish, which was "beyond all possibility." He warned her that a thousand unforeseen difficulties could arise. God knew he had learned that in only six months in Missouri. There would be delays, physical privation, and the more painful deprivation of spiritual consolations. "Expect them all," he told her hardily:

But you will get used to the circumstances. It is necessary to break new ground before you can plant it. You and I perhaps will pass our lives in this unrewarding work; our successors will reap the reward in this world; let us be content with the hope of reaping ours in the other.[33]

No words were more prophetic than this closing of a letter which never reached her until she had for four months experienced its implications herself at St. Charles.

When by July no word from DuBourg had reached Lower Louisiana, the Religious of the Sacred Heart determined to go to St. Louis without further delay, and boarding the steamboat *Franklin* on Sunday, July 12, they started upriver. A fellow passenger, a Benedictine named Benedict Richard, was destined to become their first chaplain, but it is doubtful that either the nuns or the priest suspected it, for when the *Franklin* reached Kaskaskia in early August, Richard left them. They met their first American-born priest at Ste. Genevieve, where Father Pratte came down to greet them and win their hearts with his youthful enthusiasm. At last on August 21 the *Franklin* dropped anchor at St. Louis. It was late in the day, but the captain insisted on escorting Madame Duchesne and Madame Octavie Berthold to meet the bishop.

For the first time the two French gentlewomen came face to face with the reality of a frontier mission when they entered DuBourg's "episcopal palace." None of the "necessary repairs" DuBourg had so cheerfully anticipated in January had yet materialized. They found him living in one poor room which served as dormitory, refectory, and study for the bishop and four or five priests, several of whom were sick; his church nearby was a "hut of wood with holes throughout."[34] Yet his spirit was as lively, his greeting as cordial, his air as impressive as when they first met in Paris. He went in person to conduct them to the home of their temporary hosts, the General Bernard Pratte family, with whom they were to remain for the next three weeks, as generously entertained as they had been by the Ursulines in New Orleans. The Pratte home and general store were a block and a half away from the church and rectory and that much nearer the river, and it was a pleasant stroll in the August evening remote from the humidity and threat of yellow fever ever present that month in New Orleans.

Their stay in St. Louis gave the nuns an opportunity to see some of the reasons why DuBourg was not fixing their first convent there. The terrible inflation of prices, common to an entrepôt on the edge of the frontier eternally plagued by a shortage of housing in the face of a mushrooming population, was incredible. DuBourg had warned them before they ever left Paris not to count on him for financial aid; and Madame Duchesne had tried to collect as much as possible before they left.[35] What had seemed modest enough in francs now became perilously close to a pittance in the uncertain currencies of the trans-Mississippi west. In August 1818 there was not a single room for rent in the whole town; and even if there had been, the bishop, who was trying to remove his entire band from Kentucky just then, was virtually penniless.

Philippine Duchesne was nevertheless reluctant to go to St. Charles. Years afterward, pleading for the existence of a Sacred Heart convent at St. Charles, she cited "the great salubrity of the air, which has enabled us to escape the epidemics that have ravaged St. Louis and the beautifully

521

situated property," adding in gentle reminiscence, "Monseigneur DuBourg admired the site very much."[36] Sight unseen, in 1818, a rented house a morning's drive away from St. Louis did not appeal to her, but she relayed his reasoning to Paris with her customary forthrightness:

> He puts before us the great advantages St. Charles possesses. He thinks it will become one of the most important cities of North America, as it is situated on the Missouri River, along which the population is growing daily and which is about to give its name to a new state of the Union. No day passes without the arrival of four or five families with their belongings, who come to settle in a country which is making astonishing progress.[37]

Other locations were naturally discussed. When Madame Duchesne alluded to John Mullamphy's talk of Florissant, the bishop scotched that notion categorically, saying that any house adequate to lodging twenty-five boarders there would cost not forty but eighty thousand francs, which was simply out of the question until the women had some idea of their income from the school. Madame Duchesne herself in 1818 rejected Florissant saying, "Though the country is beautiful, it is but sparsely inhabited and we should be obliged to build there."

Her own preference was for either Ste. Geneviève or St. Louis. The former attracted her because her host's brother, Henry Pratte the pastor, had impressed her the first time she saw him. When he told her of having been cared for by nuns in Canada, of wanting nuns for his mission, of having forty girls who would have come down to the *Franklin* to meet her, all of this appeared like the invitation of a "true father and apostle." Returning down river was very appealing.

St. Louis had its own attractions, or seemed to have that summer, when a group of parishioners proposed to DuBourg on August 31 that enough pupils paying tuition of $250 could be found to support a house in that city. As Madame Duchesne described the situation to Paris:

> Mr. Bernard Pratte was willing to buy a house here such as would cost 36,000 francs to build, and then rent it to us. I

visited the house. It is very well situated and quite new, but it would need changes which we could only make if we owned it. . . . I proposed to buy it from Mr. Pratte, and I do not think my proposal was rash, for at least 7,000 francs must be left from what you sent the Bishop for us.[38]

DuBourg sympathized with the nuns' wish to begin their work in St. Louis, offering on his part the alternatives of a small lot of his own, or the four-room house he had rented for his school for young men.[39] He appreciated Pratte's good intentions. But Pratte, although working hard to get a house the nuns could use, and pupils besides his own five little girls, was unable to come up with anything concrete. The truth was that even if General Pratte were to donate a house outright within the city, the cost of living in St. Louis was still prohibitive. The costs of remodeling the house for the convent school and furnishing it for that dual purpose would swallow up the income from tuitions faster than they were paid. As eager as some parents were to educate their daughters, they would not subscribe to another episcopal building that year. Mother Duchesne had not lived in St. Louis ten days before she heard Catholics expressing discontent or outright resentment at being "over-taxed" by the construction of the new church.

If St. Louis was impracticable for financial reasons, Ste. Genevieve was undesirable for pastoral ones. Between that flourishing mission and the Barrens seminary twenty-odd miles away, lower Missouri would be well supplied with Christian models of right living. Further, across the river at Prairie du Rocher and Kaskaskia, DuBourg was sending two new priests as soon as the fall ordinations were over.[40] It was the region northward out of St. Louis which sorely needed Catholic institutions to cope with the accelerating influx of migrants. At Portage Des Sioux he was hoping to install John Baptist Acquaroni, one of the Vincentians who had come with De Andreis and Rosati in 1816.[41] A priest at this post could serve more distant families farther north of St. Charles.

Whether or not he said all of this to Madame Duchesne, she took her disappointments in good grace. To Father

Barat she wrote simply, "The Bishop who wanted us here in St. Louis is having all he can do to collect for a new church. . . . He can do nothing to help us except by his example which shows us what we shall have to suffer."[42] And to his sister in Paris, her superior, she expressed the same generous resignation, saying "You expected us to have something to suffer, and the example of our holy Bishop, whose career at Paris might have been brilliant and who chose instead poverty, labor and suffering, is an inspiration to us all."[43] Now that she was on the spot she saw the impossibility of beginning on a large scale. DuBourg cheered her by telling of the slow start the Ursulines made when they first came to Louisiana, and saying perhaps Ste. Genevieve might be her second house some day. They must love their temporary abjection; the fruits would come later. Because she was of his generation and his view of things she could say, "I go with closed eyes—Providence will clear the way if it so desires."[44]

On September 7 Bishop DuBourg, Father Benedict Richard, Madame Duchesne and her little suite left St. Louis for the Missouri River. Because Richard was a friend of Father Barat's, it suited both DuBourg and the nuns that he was to be their chaplain at St. Charles. Richard drove the women, while DuBourg either rode ahead to show the way, or rode close to their carriage to cheer them with his badinage. There was still something of the fake-minstrel making light of his flight from Issy lingering in the fifty-two-year-old prelate. Youthful gaiety was never far from the surface on these forays into an uncertain future. There was almost a picnic atmosphere as he helped the women into the ferry at the river's edge, and saw them safely out again on the other side.

Madame Duchesne was fascinated by the Indians, a race she wished to serve as missionary, and was full of questions. She later reported to Paris:

> In St. Louis a trading company has been established to regulate commerce between Missouri and the Indians beyond this territory. As a result, the savages are more friendly with the white men and come down the river. We met quite a

number who had come to confer with the representatives of the government of the United States. They followed us to the river, touched the hands of the Sisters and gazed after us until we had attained this bank. Those who ferried us across the Missouri and then put our baggage on a cart and brought it up to the house refused to accept a penny, saying that we represent Our Lord, Jesus Christ.[45]

The house to which the bishop conducted them was sheltered by fruit trees and overgrown shrubbery, the former bending under their loads of apples, pears, and Osage plums. Remote from the noise of the town, it still had a splendid view of the river, which at St. Charles was more like a bay with its own small island. The house had five small rooms and one large central one which DuBourg thought could serve as a chapel. The owner, a Madame Duquette, reserved one room for herself and could answer any questions the nuns might have in adjusting to New World housekeeping. The garden would need rescuing from neglect, but it was the sort of challenge any self-respecting French woman would entertain, as soon as sturdy workmen were found.[46]

The day after their arrival, the feast of the Nativity of the Blessed Virgin, DuBourg offered the first Mass in the new convent, and then he and Richard rode off to Portage Des Sioux to visit the Catholic mission there. On September 11, on their return, the bishop again offered Mass for the nuns and reached agreements with Madame Duchesne on the details of their religious life pleasing to them both. He left them the Blessed Sacrament for their chapel, and named Benedict Richard pastor of St. Charles with the understanding that he would say Mass in their chapel once on Sundays and also on weekdays when possible. At Madame Duchesne's insistence, St. Regis was chosen as the special patron of the house, and a shrine was to be erected in his honor.

DuBourg was delighted with the order the women had achieved while he was at Portage Des Sioux and pleased with the equipment they had brought for their sacristy. As he watched Octavie Berthold and Eugénie Audé happily putting things to rights, the sound of their laughter brought deep contentment. Philippine Duchesne had surely brought with her coworkers who were well disposed and already making strides toward perfection. He said to her approvingly, "Look at those two young women who might have shone elsewhere, and are so gay in this situation. Oh, that is splendid, splendid!" And with a grin, added, "As for you and me, we are just *old sinners*."[47]

DuBourg had lost no time in talking to the townspeople about supporting the nuns, and the village spoke of giving him a plot of ground 180-by-300 feet, but two Presbyterians were withholding their signatures.[48] He hoped to take the matter up with them when he had time, but he had none then. Nor had he time to read the constitutions of the Religious of the Sacred Heart, which Madame Duchesne was so anxious to have approved. He was more concerned just then about their inability to speak English in an area where classes were given in both English and French. He could not expect Philippine to become fluent in a new language; the age of fifty was no time to be mastering a new tongue, least of all English. He rode off toward St. Louis with a copy of their constitutions in his saddlebags and in his mind a firm determination to find his nuns an English-speaking postulant as soon as he could.

Back in St. Louis he put Duchesne's mind at ease on the score of his approbation of her society, couching his letter in the formal language appropriate to a testimonial which might be needed in the future for Roman recognition. After opening with the remark that his bringing them to his diocese was his most impressive witness to his approval, he continued:

> The Church assembled in the Holy Council of Trent, and a succession of numerous sovereign pontiffs have recognized the excellence of this celebrated Society from whose constitutions yours are closely copied; and a happy experience has demonstrated to France for some years that the same principles, the same system of action, are equally applicable to both sexes. I can therefore only thank God for what you envision for these lands confided to my care. He has gratified my desires for the Christian education of young persons

of all classes. The prosperity and advancement of your establishment will be, never doubt it, the constant object of my efforts, and I will believe the whole course of my episcopacy, however long it may last, perfectly employed if I can succeed in consolidating and propagating your institute in my diocese.[49]

He signed, "I am with respectful devotion and very paternal affection, Madame, your very humble servant." The constitutions of the Society of Jesus, on which the women's were based, were of course well known to DuBourg; and even in this first year of his St. Louis episcopacy he was determined to get Jesuits for his diocese.[50] Women of the same dedication had his heartfelt approval.

With this formal document, knowing they were opening a day school even as he wrote, he enclosed a hurried little note: "I'm busy with the prospectus. I am sending the large reliquary, the two small pictures and one of St. Charles for the parish. I have spoken to Mr. Lee for the benches. Always address him with confidence and rely still more on the zeal of your father, L. Wm. Bp. of St. Louis."[51]

Getting an English-speaking postulant took a little longer, and it was not until December 15 that Madame Duchesne noted in her journal that Mary Mullen, who spoke English, had arrived. Meanwhile the bishop had departed for the Barrens with a hasty note to St. Charles, sending his most affectionate benedictions and requesting their prayers for his journey and its outcome. While he was away the nuns were to ask Mr. Lee for anything they needed for themselves.[52]

DuBourg was in haste to return to the Barrens for several reasons, most importantly for the arrival of his recruits from Kentucky, and the ordination of Michael Portier.[53] During his stay in New Orleans, Portier had been working with the children of all colors with unusual success. By mid-April 1818 he had gathered some sixty young people into catechetical classes.[54] With the arrival of Bertrand Martial that summer, however, Portier could be spared and he arrived in St. Louis on August 18, [55] to complete his studies for the priesthood in DuBourg's crowded rectory under the direction of De Andreis, who conducted what passed for the only "major seminary" in the whole Mississippi Valley. DuBourg was anxious to ordain Portier and assign him briefly to the Fenwicks at Apple Creek where he might learn English, which he had had little opportunity to use in New Orleans.

The compelling matter in southern Missouri that September was getting some horses and wagons to the juncture of the Ohio and Mississippi in time to meet the missionaries before they headed north to Ste. Genevieve, according to DuBourg's original directions. Since writing his August letter to Bardstown, DuBourg had been made an offer of temporary accommodations for his men at the Barrens. A charitable and wealthy widow, Mrs. Sarah Hayden, had a house two miles from the Barrens church where all the missionaries could live together; this she placed at his disposal.[56] Meanwhile the people of the surrounding farms had already offered to furnish supplies of flour, butter, bacon and chickens to the missionaries. It was a far better arrangement than having the men separated in Ste. Genevieve, where they could do little to speed the completion of the seminary.

Secundus Valezano, Rosati's advance messenger, was already at the Barrens by September 26, when DuBourg sent off a hasty note that Saturday, "One more step, my dear Rosati; you are at the last station, and I greatly hope you will not be treated like Moses!" The bishop was sending eight horses and two wagons to meet them and $50 "in case of need." As was inevitable with DuBourg, his first estimate was too optimistic, and the next day an even hastier note amended it. There would be only six horses and only one wagon.[57] His estimate of their time of arrival, however, proved more reliable. When he had told Rosati in his Sunday note, "You can scarcely arrive before Thursday," he was a prophet; on October 1, 1818, the Kentucky contingent arrived—all twenty-three priests, seminarians, and brothers.[58] Save for those assigned to Flaget to assist in Indiana and Michigan, DuBourg now had all his men within his diocese at last. It was while waiting for this exciting reunion that DuBourg ordained Michael Portier on the feast of the Dedication of St. Michael the Archangel, September 29, 1818.

In the midst of playing quartermaster and housemother, and exercising more traditional episcopal functions, DuBourg learned that the Sacred Heart nuns had opened their boarding school and, it seemed, lost their chaplain simultaneously. From the Barrens he replied at once: "I approve all that you are doing in the interest of your establishment. As to money, I am sending you an order on the Bank of Missouri at St. Louis for $200 which you can cash at once. I am extremely oppressed by the unexpected departure of the Pastor."[59]

Benedict Richard's departure was only temporary, as time proved; but DuBourg was fast learning that the distances of a frontier diocese coupled with the uncertainty of transportation lent themselves to a notable spirit of independence among a clergy whose bishop was as new to the terrain as most of them were, and whose superiors—if they were order men—might live in Europe. He suspected that Richard at St. Charles, a Benedictine, and Dunand at Florissant, a Trappist, felt little allegiance to the Bishop of Louisiana and the Floridas. He was happy to be able to send Charles de la Croix as confessor extraordinary to Madame Duchesne, saying, "This young priest is an angel. He will go *at least* every month to confess your Americans. Profit from him when you wish."[60] The bishop came himself to St. Charles in November for a few days, and on the feast of the Presentation of the Virgin, the day they wished to renew their vows in union with the Society in France, he offered Mass in their convent chapel.[61]

The prospectus DuBourg had mentioned working on for the St. Charles School in September was a task he gladly undertook. The headmistress had been rather surprised to find that, although French was spoken everywhere, when it came to business, "Here everything is in English—prospectus, newspapers, bills, addresses."[62] It was a relief that the bishop was quite versed in that latter tongue, and indeed enjoyed displaying his competence in it whether in speech or writing. For him a prospectus was child's play. Indeed that very fall he was busy on one for the project which was his fourth major ambition for 1818—a school for young men in St. Louis.

When Hercule Brassac in July wrote to his friend Jean-Philippe Lalanne in Bordeaux of the bishop's plans for that first year in St. Louis he mentioned among other things an academy or college "to open by December 1 next."[63] Although DuBourg was unable to erect his own building that year, classes did begin, and even earlier than Brassac had imagined. On October 23, 1818, the *Missouri Gazette* announced: "The Rev. Mr. Niel assisted by three other clergymen and under the superintendance [sic] of the Right Rev. Bishop will open on the 16th November next, in the house of Mrs. Alverez [sic], Church Street, an academy for young gentlemen." The spelling may not have been the bishop's, but the details of the prospectus which followed were certainly the work of a man experienced in schools for young gentlemen. No pupil would be received unless he could read at least tolerably well. Latin, English, French, arithmetic, and geography could be pursued "according to the ability of the pupil and the intention of the parents." Tuition of $12 a quarter was *payable in advance*. DuBourg had not forgotten the bitter lesson of St. Mary's College in Baltimore. Nor had he forgotten boys, for the *Gazette* notice concluded: "Each pupil must have a bag to bring in to carry out his books, for the eventual loss of which the masters do not hold themselves answerable."[64]

The house of Mrs. Eugene Alvarez was only one story high and consisted of "four wretched rooms," as Madame Duchesne saw them, held together by the typical St. Louis French walls of logs placed not horizontally but vertically and an overhanging roof which protected the encircling veranda. It had been used as a school before and by the time DuBourg leased it he had to pay 2,000 francs in rental for a house which a few years earlier would have commanded only one-fifth as much.[65] As soon as the old log church could be torn down, the bishop intended to build his own school on the church property; but that prospect dimmed as work on the new cathedral slowed down. A school must, nevertheless, be commenced.

In making Francis Niel head of the new venture, Du-Bourg had chosen wisely. Before his health received a serious setback, Niel was a vigorous promoter of religious education for young males in St. Louis. The academy was scarcely four months old when he announced in the *Gazette* the additions of "an able English tutor, late a student of Maynooth, for the teaching of English, Practical Arithmetic and Bookkeeping";[66] and before long had drawn up a document getting the support of the Catholics of St. Louis for a new building. The agreement, which was signed by all the Catholic householders of the city, and even some who were only allied to Catholic families, read:

> We, the undersigned, inhabitants and property holders of the town and parish of St. Louis, Territory of Missouri, members of the Roman Catholic religion, being informed that the Reverend Francis Niel, Vicar of this parish, by the authority of the Right Rev. Bishop Guillaume DuBourg, has undertaken to erect at his own cost, on a lot forming a part of the yard of the *Presbytère,* a house to be used for lodging the Clergy of our church, and the keeping of a school for the education of youth; considering the various useful purposes of this enterprise, and desiring to protect it from all claims or molestation on the part of persons badly informed, or badly disposed, as far as necessary, we hereby express our entire approbation of the building of such a house, and inasmuch as in our said capacities we might have a right to dispose of the lot forming part of the *Presbytère,* we warrant the free use thereof for the purpose hereinabove mentioned to the clergy of our communion by the authority of our bishop.[67]

This document, made and executed on October 30, 1819, although aimed at the coalescence of Catholic support for the first Catholic school in St. Louis, suggests the rapidity with which Missouri was changing; fears of "molestation on the part of persons badly informed or badly disposed" came as a surprise less than two years after a Catholic bishop arrived in St. Louis.

Niel opened the academy's second year with an assurance in the *Gazette* that the institution's goals were the "moral and literary improvement of the pupils . . . [and] a due sense of religion, the foundation of all morality," but achieved in such a way that there would be no interference with the religious beliefs of students of other denominations. With a new building in the planning stage it was also time to think of admitting boarders,[68] but as the year 1818 came to a close only a start had been made.

As Advent began, the bishop had little cause for joy. In the first week death deprived him of Joseph Caretti, the first loss in Upper Louisiana. It was not unexpected; Caretti's health had alarmed Rosati in Kentucky early that spring and he had suggested sending Caretti to St. Louis. DuBourg replied:

> I bitterly lament the decline of the worthy Mr. Caretti. In such a situation will it be prudent for him to undertake a journey pregnant with so many hardships? I leave it to you and him to decide. For my part, I will feel extremely happy to see him and to lavish on him all the attentions to which he is entitled.[69]

Caretti had wanted to come and arrived to live out his last days in the house of the bishop he had followed so willingly from Italy so short a time before. On December 4 DuBourg wrote to the Barrens, "God has disposed of Mr. Caretti, my dear Rosati; last night (the feast of St. Francis Xavier) at 9:00 o'clock he rendered his soul to his creator, after having edified us for so long by his resignation and unalterable sweetness in the face of such keen suffering. I do not need to recommend him to your prayers and those of your community."[70] Caretti had hoped to the end to enter the Vincentian novitiate, which with such cruel irony began the very day of his death. This loss in December made the year in retrospect seem one of nothing but frustration and failure. At the start, when the bishop was setting things in motion, he had felt so confident it could all be quickly accomplished. Warmed by his enthusiasm, Flaget in Kentucky had relayed to France that spring that nothing less than "marvels from all sides" were anticipated in Missouri.[71] But even the stoutest heart may quail.

To the anguish of loss were added the physical pangs of inexorable poverty. He knew his constant harping on economizing distressed Rosati, but it was an absolute necessity. As DuBourg explained:

> I have suppressed coffee in my house in the evening, because it is twice as expensive as everything else, especially today when the scarcity of this item and of sugar, occasioned by the drop in the river's waters has made them mount to an exorbitant price. I have soups made from potatoes, or cabbage, or onions, peas, etc. and that, with a plate of meat or cheese gives us an excellent supper, with which everyone has the kindness to be content. Perhaps I will even manage to find a substitute for the morning coffee as well.[72]

The price of sugar in St. Louis was fifty cents while coffee was nearly a dollar. It was a harsh day when a man could not have his coffee to drink. The only note of cheer he could offer was to send by the first barge leaving St. Louis books for the seminary at the Barrens.

He was most oppressed by the gnawing certainty that he had no way of providing decently for any of his volunteers, but at least the seminary head was better off than his bishop. "You still have a bad year ahead," he reminded Rosati. "I, I will be lucky if I am done with trials in four or five."[73] As Christmas drew near both men wondered what they would do with the next recruits from Italy, due at any moment, and the bishop begged his younger friend at the Barrens on Christmas Eve, "Pray often for me. I am always the same, full of worries, wasting time; if I do not change, or if God does not have pity on me, I fear I shall draw down chastisement on my diocese."[74]

While DuBourg still had the use of the one escritoire in the house, he greeted Philippine Duchesne as well. Like Rosati, she had been struggling against almost insuperable odds ever since her arrival, while the bishop remained helpless to ease her lot. "How I wish it were within my power to lessen your trials," he wrote sincerely, "but it would diminish your merit, and subtract from your crown." It was the old cliché Christians gave each other, but in Missouri it was more necessary to nurture this notion that deprivation and sacrifice had value. "Beginnings," he wrote—as much to comfort himself as her—"above all in a new country, still undeveloped, are always more harsh." And then, because he knew she would not misread it, added, "They are doubly so for me, because I receive the backlash of the sufferings of all those who have wished to associate themselves with my labors."[75] For a man of acute sensitivity, being a bishop had its peculiar griefs—especially at high and holy seasons when one would have liked to be generous.

Thinking of generosity made his thoughts turn involuntarily to Mme Ghyseghem in Flanders and her continued efforts to send books to the frontier. He felt a pang, recalling her words, "Although no distance can ever separate hearts, I find being far away a very sad thing." St. Louis just then seemed harshly distant from Bordeaux and Bruges, from relatives and loyal friends. Yet Mme Ghyseghem had said in the same letter that the M. Corsélés whom DuBourg had installed as Doyen de Bruges was now in prison for having courageously refused to cease his priestly functions.[76] At least in the United States one was free to work for the Lord's vineyard. His heart lifted, as it always did, at the thought of unfinished business and a new year in which to complete it.

CHAPTER XXIII

VAST PASTURES, SCATTERED SHEEP

Geographically speaking, no bishop of the Roman Church in the United States ever presided over a larger diocese than did William DuBourg. At the time of his consecration in Rome in 1815, the Congregation of the Propaganda retained the Spanish name, Diocese of Louisiana and the Floridas, a name which comprehended a vast uncertainty as far as both regions were concerned, since the American boundaries of these territories were not fixed until after the bishop reached his diocese in 1818. In addition to these extensive and undefined responsibilities, the diocese was also understood in Rome to include, for the time being, the Illinois and Mississippi territories on the eastern side of the Mississippi River.[1] Because the bishop, out of a personal desire to accommodate the Bishop of Bardstown, Kentucky, also had priests serving in the Indiana and Michigan territories, DuBourg's pastoral interests were even more far-flung.

His reports to Rome and his letters to the other American prelates display an astonishing geographic knowledge of sea lanes, canals, roads, bayous, and population centers of the United States east of the Great Plains. For a man who for most of his fifty-two years had lived in the cities of Bordeaux, Paris, Baltimore, and New Orleans he had a phenomenal ability to master the intricacies of frontier life and travel; and he seems to have done it with gusto, in spite of his regularly recurring bouts with poor health.

As a frontier bishop in Missouri, DuBourg needed to possess an infinite capacity for adaptation to new roles, new skills, and lore more usual to a craftsman than a theologian or philosopher. Having acquired a mill soon after he arrived, DuBourg thereafter took an eager interest in everything pertaining to water wheels, grindstones, thicknesses of boards, and the quality of flour.[2] His very last letter to his successor, written as he was about to leave New York for France at the end of his American episcopacy, closed with an apology for not having attended to some mill business before departing.[3]

He learned what there was to know about the tools and materials most suited to building frontier houses, churches, and schools, splitting rails for fences, grubbing land for farming,[4] and once from St. Louis sent explicit directions for keeping water out of his new seminary at the Barrens:

> You can turn away water from the cellar, by making around the house, or the side by which it enters, a ditch about three feet deep, and right against the foundation, and filling it with clay well-moulded with water, and very solidly packed. Then make a slope from the house of about ten feet all around it and have made a small trench to carry off rain waters. You will not have a drop in your cellar. Your seminarians and workmen can do it little by little. Begin on the north side. The other sides have enough slope, as I see it.[5]

He was not one to shirk physical work himself, and when he was at the Barrens he worked along with the others to help finish the seminary.[6]

In spite of leaving behind him a reputation for always being outwitted in his deals to acquire property, Bishop DuBourg took a husbandman's view of the land. He never lost his interest in crops, gardening, tree planting. "What about that field planted with wheat?" he would inquire. When seeds were scarce he would send what he could spare from his own supply in St. Louis, or recommend getting some from Henry Pratte in Ste. Genevieve, who knew all about Missouri agriculture. "Above all," the bishop would advise Rosati, "have potatoes, string beans, and turnips."[7] Knowing that one of his priests was a medical doctor, he was delighted to send the seminary a sort of wild strawberry called *quintefeuille* which was almost as efficacious as quinquina for treating intermittent fevers.[8]

One autumn in Louisville, on his way to Washington, D.C., he sent to the seminary two hundred young apple trees grafted from the finest quality fruit, writing in his own hand complete directions accompanied by a hand-drawn chart for planting them correctly. Recalling the incident years later, Rosati mused:

> Nothing escaped him. He went into the smallest detail about anything that could be useful to his beloved seminary. . . . He did not hesitate even to stoop to designating the place where they were to be planted, . . . the precautions to be taken, etc. Is it not beautiful to see a man of this stature, raised so high by his virtues, his talents, and the high esteem that he enjoyed with the Sovereign Pontiff and royalty, reach down that far and in a certain way imitate the Providence of the Heavenly Father, Whose perfections ought to be our model, which embraces in its admirable dispositions the greatest and the smallest things?[9]

DuBourg learned all about price fluctuations dependent upon the depth of the water in the Ohio, or the thickness of ice on the Mississippi, telling Rosati one January, "You will have sugar when the steamboat brings it. The river is not navigable as you know." The bishop knew as well when sugar was cheaper at Ste. Genevieve than elsewhere; and once sent Rosati three hundred pounds of "salt of allum" because it was twice as strong as the salt from Missouri's mines. Since beds were an unheard of luxury for newcomers to the western bank of the Mississippi, Bishop DuBourg sent the Barrens ten buffalo robes, but added in mild reproach that corn-husk mattresses made good beds, too. It was simply a matter of getting the cloth from Ste. Genevieve, but it had to be heavy, tightly woven stuff, of course. He wrote to Rosati, "You talk to me, my dear, of sending you some beds, as if I could fold them up in a letter, or put them in a valise . . .; besides, in order to send them, one must have them!"[10]

All of these attempts at economizing had to be made amid a monetary situation which defied certainty. As Madame Duchesne described it:

> The money in use here is another inconvenience. Gold and silver abound in New Orleans, but are lacking up here. They use bank notes issued by individual states or even by individual people, and these notes decrease in value while you handle them. You think you have paid a debt, and the creditor comes back to say the money is no good. Almost every day one must consult a new list of reliable banks.[11]

Perhaps if Bishop DuBourg had ever had a certain income he might have eschewed all the fine details of household management with which he meant to help his recruits survive in Missouri, yet it seems unlikely; he had an insatiable appetite for learning and the range of his interests knew no bounds. He was obviously in his element instructing Rosati on the handling of a particular barrel of *vin rouge* being sent one January from St. Louis to the seminary:

> Let it rest before drawing it into the bottles, and to better clarify it introduce through the bung two or three egg whites. The day following this operation, having taken care in advance to rinse out and drain the bottles, and to fix a stopcock at about a thumb and a half above the bottom. Draw off all the troubled wine, then stop. Save this sediment to make vinegar, mixing it with any other liqueur proper for fermentation. Cork your bottles well, then lay them between beds of sand in a cool place, well shut. These precautions are necessary for wine from Bordeaux. Above all, you must draw off all at the same time and tightly cork the bottles. I am sending you a faucet and some corks.[12]

Besides these attentions to the more fleshly needs of his clerical flock, a shepherd in the Mississippi Valley had to cater to other necessities less easy to satisfy on the frontier. The task of apportioning books to everyone's requirements was a constant challenge with so much clerical mobility over such distances. The simple matter of providing Ordos seemed at times insurmountable. During his first year in Upper Louisiana, Bishop DuBourg tried getting them from John Tessier in Baltimore, but they got lost en route.[13] DuBourg yearned for a printing press of his own, particularly for the purpose of printing Catholic books in French and English to help spread the faith, and he tried to persuade Propaganda to send him one.[14] In the end, he had to do what he had done before, ordering books through Louis in Bordeaux and Pierre-François in New Orleans, and hiring his other printing done where he lived.[15]

Trying to do too much too quickly brought other frustrations. There were never enough of the things a priest needed in his church, however modest it might be. As each new seminarian was ordained, the scanty supply of vestments, vessels, ornaments and altar linens dwindled. At the end of DuBourg's first year in St. Louis, he had to beg Rosati to do what he could for poor Secundus Valezano's church, which lacked even an alb, and had no single picture. "As for a picture of the Blessed Virgin," DuBourg explained, "It has been six months since I sent one to be repaired at Kaskaskia, which I destine for his parish, and two of St. Louis de Gonzague and St. Stanislaus which are for your seminary." He advised the seminary head to write to another new priest, Pierre Desmoulins, now stationed at Kaskaskia, to try to expedite the restoration of these paintings. The bishop himself was now out of varnish, having sent all he had for work on them.[16]

The crucial decisions in a diocese that size centered on the assignment of priests where they were most needed, where there was some hope for their support, and—because DuBourg's men were almost entirely foreigners—where they could adjust with the least friction to the American environment and people. If the recruits were French or Belgian they were almost immediately useful in the first years after their arrival; if they were Italian with no knowledge of French or English, learning a second language delayed their service in parish work. The truth was that even the French quickly had to learn English as the population trends altered. Already in October 1819 an Irish Society was founded in St. Louis, and the "language question" regarding Sunday sermons all too soon became acute.[17] The goal of a native clergy was never achieved in DuBourg's time, and he was constantly placing and replacing the men he had, in his desire to have pastor and people as compatible as possible, and yet, at the same time, to set the precedents that would make the episcopacy respected for his successors.

It was an impossible dream, of course, this notion of mutually educating an immigrant clergy and a rapidly changing frontier society to each other. DuBourg's clergy were for the most part handicapped by their limited and hasty training. They could not be assigned in most cases to well-established parishes to gain experience under veteran pastors. Often there was no other priest near enough to bolster, cheer, console, or advise the newly ordained missioner isolated amid his alien congregation. There were times when ignorance of American law and customs involved the priest in court actions or his bishop in considerable embarrassment.

The society into which the missioners were thrust was not the more stable, ordered, Catholic culture from which they came. The Americans they saw about them were immersed in a materialism common to a nation growing up overnight, and the fragmentation of the Christian church was nowhere more enthusiastically proceeding than in the Mississippi Valley. At the same time the destruction of morality was nowhere more triumphantly achieved than in New Orleans and St. Louis, where theatres, balls, and other worldly diversions took precedence over religious services, and where children were educated with no concern for their virtue.

Bertrand Martial, whose professors worked with such patience in Lower Louisiana to inculcate Christian virtues in their young male students, complained, "We have not had this year a single communion, not even at Easter, in spite of our instructions and urgent pleadings." The hostility toward religion in New Orleans had reached a horrifying degree by 1822, and only a miracle, he believed, could dislodge "this enormous machine of impiety." Martial commented bitterly to a friend in Rome:

> To amuse us the collection of libertines, the scum of all the countries of the ancient world, have imported from Europe all the most filthy libels and most scandalous anecdotes against priests which they distribute with complacency to all comers. The ladies in particular are not forgotten, because society, organized expressly to paralyze the *influence,* so called, of *priests,* believes this means the most efficacious of all. The counterweight to Christian education has been found in the appeal of the regicide, apostate priest, married, the celebrated Lavanal, enthroned with scandalous pomp as Principal of the College of New Orleans.[18]

Philippine Duchesne found things little better in Missouri, where twenty-year-old Catholic girls did not know how to make the sign of the Cross, and she reported to Paris:

> There is no denying the fact that temptations are great in St. Louis, and it adds to our distress to realize what we have to fear for the girls who are still in our school. I consider St. Louis as bad as Malacca in the days of St. Xavier. After a short period of fervor, or rather effervescence, there has followed a time of great indifference as regards religion and of excess in pursuit of pleasure. Our children are taken to balls, shows, speeches, have bad books in their hands, live in idleness. Already several vocations have been undermined in these surroundings, and I foresee that here, as in the time of Jesus Christ, the poor will be chosen to work for Him in preference to the rich.[19]

Madame Duchesne believed that discipline was the only remedy in a place where "insubordination is considered a virtue." Even the orphans the nuns cared for complained about their food and work, saying that they were treated like slaves.

The term slave was another reality the European mis-

541

sionaries faced with dismay in the Diocese of Louisiana and the Floridas. Although most of DuBourg's territories where Catholics lived in any numbers became states of the federal Union during his incumbency,[20] only Illinois, which by the terms of the Northwest Ordinance of 1787 was forever free, did not have the institution of slavery firmly fixed within the social structure of the state at the time of its admission. The "Missouri question" raged during the first two years of DuBourg's episcopacy in St. Louis, the same years that his recruits were concentrated in Upper Louisiana, receiving their final ecclesiastical education and ordinations. By the time that Missouri officially entered the Union on August 10, 1821, slavery had become a national issue which Thomas Jefferson termed the death knell of the Union, while John Adams with equal prescience predicted, "The present question is a mere preamble—a title-page to a great and tragic volume."

Even before DuBourg arrived in St. Louis for the first time, the Missouri Territorial Assembly had petitioned Congress for statehood with boundaries closely resembling those of today. The question only became a burning issue when James Tallmadge, Jr., of New York proposed in the House of Representatives that an amendment be attached to the bill for statehood, limiting the further introduction of slaves into Missouri and providing for the gradual emancipation of the children of existing slaves there. By a close vote this amendment passed the House in February 1819 but was rejected by the Senate. When Congress reconvened at year's end, Maine on the Atlantic Coast was likewise petitioning for statehood, but as a free state. To Missouri's supporters this seemed a happy augury, since the happenstance balance of slave and free states in the Senate would thus continue, should Missouri be permitted to retain slavery. The Missouri question was then postponed until February 1820.

The question was reopened when J. B. Thomas of Illinois offered an amendment leaving Missouri a slave state, but proposing that the remainder of the Louisiana Purchase be divided at the 36°30′ latitude making all north of that line except Missouri free, and all south slave. DuBourg confidently told Rosati on February 29, "There is scarcely any doubt that this Territory shall be admitted this year among the States of the Union. This is an affair of the utmost importance."[21]

On March 25, 1820, a handbill happily went the rounds in St. Louis, announcing that the Missouri state bill had passed without any restriction as to slavery. A traveler carrying a copy of the *National Intelligencer* of March 4 had brought the news, now three weeks old.[22] On March 3, Maine had indeed been admitted as a free state in a separate bill; but Missouri on March 6 was merely authorized to form a constitution with no restriction on slavery. A constitutional convention opened on June 12 in the "Mansion House" of St. Louis, and Madame Duchesne informed her friends in France:

> At present the laws of the state are being drawn up. The most disputed point and the one that has caused the greatest conflict concerns the admission of slavery. It seems that all who now own slaves will be allowed to keep them and that the children of their slaves will belong to them, but there can be no more African slave trade. We do not want slaves and we have no money to buy them, yet we scarcely know how to get along without them. . . . No one wants to hire out as a domestic servant; all want to be on the same social level.[23]

By July 1 the convention had drawn up a government of three branches according to the American tradition, [24] and on September 19 the General Assembly met in the Missouri Hotel to adopt the Great Seal of Missouri, and establish St. Charles as the state capital.[25] But in Washington on December 9, Senator John Henry Eaton of Tennessee moved to postpone the Missouri question once more, and Colonel Thomas Hart Benton of Missouri was heard to mutter that in its present shape the Missouri constitution would not be well received.[26]

The colonel from Missouri was quite right. The snag was that part of the state's constitution which empowered the legislature to exclude free Negroes and mulattoes from the state of Missouri. On March 2, 1821, Congress asserted that Missouri could not enter the Union until her constitution was free from any provision abridging the privileges and immunities of citizens of the United States. Altering the Missouri constitution proved a more protracted procedure than producing it had been; it was August 10, 1821, before Congress consented to admit Missouri and only in November would Governor Alexander McNair proclaim admission formally at the new seat of government at St. Charles,[27] that settlement for which the Bishop of Louisiana had predicted a future when he first located the Sacred Heart religious there.

Perhaps if DuBourg had kept them at St. Charles in 1819, their futures might have turned out differently. Neither the bishop nor Madame Duchesne was completely certain about the wisdom of leaving the house across the Missouri River after only one year. The plan had evolved gradually from Duchesne's idea of dividing her society into two groups. They had made some good friends in St. Charles who would still support sisters in charge of a day school; as for Florissant, a lingering hankering convinced Madame Duchesne that it would prove a much better location for her boarding school, and she said as much to the bishop. He replied:

> I heartily approve the plan of dividing the community and leaving only a free school at St. Charles under Mother Eugénie, Sister Marguerite, and Miss Mullen. The boarding school will be far better situated at Florissant. There the property is assured you. I will give you the greater part of the money needed for construction; day-labor is cheap in the locality. To oversee the work you will have the Prior, a man more experienced and more active than any in St. Charles. Material is abundant and not too expensive; firewood will cost you almost nothing; and you cannot fail to draw a large number of pupils for the boarding school, which is a more important work than you seem to realize, for it is from the education of the upper levels of society that reform must come, and they are just as ignorant as the lower classes.[28]

It seemed to DuBourg the right time to consolidate the work of the Religious of the Sacred Heart in the northern part of his diocese. As was inevitable when he approved a plan, he added, "For my part I am quite decided on this point. If you on your part are determined to follow my advice (I give no orders in this matter), then we must get to work and lose no more time." In February they met in Florissant to survey the scene and discuss further plans.

The property the bishop offered the nuns was not part of the farm he had acquired in Florissant in the hope of providing a bit of income; rather it was a separate plot in the village, originally intended for a church.[29] The bishop showed Madame Duchesne and her companion a sketch of his plans for both church and convent on the property. He had no firm sources of money to carry out the project except the original sum the Paris house had furnished for the American venture of the Religious of the Sacred Heart; the rest would have to be borrowed.

The women returned to St. Charles now apprehensive about a move to Florissant. Madame Duchesne confided to her journal, "Fear of expense . . . terrifies us, and we have begged the Bishop to let us remain at St. Charles in the house the townspeople wish to build for us on property they are willing to give us."[30]

The superior of the convent reckoned without her superior, the Bishop of Louisiana. Once a plan became clearly defined in his mind, DuBourg cared little for expense. He never could believe that if a plan were God's work God would not forward it; and the corollary was as clear: having put one's hand to the plow, looking back was a waste of time. When he came to St. Charles to make a retreat at Benedict Richard's house, Duchesne complained, "He spent one whole day upsetting all our plans, as well as the desires of Fathers Richard and Acquaroni, who have simply exhausted themselves in their efforts to get us firmly established at St. Charles."[31] As far as Bishop DuBourg was concerned the die was cast for Florissant; and St. Charles was to be closed since he now had become convinced that the number of religious was too small for both places. On July 29 Madame Duchesne wrote to Madame Barat, "The new house at Florissant is progressing. They say we can move into it by December 1."[32]

August 31, 1819, was Prize Day at the convent school; and when Bishop DuBourg arrived the day before, he was accompanied by two priests, one whom Madame Duchesne would get to know well in the future, and one whom she had known well in the past. Charles de la Croix was the man who was to supervise the removal from the house on the Missouri and eventually become pastor of St. Ferdinand's Church adjacent to the Florissant convent. Bertrand Martial was the companion of the voyage from Bordeaux in 1818. Companions of ocean voyages are united by distinctive bonds, even if some—like Martial—have been victims of *mal de mer*. He had come up from New Orleans in July for a conference with DuBourg,[33] and found himself like Madame Duchesne facing a change of location; that autumn he was to try a school for boys in Baton Rouge.[34] His companions of the voyage were delighted to see him again. For the bishop, Prize Days were always happy occasions.

> Presiding at the distribution of prizes . . . he congratulated Miss Odile DeLassus on winning highest honors and complimented the children on their good manners as well as on their recitations and singing. He was sincere in his praise and expressed great satisfaction at all that had been accomplished in the classes. Then he spoke with regret of the necessity which forced the nuns to leave St. Charles.[35]

For the women who had started the school rather reluctantly in that location, it was an occasion of mixed emotions. The previous night their bishop had broken the news that the Florissant house was not yet ready for occupancy, but since the lease on the Duquette house expired on September 6, they must move and temporarily stay in the log house on his farm. He was not perturbed; he had witnessed three such premature removals in the past—the minor seminary's move from Pigeon Hill to Mount St. Mary's, Mother Seton's move from Paca Street to St. Joseph's House, and more recently his own recruits from Bardstown to the Barrens. Content, he rode off the following day on horseback, with Charles de la Croix and Martial in their carriage behind him.

His journeys to the Barrens and to Florissant in July and August deprived Bishop DuBourg of the marvelous liturgies on August 8, when Benedict Flaget took eight hours to dedicate his cathedral, and those of seven days later needed to consecrate John Baptist David as Bishop of Mauricastro and Flaget's coadjutor. Flaget had hoped to have the Bishop of Louisiana at Bardstown to assist at the dedication of his magnificent new cathedral named in honor of St. Joseph,[36] but DuBourg's seminary building was still not complete that summer, and Flaget's old comrade, instead of preaching in elegant robes in Kentucky, was in Missouri sweating profusely as he worked side by side with his seminarians and layworkers to make habitable the first house of the Congregation of the Mission in the United States.[37]

Bishop DuBourg envied Flaget his coadjutor. Flaget and David had worked together for so long they had perfected the ways in which they complemented each other. In these sprawling western missions it was virtually impossible for one man to perform all the episcopal functions required of him. The Bishop of Louisiana, whose own diocese was the most extensive of all, had quickly come to think of a second bishop's assistance, whether it be that of a simple auxiliary or that of a genuine coadjutor with the right of succession at the death or resignation of the incumbent.

Reporting to Archbishop Maréchal on May 7, 1819, Bishop DuBourg first reassured Maréchal that for the moment there was a priest at Natchez, Mississippi, and then set forth his thoughts on asking the pope for a coadjutor immediately:

> The condition of my diocese is such that if I should die before having provided for the succession and having trained the successor for it, it would inevitably fall back into chaos. Besides, my health although good does not sustain long trips on Horseback. I need a coadjutor young and strong enough to spare me these. *Just between us,* it is Mr. Rosati I propose to ask for. He is a man who knows the situation perfectly and has the ecclesiastical virtues and usages. His nomination can only be acceptable to Rome where he has the advantage of being already well-known and would double the already

lively interest the venerable Congregation takes in the establishment of my diocese.[38]

Five days later DuBourg recommended Rosati to his friend
Cardinal Litta, saying that no one appeared more worthy
than this Neopolitan, a most distinguished priest of the
Congregation of the Mission who lacked nothing which
could enable him to easily gain the respect and love of all.[39]

Because DuBourg was accustomed to revealing all his
ideas to Litta, he presented the situation in New Orleans, as
he understood it to be from the reports of his clergy there.
Apparently the trustees, once so inimical, were now less
hostile, largely through the influence of a "very dear friend
the Reverend Mr. Martial." Furthermore, the Reverend Mr.
Moni, who acted as vicar general in Lower Louisiana in the
absence of Louis Sibourd, had "completely captivated"
Père Antoine and was now his first assistant at the cathedral. It occurred to Bishop DuBourg that making Sedella an
auxiliary bishop—both as a sign of approbation and as a
means of confirming this new bond of union—might be a
profitable strategy. He reasoned that:

> As after such a long vacancy, after such deplorable quarrels,
> after so many denunciations directed against their actual
> bishop and even against the Roman See, the inhabitants not
> only do not feel the need of a bishop, but even show them-
> selves disinclined to receive any bishop, no one appears to
> me more suitable, than Père Antoine to conciliate and gradu-
> ally accustom the minds of men to the episcopal dignity and
> the authority of the Sovereign Pontiff. The way being thus
> paved by him, any prudent man, after his death, will with
> little trouble take his place.[40]

If a brief for Sedella made it clear that he was a bishop *in
partibus* exercising jurisdiction within the diocese only by
delegation from his ordinary, it should work. Because of his
advanced age he would not be able to go beyond the city.

Sedella would be in no sense a substitute for a coadjutor. With his deficiency in learning and his past reputation
he was unsuited to administering a diocese. DuBourg still
needed a genuine coadjutor. "I fear that my petition may

seem exorbitant to the Sacred Congregation," he admitted candidly, "as the case of two titular bishops being given to help one ordinary, if there be any at all, must be very rare indeed. But I would ask the Most Eminent Fathers to consider that to extraordinary evils extraordinary remedies are usually applied."[41]

In May 1819 that reasoning and request were not without merit and might have worked out, if Père Antoine had indeed been reformed. The trouble was that DuBourg, who had not been in New Orleans since May 1815, was relying on the reports coming to him from priests who were new to the scene and unfamiliar with the devious ways of the pastor of the cathedral parish. DuBourg's trusted vicar general Sibourd, who had known New Orleans and Sedella even longer than the bishop, had left Lower Louisiana the previous June for medical treatment which could preclude his ever returning.[42] From Philadelphia Sibourd notified DuBourg of the arrival of four more recruits from Italy—a priest, two clerks, and a brother—and furnished the money for their trip west in return for five hundred Masses.[43] But Sibourd knew no more about New Orleans that winter than did his old friend in St. Louis. It was not until Sibourd returned to his post in Louisiana in the spring of 1819[44] that DuBourg learned that Sedella was no more trustworthy than in days past. What was worse, someone in whom DuBourg had confided had a loose tongue, and Sedella had heard he was nominated and was anticipating his appointment.

Bishop DuBourg was aghast. By the time this news reached him he had already written his letter of May 12, and it was on its way to Rome. He hastily penned a confidential letter in French to Cardinal Litta explaining the whole sorry situation:

> I turn to you with the confidence of a child towards its Father, and conjure Your Eminence to save me from the consequences of this false step. I have had the honor of communicating to you the success of one of my virtuous coworkers, in restoring order and regularity in the principal church of this diocese. One of the scandalous priests who

549

disgraced the priesthood, has at last been dismissed by my orders. I placed there three excellent curates, who gained for themselves the universal esteem, and I having consulted several of my Venerable Brethren, came to the conclusion that to consolidate the good work, it was advisable to grant to the head of that Parish an eminent dignity.

In the same mail he sent a more guarded, formal Latin letter to be read by the whole Congregation.[45]

It is not certain which of his Venerable Brethren the bishop had consulted, save for Bertrand Martial who is on record as having "strenuously and formally" opposed the nomination.[46] Whoever the bishop's confidants may have been, someone had not exercised much judgment in letting the Capuchin know of the nomination. It made DuBourg's position unenviable, to say the least. It was bad enough to appear so changeable to the cardinals of the Sacred Congregation in Rome; it was even more dangerous to risk Sedella's vindictiveness in New Orleans, where the good of the Church could suffer. Yet, as DuBourg told Cardinal Litta, "An important dispatch just received from that quarter, convinces me that I was deluding myself, and that this promotion would entail the most disastrous consequences."[47] Privately the bishop may have regretted the price of collegiality, of letting his priests know his thoughts and asking their advice.

The most Bishop DuBourg could hope for was that his May letter would not reach Rome until Cardinal Litta could read the more recent one of June 7 and could suppress his nomination of Sedella before it ever reached the Congregation of Propaganda. Failing in that, the second best solution would be to have Propaganda notify Sedella that he had been nominated, but that his advanced age precluded his being of any assistance to the Bishop of Louisiana in his travels. In any case, DuBourg pleaded with Litta to delay Rosati's nomination as coadjutor, if it had not yet been confirmed. "I am walking on fire under deceitful ashes," he said painfully.[48]

The return of his oldest and most trustworthy friend and co-worker suddenly seemed to DuBourg to offer a partial solution to his pressing need for assistance. Again he wrote confidentially to Cardinal Litta:

> For five years I had at New Orleans, in the person of Mr. Sibourd, a vicar general who by his prudence and great virtues won the esteem of all, even of my enemies. The fortitude with which he devoted himself to his dangerous and disagreeable post, his many qualities which enable him to fill it well, induced me at an early date to take him into consideration as my Coadjutor, when God who, to try us, seems to play with our apparently best concerted plans, sent him an illness which forced him to leave. . . . Now since the good God has made the worthy man well and, against all expectation, even his own, has led him back to us under these painful circumstances I have no doubt but that he is the person upon whom He wants this dignity to fall.[49]

Bishop DuBourg did not realize that Cardinal Litta was no longer Prefect of Propaganda, having been made Cardinal Vicar of Rome; but his friend was still as kind as ever, and as sympathetic to DuBourg. As soon as he received the frantic appeals of June, Cardinal Litta from Cantalupo quickly forwarded DuBourg's requests to Carlo Maria Pedicini, the Secretary of the Propaganda, strongly recommending his cooperation, saying:

> You will see that it is very necessary that the contents of the letter should not be made known to others, except to the Cardinal Prefect and to you; if the foregoing letter of which the Prelate speaks, has not yet arrived, so much the better for the affair. The Congregation should pass the opportune resolutions without compromising the Bishop who recommends that the affair remain secret and that his letter be burned.[50]

Francisco Cardinal Fontana, who had replaced Litta, at once sent Bishop DuBourg the kind of letter he had requested; a formal rejection of his nomination of Sedella on grounds of age, it was accompanied by the suggestion that if DuBourg really needed an episcopal assistant he should propose a younger candidate.[51] Later, on December 11, 1819, Fontana wrote in more detail replying to other diocesan questions DuBourg had raised, and informed him that since Cardinal Litta had already written to the Bishop of Louisiana on the coadjutor affair Propaganda would wait for DuBourg's reply, "so that when the difficulties in the way are removed, the choice may be made with due care." Meanwhile, since Louis Sibourd had formerly had the care of souls in the Island of Saint-Domingue, Propaganda would like information from him concerning the present state of the Catholic religion there and the proper means for providing for its spiritual needs.[52]

The sensible proposal that he consider someone younger than himself left DuBourg in something of a quandary in 1820. As he pointed out to Cardinal Fontana, he had only three priests whom he deemed fit for the office of coadjutor: Sibourd, Martial, and Rosati. Martial and Rosati were both younger than their bishop, the first by nine years and the latter by twenty-three; both were remarkable for piety, intelligence and administrative skills. But neither could be spared from their present assignments. "As the Rev. B. Martial and the Rev. J. Rosati have undertaken under my auspices, the one the foundation of a college for the religious and literary education of boys in Lower Louisiana, and the other that of an Ecclesiastical Seminary in Upper Louisiana, these works which are, I shall not say very useful, but really necessary above all others, will fatally crumble if these two gentlemen are taken away."[53] That left only Sibourd. From DuBourg's view the age of Sibourd was less important than the fact that he was a man of virtue and experience and, particularly, since a principal reason for having a coadjutor was to gradually reconcile minds in Lower Louisiana to the government of a bishop, it was of the utmost importance to select a man to whom they were accustomed.[54]

The Prefect of Propaganda found no fault with DuBourg's motives in suggesting Sibourd, and replied, "Although Your Lordship is still young in years and enjoying good health, in view of the importance of the reasons which you advance, the S. Congregation will not refuse to give you a Coadjutor to assist and aid you in the administration of your vast Diocese, particularly the southern part of it." But given Sibourd's age Fontana wished to know more about him. What of his zeal, his prudence, and his knowledge? "I wish you to give us full information touching his merit and qualifications before we can consider the question of his appointment."[55] And there matters stood, as the Bishop of Louisiana began his preparations to descend the Mississippi to visit for the first time as its bishop the see city of his diocese.

CHAPTER XXIV

New Orleans Revisited

In addition to coadjutors, there were many other
things on the bishop's mind that summer of 1820. News
filtered through from Baltimore that Pierre Babad, yielding
at last to Tessier's pressuring, had left to return to France.[1]
Archbishop Maréchal, amid his perennial complaints to
France against DuBourg, Dubois, and Bruté, had long since
said curtly, "I will not speak of Mr. Babade; he is a zero."[2]
Babad's old enemy, alcoholism, had eroded his usefulness
to such a degree that Tessier feared some scandal would
harm the cause of religion. DuBourg, the year before, had
suggested to Tessier that perhaps Babad and James Hector
Joubert might go to Florida as missionaries.[3] DuBourg had
not yet been able to do anything for that part of his diocese;
but it was too late to interest Babad in new challenges.

Thinking of Babad inevitably directed the bishop's
thoughts to Emmitsburg and that uneasy summer when
Babad had so keenly wanted to direct the spiritual lives of
Mother Seton and her community. DuBourg was delighted
to have learned from Bruté so recently how well things were
now going in Emmitsburg. He told his Little Brother: "The
good news of the mountain and the valley fill me with joy. Be
assured that my heart is always there. Are they not my

children? *Majorem non habeo gratiam quam audiam filios meos in charitate ambulare.* The day that I can have a swarm of bees from that precious hive of St. Joseph will be a great day for me." He sent a very special greeting to Mother Seton as he closed his letter with the command, "Distribute most tender benedictions among the Eaglets of the mountain and the Doves of the Valley."[4]

Hearing from Bruté was always diverting; Bruté was usually *au courant* where news of France was concerned. According to his recent garnerings, the duc de Rohan Chabot, who had been rumored dead, was instead very much alive and entering the priesthood. The Bishop of Louisiana was pleased to reciprocate with the only French news he had, news of Bruté's friend Féli. "While waiting for the second volume of *l'Indifférence,*" he announced, "Mr. de Lamennais has given another very interesting one on the state of the Church in France since the middle of the last century. I do not know a single other thing about France if it is not said in the public newspapers."[5]

By October 7, 1820, the bishop felt certain enough about his forthcoming episcopal visitation to warn Rosati at the Barrens that at long last he meant to visit Lower Louisiana. He was planning to leave in November, but before then he must go to Old Mine for confirmations scheduled for the following Sunday, October 15.[6] Father Henry Pratte from Ste. Genevieve had been intermittently serving a congregation there and recently they had built a little log church where Pratte was going to meet DuBourg and assist in the confirmations.[7]

The meeting at Old Mine that October never took place. Before the bishop closed his note to Rosati he had to add that Felix De Andreis was seriously ill, and three days later sent a hasty bulletin that he feared this time their fragile saint was dying. "Do what you think best about coming," he told Rosati.[8] Before the news could reach Perryville, De Andreis was dead in St. Louis at the age of forty-three. The loss of this man was irretrievable. He was not only the superior of the Congregation of the Mission, DuBourg's only order of religious men in the diocese, but he was also the bishop's vicar general in Upper Louisiana, and his presence in the rectory in St. Louis was a beautiful model for priests and seminarians alike.

Bishop DuBourg hastily got out a circular to the clergy on the death of De Andreis on October 15, and then wrote painfully to Rosati:

> God has disposed of your Father, and my holy collaborator, my dear friend. What can I say to console you for this irreparable loss when I myself am drowned in grief. . . . I send you his precious relics. They naturally belong to you; but I swear it is a sacrifice I am making for you. I will send his papers and clothes. As for his crucifix, he specially bequeathed it to you in publicly naming you Superior.

Now that Rosati was the head of the Vincentians in Missouri he would need an assistant as useful as he had been to De Andreis. "It is most urgent," DuBourg advised him, "that you write to Rome for two subjects of merit, although not too old, if you desire as much as I do that your Congregation survive; for after you we have only young people."

DuBourg's thoughts leaped ahead to De Andreis's final resting place, which should be that of a future saint, and he ordered Rosati to place the holy body so that it could be raised when necessary. The bishop preferred a "large tomb of brick well-cemented with mortar, with a cross above and with an inscription," a shrine to which the seminarians could be led on Sunday evenings, and the congregation from time to time. He drew a neat picture of the tomb he had in mind. Father Acquaroni would accompany De Andreis to the Barrens, stopping en route at Ste. Genevieve where Father Pratte would hold a service for him at eight o'clock in the morning.

DuBourg knew only too well how his young seminary rector was feeling and said: "I bless you with all my heart, and beg you in the name of God not to abandon yourself to grief. Those who have no hope behave thus. Do not fear your charge. It is God who gives it. He will give you the strength to bear it."[9]

The death of Felix De Andreis was the worst loss the

diocese had yet experienced, not only because of his person and the loving reverence it evoked in everyone, but because the very future of the seminary was at stake. The bishop wrote at once to the Vincentian head in Rome asking for two subjects capable of being superior, and forwarded Rosati's like petitions as soon as Acquaroni returned with them from Perryville. DuBourg still hoped to leave for New Orleans sometime in November and have a meeting of his priests of Lower Louisiana.[10] As for Upper Louisiana, he enjoined Rosati, "Remember you are vicar general."[11]

Bishop DuBourg might have begun to wonder if he were meant to leave St. Louis that year, for at the same time that De Andreis became mortally ill, over in Florissant Madame Duchesne also appeared to be dying and received Holy Viaticum. DuBourg brought his own doctor to treat her delirium which eventually surrendered to three blisterings and two mustard plasters.[12] It was November, however, before she was truly convalescent and could announce pertly, "Monseigneur has ordered me to take care of myself and I am doing so quite simply."[13] In the meantime, Madame Octavie had fallen and broken a bone in her leg which would keep her bedridden for thirty or forty days.

It was not easy for the Bishop of Louisiana to collect his thoughts to compose his *mandement* on marriage,[14] while riding his horse back and forth to Florissant, sorting out De Andreis's books and possessions in St. Louis, getting his late vicar general's trunk off to the Barrens, and re-arranging his clergy to the best possible advantage among seminary, college, and mission parishes in Upper Louisiana during his absence. Yet, all of these tasks were accomplished and on November 18 the somewhat flurried prelate bade the ladies of the Sacred Heart adieu.

DuBourg's companion as far as Ste. Genevieve was to be Andrew Ferrari, who had come in from the Indiana mission to take his Vincentian vows at the Barrens seminary. From Ste. Genevieve Ferrari would be replaced by a seminarian eager to go to New Orleans. It was like DuBourg to arrange in advance that the horse young Vincent rode up from the seminary to the steamboat would carry Ferrari back to the Barrens. Perhaps Rosati could come along to supervise this exchange on November 21 and embrace his bishop.[15]

Sunday's departure from St. Louis surprised DuBourg. It seemed that news of his intended journey had quickly spread, and rumors began flying that he was deserting Missouri for Lower Louisiana. Early Sunday morning he found his house besieged by people with tears running down their cheeks. He had to reassure them from the pulpit that he would return. Thus appeased, the "most distinguished French and American citizens of the town" had then escorted him to the steamboat. All of this, he confessed to his family afterward, "was very sweet to me."

In spite of being stranded twice on sandbars and losing a rudder to a tree stump, two days out of Ste. Genevieve his steamboat had reached New Madrid, where Bishop DuBourg intended to make his first visit. The facility with which he could grasp the elements of a new situation is apparent in his reflections sent to Rosati from that river port just north of the Kentucky-Tennessee border:

> These poor people, in all sixty Catholic families have been in the last twenty years without any religious assistance whatever, no marriages, no baptisms, no sacraments. Still they wish to have a priest; but I do not think they have the means to support one; neither do I believe that it would be good for a priest to stay here. Nevertheless, I deem it necessary that a Missionary should come here 3 or 4 times a year. Mr. Robert McCoy, at whose home I am now, will give him lodging and board. He has a nice hall where Mass may be said. The congregation will give the Priest $70 every time he comes; he shall remain each time a fortnight to instruct, etc.[16]

Such a missionary could also serve Cape Girardeau and more isolated Catholics twenty-nine miles from there. His first thought, he told Rosati, was to give the assignment to Antonio Potini but on thinking the thing over concluded that Francis Cellini would, because of his more mature age, be more suitable. Cellini was not only a priest of strong will but also a medical doctor to whom Rome had granted permission, upon the bishop's request, to exercise both professions.[17]

In this manner the bishop descended the meandering river, visiting parishes, conferring with clergy, preaching, confirming, and evaluating the condition of his diocese since he had last visited the Catholic centers of Lower Louisiana as administrator apostolic.[18] It was a relief to rest briefly at the home of his niece, Aglaé Bringier, near Donaldsonville. Her father-in-law, Marius Pons Bringier, had died earlier that year leaving a vast plantation in St. James Parish. Her husband Doradou was very busy preparing for the sale of his father's estate, set for the second Monday in January; and as one of the executors he had been running advertisements in the New Orleans newspapers since early October.[19] The plantation mansion was famous throughout Lower Louisiana as *la Maison Blanche* and DuBourg came to know it well as the years passed, sometimes dating his letters at the "White House."

At Donaldsonville the bishop was only sixty-odd miles from New Orleans, and his pulse quickened with a blend of anticipation and apprehension. He had dear friends and relatives he yearned to see. Pierre-François was now in partnership in the firm DuBourg & Baron, which offered for sale ships' cargoes from France, bills of exchange on Philadelphia, Bordeaux, Paris and London, and on occasion even real estate in New Orleans.[20] There was faithful Sibourd, and the bishop's most generous benefactors at the Ursuline convent, all eagerly awaiting his arrival. But there were also the *marguilliers* and their idol Pére Antoine.

Describing his trip for Louis and Victoire in a letter dated January 1, 1821, which was subsequently published in his *Notice sur l'état de la mission de la Louisiane,* DuBourg revealed his complete surprise and elation over the rest of his progress downriver.

> On December 6 I arrived at Doradou's. No one in Lower Louisiana knew that I was coming . . . . I surprised our dear children, who ate me up with caresses. It was from there that I announced my approach to all the priests and dear Ste. Colombe by a circular prepared in advance, fixing my arrival

in the city for December 23, wishing to use the interval to visit some parishes. The pastors of the neighborhood quickly came, and I was not long in seeing that God had prepared hearts for my visit. The next Sunday, the second of Advent, I went to Assumption Parish in the bayou of La Fourche, served by two fervent missionaries, Messers Bigeschi a veritable apostle, and his assistant good Tichitoli. The pastor at the head of 60 to 70 militiamen on horseback came to meet me at the edge of the parish and a general discharge of musketry on my arrival at the Church was the loud expression of the fidelity to the faith of these good and simple inhabitants. I stayed there three days which were days of rejoicing.

Wherever he went his recital reiterated welcomes of this sort.

In each place DuBourg visited, he confirmed those who were prepared and promised to confirm others on his trip back up the Mississippi. He was delighted to see the new churches already built by his European recruits, Joseph Bigeschi at Assumption and Secundus Valezano at Donaldsonville. The latter, the Church of the Ascension of the parish of Aglaé and Doradou, "was built in exquisite taste, and decorated with all possible elegance." He visited next St. James of Cabahannocé and then St. John the Baptist at Edgard, where to his delight he found Modeste Mina the pastor smiling amid Pierre-François, his daughter Noémi, and the first assistant of St. Louis in New Orleans, Louis Moni. The three days spent at Edgard were ones of "piety and fête" during which three barrels of powder were exhausted in the discharge of cannons announcing the "excellent dispositions of the inhabitants." Best of all there was his brother with all his news of New Orleans.

The city had not changed much in five years. There were the same petty bickerings in politics, the same attempts to change the location of the capital, this time to St. Francisville[21] on the eastern bank of the river—a proposal even less likely to succeed than the previous ones recommending Baton Rouge and Donaldsonville. The state legislature had spent November arguing whether or not to express appreciation to the outgoing Governor Villére. They had not thanked Claiborne; why should they thank Villére? Let the *people* reward them by re-electing them or giving them some other high office. One senator remarked angrily that their chamber had spent the previous session wrangling over the matter of a sword for General Jackson; getting a vote for Villére would likely be equally expensive.[22] The big names were still the same. True, J. Roffignac was now mayor but James Pitot was still a judge and Edward Livingston still a man to be reckoned with.

The steamboat, however, had made changes. The Orleans Navigation Company, to which Pierre-François had once belonged, was now under attack. When its charter had been granted with the right to exact tolls, steamboats were unknown. Now, instead of facilitating trade the company was a hindrance.[23] The city newspapers also increasingly carried notices of the sinking of steamboats due to fire, running aground, and other causes. That winter the *Teche* which operated between Attakapas and New Orleans barely escaped when three flatboats with cargo still on board were destroyed by fire.

As far as the newspapers were concerned, religious news was of no interest. As the year 1820 came to its close, the editorial columns debated the benefits and delights of masked balls, and two days before Christmas great advertisements began announcing the Grand Balls at St. Philip Street Ballroom and the Jefferson Ballroom, both extravaganzas running from December 23 through Christmas night. When revellers had sufficiently recovered from these excesses, the races at Live Oak track began at noon on New Year's Day.[24] There would not be one allusion to any church service, least of all any notice of the return of Louis William Valentine DuBourg. One must go to the bishop's report to Bordeaux for the details of his arrival.

His letter of January 1, 1821, continued:

> The head of the Cathedral clergy P. Antoine and Mr. Sibourd and a great concourse of citizens had prepared to come to meet me two leagues from the city. P. A. particularly was

manifesting the most lively anxiety that nothing should be lacking to honor my visit. His purse was liberally opened to pay the costs of the preparations.

I arrived Friday to dine with the MM. Labranche who had united their whole family. I found there good Mr. Martial. That night we went down to Mr. D'Etrehan's who was expecting us and put out everything to show us his joy. He had invited many people for Saturday the 23rd to a great dinner, after which I was to be taken to the city in a great cortège. I had the malice to play a joke which disconcerted all their plans. I left early in the morning with a single priest *incognito*. I entered the city in a closed carriage at the hour that they were leaving to come get me. I fell upon P. A. like a bomb. The surprise, the emotion soon gave place to the kindest sentiments. I wished to avoid the appearance of an entrée which would have an air of a triumph. Everyone ended by applauding the motives of my artifice.

The 4th Sunday of Advent, Christmas Eve, the church was crowded at my entrance, I forbade them to carry the dais, but I could not prevent all the clergy coming to meet me at the door. Tears flowed on everyone's part at the comparison of the past with the present. I assisted in pontifical vestments at the high Mass celebrated by P. A. having for assistants at the throne MM. Sibourd and Martial in capes and rochets. (I had furnished P.A. with the same costume which he had received with delight.)

On leaving after Mass I went to visit the pastor and his assistants, and afterward received visits from very distinguished persons. Christmas day I said my first two Masses at the convent, and I celebrated pontifically at the Cathedral where the crowd was even greater than on Christmas Eve. . . . In the midst of it all, not a guard, and nevertheless perfect order reigned, a silence, I will even say that made me weep. I took chocolate with P. A. who has made me six visits since.[25]

To the Ursulines it seemed that their own Francis de Sales had come home. A week from the emotional reunion of Christmas the minutes of the nuns read:

The first day of January, of the year 1821, Monseigneur Louis Guillaume Valentin Dubourg, our most illustrious

Bishop entered our Monastery, accompanied by his Vicar
General Mr. Louis Sibourg to convoke a special chapter
touching on the purchase of the Military Hospital built on
our land to which our first Mothers had certain rights.[26]

The old dissatisfactions of the nuns with the proximity of
government properties were complicated just then by two
new circumstances: the city's intention of building new
streets cutting through their section of the city, and the
federal government's announcement that the military hospital was for sale. They were virtually an island as it was, and
Bishop DuBourg advised them to acquire the hospital. With
that decision reached, the same meeting considered the
advisability of moving to the property they had acquired
from François Dupplesy a little distance below New Orleans in 1818. This, too, was decided upon, with the intention of giving to the bishop and his successors their present
convent once they were settled in their new home.[27] Although it would take time to build on the country property,
the prospect for DuBourg of eventually having an episcopal
"palace" was cause for great elation and made him feel that
he was one step nearer a permanent residence in his see city.
It was with more than ordinary optimism that he turned his
attention to one of the purposes of his visitation, a conference of the clergy of Lower Louisiana.

This so-called "synod" is almost undocumented, and
in the history of the Diocese of New Orleans—which begins
its synods with that of Leo de Neckere—goes unrecog-
nized.[28] The fact that the conference of 1821 called only for
the clergy of one part of the Diocese of Louisiana and the
Floridas may account for the cloud of uncertainty which
still hovers over it. Certain details, however, exist; and it is
clear that the bishop himself used the term synod when
alluding to the conference both before and after it met.

In two years in Upper Louisiana the bishop had come
to realize that there was not enough support for the seminary among the congregations who did not even want to
support their churches. The older, more prosperous par-

563

ishes of the south were better able to come to his aid. On October 27, 1819, DuBourg had told Rosati:

> Perhaps I am deceiving myself, but I hope that in a synod which I count on holding there I will make my priests enter into my views, and whether by themselves or by regular collections which I will establish in the churches, I will assure the seminary sufficient help, that is to say from 1500 to 2000 gourdes a year. Pray for the success of this entreprise.[29]

The second time DuBourg mentioned the conference was his letter to Propaganda afterward, in which he spoke of the warm reception he had been given in New Orleans that winter and explained:

> This example has given the tone to the whole city, so that I was not afraid to celebrate publicly a synod in that same city where a year ago, merely to show myself would have meant extreme danger. This Synod was made up of some twenty priests from Lower Louisiana. All manifested in unison both their obedience to me and their zeal for the maintenance of Ecclesiastical discipline.[30]

The third time DuBourg himself alluded to the synod was in 1829 when Propaganda inquired what he had done about feast and fast days, and he replied that he had made public in his synod the pronouncements signed by Pius VII, applying to Louisiana the reduced number of feasts prevailing in Baltimore and preserving the Spanish custom of eating meat on Saturdays.[31]

A fourth detail regarding the synod comes from Rosati, who as Bishop of St. Louis in 1827 told his pastors that DuBourg's synod had ordered that on Christmas day a collection would be taken up for the benefit of the seminary. Rosati in his "Recollections" furnished one final detail: that DuBourg assembled his clergy "in a synod for five days and made some very useful rules for his diocese."[32]

From this scanty evidence it seems that the "synod" was in reality a briefing session held by an episcopal superior for the enlightenment of his subordinates, rather than an enacting council. Given the circumstances, it could scarcely have been otherwise. The few old priests left over from the Spanish regime were either inactive, ignorant or immoral; the newer ones were all foreigners too lately come to the United States to have valid judgments about the Catholic Church in that country. DuBourg, who had known the Church under John Carroll of Baltimore, was the only one of the Diocese of Louisiana except Louis Sibourd who had any American precedents to strive to uphold. A minimum of uniformity was the most he could hope for in these widely scattered missions tended by men who might see their bishop only once a year.

News of the synod eventually reached *l'Ami* in Paris, as most news of the Louisiana mission did,[33] and Bishop DuBourg's friends could learn that:

> Monseigneur the bishop has held in New Orleans a diocesan synod, and has admired the zeal of the pastors of that part of the diocese, who having learned of the needs of the seminary have resolved to send every year from New Orleans a sum for that establishment. This proof of their charity is both honorable on their part as well as reassuring to that house; for Upper Louisiana, where the seminary is established is not rich and offers few resources.[34]

The item adds little to the story of the synod, but the remark about the disparity in support for religion between Upper and Lower Louisiana was a truth which increasingly colored Bishop DuBourg's thinking about the best interests of the whole diocese after his first episcopal visitation of Lower Louisiana.

In February the bishop's spirits were high as he added a page to a letter Sister St. Michel Gensoul was kindly writing for him to Florissant, and he told Madame Duchesne:

> Madame St. Michel doubtless has informed you of the good reception which God procured for me in this part of my Diocese. It greatly surpassed my hopes. Episcopal authority is today respected and recognized by even those who were its most ardent detractors. I have reason to hope for the happiest results for religion.[35]

He was even looking forward to a time when her Sacred Heart community might start a house in New Orleans, but he reminded her that God's works took time. Although he and she might not live to see them perfected, "Let us think ourselves happy," he said as always, "to begin them under His direction."

He had been very moved by her letter describing how he was missed in Missouri. He assured her that he was living in an excellent quarter of the city, governed by three good priests, and had found six to seven hundred people well prepared for confirmation. As for herself, "You know I told you on leaving you: *Erunt oculi mei et cor meum ibi, cunctis diebus.* It is the truth."[36]

DuBourg's high spirits—which easily erupted at the least encouragement—were not the total man. Underneath the exuberance, the over-optimistic predictions, and inevitable superlatives, there always resided a bedrock sense of reality, an ability to endure keen disappointments, and a permanent conviction that God's ways were not necessarily man's. To be sure, he was astonished and delighted to be welcomed back to New Orleans; but he was not overwhelmed. When he wrote of his reception to Bishop Plessis of Quebec on February 25, 1821, he continued:

> Now that things begin to be organized on the Missouri side to prepare an enduring establishment, the hearts of my Louisiana children are open to receive me and cause me to forget by their cordiality all past prejudices. Yet how many things are everywhere to be done! How many places destitute! How much ignorance to dispel! How many evils to repair! You are quite right, my lord, that I am only preparing the way for my successors. Pray that I shall so acquit myself as not to increase the difficulties for them.[37]

Even before writing to Duchesne and Plessis, the bishop had resumed his episcopal travels with a visitation of Bayou La Fourche southwest of New Orleans, going down the bayou to Thibodauxville, where on February 14, 15, and 16, he confirmed 387 people and made an official visit to St. Joseph Church. While visiting Catholics along Bayou La

Fourche, the bishop made a second stop at the Church of the Assumption at Plattenville. He had been there briefly in December on his way to New Orleans and had been importuned to rededicate the church; but he wished to reach his see city for Christmas. Now in February 1821 he returned to consecrate the church and make an official visit of the parish.[38]

As March began, the bishop together with Louis Sibourd headed for St. Martin des Attakapas, where Father Marcel Borella, an assistant at the church, was added to the party as secretary pro tem. Moving into Opelousas Parish to the north, they first visited Grand Coteau where the wealthy widow of Charles Smith was accustomed to receiving ecclesiastical visitors. The bishop had met her first in 1814 at the baptism of her nephew Charles. Her husband in the intervening years had built a fine church and presbytery to which he added "the necessary vestments, linen and ornamentation not only for the decency, but also for the splendor of the religious rites." For the support of this church dedicated to St. Charles Borromeo, Smith had attached eighty acres of prairie and fifty of woodland. He had died the year before DuBourg's visit, but Mary Sentee Smith had scrupulously carried out his wishes for the completion of the work.[39]

DuBourg had made Hercule Brassac pastor of St. Charles, and he had been formally installed on October 23, 1820, the same day that the church was dedicated. DuBourg had not been able to come downriver as early as October and he had named Gabriel Isabey, O. P., the pastor of St. Martin des Attakapas to stand in his stead. With Flavius H. Rosti of St. Landry of Opelousas assisting, everything had been done quite properly.[40] Although the anniversary of Charles Smith's death would not occur until April 1, the bishop offered an anniversary Mass for the generous patron who was buried in St. Ann's Chapel of his benefaction, after which DuBourg confirmed eighty adults and defined the parish boundaries.

Mrs. Smith was as generously inclined to aid religion as her spouse had been, and DuBourg had learned through Brassac that, for the purpose of establishing a girls' school, she wished to add to her husband's bequest a donation of some 400 acres of land adjoining the church property. In the summer of 1820 DuBourg's first thought had been to get some of Mother Seton's daughters for Grand Coteau and he had written to Bruté in Emmitsburg:

> Widow Mrs. Charles Smith of Opelousas is busy construct- ing a house for some religious who will take charge of education. She will furnish everything, travel, furniture, liv- ing, etc. The region is healthy and superb. Tell me if I could obtain 4 or 5 good subjects capable of teaching. At least one would have to know French well. And at this distance they would need to be full of virtue. The Widow will retire herself among them; and if God preserves her, she will do much good for this establishment. She already has some right to the gratitude of that of St. Joseph.[41]

The hope of getting Sisters of Charity from Maryland had not been fulfilled, however; and in the spring of 1821 the bishop's thoughts turned elsewhere. Widow Smith was al- ready "building, inclosing, and furnishing a two-story build- ing" at Grand Coteau, and what better place for Madame Duchesne's second house would he find? Here she would be provided money for traveling expenses for four nuns from France as well as their support during their first year in Louisiana. Divine Providence in this instance seemed no laggard at all where the Religious of the Sacred Heart were concerned. "This institution established in a locality al- ready well peopled and far distant from any similar institu- tion" promised even greater advantages than New Orleans where the Ursulines monopolized female education for Catholics.[42] As far as he was concerned the decision was made.

On March 11, the bishop's party pushed on to St. Landry's Church in Opelousas, where DuBourg wrote in the parish records: "I have confirmed only some forty adults, the great distance preventing many others, who have been prepared, from coming for the ceremony. I have found a great deal of improvement in the dispositions of the par- ish; but ignorance is still causing much harm." He urged the parishioners to build a new church and recommended to the pastor, Father Rosti, that he keep better parish records.[43] Turning eastward once more the bishop reached Pointe Coupée, an area which had been almost abandoned by priestly visitation for the past four years. As a result of this visit Bishop DuBourg notified Antoine Blanc that he was the new pastor of St. Francis of Assisi Church of Pointe Coupée and would also be responsible for Catholics in Feliciana and Baton Rouge, until pastors could be found for those parishes.[44] Father Blanc, who had originally been on loan to Flaget for Vincennes, was an admirable choice for the assignment, having been working in that county since the previous August. In two years' time after becoming pastor he had completed two new churches, a St. Francis and a St. Mary's Church at False River.[45]

From Pointe Coupée the visitation headed north toward Natchez, Mississippi, where DuBourg had been having some difficulty in getting anyone to remain. He had first tried to get De Crugy to accept the post,[46] but failed because of De Crugy's objection to living among English-speaking Catholics. The bishop then tried to get two well-recommended Irish subjects for Natchez,[47] but that hope was blasted. In 1821 there was at last someone at Natchez to assist the bishop in his confirmations. Constantine Maenhaut, a Belgian who had sailed from Bordeaux with DuBourg on the *Caravane,* was willing to try the Natchez mission after his ordination. Within two years he would grow dissatisfied and ask to resign.[48] The Natchez mission simply did not have enough challenge for men of talent and zeal; there were too few Catholics to support a genuine parish, and the climate did not agree with Maenhaut's health. Natchez would continue to plague Bishop DuBourg intermittently as long as it was assigned to him. In the spring of 1821, however, he gave a mission there, preaching as eloquently in English as he had done in French elsewhere along the way. At its close he administered confirmation assisted by both pastor Maenhaut and a Spanish priest in Natchez at the moment.

Eventually DuBourg's mail caught up with him and he

learned at last of the death of Elizabeth Seton in Emmitsburg. He had been forewarned the previous autumn by
Bruté, who had given her the last rites on September 24,
1820. Bruté had then suggested to her that he might write to
some of her friends thanking them for their affection and
attention; she had named some, Bruté named others. Du-
Bourg's name was there along with Sibourd, Flaget, David,
Filicchi, and the Archbishop of Baltimore.[49] But she had
rallied in October, and, as far as DuBourg knew, her son
William was the Seton probably dead in 1821, for the *Gazette de la Louisiana* on April 28, 1821, ran a long story on
Seton's ship, the *Macedonian*. This trophy of the War of
1812 had sailed from Boston in 1818 to make a two-year
cruise destined for Valparaiso, Chile, and eventually the
Pacific coast as far north as the mouth of the Columbia
River.[50]

The voyage had seemed doomed almost from the first.
Off the coast of Virginia the *Macedonian* ran into storms
that forced her into Norfolk for repairs. In April 1821 the
Gazette carried news of another disaster off the coast of
Callao, Peru, where part of the crew were massacred. No
names were given, but young Seton could have been a
casualty.[51] What was beyond doubt, with the arrival of
Bruté's letter, was that Elizabeth Bayley Seton had died on
January 4, surrounded by her Sisters of Charity but without
a priest present.

Bruté had been very distressed by this last fact. It
seemed to him that "souls joined together to live the most
holy lives they could, and who certainly died the most holy
lives" deserved to be attended by priests, especially when
they were only two miles away. Recently, John Dubois, the
women's superior, had ruled that when the sacraments had
been administered one could no longer call during the
night—"that the dying therefore do not have the help &
assistance of the priest." Bruté said in great distress:

> According to the new rule, the Mother was about three
> hours in her last agony before they called the assistant,
> preserving her consciousness until the last sigh & preparing
> herself, with the saintly manner which I've given you an

account of, but she could equally have been exposed to the temptations which in the most pious houses, the most religious souls, the most humble, the most loving are often permitted to experience.

Then he added bitterly, "I found her dead . . . . I do not find this rule better."[52]

DuBourg's last visit with her had left them both reconciled. When he sent a copy of his Lenten pastoral letter to Emmitsburg in 1820 she had forwarded it to Antonio Filicchi in Livorno, saying, "It just struck me, dearest brother, that it would be a curiosity to you to possess Mr. DuBourg's Mandate from Louisiana. . . . Your dearest Amabilia who keeps Lent so strictly will see what a miserable idea of penance is held in this county—and you will also see what the truly zealous Bishop is doing."[53] The bishop did not doubt that the valiant little foundress from New York had died a holy death. One dies alone, no matter how filled or empty the room. The pity was not that Bruté had arrived too late, but that she had died so young. Summoning up the accomplishments of her dozen years as a religious superior, it was awe-inspiring to imagine what she would have done had she been permitted to live. Well, "Eternity" had ever been her favorite word, and now she had her heart's desire.

It was late May before DuBourg reached southern Missouri and June before he was back in St. Louis. On board the *Hecla* from New Madrid he had leisure to reassess this first episcopal visit to Lower Louisiana. He realized that he would never have enough priests to satisfy his needs. As he told Maréchal afterward, "It needs a host of veritable Apostles here."[54] He was satisfied that the men he had were doing good work in most cases. If his envoy to Europe in 1821 had all the success DuBourg anticipated, both the manpower and financial situation would be vastly improved for the Diocese of Louisiana and the Floridas. It is to this envoy that attention now turns.

CHAPTER XXV

O ABSALOM, MY SON

The crisp, bright days of autumn were always bracing, and back in the second October of his Missouri episcopacy DuBourg had been more than usually optimistic, writing jubilantly to Simon Bruté at Mount St. Mary's in Emmitsburg:

> The prospect for subjects for our State is already rather promising for so little time. A very distinguished one aged 26 has just come to me. A Roman count, sharing richly the gifts of fortune, uniting an admirable physique to wide knowledge, above all, to that of the world and the three languages Latin, French, and English, a rare devotion and modesty. He will be, I believe, an acquisition of the first rank. He has already made his studies for the ecclesiastical state, even part of his theology. Family circumstances compelled him to suspend them; and for 6 years he has traveled all over Europe and North America as an observer and man of quality. Having arrived in New Orleans he was inclined to return to Rome, when the needs of this diocese, the hope of being useful to it, and the respect with which he saw himself surrounded revived in him his former tastes and decided him to settle in Louisiana. He is here to finish his studies.[1]

Count Angelo Inglesi had been well received in New Orleans, and Louis Moni, DuBourg's first assistant at the cathedral there, had enthusiastically recommended him to the bishop in St. Louis. In no time Inglesi, "because of his education and conversational ability which had always been highly regarded by the French, was able to gain access to the fashionable society of this growing town on the Mississippi."[2] That he should wish to become a priest seemed almost too much to believe.

Discussing this splendid new prospect with Rosati, when the head of the Barrens seminary was in St. Louis, DuBourg decided that Inglesi should complete his studies with De Andreis and DuBourg in St. Louis, and on October 8 the bishop happily announced to Rosati, "Mr. Inglesi arrived at our house a little while after your departure. He is an accomplished subject, determined upon the ecclesiastical state. God grant his perseverance. *According to all reports* such an acquisition will be a great stroke of divine Providence for us."[3]

The saintly, gentle De Andreis was equally impressed with the striking newcomer, in no time extolling Inglesi's remarkable astuteness, his cleverness in business matters, and the way he had endeared himself in New Orleans before coming to St. Louis. That a young man so widely traveled— in Russia, Germany, Ireland and England—should have chosen St. Louis seemed to De Andreis reason to thank God for having "sent to his bishop in his hour of need such an outstanding man."[4]

DuBourg was determined to add Inglesi to his clergy as soon as possible, and on October 31[5] tonsured him with the intention of making him a subdeacon during his "Christmas ordinations."[6] In fact, already in November the bishop had completed his plans for Inglesi's future and confided in Rosati, "I count on ordaining Mr. Inglesi priest at Easter and sending him on his way to Rome. . . . I have reason to believe that this trip will be of the greatest advantage for the mission, to which this excellent young man is quite devoted."[7] DuBourg had in mind a repetition of his own triumphant "begging tour" five years earlier, with his personable new priest in turn attracting recruits, collecting money, gathering paintings and altar ornaments for churches yet to be built. He wished no one to know of his plans just yet, but was telling Rosati in advance so that he could prepare whatever reports and letters he wished to send by Inglesi.

Such was his confidence and impatience, the bishop did not wait for Easter, which came in the first week of April. On March 19 he made Inglesi deacon, and the day after ordained both Philip Borgna and Angelo Inglesi to the priesthood.[8] Philip Borgna remained in St. Louis for Holy Week to participate in the beautiful liturgies, and to offer Mass on Holy Saturday at the convent chapel in Florissant for the Religious of the Sacred Heart; but Angelo Inglesi, after offering his first Mass at the convent on March 21, was preparing to depart for Ste. Genevieve and thence to New Orleans. "If they give him a day," DuBourg told Rosati, "he will go see you; but I fear he and you will be deprived of this pleasure. You can send me your letters. I will have them reach him in New York."[9]

In January DuBourg had anticipated going downriver with Inglesi, making some episcopal visitations en route,[10] but by March that plan was no longer possible. Felix De Andreis, his beloved vicar general, was very ill, and the visitation of Natchez would have to be deferred.[11] Thus Inglesi set off alone for Ste. Genevieve amid four large trunks, four small boxes, one large bag, and a bell—all to be left at Henry Pratte's rectory, destined for Rosati at the Barrens—while in addition to his own luggage Inglesi clutched a letter of introduction from DuBourg to the European friends and dignitaries whom his emissary might approach.[12]

In New Orleans his new-found dignity added to the respect Inglesi had previously enjoyed. Louis Sibourd was always talking about him after his departure[13] and Bertrand Martial, even after working to discredit Inglesi a few years later, admitted, "I esteemed him, and esteem him still."[14] In the bishop's own family, of course, the new priest was warmly welcomed. On April 29 he attended the wedding of Marie Antoinette Charlotte DuBourg to Horatio Davis at St. Mary's Church, along with Flavius H. Rosti, the pastor of Opelousas, and the bride's relatives.[15] To Pierre-François DuBourg, any friend of the bishop's was a friend of the family.

There remains no doubt about the sentiments of William DuBourg as his protégé set out for Europe from New York with dispatches from the American bishops for Rome, for he told Bruté afterward:

> Yes, my friend, our good Italian *seigneur* is ordained a priest. God in his mercy has given him to me. His devotion, his humility equal at least his other great qualities. *Neminem habeo tam unanimem.* He is en route to Rome on his own business and the affairs of the mission. I will count the days until his return, which I do not hope for until the spring of 1822. He must have embarked from New York toward the end of last month. . . . I regret that he could not pay you a little visit.[16]

The letter of introduction DuBourg gave Inglesi for Cardinal Fontana in Rome began:

> The bearer of this letter is the Illustrious Rev. Angelo Inglesi, who, coming to New Orleans after much traveling, and resolved to devote himself and all his goods to the Church, reported to St. Louis, and after a probation of eight months, during which he gave remarkable marks of virtue, and became attached to me by the closest bonds of friendship, was regularly ordained to the priesthood *sub titulo Missionis.*

And, after touching on some diocesan matters, the letter concluded:

> I wish that Rev. Fr. Inglesi could be heard, as he is quite thoroughly conversant with the condition of the Diocese, and public opinion here, and is able to tell many things worth knowing and to make prudent and most useful suggestions. When he has finished in Rome, his intention is to go through the various countries of Europe to collect new alms for helping this poor mission, then to come back as soon as possible to New Orleans, where he has decided at my suggestion to start a new parish for English-speaking Catholics.[17]

It seems unlikely that any bishop before or since has put such confidence in a young man known only eight months and ordained only one.

The Reverend Angelo Inglesi arrived in Bordeaux in mid-August, according to Louis DuBourg, who reported

575

that after having stayed with the DuBourgs from August 15 to September 19, he had left for Toulouse and from there had gone to Montpellier, where Victoire, who corresponded with him, had written to Inglesi. But DuBourg's proxy had already left for Paris, spending only one day en route at Lyon. Louis attributed this haste to Inglesi's setbacks encountered in southern France because of the grape harvesting, which rendered all the towns "deserted by almost all the proprietors."[18] Inglesi, who had decided to collect first, before going to Rome, found little reason to linger in the Gironde or the Midi.

Paris was very quickly apprised of his arrival when *l'Ami* on November 25, 1820, announced:

> Father Inglesi, a missionary from Louisiana, has just arrived in Europe. He has been sent by Bishop DuBourg for the interests of the mission, and proposes to publish some details which can not fail to offer great interest on the situation in that country. . . . Father Inglesi has had the honor to be presented to the King in a special audience, and to thank His Majesty in the name of the bishop, for the pictures which he has consented to send to decorate the churches of that country. He has also had the honor to be admitted recently to offer his homage to the Princes and Princesses.[19]

Obviously, the charm and brilliance of DuBourg's protégé was as captivating to Parisians as it had been in the Mississippi Valley. Félicité de Lamennais was glad to see that French charity and zeal were not extinguished, and was reminded of DuBourg's own trip five years earlier when the bishop had found "rather important resources." Félicité reported to Bruté, "We have seen here M. Inglesi; he has done some good business for the mission of Louisiana. He should repass through this country on his return from Rome."[20] Before the year was ended Inglesi had received from three families alone—Montmorency, Rochefoucauld, and Cayla—30,000 francs.[21]

As the new year began, *l'Ami* brought Paris up to date on the Louisiana missioner's activities: he had just gone to the home of la Marquise de la Tour du Pin on the very day, as luck would have it, on which *Madame*, the duchesse d'Angoulème, had gone there to see some objects on display for a charitable sale. The duchess, noticing that Inglesi was very attracted to a beautiful white velours chasuble, as well as a handsome portrait of herself, bought both vestment and likeness as a gift for him. *L'Ami* continued:

> The royal family has already given several proofs of the interest it takes in the Louisiana mission, and the religious public will share this interest, especially when it reads the *Notice sur l'état actuel de la mission de la Louisiane* which is now appearing, and of which we will soon speak at greater length. It is announced that on January 25 there will be a charitable assembly in favor of this mission at which M. *l'abbé* Maccarthy will preach.[22]

DuBourg could not have managed things better himself. He, of course, had written the *Notice* in advance; but the coup of getting the celebrated Nicholas Mac-Carthy, the brilliant Jesuit orator, for the fundraising affair was simply splendid.[23] No one could resist Mac-Carthy's impassioned appeals. Inglesi left Paris for Rome in triumph, after having once more been received by Louis XVIII in a special audience the Saturday prior to his departure, February 18, 1821.[24]

Instead of going to Italy by the French route, Inglesi, who had a keen eye for the main chance, proceeded to Holland and from there to Laibach where the sovereigns of Europe were assembled from January to May 1821. "He was received there in the most distinguished manner by all the allies; and particularly so by the Emperors of Austria and Russia."[25] From the latter rulers he received 40,000 francs which added to the 1,085 francs garnered in Holland certainly justified his choice of routes. As he descended into Italy he received from the duchess of Tuscany 11,474 francs and from the duchess of Lucca 5,100 francs.[26]

During this first year of Inglesi's tour, Bishop DuBourg in the Mississippi Valley received, after the customary delays in European mail directed to St. Louis, only news calculated to raise his fondest hopes. Inglesi was vindicating all the bishop's trust and predictions. The reports of his collections were exhilarating and the prospect of a dozen or so new missioners most gratifying to a shepherd only beginning to realize how vast was his pasture, how scattered his sheep.

The only qualm DuBourg had just then was that, as bishop, he might have violated canon law in ordaining the young man so hastily. The letter Inglesi carried to Propaganda raised this question:

> In this regard I wish to submit a doubt to Your Eminence:
>
> In the matter of promoting strangers to Sacred Orders, there is no sufficient unity of views among the American prelates. The Archbishop of Baltimore follows an opinion different from that of the others; for he, according to the Constitution of Innocent XII, requires a domicile of ten years; all the others think it sufficient that the candidates bind themselves by oath, and that there be no doubt concerning their intention to remain permanently. This common opinion was advocated first by the late Most Rev. John Carroll . . . and practically all the Bishops of this country adopted it, basing their view on the following two reasons: first, the necessity of these missions and, second, the poverty of the churches and of the candidates as well, which does not allow the latter to bear the considerable expenses entailed by so many years of probation. . . . Furthermore we deemed it a strong argument that the aforesaid rule of Innocent XII seems to be laid down only for Catholic countries and that it could scarcely be supposed that that great Pontiff ever had in mind to extend this rule to missionary countries, where it can be observed only with the greatest difficulty.[27]

Although Cardinal Fontana's reply was to put DuBourg somewhat sheepishly at ease,[28] he did not wait for it before going even further and proposing Inglesi for the coadjutorship.

Arguing that since both his former nominees had proved too old for Propaganda's acceptance he now hoped a younger man might find more favor, he presented his case in these revealing words:

> Such a one, unless affection misleads me, I have found in the person of my most beloved son, the Rev. Angelo Inglesi,

whom Divine Providence has placed by my side to be to me a comforter in my sorrows and the staff of my coming old age. To tell the truth plainly, never did I have anyone so congenial to me, and who ever showed greater affection for me and greater solicitude for my flock. This solicitude it was which, when he saw me destitute of almost every means of either supporting myself, or of promoting the interests of our missions, led him to Europe, in order that both with his own fortune, which is not small, and with the offerings that he would beg from the faithful he might supply our want. . . . I believe that Your Eminence is aware of the journeys he has already undertaken . . . of how worthily he has acquitted himself of his mission, and of the honors bestowed upon him everywhere, even by the greatest princes and potentates. . . . All this evinces certainly a prudence beyond his age and leaves no doubt this new Timothy will so conduct himself in the Episcopate that no one shall despise his youth.[29]

DuBourg was by nature headlong. Before his nomination could possibly have reached Rome, he had to tell Inglesi what he had done and, so persuaded of his friend's modesty, beg him to accept the position of coadjutor. From the steamboat *Hecla* near New Madrid on May 22, 1821, he wrote:

Fearing that you may already have departed from Rome before this letter reaches you, I have decided to inform you without further preamble, that it is yourself that I have designated to be my coadjutor. I believe it to be the will of God over you. . . . If therefore you receive your institution, after humbling yourself before God, submit to the orders and wishes of your brothers of Louisiana (of whom a large number have spoken to me on this subject in your favor) and to the decision of the Holy See, and receive as soon as possible the holy unction, which will be for you a new source of grace, of light, and of benediction, in completing your glorious enterprise. Whatever consolation I might experience in conferring the holy unction on you myself, I believe it to be more proper you should receive it in Europe.[30]

Meanwhile, the heir-apparent to an episcopal throne in Louisiana was blithely on his way to the heart of Catholic

Christendom where he arrived in May, causing Propaganda to notify Cardinal Consalvi on May 15 that Inglesi had brought among other things fresh information on the Diocese of New York.[31] When Inglesi presented DuBourg's question regarding his hasty ordination of his young friend, Propaganda in a general congregation decided in DuBourg's favor; the pope sanctioned it,[32] and Cardinal Fontana on July 21 wrote to the Bishop of Louisiana and, mentioning Angelo Inglesi by name, told DuBourg that he had been granted a *sanatio* and was absolved from all censures related to ordaining priests in violation of the Constitution of Innocent XII.[33] On August 4 Cardinal Consalvi sent to Inglesi contributions from both the pope and himself for the Louisiana mission fund,[34] after which Inglesi departed for Naples from which city he notified Propaganda on September 1 that His Majesty the King regretted that his financial situation did not permit him to encourage "the fine enterprises of my Bishop."[35] Some recruits for the mission, however, responded to the young priest's pleas; and with this accomplished, Inglesi returned to Rome and disaster.

In September 1821 ambassadors to Rome were dispatching to their own capitals brow-raising reports that Inglesi had been surprised in bed with a woman by her cuckolded husband.[36] Propaganda, on September 22, held a particular congregation to deal with the reports of the misconduct of Father Angelo Inglesi, reporting to the Secretary of State that he was to be sent back to Louisiana and that Bishop DuBourg was to be informed. The money collected by him was to be confiscated and the nuncios of Paris and Vienna were cautioned against permitting any further collections to be taken up by Inglesi.[37] That very day Consalvi wrote to DuBourg notifying him of his agent's conduct and saying that there were most solid indications to persuade Propaganda that he was culpable.[38] If there had been modern communications, the Inglesi affair would have ended that autumn. But there were not.

Inglesi quickly sent DuBourg his own account of what had happened, and enclosed a confession of intrigue by the woman involved. The account was so improbable that it could have convinced no one save a partial friend. Du-Bourg, nevertheless, cited it in Inglesi's defense to both Vatican officials and his own clergy in Louisiana, adamantly insisting:

> Father Inglesi from the Torlonia Bank had withdrawn $10,000 . . . for the payment of his brother's inheritance. Seeing this, a clerk of the bank concocted a plan. He insinuated himself into Inglesi's friendship, paid him many kind attentions and offers of services, and when Mr. Inglesi indicated that he desired a lodging in a healthy, quiet neighborhood the clerk offered him one in his own home. Inglesi accepted and brought his money and his effects there. A few days later the clerk absented himself in the evening, having agreed upon it with his wife that at about 9 o'clock she would enter the apartment of Mr. Inglesi, do what she could to seduce him, that in one way or another she would stay there until 11:00 when the husband would return, surprising them and frightening Inglesi to the point where he would find it wise to save himself and his projects at the price of all his money. On the evening in question, Providence permitted that Inglesi only entered his apartment a little before 11:00. The wife went quickly to his room, and whether from stratagem or horror at her crime, on entering she fell on a trunk saying she was ill. Mr. Inglesi ran to his armoire for a bottle of eau de cologne and at that moment her husband entered emitting fire and flame. Disconcerted by what he saw, he showed some embarrassment. Mr. Inglesi easily took advantage of this to escape from the room and leave the house. Early the next morning he sent for his trunk, which the clerk refused to surrender. Inglesi without losing any time ran to Cardinal Consalvi, who made the clerk return it. The cunning scoundrel, frustrated, quickly spread the calumny which was avidly accepted and believed even by many honest folk.[39]

The Prefect of Propaganda had likewise received from Inglesi a copy of the wife's confession of intrigue against him dated December 28, 1821,[40] but, unlike DuBourg, Consalvi doubted its authenticity and added that even if Inglesi tried to use it to justify himself of the grave misdemeanor imputed to him—wrongly or rightly, Consalvi did not know—"still he exhibited other signs of levity and impropriety, both by taking part in dances and by a mode of dress in no way befitting an Ecclesiastic." Clever and skillful in business as Inglesi might be, Consalvi warned DuBourg, he bore watching and his character needed careful investigation."[41]

That "clever and skillful" young man, having presented his American bishop and Roman Church authorities with letters designed to clear him of the charge of adultery, left the Eternal City and headed back to France as though his tour had been quite uninterrupted. The *Gazette* of the Grand Duchy of Tuscany carried an item dated at Florence on January 18, 1822, announcing that Inglesi had "obtained from the Grand Duke a handsome donation and proceeded thence to the court of Lucca, whose Sovereign also contributed to his mission." He successively visited the courts of Parma and Piacenza, of Piedmont and Turin where he was received by the king and queen.[42] The Piedmont *Gazette* of March 2 reported that the Abbé Inglesi, being near the end of his European tour, on his way to France, at the capital of Piedmont had the honor of a private audience with the august sovereign, "who received him with much kindness, and showed great satisfaction at the progress made in the Mission of Louisiana, which likewise has been assisted by some zealous Piedmontese priests."[43] On the same day this news appeared, Inglesi in Turin was addressing the Holy Father in Rome, expressing his fidelity to the pope, and enclosing a printed paper showing the names and amounts of the donors to the Louisiana Mission.[44] In Turin Inglesi likewise addressed a letter to the general public, thanking all who had contributed to the mission.[45] By April he was back in France, ready to take part in the creation of the Society for the Propagation of the Faith at Lyon.

Although disquieting rumors about Inglesi had reached Lyon that winter,[46] they were not enough to counteract the irresistible force of Inglesi's distinguished manners and the charm of his own personality. On his previous visit to Lyon, brief as it was, he had been received by the Petits, Father Jean Cholleton, and their friends as the vicar general of

Bishop DuBourg, whom they revered and for whose diocese they had been collecting funds even before Inglesi's arrival.

Angelo Inglesi's second appearance in Lyon took him to the Petits' home where he was sure of a warm welcome and where, according to the *Annales* of the Society, "beginning at this moment, M. Didier Petit, who for a long time had identified himself with the thought, work, and pious desires of his mother, took a more active, if not a preponderant part, in the work which Providence prepared."[47] Petit, inspired by Inglesi's vivid account of the needs of Louisiana, especially the lack of any regular support for a bishop and the imperative need for a permanent organization in France, called together some friends to discuss the "project of Father Inglesi." From this meeting emerged the Society for the Propagation of the Faith.

The origins of the society are actually rather diffuse, traced by one historian as far back as 1632.[48] Its emergence in 1822 may be more immediately attributed to the remarkable flowering of lay organizations and charities under the restored Bourbon monarchy[49] and to the particular energies of Pauline-Marie Jaricot, the widowed Madame Petit, and Benoît Coste, all of Lyon. Jaricot contributed a method of raising funds from the working people—her "penny-a-week for the Foreign Missions" idea which organized contributors first in groups of 10, then 100, and even 1000. Petit, who had seen something of the American mission field herself in Maryland, and had learned even more through her correspondence with DuBourg and Flaget, kindled a special enthusiasm for the American missions among the upper classes of France. Coste, a silk merchant of Lyon, held that the society should be truly universal, concerned with evangelizing every portion of the world.[50]

These three elements were synthesized on May 3, 1822, by the creation of the *Association de la Propagation de la Foi dans les Deux-Mondes* directed by a central council chosen that day with Didier Petit de Meurville as secretary.[51]

In its obituary *Notice* in the *Annales* at the time of DuBourg's death, the Association took issue with another obituary crediting the bishop of Louisiana with founding their society, saying, "We simply remark that Mgr. DuBourg is by no means the founder of the Association for the Propagation of the Faith. The interest which his mission inspired had no doubt great influence upon those who did establish the society; hence it was founded in part for him, but not at all by him."[52] DuBourg himself believed it was Inglesi who deserved the credit. Whatever its lines of connection with DuBourg or Inglesi, the association was to be an immediate godsend to the American dioceses of the Midwest, with one-third of its first money going to Louisiana, one-third to Kentucky, and the remainder to the Far East.

DuBourg, during the first part of the year 1822, was living in New Orleans still unaware of Inglesi's fall from grace in Rome. Whether he should have believed so or not, he was under the impression that his admiration for Inglesi was shared. His most influential European recruit in the city, Louis Leopold Moni, whom Père Antoine had welcomed as his first assistant at the cathedral, had written to the Marquis of Lopri in Rome attesting:

> Mr. Inglesi, to whom the most liberal offers have been made, and who had it in his power to select a most desirable situation in this country as a layman, had preferred dedicating himself to our mission and has embraced the ecclesiastical state. I can assure Your Excellency, that he has done and can do much good to our religion. All the good men of this country are anxious that he should return to us as a bishop; it will not be difficult at Rome to become acquainted with his merits and to obtain his favor.[53]

Unknown to the bishop, however, other reports were reaching Rome conveying quite another view, and when Cardinal Consalvi wrote to DuBourg on April 27, 1822, he rebuked him:

> One thing . . . vexes me very sorely, namely that we heard from New Orleans that, as the rumor was spread there that Your Lordship wanted [Inglesi] as Coadjutor, a great deal of trouble arose throughout Louisiana, and all the missionaries were so downhearted that some left the Diocese, while others, forgetful of their former zeal and solicitude, became

slack and careless in the discharge of their duties. Wherefore I earnestly beg you in the Lord to do everything in your power to suppress that evil rumor, and to recall the clergy to their duty, in order that what you have built up with so much pain and care may not, on this account, fall in ruins. Trusting that you will spare no efforts to this end, I pray Almighty God to keep Your Lordship yet many years, and in good health.[54]

DuBourg did not receive this galling reprimand while he remained in New Orleans, but he was beginning to perceive for himself that someone was busy stirring up opposition to Inglesi and the bishop's wish to have him as his coadjutor.

Rome's informant and the fomenter of opposition in New Orleans proved to be Bertrand Martial, the eminent educator from Bordeaux whom DuBourg had coaxed away from Archbishop d'Aviau in 1818, and who was in 1822 conducting a school for young men in one of the buildings still standing on the Ursuline properties below the city. In his letters to Rome DuBourg had praised Martial extravagantly for his good influence in Louisiana, only to find him now his bishop's severest critic. Martial's channel to the Congregation of the Propaganda was through a Bordeaux friend, B. Billaud, who worked in the French Embassy in Rome. Although Martial at first told Billaud his letters were in confidence, his reports from the beginning found their way to Consalvi, as the cardinal's letter of April 27, 1822, indicates.

Prior to his arrival in New Orleans, DuBourg had written to his clergy for their opinions on making Inglesi his coadjutor. The bishop was surprised and wounded to discover that opposition existed in Lower Louisiana, particularly that of Martial who, unknown to DuBourg, reported to Rome:

> The opposition which manifested itself at the time when it appeared that he wished to have Mr. Inglesi for coadjutor so distressed his soul that he hurled a circular at them to inspire terror; but he was sorry for it when he saw the effect it had produced. Thus great-spirited men sometimes make great mistakes. It left in the heart of a certain number of the

missionaries a wound difficult to heal. I have tried to prevent the departure of some; they replied one must save oneself.[55]

Only Martial's version of the circular's effect remains; the circular is no longer extant.

Another major error in Martial's eyes that spring was DuBourg's attempt to wrest the control of the cathedral away from the *marguilliers*. Again there exists only Martial's view:

> Persuaded that he had some influence, he tried to provoke the Legislature into changing and enlarging the trustees of the Cathedral. A simple suspicion that he was after something in the proposal made to the chamber brought him the humiliation of having a list of 12 trustees accepted against him, his adherents and against the priests. . . . But it is hard to persuade him that he is disliked.

DuBourg's own correspondence that spring reveals nothing of these difficulties, nor any discouragement. By the first steamboat able to head upriver, he was sending two new seminarians to Rosati, reiterating:

> Mr. Inglesi will bring us people. He is not yet a bishop; he does not even want to hear about that. He is very annoyed at having written me a certain letter, the contents of which I mentioned to you. He has notified me that he would be returning at the end of the year. I do not tire of admiring his devotion and his zeal. But as you can imagine, the disappointment causes me some concern. It doesn't matter! God knows what is best. One must not lose heart.[56]

The bishop had been refused twice before in this matter of securing a coadjutor.

While Bishop DuBourg journeyed northward by installments, busying himself with pastoral cares, Bertrand Martial continued his evaluations of his ordinary in correspondence with Rome. He was, he told Billaud, disgusted that the bishop tolerated the outrageous flaunting of religion in New Orleans. His priests had, by word of mouth and letter, addressed to him "lamentations" against these evils, but the bishop did not refrain from counseling that in regard to marriage, baptisms, and burials they tolerate the old customs inherited from Spanish times. Indeed, the bishop further took it upon himself to interpret the decrees of the sovereign pontiff on Freemasonry to suit himself. "Are we establishing or destroying Religion in this country?" Martial demanded.[57]

The schoolmaster did not perceive, as the Bishop of Louisiana had learned from Cardinal Litta during his years in Europe, that "it is sometimes necessary to bend the ordinary rules to prevent people from apostatizing." Martial did not realize how carefully and at what cost the bishop had striven to prevent outright schism in New Orleans for the past ten years. At the moment, he was more avidly curious about Inglesi, that facile orator and fundraiser. Rumors from Europe raised so many questions. It was, he assured Billaud, imperative for Religion that all this be cleared up.[58]

In the midst of writing this request for precise information on Inglesi, Martial was thrown into near-panic by news of his bishop, and he resumed his letter:

> I retake my pen, my very dear friend, to give you news I can neither confirm nor refute. . . . A Gazette of St. Louis says that Mgr. DuBourg is dangerously ill. Great God, what will become of the mission if he should die? Rumor is circulating already that Mr. Inglesi is the principal executor of his will together with MM. Rosati and Niel, neither versed in the affairs and chicanery of the world. Desolation has come upon us. To this great affliction it must be further added that the cabal, or society formed to destroy Catholicism in this region holds its sessions daily and has just put in the papers an atrocious article against the bishop, the priests, and even the Sovereign Pontiff whose alleged ambitious despotism extends beyond the seas. The ecclesiastics of the city seem to want to sign a response to give the lie to the calumnious deeds imputed to Mgr. DuBourg.[59]

Momentarily, imagining the diocese without him, Martial sensed something of the genuine worth of his bishop.

DuBourg did not die that summer, although he had been ill ever since his return to St. Louis. For more than a month he had been unable to recite the Office, and had scarcely been able to eat. The nervous attacks which recurred two or three times a day made any effort to work or write nearly unbearable, he told Rosati;[60] and to his faithful friend, Sister Margaret George in Emmitsburg, he commented wryly, "Alas, my dear child, we are poor crazy machines, which require constant attention to keep them going. Let us not lose courage; our very infirmities will serve to consolidate our virtue, by affording it a continual exercise."[61]

It was not the best of times to receive from Martial a letter passing on the tale of Inglesi's adultery in Rome, and DuBourg replied with some coolness: "You will learn with pleasure these infamies are the result of a most abominable intrigue." He had at hand the Perret woman's confession, which he repeated in detail for Martial, trusting it sufficiently cleared Inglesi. As for Martial's other canard about Inglesi's misuse of mission funds, DuBourg asserted, "This great exposé is nothing more than an invention of a Gazette of Genoa, whom Mr. Inglesi has forced to retract. There is not a grain of truth in it, you see, my dear friend; you have built upon a crumbling foundation."[62]

It was with enormous relief and a feeling of being vindicated that DuBourg learned that on July 11, 1822, Inglesi recruits had finally arrived in New Orleans,[63] and he wrote triumphantly to Rosati:

> Good news! 5 or 6 subjects have just arrived from France for the Seminary, of whom one is a subdeacon and the others in minor orders. There is also a deacon; but as I believe him ripe for the Priesthood, I have ordered that he come here directly. The others will stop at Ste. Genevieve, whence the Pastor will lead them to you. I don't know yet how we will provide for the needs of this addition to the family; but God sent it to me, he will provide.[64]

It was a notable band. All, ironically appear to have been recruited as Inglesi made his way back to Bordeaux after his expulsion from Rome.[65] In the summer of 1822 DuBourg only knew what a joy it was to tell Rosati proudly, "This reinforcement which has just arrived from Europe is the precursor of another composed of 4 or 5 perhaps 10 priests. You surely understand that it is the indefatigable Mr. Inglesi who sends them to me. I expect him himself at the end of this year."[66] When the bishop wrote to Propaganda a few days later on diocesan matters he added a plea in defense of Inglesi.[67]

With the bishop's health restored, Martial resumed his lengthy reports to Billaud. Aggravated at all the attention Inglesi had attracted abroad and by the "articles multiplying in France and America," Martial commented sourly, "His praises never cease." The new arrivals from Italy and France, however, told different stories. M. le comte Inglesi was robbed in Genoa by a bank failure and then robbed again near Rome . . . having saved only a snuffbox adorned with diamonds which the Emperor Alexander had given him in gratitude for Inglesi's overture made for the reunion of the Greek and Latin Churches. Inglesi's clothes and behavior had not only shocked Rome but Paris, where at a wedding ball he proposed to celebrate the Sacred Mysteries the next day in the same house, on the pretext that the dancers would be too tired to go to church to satisfy their Sunday obligation. The pastor from whom Inglesi had demanded a chalice and other requirements of a Mass had most properly refused.

Nothing was too petty to report as Martial's indignation mounted. All of it only proved how DuBourg had demeaned himself. "This is what he's reduced to," Martial sneered, "a bishop holy and learned, but whose heart is too tender and weak—cajoleries, handkissing, little attentions hold sway over him." If this bishop with his great virtues and knowledge had so much difficulty running the Diocese of Louisiana, what would become of it if Inglesi ever took over? Martial hoped that Propaganda would not be dazzled by the flash which had only glistened in the eyes of one weak bishop.[68]

Martial was by now no longer content to present his dissatisfactions to Rome, he admitted to Billaud. He had written to d'Aviau in Bordeaux who, according to Martial, had agreed that Inglesi should not be DuBourg's coadjutor, that at DuBourg's death his missionaries would abandon Louisiana rather than be governed by Inglesi. Having learned from Philip Janvier, who conducted some Canadian nuns from Quebec to New Orleans, that a man named Inglesi had lived for some years in that diocese, Martial then determined to quiz the Bishop of Quebec. He justified his action to Billaud, saying:

> The story reports that [one Mr. Inglesi Italian] came to Canada with the Duke of Richmond, governor, served first as secretary then as soldier. He presented himself to the Bishop saying he was a subdeacon in order to be admitted to the seminary and receive the other orders. The prelate who I dare say does not ordain so hastily, engaged him to conduct himself properly, and after suitable instruction would consider his request. Time perhaps seemed too long to that individual and believing he would do better he joined the theatre to play roles of a comedian; he married and lived eight months with his wife who is well known today as Made. Inglesi, then he disappeared.

Everything about the story and the physical description of the man convinced Martial that this Inglesi was the same fellow who had promised to get DuBourg a cardinal's hat from Rome and build him a new cathedral at Inglesi's expense. "All that seemed to me extravagant," Martial said disapprovingly, "and very suited to establishing a schism in the very city of New Orleans." Consequently he had just written to Bishop Plessis "in order to obtain from him all the necessary information and documents to support it." But DuBourg was to know nothing of all this. "I have already rigorously forbidden individuals who know the secret to tell it," Martial said piously, knowing that the blow to the heart of a bishop "so good, so holy, so confident is quite capable of killing him." Meanwhile he begged Billaud to see to it that the French Ambassador to Rome consult with Cardinal Consalvi over what must be done. "I have not yet the proofs in my hand and could not have them before the end of January 1823," Martial reminded him, "but the business seems so important to me I believed I must not wait any longer to inform you for it would be the case of saying *periculum in morā.*"[69]

As for his letter to Quebec, signing himself "Vicar General" Martial craftily wrote, as if empowered to do so:

> This young man, said to be a Roman count . . . has left some very disquieting doubts about the truth of his stories. The need to return to his homeland on family business precipitated his ordination to the priesthood and did not permit our prelate to get the customary information and attestations; his words alone were believed. What has just been told us by Mr. Janvier makes it our duty to address Your Excellency directly to obtain the most accurate information on the life, habits, and engagements contracted by the individual in your diocese.

Martial explained that letters from Rome seemed to confirm suspicions about Inglesi, and in closing he requested that Plessis "send to New Orleans all the facts which could clarify the conduct of this truly extraordinary man who has kept us alarmed for two years."[70]

Growing apprehensive that he might not have affixed the proper postage to this first appeal, Martial again addressed Plessis ten days later. This time throwing caution to the winds he told the whole saga of Inglesi, how Inglesi had arrived in New Orleans without funds, claiming that his valise had been stolen, how he had ingratiated himself with Father Louis Moni at the cathedral, "with a very mysterious air," how Moni with all his customary good heart and enthusiasm "took charge of recommending him to Du-Bourg," how the bishop had received Inglesi as one sent from heaven and had made him his most intimate friend. "A fine height, manners and an air quite distinguished, a certain facility with French and English, an easy smile, little courtesies, and a certain familiarity with society, all these qualities were more than enough to seduce the holy Prelate" into asking for Inglesi as his successor. In short, Martial said, "The infatuation is such that nothing save the details we are awaiting from you will convince him of the miserable abuse made of his good heart." Again Martial made sure Plessis's reply would come to him, saying that since DuBourg was traveling on business all the desired information should be sent to Martial's address.[71]

Having already written to Bishop DuBourg of the truth about Inglesi on October 3, 1822, the Bishop of Quebec may have wondered why DuBourg's vicar general was still in ignorance; or he may have preferred to be sure the bishop of Louisiana received that news before any of his subordinates. In any case, Plessis did not reply to Martial's pressing inquiries until March 5, 1823.[72] And so the year 1822 ended with neither Martial nor his bishop aware of the precise proportions of the deceptions to which DuBourg had succumbed. But DuBourg knew what Martial did not: that Inglesi would never be coadjutor in Louisiana; that, learning of Rome's disapproval of Inglesi, the bishop had already proposed Rosati, the man he had believed worthy in every regard from the first.

On January 29, 1823, Bishop DuBourg, in Washington, D. C., on business for his diocese, was contentedly writing two letters to Lyon in France: a rather formal one to the new Association for the Propagation of the Faith expressing his deep satisfaction that such a society was at last a reality—confident that its contributions would forward the cause of religion in Kentucky and Louisiana—and one to his good friend Didier Petit, the association's secretary. In the first he reported that he was sending a copy of their plan to Flaget, who would correspond with them directly on the labors and great designs of the Diocese of Bardstown; and he apologized for not answering Petit's letter sooner, explaining:

> The reason of this delay will appear quite simple, when you learn that successive removals have prevented its reaching me sooner. Addressed last July to New Orleans, it traveled after me to St. Louis, four hundred leagues higher up, and from that followed me four hundred leagues to the east, to the capital of the United States, where business of great importance has forced me to spend the winter, where I finally received it, two days ago.[73]

To Petit as a friend DuBourg wrote more somberly:

> You asked me in your last if I had no trials. How can you imagine that I have not and of the most bitter kind? One would have to be made of marble, while I am made of quite different stuff. Would it remedy them to relate them? That would be making two people unhappy instead of one. . .

He had no right to complain; he believed as always that God also sent consolations, that of seeing "little by little, order coming out of chaos, light from darkness; of seeing good principles established, education propagated, and the knowledge of Christianity and its duties encroaching day by day, upon the territory of ignorance." Certainly when contrasted with his situation five years ago, Louisiana offered much more cause for hope and joy than for discouragement and sadness. His goals remained the same:

> To increase the number of good priests to form a native clergy . . . to disseminate the means of Christian education, to build little churches . . . in the most neglected places, even if they were only of logs; and to try to maintain the traveling missionaries who go about the country preaching words of charity.[74]

It was the last mood of hope and joy the bishop was to experience for weeks to come.

Like the letters from Lyon, Plessis's letter of October finally caught up with DuBourg in Washington with its soul-piercing query:

> But what story are they telling me here? That an Italian named Inglesi has become your coadjutor? You must have been singularly deceived, if it was the Angelo Inglesi who lived some years in Canada, calling himself a subdeacon ordained at Perugia & not proving it, arrived here as a soldier in an English regiment, then buffoon, then adventurer, then wine merchant, then bankrupt, having married or pretended to marry in Quebec a Catholic woman before a Protestant Minister, then wishing, without success, to marry another after being cast off by her. It seems to me unbelievable that such a man without papers, without permission to leave, without ecclesiastical knowledge & without testi-

monial could have imposed on you to the point that you not only ordained him but would also have dreamed of making him your successor. I do not know who could have started all this story, and you would give me great pleasure, my dear bishop, in telling me the truth about it.[75]

DuBourg was shaken beyond description, scarcely able to hold the pen with which he wrote to Louis in Bordeaux, scarcely knowing what he was saying to his brother:

> I am writing to you in a moment of most bitter anguish. For some time every mail has brought me some new stab of the dagger, in casting horrible suspicion on Mr. Inglesi. I have resisted them until now. I can no longer. I dare not pronounce him guilty. *If he is, he is a miserable wretch.* But if he is, am I to permit him to return to my diocese, where his misconduct would soon be known? Without a doubt, no.

He was searching desperately for some way to believe that an inquiry might exonerate his protégé, saying, "Poor young man! If he is innocent, he is to be pitied. But what anguish these doubts cause me! And what frightful harm his presence would do to Louisiana, if there remained the least cloud on his innocence." He begged Louis to do all he could to find the truth. He wished also that Louis would write to Inglesi and tell him of the embarrassment in which the bishop now found himself. Louis was also to send to Baccari, the Vincentian superior in Rome, a copy of the bishop's letter and beg him to make inquiries.[76]

Engraved on his heart were Plessis's words: "It seems unbelievable that such a man could have imposed on you to the point where you not only ordained him but also dreamed of making him your successor." His humiliation returned in nauseous waves whenever he thought of it. He, William DuBourg, who had so revered priestly orders, who had gone to such lengths to pick only the finest men he could find in Europe, to have ordained a scoundrel? He must try to accept the fact that it could be true. As his more turbulent emotions began to subside, he wrote again to Louis on February 10, "I wrote you two or three days ago in a veritable attack of mental turmoil, which you could have guessed by my style. I am more tranquil today, and after ceaseless and profound reflection on the subject of my previous letter, here is the final result."

In the first place, Inglesi must at once make every effort to reinstate himself with his Roman superiors, Propaganda, and bring or have sent *authentic proof* that he was completely rehabilitated in their eyes. Nothing must prevent him from doing this; he owed it to Religion as well as to himself. If he did not succeed in this, what would become of him? Stay in Europe, or return to America? The decision was Inglesi's, but always on the condition that if he had no authentic document attesting his innocence his return to Louisiana could mean only that he retire to the seminary, to live in solitude far from any person or occasion which might compromise Religion.

The bishop was still, in spite of himself, thinking of Inglesi as a sincere priest, believing he could "certainly be innocent before God and not have means to justify himself before men." A retreat from the world would present an opportunity to advance in ecclesiastical knowledge and sacerdotal virtues. If he *had* committed sin, his retreat would be a means of expiation whose duration would be left to the judgment of his bishop. Innocent or guilty, however, should Inglesi return he was absolutely forbidden to land at New Orleans. Arriving at New York or Philadelphia, he was to travel *incognito* to Ste. Genevieve *without going to St. Louis,* and get a horse to ride directly to the Barrens, where DuBourg would come to see him and decide his future. Cringing as he was from the possibility of Inglesi's guilt as a priest, DuBourg was not yet ready to face the complacent looks of triumph of Martial or others who had followed Martial's lead.

As he repeated his directions to Louis for notifying Inglesi and Baccari, for giving each copies of his two letters, suddenly all the implications of Plessis's description hit home, and he added an agonized postscript for Louis's eyes alone:

There is in all this affair a Mystery which escapes me: it is not just misconduct they accuse M. Ing. of, they traduce him as an impostor and a *Chevalier d'industrie*. Great God! is it possible that a character so perverse is concealed beneath such a winning exterior which won him all hearts here and in France? All is possible however. He would not be, then, what he said he was, son of an illustrious family, removed from England to Rome at the time of the Stuarts; his father and brother after him would not have been Minister from Sweden to the Holy See; he himself would not have been a knight of Malta, he would not be the sole heir of an uncle who died possessed of a great fortune, he would not have made his studies at the Seminary of Perugia, the widow and children of his brother would not hold a distinguished rank in the nobility of Rome. If all of that was imposture, then what was that about the 10,000 *Roman scudi* which he received from the Banker Torlonia in Rome, and which he told me was a payment for his family? Certainly all these points must be cleared up; it is very easy to get authentic documents on each one of them. But if, unhappily all is false, what hardihood, what audacity in this man to have dared to go to Rome, to present himself with letters from me which could instantly prove that he had deceived me and was a thief! Little accustomed to intrigues, incapable of pretenses, and under the appearance of· trustworthiness, I am completely confounded, and I lose myself in my thoughts. What an astonishing role this man must have played! Oh! if it *was* that, it is not to my Seminary but to a Trappist monastery he should go to cleanse himself of his shame and do penance for his crimes.[77]

As soon as these letters arrived in Bordeaux[78] Louis undertook his brother's commissions. Louis was less shaken by the content of his brother's letters because he had been prepared by letters from Baccari in November and December 1822 alluding to Inglesi's conduct in Rome, and from "divers other sources"; but knowing his brother's sensitivities, Louis was not less afflicted by the keen chagrins he knew the bishop was enduring.[79]

Louis's first task was to get copies of the letters to Inglesi who was traveling in southern France. As luck would

have it, Inglesi wrote from Marseilles on April 4 that he was
planning to come to Bordeaux to send a second group of
recruits to Louisiana. His real object in coming, he asserted,
was to persuade Louis and Victoire of his innocence; already in Rome those false rumors had "fallen into the
water," but in Paris there were still some, he said airily, who
did not wish to be disabused. Louis replied on April 11,
sending copies of the bishop's two letters and trying to
make Inglesi abandon any further hope of being believed.
Inglesi then deluged Louis from Marseilles with daily letters
of regrets, of willingness to conform, of resignation to suffering in solitude, and finally of his despairing illness. Louis
on May 2 told Inglesi bluntly that he must pursue the
Roman testimonial or protestations were of no avail; on May
6, he forwarded the bishop's letters and request to F. A.
Baccari in Rome.[80]

Another group of Inglesi's recruits actually did sail for
Louisiana that summer.[81] Inglesi himself reached Philadelphia on August 24, 1823, "rich in ready money in priestly
vestments in pictures and in sacred vessels—the apparent
result of his begging in Europe."[82] The next day he presented himself to the vicar general of the diocese, whose
bishop, Henry Conwell, was absent. Bishop DuBourg's orders were thus flaunted from the moment of Inglesi's arrival
in the United States. Instead of traveling incognito as a
layman directly to Missouri and the Barrens seminary, Inglesi not only announced himself at once but also plunged
immediately into the maelstrom of the bitterest schism the
Church in Philadelphia had yet endured. On August 28 the
trustees of St. Mary's Church, the church in schism and the
bishop's cathedral, addressed to Vicar General William V.
Harold this notice:

> The Rev. William Hogan having resigned the duties of pastor
> of the Church of St. Mary's, which resignation had been
> admitted by us, we have this day nominated the Rev. A.
> Inglesi, and requested him to officiate at said church. Mr.
> Inglesi being a regular Roman Catholic clergyman, duly
> authorized to celebrate divine offices, and officiate as a
> priest, within this diocese, and in all respects acceptable, we

respectfully trust that this arrangement will put an end to all future dissensions in the church.[83]

It is not necessary here to enter into that complicated story known as the Hogan Schism;[84] it is enough to say that Inglesi's involvement in it would remove any doubt possibly remaining in DuBourg's mind about the character of the man he had trusted profoundly.

Endowed with every grace save candor, without a qualm on September 12, 1823, Inglesi wrote to Rome describing the critical situation in Philadelphia, announcing the invitation of the trustees to become the pastor of St. Mary's Church, and saying he would be willing to accept if Propaganda approved.[85] Two days earlier he had written to DuBourg asking for an *exeat* from the Diocese of Louisiana to enter the Diocese of Philadelphia.[86] It was this incredible request which led DuBourg to issue his circular to the American bishops on October 20, announcing:

> An Italian Clergyman, ordained by me and then sent by me to Europe on an errand which supposed a degree of confidence, to which he unfortunately did not prove himself entitled, lately arrived in Philadelphia; and as he knows that he would not be well received in this his adopted Diocess, he may probably apply to your Reverence for admission into yours. I would be sorry to take down the character of a Priest; but duty to Religion compels me to invite you to be on your guard. I have strong reasons to believe him unworthy of any trust; yet I would not wish you to make any other use of my name than by requesting of him as a preliminary to any faculty in your diocess, to exhibit you *fresh credentials* and *demissorials* from me . . . .
>
> Be pleased to keep this entirely to yourself, or if you think it necessary to communicate it to your Vicar general, enjoin on him the same discretion. I fear he would give some great scandal.
>
> His name is A. INGLESI, once alas, very dear to me for his apparent virtues. Never did a man practice upon a Bishop so sacrilegious an imposition. May the all-merciful God forgive me his ordination, which I will always regard as a stain on my episcopacy.[87]

When this circular appeared in the Philadelphia *Democratic Press* on November 22, Inglesi wrote reproachfully to DuBourg, "How could you have accused me, without allowing me the privilege of being heard?" After all he had done for the Louisiana mission, he would not have expected DuBourg to deprive him of the consideration he deserved. He warned the bishop: "I have . . . informed the public . . . that I should expect from your Lordship an explanation of that letter; and if you shall confirm what I cannot believe, I shall have recourse to the means which the justice of my cause, and the truth of my innocence will dictate. I shall, if it be necessary, go to New Orleans, to obtain from your justice the reparation of my honour."[88]

The bishop replied, "My hand as well as my heart, refuse this sorrowful task; but you make it my duty, in complaining of my severity in terms which might be thought to convey a reproach of ingratitude." He still wished to be mistaken about Inglesi, but he cried out, "Why does not he whom you call Father who was and will yet be one, God knows! with more than former tenderness, deserve that you should dissipate his fears? Would you rather sacrifice his friendship for ever, than impart to him your means of justification?"[89]

In publishing his vindication of himself in Philadelphia in 1824 Inglesi cited both letters—his and Bishop DuBourg's—as proof that DuBourg still believed him innocent, and had only issued his circular out of fear of losing Inglesi from his diocese. Such was the intricate maze of that young man's mind. The ties between him and the man he had betrayed, however, were broken beyond mending. Before the year 1823 ended, Propaganda replied to Inglesi's request for St. Mary's pastorate with a categorical statement that Rome was fully aware of his misdeeds in Quebec, Louisiana, Rome, and Città de Pieve; that he was unworthy to exercise the priestly ministry, and that he should return to Europe and retire from the world.[90] Propaganda also notified the vicar general of Philadelphia that Inglesi was interdicted from exercising the ministry throughout the diocese.[91] Although he did not leave Philadelphia at once,

Inglesi's role in American Church affairs was played out; the curtain had been rung down.

Bishop DuBourg's own connection with the Philadelphia schism ended in December 1823 when he replied to Richard W. Meade, one of the schismatic trustees of St. Mary's Church who had hoped to win DuBourg's mediation in some fashion. DuBourg declined, pointing out, "A stranger to the Ecclesiastical Province on which Philadelphia depends, I have no vote in its affairs and for me to propose, as you hint it, a meeting of its bishops on that business, would be an unjustifiable, nay probably dangerous interference." He did not hesitate, nevertheless, to remind Meade that bishops had rights "firmly rooted in the very constitution of the Church" which they could not surrender:

> Of this kind certainly are the rights of officiating and presiding in the church assigned to him by the Pope for his Cathedral, of partaking in its income, of appointing proper pastors, and finally of deposing, suspending, interdicting, excommunicating any Priest whom he may judge worthy of those censures, save the right of appeal to the Metropolitan & from this to the Holy See.[92]

Meade could not know how acutely DuBourg had suffered in trying to retain these episcopal rights in New Orleans, nor could the Philadelphia trustee realize how heartfelt was DuBourg's advice that Meade and his fellow trustees acknowledge their bishop's rights, nor how sincerely he exhorted, "Pride is a bad counsellor. When in the heat of controversy we have exceeded the lawful bounds, to retrace our steps is rather honorable than degrading, as it is the sublimest effort of virtue." Their own Bishop Conwell was the trustees' natural mediator, and they should approach him openly and frankly in a spirit of mutual sacrifice.[93]

In regard to his own dilemma, the Bishop of Louisiana had months ago made up his mind. On first learning the news about Inglesi in February he had instructed Philip Borgna, who was going to Rome:

Make known to the Card. Prefect by what artifices the notorious Inglesi magnetized me, and Father De Andreis and all, both priests and lay people, who knew him here. Say that I acknowledge my mistake and deplore it, and that such is the confusion and sorrow into which this sad disclosure has plunged me, that I have several times been tempted to beseech His Holiness' permission to retire in order that I may express my deep sorrow for this fault; that only the fear to see my Diocese lost by that request prevented me; but that if His Eminence deems it fit to relieve me of a place of which I made myself unworthy by such great imprudence, I am ready to resign, and will be most thankful to him.[94]

Since then Inglesi's conduct in Philadelphia had only augmented that sorrow and made DuBourg feel his own guilt more agonizingly. On March 8, 1824, the bishop reported to Propaganda on the events since Borgna had arrived in Rome: of DuBourg's circular to the Bishops of Philadelphia, Boston, and New York, revealing Inglesi's true character; of Meade's request that the Bishop of Louisiana mediate the schism in Philadelphia and his own reply; and, particularly, of his own determination to resign as Bishop of Louisiana because of his tragic blunder in regard to Inglesi.[95] Until his resignation should be accepted, there were many projects in the Mississippi Valley to be consolidated. No matter what humiliations God permitted a man to bring down on himself, the work of His vineyard must go on.

CHAPTER XXVI

SEEDING NEW FIELDS

Focusing the glare of the spotlight on scenes from Inglesi's sorry scenario obscures the larger drama in which DuBourg remained the protagonist. During the long months from Inglesi's arrival on the scene in 1819 until the ultimate confirmation of his imposture in 1823, the bishop was continuously occupied with matters of importance to religion within his diocese. To men of character the pain and disappointments which inordinate attachments bring do not alter the steady, strong-flowing current of their purposes, particularly when these are devoted to the service of God.

To be sure, for DuBourg the Inglesi affair never quite ended. As bishop, he never forgave his own folly in ordaining Angelo Inglesi; as a Christian, for the man whom he had imagined as the filial prop of his declining years, he retained a tender pity and hoped for his conversion. Two things sustained this hope, he told Peter Caprano, the Secretary of Propaganda: the fact that in the Philadelphia trouble Inglesi had not accepted the pastorate of St. Mary's Church, and, particularly, that "he did a great deal for the missions at large by promoting and stimulating the institution of the Society for the Propagation of the Faith, which . . . has since spread wonderfully through the largest cities in France and of some other countries."[1]

The Widow Petit in Lyon, who had known the bishop's heart for a quarter-century, encouraged him to continue to hope for the unfortunate young man's reform. "What will become of him?" she mourned. "If only God would touch him and convert him! Every day I pray Him for it with all my heart, but with a feeling so painful that my whole body shivers each time."[2] The important thing, however, was that the work in Louisiana must go on, as it had in the past.

In 1821, when Angelo Inglesi was having such success collecting men and money in Europe, the Bishop of Louisiana had been energetically promoting the spread of the Religious of the Sacred Heart to Lower Louisiana. He had scarcely put foot on terra firma on his return from visiting that region in June 1821 when he set out for Florissant. He was in an irresistibly persuasive mood, as he regaled Madame Duchesne with the details of Mrs. Mary Sentee Smith's offer of a place at Grand Coteau. On his departure Madame Duchesne wrote in her journal, "We have accepted, and Monseigneur, who had already arranged for his niece to keep at her home the two religious who are said to be coming from France, thinks that one of us should go down to Opelousas to await their arrival. . . ."[3] Aglaé Bringier, like her Aunt Victoire, was easily drafted to support the lightning proposals of their eternally energetic episcopal relative.

In reporting Mrs. Smith's offer and the nuns' acceptance to Madame Barat, Philippine Duchesne made a very strong case for a house in Grand Coteau: first, that a Louisiana house would help support the one in Missouri: second, that the milder climate "agrees with some temperaments"; third, present debts could more quickly be paid off; fourth, with five good novices Florissant could still accept new postulants. She climaxed her defense, "Then too, we should be able to double the number of new religious, of pupils, and of poor children, and to spread devotion to the Sacred Heart of Jesus and set up new altars in His honor."[4] Like the bishop, she could marshal her persuasions well.

If her arguments were heartfelt, she was nevertheless unprepared for the speed with which her bishop decided to execute the plan. After an acquaintance of four years, she should not have been. Louis William DuBourg, Bishop of Louisiana and the Floridas, was incapable of marking time. When with Father Joseph Tichitoli he returned to Florissant on June 16 to celebrate the feast of St. Francis Regis at the convent, and give the veil and holy habit to Mathilde Hamilton, Bishop DuBourg resumed the discussion of Grand Coteau with undiminished fervor. Two weeks later all discussion ended. On July 30 DuBourg arrived to announce that Madame Eugénie Audé should be ready by August 5 to leave for Lower Louisiana, that he was reserving two places on the *Rapide* for that Sunday.[5]

Again, as highhanded as he may have seemed, the bishop had his reasons. Father Andrew Ferrari, C. M., whom the Religious of the Sacred Heart knew as their excellent retreat master, was taking the same boat, as was a group of schoolboys from DuBourg's college in charge of a respected Negro woman, who promised to take good care of Madame Audé and her companion. The bishop had already written to both Mrs. Smith and Father Hercule Brassac at Grand Coteau letters of introduction for their arrival. He did all that he thought would ensure them a pleasant trip and a safe arrival; from his meagre store he gave what he could for the new house. Madame Duchesne assured Paris, "Monseigneur added some books, vestments, candelabra, and four handsome pictures. . . . He would have given her his whole house, had he been able to do so."[6]

DuBourg was quite aware of the void Eugénie Audé's departure left. She was the jewel of the American motherhouse; as Madame Duchesne said sadly, "She was my right arm." He was keenly moved to receive from Florissant a note thanking him for his thoughtfulness toward her and replied swiftly:

> You speak to me of your gratitude and that of Me. Eugénie. As bishop I am very in arrears with you; and by what care could I ever repay myself the good you have done in my diocese? I would have given all I had to this excellent young person, if she could have carried it away. We will have occasion to get to her what she will need.[7]

He would bring over on Monday newly ordained Aristide Anduze to offer his first Mass at the convent chapel, and suggested, "It seems to me you could permit the students to hear the Mass with you from your room." He always liked to have young people share the special joys of the Church's liturgies on these occasions.

He returned again in September with Rector Rosati from the Barrens seminary to chat with two postulants who were having trouble adjusting to a religious life,[8] and was pleased when Rosati said enthusiastically that Perryville ought to have a Sacred Heart school before long. Perry County had recently been formally organized as a political entity, and the future of the area around the Barrens seemed more promising than ever.[9]

In October the bishop brought Madame Duchesne other visitors. A fellow Sulpician of former years, Gabriel Richard, the famous missionary of the Detroit Territory who would soon become the first Catholic priest to sit in Congress,[10] was visiting St. Louis and had business with her. Richard had a few religious women in his jurisdiction who needed a superior and asked Madame Duchesne if she would furnish one. DuBourg was unenthusiastic and told her, "There would be more difficulty in this project than appears at first sight. But I am convinced that when the time comes for executing the project you will do nothing without counsel. Until then I urge you to contract no promise in order not to embarrass yourself."[11] With Madame Audé just gone to Grand Coteau it was no time to deplete Florissant further.

The bishop's more pressing concern just then was Grand Coteau and Audé's uneasiness over the title to the property of her school, and he assured Duchesne, "I will not delay seeing Me. Eugénie and put her mind at ease over the donation of Mrs. Smith."[12] Having been in St. Louis little more than four months, he now prepared to go downriver again.

As usual, under pressure his mind worked with amazing speed. At the convent in early October he called a conference of his college priests together with John Baptist

Acquaroni from Portage Des Sioux. Francis Niel reported that the people running the college had all signed an agreement that they would work only for the good of that institution, renouncing "any claim or retribution for the services . . . rendered . . . satisfied to receive . . . no other recompense than food and raiment," and promising that on leaving—either voluntarily or by dismissal—would not "claim or be entitled to, any kind of remuneration whatsoever." This remarkable document was signed by President Niel, Aristide Anduze, Leo Deys, Edmond Saulnier, Samuel B. Smith, and E. de Geyter as well as two workers, one male and one female, who simply made their mark.[13] It appeared that Niel had forestalled unforeseen financial tribulations for his school for the coming year.

DuBourg provided for the convent by giving Father de la Croix "all the powers of a vicar general" for that house, and in his absence provided that Francis Xavier Dahmen would substitute for Charles de la Croix.[14] It was not to the bishop's liking to miss the dedication of the fine new Church of St. Ferdinand that fall, as he had missed the laying of its cornerstone in February.[15] He had resolved to put the axe to the roots of trusteeism in Missouri on the occasion scheduled for November 21. Instead, on October 11 he feverishly wrote out decrees on both trusteeism and pew rents to be read at the consecration and had Gabriel Richard sign as one of his witnesses. The former decree said categorically that the "powers of the trustees named by the parish shall cease from the moment of the blessing of the new church," and that Charles de la Croix, the pastor, "shall be the sole trustee under our authority."[16]

Two weeks before these regulations could be announced, the Bishop of Louisiana was baptizing members of his flock at St. Gabriel's Church in Iberville, Louisiana, some twenty miles below Baton Rouge,[17] and by the day after Christmas was writing confidently to Madame Duchesne from Grand Coteau, "It is still a little flock, but it will grow, and the limitless devotion of Mrs. Smith leaves me without any anxiety for its solidity."[18] On December 30, 1821, he was in Lafayette, Louisiana, blessing the new Church of St. John the Evangelist with the assistance of

Hercule Brassac and Marcel Borella.[19] It had been a long and tiring year, with so much travel, but so much more needed to be done.

His most loyal and generous friends, the Ursulines, were about to embark on a major building venture on property they had owned since 1818 about three miles down the river from New Orleans on the same side of the Mississippi. Mother St. Michel Gensoul would not have the satisfaction of supervising this long-awaited enterprise. She was tiring with age and poor health, and her successor would already have been chosen during the Octave of St. Ursula in 1821, but learning that their "most illustrious prelate" was coming in the new year the nuns deferred their election until February 6, 1822. On that day, Sister St. Joseph de Laclotte— whom Victoire had befriended in Baltimore a dozen years earlier—was elected; in the presence of the bishop, Louis Sibourd, and Benedict Richard, who was now the Ursulines' chaplain,[20] she received the pledge of submission from her sisters. At least in *that* house DuBourg could rely on constant support.

With the prospect of a larger, new home outside the city, it became urgent to secure more women for their expanding work. DuBourg the previous summer had asked Bishop Plessis of Quebec for some women to augment the New Orleans house, explaining that the old nuns were dying off and the new ones were still too young for the responsibilities ahead. He continued:

> It is indispensable for the maintenance of the institution that there should come to it three or four religious already professed, of mature age, that is to say about forty and forty-three years old of proved judgment and virtue, who could fill the gap which separates the old from the young. . . .I have been told that in Canada there are two large houses of the same institute, one at Quebec, the other at Three Rivers.[21]

The superior at New Orleans had written to both houses, Sibourd had written to the pastor at Montreal in their behalf, and DuBourg felt that a word from Plessis would serve to reinforce their pleas.

Plessis had responded quickly, promising to get Du-

Bourg several subjects for Louisiana. In February 1822 DuBourg began to make arrangements for their trip from Canada to New Orleans, notifying Plessis:

> The Abbé Janvier, one of my priests, a most prudent and virtuous man, is preparing to leave Detroit (where he has been for three years with my permission) in charge of three nuns destined also for the convent in New Orleans. . . . I advised him to go with his companions to Montreal. . . . Your nuns should go to the same place, whence they will all travel together, in care of Mr. Janvier . . . as far as New York, and thence here by sea.[22]

Andrew Morris, that staunch old friend of other days, would procure suitable lodgings for the ladies in New York City. Janvier's party should not arrive before late fall in order to avoid the yellow fever epidemic common in New Orleans.

DuBourg could not wait to pass on this good news to Madame Duchesne, saying expansively, "The Ursuline ladies are expecting a reinforcement of three professed Ursulines from Quebec and three of the sisters of Mr. Richard from Detroit." He knew that she would rejoice that the women to whom she could not furnish a superior, when Gabriel Richard made the request, would be able to preserve their vocations in New Orleans.[23]

The bishop was enormously touched and elated when on Tuesday of Holy Week the Ursulines confided to him the "full and absolute" direction of the construction of the new convent.[24] They had already promised him their present convent for his residence, and as he headed for St. Louis at the end of May[25] he was at peace with himself and his accomplishments. A fine new church dedicated to St. John the Baptist had been consecrated on the fourth Sunday in Lent at Edgard on the "German Coast" of the river, a ceremony performed in the company of some of his most trusted missionaries.[26] Best of all, on April 18 Charles de la Croix had left for a mission to the Osage Indians.[27]

On the very heels of his consecration in Rome, DuBourg's thoughts had leaped ahead to the Indians within his jurisdiction, and on October 5, 1815, he had asked Archbishop Carroll to pass on his ideas to President Madison, whose "solicitude" for the civilization of the tribes might induce him to favor for Catholic missionaries gifts of land and government subsidies like those offered to "any zealous minister."[28] It was no mere passing fancy, for on February 5, 1816, having learned of John Carroll's death the previous December, DuBourg quickly approached the archbishop's successor, Leonard Neale, on the same subject, saying that in his last letter to Carroll he had particularly expressed his hopes of obtaining a small colony of Jesuits and Camaldolese monks "destined to form a permanent seminary of missionaries for the poor Indians." He reiterated his desire for government lands and subsidies for work among the Florida and Missouri Indians. He knew this to have been "always a favourite scheme with Government, and that provisions of this kind, for the same object, had . . . not only been preferred, but actually supplied to the late Rev. Mr. Rivet at Illinois, and the Rev. Mr. Richard at Detroit." Giving Neale his Bordeaux address, he asked him to promote this idea.[29] By the time DuBourg returned to the United States, Neale was also dead, and Madison had been succeeded by James Monroe; but the two proposals, one for Jesuits and the other for government support, remained firmly fixed in DuBourg's thoughts for the future.

The challenge of "hundreds of Indian tribes that seem but to wait for instruction in order to embrace the faith"[30] was not only in the bishop's mind as he took up the shepherd's crook in St. Louis in 1818; it also appealed to many European missionaries opting for the United States in the early nineteenth century. Felix De Andreis, while remaining in Kentucky with Flaget in 1817, confessed:

> I feel strongly impelled to devote myself, in a particular manner, to the conversion of the Indian tribes who live beyond the Mississippi. Here in Kentucky no trace of them remains, while, on the contrary, the Mississippi, which serves as a boundary to the United States . . . flows by St. Louis, and makes of it the central point of all these savage nations. Among these, so far, the light of the gospel has never penetrated, though they seem well disposed to receive it.[31]

He envisioned establishing a seminary for Bishop DuBourg, entrusting it to Father Joseph Rosati, and then wending his way along the banks of the Mississippi and Missouri Rivers, preaching the Gospel to the Indians. In the interim, he intended to have the catechism translated into their language.

De Andreis soon discovered the difficulties of such a task, and told a friend in Italy:

> With the assistance of an interpreter, I have made some attempts to arrange their principal language according to grammatical rule. It is a difficult undertaking, as my interpreter, knowing nothing of such laws, cannot translate word for word, nor supply me with equivalent expressions for every idea. However, I have begun a small dictionary, and made some translations. Their scarcity of ideas renders their language poor in words. They are constantly obliged to express themselves with the aid of circumlocution, especially on the subject of religion.[32]

Acting as DuBourg's vicar general, training novices for the Congregation of the Mission, and teaching seminarians, left De Andreis little time for Indian missions; nevertheless, *l'Ami* noted:

> M. de Andreis has baptized several times at the high Mass as often as he could enter into the habitation. He explained one after the other, the baptismal ceremonies to the people assembled. These adults were savages, or semi-savage, or of all sects and nations.[33]

The year after De Andreis and DuBourg settled in St. Louis, John C. Calhoun circulated a letter from the War Department in Washington announcing that Congress had voted an annual appropriation of $10,000 for the "civilization" of the Indians. Educational institutions undertaking such work could apply to the Secretary of War for funds from this appropriation.[34] Unfortunately for Missouri, DuBourg would need a school and missionaries to staff it, before he could take advantage of this offer; and in 1819 neither his school for boys in St. Louis nor his seminary for priests had yet a permanent home.

In the summer of 1820 the subject of Indians was on everyone's tongue and Madame Duchesne wrote to Paris:

> An event that gave me the greatest amount of pleasure recently was the deputation that reached St. Louis from the Osage Indians a savage tribe. The chief came to ask Bishop DuBourg to pay a visit to his people. The Bishop is going there next month with some Missouri River traders who have promised to help him in every way so that he may be treated with respect among these peoples, something like the way the Portuguese merchants helped St. Francis Xavier. . . . Monseigneur gave this Indian chief a crucifix, which he accepted very reverently. He then went into a store. The merchant who owns the place wanted to see whether or not he really valued the crucifix, so he offered him in exchange for it a very handsome saddle, then some liquor, then a big sum of money. The Indian refused all three, saying he would not part with the gift which he had received from the man who talked with the Author of Life.[35]

The deputation of chiefs headed by Sans-Nerf had been encouraged to come by the Indian agent William Clark, and their arrival was enormously fascinating to DuBourg's Italian and French recruits, both those who were actual eye-witnesses and those who listened avidly afterward. One of these described the event in detail:

> They all visited our Bishop, whom they call the "Chief of the Black Robes." As they have a high opinion of him they came in full dress. Their copper-colored bodies were coated with grease, their faces and arms were striped in different colors, white lead, vermillion, verdigris and other colors formed a great variety of furrows, all starting at the nose. Their hair was arranged in tufts. Bracelets, earrings, rings in their noses and lips completed their head-dress. Their shoes are made of buckskin which they ornament with different designs in feathers of various colors; hanging from their robes are little pieces of tin shaped like small pipes. These are to them the most beautiful ornaments. Their great object is to make a noise when they walk or dance. Their heads are ornamented with a sort of crown in which are mixed up birds' heads, bears' claws and little stag horns. A woolen robe hung over the shoulders covers nearly all the rest of the

body; and again, to this robe are fastened the tails of different animals, etc. Such is the attire in which the chiefs of the Osages paid their respects to the Bishop of Louisiana. He has in his room a handsome crucifix of ivory, a small picture of St. Thomas and a few other paintings. The sight of the crucifix struck them with astonishment. They gazed at it, their expression wondering and softened. The Bishop profited by this occasion to announce to them Jesus Christ.[36]

Before leaving, Sans-Nerf said to the bishop through an interpreter that he would be well received if he would come to their homes, that he could "pour water on many heads." The bishop promised to do so, and gave each chief a little crucifix and a medal which he hung around their necks with the admonition to guard them carefully.

When the Osages departed, one of them forgot to go through the ceremony of handkissing, which was a symbol of friendship to him, and when he was some distance gone recalled his omission and "turned back immediately, running all the way, and uttering loud cries, kissed the Bishop's hand and departed once more."[37] The esteem the Osages retained for DuBourg after this meeting was demonstrated not long afterward when the seven Osage chiefs visited the nation's capital.

> Being in Washington as guests of the Government each was the recipient at the hands of President Monroe of a superb uniform and a silver medal. At the banquet tendered the chiefs the President drank to the health of George Washington while the distinguished guests who followed him also proposed the health of some American celebrity. When it came to Sans-Nerf's turn, there was a general expectation that he would propose the President's health, but to the great surprise of the gathering he exclaimed, "I drink to the health of our good Father, the chief of the Black-robes, who lives in the village of the Chouteaus."[38]

When Bishop DuBourg in 1820 promised the Osages he would visit "those immense forests" west of St. Louis he had intended to take with him his vicar general and superior of the Vincentians, Felix De Andreis, who exclaimed

joyfully, "Alleluia! Deo Gratias! At length we are to commence a mission among the savages. I am to have the
happiness of accompanying the Bishop to visit these unfortunate people."[39] Instead, the bishop had the dreadful un-
happiness of burying Father De Andreis only a few weeks
later, and the visit to the Indians had to be shelved for that
year.

While DuBourg was visiting Lower Louisiana in the
months following De Andreis's death, the Indians remained
on his mind, and he pleaded with Propaganda to get him
some Jesuits to serve his Indian missions. If he could have
Father Barat from Bordeaux and five or six of his colleagues—perhaps augmented by two or three from Maryland—he could manage. Otherwise, the Protestant
missionaries might win out in the end.[40] In fact, while Du-
Bourg was still in the New Orleans region a feature in the
Gazette de la Louisiane datelined Philadelphia, March 16,
1821, described the triumphant send-off of the "Great Osage Mission Family." Arriving from Trenton, New Jersey,
this intrepid Protestant missionary group had spent a week
in Philadelphia, featuring a different preacher and prayer
leader in each pulpit, and collecting a total of $1,745.01,
after which their wagons headed west for Pittsburgh and
beyond.[41] It was this degree of zeal which could outdistance
hesitant Catholicism, and the Bishop of Louisiana knew it.

The Congregation of the Propaganda in Rome was not
deaf to DuBourg's entreaties, and Cardinal Fontana
sounded out the Jesuit General Aloysius Fortris,[42] but to no
avail. Fontana notified DuBourg that summer:

> I did not fail to recommend warmly to the Superior General
> of said society. But from the answer returned by him, a copy
> of which I enclose, you may easily understand that, by
> reason of the scarcity of laborers, he is for the present
> unable to undertake this noble work. It accordingly devolves
> upon you to adopt other means. . . . No work, indeed, is
> holier and more apostolic than that of turning barbarous
> nations, plunged in the darkness of error, to the light of truth
> and the path of eternal salvation. What I know of your
> solicitude and zeal assures me that you will not neglect these
> means.[43]

The only "other means" available to the Bishop of Louisiana was to send some one of his already overworked priests on a brief mission to Indian country.

On January 30, 1822, Father de la Croix wrote to Rosati at the Barrens:

> Madame Auguste Chouteau told me that her husband will be here in eight or ten days and that he hopes to leave for the Indians in the month of March. As I am to leave with him, according to the instructions of Monseigneur, our worthy Bishop, I beg you as a favor to send me Mr. Dahmen for that time, as I have quite made up my mind to leave with Mr. Chouteau . . . . I beg you, Monsieur, not to forget the crosses and medals which you promised me for the Indians.[44]

Rosati of course complied, and on April 16 Madame Duchesne told a friend, "Tomorrow our chaplain leaves for the Osage mission. A Lazarist priest will replace him."[45] On April 17, 1822, DuBourg's first missionary set out for Osage country, where over 5,000 Indians—the Great Osage, the Little Osage, and the Arkansas—awaited the Gospel message.

The priest whom the bishop liked to call his "Angel" found this an almost thankless assignment. He reached his destination just as the Indians were about to set out on a hunting expedition and he had time to visit only one village. After traveling twelve days on horseback, across prairies broken by forests and streams,[46] he was bitterly disappointed to reach so few hearts, to "pour water" on so few heads. Bishop DuBourg, nevertheless, wearing his customary rose-tinted spectacles, was elated at this first beginning, and announced to Margaret George, his devoted friend at St. Joseph House in Emmitsburg:

> An establishment is now in forwardness for the Osage nation, in which the first Catholic missionary has been received with the most glowing effusions of love and confidence, whilst the [Presbyterian] Missionaries, tho' strongly supported by Government, are pining in neglect and inaction. The Indians have their old traditions of the *Robe noire,*

614

of the cross, of Catholic rites; nothing but that will satisfy them.[47]

Knowing how his friend at the Mount was always talking about going off to be a missionary,[48] the bishop added, "Show this to my good friend Mr. Bruté; I know how much he will be interested in this prospect; and his prayers will contribute not a little to realize it."

Father de la Croix set out again on July 22, again leaving his Florissant flock in the hands of Dahmen, who this time had occasional assistance from Aristide Anduze and Hercule Brassac.[49] Pushing beyond the first village he had visited, the missionary traveled along the banks of the Missouri River "a hundred leagues beyond the nation of the Osages, among a great number of other savages."[50] One tradition has him reaching as far as the mouth of the Kaw River, near the site of today's Kansas City. Between August 11 and 16 he baptized thirteen people saying later:

> The day for baptizing having come, I fixed up my altar as well as I could. The chief ornament was a handsome banner from Madame Duchesne, showing a beautiful picture of the Blessed Virgin embroidered by the young Ladies of the Sacred Heart Boarding School. It was an object of delight to the Indian women.[51]

At the principal village of the Osages he addressed a great council of the nation.

The excessive heat of the prairies in summer, however, soon levied its toll on the missionary and the fever, "from which he suffered almost constantly . . . . prevented him from prolonging his sojourn and obliged him also to abandon his intention of building a church in that part of the country."[52] It was some weeks before he quite recovered and found time to write to Rosati:

> It is now four weeks since I returned from my second visit to the Osage. Again I was received very well by the natives. I saw the entire nation. I had the good fortune to speak to them in a great council in which all the chiefs, natives and fighting men were assembled. I spoke to them in surplice

and stole and with a crucifix in my hand (whereat all seemed to be greatly pleased) in presence of two Presbyterian ministers. The Osage nation is ready to receive Catholic missionaries as soon as the Bishop can send them some. The heat, thirst and fatigue made me fall into a fever. I traveled from three to four hundred miles while so indisposed. The good God gave me strength enough to reach Florissant and I begin now to feel better. I had the happiness of saying Mass eight days after my arrival here.[53]

One small detail of his trip, which the valiant missionary neglected to mention, was its ecumenical overtones; the Catholic priest left his altar equipment and liturgical vestments with the Presbyterians at their Harmony Mission, where Jesuit Father Charles Van Quickenborne found them five years later on his own first visit to the Osages.[54]

In the January following her chaplain's safe return from Indian territory, Madame Duchesne speaking of their bishop's peregrinations remarked, "Our *Seer* is away just now. I think he went to Baltimore to straighten out a misunderstanding with his colleagues or to ask the Jesuits to help with the missions to the savages. I feel that nothing can be done without them."[55] The bishop had been joking with her about the questionable odor left behind his departures from Baltimore's Saint-Sulpice. Actually, he was sure of his welcome this time, for Tessier, months before his arrival, had written warmly, congratulating the bishop on the success religion continued to have in Louisiana and offering him hospitality when he came in the autumn of 1822.[56]

Bishop DuBourg started his trip east in October, going by way of the Barrens seminary to see how the new men Inglesi had recruited were faring. One of them, John Mary Odin of Lyon, wrote back to Jean Cholleton at St. Irenaeus:

The 10th of October we had a visit from Bishop DuBourg. He showed much kindness to me and M. Blanc (whose brother is already in Louisiana) and on the 12th he ordained one subdeacon and the other deacon. I could never tire of admiring the sweetness, the goodness, and the great qualities of a holy bishop. He was suffering a little but he refused all the remedies one could get for him. He shared at our table the poor food we are served; but the meagre fare did nothing to take away the gaiety which you know in him.[57]

Although the bishop was still feeling some lingering effects of his summer illness, he was in good spirits as he started up the Ohio River with Aristide Anduze, who accompanied him. Young Anduze had come to Missouri in 1820 at Bruté's suggestion. He had begun his studies at Mount St. Mary's in Emmitsburg, where he was the first to enter the course in theology after Archbishop Maréchal granted permission for a two-year course at the Mount.[58] On June 23, 1819, Bruté recommended him to the archbishop as acceptable for study in the major seminary in Baltimore,[59] and on June 28 Anduze entered St. Mary's Seminary, where he was listed as Matthieu Bernard Anduze. The seminary list of seminarians says only that "having given some dissatisfaction, he asked to resign the 21 of January 1820."[60]

In mid-July, announcing young Anduze's safe arrival in Missouri, DuBourg commented approvingly to Bruté, "He is very tenderly attached to you. I hope he will settle here. He evinces the best of aptitudes, and especially the one I prefer to all others, candour."[61] After his ordination Anduze was assigned to the faculty of the College of St. Louis,[62] which since the fall after his arrival occupied the new two-story brick building standing on the site of the old log cathedral. The bishop came to rely on him as a part-time secretary while the two men lived in St. Louis.[63] Bruté would be glad to see Anduze again and would offer him hospitality at the Mount, if needed.

Since none of their former plans to meet had yet materialized, DuBourg intended to visit Flaget en route to Baltimore. From Louisville on October 30 DuBourg told Rosati:

I am enchanted with all that I see in this diocese. The establishment at Bardstown is prodigious. I have noticed the large part Monseigneur draws from the Sisters, particularly those of Mr. Nerinckx. The thought has come to me to ask for some for the Barrens. These daughters would be a treasure of edification: they instruct young people, and further, they furnish clothing for the Seminary without costing it anything, so to speak, because they also cultivate their land. I have not wished to do anything without consulting you; if you want them, speak about it to the Congregation, and write to Mr. Nerinckx. It would be a matter of constructing some buildings, for which I believe that the Congregation would take pleasure in aiding you. It's a matter for reflexion. Another great advantage one could reap from these holy daughters is that as they multiply they would be found excellent servants for the colleges. Monseigneur has seven of them in his establishment at Bardstown.[64]

The spur of Flaget's accomplishments, and the excitement which always accompanied new plans for his own diocese, compensated Bishop DuBourg somewhat for the miseries of this first leg of his journey east of the Mississippi. As he told Rosati, "The weather having been abominable for some days kept us in an inn three days. But good comes from evil. This rain has given water to the Ohio, which permits steamboats to navigate." As primitive as these vessels still were, they were better by far than overland travel. Embarking for Wheeling on October 30, he hoped to be in Baltimore between November 10 to 15.[65]

The delay in Louisville at least gave DuBourg time to get Rosati two hundred splendid apple trees and write out full directions for their planting and care; and he opened up a correspondence between Portier in Louisiana and a purveyor of beeswax in Louisville so that Bigeschi at La Fourche could have the wax he was pining for. The wax could be sent free to New Orleans where they could pay for it when they were able. The bishop was always relieved when payments could be delayed.

The original motive behind DuBourg's going east that autumn was the matter of the Ursuline property within the city of New Orleans which the nuns wished to bestow upon the Diocese of New Orleans in the persons of Bishop DuBourg and his successors. Before going ahead with his plans for the property to become his, DuBourg wished to have a categorical assurance from the government of the United States that the property at issue was in fact the Ursulines' property to transfer. On the completion of this "principal and all-important" business, the Bishop of Louisiana returned from Washington to Baltimore to hear what he thought was very good news. He swiftly passed it on to Rosati on December 3:

> Two excellent subjects, advanced in their theology, request entering my diocese, and being admitted in your Congregation. One, the nephew of the late Bishop Egan of Philadelphia, has been raised since his infancy in the Seminary in Emmitsburg, where he has been teaching for 5 or 6 years. He was born in Ireland. His father had his domicile and left his properties in Baton Rouge. Just between us his departure would greatly displease and frustrate many hopes here, for he is very esteemed: but 1st he believes himself from my diocese (*ratione paterni domicilii*), 2nd he has satisfied that of Baltimore for the education which he received there—3rd he wishes to enter Religion and believes himself called to your Congregation. He has written me on all that. I have replied without encouraging him too much, counseling him to remain where he is, at least until he is certain of his vocation, in which case I will send him to you for admission.[66]

Michael de Burgo Egan, who had been teaching with Bruté at Mount St. Mary's, may have had further reasons for contemplating leaving Emmitsburg. For some time both John Dubois and Bruté, who loved the Mount dearly, had been trying to keep the institutions there alive in the face of Maréchal's determination to suppress the college. Bishop DuBourg had been installed in St. Louis only a few weeks when his Emmitsburg friends found themselves compelled to defend their schools from Baltimore's attacks. Dubois, who was very garrulous on paper, was in February 1818 already beginning those voluminous letters which so irritated the Archbishop of Baltimore.[67] Bruté in May, in an emotional outburst to one Sulpician recently come to Baltimore from France, exclaimed, "It is very Sulpician to destroy! For destroyed you must be, dear friend, as quickly as Emmitsburg is destroyed; and destroyed you can't be so long as Emmitsburg lasts."[68]

During the five years since then, Bishop DuBourg had been aware of an increasing bitterness in Emmitsburg. At the start he had simply commented, "I hear strange accounts about our dear foster-child of the Mountain. . . .I still hope that Divine mercy will direct everything for His greater glory";[69] the next year, however, he reacted more particularly to the news which continued to reach him, telling Bruté:

> I have in the course of time learned of the decision of our Gentlemen on the Seminary of Emmitsburg. It would have been quite useless for me to propose my advice on an affair to which they have never failed to regard me as a stranger. However having had occasion to write to Mr. Tessier, I told him my way of thinking, based as much, I believe, on reason as on the sentiment of predilection which I have always had for that house. A letter of Mr. Dubois informed me that the Superior General had upheld it; but that a difference of opinion exists between the Gentlemen of Baltimore and himself on the subject of the property and responsibility. No one more than I would rejoice to learn that all was finished to the reciprocal satisfaction of both parties. I would regard the fall of that institution as a veritable calamity. Its progress and that of our good Sisters fill me with joy and consolation.[70]

Now, in 1822, face to face with Bruté and Dubois, the bishop learned of the most recent developments—that the college at the Mount was completely divorced from the Sulpician seminary in Baltimore, not only financially as it had been for over two years, but spiritually as well, with Tessier no longer making visitations there. Dubois, its head, was trying in every way he could to find a way to keep the college alive, even "parleying with his confreres for reunion with Baltimore and a *modus vivendi.*"[71] On his return to Baltimore DuBourg wrote to Bruté at the Mount a somewhat guarded note of consolation, "I have seen here someone whose head seemed overheated by a letter of our friend [Dubois]. However, I have seen with pleasure that they render him justice, which leads me to hope that he will obtain a favorable compromise."[72]

The uncertainty of the Mount's future and the wrangling between the Gentlemen at Emmitsburg and those in Baltimore made Saint-Sulpice less likely to attract men just then, and Michael de Burgo Egan suggested to the Bishop of Louisiana that December another candidate for his diocese, whom DuBourg described to Rosati as "Irish, taking exception to the general rule, full of humility, talent, and learning, who is free to choose his diocese." His name was John Baptist Purcell. DuBourg advised Rosati that if Egan and Purcell wrote to him about coming to the Barrens he should make clear to everyone who might see his letter that neither Rosati nor the bishop had influenced these young men in their decision. "I assure you I am as innocent as you are," he insisted. But he knew Maréchal's penchant for seeing intrigue in anything involving the Bishop of Louisiana. There is no question that DuBourg would have been delighted to get Egan or Purcell, or both. Louisiana sorely needed English-speaking subjects, and, in spite of the prejudices against the Irish in some quarters, he was sure that Providence in addressing these two to him was making "two immeasurable gifts."[73]

As Advent approached its climax in 1822, the Bishop of Louisiana and the Floridas found it easy to count other blessings Providence seemed to lavish on his ministry. Certainly it was good to see again old friends in Washington and Maryland. It was delightful to find that "le petit Bernabeu," who had been one of his first pupils at St. Mary's College, was now Don Juan Bernabeu, the Spanish Consul in Baltimore, graciously willing to assist DuBourg in a matter involving Spanish tact and diplomacy. That winter a ship destined for New Orleans and carrying the remains of an early Roman martyr Saint Simplicius, intended for DuBourg's cathedral, had been intercepted and was being detained in Puerto Rico as a lawful prize. DuBourg requested Bernabeu to assist, "through some friend or suitable person," in the recovery of the precious relics.[74]

It was pleasant to think that his former young connections were proving so useful to their nations, as well as to the clergy when occasion demanded it. Dear Guillemin had been serving as French Consul in New Orleans since 1819, and a Menou was presently chargé d'affaires in Washington. None of this, however, was relevant to the business Du-Bourg intended to pursue in the new year. In Missouri, Indian tribes were still waiting.

CHAPTER XXVII

JESUITS FOR INDIAN MISSIONS

While DuBourg had completed his first business with the government in Washington by 1823, his second business, which, as Madame Duchesne had predicted, was to seek Jesuits, became a much more complicated set of negotiations than he could possibly have imagined, negotiations which detained him in the East until the end of March. In retrospect he chose to attribute the outcome as completely due to the workings of divine Providence, telling his brother Louis, "God in His infinite goodness has brought about one of those incidents which he alone can foresee and whose results He alone can direct." More to the point, he explained, "I have delayed, partly on account of the bad roads, but more especially in order to see the end of a negotiation which I had begun with the government on the one hand, and with the Jesuits on the other, for the establishment of Indian missions on the Missouri and the Upper Mississippi."[1]

The course of Bishop DuBourg's negotiations with the government, thanks to the publication of the *John C. Calhoun Papers,* is easy to trace. Following Calhoun's first circular on federal aid to Indian "civilization" in 1819, additional regulations had made applications for this aid somewhat easier. The United States government, if it had the means, and if it approved the proposal, would pay two-thirds of the expense of erecting the necessary buildings for Indian education.[2] While DuBourg was in Washington in 1822–1823, he had approached the Secretary of War on the matter of getting federal aid, and Calhoun suggested that the bishop put his proposals in concrete form for the record. On February 15, 1823, DuBourg wrote:

> Encouraged by the friendly attention with which you have been pleased to honour my advances for the establishment of Catholic missions among the native Indians of Missouri, I gladly meet your kind invitation, in submitting some considerations on that important subject, which, if approved, may serve as a basis of the concessions to be made by Government for the support of those missions.[3]

He began by pointing out that the federal regulations adopted for the civilization of Eastern tribes were premature for the Western and more remote Indians. As long as these latter had wide hunting ranges open before them they were not readily brought to set any value on the pursuits of civilized life. Rather, they positively resisted the introduction of teachers of arts and sciences among them. Instead, "the work of civilization should commence with humanizing them by the kind doctrines of Christianity," instilled by missionaries whose unremitting charity would subdue the ferocity of their hearts, and by degrees "assimilate their inclinations to those of their fellow Christians."

He therefore proposed sending a few missionaries, by way of trial at least, among the Indians of Missouri. Since he understood that money was very limited and to a great extent already allotted, he felt extremely delicate about making any specific request, contenting himself with the observation that a missionary could scarcely survive on less than $200 a year. He closed with three questions: what allowance would the government grant each missionary; to how many might that support be extended; and, in case establishments were made, what aid in either money or lands would be afforded.[4]

Bishop DuBourg received a prompt reply. Calhoun notified him that President James Monroe had approved a federal grant of $200 toward the annual support of as many as three missionaries if they were sent to remote tribes beyond the Osages and the line of military posts. Funds would be paid quarterly. Calhoun enclosed printed regulations regarding government support for buildings, and told DuBourg his missionaries should report their work, and secure their passports from Indian agent William Clark in St. Louis.[5]

In a subsequent exchange between the bishop and the Secretary of War, DuBourg got Calhoun's promise to support four, not three, missionaries while Calhoun designated three mission posts: at Council Bluffs, River St. Pierre, and Prairie du Chien. From the Visitation Convent in Georgetown on March 10, Bishop DuBourg sought written confirmation of this oral agreement and requested that General Clark in St. Louis might assist in conveying the missionaries to their posts.[6] Calhoun's letter the next day extended the encouragement of his February 20 letter to four missionaries and enclosed a copy of the letter to William Clark which DuBourg had requested.[7]

It is possible to wonder, at this point, how DuBourg could talk in terms of four missionaries and three posts in a matter of a few weeks' discussion with Calhoun. The explanation lies in that marvelous "incident" as he called it, the acquisition of a band of Jesuits for his diocese. Divinely smiled upon or not, the train of events attending this acquisition could scarcely have been maneuvered by Bishop DuBourg alone.

Back in 1817, while DuBourg was yet in Europe, Charles Nerinckx had recruited several Belgians who, on arriving in Baltimore, had decided to join the Jesuits and went to Whitemarsh for their novitiate. In 1820 Nerinckx again went to Europe, this time gaining seven more recruits who likewise resolved to become Jesuits, likewise went to Whitemarsh where since 1819 Charles Van Quickenborne had been master of novices.[8] At the time Bishop DuBourg came East, this Jesuit novitiate, virtually a Belgian enclave,

was on the verge of being closed. There was talk of removing it to St. Thomas Manor, or of the Belgians' returning to
Europe. A Jesuit historian comments ambivalently, "Bishop
DuBourg, on being advised of this critical state of affairs,
proposed or had proposed to him a transfer of the novitiate
to his diocese, with the design of realizing through their
agency his program of missionary enterprise among the
Indians of the west."[9]

The very name Whitemarsh was a cause for hottest
controversy just then between the Society of Jesus and the
Archbishop of Baltimore.[10] Maréchal had recently returned
from Rome with a papal order that the Jesuit Whitemarsh
plantation be given to him to support him in his office as
archbishop, an order which the Jesuits rejected. Whether or
not DuBourg knew about Maréchal's controversy with the
Jesuits before he came to Georgetown in November 1822,
he certainly knew of it before making his own arrangements
with the Jesuit superior, Charles Neale, in March 1823. On
his arrival in Washington the subject was already creeping
into conversations, and he wrote to Tessier in Baltimore
that he feared a violent storm might arise over Rome's
decision on Whitemarsh. He exclaimed, "Please God the
public papers will not propagate scandal further!" The
Jesuits were complaining of having been condemned without being heard in Rome, were protesting the verdict, and
were ready to submit to an interdict sooner than abandon
their right to their property or sanction what they judged a
usurpation. The Bishop of Louisiana recommended loftily:
"Let our Gentlemen remember they are priests, French and
Sulpicians, and scrupulously avoid giving this affair any
suggestion of national interest or self-interest. Let us give to
religious and laity alike the example of respectful silence in
a matter which does not concern us."[11]

Tessier replied serenely that he did not think the archbishop had any intention of taking any striking measures
against the Jesuits, but that if they did not accord him what
he demanded, he would leave it all up to Propaganda. For
the rest, Tessier believed the matter did not seem to "make
much noise" in Baltimore.[12] Bishop DuBourg's seasonal

greetings to his episcopal confrere that December made no allusion to any Jesuit matters concerning either prelate, and were largely pious generalizations. The closest DuBourg came to anything of substance was his wish, "May you especially soon see an end to those sad differences which retard the consummation of the work you have so well begun for the consolidation and independence of your see."[13] And even this remark could have alluded to troubles in the suffragan sees of the Archdiocese of Baltimore.

Precisely when Bishop DuBourg himself began negotiations with the Jesuits in his own interest is not clear. Since he stayed in Georgetown during his first business with the government in late November, it is possible that he quickly learned of the imminent closing of the Whitemarsh novitiate. The new procurator of Georgetown College after September 1822 was Benedict Fenwick, whom DuBourg had had in class in 1805 and whom DuBourg would consistently support as a candidate for bishop in coming years. Although disparate in age, they liked each other's style and tended to view things in the same light. They remained on the same side of the Jesuit-novitiate issue that winter.

It is certain that by the first week in March 1823, talk of Bishop DuBourg's affairs had reached the Archbishop of Baltimore, and it is also certain that when they met, their discussion had not been a pleasant one. Maréchal was incensed at what he saw as the draining of his diocese to fill up DuBourg's. It seemed always to be DuBourg's lot to provoke Maréchal inadvertently while pursuing his own admirable goals. Although DuBourg was singularly obtuse while immersed in his own affairs, he did not enjoy being disliked or accused of giving offense, and before leaving again for Washington wrote to Maréchal trying to present his view of the situation. He had known none of the Whitemarsh novices in advance, nor had he known any of their plans. Neither he nor they, furthermore, had known anything of their novice-master's plans for them. Perhaps all the young Belgians would persist in their vocations; perhaps some would become diocesan clergy. "In the last hypothesis," he declared, "I don't want one of them." But if they were determined to become Jesuits and serve Indian missions, DuBourg said he could not see what right Maréchal had to oppose it, reasoning:

> These young men are strangers. They have cost the diocese nothing as such. They came to America to be Religious; they have persevered for 16 months in this determination. I can't quite see what you could found your right upon to object. However, I certainly do not attach as much importance to acquiring some subjects as to preserving charity, and consequently I hold only to what can be done without detriment to the unity which should exist between us. For that reason please make clear, without subterfuge, if you insist that I do not change any of these young men, or if you would find it acceptable that a certain number accompany me; for example, 3 or 4.

As for the Maryland seminarians, Egan and Purcell, he was quite disposed to refuse their services, since Maréchal objected.[14]

Back in Washington in mid-March, the Bishop of Louisiana had reached his decision. With the assurance of government aid, he felt no hesitancy, telling his brother Louis, "For an enterprise such as this, it was essential that I should have men especially called to this work."[15] There was nothing to be gained by further delay, and he notified Calhoun of his plans for the novitiate in Missouri, indicating that its site would be his farm in Florissant, fifteen miles from St. Louis and one mile from the Missouri River, that great highway to Indian territory. As he wrote, his dream expanded with his phrases and he concluded:

> Seven young Clergymen, from 22 to 27 years of age, of solid parts & an excellent classical Education, are now ready to set off at the first signal, under the guidance of two Superiors & Professors, and with an escort of a few faithful Mechanics & husbandmen, to commence the foundation. I calculate at about two years the time necessary to consolidate it, and to fit out most of those highly promising Candidates for the duties of the Missions, after which they will be anxious to be sent in different directions, according to the views & under the auspices of Government, whilst they will be replaced in

the Seminary by others, destined to continue the noble enterprise.[16]

Two days later Bishop DuBourg and Charles Neale, the Jesuit superior of the Maryland Province, signed a seven-article agreement providing for the removal of the White-marsh novitiate to Florissant.[17] On March 25 DuBourg deeded to Francis Neale "350 acres more or less" in Floris-sant to take effect as soon as DuBourg was notified that the pope ratified the agreement, or concordat, entered into by Charles Neale and DuBourg on March 19, 1823.[18]

Midway between these two agreements with the Jesuits, the Bishop of Louisiana revealed his decision to the Archbishop of Baltimore. Writing from the Visitation Convent in Georgetown to "My Lord and very dear Brother," DuBourg explained:

> After the harsh *explications* we had together in Baltimore, where . . . I was not fortunate enough to persuade you of my innocence in the business of the Jesuits, I came here firmly decided not to accept any of their propositions. Thus on my arrival I said so to Father Benedict Fenwick who left at once to carry my resolutions to his Superior. Two days later I saw Father Van Quickenborne arrive at my door from Port To-bacco and to my inexpressible surprise informed me that he had been ordered by his superior to leave with his *Socius* and all his novices. At first I understood nothing of what he was saying, knowing in advance that the plan of the Superior was to destroy the novitiate. He explained it to me saying that when the news had been brought to White-Marsh the novices declared they would die sooner than leave the So-ciety, and that in consequence the Superior had decided to save them and have them leave with their Masters to go make a foundation on the Missouri. . . . I argued against the project; Mr. Van Q. responded that he knew only the voice of his Superior to whom he had vowed obedience. . . .Shortly afterward, Father Ben. F. arrived to confirm these arrange-ments.[19]

From the other-worldly view so natural to his lips or to his pen, Bishop DuBourg told Maréchal:

I reflected that Providence seeming to act in this affair to procure for a throng of unbelieving nations scattered through my diocese the benefit of the faith, which I could not hope to be able to procure otherwise, I did not have the right to oppose what I had done nothing to obtain. . . . I believed I saw in this outcome the accomplishment of that remark of the Pope, addressed to me when I had the honor of seeing him for the first time and exposing the condition of my diocese: "You need Jesuits," words which by odd coincidence were repeated to me here by the Secretary of War while discussing with me the Indian missions.[20]

DuBourg was also a man of a ready, self-justifying logic. Surely the Jesuits had a right to dispose of their subjects for a work peculiarly suited to their destiny, he reasoned. Benedict Fenwick had told him that Charles Neale was simply following the wishes of their Father General in Europe, who several times had expressed surprise that the American Jesuits had not yet begun work among the Indians of Illinois, where the tradition of their labors was still preserved. How could DuBourg be expected to resist pressing offers made him to accept Jesuits in Missouri? Besides, opposition would have been useless; the novices would simply offer their services elsewhere. "Thus," he told Maréchal neatly, "I would lose them for my diocese without you gaining anything for yours."[21]

Taken all together, these considerations had persuaded DuBourg he was doing the right thing, and he hoped there need be no abatement of the bond of fraternal charity which ought to unite shepherds employed in different aspects of the same work. He told Maréchal he was confident that the "new arrangements" would not alter their friendship.

They were two quite different men, these Sulpicians become bishops. Once William DuBourg had summoned an array of propositions to support a step he meant to take, and did take, that ended the matter for him, as to both those who sided with him and those who opposed him on the issue. With Maréchal it was different. His mind, his charity, could accept opposition in theory. But in retrospect, his nature required that he see himself as a victim of conniving and cabal. To his sympathetic friend Garnier in Paris, he unburdened himself on March 25, 1823. Instead of giving a history of his recent voyage back from France, the archbishop began, he would treat of affairs infinitely more important, particularly an event giving him great affliction:

> Bishop Dubourg, who was very bored at St. Louis, has come to pay us a visit. He was accompanied by a young priest who was driven out of the Baltimore Seminary for reason of bad habits. From here he took refuge in St. Louis where, to the great astonishment of those who knew him, he was precipitately ordained. Bishop DuBourg, having this intriguer with him, used him to excite heads first in the Minor Seminary of Emmitsburg, and then here in the Major Seminary. . . . No little care was needed to restore the calm disturbed by these secret and seductive discourses.

Having upset both Sulpician seminaries DuBourg then took off for Washington where by means of a lawyer he got government aid for missionaries to live among the Indians. Soon he had to have Jesuits. Maréchal continued balefully:

> To procure them he seized on a circumstance which appeared favorable to his designs. He saw that the Jesuits were divided into two distinct parties opposing one another, the American Jesuits versus the Flemish Jesuits. Since a revolution which occurred last year in the Society, the Americans possess all the offices. Bishop DuBourg having learned that there were seven young Flemings under the supervision of two priests of their nationality at Whitemarsh, found a young American Jesuit who has persuaded Father Neale to get rid of them all, freeing them for the Bishop, who takes away with him these 9 ecclesiastics to whom others from one side or another will be united en route.

All decent, sensible people, of course, deplored this seduction of subjects from the jurisdiction of the archbishop, who had tried in vain to prevent it. Then, suspiciously, Maréchal added, "I would not be surprised if the young intriguer of whom I spoke above were not to play in Europe the role of Inglesi." Whether Maréchal meant Benedict Fenwick, that Jesuit intriguer, or Aristide Anduze, that confounder of seminaries, is not quite clear. In any case, the Archbishop of Baltimore profoundly hoped that people in France would remain *en garde* against DuBourg's version of things "represented in very beautiful colors" but which Maréchal dreaded "in the end will be prejudicial to the prosperity of religion."[22]

The Jesuit agreement with the Bishop of Louisiana was certainly not a premeditated plot to denude the Archdiocese of Baltimore of its clergy. It was rather a coinciding of needs on both sides. As Benedict Fenwick explained to the Jesuit General in Europe, the missionaries were sorely needed in the Diocese of Louisiana, and the availability of government support was most opportune. DuBourg had always been anxious to establish the Society of Jesus in his diocese, and the financial situation of the Society in 1823 demanded that some of its members be placed somewhere offering a sound means of support. Because the Belgian Jesuits had not yet become accustomed to the Anglo-American culture of the East, the Franco-American Missouri mission field offered them a better chance to work usefully. "These were the chief motives," according to Fenwick, which had induced Charles Neale to accept the offer made him by the Department of War and to accede to the wishes of DuBourg. There was one thing further, Fenwick believed:

> A fifth motive might be added, which might have also contributed to influence his determination as he apprehended at that time persecution on the part of the Archbishop of Baltimore in consequence of his refusal (a thing he had no power to grant) to surrender the [Whitemarsh] Plantation to him. . ., viz.: The obtaining in a New Diocese an Asylum where the Society . . . would experience no interruption, & where its members would have no other enemies to encounter but such as are equally enemies to God and his holy religion. . . .[23]

If Fenwick's evaluation be accepted, Maréchal himself may have been the catalyst in the novitiate's departure.

In March 1823, however, that master plotter and conniver, the Bishop of Louisiana, was back in the federal city, typically trying to stretch his luck. Having won from President Monroe the concession that an Indian school in Florissant could be substituted for missions in Indian territory, with federal funds beginning with the opening of the school, the bishop now pressed for having his Flemings paid from the time of their departure from Maryland.[24] This time the bishop had gone too far. The Secretary of War replied succinctly that under all the circumstances he thought it proper to defer any decision on the Reverend Mr. DuBourg's request.[25]

By then it was Holy Week and DuBourg, who meant to leave for St. Louis on Easter Monday, had many loose ends to tie up. On Tuesday he requested the French chargé d'affaires, Count Jacques de Menou, to notify Calhoun of the Flemings' departure, which would follow the bishop's by two weeks.[26] Most of Holy Saturday he spent writing his detailed report to Propaganda of his activities in Washington. His reason for going in the first place, he stated, was that:

> The Ursulines of New Orleans had been given, over eighty years ago by the French Government, to which Louisiana then belonged, a tract of land in the midst of the City, on which later on . . . they had built a large Monastery. Two years ago, however, as a consequence of a clerical error in the deed, the American Government claimed back one-third of the property. Although several times the nuns entered a reclamation in writing, their claim received no acknowledgment. I was advised, therefore by the lawyers to come to the seat of the Federal government. . . . This piece of property, indeed, is so valuable that I deemed that no effort should be spared to have the wrong righted.

He then reported the Ursulines' decision to move to a new location and their gift of the old convent to the bishops of New Orleans, which had added another complication. "I was afraid that, as they had been given this property by a former Government *for a special purpose,* if they left it the American Government would claim it back," he explained. Happily, in Washington, the bishop had both his petitions regarding the Ursuline property "graciously granted."[27]

He then gave the details clarifying his acquisition of the Maryland Jesuits and enclosed copies of his agreements with that province requesting Propaganda's approval. This left only Easter Sunday for the remaining correspondence in behalf of his mission band: an explanatory word to Father Van Quickenborne about their journey, a letter of introduction for him to present to Bishop Conwell of Philadelphia requesting the privilege of taking up a collection in the diocese to defray their expenses west, and a hasty note to Father Francis Roloff at Holy Trinity in Philadelphia.[28] Du-Bourg knew he was imposing on old friendship when he asked Roloff to accompany Van Quickenborne around the Diocese of Philadelphia to any house—Protestant or Catholic—where the Jesuit might collect the "widow's mite," but he knew Roloff's zeal and that the "dread of some rebuffs" would not cool it. A last, most lengthy letter was addressed to the Father General of the Jesuits in Rome to describe the recent negotiations involving the Flemings.[29]

It was the old story over again for the Bishop of Louisiana, trying to found a new institution with no money of his own, and feverishly tending to last-minute details before setting out on an arduous journey at the earliest possible moment permitted by road, river, and weather. On March 31 John Tessier noted in his diary what was to be the final departure of Louis William Valentine DuBourg from St. Mary's Seminary in Baltimore.[30]

At Wheeling on April 11 he penned a hasty letter to Don Juan Bernabeu explaining, "I have just heard through the Archbishop of Baltimore, who had heard from you that the holy body had been taken with a solemn escort of clergy and laity to the Holy Cathedral of Saint John of Puerto Rico, and it was to stay there with all reverence until it was claimed by me with the naming of someone in my confidence to whom it could be handed over with complete safety." Since DuBourg knew no one on the island, he hoped Don Juan as Spanish Consul would lend his influence with the political authority, Francisco Gonzales de Linares, to get "this holy relic" into trustworthy hands so that it could be sent "with all safety on the first boat which leaves that port for New Orleans."[31] The remains of Saint Simplicius had almost been forgotten in the press of Indian affairs.

By April 13 the bishop had reached Cincinnati where he planned to spend a few days, primarily to give Charles Nerinckx time to bring some Sisters of Loretto to Louisville, where DuBourg would meet them and conduct them to the Barrens. While DuBourg was away Rosati had acted swiftly on the bishop's suggestion of October about having Lorettines in Missouri, and by November 24, 1822, had begun preparing for their arrival. Rosati told Baccari in Rome:

> The support of the Sisters will be provided by their own labors and those of the children, as well as by the contributions of the parents who send their children to the Sisters to be instructed. . . . The monastery will be scarcely a quarter of a mile from the present church. . . . I have already seen them in Kentucky, having frequently heard their confessions, preached and said Mass in their chapel. Therefore, I have occasion to admire their regularity, fervor and austerity.[32]

Bishop DuBourg now in April sent Anduze on ahead to the Barrens to warn Rosati of their imminent arrival saying, "I will disembark at the home of the widow of Judge Bird, where I will deposit them and come immediately to the Seminary in order to send them some means of transportation. I presume we will arrive 8 or 10 days after this letter." Anduze would await the bishop at the Barrens, and in the meantime, Rosati would be wise to have everything ready in advance for the ordination, the bishop suggested.[33]

The brief respite in Ohio gave DuBourg a chance to visit with Edward Fenwick, O. P., who had been consecrated Bishop of Cincinnati the year before and was preparing to go to Europe soon in the interests of his diocese.[34] Fenwick was a veteran frontier missionary and like DuBourg, Flaget, and David saw the Church's work from that point of view. DuBourg was delighted to brief the Dominican prelate on European recruitment, and told him to be sure to look up Widow and Didier Petit in Lyon, among others. It was pleasant to feel like a senior adviser to a new bishop.

When DuBourg reached Louisville he found to his elation that Flaget had come up from Bardstown to get all the news of the Baltimore-Washington sojourn as well as to explain why the Lorettines were not leaving Kentucky just then. In November the original idea had been that four or five of these nuns would go to the Barrens; but Nerinckx their founder had changed this plan, telling Bishop DuBourg in April that this number was not sufficient to do their work well. A sisterhood should have a superior, a cook, two more to teach, and sisters for the garden and other manual work.[35] The thirteen women Nerinckx destined for Missouri thus did not leave Louisville until May 13, 1823. Following the usual course of events in the Diocese of Louisiana, the house meant for their convent was not ready on their arrival, and once again the generous Sarah Hayden came to the rescue, offering her hospitality, this time entertaining her own daughter, Sister Mechtildis, among the rest.[36]

While in Louisville Bishop DuBourg preached to a large audience in the courthouse, where his interpretation of the Scriptures and explanation of the sacrament of Penance was delivered with all his usual eloquence.[37] Then he hastened to the Barrens to ordain John Audizio and to charge Rosati with getting the Lorettines settled. After an absence of six months, he finally headed for St. Louis.

Bishop DuBourg spent very little time in Missouri that spring, and when he visited Florissant he seemed to Madame Duchesne very preoccupied. She commented later, "He came on the feast of the Ascension to give confirmation in our church and first Communion to 14 children, boarders and day pupils, left the next day, and that was the extent of his visit. He made far fewer inquiries than usual about what concerns the convent." Yet, at the end of this short visit, she knew that the Jesuit Flemings were coming "in complete dependence on Divine Providence," and were perfectly happy about it. She knew, too, that "as he was passing through Kentucky, Monseigneur secured twelve of the Sisters whose order was established in that Diocese by Father Nerinckx" and whose rule was very severe.[38]

Two days later the bishop notified Rosati, "I leave tomorrow for Louisiana." In Florissant he had found his plantation meant for the Jesuits "somewhat in disarray" and instead of giving the Negro workers there to Rosati, as he had planned, he told his friend at the Barrens, "I believe I must in conscience put my Negroes there for the conservation of the property and the advantage of Religion," at least until his Maryland missionaries got settled.[39] On May 11 he was on a steamboat headed south.

The Jesuit pilgrimage under Charles Van Quickenborne began on April 11 and ended on May 31, 1823. The band included some remarkable men, among them Peter J. DeSmet, the future missionary to the Indians of the Pacific Northwest, and Peter J. Verhaegen, the future first president of St. Louis University.[40] In addition to the two priests and seven novices, the band had three lay brothers, and three couples of Negroes. In the absence of the bishop they were welcomed to St. Louis by the five priests who ran the college. Father de la Croix came over on June 2 to conduct Father Van Quickenborne to Florissant and show him around the plantation with its three log cabins, the largest of which had once housed the Religious of the Sacred Heart while their own convent was being finished. The Jesuits turned the first spadeful of dirt for their monastery on the feast of St. Ignatius, July 31, 1823.[41]

Meanwhile, the novices slept in the loft of the log house, while Fathers Van Quickenborne and Timmermans used the first floor for part chapel, part dormitory. They were following already in the footsteps of their new bishop whose first years in St. Louis had been scarcely more luxurious. Madame Duchesne and her sisters were overjoyed to have the Jesuits nearby and "placed at their disposal an old structure which stood a few yards south of the church and was being used by the nuns for a school. With their inimitable Superioress in the lead, the nuns outdid themselves."[42] The young Flemings were lodged, fed, and fussed over as they had not been since they left home.

Father Van Quickenborne wrote to Bishop DuBourg of their cordial and affectionate reception in St. Louis by Francis Niel and his colleagues, and of his negotiations in Florissant with Hugh O'Neil, the farmer who had been cultivating the bishop's farm. "The liberality and generosity of your Excellency toward us has agreeably surprised us," he said. They had a wagon, a carriage, a couple of beef and several cows, a good number of pigs and some implements which put them in condition to work the farm and make it produce something even that year. "I hope that for all these favors your Excellency will find in us ministers who will be for you a subject of contentment," he said gratefully.

Van Quickenborne had found the Indian agent, William Clark, as good as his word, when on June 2 he had promised Calhoun, "In relation to the permission granted to Bishop de Burgh to send missionaries into the Indian country, every due attention shall be paid by me to promote the humane objects of the government as far as it is possible."[43] The Jesuit reported:

> He has encouraged me in a singular manner. He strongly approves the plan and will write to the government to have it on a larger scale. He has given me instructions which will prove very useful & he believes that this autumn we will have 6 Indian children. It seems he wants us to do well & that he is interested in the success of our undertaking.[44]

One thing distressed Van Quickenborne, however. Charles de la Croix who had been the convent's chaplain was determined to leave Florissant the following week, and the Jesuit novice master explained, "I find myself perplexed as to the direction of the convent. Our holy institute forbids me to take on such work." He would continue as Father de la Croix had done while waiting to hear from his superior in Maryland. Van Quickenborne was afraid that the Sacred Heart nuns had been too anxious to have Jesuits, and may have expressed their sentiments "with imprudence." Meanwhile, the two Jesuit priests would serve Florissant and the convent, as well as St. Charles, Portage Des Sioux, and Dardenne once a month.

DuBourg's Jesuits faced many uncertainties their first year in Missouri. After their departure from Whitemarsh, Charles Neale had died, to be replaced by Francis Neale. Living at St. Thomas Manor, the new superior of the Maryland Province was besieged with questions from Missouri. Could Van Quickenborne act as chaplain to the convent? What was he to say to government officials who wanted him to educate Indian youth? How should he deal with the mission churches at St. Charles, Portage, and Dardenne which were controlled by trustees? When would he get any money from the War Department?

Benedict Fenwick, who had gone at the death of Charles Neale to console the Carmelites at Port Tobacco on the death of their founder, passed this all on to DuBourg in New Orleans, when writing to answer some of the bishop's own questions on Jesuit matters. DuBourg was most concerned about getting some assistance for Van Quickenborne and Timmermans, and asked if John Theodore De Theux could be sent. Fenwick felt confident that the Maryland Jesuits would leave no stone unturned to promote the work in Missouri as soon as they could; but regretted to say, "At present we are too shackled to afford any aid." As for De Theux, he had never petitioned to go on that mission so far as Fenwick knew, but he might do so later. In any case, in the course of a few years—after the ship was under way— members would not be lacking. For the moment, she was just launched and the important thing was to keep her afloat. "I entertain no doubt that a favorable gale will come in time which will waft her even beyond the Rocky Mountains," Fenwick predicted.[45] Bishop DuBourg may have winced at this view, the metaphor was of the sea, instead of the farm or pasture, but it was the sort of thing he was always saying to Rosati and Duchesne when he had no material assistance to offer: "We can only commence the work."

Fenwick was more generous with his news. Of Maréchal he said:

> It appears that the storm only threatened while the thing was in agitation; after the line of march was taken up it com-

pletely subsided. A shrug of the shoulder was all that was manifested whenever the matter happened to be mentioned. As to our dispute about Whitemarsh, that affair seems to have gone completely to rest. The A. B. has been heard to say that he intends to think no more about it. For my part I have always heard it said that the greater the calm before an earthquake, the more tremendous was the explosion. Nothing has been heard yet from Rome. I shall give your Lordship early information of whatever may reach us from that quarter.

From his brother in Rome he had learned that it was rumored Pius VII was not likely to live very long, but whether a new pontiff would be more favorable to Maréchal or the Jesuits in the Whitemarsh business, Fenwick could only conjecture. He closed warmly, using French, "Be persuaded that however wicked and bad a Jesuit . . . I will always be all for you."[46]

At year's end, it seemed that the good ship at Florissant was not even launched. On December 12, 1823, Van Quickenborne wrote a devastating criticism to Maryland of the chasm between what Bishop DuBourg had promised and what was the actual state of affairs in Missouri. The farm was only two-thirds as extensive as described; there was still a mortgage on it; the bishop still held title to it. St. Ferdinand's Church still had a debt on it of $350. The bishop gave nothing to the Jesuit establishment. Inglesi who worked such wonders in the courts of Europe and from whom the bishop had expected $50,000 had blasted all his hopes. The properties at St. Charles and Portage did not provide the income Van Quickenborne had anticipated. Further, General Clark had informed him that until he actually had Indian boys in his school no government aid would be given. Clark had offered him two Indian boys that fall and was again urging him to take them, but Van Quickenborne adamantly held that "to take any without being paid for, is a thing which forbids itself." He concluded that he would consent to begin anything new or to enlarge their sphere only under pain of obedience.[47]

Two of the Jesuit complaints were due to circumstances which only time could remedy. Until Rome approved of the Jesuit establishment, the arrangement agreed to was that the bishop should retain title to the land. DuBourg had done all he could in that regard. Propaganda notified him that his project for an Indian Jesuit mission would be examined and in due course the decision would be announced.[48] That was in July. By February 1824 the cardinals considering the matter had received an additional appendix necessitated by a letter Maréchal had written to Cardinal Fesch condemning the "intrigues which assuredly one would not have believed DuBourg capable of"; Maréchal accused his Louisiana confrere of stealing away De Theux, who had just announced that he, too, was going to Missouri.[49] The Bishop of Louisiana could only wait upon the cardinals in Rome and their decision, after pondering the charges of the Archbishop of Baltimore.

The actual payment of federal aid was likewise contingent on an agreement between DuBourg and Calhoun that a school could be substituted for missions in Indian territory. It was not until May 1824 that the first two Sauk boys were accepted at Florissant, to be followed in June by three of the Iowas. Even then the War Department told Van Quickenborne that the $800 originally anticipated could not be paid to a school with only five pupils. Instead:

> The Secretary however, directs that the most that has ever been allowed for this purpose be allowed to you, which is one hundred dollars for each youth, which will be increased at that rate 'til you shall have received Eight, when the increase of appropriation will have reached its limits. A remittance of five hundred dollars has been made to General Clark to be paid to you in conformity with the above decision.[50]

DuBourg did what he could to get the money for the school, once it began, writing to Calhoun, by then Vice President of the United States, protesting the failure of the government to live up to its "sacred obligation" and expressing his confidence that the Vice President would see to it that his pledges as Secretary of War were redeemed.[51] The bishop also urged Thomas Hart Benton, now Senator from Missouri, to remind Calhoun that as of December 9, 1824, the Indian school at Florissant had received no reimbursement; Benton complied with his request in the matter.[52]

The other complaints of Father Van Quickenborne were more reasonable; although if he had known the bishop better he might have been prepared for the discrepancies. DuBourg always enlarged upon things. He described them as he hoped they would be some day. When he told his brother Louis that he had gotten federal aid it was "four or five" missionaries, not the actual four. The deed to the Florissant farm stated "350 arpents more or less." As for mortgages, everybody had these, and the bishop always expected, somehow, to pay them off before transferring the particular land in question. St. Ferdinand's Church was surely nothing to fret about.

On June 12, 1823, Father de la Croix wrote into the Baptismal Record of the church that after paying $6,000 for the new church he still owed $355, "which Mr. Van Quickenborne has the goodness to assume."[53] As pastor, Van Quickenborne was sole trustee, thanks to DuBourg's perspicacity the year before, and could easily pay off the church debt from pew rents.

The Bishop of Louisiana sincerely cared about the people he brought to his diocese. His was a most generous heart; his difficulty was that he had no purse to match it, and never would have. When Francis Neale was succeeded by Francis Dzierozynski, it was the bishop who had reason to feel apprehensive. DuBourg had hoped from the beginning that the Jesuits who came to Missouri could become a separate province; but the American superior declined to make, or postponed, any promise to send a separate superior to Florissant. When Father Timmermans died at the end of May, just when St. Regis Seminary for Indian boys was becoming a reality in 1824, Father Van Quickenborne was the solitary Jesuit priest left to handle all the work; and when a year later he still had been sent no associate, DuBourg wrote urgently to Dzierozynski that the burden resting on Van Quickenborne's shoulders must be lightened or he would collapse from sheer fatigue in a year or two. DuBourg said frankly that he was apprehensive about the properties promised to the Jesuits. Should St. Regis fail, he asked, "Would it be just that the diocese should lose the property I have given for that express purpose?"

The Bishop of Louisiana, when believing himself or a co-worker unjustly treated, could always take a high tone, and his peroration ended:

> My devotion to Yr. society has been everywhere known, ever since I could form an opinion, but allow me to tell you that I never could approve of policy which everywhere shrouds all its steps in an impenetrable mist. If I, a steady friend, if ever you had any, feel shocked at it, what must be the feeling of its enemies and what scope does not this *appearance* of duplicity give them to justify their inveteracy against it.[54]

It was quite normal for him to close this letter with cordial greetings to the Jesuits at Georgetown whom he assured of his sincere attachment in spite of "the appearance of severity in the above lines."

Father De Theux was, of course, permitted to come to assist Van Quickenborne, and the Jesuits remained in Missouri. The Indian school was not, however, the solution DuBourg had hoped, and it was closed in June 1831.[55] But by that time the Bishop of Louisiana had become the Bishop of Montauban in France, and the men he had brought to Missouri were serving Indians farther west than he had ever dreamed.

CHAPTER XXVIII

EPISCOPAL CONFRERES

It was early June and the Bishop of Louisiana was writing to congratulate the Archbishop of Baltimore for his fine pastoral letter[1] on the occasion of the consecration of the Baltimore Cathedral on May 31, 1821. DuBourg could remember the days in Baltimore when he had been involved personally in the cathedral's beginnings, when the Sulpicians had intervened to get the location changed to the cathedral's present site. Carroll and Latrobe, who had conceived and begun the work, were now both dead; but the Bishop of Louisiana would always think of the cathedral as a monument to those two men whom he had known well in other days. As he reminisced he found himself telling Maréchal:

> I take as much share in this success and in that of all your undertakings as if I were personally involved. And are we not thus in all that consolidates Religion, and turns to the greatest glory of our common Master? The episcopate is one, as is the faith. Unhappy the man who isolates himself from the great interest which ought to unite us all in the same cause.[2]

In retrospect, DuBourg's words seem oddly prophetic. His statement on the nature of the episcopacy was a view that DuBourg was to hold throughout his years in office as bishop; but time would prove that it was a view not always shared by the Archbishop of Baltimore when interdiocesan relations involved the Bishop of Louisiana.

As a member of the American hierarchy, DuBourg occupied a somewhat anomalous position as the only bishop not a suffragan of the Archbishop of Baltimore. He was also the only American consecrated in Rome and thus the only one whose first episcopal relations with Propaganda and the pope had been person-to-person. Cardinal Litta had encouraged DuBourg's "confidential correspondence" on American ecclesiastical affairs,[3] and after Litta left Propaganda DuBourg continued to address confidential as well as formal letters to Litta's immediate successors Fontana and Consalvi.

DuBourg's relations with his episcopal confreres were also colored by his affinity with the bishops of the frontier. Long friendship, past collaboration, and a coincidence of episcopal interests naturally drew DuBourg, Flaget, and David together. The three men had lived on the East Coast in the era of John Carroll; they were familiar with his methods of dealing with the complexities of governing the Church in the United States in its foundation period. In addition, as frontier bishops they shared experiences quite foreign to the eastern seaboard prelates. In some ways the western bishops were the least provincial of the American hierarchy of the 1820s; they knew both sides of the Appalachian Mountains.

Flaget's friendly assistance did not end with settling DuBourg in St. Louis in 1818. The Bishop of Bardstown already had consulted with the Bishop of Quebec on matters involving their border regions, and he did not hesitate to suggest to Plessis the implications of DuBourg's arrival. Flaget pointed out that no papal bulls determined the limits of DuBourg's vast diocese, and that politically the boundaries of the Louisiana Territory were still being disputed with Spain and England. As for the care of souls, Flaget told Plessis, "My opinion is that you, My Lord, with Mgr. Du-Bourg and myself should determine . . . the boundaries between the English and the Americans, between the Americans and the Spaniards."[4]

Flaget anticipated correctly that the Anglo-American border would soon be defined, and that eventually new dioceses would be created around the Great Lakes. Nevertheless, according to the most recent maps available in 1818, there was still between the sources of the Mississippi and the St. Lawrence River a very large area which Flaget believed was not assigned by Rome to any bishop. On Flaget's advice DuBourg approached Bishop Plessis, requesting an exchange of power and responsibility in the remote areas of their dioceses visited only occasionally by priest or bishop. "I do not believe that formal letters of vicar generalship are essential here," DuBourg ventured. "I shall be satisfied therefore to beg you to accept, and to exercise in all cases, according to your discretion, all the faculties that I possess in my diocese."[5]

An historian of the relations between Quebec and the American bishops calls it "providential" that Plessis occupied the ancient Canadian see at the time the Church in the United States was establishing its hierarchy.[6] During DuBourg's five-year residence in St. Louis, Plessis often seemed nearer and more sympathetic than Maréchal in Baltimore. Certainly the correspondence DuBourg began with Quebec in 1818 was to prove that even across national borders episcopacy could be "as one."[7]

DuBourg quickly entered into the west's spirit of optimism. He was scarcely ensconced in St. Louis when he rather casually informed Maréchal in a postscript:

> I don't know whether I told you in my last that it has been discussed between Bishop Flaget and myself to ask Rome for new definitions of our respective dioceses and probably the erection of a new See at Detroit; perhaps a second one on the Ohio. I would also like to be able to ask as well for the division of my diocese but that seems to me premature. We will send you our work on the first objective, when it is done, for your approval as to the part which is in your archbishopric.[8]

All together, during the years of his American episcopacy, DuBourg in concert with the other western bishops considered the advisability of creating four new sees within the

Province of Baltimore. Only one of these, Ohio, emerged in DuBourg's time; but the debates over all four caused, on occasion, ill-feeling between the Archbishop of Baltimore and the western bishops. Maréchal suspected that the proposals for new dioceses emanated from DuBourg, and as time went by he became convinced that there was a western plot to dismember his archdiocese. He was mistaken. If on occasion the western prelates seemed to speak with one voice, they were still strong-minded men who could sharply disagree. There was never a "western bloc," least of all a cabal, committed permanently to any one goal save the good of religion.

The idea of creating new sees from the Diocese of Bardstown originated with Flaget, who wished to relieve himself and David of some of the burdens of a jurisdiction encompassing the Northwest Territory. As the idea took shape, Flaget wrote to Maréchal on March 7, 1820, seeking his support for two new sees. Flaget also gave the archbishop the names of the candidates upon whom he had reached agreement with both David and DuBourg. For Ohio, they preferred either Benedict Fenwick, a Jesuit, or Edward Fenwick, a Dominican; for Detroit they recommended Prince Demetrius Gallitzin of Pennsylvania.[9] Maréchal agreed that he could see some need for a diocese in Ohio, but he regarded one for the Detroit Territory as premature. As for candidates, he rejected Flaget's out of hand. Benedict Fenwick could not be spared from Charleston, a perennially disturbed congregation, and Gallitzin was needed in Philadelphia. In his correspondence with Rome, Maréchal eventually, after meeting him, came to favor Edward Fenwick for Ohio; for Detroit—should Rome create the see—the archbishop proposed Gabriel Richard, a Sulpician who already worked there, DuBourg's seminary head Joseph Rosati, C.M., or a priest from Montreal.[10] Thus began the episcopal game of nominating suitable candidates from any diocese not one's own. No bishop wished to lose a good man. The agreement on the Dominican Fenwick was possible because he was already working in Ohio in Flaget's interest.[11]

The western bishops still favored a diocese for Detroit,

and they nominated John Grassi, the former Jesuit superior and president of Georgetown. Flaget, whose desire to protect his own diocese rivalled any bishop's, wrote contentedly to France, "Already sent to Rome—if they are not already arrived—are letters making two new bishops, one for Detroit and the other for the State of Ohio."[12] Flaget was not gifted with prophecy, for at the same time he was writing to France, Maréchal was writing to Rome, reiterating his opposition to Detroit, but suggesting a new diocese at St. Louis. The result of these conflicting recommendations to Rome was that on May 21, 1821, only one new diocese was created and Flaget, who had chosen the see city himself, consecrated Edward Fenwick Bishop of Cincinnati. Even before his consecration, Fenwick joined in writing to Propaganda in favor of a diocese for Detroit.[13] The western bishops now numbered four.

During the next four years proposals and counterproposals were sent to Rome from Bardstown, St. Louis, New Orleans, and Baltimore. By 1824 both Maréchal and his suffragans were in agreement over Gabriel Richard for Detroit, but they differed over Indiana. Maréchal wanted Guy Chabrat for Vincennes; Flaget would not hear of losing him. Flaget countered with a proposal to nominate Antoine Blanc, one of DuBourg's most valued priests.[14] By this time DuBourg, who was living in New Orleans, was much more interested in preventing the division of his own diocese prematurely. When Flaget approached him on the matter of a see at Pittsburgh he replied guardedly:

> Should you judge it opportune to request the erection of a see at Pittsburgh . . . I will unite with you; but 1st you should define very distinctly the boundaries of the new Diocese; 2dly. The Archbishop and the Bishop of Philadelphia, who are both interested, should be consulted, and should unite in the petition. . . .[15]

If Pittsburgh should become a diocese, DuBourg would prefer to see Gallitzin rewarded with the miter "in consequence of his long and useful service, for the good he has effected in those regions"; but the Bishop of Louisiana was beginning to realize how much animus was roused by these disagreements over future dioceses.

Maréchal told his western suffragans that if they wished a new see at Pittsburgh, and if the Bishop of Philadelphia also recommended it, he would agree.[16] But when he wrote to Rome he denounced DuBourg for having a part in the Pittsburgh proposal, saying:

> As for the erection of a see at Pittsburg, I have never spoken of it to Mgr. of Philadelphia. But I know his piety as well as my own, he will be ready to listen to all proposals advised by his confreres *members of the Province of Balt.* . . . Its erection definitively must depend on us; and Mgr. DuBourg who is a stranger to our Province, in writing secret letters, not to Mgr. of Phil. and to me but to my suffragans, is in my eyes as in the eyes of the Holy See guilty of conduct both irregular and indecent.[17]

While the western bishops were more vitally concerned in the proposals for new sees beyond the mountains, all the bishops were seriously involved in filling the vacancies in the older dioceses in the East and the creation of new ones there. When Rome desired information and suggestions regarding these matters, Propaganda customarily sent all the American bishops requests for advice and recommendations. In the case of New York, however, since the creation of the diocese in 1808, Rome had twice consecrated Irish Dominicans unknown in the United States. Luke Concanen had never been able to sail for his diocese because of the Napoleonic Wars, but his successor did arrive. While DuBourg was on his way to Rome in 1815, John Cheverus of Boston notified Plessis, "They expect daily the most Rev. John Connolly consecrated at Rome Bishop of New York last November. He is a Dominican and lived thirty-seven years in Rome."[18] The new Bishop, totally unfamiliar with his new jurisdiction, quickly encountered difficulties in New York,[19] and Cheverus commented morosely, "The Bishop of New York does not understand this country."[20]

From St. Louis in 1820, DuBourg more vigorously told Plessis that the only efficacious way to remedy New York's troubles would be to give the new bishop a coadjutor, to whom Connolly could abandon the details of administering the diocese. For that post DuBourg envisioned Peter Kenny, the provincial-visitor of the Jesuits in Maryland, saying:

> He is an Irishman, an essential thing for the removel of national jealousy; but, if I may believe all reports of him, he is a man of talent, and of rare vigor and prudence. Your lordship must surely have heard of him. If as I believe, your advice has been asked, you will perhaps judge it proper to support mine. In this I do not fear the reproach of meddling; the episcopate is one.[21]

When Connolly died, after an unhappy decade of misunderstandings, Propaganda on May 7, 1825, requested the American bishops to propose names of qualified candidates for the vacancy at New York.[22]

DuBourg replied at once:

> Of all the priests I know, by far the most suitable, or better still, the only one truly and all around suitable, seems to me to be the Rev. Benedict Fenwick; he is about 45 years of age, has belonged for a number of years to the Society of Jesus, was at one time Pastor of New York, then later vicar general of Charleston, and afterwards Superior of the discalced Carmelite nuns, and is now President of the College of his Society at Georgetown, Maryland. His incomparable prudence and skill in dealing with men, his remarkable piety and rare eloquence are acknowledged by all; and, besides, for two reasons, in my opinion, he should receive the preference for the See of New York: first he is a native of America, and thus in that unhappy Diocese, lamentably torn by so many foreign parties, is most capable of conciliating to him all opinions and wills; secondly, in the city of New York he counts as many friends as there are inhabitants, irrespective of religion or nationality. People still remember the zeal and success with which he labored in that vineyard for a number of years, and the spiritual fruits which he reaped there, in particular the conversion of three Anglican ministers, two of whom were later promoted to the priesthood.[23]

DuBourg gave as his other choices: Demetrius Gallitzin, a missionary of Pittsburgh named McGuire, and John Power, whom he believed to be the administrator of New York. He had nominated Fenwick consistently for the episcopacy since 1819 and had not yet learned that his favorite candidate had already been named to Boston and would be consecrated the following month.[24] New York meanwhile remained vacant until DuBourg's old friend John Dubois of Mount St. Mary's in Emmitsburg became Bishop of New York in 1826.

The Philadelphia story was not very different from that of New York. When it was learned that Philadelphia, vacant since the death of Egan in 1814, was likewise receiving an Irish bishop, there was general agreement with Cheverus's view that, "As we are situated in this country, a stranger finds himself from the first contradicted, etc. and perhaps unable to do any good at all."[25] Henry Conwell arrived in Philadelphia in November 1820 and immediately entered upon a reign of almost uninterrupted schism.

DuBourg, who had the previous year recommended Benedict Fenwick as "the only possible candidate,"[26] commented to Plessis:

> We have not been able up to the present to prevent entirely the danger of having nominated men who are totally unfit to govern these republican dioceses. You have had an opportunity to see the bad effects of this. I should have been very glad if you had made known what you thought of it at headquarters. Such observations coming from a prelate who was stranger to the situation would have double weight.[27]

But Plessis had already returned from his visit to Rome, and things in Philadelphia deteriorated rapidly. Even the archbishop of Baltimore was calumniated in the Philadelphia press, and DuBourg wrote sympathetically to Maréchal:

> I have read recently in the *Aurore* of Philadelphia a diatribe addressed to your lordship which has afflicted me profoundly. If it were only a question of personal injury, it is something we should expect and to which a good bishop can

scarcely take offense. But what desolates me and what must give the most painful grief to your soul is the schism which has produced this detestable publication. This poor church of Philad. is most unfortunate.[28]

Plessis, who, with Cheverus of Boston, respected Bishop Conwell, told DuBourg, "I do not know a more worthy man, but he could not be worse suited to this thorny situation. The finest qualities are of no use to one who does not know the country where he is sent to govern as head."[29]

The Bishop of Louisiana was beginning to suspect that there was a faction influential in Rome eager to install Irish prelates in preference to the pioneer bishops, who were preponderantly French. He begged Plessis to add to the information he sent to Rome a warning to the Prefect of Propaganda that he mistrust the calumnious reports which sought to prejudice Propaganda against the French bishops. He said defensively:

> If it were only a question of myself, it would not cost me a great effort of modesty to acknowledge myself vanquished by those accusations; but, my God! what can they say of my venerable colleagues of Baltimore, of Bardstown, and of Boston, that would not be to their advantage! It is only necessary to see what they have done and to remember the numberless difficulties that they had to overcome. The thing speaks for itself to those who are its witnesses . . . but these saintly bishops will not speak in their own defence, and at a distance the most malicious calumnies acquire weight.[30]

Plessis had already more than a year earlier tried to scotch just such calumnies, telling Prefect of Propaganda Fontana:

> I believe it is my duty to reiterate to your Eminence that the Catholics in the United States have, in general, much respect and affection for their French bishops, and if there are complaints against them they are made by Irish monks, ambitious vagabonds, who to the misfortune of these dioceses, would occupy the first places.[31]

That had been written on September 6, 1820; but the ambitions of Philadelphia's Irish priests had not altered judgments since then, nor made life easier for the city's Irish bishop.

DuBourg in 1823 had personal reasons for writing to Conwell directly, first in behalf of Van Quickenborne and the Belgian Jesuits, and again more painfully to reveal Inglesi's true character. His letter to Meade in December 1823 showed his unwillingness to add to Conwell's distresses by intervening in the Philadelphia controversy. He did, however, voice his opinions on Philadelphia to Propaganda the following spring, when he said that the chief obstacles to peace in that city were the priests who had the most influence on Conwell. He suggested that they should submit their grievances to a panel of bishops, or that Conwell should remove the trouble-making priests.[32] Secretary Peter Caprano replied that until DuBourg named the priests the subject could not be broached to the Bishop of Philadelphia nor to Propaganda. "Meanwhile I can not help telling you," said Caprano, "that it appears to me very hard to persuade the Bishop to do as you suggest." If they enjoyed Conwell's friendship would he be likely to remove them? Caprano doubted that concord could be that easily restored. "My sole intention in writing this, pray believe me, is simply to let you know the difficulties which arise in my mind in connection with the affair," he concluded.[33] Caprano's doubts were not idle ones; the schism in Philadelphia continued for another five years. On the eve of DuBourg's sailing for France he had come to agree that Conwell's transfer from Philadelphia might be the best solution.[34]

A third Irish prelate taking office during DuBourg's American episcopacy, John England, was more successful in taking control of his diocese, the newly created See of Charleston which included the Carolinas and Georgia. Arriving in Charleston on December 30, 1820, he began the new year by writing letters of courtesy to all the bishops of the United States, including DuBourg.[35] With England's diocese adjacent to Florida, the Bishop of Louisiana decided to ask the Bishop of Charleston to exercise the powers of vicar general there.[36]

While the northernmost part of his diocese involved

DuBourg with Plessis of Quebec, the southern coast, "The Floridas," raised questions of jurisdiction with the Diocese of Havana and its head, Juan Jose Diaz de Espada y Landa. While he was still in Europe in 1817 DuBourg had tried to begin negotiations by preparing for the king of Spain a memorial on the subject of the Floridas.[37] Unfortunately the Spanish Ambassador to the Vatican was unable to forward the memorial prior to DuBourg's departure,[38] and on his return to the United States DuBourg temporarily took the precaution of adding his authority to the faculties of the Spanish priests still serving in Florida under Espada.[39]

The purchase of east Florida by the United States in 1819 did not immediately clarify DuBourg's position, for he reported to Cardinal Fontana in 1820 that the Bishop of Havana refused to give up his jurisdiction in Florida in the absence of a royal decree from the king of Spain.[40] At last in 1822, with the withdrawal of the Spanish troops, Spanish ecclesiastical jurisdiction ceased, and the Bishop of Havana recalled those priests who were subject to him.[41] Once DuBourg had John England's consent to act as vicar general in this most distant part of the Diocese of Louisiana and the Floridas he felt more certain that priests would visit the region with some regularity.

Bishop England, who prior to his arrival in the United States had had some experience in journalism, on June 5, 1822, founded a newspaper called the *United States Catholic Miscellany.* It was the first Catholic newspaper to survive, with a few brief suspensions, until the Civil War. Although Archbishop Maréchal liked to report it to Rome as "a very bad one," which as time went on was "going from bad to worse,"[42] the *Miscellany* proved to be a leading influence on Catholic opinion during DuBourg's years in Louisiana, and on occasion it carried his name.

On April 5, 1824, England preached a sermon at Warrenton, Georgia, which caused something of a furor when a Georgia newspaper published at Mount Zion, the *Missionary,* attacked the Catholic bishop for his views. The resulting exchanges, which the *Miscellany* carried under the title,

"Controversy with the Mount Zion Missionary," lasted until 1825.

In his retort to the *Missionary*'s attack, Bishop England included an imaginary dialogue between General Jackson and Bishop DuBourg which poked fun at the Protestant notion that "the Pope has temporal power over all goods and possessions of all Christians, to dispose of them as he pleases, including the transferring of kingdoms from one to another." England had DuBourg defending the pope's right to give Louisiana to the Duke of Wellington, and even to donate the American republic to King George IV of England. The Bishop of Charleston inquired caustically, "Does anyone imagine that Bishop DuBourg would be the fool, the simpleton, this exhibition would designate? Yet, yet if the principle of the *Missionary* were true, such would be the language of the Bishop."[43]

It was the sort of literary controversy DuBourg himself had enjoyed in his Baltimore days, when retorting to the *Strictures* attacking his college and the Church. Both England and DuBourg were men who enjoyed a way with words. There may have been a tinge of wistfulness in Bishop England's complaint to Bishop Rosati on December 29, 1826, that when DuBourg returned to France he had left England in the dark about East Florida.[44] Their exchanges had lent a zest not easily replaced. Years after DuBourg was in his grave the Bishop of Charleston remembered him as "a man of most extensive views."[45]

The fourth Irish prelate sent without warning to the United States enjoyed a short-lived term. In his letter of June 11, 1821, congratulating Maréchal on his pastoral letter, DuBourg had added, "I see you today relieved of a large part of your anxiety by the erection of the new Sees in Virginia and the Carolinas. Limited to the single State of Maryland, with the admirable help with which you are surrounded there, what wonderful things will you not accomplish, for which may God preserve you."[46] While the creation of the Diocese of Charleston and the competence of John England may have relieved Maréchal of some anxiety, the erection of the new see of Richmond at the archbishop's very door was not to be tolerated. While Maréchal was in Rome in 1822 he got the Virginia see suppressed. Bishop Patrick Kelly, although nominated for another American see, demurred, and he soon ceased to be of interest to the American bishops.

Bishop DuBourg's relations with the Diocese of Boston, so far as any remaining evidence can tell, seem to have been rather tenuous. From DuBourg's view, New England was not an area with enough Catholic growth to challenge his fertile imagination. After Cheverus went to Montauban as bishop, DuBourg asserted, "None of us indeed has the least doubt that the smallness of the Diocese of Boston was the chief cause why the Right Rev. Cheverus lent a most willing hand to his transfer there."[47] Certainly the Bishop of Boston did not "lend a most willing hand" to his recall to France;[48] yet it is true that Cheverus was not, like Flaget and DuBourg, fascinated by planning new dioceses for new bishops. Indeed, he complained that Rome was making too many bishops as it was. When he heard talk of a second metropolitan see west of the Appalachian Mountains, Cheverus told Maréchal, "I have expected for a long time to see Mgr. DuBourg archbishop and I even believed Mgr. David was consecrated to speed the event." Then he added doubtfully, "If this plan should take place all we can do is pray that it will contribute to the glory of God and the spread of Religion."[49]

The Bishop of Boston was content to second his archbishop's proposals, whether they were designed to delay new sees in the West, suppress dioceses in the East, or secure seats for his candidates on episcopal thrones both east and west of the mountains. When DuBourg, Flaget, and David in 1819 had wanted Benedict Fenwick for Philadelphia, Cheverus agreed with Maréchal that the Jesuit should be left in Carolina where he was then working "such wonders as he did at New York."[50] To the end of his stay in the United States, the Bishop of Boston remained Maréchal's staunchest ally.

When on February 22, 1824, Bishop DuBourg was

requested by Propaganda to recommend someone to fill the vacant See of Boston, he replied at once in a letter presenting a novel idea. He argued that New England had too few Catholics to warrant a separate diocese, that John Carroll, the first Archbishop of Baltimore, had favored uniting New York and Boston into one diocese, and that whoever replaced Cheverus should be appointed with the stipulation that, after the death of Connolly, New York and Boston would become one see. From a man so happily engaged in proposing new dioceses for an area he knew, the suggestion must have come as something of a surprise in some quarters. For Boston he wanted Benedict Fenwick, and added as second choice Gallitzin.[51]

The bishops all knew that Cheverus wished his own nominee, William Taylor, to succeed him; and John England, out of old friendship, likewise favored Taylor. Maréchal hedged. He knew Cheverus wanted Taylor, but he also knew that Taylor had been insubordinate to episcopal authority while serving in New York. Connolly and Conwell would never support the nomination; nor would the bishops of the West. Maréchal "at first adopted an evasive attitude, and finally came out for Father Taylor only when it was too late. . . ."[52]

DuBourg's idea of uniting Boston and New York received short shrift, with Maréchal telling Cardinal Fesch:

> It is quite true that Mgr Carroll originally thought it was not useful to erect a see at Boston. There were in Boston at the time only 150 to 200 Catholics; and N. Y. had only a 20th part of what it has presently. But times are quite changed. A bishop full of talent and vigor would have difficulty governing this diocese which includes northern New Jersey.[53]

DuBourg's undeviating insistence that Benedict Fenwick was the nation's outstanding candidate for episcopacy at last won almost unanimous approval.[54] "Bishop DuBourg, in particular, had urged Father Fenwick very strongly as one 'adorned with the principal gifts that become a bishop; namely, piety, zeal for the glory of God, exquisite prudence, and rare eloquence,' and eligible especially through the fact that he was born an American."[55] It would prove one of the rare causes for Louisiana's elation as 1825 ended to learn that on November 1, 1825, Benedict Fenwick was consecrated second Bishop of Boston in the Baltimore Cathedral by Archbishop Maréchal, assisted by Conwell of Philadelphia and England of Charleston "amid an immense concourse of people." Although the Bishop of Louisiana was not present, his sentiments were not unlike those of a fellow Sulpician who found it grand indeed, saying, "It was a universal joy, I don't believe there was a dissenting voice. I felt happy beyond measure."[56]

With recurring frequency and discordance, one ominous note sounded throughout these episcopal orchestrations. It was Maréchal's suspicion that Baltimore's interests were being undermined by his fellow bishops, who were all, with equal courtesy, asked by Rome to inform and advise regarding American Church matters. Maréchal would have preferred the archbishop to have the preponderant influence in filling vacant or new sees.

Flaget, who had shared in the first Baltimore council of bishops in 1810 under the aegis of John Carroll, felt that Maréchal should follow Carroll's example, arguing that in six or seven sessions the bishops in council would agree on policies ten times more effectively than by writing fifty letters.[57] Flaget shared with Plessis the view that all the American prelates who knew the mentality of the people must share in the nominations. Plessis did not hesitate to express his views to Rome, both directly and indirectly, telling Propaganda that it would be useful to have the metropolitan consult with the other American bishops before proposing candidates to new or vacant sees.[58] Plessis said as much to DuBourg as well on May 10, 1822.[59]

After Maréchal confided in Plessis his intention of going to Rome, the Bishop of Quebec heartily approved, but he told Maréchal bluntly, "My position is so different from yours that I have no reason to join you in a request for the right to nominate or present for vacant sees and to determine upon the erection of future bishoprics."[60] In Rome Maréchal was directed to seek the counsel of his suffragans, and he told Plessis rather stiffly on his return:

Cardinal Fontana was assuredly mistaken about the nature of the request I made him in regard to the nominations to the bishoprics in my province. I never asked of the Holy See the right of nominating, either absolutely or as a privilege. The favor that I solicited for the good of religion was that Propaganda will write to us and listen to our reasons before it proceeds to nominate men recommended only by intriguing monks at Rome, or by foreign bishops who have no knowledge whatever of our ecclesiastical affairs.[61]

When Flaget learned that the suffragans were now assured a voice, he conveyed to Maréchal his delight that "the metropolitan would now be the center of correspondence for all the bishops in determining candidates for the episcopacy."[62]

Improving relations with his suffragans did not alter Maréchal's attitude toward DuBourg, however. When Plessis advised Maréchal to get an agent to represent him in Rome, one of the archbishop's first requests to Agent Robert Gradwell—after asking for a copy of the brief establishing the new Diocese of Cincinnati—was to find out what proposals DuBourg had made to Propaganda in particular, how many sees had he recommended, where were they to be located, and who were the men he favored as new bishops.[63]

While Maréchal was in Rome in 1822, he established a connection with Cardinal Fesch, whom he could also use as a channel for an exchange of information about DuBourg's activities, telling Fesch, "He has the miserable weakness of wanting to be Archbishop."[64] After DuBourg removed the Belgian Jesuits from the Archdiocese of Baltimore in 1823, Maréchal's bitterness festered, and by August of that year DuBourg had become almost an obsession in the correspondence between Baltimore and Rome. Gradwell was enjoined to frustrate DuBourg's crafty schemes to lure priests away from Baltimore and make bishops of Maréchal's men.[65] Fesch was urged to get DuBourg censured and have the Jesuits forbidden to leave the archdiocese without the consent of both Maréchal and the pope. To Propaganda he wrote much the same thing.[66]

On August 7 Maréchal warned Gradwell that Philip Borgna, "another Inglesi," was going to Rome to forward the insidious designs of Louisiana's bishop. Poor Borgna, whose health had suffered from a recent yellow fever epidemic in New Orleans, was returning to his homeland to visit his family and his Vincentian superior in Rome. He had indeed carried lengthy instructions from DuBourg, but they were all related to his own diocese.[67] The Archbishop of Baltimore was nevertheless persuaded that Borgna's trip was part and parcel of a plot to weaken the metropolitan see of Baltimore, and he begged Gradwell to ensure that Propaganda reject any measure of DuBourg's that touched on Maréchal's jurisdiction. "After his having last winter enticed nine subjects away from Baltimore, this would deal me a mortal blow if this prelate removed others," he assured Gradwell. "I am in extreme penury. Virginia is almost without pastors."[68]

It was quite true that DuBourg had sent to Propaganda names of priests from the archdiocese as possible candidates for the episcopacy, just as Maréchal had sent names of priests from the diocese of Flaget's and of DuBourg's. From the beginning he had favored Benedict Fenwick. More recently DuBourg had proposed two others from the archdiocese as possible choices, should the Floridas be taken from the Diocese of Louisiana and the Floridas. These two he had reason to know were men for whom Maréchal had little fondness. Enoch Fenwick, a Jesuit like his brother Benedict, was a priest whom Maréchal was relieved to have recalled to serve as president of Georgetown. Simon Bruté was a Sulpician who annoyed the archbishop by his constant defense of Mount St. Mary's in Emmitsburg, and who had already talked of leaving Maryland for the foreign missions.

During the months that DuBourg learned of his "Little Brother's" growing distress over Maréchal's intentions for the Mount, the Bishop of Louisiana four times sent Bruté's name to Rome: on May 30 and September 5, 1822; and on March 8 and June 14, 1824.[69] It may have been DuBourg's impulsive way of trying to bolster his friend's morale, for he seems not to have expected Bruté's appointment most of the times he proposed his name. After the first nomination, DuBourg told Bruté frankly that he would not have done it earlier, saying, "At that epoch, which was that of my great trials, my greatest difficulties, I would have feared to have you near me for fear that you would want me to go faster than, in my opinion, I ought."[70] After his September 5, 1822, nomination of Bruté as his second choice for his coadjutor, DuBourg confessed to Rosati, "I do not think Mr. Bruté would accept the nomination."[71]

Whatever DuBourg's motives may have been, Maréchal was uneasy that the names of Enoch Fenwick and Bruté had been sent at all, and as soon as he learned of it he wrote fearfully to Cardinal Consalvi, "The good of religion demands that I should know who it is that may attempt in the future to deal a new and grievous blow to the Church of America." He opposed both Enoch Fenwick and Bruté, and warned Consalvi against DuBourg, "His temperament is such that the Sacred Congregation should exercise the greatest caution when it lends an ear either to what he reports or what he plans."[72]

That same month the archbishop wrote aggrievedly to Cardinal Fesch:

Without doubt you have been informed of the conduct of Mgr. DuBourg, during the stay he recently made in my diocese. By intrigues which assuredly I never could have believed him capable of, this *prélat projecteur* has succeeded in kidnapping a good number of my subjects. Here is another act allied to the first *embauchage*. I have just received a letter from Père DeTheux who informs me of his departure for Missouri. Thus it is that this religious abandons a numerous parish which I had confided to him without my knowing how in the world the post he is deserting will be filled.[73]

Maréchal had every right to protest the transfer of a member of a religious order by his superior without consulting the ordinary of the diocese. An agreement on this subject had been reached in John Carroll's time, and Maréchal in 1818 had published the decrees of 1810.[74] It was properly a matter between the Archbishop of Baltimore and the superior of the Society of Jesus. The real scapegoat, nevertheless, for Maréchal was DuBourg.

It is not possible to determine how much of Maréchal's protesting to Rome over the Jesuit affair may have reached DuBourg's ears. For DuBourg, the Jesuits were in Missouri to stay. The Bishop of Louisiana remained, however, deeply concerned over the appointments of new bishops, for the episcopal succession was critical to the peace and welfare of the Church in the United States. He had expressed his first apprehensions in that regard to Plessis early in 1821, adding:

> As for me, I tremble to leave my see unprovided for at my death. For all the institutions in this section rest absolutely on the bishop; and one who does not enter into the views of his predecessor may in a year destroy a century of effort and of forethought.[75]

In the four years that followed, DuBourg had done a great deal of mulling over the matter and, during his episcopal visitation of the western Louisiana wilderness, finally came to a decision to express his views to the American bishops. From Natchitoches on October 4, 1825, he wrote a lengthy letter which began:

> About one year ago, if my memory serves me well as to time, I received an invitation from Propaganda, which I must suppose to have been addressed also to every Bishop in the United States to give my opinion for the appointment of a successor to Fr. Cheverus in the See of Boston; and just now a similar one has reached me, respecting that of New York. . . . From this it is natural to conclude that the Sacred Congregation has come to a settled plan, not to proceed henceforth in the American nominations, but upon the joint suffrages of the American Bishops.

The plan, no doubt, was a very correct one from every point of view. The difficulty was in carrying it out. The present method had not worked, with each bishop privately sending his own nominations. These isolated opinions, DuBourg noted, could only perplex Propaganda, particularly since each candidate could conceivably get only one vote in his favor, "the consequence of which must be an indefinite protraction in the appointments, the greatest calamity that can befall our infant Churches."

DuBourg then said that although he personally was willing to travel any distance on an errand of such interest to religion, he proposed:

> The Archbishop, or in case of his absence, or death, the eldest Bishop might be commissioned by the Holy See, in the emergency of any vacancy, to confer by letters, with his colleagues to suggest to each of them his own ideas, to receive theirs in return, and in case of such division of opinions as might embarrass the nominations, to acquaint them . . . in order that, upon a new consideration . . . the Bishops might . . . modify their former opinions, and join in making a common return.

He realized that a short cut would be to give every bishop a coadjutor to succeed the incumbent on his death, but could see many objections.

He closed his letter on the subject saying that he knew he would be accused of intruding, that the initiative in the matter could with more propriety have been taken by someone else. He admitted he had refrained in the past for this very reason from presenting his views. Nevertheless:

> Recollecting the word of St. Cyprian, *Episcopatus est in solidum,* which is particularly enforced in the application made to each of us by the Holy See, I have concluded that every member of the Episcopal body is strictly indebted to all of his Brethren for a candid disclosure of all his own views toward the consolidation and advancement of the common interest.

In the spirit of this conviction, he told the bishops he was sending his views to Propaganda and was enclosing the names of his nominees for the vacant see of New York.[76]

The plan he favored as practicable was the one he had seen in operation while John Carroll was archbishop. When

Egan of Philadelphia died in 1814, letters to the suffragans had gone out, candidates had been narrowed down to David and DuBourg, and everyone had been notified; that neither nominee had been appointed was due to circumstances that had nothing to do with the method.

When Bishop Flaget responded to DuBourg on January 18, 1826, he said he had passed on to Edward Fenwick the copy of DuBourg's letter as requested and attached the reflections which the Kentucky bishops had made on his propositions. They agreed with DuBourg that if on the death of a bishop a meeting could be held "the choice would be made in two or three sessions, while six months would not suffice to do it by correspondence." However, since the first method offered extreme difficulties, another would have to be chosen. Flaget likewise felt a polling should be taken with the archbishop sending the bishops the names of those subjects which seemed to him worthy of the see.[77]

Although the first part of Flaget's letter was personal, relating to matters of interest only to Flaget and DuBourg, the latter when sending Propaganda his nominees for New York enclosed the whole letter saying:

> I received lately from our Right Rev. Colleague of Bardstown a letter, of which I thought it my duty to forward the original to your Grace, in order that you may understand in a better and shorter way the consensus of opinion which exists among the Bishops of the United States, regarding the appointments to the vacant or recently established Episcopal Sees. This letter is a reply to one of mine, in which I was setting forth to my brother-bishops my views on the subject; this my letter I enclose herewith in English, just as it was written.[78]

It was as forthright as he knew how to be. Rome could read for itself what both men had actually written.

When Maréchal first touched on the subject when writing to Fesch, he spent more time on the suggestion of a coadjutor for every bishop, saying at the outset that it would be perfectly useless to try to get the Holy See, as a general rule, to give each bishop a coadjutor. In cases where coadjutors were to be granted, he said, the choice should always be made with the concurrence of the archbishop or two bishops nearby. Then he reverted to his *bête noir:*

> I still tremble at the mere thought that Mgr. DuBourg asked for Father Inglesi for his coadjutor, not one time but repeatedly, that he represented this adventurer not only in every seductive color of his imagination but applied to him the tenderest terms of St. Paul to Timothy. Happily I found myself in Rome at the time and decided the choice of Rosati.[79]

On the subject of his own leadership in selecting suitable candidates Maréchal complained:

> When I was in Rome I tried to obtain a decree from the Holy See conferring on the archbishop in union with his suffragans the exclusive right to present bishops for vacant sees and those to be created. My request was in the process of being granted when unfortunately the enormous scandals of Father Inglesi broke out. The Cardinals who were members of the Propaganda had at hand the letters of Mgr. DuBourg supported by others of respectable authority. . . . In vain I pointed out that the bishop of N. O. did not belong to the Province, that his inconceivable imprudences should not prejudice [illegible] my request. . . . You perceive, Mgr., the danger to which the Church in America would be exposed if the See of Baltimore had a prelate of the sort of Mgr. DuBourg?[80]

By the summer of 1826, the Archbishop of Baltimore was determined that DuBourg's influence must be limited to his own diocese, which would include the states of Mississippi and Louisiana; he had already recommended to Propaganda that Auguste Jeanjean be made DuBourg's coadjutor for the Diocese of New Orleans.[81] Although at the time stipulated for the division of DuBourg's diocese the Bishop of Louisiana had been given by Rome the right to choose whatever diocese he preferred, Maréchal in advance had seated Rosati permanently in St. Louis. Maréchal not only asked Fesch again to oppose any plan DuBourg might suggest which would dismember the Province of Baltimore;

he demanded in addition that Fesch reject the names of priests submitted by the Bishop of Louisiana for vacant sees.[82] "Clearly," Maréchal's biographer says, "Archbishop Maréchal had become completely opposed to any influence DuBourg might have in the American Church."[83]

The decision regarding the method by which American nominations to Rome were to be made were finally worked out under Maréchal's successor, Archbishop James Whit-field,[84] who, unlike Maréchal, called two councils in swift succession and invited DuBourg's successor Joseph Rosati, to participate.[85] In the end it was DuBourg's adherence to Saint Cyprian's injunction, *Episcopatus est in solidum*—his conviction that the episcopacy, like the Faith, was one—which triumphed.

CHAPTER XXIX

A COADJUTOR AT LAST

While DuBourg may have seemed like a thorn in the flesh to Maréchal, there were times when the archbishop's advice to Rome needlessly complicated the administration of the Diocese of Louisiana for DuBourg. The first of these occasions arose from Maréchal's desire to rid himself of the southwestern part of his diocese, where DuBourg had accepted the responsibility of acting as vicar general. As Rosati recalled the episode:

> Msgr. Maréchal had made a trip to Rome on the business of his diocese. He had resigned into the hands of the Holy Father, Pius VII, the jurisdiction and spiritual care of the territories of Mississippi and Alabama which were attached to his See. He suggested to the Sacred Congregation of Propaganda the erection of a Vicariate Apostolic for this region and proposed Mr. Rosati for that position. The Sacred Congregation asked the Holy Father to grant the request. . . .[1]

The request had been granted; the vicariate had been created; and Rosati was named the bishop in charge.

At first glance, Rome's action in 1822 might seem to have involved only Rosati's loss to DuBourg's diocese. It was, in fact, a more complex situation because of the Florida question. Before the Spanish troops and clergy ever withdrew from Florida in 1822, Cardinal Fontana had already suggested to DuBourg that his diocese might well be divided into three parts, with Florida a separate see. Fontana worried, as DuBourg did, about the distance of that region from DuBourg's center of activity. "Whenever you consent, as I hope, to come to this dismemberment," the cardinal added, "the Right Rev. Patrick Kelly, Bishop of Richmond, would seem to be most suitable. . . . as the Sacred Congregation has for grave reasons decided to transfer him to another See. . . ."[2]

On receipt of this letter DuBourg replied with alacrity:

> Much joy was afforded me by Your Eminence's letter of last October, because, above all, it gave me a certain hope that before long the Floridas will be withdrawn from my jurisdiction, as I had often earnestly requested your regretted predecessor, His Eminence, Card. Litta, and even the Holy Father himself. Not only, therefore, insofar as I am concerned, do I give my consent to their erection into an Epicopal See, but I repeat my prayer that this be done as soon as possible. . . .
> The limits of this new Diocese might include the present *Territory of the Floridas* and the State of Alabama. The title and the See, I think, ought to be the town of Mobile, as it is on the borders of both territories.[3]

Although DuBourg had no objection to Kelly,[4] Kelly objected to accepting Florida, and learning of this DuBourg then suggested that Propaganda consider Benedict Fenwick's brother Enoch for Florida.[5] During the summer and fall of 1822, having heard nothing to the contrary, DuBourg assumed that the idea of a diocese or vicariate combining Florida and Alabama was still in favor at Propaganda, and he continued to write to Rome on the subject. He relayed the opinion of the Governor of the Florida Territory that Pensacola was preferable to Mobile for a see city, but he himself recommended that this decision be left to the bishop whom Rome would name to the diocese.[6]

During his stay in Bardstown on his way east that autumn, DuBourg discussed the Florida matter with Flaget and David, who willingly notified Rome that they endorsed DuBourg's views on both the combining of Alabama and Florida into a new diocese, and on Enoch Fenwick for its head.[7] DuBourg, who had recently renewed his plea to Rome that Joseph Rosati be made his coadjutor, with permission to reside at the Barrens seminary as its head, found his Kentucky friends in complete agreement on that subject as well. Bidding the Damon and Pythias of Bardstown an affectionate farewell, the Bishop of Louisiana lightheartedly rode off for Louisville, happily anticipating the day when he would be free of Florida and have an episcopal assistant of his own in what remained of his extensive diocese.

It is easy to imagine the shock Bishop DuBourg sustained when, on reaching Baltimore a few weeks later, Maréchal informed him that early that summer Propaganda had created a Vicariate Apostolic of Mississippi and Alabama, to be headed by Joseph Rosati, Bishop of Tenegra *in partibus infidelium,* and that the letters of Pius VII to Rosati[8] announcing this had already been dispatched to the Barrens by Maréchal, who had brought all the pertinent documents from Rome, The Bishop of Louisiana was not only still saddled with the distant Florida Peninsula but was also now deprived of his vicar general in Upper Louisiana, the rector of his seminary, and the superior of the Congregation of the Mission whose members were the heart of his clergy in the whole diocese—and this without one word of consultation on the part of Propaganda or warning from Maréchal who was in Rome when the decision was made.

To be sure, Mississippi and Alabama were within Maréchal's jurisdiction, but he had never wanted the responsibility for that part of his diocese and had quickly passed it on to DuBourg. The Bishop of Louisiana would have been happy to be freed from this extra burden, but not at the cost of Rosati. He had no intention of accepting this new state of affairs, and he wrote speedily to the Barrens:

> I learn on my arrival here, my dear Monsieur Rosati, of your nomination to the See of Tenegra and to the administration of the two States of Alabama and Mississippi. This news would drive me mad, if I believed for a moment that you

would accept. I am writing to Propde. and I send you a copy of my letter. I am writing also to Mr. Baccari. I pray God will direct your response; but in my opinion all is lost for the whole of Louisiana, if the thing goes into effect. Apart from the damage to Religion, what an injustice to me! What cause for discouragement to all Bishops. God keep me from thinking that this affair will be consummated! If I believed it I would not return to my Diocese but would go place my resignation at the feet of the Pope.[9]

Flaget on hearing the news in Bardstown was as outraged as his friend and wrote immediately to Propaganda of his pain and surprise. He said bluntly that the new jurisdiction had been formed without the advice of the men who, far better than Maréchal, knew the territory involved, the number of Catholics there, and the means for supporting a bishop. Further, Flaget asserted, the harm inflicted by Rosati's removal from Missouri would far outweigh any good he might do in Mississippi, where he would be quite wasted.[10]

To Maréchal, Flaget protested indignantly that the suffragan bishops had not been consulted on this preposterous proposal. The Bishop of Bardstown said that he, for one, would never consent to the nomination, since Rosati could do no good in Alabama and Mississippi and, in addition, if he were taken from Missouri it would destroy DuBourg's diocese and DuBourg would resign.[11]

Flaget took it for granted that Maréchal was behind Rosati's nomination and said so. The Archbishop of Baltimore tried to shrug off the accusation, lightly accusing Flaget himself of being indirectly to blame for the recent developments. If Flaget had not aided and abetted DuBourg's settling in St. Louis, Maréchal quipped, Rome would not have found it necessary to provide for closer supervision of Alabama and Mississippi.[12] It was a specious argument which did not concern DuBourg, who was single-mindedly determined to nullify the vicariate and Rosati's appointment.

Following his letter to Rosati, DuBourg next addressed Rosati's Roman superior, F. A. Baccari, pointing out that

Rosati's transfer would be disastrous to everything they had accomplished so far, and begging for Baccari's support in preventing it.[13] He would enclose his letters to Propaganda and asked the Vincentian superior to read them before passing them on. He next penned an impassioned letter to Propaganda asking, "Oh! Your Eminences! What have you done? Who ever prompted you with this advice to take from the poorest of Bishops the last and only anchor of his hope? . . . Here I am prostrate on the ground . . . and I am not going to rise until you revoke this nomination."

He pointed out to those who may not have known it that he had accepted the episcopate in 1815 only on the condition that priests of the Congregation of the Mission would help him. With De Andreis dead, Rosati was the only one left to build up that congregation in the United States and conduct the seminary. In the states of Alabama and Mississippi there were only two Catholic congregations, Mobile and Natchez; both were easily looked after by the Bishop of New Orleans or his vicar general because of proximity. "As a matter of fact," he said, "I had provided for the two aforementioned parishes . . . by establishing in each of them an excellent priest." Since neither of these places could support a single priest properly, how could an administrator survive?[14]

Then he reminded the cardinals of their proposal to erect a see in Florida. "This proposal not only did I consent to, but in fact I had repeatedly suggested it myself," he continued forcefully, "as may be seen from various letters of mine possibly preserved in the Archives of the S. Congregation." He had further even proposed a candidate for the see, the Rev. Enoch Fenwick, S. J., from Maryland.[15] Rome's plan was based on complete ignorance of the locality. Mobile and Natchez were three hundred miles apart; geographically Mississippi belonged to the Diocese of Louisiana, while Mobile—lying on the same bay as Pensacola—belonged to Florida. It was a cogent summary of the view from Louisiana; it was a view which should have been requested before the fact.

On January 23, 1823, the innocent object of all this

feverish correspondence, Rosati himself, received the packet of Roman mail which Maréchal had forwarded after his arrival in New York on November 22, 1822.[16] Rosati's emotions were even more intense than those of DuBourg and Flaget, and he told Baccari, "I did not hesitate for a moment to resolve to refuse a burden which is beyond my strength in every regard. To this end I warmly recommend myself to you, in order that you may obtain that the Holy Father and His Eminence Card. Consalvi, grant me the favor of accepting my refusal."[17] He was writing with tears in his eyes, scarcely knowing what he was doing.

It was the beginning of another barrage of letters, this one going to Consalvi, Caprano, DuBourg, Flaget, and Rosati's brother. To his family Rosati confessed, as his first month of violent trepidation ended, that his appointment was "the most calamitous" event of his life. "I am waiting most anxiously for the answers from Rome," he wrote apprehensively, "and I shall not recover my composure until I see my wishes fulfilled."[18]

When Philip Borgna passed through Missouri on his way to Rome that April, Rosati gave his fellow Vincentian the papal documents to return to Propaganda, urging Borgna to spare no effort in his behalf. To Consalvi himself, Rosati wrote on April 2 that he still persevered in his resolve to escape the Mississippi-Alabama assignment. Borgna had confirmed what DuBourg had already reported: that in Mobile the number of Catholics would scarcely support a single priest, and that in Natchez the thirty families were incapable of supporting their present pastor Maenhaut, who intended to leave as soon as he had permission. Rome ought to question, Rosati believed, the expediency of establishing a bishop in an area where there were no means of "keeping up his dignity," or furnishing even the bare necessities of life.[19]

In the end, it was DuBourg's December protest, supported vigorously by Baccari in Rome as well as by Flaget and David from Kentucky, which determined the outcome.[20] Instead of administering the Alabama-Mississippi

vicariate, Joseph Rosati was to become DuBourg's coadjutor in the Diocese of Louisiana and the Floridas. When
Baccari relayed the news to Rosati, he defined the terms of
the solution, saying:

> This morning Msgr. Caprano, the Secretary of the Con-
> gregation, told me that the Sacred Congregations had taken
> into consideration Msgr. DuBourg's representations and
> those that I had made myself, and had decided that you
> would not be removed from the area where you are, that you
> would continue to be in charge of our house and mission
> until told otherwise, and that at the same time, as Msgr.
> DuBourg's Vicar General and Bishop *in partibus,* you would
> exercise episcopal functions there and that thus you would
> live in Louisiana.[21]

As soon as the Bishop of Louisiana received the Roman rescript confirming Baccari's news of Rosati's appointment, he wrote jubilantly to "Monseigneur and beloved
Brother":

> The die is cast and divine goodness has at last granted my
> wishes. I have just received the *Mandatum Apostolicum* for
> your episcopal consecration under the title of Tenegra as my
> Coadjutor. . . . It is no longer a question of refusing; for the
> document is imperative. Whatever the fright with which you
> are seized at the thought of the Episcopat, fright certainly
> justified and which I will take care not to discard, knowing
> myself as I do both the perils and the difficulties of this
> charge, it only remains for you to bow your head under the
> yoke imposed upon you.

The Roman document, DuBourg reminded Rosati, was "all
the more precious and sacred as the last will and testament
of Our Holy Father who survived its expedition by only 35
days." DuBourg had not yet had time to think what they
would do about the consecration, but meanwhile Rosati
must announce his appointment to the seminary at the
Barrens. "I am going to tell it to St. Louis and Florissant,"
DuBourg ended. "Adieu; my heart is very solaced. I really
needed it."[22]

In retrospect, it is not quite clear what part the Archbishop of Baltimore may have intended to play in the business. It would be easy to view Flaget's accusation as proof of Maréchal's imputed tendency to ignore his suffragans, or as one more thread in the rough cloth of his disdain for DuBourg. The actual sequence of events leading to the creation of the vicariate in 1822 began with Maréchal's note of June 1, 1822, written to Propaganda while he was still in Rome. It announced his intention of relinquishing all claim to jurisdiction over the states of Alabama and Mississippi. He gave as his reasons the distance of the region from Baltimore and his inability to provide for the spiritual needs of the Catholics there. He suggested that these states be either assigned to the nearest bishops or that they be made a separate vicariate. The latter suggestion was quickly adopted at a general congregation of Propaganda on June 8.[23]

A brief of July 14, 1823, which subsequently suppressed the vicariate, states that the new jurisdiction was created "consequent on the fact that the Archbishop of Baltimore had surrendered his spiritual rule over those territories."[24] The formal implementing documents were issued on August 13, 1822, to be brought to the United States by Maréchal. One historian comments, "It is hard to believe Propaganda confided to the prelate documents of such importance without acquainting him with their contents; and if he was privy to the transaction, as appears quite probable, then there can be little doubt that his consent had been obtained, or at least his objections overruled."[25] A more recent historian goes even further, holding that in the light of the archbishop's expressed views of that region later, Maréchal was the "real author of the vicariate."[26] Certainly Rosati believed Maréchal responsible for his nomination.

In addition to the question of the archbishop's responsibility for its creation, there remains some uncertainty about his part in having the vicariate suppressed. The second Maréchal letter to Propaganda associated with the Alabama-Mississippi matter, written from Baltimore at DuBourg's request on December 2, 1822, has led to the notion that Maréchal, DuBourg, and Flaget reviewed the whole matter and "their reports were unanimously against the erection of the new Vicariate Apostolic."[27] As Rosati understood it, DuBourg "earnestly begged Msgr. Flaget to join him and even got Msgr. Maréchal, who was now better informed on the state of affairs, to write in his favor to the Sacred Congregation of Propaganda."[28] Maréchal's letter of December 2, did not in fact attack the vicariate or recommend its suppression. Instead, Maréchal began by saying that the Diocese of Louisiana was not within his province and he therefore had no right to speak; but since DuBourg had now given him leave to do so, he could answer with greater assurance that he approved of DuBourg's request to have the division of his diocese deferred and Rosati made his coadjutor.[29]

If DuBourg, like Flaget, believed Maréchal to have been at fault in the vicariate matter, it does not show in his correspondence during those months of uncertainty. His spirited protest to Rome leveled no accusations against the archbishop. Writing to Plessis not long after the news of the vicariate reached him, DuBourg's references to Maréchal were generous:

> You no doubt know ere this of the arrival of our dear Archbishop. One of the first results of his return was the submission of the schismatic priest of Philadelphia. It is to be hoped that the party will follow the example of this leader. The Archbishop has come back with a judgment from the Pope granting him for his episcopal residence a magnificent property of the Jesuits, valued at eighty or one hundred thousand dollars.

After closing with his customary sentiments of respect and attachment, he added a postscript:

> I forgot to tell you that among other good things that the Archbishop obtained at Rome, were the suppression of the See of Richmond, cut off of his diocese without his consent; and the most severe measures against the admission of unapproved priests to the United States. A law for episcopal nominations was also made.[30]

If he were harboring any ugly suspicions or resentment against his Baltimore confrere, the Bishop of Louisiana had them under firm control.

His letter to Rosati of February 6, 1823, displays a similar absence of animus:

> Although I have had no letters from you since the packets from Rome arrived, I have some idea of your situation. Mine would be very sad indeed in so far as I could believe that such a nomination could take effect; but in truth, reflecting on it since has convinced me of the utter absurdity of this measure, and since I have been able to succeed in having Mgr. the Arch. and Mgr. Flaget write in the same sense as I, I am more tranquil. The letter of the latter, above all, is as forceful at least as mine.[31]

His optimism was vindicated when he received from Rome the news that his protests had been heard. He wrote at once to Maréchal: "I have just received from Rome a brief of last July 15 revoking that of the preceding month of August by which Alabama and Mississippi were erected as an apostolic vicariate . . . that is to say, as his eminence Card. Consalvi expressed himself in a letter accompanying the brief, restoring to you Alabama and Mississippi, reserving to you the right to have them administered by me or the Bishop of Charleston as your vicar general." Doubting that the powers he was exercising in these states were valid until Maréchal confirmed them again, DuBourg asked Maréchal to express his wishes in that regard. He then went on to the heart of his concern:

> By this brief Mr. Rosati is given to me as coadjutor in accordance with my wishes, after the serious reasons which you had the kindness to support, with the express clause that this immense diocese will be divided in two at the end of three years, and that . . . Mr. Rosati will be titulary of that one of the two divisions I deem fitting to surrender to him. There's a solution which fully satisfies my spirit and my heart, and in which I believe you share.[32]

No one could guess from this letter that DuBourg felt any bitterness at having spent a year of needless uncertainty over the future welfare of his diocese.

Rome's decision in July 1823 to give DuBourg a coadjutor ended a question which had been hanging fire since
the bishop first broached the subject four years earlier, with
Rosati in mind for the office. With the shocking discrediting
of Inglesi, DuBourg had needed to reassess his candidates,
and he passed on some of his thoughts to Plessis:

> I have cast my eyes on two men, one French, the other
> Italian; the one a Sulpician, who has been in Baltimore for
> twelve years, and is a man of universal knowledge, of emi-
> nent sanctity, whose zeal was in the past considered exces-
> sive, but which age and experience have toned down to the
> proper degree; for the rest, possessing in a high degree the
> power of making himself beloved, because his heart is the
> tenderest and humblest that I know of, blessed, finally, with
> strength proportioned to the immense labors he would have
> to undertake. He is Mr. Simon Bruté, of Rennes, about forty-
> two or forty-four years of age. The other is a disciple and
> child of St. Vincent de Paul, superior of my seminary and my
> vicar general, only thirty-two years of age, but with the
> wisdom and maturity and poise of a man of fifty. He is Mr.
> Joseph Rosati, a Neapolitan.[33]

Both men were loved by the Louisiana priests who had
come from Europe, Bruté for befriending them in Baltimore
on their arrival, and Rosati for working with them so cheerfully on the mission. The humility of both men presented a
difficulty, but the pope would surely be able to "gain this
important victory over their modesty." DuBourg suggested
ingratiatingly to Plessis, "If I did not dread to abuse your
goodness, my lord, I should beg of you to mention all this to
the Cardinal, as things about which I have consulted you,
and upon which I await also the advice of Bishops David,
Flaget and Fenwick before making a definite decision."[34]
Writing to Rome in May 1822, DuBourg was still suggesting
either Bruté or Rosati[35] and had only in October—with the
approval of David and Flaget—fixed upon Rosati alone.[36]
When DuBourg was in Emmitsburg in November and
related to Bruté the most recent developments in the coadjutor matter, Bruté was dismayed to learn that his name had
been mentioned at all. DuBourg reassured him with the
promise that in his next letter to Rome he would remove

Bruté's name categorically from consideration. DuBourg's lengthy protest to Propaganda from Baltimore on December 6 closed with keeping his pledge to Bruté, and urging once more his designs for Rosati, as he explained:

> I have already asked for Mr. Bruté, a most deserving priest of Saint Sulpice, as my coadjutor out of fear that Mr. Rosati, if he were chosen for this duty, would be removed from the government of his Community. Now, however, since [Rosati] has already been nominated bishop, I asked that Mr. Bruté be removed from consideration and Mr. Rosati himself be assigned as my coadjutor and that at the same time he continue to be in charge of his Congregation until another is ready who can succeed him in that office. Thus all things will be settled by a simple move.[37]

To Bruté he sent off a hasty note saying:

> Calm yourself, my dear friend, I have already written according to your wishes. The only danger there is, is that in the interval between my first and second letter the affair might have been decided; but in such a case you could give your reasons for not obeying the first decision. I have reason to believe you will not be put to the test.[38]

The news of Rosati's appointment in 1823 gave as general satisfaction to Bruté as it did to the Bishop of Louisiana, who was now busily planning his coadjutor's consecration.

By the end of December, DuBourg had firmly decided that he wanted the ceremonies to take place in Louisiana rather than Missouri. He had some personal reasons, he admitted; his health had been bad for a month and the expenses of a trip from New Orleans to St. Louis were oppressive. The real reason, however, was that he wanted Rosati to meet as many of the clergy as possible and the priests in Lower Louisiana wanted to attend. He was tentatively thinking it would be appropriate to have the consecration on Rosati's feast day. Steamboats should be running by then; Rosati could rest up for a while at Aglaé and Doradou Bringier's home near Donaldsonville and then make a retreat with Father Charles de la Croix, now pastor at St. Michael's Church six miles away.[39]

On New Year's Day DuBourg told Rosati he had been having second thoughts about the date of the consecration. His first choice, which fell on a Friday that year, would leave too little time for priests to get back to their parishes for Sunday. Sundays were out, of course, since too few priests could attend. If they waited for the feast of an apostle that would take them into May. As a result he had decided upon the feast of the Annunciation, March 25.[40] The location would be the Church of the Ascension in Donaldsonville.

DuBourg then attended to a task he always enjoyed, the writing of a pastoral letter; this time his pleasure was keener than usual since he was announcing the forthcoming consecration of a coadjutor bishop, an event he trusted would furnish an historical date for the annals of the Diocese of Louisiana.[41] He was particularly happy that he would be consecrating Rosati, who had been his first choice in 1819 and his consistent choice for the last two years. His other three nominees had been not so much for the office as for personal reasons: Sibourd for his loyalty and long service, Bruté for his genius and misery in the Archdiocese of Baltimore. The thought of Inglesi could still wrench his heart and turn his stomach; DuBourg had wanted this wealthy, talented, ingratiating young Roman nobleman—as he had believed him to be—for the joy he could bring the bishop, less for the best interests or the diocese. Providence had made the fitting selection. De Andreis had foreseen it already in 1818 when he said, "Father Rosati promises great things. He is young, strong, healthy, disinterested, full of zeal and very talented. . . . I am certain that as soon as possible he will be summoned to the episcopacy."[42] That time had now come.

Since this ceremony had never been seen before in Louisiana, and was not likely to be seen again soon, DuBourg meant it to be as impressive as he could manage. He told Rosati to be sure to bring the large Pontifical from the seminary when he came downriver. It would have been more edifying to have two bishops; Rosati had particularly hoped Flaget could come. But Flaget had begged off on February 2, 1824, saying that his presence would be "almost useless," pointing out:

In fact, when the Bishop of Philadelphia was consecrated, although the coadjutor of our archbishop was in Baltimore, he had nothing to do with the ceremony; for all our rubricists agree that it is better for two priests to assist the new bishop, one by the bishop on one side and a single priest on the other. The rubrics not having changed since this time, I do not see how I could be of any use to you.[43]

DuBourg chose as his two assisting priests Louis Sibourd, his faithful friend and vicar general in the South, and Père Antoine, the priest in longest service in New Orleans and pastor of its cathedral. The choice of Antonio de Sedella was not as odd as it might seem. DuBourg was not a man who nurtured grudges; he was too busy with new plans to further the good of religion and the glory of God. He was in addition a man of common sense and would avoid, when he could, giving offense needlessly. Père Antoine still had a firm hold on the hearts of the *Orléannais,* and to denigrate the Capuchin could cause some of the hatred for the bishop to spill over on his coadjutor. More than anything, perhaps, it was DuBourg's view of the Church that those who served her to the end earned recognition. However lax the old Capuchin had been in those times of transition, he had kept the Church alive in a city where her enemies daily multiplied. Certainly in recent times he had welcomed Father Moni and DuBourg's other good assistants now serving at St. Louis Cathedral, while concerning himself more with good works and almsgiving to the city's poor.[44]

Rosati's attending priests were to be Edmond Saulnier, the pastor of the cathedral in St. Louis, Missouri, and Charles de la Croix, formerly of Florissant but now pastor of St. Michael's in LaFourche, Louisiana. It was like Du-Bourg to have another old Capuchin, Father Bernard de Deva, as another assistant in the ceremonies. Aristide B. Anduze, now at St. James Parish in Louisiana, was to be the homilist; and Hercule Brassac would serve as master of ceremonies.[45] With the date fixed in March, when weather along the Mississippi could be uncertain, DuBourg advised Rosati to start early in the year from the Barrens. Realizing that it would be more convenient for Rosati to make his headquarters where he was to be consecrated, DuBourg had by now decided that the bishop-elect should stay with Brassac in Donaldsonville rather than at the Bringiers', nine miles to the south on the opposite side of the river.

DuBourg himself did not reach the Bringier settlement until two days after Rosati's arrival. The bishop was just riding in from New Orleans when Brassac arrived at "the Hermitage" with Rosati in tow. The old friends enjoyed a pleasant two days, sharing each other's company and conversation, before Rosati went off to his retreat.

On the eve of his consecration, Rosati returned to Donaldsonville, where, as he later noted in his diary, he found:

> The Rt. Rev. Bishop of New Orleans and most of those who had been invited to the Consecration. Everything in the church was in readiness; the joyous peal of the church bell, the roar of the mortar, the sound of innumerable pipes first from the houses near the church, then from every other house inside and even outside the Parish of the Ascension heralded to all the faithful the morrow's celebration.

It was the way the frontier French celebrated every grand occasion: with bells, cannons, fifes, and drums.

Although there were torrential rains on March 23, the sun on the feast of the Annunciation rose "in brightness, drying the country roads, lending to every color a wondrous brilliancy." Creoles loved a parade, and to those watching who were not Catholics this one must have seemed wondrous indeed, with thirteen priests following the choirboys, then the bishop-elect, and then DuBourg in his elegant array, all moving through the bright, crisp air toward the church, one of the loveliest on the frontier. The Church of the Ascension, built only a few years before, was "very handsome, of brick with three aisles the roof of which is supported by columns quite tastily finished"; it was a place DuBourg knew almost better than any other between St. Louis and New Orleans.

The Bishop of Louisiana had not been well that winter, and the ceremonies of episcopal consecration were taxing even for a man in the best of condition. Flaget had taken eight hours, he said, to consecrate his own coadjutor in 1818. Yet, as DuBourg rested during Anduze's splendid sermon, he was content.[46] The previous year's anguish and apprehensions over Inglesi, the tension of waiting for Rome to undo the naming of Rosati to the vicariate created to relieve Maréchal of his responsibilities, all were swept away in the joys of this high watermark of his American episcopacy.

As he relaxed briefly at the Bringiers' afterward, DuBourg mused over the ways in which this consecration had silenced questions which had plagued him for so long. The brief making Rosati a bishop had been accompanied by a stipulation that the Diocese of Louisiana would remain undivided for three more years. For that duration DuBourg need not fret over the separation of regions so interdependent in the bishop's eyes. Nor would he waste time speculating about future archiepiscopal provinces in the West. It was enough, for the moment, that he and Rosati would share the responsibilities of Upper and Lower Louisiana.

Separating Upper and Lower Louisiana into two dioceses, with respective bishops at St. Louis and New Orleans, was a matter which had hung fire since 1819, and it was an issue on which DuBourg had remained more than usually consistent. His opposition to such a division had been clearly expressed to Propaganda on April 5, 1820, when he argued that it was premature, since for some years to come Upper and Lower Louisiana would be necessary to each other. The state of Missouri was still too young to provide a bishop much work; there were only seven or eight places which could afford—and that poorly enough—to maintain a priest. In those days, too, Sedella was still capable of making the situation of a resident bishop in New Orleans extremely unpleasant. "Owing to these conditions," DuBourg told Propaganda, "it seems to me, your Eminence, that it is better to leave the Diocese as it is, giving the Bishop, however, a coadjutor with whom he may share his income and his work."[47] As was his habit, in case his first letter might be lost in transit, when he found time later in the month he wrote again in the same vein. This time his objections were more cogent:

> A division of Louisiana is in no wise advisable, at least for yet a good while. For Lower and Upper Louisiana are so necessary to each other, that if they be separated, the latter could not get temporal, and the other spiritual help. The Episcopal *Mensa,* and the support of the seminary are somehow supplied by Lower Louisiana; from Upper Louisiana alone can priests be supplied. Each one, therefore, needs the society of the other; hence, if a division is made, both must of necessity suffer. At some future day, perhaps, it will be possible to make this division, otherwise desirable, without such great detriment; yet it will always be profitable to proceed slowly in a matter of such importance, lest, under the specious appearance of greater utility, the strength of both parts be impaired. For the present at any rate, it is evident that the division would be a calamity.[48]

Cogent or not, these arguments did not sway Propaganda immediately, and DuBourg had reason to believe he knew why. On August 6, 1821, he wrote bluntly to the Archbishop of Baltimore:

> I do not know whether I ought to disbelieve the news I receive from Rome, that you have recommended the division of my diocese. Should I not have a right to be surprised at this solicitude for a Church which does not belong to your Metropolitan province? But I would be astonished that you could believe that you knew better than I the interest of my diocese. I therefore very much doubt the accuracy of the report, and I will doubt it until your Excellency is pleased to tell me that it is so.

DuBourg continued with the reasons he had already given Rome for deferring the division, adding that the Mississippi River made it possible to get from one end of the diocese to the other and made episcopal visitations once a year without inconvenience. He then came to the point of his letter:

> If it is true that your Excellency has given Propaganda advice different from mine you will oblige me by telling the reasons which I absolutely can not guess and which might, if

communicated to me, prove useful to my diocese. I will observe only that in such a case it would be suitable, before writing to Rome, that you have the kindness to give your ideas to me myself.

The Bishop of Louisiana was of the opinion that fellow bishops ought to avoid embarrassing Propaganda with "having to decide between our opinions, whose divergence could delay its resolutions." For himself, he confessed, he would like to be able to recommend the division of Louisiana. "It is so sweet," he said pointedly, "for a Bishop to have his responsibility diminished!" He closed with reiterating his conviction on the subject of bishops:

> But what is most important to the common good, as to general satisfaction, is the union among the Bishops, above all among those who formed in the same school ought to be animated by only one spirit. How annoying it would be if in Rome they suspected the least coolness among them! For that will surely happen if we do not agree in what we have to propose for one another's dioceses.[49]

Propaganda had certainly been listening to someone opposing DuBourg's view, for in June a letter had already been dispatched to Louisiana coolly asserting, "Your Lordship is not so broken down either by age or ill health as to need a Coadjutor just now. . . . It would be to the utmost interest of the Diocese if it were divided. . . ."[50] In October Cardinal Fontana repeated his position: DuBourg's diocese ought to be divided into three parts, Upper Louisiana, Lower Louisiana, and the Floridas.[51] DuBourg had rejoiced at the prospect of losing the Floridas, but he remained adamant on the subject of Louisiana. The time had not yet come, he insisted, for a separate diocese at St. Louis; there was still no income for a bishop there. The properties he had acquired in the hope of furnishing some revenue were still not fully paid for, and he could not agree to a division of Louisiana until his finances were on a firm footing.[52]

Propaganda began the year 1822 with a somewhat ambiguous remark: "In regard to the division of your vast

Diocese, the proposals made do not appear to have as yet attained maturity," followed by the courteous assurance, "Whatever course of action the S. Cong. resolves to take about the Floridas, I shall let you know at the first opportunity."[53] By spring, Ercule Cardinal Consalvi, the acting Prefect of Propaganda since the death of Fontana, wrote more forcefully that he had not had an answer from Louisiana on the division question and demanded a speedy reply. He hoped that DuBourg would find it agreeable to take one part of the diocese and have Sibourd or Rosati take the other.[54] Apparently a decision had been made whether DuBourg advised it or not. Knowing the Archbishop of Baltimore was in Rome that spring, the Bishop of Louisiana may have wondered if Maréchal had any connection with Consalvi's seeming urgency.

Maréchal was without question enjoying himself in Rome in 1822, telling Antoine Garnier in Paris, "All the prelates of the Propaganda are perfectly disposed in my regard."[55] His business was temporarily set back by the death of Cardinal Fontana, but he assured his French friends that "all the kindnesses which the Holy Father never ceased to lavish . . . the demonstrations of love and attachment of the cardinals" made his six months seem only a day, and on his departure he could not refrain from "bursting into tears."[56] He was really in his element when Cardinal Consalvi, who succeeded Fontana to Propaganda, requested his opinions on Bishop DuBourg's proposals, and he quickly disposed of that intriguer's jurisdiction. Rome should establish a new see at St. Louis and make DuBourg its bishop, while Rosati should be made Bishop of New Orleans with temporary jurisdiction over Alabama and the Floridas![57]

DuBourg, knowing nothing of this, remained determined to prevent the divorce between Upper and Lower Louisiana; he wrote as firmly as ever on September 5, giving Rome again all his reasons for requesting a postponement.[58] He told Rosati rather wearily, "I have written anew to prevent the division of the diocese as premature. My letter was most strongly worded. It was the fruit of most serious reflection; and my soul is much more tranquil since I wrote it."[59] In the end, with the enthusiastic support of Flaget and David and the guarded agreement of Maréchal, he had won his point in 1823.[60]

The question of a metropolitan province for the dioceses beyond the mountain, like the division of the diocese, receded into the background after Rosati's consecration. The notion of a second archbishopric in the United States appeared as early as 1819 when, according to Flaget's biographer, "a correspondence was opened between Flaget and DuBourg on the establishment of an archbishopric in the West, consequent upon the erection of Cincinnati into a see," with DuBourg suggesting either Bardstown or St. Louis as the seat of the archdiocese.[61] During the years prior to 1823, when the bishops of the West had felt isolated by geography and the distinctive nature of their problems on the frontier, the idea of a central clearing house was appealing; the western prelates had exchanged random thoughts on the subject with each other and with Propaganda. Yet there was never any wholehearted effort made to achieve this goal; least of all was there agreement on the best location for a metropolitan see city. With Flaget the notion stemmed primarily from his dissatisfaction with Archbishop Maréchal's reluctance to consult his suffragans. When Rome directed Maréchal to seek the counsel of his suffragans, and that information reached Kentucky, Flaget quickly revised his thoughts about a western archdiocese. David his coadjutor had never felt any sincere desire for it, certainly not if it were to be located in New Orleans or St. Louis. He told Maréchal in 1820, "New Orleans would not suit us so well as Baltimore for a metropolitan see. . . . Mgr. DuBourg could, if he so wished, establish an archbishopric in his own immense diocese. . . ." David held that there would be time enough later to consider a second one "this side of the mountains."[62] Talk of a western metropolitan faded in Kentucky after 1822.

With DuBourg the idea of a trans-Appalachian archbishopric was merely a randomly recurring dream of the future development of the Church in the West. His letter to

Propaganda on April 25, 1820, suggests how nebulous his own ideas were:

> Now touching on the erection of a new Metropolitan See
> . . . the Bishops' prevailing opinion is that the *city of St.
> Louis* should have the preference above all others, on account of its geographical position, as well as the increasing population and appreciation of the surrounding country. There can be no doubt that the creation of another Archbishopric is destined to serve greatly the interests of religion.[63]

In 1822 a small difficulty interfered, he granted: St. Louis was not yet even a diocese. If that could be remedied, the Diocese of St. Louis might include western Illinois, while eastern Illinois and Indiana could constitute another new diocese. But all that, he admitted, was a matter not ripe for consideration. The only point on which he seemed certain was that the new province "might properly have as suffragans all the Episcopal Sees this side of the Alleghenies." A month later in concert with Flaget and David he signed a joint appeal for a new archdiocese, giving as the reason the distance from Baltimore which made it difficult to attend synods.[64] No see city was suggested at all, but Flaget and David told Maréchal separately that Bardstown and Louisville would have their preference.

None of the western bishops made any secret of these occasional and fleeting thoughts on the subject, even inviting Maréchal to join them in sending petitions to Rome when Inglesi went over in 1820.[65] The Archbishop of Baltimore, however, who had a monopoly of that rank, had preferred to send his own views separately, not surprisingly disagreeing with his western confreres. A second archdiocese was premature; but, he offered grandly, sometime later there might be three, not one. These should be located at Bardstown, Charleston, and New Orleans. As for St. Louis, where DuBourg was presently located, it sufficed to make that a diocese in the future.[66]

After DuBourg learned that the Ursulines meant to give him their old convent as a bishop's residence, he began mentioning New Orleans as a possible metropolitan see.[67] Cardinal Consalvi had replied to this *volte face* politely, saying that he had made "good note" of the recommendation and would see that the other cardinals were asked for their opinions.[68]

That had been in the autumn of 1822. Since then, the appointment of Rosati and his consecration, coming so soon after DuBourg's removal to New Orleans as his permanent residence, had relegated daydreams of future archbishoprics into the background of DuBourg's waking thoughts. Even though to the end of DuBourg's American episcopacy the Archbishop of Baltimore remained haunted by the spectre of an archiepiscopal rival in the West, beyond the mountains it was never a burning issue after 1823. The Bishop of Louisiana had far more pressing, practical matters to confront in Lower Louisiana, where he was to reside for the next three years.

CHAPTER XXX

AN EPISCOPAL RESIDENCE
IN NEW ORLEANS

Even before receiving Rome's assurance that he would
have Rosati for a coadjutor, the Bishop of Louisiana and the
Floridas had already decided to make his episcopal residence in Lower Louisiana for the rest of his tenure. When
he returned to Missouri from Maryland in the spring of
1823, Madam Duchesne, who was a keen observer, had
noticed that the bishop was more preoccupied than usual.
His visit to her establishment had been almost perfunctory,
with far fewer questions about their concerns. She had
commented in her next letter to Paris, "People say he is no
longer our Bishop, and as a matter of fact he signs himself
Bishop of New Orleans, now, and not Bishop of Louisiana,
as formerly."[1] The Florissant superior of the Religious of
the Sacred Heart was only speculating about DuBourg's
intentions, for he had said nothing about them prior to his
hurried departure for the South on May 11. It was not until
she got his letter of July 12 written from Côte d'Acadie that
she realized how correctly she had sensed what lay behind
his behavior on his last visit to St. Ferdinand. He began:

> My heart was quite shaken, my dear daughter, when I took my leave of you, leaving you in ignorance of the plan I was to execute two days later. I thought I had to act thus in order to control your feelings and mine, not doubting that you would give my reserve the most favorable interpretation. Here we are separated until springtime. It is a grief with which I must familiarize myself if I want not to succumb to it.[2]

Until he obtained a coadjutor it was absolutely necessary that he reside, at least the greater part of the year, in the most populous region of his immense diocese. He reflected ruefully, "What is doubly inconvenient for me is that my mind and heart are always drawn violently toward the extremity from which I am distant and can thus enjoy no repose." Nevertheless, he assured her in phrases she knew so well that in spite of this mélange of uneasiness and sense of duty he was confident that his diverse enterprises were "manifestly the works of God miraculously formed and sustained."

He saw the arrival of the Jesuits as an excellent omen for both his diocese and for her society. She knew he would not lose sight of their needs, but for the moment it was God's will that the bishop could not supply them. He was writing to Van Quickenborne to overcome all his scruples in regard to directing the Florissant convent and hoped the Jesuits could care for her house as she desired. He comforted her:

> Don't get discouraged, my dear daughter, by the decrease in your boarding school; that is due to the circumstances of the moment. Let us envision the future, in which your house must necessarily be the resource of the state of Missouri. While waiting, your ministry among the poor girls will not be sterile. As for the means of survival, God will not fail to provide. The house at Grand Coteau can already come to the aid of yours; and I am going to propose to you a third, which by its double yield, spiritual and temporal, will perhaps be of greater benefit than the other two.

He was not talking of New Orleans, that "foyer of yellow fever," he explained, but of a finer, more beautiful, rich, and

690

healthy part of the river valley twenty-two leagues above the city. "As soon as I have your approbation," he urged enthusiastically, "I will push the enterprise which will rest until then."[3]

Being DuBourg, he did not rest long but already in August was pressing her for a reply, arguing with his customary optimism, "The projected establishment by its situation promises to be the most flourishing of its kind which exists in America."[4] He was going to Grand Coteau in September for Prize Day at the urging of Madam Eugénie and all the students, and he did not doubt he could sway the headmistress of that house to his designs. But the summer of 1823 was no time to do anything but dream of further expansion.

DuBourg had reached New Orleans in early June to find the Ursulines, delighted with the bishop's success in clarifying their property titles in Washington the previous winter, already busy with their new convent below the city.[5] His mind was teeming with all the implications this project had for the future, as he wrote to Rosati:

> The construction of the new monastery of the Ursulines of N. Orl. advances rapidly and gives me the hope of taking possession of their present dwelling in 8 or 10 months. All is arranged for the reestablishment of the College in this fine property in a manner to assure the Bishop of his living, and revenue for the Church. The profits from the institution, which promise to be flourishing, will also be put in common for the needs of the Diocese, the Seminary being the first and the Missions the second. But before realizing these fine hopes there will still be expenses for making the establishment. Mr. Portier will turn over to the College all the funds of his school, which numbers 180 students, and all his equipment which is rather considerable in Servants, furniture, library, etc. But he is still not free of debt, although only a little remains.[6]

It was, as it always was, exhilarating to plot the future; as always, DuBourg remained undaunted by the thought of new debts; and, as always, the barest hint of new income promised the resolution of all his financial needs. He was probably never more sanguine about progress than in the midsummer during which Rome granted him a coadjutor and permitted the Ursulines to give him an episcopal residence.[7] He promised Rosati happily, "If all should succeed, 1823 would be a fruitful year."[8]

Living in New Orleans added new zest to everything. The proliferating press, the bustle in the streets, the activity of an international seaport, all made the city more cosmopolitan, and kept the mind more active. Louisiana had been a state almost a decade longer than Missouri, and since the War of 1812 the political life seemed more sophisticated. Celebrations of the Fourth of July were signs of the times, with newspapers carefully announcing the order of the day in minute detail. The cathedral became the core of the annual gala, with a *Te Deum* followed by the reading of the Declaration of Independence in both English and French and spirited addresses by notables of city and state. Ladies accompanied by their escorts were permitted to take their seats at 10:00 a.m. with the general public surging in after 11:00. The procession to the cathedral formed at the Government House and was preceded by resplendant military escort and grand marshal. Then came Governor Robertson and his suite, the Secretaries of State and Treasury, the Mexican Ambassador and his suite, judges and court officials, consuls of foreign nations, the reverend clergy, orators, and finally the officers of the Army, Navy, and Marine Corps, the Masonic Lodges, and the Volunteer Corps.[9] It was typical of the city, however, that in the same week in July the *Gazette de la Louisiane* devoted even more space to the political opinions of Félicité de Lamennais and Alphonse Martainville and attacks on the French ministry of Count Joseph de Villèle and Jacques-Joseph Corbière.[10]

DuBourg found that the same notable names remained on people's lips. The election of the hero of the Battle of New Orleans to the United States Senate, and the election of Edward Livingston to the lower house of Congress were duly hailed, with the latter given a splendid dinner at Elkins's Coffee House on the eve of his departure for Washington, "a fitting tribute of respect to the lawyer of longest standing in Louisiana."[11] The common man, however, was becoming more critical and more vocal about his dissatisfactions nearer home. The Company of Louisiana Guards meeting at Richardson's Coffee House on August 2, 1823, voted unanimously not to obey the orders of their major, a Frenchman named Cavellier, or any other foreigner not a naturalized citizen of the United States at the time of his appointment. Of the sixty signatures to this protest, Louis Tulane's was the only name of French origins.[12]

This growing consciousness of nationalism was only part of a more general desire to be heard. A group of malcontents at Elkins's Coffee House drafted a protest to the Postmaster General decrying the dreadful situation in the mails.[13] By indirection, private religious education came under attack that summer when the *Gazette* published lengthy articles supporting public education, citing the statistics of those educated in the public schools of Boston and New York.[14] The most civic-minded rhetorical complaint came from "Bonum Publicum," who addressed the editors in October, denouncing the daily interments at the Old Catholic Cemetery in Basin Street, and demanding to be told why Mayor J. Roffignac, who while president of the Board of Health had termed the custom a "nuisance and hotbed of infection," as mayor had done nothing about it. The *fabrique* of the Catholic Church, "Bonum Publicum" asserted, while hurling denunciations continued "cruelly and wantonly" their shocking custom of exposing the contents of graves as they deposited dead bodies daily in the Old Cemetery, awaiting "the autumnal fire which casts the ashes of the poor to the four winds." Petition after petition had gone to the city council. The legislature had authorized the city to give ground for a new cemetery, and to fine violators five hundred dollars after June 1, 1823. Yet nothing was done![15]

While these political affairs at home and abroad shared the attention of the reading public, the generality of the inhabitants of Lower Louisiana were more concerned year in and year out over economic conditions and the ever present threat of yellow fever each summer and fall. In his

August letter to Florissant, the bishop had reported gratefully, "No sickness in the city at present. We hope we are rid
of it this year"; and this hope was fulfilled, for young Theodore Seghers, who had studied under the Sulpicians eight
years earlier, wrote to Maryland on October 6, "At present
there is not much yellow fever here, and it is hoped it will
not increase." Seghers thought that they owed their respite
in New Orleans that year to the heavy rains, "even a little
hurricane," which purified the air, and to the fact that city
residents were more careful. The weather, together with the
lazarets and strict quarantines had saved them from the
horrors of 1822.[16]

Unfortunately, the economy of Lower Louisiana was
less consoling that year. Seghers somberly noted, "The port
is completely empty, with only two or three little two-
masted craft."[17] As August began, the *Gazette* lamented:

> Never in twenty years has the port of New Orleans counted
> so small a number of ships as today. Almost all the rich
> cargoes have departed and we have left enough foodstuff to
> fill another thirty or so. How is it that with a rather consider-
> able commerce every one cries misery and that hard cash
> has almost disappeared?[18]

Part of New Orleans's difficulty was that in the years of
DuBourg's residence, "King Cotton" was becoming more
securely enthroned. American exports in cotton between
the year of DuBourg's synod in 1821 and his departure in
early 1826 grew by some 130,000 bales, and New Orleans
led all the exporters including Charleston, Savannah, and
Mobile.[19] The disadvantages of a one-commodity economy
were beginning to be felt.

Times were hard all over, however. The religious of the
Visitation Convent in Georgetown had once had forty
pupils, now they had only nineteen without any hope of
increasing the number, for the money shortage was felt in
the East as well as in the Mississippi Valley.[20] By November
6, 1823, Archbishop Maréchal in Baltimore was contemplating sending Visitation nuns to Canada, telling Plessis:

694

You doubtless know, my Lord, the hard times that are weighing upon us now in America. I have never seen anything so distressing. The wealthiest families are suffering to a degree that I would not have believed possible. My dear Visitation nuns feel the effects very keenly. They get no more sewing to do. Because of lack of means, parents have been gradually obliged to withdraw their children. While in regard to money due, it is useless to press for payment.[21]

It was impossible for Maréchal in his poverty to help them. Would Plessis be willing to take twelve to fifteen from the American motherhouse? "Your diocese," Maréchal urged ingratiatingly, "would be the gainer by our loss at a time when we are experiencing the most lamentable misery."[22]

The indomitable Bishop of Louisiana, impervious as usual to the absence or presence of hard cash, was by the end of 1823 blithely going ahead with his intentions of starting not only a third establishment of Sacred Heart nuns, this time at La Fourche, but also dreamed of a second house of Vincentians, this one to serve Lower Louisiana. His diocese was scheduled to be divided at the end of three years and there was still much to be done in the southern part which had no seminary or religious order of men. The Protestants were not losing heart. In August the Methodists had engaged the upper part of a large house in rue Poydras and announced that it would be open for religious services every Sunday at ten in the morning and four in the afternoon.[23] In December the Presbyterians met to elect a board of trustees and a treasurer and discuss ways to raise money for their house of worship.[24] It was no time for any other shepherd of a flock to show himself fainthearted.

If pressed, however, DuBourg would have confessed to a sense of relief that his Jesuits were safe in Florissant that summer and not in Indian territory, for on August 7 a steamboat was engaged to transport the First Regiment of U.S. Infantry from Baton Rouge to St. Louis in the face of increasing hostility from the "Savages upon the upper Missouri." The *Gazette* assured its subscribers, "From Mr. Calhoun, the ablest member perhaps, of the present cabinet, the army and the frontier inhabitants may expect measures at once prompt and efficient." Indeed, on August 12 two steamboats were believed en route to Council Bluffs, and part of the troops at Pensacola had received orders for similar movements.[25] If Calhoun had gotten his way earlier, DuBourg reminded himself, one of the Whitemarsh priests might have been sent to Council Bluffs.

These alarums and excursions notwithstanding, the Bishop of Louisiana had innumerable duties to perform, among them his episcopal visitations. In 1823 they proved later than intended. He had gone to *Maison Bringier* in June to enjoy "some rest and rather good health" among Aglaé's growing family, telling his brother Louis:

> I have a pretty separate house where I enjoy a peace I had not known for many years. These dear children overwhelm me with attentions. On Sundays a considerable crowd comes to my chapel. I am preparing my youngest niece, with two other young people, for First Communions on September 8, after which I will go to visit Natchitoches, Ouachita, Attakapas, Opelousas, and other parishes in Louisiana.[26]

Involuntarily recalling the dreadful summer of the previous year, his painful attempts to discount the rumors about Inglesi, the horrible attacks of nerves three and four times a day, he hastily reassured Louis, "This summer I am enjoying rather good health; I owe it, I believe, to the repose of body and soul that I have achieved. Another summer like the last one would have finished me." Actually his health was the result, not the cause, of his lingering at Aglaé's just then. As he told Rosati, "The great heat and inundations have forced me to defer until autumn the visitation intended."[27] September's weather proved little better. A terrible storm destroyed at least half the cotton crop near Baton Rouge, and there were heavy rains throughout Lower Louisiana that month.[28]

It was not until October that his journeying began and he could fit in some of the ordinations anticipated. At Iberville he visited St. Gabriel's Church and at Pointe Coupée the two Blanc brothers at St. Francis of Assisi. Jean-Baptiste Blanc who was to be ordained was staying with his brother Antoine until Lawrence Peyretti would arrive in Donaldsonville for their ordinations.[29] As it was, communications were delayed and the bishop wrote to Rosati afterward, "I ordained M. Blanc October 24 at the Church of Donaldsonville, assisted by eight priests and an immense concourse. The two brothers seem very happy and full of courage. They have had a second church built in the parish of Pointe Coupée to facilitate services.[30] Peyretti would have to come later.

DuBourg then visited the interior of La Fourche, where he confirmed 365 people and found himself quite content with conditions at both the Church of the Assumption and St. Joseph's. Fathers Potini and Rosti for the moment gave satisfaction, and Potini particularly seemed to be maturing and was "reducing to silence" some of the trustees who had been opposed to him at first. Father Tichitoli and his two confreres appeared "very edifying, very united, and very exact in their rules."[31]

It was back in Donaldsonville that the news caught up with DuBourg that Pope Pius VII had died. The pontiff's death had occurred on August 16, but New Orleans learned of it at the end of October when an item of September 5 was forwarded from Liverpool, England.[32] The last news the bishop had had of the pope had been in July, when he told Rosati, "The Pope has made a promotion of Cardinals which brings the Sacred College today to 68. Cardinal Consalvi was very sick and was despaired of last April. Mgr. Pedicini has received one of the hats. Mgr. Caprano replaces him at the Propaganda."[33] It was odd to realize that for three months prayers for the pope in the Mississippi Valley had been for a man since gone to his reward. For William DuBourg it was more than the loss of a good man. Pius VII had been his friend, had made him a bishop, had wished his mission Godspeed when they left Rome eight years ago. The portrait the Holy Father had given him was DuBourg's most prized possession.[34]

On his way south in November 1823 the bishop's thoughts were on the *mandement* he would issue on the subject of the pope's death. He was grateful for the companionship of Charles de la Croix. The former pastor of St. Ferdinand's in Florissant had quickly come to feel unneeded, once the Jesuits arrived, and was now going to work in Lower Louisiana. DuBourg, who was already sure there would be a third convent of the Sacred Heart nuns near St. Michael's Church in the county of St. James, was assigning Father de la Croix to that church. Arrived at St. Michael's, with the faithful Belgian serving as his secretary, the bishop issued his pastoral letter on prayers for Pius VII and for his successor.[35] A few days earlier he had sent Rosati the news of the pope's death saying, "Have a funeral in all the churches of Upper Louisiana."[36] Now, writing his own pastoral on Pius VII, DuBourg found it rather appropriate that his coadjutor's first administrative act should be a circular ordering prayers for the late pope and for his successor Leo XII.[37] Leaving St. Michael's, DuBourg returned to New Orleans for Advent and Christmastide.

The bishop had admonished Rosati in October, "Let us remember, we do not say the beautiful words of the psalm in vain when we say, 'Why are you sad, oh my soul? Trust in God, etc.' As harsh as our situation is, it is at least a little more reassuring than it was 4 or 5 years ago. . . . He who has begun the work will perfect it."[38] Yet there were moments when even DuBourg had his qualms, especially when he thought of St. Louis where it seemed that all his efforts of the past five years had been in vain. A year ago, while DuBourg was in Maryland, the Missouri State Legislature on December 17, 1822, had authorized the trustees of St. Louis Parish to sell as much of the church block as was necessary to indemnify themselves for the money advanced for the building of the church, forty-five hundred dollars of which was still owed them. Madame Duchesne, who heard all sorts of rumors in Florissant, wrote to her French superior:

> Things are going badly for religion in St. Louis. As the debt
> on the church has not been paid, those who hold the mor-
> tage want to sell the property of the presbytery, including the
> Bishop's house and garden, etc. Monseigneur is in Bal-
> timore just now and the priest who holds the power of

attorney for him dares not make a move to buy the church and shoulder the debt. All this is a bitter blow for Monseigneur and his priests, toward whom these men are acting with the greatest ingratitude, having given them no remuneration for their services. I was told that the Bishop might be forced to come here to live—perhaps these people were just sounding me out.[39]

St. Louis Catholics were still not inured to the reality that they must support a church if it were to survive. The Spanish government until 1804 had provided church and clergy; the tithes of the congregation had remained normal for years. Following the American acquisition of the Louisiana Territory, religious institutions had languished, and the occasional visits of itinerant missionaries during the fourteen-year interim preceding DuBourg's arrival had built up no habits of assuming responsibility for the regular support of a building or a pastor. With the arrival of a bishop who tried to provide a church, school, seminary, and convent simultaneously, the people were totally unprepared for the burdens these institutions entailed.

Francis Niel, who administered both church and college, tried to satisfy his creditors, "living personally like a beggar," but the offerings of the parishioners were quite inadequate. Even had good will existed, the economic situation after the Panic of 1819 would have dispelled it. Niel tried without success to institute two lotteries to save the church block.[40] Auguste Chouteau the city's founder, his stepbrother Pierre Chouteau, and Bernard Pratte were determined to recoup their losses, and on September 16, 1823, Sheriff John K. Walker offered for sale four lots of the church block facing Walnut Street. "Probably at the request of Bishop DuBourg," Niel bid for the lots and acquired them for $1,204. This purchase, while temporarily retaining the church block intact, did little to satisfy the larger claims of the creditors. Nor did it ameliorate Niel's own financial situation as pastor. No matter what resolutions the wardens of the parish passed regarding his salary, the church collections went first to pay debts which the building committee had contracted on the church.[41]

Administering a church and a secondary school were

becoming too much for Niel, whose health no longer supported such responsibilities. In October after he retrieved the church lots, Niel announced that he was placing the administration of the college in the hands of two newcomers to the faculty. François de Maillet was one of the Jesuit novices who had come from Whitemarsh; Elihu Shepard, a married man and a Mason, was from New England and had moved to St. Louis less than a year before. The new prospectus announced in the *Missouri Republican* in December was the work of these neophytes. By April 1824 Niel turned over the college finances to a public accountant, P. Walsh. The original notion DuBourg had cherished—a school run by ecclesiastics rearing Christian boys who might develop vocations to supply a native clergy for Missouri—seemed to be vanishing, especially after Niel made a contract with the city government to educate poor boys, and St. Louis College became the first school west of the Mississippi to receive municipal tax support.[42] At least Rosati's college at the Barrens was the sort of school the bishop approved. Started in November 1822 and run by Vincentians, its enrollment in a short time had reached well over fifty students.[43]

Bishop DuBourg's relations with the church trustees of St. Louis were not improved by his removal to New Orleans, and were particularly exacerbated by his attempt to remove his possessions in books and art works for his chapel and residence in New Orleans. Perhaps if he had been able to take them with him when he left St. Louis in 1823, there would have been less outcry; but the Ursulines had not yet moved from his future residence, and even while he was in the East in 1822 Madame Duchesne had heard that "the lawyer for the Bishop's enemies has said very violent things against him. They went so far as to say that the King of France had made his gifts, not to Monseigneur, but to the city of St. Louis."[44] When DuBourg did send for his property, there was a real furore and no one dared to comply with his request on December 28, 1823.

On April 24, 1824, the Bishop of Louisiana, who preferred peace and good will, wrote to the trustees patiently explaining his reasons for making his residence in New Orleans. His age and infirmities did not permit him to continually travel the immense extent of his diocese; the pope had kindly given him a coadjutor to administer the upper part of the diocese; indeed, Rosati had just been consecrated. DuBourg had not ceased to be interested in them; surely the sacrifices he had made for the Church in Missiouri, without any recompense, were a proof of his devotion. He hoped to visit them again in the coming year. As for the adornments of the church in St. Louis, he stated;

> I leave to Mgr. Rosati my Coadjutor, and presumptive heir in the State of Missouri, to be transmitted to his successors in the same State, the organ which I have placed in your Church, a beautiful set of candlesticks with the cross for the altar, a processional cross and candlesticks for the acolytes, two censors with gold chains, a beautiful altar lamp, sacred vases, an aspergillium, a number of fine ornaments and church linens, my furniture, 9 servants large or small. . . . in a word almost all I possess in that quarter.[45]

All of this was being given for the sole purpose of facilitating religious services in their church and diminishing the cost to the inhabitants. Was it necessary to prove his attachment to the church that he give as well his own pictures and books? "In truth I do not know what use my library would have for the people of St. Louis," he said practically, "being uniquely composed of Ecclesiastical authors." Besides, he had need of them and could not do without them. For the time being he would share his paintings with them: five for himself, and five for the church at St. Louis with the understanding that if he ever had another cathedral he had the right to withdraw the paintings from the St. Louis church for his new one. He concluded, "This is to tell you that I have and that I will always have for the faithful of Missouri all the attachment of a Father; and for you, Gentlemen, personally and in your quality as Representatives of the Church of St. Louis all the esteem and devotion you could desire and expect."[46] This reasonable approach was wasted on the trustees, but in June 1824

Edmond Saulnier, who assisted at both the church and the college, did send seventeen boxes of the bishop's books downriver to New Orleans.[47] There the matter of the bishop's belongings rested.

Uneasiness over St. Louis revived, when on the eighth of September, Niel, who had had an attack of what seemed to be apoplexy the previous winter,[48] asked Bishop Rosati for permission to go to Europe to recuperate and raise some money to free the church lots from the mortgage still threatening foreclosure. The people were embittered, he reported, and would not help.[49] Rosati referred him to Bishop DuBourg, who refused to have any part in sponsoring another begging trip to Europe, given the circumstances existing by 1824.

In the first place he had been badly burned in the Inglesi affair; he was still being dunned by French aristrocrats who believed they had bought land in Missouri. Further, he believed that since the Society for the Propagation of the Faith was already generously supporting American dioceses in the West, it would weaken French enthusiasm to have other supplicants seeking their aid. Bishop Fenwick of Cincinnati had found generous support on his trip by appealing to that society; DuBourg felt that Bishop Rosati himself ought to go eventually and have the same success.[50] Finally, by 1824 DuBourg had very little faith left in Niel's business acumen. Neither the parish nor the college of St. Louis had prospered in recent times, and one suspected that more than poor health was responsible for important matters going unattended.

In the same letter advising Rosati to go to Europe, DuBourg had expressed his uneasiness about the church property in St. Louis. He had heard that there were still threats to take it away. He urged Rosati:

> Try to settle this matter. You could compromise with these Gentlemen for the sum of $2500 payable by you in annual terms of $500 without prejudice to what they could recover from the pews in accordance with their claims. Only my signature is necessary, which I give for a guarantee of yours; but on the condition that the title is immediately passed to

you. You will have to be on the spot to handle this. . . .
Speak of this to no one; above all do not use Mr. Niel for any
transaction. He doesn't know the first thing about it. Handle
it yourself with the gentlemen of St. Louis.[51]

When Niel importuned Rosati again to let him go to Europe,
describing the bad state of his health and assuring Rosati
that Bishop DuBourg need have no fears that he would
pretend to be going to collect money,[52] Rosati decided on
December 4 to grant his permission.[53] With Niel determined
to go, and Rosati permitting it, Bishop DuBourg conceded
gracefully on December 28 and told his coadjutor:

> I authorize you to arrange this matter with this good Niel, as
> you judge fitting. You can give him his *exeat,* or his *tempo-*
> *rary dimissory,* with all the recommendations which his
> conduct merits. But if you authorize him to make any collec-
> tion, let it be only in your name, as Administrator of the
> Catholic Church in the State of Missouri. I am distressed at
> not being able to give him the money for his trip; even more
> so for not being able to furnish Mr. Janvier to replace him.
> The thing is entirely *out of the question.* Please write to Mr.
> Niel at once comformable to these arrangements. I infinitely
> regret losing his services for that part of the Diocese. In spite
> of its needs, I am not of the opinion that he should be in
> charge of collecting. Do what you wish, but only in your
> name and without any mention of mine.[54]

With Niel leaving St. Louis, his responsibilities were
transferred to the reluctant shoulders of Edmond Saulnier.
Saulnier had come from Bordeaux in DuBourg's second
year in St. Louis. Arriving at the Barrens in May 1819, he
studied philosophy there for a while under Philip Borgna.
DuBourg then assigned him to the college at St. Louis,
where he began to teach, at first continuing his own studies
under Felix De Andreis while the latter lived, and later as an
ordained priest.[55] It was Saulnier who presumed to send to
DuBourg on November 24, 1824, the five paintings, five
more cases of books, and the ornaments the bishop had
requested for his chapel in New Orleans.[56]
Saulnier now bore the brunt of the anger of the St.

Louis church wardens, and when he reported some of the details, the criticisms, the demands, and the arguments to the bishop in New Orleans, DuBourg lost all patience and told Saulnier:

> The truth is that I am at least very astonished to find myself treated as I am. I will not write to you further about my reclamations. I will take other means which can not compromise you; for I would be distressed that you should suffer on my account. But I believe the end of all that will be that I will leave nothing at all to the Church of St. Louis other than what I found there. All the rest being mine, I will know how to repossess it. One will then learn, but too late, he who offers to give his cloak must not be asked to give his shirt as well.

DuBourg, once he had begun, had no compunction about making his view of the whole agitation known. He found it most singular that anyone could pretend a right to his paintings since he had either purchased them or received them as personal gifts. He had paid for their freight and their customs duties, as well as the cost of having them restored. General Pratte could well remember the freight on only six of them from New Orleans, because he paid it in DuBourg's absence. It was the same for the organ and the ornaments, etc. "As for the latter, is it not a crying shame," the bishop demanded, "that my chapel used by 6 priests should be deprived while you retain an enormous supply for yourself alone?" He could only find it an injustice and ingratitude which revolted him and he could think of no other case where injustice and ingratitude had been carried to such a degree.

He did not blame Saulnier; he only reproached him for having allowed the people to intimidate him. "Continue, my good child," he said kindly, "to aid the good souls and work with zeal to convert Sinners. Sanctify yourself by obedience and fidelity to your duties." As for those who talked of getting lawyers, the bishop would use one even sooner.

It was difficult to be left in charge, DuBourg knew, and he said frankly, "I swear to you I count little or nothing on the great projects of Mr. Niel. God grant that he will not do more harm than good for the mission. I do not like a Pastor who by his silence seems to approve that his Bishop's intentions and views should be so horribly distorted and calumniated."[57]

The thought of disloyalty hurt him inordinately. He had always been easily pricked, and as he grew older DuBourg found himself even more sensitive. He ended his outburst, "I do not like to write on this subject. It is the last time I shall do so. I will act, and I will act efficaciously; that will put an end to it all."[58] It *was* the last time he wrote on the subject, but he did not have recourse to lawyers. He was much too busy with other matters in 1825 and, besides, as quickly as an animus rose it subsided.

He was sound in his judgment of Niel's prospects for bringing any notable aid to Missouri. In Europe, instead of seeking recruits for the college as his first aim, Niel sent Rosati a tiny remittance from Paris and headed for Rome. There he busied himself advising Propaganda on affairs concerning the Diocese of Louisiana, first urging a postponement of the division of DuBourg's jurisdiction, then retracting that recommendation. He prepared a memoir presenting his opinions on American Church matters, among them the qualilties which a Bishop of St. Louis should possess.[59]

Rosati viewed Niel's first remittance glumly, thanking him for this "small help" which had arrived while weevils were voraciously devouring Missouri's winter wheat crop.[60] Rosati had pictured Niel seeking recruits for the mission in France and Belgium, not playing the diplomat at the Vatican. Reprovingly Rosati suggested that Niel return to St, Louis where they might "work well together."[61]

Niel did not return to Missouri then, or later, and when three of his recruits finally reached St. Louis, Rosati commented caustically, "Instead of bringing me something, they announced that they had to borrow $120 which I have to pay back to Bp. Fenwick." At that moment the Bishop of St. Louis had exactly thirty-seven cents! As for the recruits themselves, Rosati reproached Niel, "Fr. Lutz does not want to teach; Chiaverotti is afraid of a stomach-ache; as to

Surault I will not admit him to Orders, owing to some indiscretions on his part during the journey."[62]

Niel gave Madame Duchesne even more reason to feel apprehensive about the benefits of his trip. Back in Paris he persuaded Madame Barat that she should establish a new Sacred Heart house in St. Louis, The third house at St. Michael's was just getting started and a fourth house at the time seemed to Duchesne an incredible notion. She was further concerned about the pretext under which Niel might get money from Madame Barat; and she warned Paris, "If Father Niel, pastor in St. Louis, comes to you to beg financial help, will you please state the purpose of what you give him, whether for the Jesuits or for ourselves, since we are carrying on work for the Indians. They now have ten boys, and we have six girls."[63] Someone much more devoted to the interests of Sacred Heart in Louisiana was planning to go to Europe soon to solicit for both the women and the Jesuits. As DuBourg explained to Van Quickenborne:

> Mr. de la Croix, very busy today for the establishment of the Ladies of the S. C. had asked my permission to make a voyage to Flanders next year, I promised it to him on the condition that he would work there especially for your establishment in Missouri. You can count on his zeal as on mine. I appreciate your difficulties much more than you think. . . . Meanwhile, my very dear Father, have courage. God wishes us to purchase his benedictions. Let us not look at the price he places on them.[64]

The successes of European collections, present or future, for Missouri were not in the forefront of the Louisiana prelate's mind in 1825. When he was at home in New Orleans in between episcopal visitations, he had his new residence to occupy his interest. Then there were the eminent visitors to excite the city. In April the noble Lafayette stayed at the Cabildo, where Père Antoine called upon him. The *Courier* of April 13 reported that the General remarked politely that he was proud to be of the same age as Father Antonio, who was three generations old, "for there is not much difference between us,"said Lafayette; "I am a man of 76." DuBourg did not anticipate a call from the French hero of the War for Independence, for the year before in Boston, when Father William Taylor invited Lafayette to assist at Mass at Holy Cross Cathedral, the visiting luminary had "thanked him, saying that he was to go to the Presbyterian Church." A month later in Baltimore he had accepted the highest honors of the Masonic Lodge and had further scandalized good Catholics at the Baltimore Cathedral by refusing to kneel during the consecration of the Mass, causing Charles Carroll of Carrollton to call out, "Either kneel or sit down!"[65]

Bishop DuBourg did exchange polite calls with His Highness Bernhard Duke of Saxe Weimar Eisenach, however, when that dignitary visited New Orleans. The duke called upon the bishop, bringing with him "the Colombian Commodore Jolly . . . a Frenchman fifty-six years of age, of which he . . . passed forty in the West Indies," and two of the commodore's officers. The duke noted in his account of his North American travels that DuBourg seemed to be about sixty years old at the time and added:

> He delivers himself very well, and conversed with me concerning the disturbance in the diocese of Ghent, in the time of Prince Broglie, in which he, as friend and counsellor of the prince, whom he accompanied in his progress through his diocese, took an active part. In his chamber I saw a very fine portrait of Pope Pius VII, a copy of the one painted by Camuccina, and given by the Pope to the deceased duke of Saxe-Gotha. The Bishop inhabited a quondam nunnery, the greater part of which he had assigned for and established as a school for boys. The Bishop returned my visit the next day.

DuBourg, who knew something of the West Indies himself and was innately a courteous host, made the naval officers feel at ease and, on leaving, one of them, an Englishman, kissed the bishop's hand. When DuBourg expressed his surprise at this mark of respect from a Protestant, the officer replied that his reverence was paid to the episcopal ring. The duke remembered afterward that "Mr. DuBourg, indeed, wore a costly amethyst on his finger as a representation of the fisher's ring."[66]

As he mused over the year just ending, DuBourg found himself thinking more of France than was his custom. Bruté's trip to France had started that train of thought, he supposed; his "Little Brother" had talked so much of the restoration government of Louis XVIII on his return.[67] Replying to Bruté's letter on February 16, 1825, DuBourg had said:

> You have seen in France many things likely to console you and raise your hopes. I know them all here in the smallest details; and I avow that it is the sweetest of all my pleasures. However, there is always a canker which works in secret and which without doubt requires continual attention and vigilance. It is to be hoped that *he who keeps Israel will neither slumber nor sleep.* I know some very good men who still are frightened to the point of announcing very great misfortunes are near. I swear that I do not share this opinion, for I see neither signs nor foundation for these fears. The government seems to be going ahead firmly and in the right direction; the army, the majority of men of property, as well as the people seem to be frankly attached to the existing order. Finances are prospering, the chambers, for the most part, well composed. Thus humanly speaking it is hard to see how a shock of any consequence could take place. But, people say, there are still great impieties which can not fail to call down new scourges of celestial justice. Oh no doubt there is much godlessness. But there is also an incalculable number of just souls certainly greater than that which disarmed the forces raised against Sodom and Gomorrah.[68]

There would always be a Moses to pray, and stand between the threats of heaven and the guilty. There was much sin, but one could not say that it was national. The court was composed of virtuous and generous men who were doing everything everywhere for all classes of people to repair the breaches made within the sanctuary in France, as well as aiding the propagation of the faith outside the nation. What was more promising was that impiety was concealing itself while everywhere virtue once more was raising its head, which had not been the case during the twenty-five years preceding the revolution. "I dare to add that with all the impieties," DuBourg asserted, "there is no nation in the world as worthy as ours, taken as a whole, of the name *Christian* with which she is honored."

He was concerned about one thing, telling Bruté:

> I believe that the sole real danger lies in the exaggeration, in the pretensions, and in the concealed egoism, which nourishes coteries and sows division and defiance even in the ranks of honorable men. I do not like exaggeration; I fear it above all in religious men, and in this regard I deplore the divergence of a Lamenaye, of a Cardl. de Clermont Tonnerre and of several others, with as much sorrow as I have esteem for their distinguished talents and for their high virtue. But this danger is restrained by the character of the king. *"Je tromperai bien des esperances, je dissiperai bien des craintes,"* was his first word on coming to the throne. His honesty effaces distinction of party; I hope that his firmness will contain the malcontents.

He had not realized how strong his optimism regarding France's future had become, how deep his love for France had remained. He said a bit apologetically, "All this, my dear Bruté, is not politics. These are the effusions of a heart eminently French and not less sacred, I hope, to the heart of a friend, whom he knows to be as convinced as he is of the great influence France has on the morality of the entire world. She has infected it with the venom of her impiety; I hope she will make reparation for her wrongs and that her return to right principles will spread them everywhere. . . ."[69]

He wished he could be as hopeful about his own diocese, especially in New Orleans. The infection of the revolution's impieties was still rampant, and opposition seemed to dog his footsteps at every turn. Opposition, in fact, had been the leitmotiv of the whole year; but it had begun much earlier, as the next chapter will show, and was not likely to disappear in DuBourg's time.

CHAPTER XXXI

LILIUM INTER SPINAS

During his New Orleans episcopacy, DuBourg had occasion to wonder if his choice of a motto for his coat of arms had been an omen; *Lilium inter spinas* expressed with such painful accuracy his situation after 1823, caught as he was between the thorny behavior of first Bertrand Martial and then Francis Cellini. The distress inflicted by these men was augmented by the bishop's sense of betrayal not only by Martial and Cellini themselves but also by his old friend Flaget who welcomed them to the Diocese of Bardstown.

Martial's defection ostensibly was precipitated by the building of the new Ursuline convent below New Orleans on property where Martial had conducted his school for almost three years. There were, in addition, undercurrents having nothing to do with a relocation of his school. It is sometimes difficult to feel at ease with those one has maligned; it is certainly easy for bishops to feel cool toward priests who have written criticisms of their ordinaries to Rome. It is not clear how much of Martial's complaining to Rome was known to DuBourg at the time he settled in New Orleans, but he soon perceived that in Lower Louisiana his clergy had been influenced by *someone's* charges that their bishop

was guilty of indiscretion in Inglesi's regard, of maladroit-
ness in business affairs, and of tolerating questionable
customs of an earlier era. Certainly in the school crisis
DuBourg believed that Martial acted underhandedly.

While DuBourg was preparing to go on his annual
episcopal visitations in 1823, Martial—long accustomed to
having a free hand as headmaster—sent a group of orphans
to Rosati's school at the Barrens. When the bishop learned
of it, he asked Rosati mildly:

> What do you make of the subjects sent you by M. Martial? I
> have seen with surprise that without consulting us he has
> given you this responsibility. Assuredly what he has sent
> you, *a Chalice and some books,* will not pay their expenses.
> If these children are good, and they show signs of a vocation,
> you could keep them; but if they are a burden to you, do not
> fear to send them back to him, but do not delay for he talks
> of returning to France in the month of March.[1]

He pointed out to Rosati that since these children were
orphans, it was indispensable to their remaining at the Vincentian school that Martial guarantee that some reputable
person would receive them and pay their passage on leaving
school, for without such a pledge Rosati would have a "most
burdensome responsibility."

By Christmas DuBourg knew something more of Martial's plans and was visibly annoyed, telling Rosati, "I repeat
my advice to you to send the orphans back to M. Martial if
you do not judge them disposed toward the Eccl. State. That
gentleman and his confreres will, I believe, all be in Kentucky in the springtime at the College of Bardstown. May he
not plague the Bishops there as he has me!"[2] Martial's
confreres were Simon Fouché and Evremond Harrissart.
The latter had come from France in 1818 with Martial and
had already gone to Kentucky in defiance of his bishop,
arguing that having once belonged to the Society of Liautard before his ordination for the Diocese of Louisiana, he
did not have to obey DuBourg. "Poor fool," DuBourg said
sardonically, "as if a group the Church does not recognize is
superior to Bishops";[3] and he ordered him to return under

penalty of suspension. Flaget notified Rosati on December 10, 1823, "Mr. Evremond left some time ago for New Orleans. Your illustrious prelate recalled him there."[4] There was little satisfaction in holding a man against his will, however, and in the end DuBourg saw all three men depart for Bardstown.

In 1824 Martial and his co-workers left with twenty boarders for St. Joseph's College in Kentucky;[5] and the following spring DuBourg told Rosati, not without bitterness:

> Mr. Martial has come to remove from 50 to 60 students from Louisiana for the Coll. of Bardst. He has taken all, good and bad, even young men 16 and 17 years old encrusted with vices. You may judge what service he is rendering that college. I expect to see half of them expelled, and the other half seeking to be recalled. On his arrival at Louisville one of them from one of our best families of St. Michael was dead, and an ugly rumor says that he was killed by one of his comrades. . . . What a harvest of chagrins for our saintly brother of Bardstown. The college here is going well in spite of these appalling intrigues.[6]

Bishop Flaget was not at all chagrined to accept "this remarkable recruitment,"[7] and willingly wrote to d'Aviau in Bordeaux to get Martial an *exeat,* which DuBourg seems to have refused his former schoolmaster. Flaget told d'Aviau exultingly that Martial, "to his great honor . . . continues with an admirable zeal to render me the most important services. Had he been born in Kentucky he could not work there with greater ardor nor show us two bishops more friendship and devotion than he does."[8] Flaget's coadjutor told Tessier complacently, "It is a very good and very generous friend that providence has given us; we owe to his zeal a very large part of the good done here. We bless the providence that did not permit him to agree with Mgr. DuBourg and let us earn his confidence and devotion at a time when it was evidently the work of God. Help us to thank him."[9] It would seem that brotherly love among members of the hierarchy did not prevent taking advantage of each other's misfortunes.

Flaget's glowing report to DuBourg of the new additions to his school must have rubbed salt in already painful wounds, for Flaget began, "You will learn with pleasure that we have from 30 to 45 of these little creoles who go to communion rather often in order to convince us that they are going because they find their happiness there." Already a little "apostolic society" had grown from four to eight, and had a splendid effect on their other comrades. Religion and piety were flourishing. "Thus, my very dear brother," Flaget concluded exuberantly, "you see how usefully busy I am for your diocese."[10]

As events proved, the arrival of Martial's recruits brought little lasting joy to Flaget and David. In less than two years, when Martial left for Europe, the "invasion of the Creoles from New Orleans" nearly brought financial disaster to the school and David complained that Martial had brought to Bardstown all the corruption of New Orleans, that the contagion was such that the college would never be cleaned out.[11] Although Martial returned from Europe in 1828,[12] he did not remain in Kentucky but went instead back to New Orleans, where he eventually became chaplain to the Ursuline convent.[13]

DuBourg's trials at the hands of Francis Cellini were much more complex and brought the bishop to the nadir of his forbearance. Like Martial, Cellini was a priest whom DuBourg had respected, appreciated, and given rather free rein. A native of Ascoli, Italy, Cellini was a thirty-seven-year-old priest before he joined the Congregation of the Mission and set out for Louisiana with two Vincentian scholastics on May 18, 1818. Arriving in Philadelphia without funds, they met Louis Sibourd, who gave them $300 in return for Masses so that they could reach Missouri. DuBourg's small rectory was as crowded as ever, and the bishop told Rosati, "I am still uneasy about your gentlemen. I fear they will arrive without our knowing where to put them."[14]

Cellini, accompanied by Philip Borgna and Anthony Potini, and a lay brother named Bettelani, arrived in Missouri on January 5, 1819, and almost immediately let it be

713

known that he had had medical training as well as his clerical education. DuBourg—knowing the scarcity of medical assistance on the frontier, where illness was so frequent and physicians so few—requested Propaganda to grant Cellini permission to practice medicine and the request was granted.[15] DuBourg's first preference, because of Cellini's maturity, would have been to assign the newcomer to Lower Louisiana, but because Cellini had been only four weeks in the Vincentian novitiate in Italy, De Andreis advised that he receive further training in the congregation under Rosati at the Barrens, where he could also learn French and English, languages he never really mastered. Cellini was a strong-willed man and was soon pressing to go to St. Louis; and DuBourg apologetically told Rosati, "I had consented to let Mr. Cellini pass Lent here, because I don't know how to refuse anything, and my first word, without reflection on the inconveniences, is *YES*. But on reflection I see that I don't know where to put him. As I will be leaving after Easter . . . he could come then and find room."[16]

While Cellini resided at the Barrens he was a hard worker, going on sick calls, hearing confessions, acting as procurator of the seminary, and starting to serve the Catholics at New Madrid some 100 miles away. After only one visit to the isolated Catholics there, he was already encouraging them to build a church.[17] In no time at all, he was requesting to be placed in Lower Louisiana permanently, suggesting—to DuBourg's uneasiness—that he and Anthony Potini, with whom he had come from Italy, be stationed together at St. Joseph Church of Baton Rouge. DuBourg hesitated, explaining his reservations to Rosati. "I tremble at the thought of leaving the seminary without a doctor; you would all become mad. I believe this consideration ought to make him give up his design. Besides, I can not help thinking that in that region his manner of speaking French would greatly injure the dignity and success of his ministry."[18] In Lower Louisiana the French language was far more necessary than in Missouri. DuBourg went on, "I fear to offend Mr. Cellini, and I would be very sorry to do it, for I love him and I esteem him too much to wish to do so. I count on his virtue and I request of him this new proof of his devotion."[19]

Cellini's request had come the summer DuBourg was very near to a nervous breakdown over Inglesi and Martial's attacks; yet his innate kindness served him well when Rosati replied that Cellini should be permitted to leave the Barrens. Three weeks after pleading for Cellini's presence at the seminary, the bishop told Rosati generously:

> I approve, my dear Mr. Rosati, your dispositions in regard to Mr. Cellini; but in return I hope you will approve mine as well. The pastor at Grand Coteau and chaplain to the Ladies of the Sacred Heart has just left his post *insalutato hospite;* you can guess who it is; you will not have trouble, for of those you know I believe he alone is capable of such a trick; he has left my Diocese; God go with him! But his post can not be left vacant, if only for the Ladies; I can not deprive them of the only recompense they ask in this world.[20]

DuBourg explained reasonably that having no other person available at that moment, and the reunion of Cellini and Potini being susceptible of postponement for a few months without any great inconvenience, he wished to notify his vicar general for Lower Louisiana of the vacant post and recommend that he urge Cellini to hasten to Grand Coteau, to fill in temporarily. Cellini would encounter no danger there; he would like the place, and the people might even want him to stay. "In that case would you not consent to his staying?" the bishop asked the Vincentian superior. "In any event, I still ask for him provisionally."[21]

With Rosati's consent to this request, DuBourg notified Louis Sibourd that Cellini was coming to Grand Coteau, but only *provisionally,* making it quite clear to Sibourd, "I destine him for St. Joseph with the approval of his Superior M. Rosati."[22] The bishop still hoped to keep Cellini content. It was in this way that Francis Cellini, apparently reluctantly, came to Grand Coteau on September 29, 1822.[23] It was a fateful day for the bishop's future peace of mind.

On his arrival Father Cellini was offered hospitality by

the widowed Mrs. Charles Smith, whose home lay midway between the church and the convent.[24] He settled in quite gracefully and before three months had elapsed was not only planning to remain at Grand Coteau permanently but was also recommending that the Congregation of the Mission establish a house there as well, explaining to Rosati:

> Mrs. Smith is ready to give us in fee simple a piece of property contiguous to that of the Ladies of the S. Heart, and she would have a house built there at her own expense, capable of housing at least thirty boarders, and I am perfectly sure she will not fail to assist us as long as she lives.[25]

Four months later he boasted, "I can assure you that she regards the Congregation as the apple of her eye and certainly could not live any more under another direction than that of one of our priests." This was just between themselves, of course; and Cellini advised Rosati self-importantly:

> I beg you not to speak of this to anyone; and if you think it fit to mention it to the Bishop, mention it as a project and without manifesting the intentions of that lady. She certainly has for the Bishop the esteem due his character, but, because she was treated a little highhandedly, she now does not wish to have anything to do with him; the motives which have led her to this course of action I have examined very carefully, and they appear to me just and reasonable.[26]

Just what this highhanded treatment suffered at DuBourg's hands may have been, the available evidence no longer reveals, and the biographer has only Cellini's word for the justice and reasonableness of that lady's attitude toward her bishop.

While Cellini was establishing himself as the widow's advisor and director, he was not ingratiating himself so successfully with others in the Grand Coteau area, for Madame Duchesne guardedly told Rosati:

> I am told Father Cellini has not adjusted himself at Opelousas. If this is so, you know it. If the choice of his successor depends on you, we would like it to fall on Father Dahmen in the event that he is no longer contented at Ste.

Genevieve. The Bishop seemed desirous of assigning him to Opelousas and has already told my Sisters how much they would profit from the choice.[27]

Francis Xavier Dahmen had often enough filled in at Florissant in the days when Charles de la Croix was pastor there, and Philippine Duchesne felt confident he would suit the religious at the convent in Grand Coteau. What little she had heard of Cellini was not prepossessing.

DuBourg was in Baltimore and Washington with other things on his mind while Cellini was assuming the role of spokesman for his patroness, and the bishop grasped very little of the situation when Rosati broached the subject during the bishop's exceedingly brief stay in Missouri that spring. Cellini himself had said nothing of it by the end of July, for DuBourg commented to Rosati, "I still do not know where things are in the Grand Coteau affair. The great heat and inundations have forced me to defer until autumn the visit to that quarter. I hope God will bless this project, which I regard as of an immense advantage."[28] Mrs. Smith meanwhile at her spiritual director's recommendation was making novena after novena to learn the will of God, which emerged more and more clearly, as Cellini reported it, as her duty "to give our Congregation the greater part of her fortune"; but she did not yet know how to do it.[29]

When Cellini finally informed the bishop of Mrs. Smith's intentions, which DuBourg found generally acceptable as he understood them, the bishop passed on his thoughts on the matter to Rosati on November 14, 1823:

> It would be to your Congregation that the donation would be made, if I approve it, and to which you would give your consent. The property of this Lady consists of fine and considerable lands, some thirty slaves, and personal property rather extensive in animals, utensils, household furniture, etc. The only reservation she would make, would be her upkeep, a little like the arrangement good Madame Hayden made at St. Thomas in Kentucky. . . . She would commence by giving by public deed only a piece of land 8 by 40 acres well fenced and cultivated. She would rent all her negroes to Mr. C. on the condition that she would live and

717

be nourished on the land by him. I would add to that, that she would have for her support the Tenth of the net revenue of the produce. The remainder she would dispose of by a will signed and sealed.[30]

DuBourg foresaw that this disposition of her property would be dimly viewed by some people in Opelousas, especially by her collateral relatives; yet, since she had already been very generous with them, she had the right to do as she wished with her own property, the fruit of her own industry. He nevertheless warned Rosati that in a business of such high consequence it was wise to consider the possible results. Thinking of the good of his diocese, DuBourg felt it prudent to have Mrs. Smith stipulate that her properties and the income from them should be applied only inside the diocese "such as it is at the present time." Above all he wished to prevent the possibility that there should ever arise between a bishop and the Congregation of the Mission "such difficulties as exist today between the Arch. of Baltre. and the Jesuits, who have been condemned by the Pope to cede to the arch. the best of their properties for his subsistence." With this in mind he believed Rosati might suggest that the tenth of the property's revenue reserved for Mrs. Smith's living should, at her death, revert to the bishop of the diocese. Secular priests would never feel obliged to support a bishop if a congregation, as rich as the Vincentians would be, were exempt from supporting him. "I do not speak for myself," he assured Rosati, "for I do not count on surviving Mrs. Smith, but I speak in the interest of religion and the lasting union I would like to establish between the Bishop and your Society." He had tried to explain this to Cellini, but that man knew nothing of the problems of church support in a republican nation where no provision was made for bishops and clergy, and it was difficult to reason with him on any subject. DuBourg recommended to Cellini's superior: "Reflect on it, and if, as I doubt not, you share my views, dictate the same conditions to Mr. C."[31]

Cellini's reaction to these suggestions was categorical: "I can not see why Mgr. DuBourg would enslave us to the

Bishop in regard to our possessions. I believe that he should at least leave our rights intact." Cellini held that the constitutions of the Vincentians guaranteed that their properties should be free and independent.[32] When Rosati visited Cellini after the former's consecration as bishop in March 1824, they discussed the Smith property but their remarks are not on record. Nor does Rosati's diary for the remainder of that spring and summer allude to any communications from Cellini on the subject. Whether the widow Smith reached her decision alone or in conjunction with Cellini, it is certain that she refused to have any dealings with either bishop. In August DuBourg wrote to Rosati, "You must have been astonished to receive no reply from Mrs. Smith. I wrote to her again some weeks ago, entirely in the sense of avoiding scandal."[33] By this time DuBourg believed that Cellini's usefulness at Grand Coteau had come to an end and he told Rosati:

> He has finished by so exasperating everyone against him that I wrote to him amicably to leave that parish. Will he do it? I have very serious fears. May God put his hand to it. . . . I have been no happier than you. This poor woman is absolutely subjugated and only has permission to read a letter or reply to it according to the good pleasure of her guide, who tells her to pay no attention to the decisions or counsels of Bishops. You have no idea of an infatuation like that. Please the Lord they do not give the scandal of leaving together for another diocese; for you know it has been openly talked of. You may judge if I am very tranquil.[34]

DuBourg had tried to be tactful with Cellini and he hoped he might ask for a dimissorial. If he did, DuBourg told Rosati, the bishop would refer him to his religious superior, the coadjutor bishop. "If he has recourse to that," he requested Rosati, "I charge you to give him one only for Rome." DuBourg then removed Cellini from his assignment at Grand Coteau and replaced him temporarily with Leo De Neckere, who happened to arrive on the scene as Cellini departed.

It was De Neckere who related the newest developments to Cellini's Vincentian superior on September 22, 1824:

> Mrs. Smith has, by a public deed made a donation of all her possessions to Fr. C., which, being known everywhere is commented upon in a manner very disparaging to Fr. C., Mrs. Sm., religion in general, and us all. Religion and its ministers are exposed to obloquy, the way Fr. C. is spoken of is horrible. . . . Mr. Perroden, who expected, as you know, one-fifth of the property, is plunged in desolation; Bp Du-Bourg has nervous fits.[35]

According to De Neckere everything was so firmly in Cellini's hands that nothing but his own relinquishing of the property could deprive him of it. There was the possibility of a lawsuit; the State Attorney General had expressed himself in very strong terms. It was a situation to give any bishop an attack of nerves.

Until the advent of Francis Cellini, Lower Louisiana, which would be DuBourg's diocese after the division scheduled to take place two years hence, had known nothing of the Congregation of the Mission as a religious group and scarcely more of its individual members, except as Bishop DuBourg assigned them to Louisiana parishes; and he had tried to send there his most mature, most prudent men. He had done everything he could to support the congregation, encouraging priests to join it on their arrival, and encouraging seminarians to enter its novitiate. The bishop and the Vincentian superior had worked together hand in glove to forward religion in the diocese and to gain support for the Barrens seminary and the development of a native-born clergy for the Mississippi Valley. DuBourg had been at great pains to place priests where they would be satisfied. As Rosati told Baccari, his Roman superior, "With regard to the Bp.'s disposing of the subjects of the Congrn., I have had sometimes to complain that I was not forewarned of the moves; but the case was urgent and I was far away; he never failed to notify me and when I insisted, he changed his policy. It is but just to add that our own men were the first to ask him for their change, some even without vouchsafing a word to me about it."[36] Now, for no reason either man could have anticipated, before Rosati had been coadjutor a full year, the whole administrative pattern seemed to be dissolving because of the intransigency of one who had recently become a Vincentian and the benevolent impulses of a wealthy widow.

DuBourg's having seized upon the arrival of Leo De Neckere at Grand Coteau as an emergency measure to replace Cellini offended Rosati, who had not been consulted. Molehills became mountains, and with communications taking so long between New Orleans and St. Louis, the two bishops were on the verge of a real estrangement for the first time since they had met in Italy in 1815. Happily, both men, in spite of tender sensibilities and volatile natures, were easily placated because of their solid friendship and even firmer commitment to God's work among men. After explanations were made—and heard—they went on as before, and DuBourg could write in mild raillery:

> You reproach me, Monseigneur, with some warmth, for having placed Mr. de N. at Grand C., which proves that you had not been properly informed. You yourself gave him that destination in concert with me. When I believed I had reason to complain of the conduct of Mr. Cellini, which coincided with the time of Mr. de N.'s arrival at La Fourche, I wrote at once to him to stay where he was and I notified you of this change, which you approved. But my letter was delayed, and Mr. de N., not knowing of the change, left before receiving it, to go to G. C. It was not I who placed him there. But if it had been I, I would not repent of it, because I believe that his presence there has done good, in making people see that all the members of your Congregation were not Cellinis.[37]

In the summer of 1824, however, DuBourg found nothing to joke about in the news of Mrs. Smith's gift to Cellini. If Cellini made a true copy of DuBourg's letter to Mrs. Smith on learning of the deed, and only a fragmentary document remains, the Bishop of Louisiana was indeed overwrought at the news. He chided the widow for putting herself entirely at the disposal of a man in whose judgment she could place no confidence. Her action would create "enormous scandal and discredit religion." That was his only concern, he insisted, but he revealed hurt and anger in the next breath. "I hear that it was to save your property from my grasp, that you threw it at the hand of a man whose intemperate disposition and open rebellion against his superiors should have been the best preservative against an excess of confidence," he said accusingly.[38] It was not his finest hour.

As usual, his body did not support him in the crisis and relaying the latest news he had of Grand Coteau to Rosati it was harder than usual to achieve any perspective, least of all light humor:

> You see that I am obliged to borrow a strange hand in order to write to you. Already for fifteen days I have been deprived of the use of my right arm & have been reduced to extreme feebleness by an abscess in default of my shoulder blade. I am not astonished that the weight of so heavy a cross as I have been carrying for a dozen years has made some impression on my shoulders.[39]

He supposed that Cellini was now back at the Barrens and that his superior knew already what DuBourg had just learned at the *Maison Blanche* of his relatives near Donaldsonville, that is, the donation Mrs. Smith had made of all her property real and personal to Cellini. "I cannot persuade myself that, while acting against all the rules of most elementary prudence and the counsels and even the commands of his Superiors, he was guided by sordid views of personal interest; I attribute his conduct to his self-sufficiency and his obstinacy; but only after proof will I bring myself to believe him capable of criminal seduction," DuBourg said plainly. Yet Rosati could surely perceive what a sensation the deed had created when it became known. The problem now was to find a solution, if that were still possible. Perhaps Rosati could persuade Cellini to turn the donation over to a few Vincentians of Rosati's choice, to make the donation clearly one to the Congregation of the Mission. Given Cellini's character, he doubted this would work; but he recommended refraining from showing any disapproval or suspiciousness toward Cellini in any case. "If nothing succeeds, after having done our duty, we must remain tranquil & abandon to providence the direction of events," he advised and affectionately closed his letter: "With the good arm left to me I press you to my left side."[40]

Suddenly Mrs. Smith had a reversal of her intentions. Taken ill that autumn, she regretted having deeded all her property to Father Cellini, and while still sick signed a paper to that effect. When De Neckere saw her during her convalescence, she earnestly begged that Cellini be prevailed upon to annul the donation in order to prevent further trouble over it. Feelings were running high against Cellini, and De Neckere believed it could be dangerous if he appeared in Grand Coteau.[41]

From New Orleans in December, Bishop DuBourg filled in some of the details for Rosati. People had feared for Mrs. Smith's life, she was that close to the "doors of the tomb." Happily she had been spared, and now her intention was to have her donation to Cellini annulled so that she could live up to the terms of her will, by which she left her mother three-fourths of her property (which the law of Louisiana guaranteed her) and left the other fourth to the Congregation of the Mission, "after having set apart from the whole that which, in virtue of her promises reverted to Mr. Perrodin, the husband of her niece." DuBourg pleaded, "This poor woman begs you to do all in your power to restore everything to its place. The difficulty will be to have Mr. C. consent to it, on whose willingness all depends. Neglect nothing which could bring this about."[42]

Like De Neckere, DuBourg was convinced that Cellini should not try to return to Grand Coteau, saying, "Madame Eugénie recently wrote me that his return had been announced and that she trembled in advance, persuaded that the public, exasperated as it was, would do something to him." DuBourg hoped Rosati would dissuade Cellini from any plan to return. "As for myself," he added, "I think I ought to forbid him, under pain of suspension of his faculties, approaching the State of Louisiana."[43]

Father Cellini did return to Missouri briefly, and Bishop Rosati used him in November to serve the Catholics scattered in Illinois;[44] but in the new year Cellini headed downriver again. DuBourg, who had not threatened a suspension of the man's faculties, heard indirectly that Cellini had gone to Grand Coteau and said apprehensively, "I greatly wish that no mishap occur to him. . . . I fear the unhappy affair. God grant it may turn to his glory.[45] Cellini later appeared in New Orleans, and DuBourg reported cryptically to his coadjutor, "I have seen here Mr. C. who stayed 10 or 12 days and made me only one visit. I learn he leaves for Europe . . . God go with him. He leaves without being regretted."[46]

It was not quite the end of the Cellini story, even then. On October 16, 1825, Propaganda wrote to Bishop DuBourg that Francis Cellini, C. M., had come to Rome complaining that DuBourg had deprived him of his parish. He now wished to go to Bardstown and was asking for a traveling allowance. DuBourg was requested to send a detailed report on this matter.[47] DuBourg's reply was swiftly composed, his quill scratching furiously as he replied in no uncertain terms, denouncing Cellini for giving scandal by living with a widow and acting as if he were the man of the house. This behavior had disturbed some parishioners to such an extent that there were threats on the priest's life. Cellini had disobeyed both DuBourg his bishop and Rosati, his religious superior. There was even some uncertainty about the man's involvement in Mrs. Smith's financial affairs. In short, DuBourg retorted, it was a wonder any bishop could put up with him.[48]

The following spring Flaget wrote cautiously to Rosati:

Mr. Celini [sic] a priest of your society, wrote to me last year as he was leaving for Rome that he would be very glad to come and work in my diocese if I wished to employ him. I answered him that, on the information that had come from him, I should esteem it an honor to possess him if his superiors would lend the helping hand. The same Mr. Celini wrote me from Rome that his superiors had permitted him to come to Kentucky, but with the condition that he continue to belong to the society of Lazarists . . . but what was not my surprise when, in conversation, he told me that he had left the society and was free.

Cellini said he had lost his papers but that Rosati knew all about it and would vouch for him. Flaget requested all the details about Cellini that Rosati could give, saying, "I want to have peace with everybody and still more in my diocese; but for this end it is proper that I be given information about the subjects that come to me 'full grown' and that I take them in the most unquestioned service."[49]

Cellini himself wrote to Rosati from Bardstown on June 14, 1826, telling of his sufferings in Europe, particularly in Rome, of his satisfaction with his situation at Bardstown. He revealed that he had left the Congregation of the Mission but had lost the papers attesting his dispensation. He now wished Rosati to assure Flaget on this matter as well as Cellini's permission to practice medicine.[50] On July 22 Rosati replied to both Cellini and Flaget. To the former he said that Baccari had written that on Cellini's repeated requests he had been granted a dispensation from his Vincentian vows. As for practicing medicine, "Remember that I gave you all your papers when you left here," Rosati reminded him, and then offered, "Best wishes for your happiness in Bardstown."[51] To Bishop Flaget, Rosati wrote charitably of Cellini:

> I am sure he comes with most pure intentions; but I found him very self-opinionated; hence his complaints. You heard, no doubt, of the affair at Grand Coteau. I am certain he is not guilty of what was then imputed to him. After this unfortunate occurrence he came here very much incensed, and left for Rome, determined to leave the Congregation. He did not live in our house there; he asked for the demission of his vows, and got it. Father Baccari wrote me about it. He is, therefore, absolutely free. I hope he may find happiness in your diocese.[52]

By July 1826 DuBourg was no longer in the United States and no longer Bishop of Louisiana; Cellini's location was no concern of his. Bishop Rosati, who was beginning to perceive the complexities of administering a diocese which was becoming two in one,[53] summarized the Cellini affair for Baccari later that summer after Cellini had settled in

Kentucky. As he had told Flaget, Cellini's intentions were good but he was too self-opinionated. Bishop DuBourg had also had good intentions and also had his own ideas. The bishop was greatly attached to the Congregation of the Mission and before his departure had made the ownership of the seminary property as secure as possible for the Vincentians. As far as the Smith donation was concerned, the bishop had wished to see it go through, but when Cellini accepted it in his own name, he did not approve of it, owing to certain circumstances which stirred much gossip. "I thought I ought in this affair to follow St. Vincent's maxim and example, and hope that Providence will help us otherwise," Rosati said. "Had Father Cellini been less precipitate, and followed my wishes, everything would have been done without noise, scandal and opposition."[54] It was a fair assessment. It accounts for Rosati's action in accepting Cellini into the diocese of St. Louis the following year[55] when Cellini—like Martial—grew dissatisfied in Kentucky.

Fair assessments of events presented in retrospect, however, do not always suggest the full force these events may have exerted on the individual participants. The Cellini unpleasantness would have been a trial for a bishop at any juncture in his career; but in the life of DuBourg it coincided with other more painful disappointments and frustrations. The onrushing events of 1825, which would have seemed fated to bring a lesser man to his knees, did in the end permit DuBourg to triumph in his defeat. But in the midst of what seemed to him attacks and betrayals on all sides the bishop was like a man tied to a tree with arrows piercing him from every bow. It was only natural that by the end of the year he should have begun to question his further usefulness in the Mississippi Valley.

CHAPTER XXXII

YEAR OF DECISION

If, as historians suggest, there is a "year of decision" in human affairs, that year for William DuBourg was 1825, for by the end of that year he had reached a firm decision to resign from his American see and return to France. Altogether during his tenure as Bishop of Louisiana and the Floridas DuBourg mentioned resigning at least seventeen times. The earliest of these were mild threats evoked by temporary setbacks or dissatisfactions with Roman proposals rather than categorical expressions of any determination to leave Louisiana. For example, in 1822 while arguing against a division of his diocese he said, "I am so thoroughly convinced . . . that I . . . am ready to ask the Holy See to accept my resignation rather than lend a hand to it in any way."[1] Again, angered by Rome's action in making Rosati a bishop for a vicariate created from Maréchal's jurisdiction, DuBourg asserted, "If this should go into effect . . . I would go and place my resignation at the feet of the pope."[2]

Then there were the times when, in chagrin and humiliation at his own folly in ordaining Inglesi, he believed he ought to resign. On February 27, 1823, he begged Borgna to notify Propaganda that "if His Eminence deems it fit to relieve me of a place, of which I have made myself unworthy by such a great imprudence, I am ready to resign and will be most thankful to him."[3] While Borgna remained in Rome DuBourg forwarded another similar letter to Propaganda, this one precipitated by the news of Inglesi's participation in Philadelphia's church affairs and the inevitable reopening of old wounds.[4]

Rome assured DuBourg that he should remain tranquil and not let the Inglesi matter be a cause for resigning from his see.[5] Yet the old shame and revulsion could return whenever news of Inglesi arrived or allusions were made to his deceit. Letters from Lyon could have that effect, as when Didier Petit, in talking of Edward Fenwick's visit, commented, "This worthy prelate does not know how much importance the French attach to the exterior. It is almost necessary to sparkle in order to collect money. I could cite a fatal example if I did not fear to open a wound we would prefer to close."[6] Didier's mother only three months earlier, reporting Antoine Blanc's French sojourn to DuBourg, had said, "We grieved with him over the chagrins you have experienced." Blanc, of course, had not gone into detail, only saying that he tried not to speak to the bishop of it in order not to renew his pains. "We asked him where the unhappy fellow was who had caused them," she added, "but he did not know."[7]

News of Inglesi was bound to recur, and as 1825 began DuBourg told Propaganda:

Although it may be burdensome to Your Lordship to hear, and it should be still more burdensome to me to speak again, of the notorious Inglesi, yet I deem it a duty of my office and of Episcopal mansuetude to communicate to Rome certain news which I have lately received about him. I heard from two excellent priests who went to see him at Philadelphia, that the poor fellow is stricken with bitter remorse and ready for anything that may restore him in peace with the Church. Although I did not give unreserved credit to this information, because at last I have come to know his hypocrisy, still, moved with pity and yet hoping for the sinner's conversion, I wrote to him to open his heart to me, offering my mediation with our common Father, in order that the door of penitence and reconciliation might be opened before him.[8]

Inglesi had replied expressing his gratitude and obedience. DuBourg had then told him such generalizations were not sufficient, that he must acknowledge the long series of his errors, ask for penance, and declare himself ready to retire to a monastery to remain at the pope's will. "In case he returns a satisfactory answer," DuBourg ended, "I think that it would be best for him to return to Italy, even under an assumed name, to seek refuge in some out-of-the-way place where he may hide himself unknown to all, after obtaining, of course, the Sovereign Pontiff's leave." In spite of the many crimes of which Inglesi had been accused, the bishop still believed there was some hope of his conversion.

It was in the wake of these reflections that DuBourg revealed most clearly the full extent of his remorse over Inglesi, this time addressing Pope Leo XII:

Most Holy Father:

Much consolation have I derived from your kind letter, by which Your Holiness commands me to be of good cheer and to persevere in ruling the flock entrusted to me. But I confess that the arrow is fixed too deep in my heart to be ever drawn out entirely. Since that day when I put aside the wise sanctions of the Canon Law and hastily ordained an unworthy man who later scandalized the Catholic world (by which action I became an accomplice of the sins and shame of that man) not alone the office of a bishop but life itself has become hateful to me. While formerly with a strong mind I bore all the labor, persecution, care and misfortune, now, crimson with shame, consumed with anguish, I hardly dare to raise my head. No wonder. The pangs of conscience torment me and I am convinced, that by that unfortunate action I have lost all esteem and confidence of my priests and I have no longer a right to demand their loyalty and obedience. I see that the hatred which, right or wrong, from the very beginning of my administration, inspired the various classes of our population against me, will never die out and that, whatever I do, the progress of religion will be thwarted.[9]

It was here that DuBourg indicated that he was in fact thinking of a successor, saying, "Any other Bishop may take my place, especially that angelic man, the Right Rev. Mr. Rosati, whom the apostolic See gave me as Coadjutor; a man, who on account of his inborn meekness and for his great knowledge and virtue is most welcome to all the clergy and who is not hated by any of the laymen; by him the Church will certainly be well provided."[10]

This petition uttered from the depths of his discouragement had scarcely gone on its uncertain way to Rome when DuBourg received a despairing cry from Inglesi himself in Philadelphia. The younger man was in debt; only money could keep him out of prison; only DuBourg could rescue him. If only he could settle his obligations, Inglesi promised, "I will leave directly for Rome, I will go throw myself at the feet of the Holy Pontiff. I will confess to him all my faults and I will submit blindly to all it pleases him to command." The only happiness he had ever known in life, he swore, was when DuBourg had made a new being of him, when he had been filled with zeal to serve the Lord, when the bishop had been a loving father to him.[11] On April 16 DuBourg forwarded this last protestation of good intentions to Rome.[12] On June 13, 1825, Angelo Inglesi was dead in Saint-Domingue,[13] some said a martyr to serving the sick during an epidemic of yellow fever.[14] Why he died on the island where DuBourg was born, like everything else about Inglesi's life, is veiled in mystery. At least on paper he had made a good act of contrition. One will always suspect that the Bishop of Louisiana redeemed him from Philadelphia. As he had once told Rosati, "I do not know how to refuse anything. My first word is YES."

DuBourg, nevertheless, did not resign his see over Inglesi. His most emotional plea, the letter to Leo XII, at the beginning of 1825, reveals more than penitence for an egregious mistake; it shows as well DuBourg's painful suspicion that he was hated, that whatever he did he would still be hated, and, most painful of all, that because of himself the progress of religion would always be thwarted. This state of affairs in and around New Orleans had been present from the beginning of his labors as an administrator apostolic in 1813, and in times of discouragement he feared it would always be so. Yet, such was his nature, in times when sheer zest for doing God's work filled him with boundless optimism, when he had on, as Madame Duchesne used to say, his rose-colored glasses, he rushed energetically ahead, spurred on by the undeniable signs of progress. It would be misreading the man's whole life to picture him, when he finally chose to leave Louisiana, as a man with head hanging in defeat, driven by the spectre of a protégé who had thrice deceived him.

The years of his New Orleans residency, 1823-1826, were years of steady progress in the cause of religion, particularly in Lower Louisiana. After his departure one of his priests wrote to a friend in France that in the Diocese of New Orleans one could count twenty parishes which, thanks to the care of Bishop DuBourg, were served by young and good priests. After listing the parishes the writer continued:

> All the parishes that I have just named, except two, St. Jacques and Pointe-Coupée, are served by priests who were placed there by Mgr. Dubourg. You can judge by that the good he achieved in New Orleans during the few years he lived there. Some of these parishes did not exist before his arrival and have been founded by him; others, where there was a miserable wooden church, maintain very pretty brick ones which he himself consecrated. I do not mention the convents of the Sacred Heart raised by his efforts. There, my dear friend, is what he has done in Lower Louisiana. It would take too long to speak of the diocese of St. Louis— where several churches were built, two houses, one Jesuit, one Lazarist, two convents of the Sacred Heart, and numbers of other enterprises useful to religion make his name ever venerated.[15]

The second convent of the Sacred Heart in Lower Louisiana, the third established in the whole diocese, was begun in 1825 near St. Michael's Church and it later gave its name to the town of Convent, Louisiana. Charles de la Croix, who had been the women's chaplain in Florissant, was enthusiastic about the new project, and DuBourg told Madame Duchesne that the good man already in January had a subscription promising more than $7,000 for this new venture. "I hope it will become the source of others and will aid you in supporting the good works you have done at Florissant," the bishop said enthusiastically.[16] Times were hard for her house in Missouri, he knew; but she could rejoice in the arrival from France of Father Louis Dussaussoy, the nephew of Madame Barat, bearing welcome letters from France.[17] DuBourg was keeping him in Lower Louisiana, anticipating that the Religious of the Sacred Heart at St. Michael's would be happy to have him.[18]

The arrival of the Lorettines in Lower Louisiana came later in 1825. DuBourg had originally asked Flaget for a nucleus from the Kentucky motherhouse but Flaget had refused to further deplete his own convent.[19] With the enlargement of the Bardstown college by Martial's transfer of so many students, the women who wove, sewed, mended, among their many other services, were more valuable than ever. So Rosati spared three from the Missouri convent and on November 27, 1825, sent them on their way to Assumption Parish at La Fourche where Father Joseph Bigeschi would welcome them.[20]

Rosati was a joy to Bishop DuBourg in other ways. Although the Barrens church really needed replacement, financially that was out of the question and so on February 13, 1825, after the high Mass the coadjutor spoke to the people about the need to enlarge the church they already had. The following Wednesday, although it was Ash Wednesday, the work was begun on a new choir and sanctuary. By Holy Week the work was finished and the church, by using the old sanctuary space for more pews, could accommodate its Perryville congregation for a few more years.[21]

With the same sort of forethought Rosati sent a mission to Arkansas. On receiving a letter from a Mr. John Mulletti offering some property for a church about twenty-five miles from Little Rock, Bishop Rosati learned that there were almost a thousand Creole Catholics who desired the services of a priest. Without hesitating, Rosati directed Father John Mary Odin and deacon John Timon to set out for

Arkansas to assess the situation there. These Vincentians visited both Little Rock and Poste des Arkansas, the latter, one of the oldest white settlements in the Mississippi Valley.[22] Rosati told Madame Duchesne on their return:

> Messers Odin and Timon in their trip to the Arkansas found the most beautiful dispositions above all in the Americans who until now profess no sect; and who are quite disgusted with some Methodist preachers; who have already established themselves in these regions. Our men were received with the greatest respect by the Savages who show an extraordinary penchant for civilization and the Catholic religion. But no workers, no means. Let us pray that the Master of the Harvest will send us some.[23]

The coadjutor was already sounding like the Bishop of Louisiana, perceiving the needs, possessing no means, and having too few workers to send forth. Reporting to Peter Caprano later, Rosati described the Arkansas trip in the same regretful terms saying,"One priest would not be sufficient in this vast territory which increases so rapidly in population. This place is more than five hundred miles distant from the seminary. . . . Till now I have not been in a position to do anything, having neither the priests nor the means."[24] At least 200 people had been baptized and many marriages had been performed; and it was heartwarming to learn that the Quapaw Indians were anxious to have a priest living among them.

Meanwhile Bishop DuBourg farther south was planning to make two taxing episcopal visitations to regions almost as remote and almost as forsaken: one to Alabama and Florida to the east, the other to Avoyelles and Natchitoches to the west. He set out for Florida in the spring of 1825 to see for himself the condition of that region since the withdrawal of the Spanish. Bishop John England of Charleston, who had been acting as his vicar general of that territory since 1823, had been able to have the parish church and rectory at St. Augustine restored for use and sent one of his own priests, Francis Boland, to Forida; but at the beginning of 1825, England had need of him at Savannah.[25] DuBourg had from his own clergy sent Constantine

Maenhaut to Pensacola, after Maenhaut grew tired of
Natchez. The first Bishop of Alabama said a few years later
of the Catholics of that region:

> Those of Mobile are an aggregation of men from every land;
> they have scarcely the shadow of Faith. Those of Pensacola
> are better. Those of St. Augustine are very well disposed,
> and judging from reports, those who live in north Alabama,
> who are all native Americans, will one day give us great
> consolations.[26]

In 1825 DuBourg was going only to the first two settlements, where the population counted very few Catholics,
and he expected rather limited rewards from his visitation.
Nevertheless on May 24 he happily announced his return to
Rosati with the words: "I am back from Florida. I have
placed Mr. Ganilh at Mobile, an important city where I hope
he will do great good. Mr. Maenhaut has put Pensacola on
firmer footing. He has been enchanted by the dispositions of
this good people and by the piety of a great number."[27]

DuBourg's second visitation—perhaps the epitome of
missionary evangelization on the frontier, with all its haz-
ards, oddities, and joys—began on Tuesday, September 13.
Aristide Anduze, who accompanied DuBourg, wrote a vivid
account of the whole journey, later printed in the *Annales* of
the Lyon Society for the Propagation of the Faith, which
preserves the flavor of a Louisiana ministry for a later
generation.[28] Father Rosti, the pastor at Opelousas, had
secured in advance a guide and horses for the bishop and
accompanied the little group as far as Bayou-Crocodile
where the visitation began in earnest. The order of the
caravan at the start began with the guide on horseback
leading by a long rope a mule carrying their provisions,
followed by a Negro servant Charles, also on horseback,
carrying a whip to urge on the laggard mule, then Anduze
with the bishop bringing up the rear. It was an order not long
preserved.

The road from Bayou-Crocodile to Bayou-Boeuf was
rather pleasant and gave no hint of the challanges ahead.
Arriving at the bank of the second bayou, the men dis-

mounted and unburdened the animals, who had all they could do to cross to the other side carrying only their saddles. For the men, the only means by which to cross the water were two huge fallen trees jutting out from either bank of the bayou and apparently almost meeting in the middle of the water. DuBourg volunteered to try crossing first, with the guide going ahead of him on the nearer tree. The trees, unfortunately, were submerged by a foot of water and by the time the guide and bishop approached the juncture in mid-stream the tree on which they were cautiously edging forward began to roll and both men plunged into the murky water. Although they grabbed and held on to the trees, they were up to their armpits in the bayou. They proceeded, nevertheless, to the other tree, and with garments sloshing they clambered up onto the other shore. Anduze simply swam across. Except for some scratches, the bishop believed he was none the worse for his wetting and good humoredly watched Charles and the guide bring the provisions across as best they could. Re-forming their single file, they resumed their progress.

The path ahead, at most three or four feet wide, crossed bogs bristling with pointed stumps of cypress trees upon which the riders might at any moment be impaled as their mounts stumbled and lunged through the unpredictable footing. The bog gave way to impenetrable thickets of cane threatening to pierce them in another fashion, and the horses could scarcely move forward while riders kept dismounting to recover their hats knocked off by the wild growth. The sun began to disappear and the guide hastily proposed preparing their beds, insisting that the tufts were strong enough to support them; but DuBourg having heard that a small Bayou-Rouge was about a mile further on insisted on going on that far. Night closed in and at one time the horses seemed to disappear in the surrounding mists; but they achieved the next bayou where they again crossed on trunks of trees and made their resting place on the other shore.

At this point DuBourg said he could no longer put one foot in front of the other and sat down on his baggage to watch the others make a rude shelter from saplings. It was, he announced cheerily, just like the one where Saint Francis Xavier had rendered up his last sigh. They had no water fit to drink, but they could build a fire to keep away marauding creatures. It was ten o'clock by that time and they took their supper of whiskey and bread. Anduze noted, "On our couch of palms we broke the bread into four equal portions and after having rendered thanks to God abandoned ourselves to providence, who favored us with a tranquil sleep and, a most remarkable thing, we were not troubled with mosquitoes." They had come fifteen leagues that day.

At daybreak, after thanking God for a site so dry, they again resumed the order of march in silence, because morning prayers were said en route. About nine o'clock they reached Petite-Prairie and got their first glimpse of the mission of Avoyelles. Here they were to learn of the fruits of the indefatigable Father J. E. Martin's zeal while they listened to his tales of the difficulties he had encountered in a place which had never had a church.

After remaining with Martin for a few days, the bishop's suite moved on, with the pastor accompanying them as far as Les Rapides, beyond which the route northwest to Natchitoches began. Now their journey was through thick pine forests constantly cut up by valleys and hills. It was here in the wilderness that they had a most moving experience, "one of the sweetest sensations of the heart of which man is capable." From a distance they glimpsed a huge wooden cross, and DuBourg called out, "There is the sign of the greeting of peace!" The cross was planted in a lonely Indian cemetery. There were no individual inscriptions, only the one on the cross: "They are no longer here." The bishop dismounted to recite the *De profundis* and then he gave absolution for the repose of the souls of "our brothers of the desert." He learned later that the cemetery belonged to two tribes, the Apalaches and the Paskaoulas, who had united their interests. They were all Christians, but deprived of instruction they had remembered only two things, baptism and prayer.

After two more days of travel DuBourg came to

Natchitoches. It was in size a vast parish, or county, but sparsely populated by French, Creoles, Americans, Indians, and a few Spaniards. Although their church had burned down, the ladies of the congregation had rivaled each other in their efforts to prepare a chapel in a large room of one of their houses. According to Anduze, "Much good was done for religion on this visit. Sixty were confirmed, who knew the catechism before our arrival; three hundred and fifty children were baptized, several marriages blessed; and arrangements were made for building two or three churches."

They had been at Natchitoches only a few days when a mulatto came to interrupt them at dinner, saying, "Monseigneur, Mademoiselle de Mezières is dying, she is having you called." The priests went at once to the bed of the sick woman, who said to the bishop, "The good God granted me thirty years ago, Monseigneur, that I pray for the grace of not dying without the sacraments . . ." She made her general confession with great calm and resignation, received the sacraments, and died a half-hour to three-quarters of an hour afterward. According to Anduze, she was Colette de Mezières, the cousin germane of Mlle de Genlis and the goddaughter of the Duke of Orleans, father of Egalité, and of Madame de Montesson, with whom the duke had contracted a secret marriage. Mr. de Mezières, father of the girl Colette, being married in this country, had had five children, three boys and two girls, who not wishing to make improper marriages were not married. The only ones left when Du-Bourg made this visit were a very old man, M. Athanase de Mezières, and Colette, who was sixty-two at the time of her death.

It was during his stay at Natchitoches that Bishop DuBourg composed his proposals addressed to all the American bishops on the selection of episcopal candidates, and his forceful letter to Rome favoring Benedict Fenwick for the hierarchy.[29] From Natchitoches, too, he sent Rosati his most recent ideas on establishing a seminary in Lower Louisiana. More important, the outcome of this visitation was the agreement that the people would build a church, that two priests would be furnished, and that later there would be two chapels between the Sabine River and Natchitoches. Between there and les Rapides three chapels were anticipated.

On his route back to New Orleans, DuBourg stopped at the newest Sacred Heart convent at St. Michael's, where Madame Eugénie and her six companions were working furiously to be ready in two or three months to receive their pupils. Their brick house was 100 feet long, with green shutters and a shingled roof. In the chill of autumn it was probable that they would suffer from the dampness, all the greater because of the proximity to the Mississippi River. DuBourg found Madame Audé in the kitchen trying to write a letter with her sheet of paper resting on the cover of an iron pot. "Mother Eugénie," he said reproachfully, "Mother Eugénie, this is not the place for you." She replied, "Monseigneur, allow me to take the liberty of saying that neither is it the place for you." They both laughed at the knowledge that in new establishments there were no proprieties, as she led him to the bare room that served as the parlor just then. "A religious of the Sacred Heart should be ready for anything, and satisfied anywhere," was a motto they both understood.[30]

He had rather hoped Philippine Duchesne herself might have headed this new venture closer to New Orleans, but the women had decided otherwise, and he conceded, "It is for you others to see what best suits the general interest of your Society in Louisiana." Yet it was a disappointment and he told Duchesne, "I confess I at first highly approved the idea of placing you at the head of St. Michael. Perhaps it was in part because I would get something out of it."[31] He was remembering one of the last times he had seen her, and how he had coaxed away from her the beautiful brocade her sister had sent her.[32]

By November 9 DuBourg was back on the Mississippi River, writing to Van Quickenborne about December ordinations and conferring with Rosati on affairs in Upper Louisiana.[33] To his surprise, on reaching St. John the Baptist at Edgard on the German Coast, DuBourg had found his coadjutor waiting to ascend the river. Rosati had been visiting the Vincentian priests in Lower Louisiana in DuBourg's absence and the two prelates had much news to exchange as they shared the same steamboat to Donaldsonville. Rosati laughingly told Madame Duchesne later that DuBourg had returned from his strenuous tour of duty with "an embonpoint such as I have never seen on him."[34] If his midriff was a trifle heavier, DuBourg's spirits for the moment were certainly lighter. He felt that the visitation had accomplished a great deal, and it was reassuring to learn that De Theux was at last arriving at Florissant to assist Van Quickenborne, and that some of the novices at St. Ferdinand could be ordained priests at Rosati's hands during the coming Ember Days. If only his dream of a seminary for Lower Louisiana could come true, DuBourg thought restlessly as the skiff carried him from steamboat to shore at Donaldsonville, he could regard the division of the diocese in 1826 as timely, or at least acceptable.

A second seminary under the direction of the Congregation of the Mission had been a dream for over three years, and had taken many forms. At the end of 1822, DuBourg was considering such a beginning at La Fourche, Louisiana.[35] There were some disadvantages in that location: bayou country presented the danger of yellow fever, swarms of mosquitoes, and damp, swampy ground in winter. Yet a retired old Capuchin, Bernard de Deva, had property in that area which he talked of giving to the Church for some establishments there. Then in the summer of 1823, when rumors of Mrs. Smith's intended generosity to the Vincentians reached the bishop, his thoughts rushed to the possibility of Grand Coteau as a better location. John Mary Odin, a Vincentian novice at the Barrens, told Jean Cholleton in Lyon that August:

> A lady of Opelousas, a parish in Lower Louisiana where there is a community of Ladies of the Sacred Heart, has given a rich donation to establish a seminary in their parish. Mgr. has this establ. very much at heart; he wishes to put there some Lazarists, and make a retreat house for priests, who always in the midst of the world, a great distance one

from another, would be very relieved to reenter from time to time into the solitude to take stock of themselves.[36]

If Odin was correct about the bishop's thoughts, DuBourg entertained them very fleetingly for on his return from a visitation of La Fourche he told Rosati that he was convinced the Vincentians must have at least one house in Lower Louisiana and it should be at Assumption in La Fourche for three reasons: the area generally was inhabited by excellent Christians; it was the only place in the state which offered any hope of vocations to the priesthood; and it was centrally located within the state and of easy access—three advantages Opelousas did not offer.[37] In addition, he believed the area would be suited to a school for girls run by sisters. He was envisioning a Catholic center of many institutions from which would radiate Christian principles and example which would gradually penetrate the more godless settlements and cities.

When Rosati showed a reluctance to consider a second Vincentian house, DuBourg urged him not to be too hasty in deciding against it, arguing: to restrict the congregation to Missouri, a very narrow and impoverished area for Catholicism, would expose his few seminarians to die of hunger; it would negate the agreement the bishop had with the congregation to train men for the diocese; a house in Lower Louisiana would resolve the problem of sending a Vincentian visitor to supervise the Vincentians working there. "A little time and patience are the only things needed," DuBourg urged. "We will talk all about it at our ease."[38]

The dream required, however, more than time and patience; it needed Rosati's consent, and, as both a religious superior and a bishop, DuBourg's coadjutor in the two years which followed became less pliable, more protective of his congregation and more defensive of the interests of upper Louisiana which was soon to be, everyone expected, his own diocese. DuBourg likewise became more insistent that the future truncated Diocese of New Orleans must share in the establishments he had created when the diocese was one. He was adamant on the subject of a seminary; if

Louisiana could have no nursery for vocations, a division of the diocese should be delayed.

As 1824 began, even while concentrating on the plans for Rosati's consecration, DuBourg had continued his plea for Vincentians for Louisiana, reminding Rosati that Bernard de Deva was willing to give 1,000 acres of fine land for that purpose. Philip Borgna was bringing two or three more Vincentians from Europe and DuBourg grandly suggested that there might even be two new houses, one at La Fourche and one at Grand Coteau.[39] Rosati, as Vincentian superior, began to fear that DuBourg intended to denude Missouri of priests while building establishments in Lower Louisiana. Although this fear may have been excessive—the evidence of the St. Louis catalog of clergy and Rosati's own diary shows seventeen priests serving in that diocese as DuBourg returned to France in 1826—Rosati increasingly emphasized that members of the Congregation of the Mission could not be put to work in parishes distant from the motherhouse for long periods of time.

DuBourg was stung to the quick when, before Rosati had been coadjutor a year, their disagreement over Leo de Neckere revealed Rosati's apparent determination to recall Vincentians from Lower Louisiana. Insisting they were still friends, DuBourg told Rosati:

> What has affected me otherwise, is the announcement you enunciate of withdrawing all of your subjects from this part of my diocese, destined soon to form the entire diocese. Do you think this just, after our agreements, after the sacrifices I made to you of my best Ecclesiastics, on the express condition that I would not be deprived of their aid, after the protestations and promises from you, so often repeated, and founded on what I always tried to do for your Congregation? Suddenly all this is forgotten, I swear to you it was the last trial to which I expected to be put. Oh, Monseigneur, affliction is a very bad counselor since it loses sight of so many strong ties.[40]

He could understand that Rosati did not like having Vincentians permanently stationed far away from their religious house; but an establishment at La Fourche would have been a solution. "Will I have the sorrow of seeing dry up at its roots a Diocese I have watered with so much sweat, so many tears?" he demanded. In that case, it would be necessary to withdraw his own clergy from Missouri to replace those Rosati recalled.

These recriminations over assignments of priests were soon straightened out with DuBourg saying penitently, "My good and very dear Brother, your last two letters filled my soul with sorrow, by manifesting to me the pain with which your own soul is filled. There was a misunderstanding; and yet our hearts were made to live in unison. Now all is cleared up." He closed his apology with the words, "Would that I could give wings to this letter so that you may receive the consolation and hope that nothing is changed in your regard in the heart of your good friend and brother."[41] DuBourg resumed his plans for achieving a seminary in the south.

In the spring of 1825 DuBourg wrote to Rosati blithely: "Today all is clear. The Seminary will be established at La Fourche. Your Congregation will direct it as well as two or three neighboring parishes."[42] Uneasily Rosati proposed that they meet to talk face to face about the matter. To this DuBourg readily agreed, suggesting Donaldsonville in order to avoid New Orleans' heat. The meeting took place there on August 16 and Rosati in his diary later revealed its emotional aspects:

> The Bishop and I had a long and exhaustive talk about the matter which had brought me on this journey. He, moved by the great difficulties besetting the progress of the Seminary at the Barrens on account of the latter's scanty income; wishing moreover, to provide Lower Louisiana with another Seminary of our Congregation, spoke at length of the necessity of such a foundation, affirming that it would prove most helpful even to the churches and the Seminary in Missouri. His opinion was, therefore, that I should as soon as possible, devote all my energies to this foundation; that I should leave in the Seminary at the Barrens one, or maybe two, priests, with the boys of the lower classes, and go with all the rest to Lower Louisiana, to conduct the Seminary and College

there to be erected. My soul was pierced to the quick at hearing this; and I represented to the eager prelate the dismal condition into which the church of Missouri was to be plunged, destitute as it would be of all spiritual help. But on his retorting with vehemence that my refusal to consent . . . was tantamount to bringing ruin upon the whole Diocese, I found it impossible to resist any longer; I gave my consent. . . .[43]

Rosati had reacted under pressure against his better judgment and when the two men met again on the steamboat in November, Rosati candidly told DuBourg of his change of heart. He had been recently talking to the Vincentians in Lower Louisiana that autumn and would now likewise consult those who were his council for the Barrens seminary. On their decision would depend the issue of a second house or the removal of the Barrens one to Louisiana. The seminary council voted unanimously against DuBourg's proposals.[44] It was their view that the time had not come to start a new house anywhere; there were too few Vincentians for two houses and to remove the first one would leave Missouri virtually abandoned.[45] In defending their decision to his Roman superior Rosati asserted that to decide otherwise would leave the Barrens with no subjects and Upper Louisiana without priests.[46]

As for DuBourg's claim that the divison of the diocese should be postponed, Rosati told David of Kentucky defensively, "The more I consider it the more I feel inclined not to accede to the proposals Mrg. DuBourg made to me." It was not self-love, Rosati insisted, but a concern for the people of Upper Louisiana and a desire to do something for the Indian missions which dictated his position. There was a future ahead for that part of the Church, but it would all be engulfed in Lower Louisiana if DuBourg had his way.[47] The bishops in Kentucky quite agreed with Rosati.

Whether DuBourg knew it or not—his existing letters do not indicate—Flaget once again sympathized with those who differed with his old friend and confrere, the Bishop of Louisiana. In February 1826, speaking for himself and David, Flaget wrote to Baccari in Rome, "It is our firm conviction that the projects explained by Bishop DuBourg to Bishop Rosati are prejudicial in every respect." Flaget opposed the transfer of the major seminary and the postponement of the division of the diocese. He further favored Rosati's recall of his clergy from Lower Louisiana, and said in closing: "This is our conclusion, grounded principally on the perfect knowledge we have of Bishop DuBourg. When Father Martial . . . arrives in Rome, you may get more information touching Bishop Rosati's situation, which will enable you to take prompt measures to extricate him from his painful position."[48]

Flaget's meddling was wasted. On receipt of Rosati's news of his council's decision DuBourg on December 9 had already replied serenely, "I have said Fiat to the deliberation of your Council. Having few years to live I will probably not see the extinction of the Diocese. And if I see it, I will have nothing for which to reproach myself." He accepted without rancor the fact that the time was not right for dreams to materialize, telling Rosati:

> This has been a disastrous year everywhere. Up there you are ruined by drought; here we are by the bankruptcies, which threaten to destroy most of the houses of commerce. According to last reports it is not a time to begin any enterprise. But let me hope that when the time comes I will find favorable dispositions in you and your council; above all if, as my plan has always been, and as I still have hope of realizing, I may form here for you an establishment free of all obligations and of all debts.[49]

The dispelling of the dream of a seminary for the Diocese of New Orleans in the near future was the catalyst which produced DuBourg's firm decision to resign his American see and return to France. Beginning on December 20, 1825, he began his bombarding of Rome with earnest requests that he be permitted to resign.

His defeat over the seminary was, nevertheless, only the catalyst and not the underlying cause for his departure. Writing to his former Sulpician superior in Baltimore in the early part of the new year, Bishop DuBourg said somberly,

"Nothing new in this quarter that could interest you; for scandals and afflictions are nothing new for me; each new distress finds me, however, equally sensitive, and with this aggravation, that little by little by force of constant rubbing, resilience is worn out and the soul no longer has the force to resist. Pray for me."[50] He was sixty years old that February and was faced with the realization that his extensive plans to promote religion in the Mississippi Valley, and he remained certain that the plans were sound, could never be properly effected by the man who had conceived them—that it was he himself who was the impediment to the Church's best interests. As he mused over the past months everything pointed to this conclusion.

He had not withdrawn over the Inglesi blunder, but he could not escape his conviction that he had lost all the esteem and confidence of his priests, that he no longer deserved their loyalty.[51] In reality the clergy in Louisiana had not suffered at the hands of their bishop. Inglesi had never become their superior; he had never returned to the diocese in which he had spent only a few months. The ill feeling that men like Bertrand Martial and those close to him nurtured should have been quickly dispelled by the nomination of Rosati, whom they all ardently desired as coadjutor.

DuBourg's handling of the Cellini affair, on the other hand, may have temporarily offended some of the Italians in Lower Louisiana like Potini and Bigeschi.[52] Yet there were no wholesale defections on that score. Antonio Potini's trouble was not with his bishop but with Father Flavius Rosti, whom Rosati, at DuBourg's request, recalled to Missouri; Potini was still working at St. Joseph's Church the year DuBourg returned to France. John Acquaroni, who had tired of the Portage Des Sioux Mission in Missouri, was permitted by his bishop to replace Borgna in New Orleans when the latter left in 1823 to visit Europe. DuBourg was not pleased with this solution for, as he told Rosati, "Acquaroni is a child, indiscreet to the point of making himself despised. I would be very relieved if you recalled him as soon as possible."[53] Even then the bishop had tried to spare his priest's sensitivities. Acquaroni's health settled the question. By the end of 1823 he was clearly suffering from what doctors called *lepre scorbutique,* whose symptoms he had displayed at Portage. His health demanded a change and he eventually returned to Europe.[54] Joseph Bigeschi had remained DuBourg's strongest supporter in the La Fourche project and only began talking of leaving Louisiana after the Vincentian decision to postpone it; he was still actively at work in Louisiana when DuBourg left in 1826. He had worked very hard to help the Lorettines settle in Louisiana and DuBourg praised him to Rosati on February 4, 1826, "Mr. Bigeschi is doing many things [for them]. He neglects nothing for the comfort of their establishment, nor for its elegant simplicity, and he provides generously for all their needs until they can provide for themselves."[55] Philip Borgna remained loyal to his bishop in New Orleans, and on his return from Europe brought two other priests as well as two younger ecclesiastics.[56]

One suspects that the legend of the wholesale desertion of DuBourg's clergy emerged from rather scanty evidence: Maréchal's gratuitous comment to Fesch on July 11, 1823, that DuBourg had lost the confidence of the clergy and laity of New Orleans; DuBourg's own assertion in his letter to Leo XII that he felt he had forfeited his clergy's respect and loyalty; and Bertrand Martial's claims in 1822 that he could not prevent some priests from deserting over the Inglesi matter. The truth is that DuBourg lost more men to death than defection. As Madame Duchesne was fond of saying, it was a harsh country. Not everyone could bear it.

One of the deaths most painful to DuBourg in 1825 was not that of a priest but of a young layman who had once attended a Sulpician school in Maryland, Edouard Seghers. He had been ill six months with what seemed to be a cold in his chest. His brother Theodore had tried to persuade him to try the cure Dr. Chatard had used in Baltimore, but Edouard had faith in his own New Orleans doctor and refused his brother's advice. He was obviously losing ground in February and DuBourg was in and out of the house until he died. On February 22 Edouard went to confession and received communion the next day; he seemed to be improving for a while. But his illness was too far advanced and when the bishop returned on March 1 he administered extreme unction and read him the prayers for the dying. At half past midnight young Seghers died. "How I would have wished Mr. Chatard to have been here," Theodore cried.[57] The thought of that good doctor, of the college, of those days two decades ago, was all the more poignant because of the death of a virtuous young man in his prime in a city where virtue was so little valued.

The end of his year of decision brought DuBourg a loss which he had only sensed at first and found confirmed later. On December 5, 1825, the gallant, merry Victoire-Françoise Fournier died at the age of sixty-two at the home she and Louis shared in St. Seurin Parish in Bordeaux.[58] She had been ill for some time and when DuBourg wrote to Tessier he had added:

> I recommend particularly to your prayers and beg you to have recommended to the Sisters of Charity, my sister Mde. Fournier, long since attacked by a fatal malady, and I have too much reason to believe she no longer exists. I ask also the prayers of your Gentlemen, of Mr. Chévigné and all our good friends of Emmitsburg & Baltimore, to whose memory I wish to be recalled.[59]

It was one of the penalties of living in the Mississippi Valley where communications with the outside world could be so uncertain that when one prayed for a beloved sister he was constrained to think of St. Paul's phrase, "Whether in the flesh or out, I know not." The long uncertainty over Victoire's suffering had been a strong undercurrent in the river of his other woes of that year. What dreadful irony that just as he reached his decision to return to France she should have been gone forever.

CHAPTER XXXIII

THE RETURN TO FRANCE

The Bishop of Louisiana by the end of 1825 was clearly determined to resign, and his letters of resignation present the sum of his reasons for reaching this decision. Earlier in the year he had mentioned his sense of having lost the esteem of his fellow workers and his conviction that his coadjutor Rosati would more effectively serve the Church in his stead. Now in December he spoke of a specific matter: his fear that personal antagonism toward himself might harm his family. It was a larger family than before; Pierre-François's daughters were married and the number of grandchildren was increasing. The DuBourg name was more prominent now that Arnould was a justice of the peace and Pierre-François was consul for Sardinia in New Orleans;[1] and the other men in the family although not bearing the name were equally jealous for the DuBourg reputation. When the bishop was publicly calumniated tempers rose. As DuBourg saw the situation, "A longer stay in this country is incompatible with both the good of Religion and the safety of my family." In the letters stressing this point,[2] he told Rome, "How long I shall be able to restrain my natural defenders, I know not; but the mere thought that on my account blood—the blood of my relatives—may be shed does not leave me a moment's rest."

There were two developments in particular which had augmented high feeling in the city. The first was the Ursulines' move to their new convent, leaving their old one in the city to the bishop. DuBourg was delighted with the prospect of having not only a residence for himself and his priests but also the small but regular income from the college also housed in the former convent. Aside from the generous aid of the New Orleans nuns and the Society for the Propagation of the Faith in France, the bishop had never enjoyed any financial certainty during his residence in the Diocese of Louisiana.[3] He had told Louis jubilantly in the spring of 1824:

> The new monastery of the nuns of Ste. Ursula will be ready by the month of June. I must set about locating myself and the college in the old one. It is a fine house, capable of holding one hundred boarders, with all the necessary halls, rooms for masters and servants, and a fine and complete apartment for the bishop, who will have his special entrance and stairway. The city, in general, looks with pleasure upon this establishment. The Mayor came to present his thanks to the religious. There being no public college now, all look to us to provide them with one.[4]

The mayor of the city may have been pleased, but there were others who were not. The very thought that DuBourg had an *évêché* roused the *marguilliers* and the bishop's enemies to a fury not displayed since they had believed he was to preach in favor of the Bourbons in 1814. As one Louisiana historian commented:

> It is not surprising to find them explosively condemning Bishop DuBourg in the newspapers and pamphlets like *Nos Libertés Vengées* and charging that he had either deliberately robbed the Sisters of their property or insidiously prevailed upon them to forfeit it to him, interloping foreigner that he was, seeking to enrich himself, lining his purse and that of the clergy, and ready to make his escape, well fixed, as soon as there was a chance! As to the Ursulines, they had abandoned their post; they had forfeited their right to the

property and it was by all rights civil property, reverting to the government. They had been buried by the scheming DuBourg in a cypress swamp—about 30 squares below the city! They had placed themselves out of reach of the civil and police authorities, unprotected too, in a swamp where any scalawag might harm the girls going to school. But worse, they had gotten away from the city where they were supposed or obliged to give free instruction.[5]

Small wonder that the bishop's relatives were incensed and the prelate himself heartsick that his most loyal friends in the city should suffer attack on his account.

The second violent outburst attacking the bishop was provoked by his refusal to give a place to a newcomer to Louisiana. He told Propaganda in February 1826:

I had a great deal of trouble lately to stop my nephews nay even my dearest brother from taking revenge of those who attack me; and now scarcely a week passes by that I am not grossly insulted in the newspapers at the occasion of that miserable Spanish priest, (Sigura), who was foisted upon the church of one of the suburbs by the trustees; even though this man is utterly despised by his abettors, yet these, out of hatred towards me, make themselves openly his supporters.[6]

The Segura affair had developed during the summer of 1825. Between his visitations in the spring and fall DuBourg remained in New Orleans attending to diocesan business, presiding at final vows at the new convent,[7] making another effort to get his possessions from St. Louis,[8] seeking a renewal of his faculties from Rome,[9] and preparing for his absence during the visitation at Natchitoches. In June a Father Segura arrived in New Orleans and requested permission to officiate. He had come from the French Diocese of Aire, admitting that because of an intrigue against him he had no *exeat,* but claiming that his bishop had not censured him. Bishop DuBourg promised Segura that he would write to Aire, and in the meantime Segura could offer Mass but perform no other functions.

While away from New Orleans DuBourg was astounded to receive two letters from Destrehan on the German Coast, one from Segura and one from the *marguilliers* of the Church of St. Charles Borromeo there, announcing that Segura was their pastor and seeking the bishop's approval. On returning to New Orleans the bishop had laid the matter before his council, which consisted of the pastor of the cathedral parish, Sedella, the vicar general of the diocese, Sibourd, and the chaplain of the Ursuline convent, Richard. The council unanimously concurred with DuBourg that without an *exeat* Segura could not be installed as pastor. Ignoring the bishop and his council:

> The St. Charles church wardens adopted Father Segura and let loose a barrage of letters and articles in newspapers of New Orleans . . . stating that in the United States of America the voice of the people was sovereign, that the use of the term "hierarchy" was contrary to principles of American democracy, that the people had a voice under American institutions to choose their pastor, that Father Segura was a regularly ordained priest, hence did not need the approval of foreign interlopers, nor did such foreigners have any right to interfere with the practice of religion.[10]

Just why the bishop, who had been in the United States since 1794 and was of French origins, as were so many New Orleans families, should have been dubbed a "foreign interloper" while Segura, a Spaniard newly arrived from France became the symbol of American democracy at bay remains enigmatic. But fanatics are no respecters of reason, and their scurrilous attacks on DuBourg in this instance made it very difficult for the bishop to dissuade his hotheaded nephews from challenging to a duel the editors who printed the calumnies, a tragedy which would have brought disgrace to both the Church and himself.[11] It is not surprising that DuBourg's letters of resignation cited the feelings of his relatives in the face of these attacks as an influence upon his determination to resign.

The bishop's chagrins of 1825 were not yet over. The Archbishop of Baltimore had been busy once again, rearranging Church jurisdictions within the superintendence of the Bishop of Louisiana and the Floridas. In December, just as DuBourg was adjusting to Rosati's *fiat* regarding the seminary, recoiling from the vilification of the press in his see city, grieving over Victoire's terminal illness, and painfully concluding that for the good of religion he must resign, he received the news that Michael Portier, the head of the college which was to provide a bishop with a small income, had been made a bishop and appointed administrator apostolic of a newly created Vicariate of Florida and Alabama.

DuBourg who had known nothing in advance of this proposal was aghast. He had only recently been, at the cost of great effort and indebtedness, able to convert the former Ursuline convent into part residence, part college. Only that year he had commented, "The college prospers. . . . We number 36 boarders; day pupils number from 130 to 140. It is a great good for the city to accustom men early to seeing and coming in contact with good priests; from esteem for its ministers one passes easily to esteem for religion; there was no other way by which to establish this."[12] With Martial's school removed to Kentucky, the thought of losing Portier was not to be tolerated.

The dismay with which DuBourg contemplated this disruption of his plans was not long in giving way to deepseated anger, when he learned that a full year earlier the "decisions had been made and approved that would transfer Michael Portier from his tasks in New Orleans. . . ."[13] The western bishops and Maréchal had all long since recommended men for Florida. DuBourg, Flaget and David favored Enoch Fenwick, with DuBourg adding Simon Bruté as a second choice. Maréchal had rejected both of these, proposing instead Benedict Fenwick, Portier, and Guy Chabrat. It was not until December 20, 1824, however, that in a general congregation Propaganda effectively discussed who should be made vicar apostolic of the proposed jurisdiction which united Florida and Alabama.

Bruté was ruled out on the grounds that in spite of extensive knowledge, piety and virtue, his zeal was exuberantly excessive. Enoch Fenwick, whom Archbishop Vincenzo Macchi—on the basis of reliable reports—described as fit in every way for such an appointment, was undermined by Maréchal. The Jesuit who had served as secretary to the late Archbishop John Carroll was now pictured to Rome as "completely lacking in that piety and doctrine that are required in a bishop." Obsessed with his notion of DuBourg as an intriguer, Maréchal had done his best to undermine Louisiana's suggestions, writing to Propaganda in feigned ignorance, "Who dared to propose such men? I do not know. But whoever it might be, either he is a secret enemy of the Church, or at least one who has judged the situation with utter incompetence."

Maréchal's own first choice, Benedict Fenwick, was ruled out by the congregation, whose cardinals reasoned that it would be difficult to secure permission from the General of the Society of Jesus for Fenwick to become vicar apostolic. Rome was well aware of the feud between the Jesuits and the Archbishop of Baltimore over his financial support. Instead, Propaganda followed Maréchal's second recommendation:

> Equally fit is Father Portier who at present exercises the Sacred Ministry in a most praiseworthy manner in the Cathedral Church of New Orleans. He is learned, pious, prudent, kind and has great respect for ecclesiastical discipline. Unless I am mistaken he was born in the Diocese of Lyon, in France and is about 34 years of age.

Without any documents for Portier, however, Propaganda's appointment could not be made official. Inquiries were then sent to Lyon and Baltimore on June 25, 1825. Maréchal's only firsthand knowledge of Portier, which included neither his first name nor age, was based on Portier's less than two months' stay in Maryland in 1817, when he lived either at Mount St. Mary's in Emmitsburg or at Charles Carroll's country estate, and was not yet a priest. The Archbishop of Lyon, Jean-Paul Gaston de Pins, who could furnish Portier's first name, vouchsafed the opinion that the candidate was "most skilled in theology, conspicuous in piety, with an eager zeal for God's glory." It was an opinion widely circulated in Lyon, formed from the many letters DuBourg had written to Jean Cholleton at the semin-

753

ary, and to Didier Petit at the Society for the Propagation of the Faith. To the bishop in Louisiana, whose subject Portier had been for eight years, no inquiries were sent.

The Archbishop of Baltimore on August 25 finally furnished Portier's baptismal name and a further speculation that his candidate was "about thirty-two" years of age. (Portier was actually twenty-nine at the moment of that writing, having been born on September 7, 1795.) By the time this information could reach Rome, Leo XII had already issued the apostolic brief making Portier titular bishop-elect of Olena, and on the same day he had declared Alabama and the Floridas an apostolic vicariate with Portier as its administrator.[14] Seven days earlier, without his knowledge, Bishop DuBourg had been made vicar apostolic of Mississippi![15] On September 3 Portier's faculties and briefs were despatched, and only then did Propaganda notify DuBourg of Portier's appointment.[16]

While the letters sent from Rome the first week in September 1825 were finding their way to New Orleans, the Bishop of Louisiana was making his hazardous visitation of western Louisiana and, ironically enough, composing with the best of intentions his letter to the American bishops on proper ways of nominating bishops for American sees.[17] What must his thoughts have been when the week before Christmas he sat down to acknowledge Propaganda's notification of Portier's appointment? His letter of December 20, 1825, sheds very little light, filled as it was with other matters including the death of Inglesi, DuBourg's concern for his family, his own desire to resign.[18] The shock of the news may have numbed him momentarily. In any case, he refrained from comment.

After two months had passed, however, he determined to speak his mind fully and he did. Addressing Archbishop Peter Caprano, the Secretary of the Propaganda, on February 17, 1826, he presented a cogent case against the actions of Rome in regard to part of his diocese and the disposition of one of his priests. He began:

> I had resolved not to write about the recent institution of a Vicar Apostolic. . . . However, I would consider it a breach of duty on my part if I kept silence any longer. I have long

since manifested more than sufficiently that not only was I not averse to the separation of Florida from my jurisdiction, but even that this was all along one of my great wishes. That Alabama be joined to Florida under one and the same Vicar Apostolic, nothing, in my opinion, is more desirable. But there are two points on which it seems to me action was taken prematurely.

1. There should have been made some inquiry as to whether there are at hand the means to support both the Vicar Apostolic and his missionaries. On this subject I may—and must—say openly that with the exception of two or three parishes which can each actually support one priest, and that with difficulty, no means whatever are to be found in that immense territory to foster the development of Religion.

2. In regard to the designation of the person, it seems to me that the S. Congregation has been induced into error by anyone who proposed to it the Rev. Michael Portier. I have a suspicion it was deliberately intimated that that priest belongs to the clergy of Lyon; this was done clearly in order to prevent the S. Congregation from consulting me about the qualification and fitness of the candidate. The assertion is true, insofar as his birthplace is concerned; still, if that gentleman had told the S. Congregation that this young man has been incorporated into my Diocese since he was twenty years of age, has lived constantly under my very eyes, was promoted by me to Sacred Orders, I am convinced that informations would not have been sought elsewhere. Now had I been asked these informations, the affair would have stopped right there, as I owe it to truth to declare, that virtuous and talented as the Rev. Michael Portier is, he is still far from possessing that gravity, moderation, self-control, ecclesiastical knowledge, prudence and experience, which a Bishop must have, particularly in this country, where he has to reckon on himself alone.

It was not surprising, DuBourg explained, because in the six years since his ordination Portier had exercised the sacred ministry scarcely two years, the rest of the time teaching in a primary school. Among DuBourg's friends there had been utmost surprise at the news that this particular young teacher was now a bishop. When Portier asked DuBourg if he should accept the appointment, DuBourg continued, "I have considered it my duty as a father to let him know plainly what I thought about his fitness and the weight of such a burden. Whereupon without any hesitation he has sent back the Apostolic letters with his excuses."[19]

Rome's action had been premature for precisely the reasons DuBourg gave, as a carefully documented history of Portier's early years as vicar apostolic demonstrates.[20] Flaget was incensed at Portier's appointment and told Maréchal forcefully that it would need a miracle for Portier to accomplish anything in that region.[21] DuBourg's visitation the previous spring certainly had led him to a similar conclusion.

There is equal sense to DuBourg's assertion that he was the one prelate who really knew Portier's priestly career and capabilities and should have been consulted. If this letter to Rome had been the only one DuBourg sent, history would have little to complain of in regard to DuBourg's attitude. But two more letters alluded to the matter, especially to Portier's qualifications, and these have left an opportunity for the claim to be made that the Bishop of Louisiana was much too sensitive, too harshly critical, and therefore less reliable as a judge of the decision reached in Rome.

Ten days after his first letter to Propaganda on the subject, DuBourg wrote again and spoke of Portier's fitness, saying that he had been guilty of acting "disrespectfully and even insolently" toward his bishop. DuBourg added, "In saying this my intention is not to give the impression that Fr. Portier is lacking in faith or virtue; but he is given to levity, inconsiderate, restive, affecting independence, purposeless, devoid of firmness and ever ready to veer with every wind."[22] These criticisms may hint at two main reasons for the bishop's dissatisfaction: the witty tongue which is a delight if one is not the victim, and a willingness to change sides.

Portier was ordained a year when he told Rosati, "He is a terrible man, our Bishop, he is good, he is kind, he is all that one would want, and he is such that I obey him in spite of myself, that I suffer in spite of myself, and in spite of myself I am assistant at a cathedral where we only make money."[23] For the moment he was the bishop's man, even to the extent of talking like him: "We walk on half-heated cinders that one day may give way under our feet and show us an abyss and a volcano."[24] It was one of DuBourg's favorite metaphors for the slumbering hatred of the *marguilliers* and godless men in New Orleans.

Portier, however, quickly came under the influence of Bertrand Martial and, like Martial, questioned the bishop's policy of avoiding provocations of overt violence by refusing to extirpate immediately all the old customs Catholics enjoyed in New Orleans. It was not long before Portier was talking of his "torture" and "despair" at having to close his eyes at abuses he was expected to tolerate. "I well know," he told Rosati, "that one may give very pious advice and preach eloquently for the good of religion, but our good old St. Paul settles all our difficulties with only one word *non facimus*."[25] If Portier shared Martial's views in 1822, when the latter indulged in his lengthy criticisms of DuBourg to Rome and Quebec, this would not have strengthened the rapport between bishop and college head during DuBourg's first months of residence in New Orleans. Yet, while Martial took his students to Kentucky, Portier moved in with DuBourg when the remodeled convent was ready for occupation and was building up a successful college there, to the bishop's great satisfaction. The men were not in any sense enemies.

DuBourg's third letter to Caprano, with its quite gratuitous derogation of Portier, is less easy to understand except as a revelation of how acute was the bitter humiliation DuBourg was suffering at the indignity Propaganda had dealt him, and his association of Portier with that humiliation. On March 10, after again pointing out that no one other than himself and his coadjutor was competent to speak about Portier's qualifications, the Bishop of Louisiana said meanly:

> No sooner did the first rumor of his appointment reach here than most of his friends and fellow priests could not help

laughing heartily over it; but what saddened me yet much more, laymen and women, even among those well disposed, manifested their wonderment, that a young man, whom nothing singles out and recommends particularly among his fellows, and who had no experience, should be raised to such a high and difficult position. Some did accuse me of this decision, whom I could scarcely convince that I had absolutely nothing to do with it, and had never been consulted about it. When good and religious people are feeling that way, what can you expect of the men of loose morals and of no religion, so numerous in this part of the country?[26]

It was unworthy of him, particularly if he knew Portier had returned his bulls to Rome in January, as DuBourg's letter of February 17 indicates. The only remaining reference of DuBourg's to the matter is alluded to in a letter from James Commiskey of Philadelphia to A. Elder at St. Mary's Seminary in Baltimore in which Commiskey reported:

> The Right Reverend Bishop Duburg left us this morning on his way to Rome. He is all alone and seems to be in good health & spirits. Says that the Rev. Mr. Portier whose Bulls had arrived has given in his *nolo episcopari* and that the whole was a mistake on the part of his Holiness.[27]

DuBourg was wrong. On March 18, 1826, Propaganda informed Portier that the pope had directed that Portier's documents were to cross the ocean for a third time and that under obedience he must accept them this time.[28] They reached New Orleans in June, but by then the Bishop of Louisiana was on his way to France. Had he known it, the Archbishop of Baltimore would have been elated to realize that he had had the last word on Portier. In notifying Propaganda of DuBourg's departure he reinforced his recommendation of Portier:

> It is said that the nomination of Portier to the spiritual rule of the Floridas displeased the Rt. Rev. Dubourg. Certainly not by reason of the defect of those virtues that are required in a bishop. He himself constantly covered Portier with praise above all the other priests of his diocese. In every place that he has lived, whether in France, or in our America, he has

won the respect and good will of all. Especially has he shown a marked example of humility to the Bishop of New Orleans at whose request, even though he was capable of teaching Philosophy and Theology, he did not hesitate to organize a school in which he taught the elements of language to young boys in order that he might at the same time inspire them with the principles of religion. He is indeed only 33 or 34 years of age. But Dr. Dubourg surely knows that both an active mind as well as an active body is of first necessity in a diocese of North America, so long as they be accompanied by seriousness and dignity.[29]

As before, he had to stretch the little he knew about his candidate, making him even older than ever, not knowing he had already won and that his imagined adversary of the past decade was gone beyond his ken.

Except for confirming it, Maréchal's influence in the Portier affair had little to do with DuBourg's decision to return to France; it had already been reached. The real reason for DuBourg's decision was his deep-rooted concern for the episcopacy, the authority of the Church, and his conviction in 1825 that he himself, through no fault of his own intentions, was contributing to undermining that authority. As he was to say later in justifying his resignation: the foundations had been laid, probably better than another man might have laid them, and his successor would have in his hands all the elements needed to exercise the ministry without having to struggle against the personal opposition which DuBourg had faced.[30] Those who had worked with him in New Orleans and St. Louis could testify that he unwittingly aroused opposition and even hatred among trustees and other laymen.

It was more than vilification of himself personally, however, that DuBourg believed was at issue; it was the prolongation of disdain for the episcopacy. He had seen in Belgium in 1817 his friend Maurice de Broglie, the Bishop of Gand, undergo harassment within his diocese after the Restoration settlement altered the political situation. Knowing Broglie to be a devoted servant of the Church, the pope had refused his attempts to resign; but in the end the Bishop of

Gand returned to France, writing to his flock from his exile that, like Saint Athanasius, he believed it wise to flee a persecution that was directed against himself personally lest it come to be directed against episcopacy and the Church.[31]

Genuine concern for the dignity of the Church and respect for the episcopacy were nothing new to DuBourg in 1826. Ten years earlier, during his stay in Europe, DuBourg in reporting the most recent hue and cry provoked by Sedella had described the flaunting of papal documents in a public café and Sedella's sneering boast that he, the pastor of the cathedral parish, had nothing to do with the pope nor bishops of his making.[32] In the face of such insubordination, DuBourg's arrival in New Orleans could only have jeopardized the respect due the episcopal dignity. It was a danger, he had insisted in 1816, "which ought to be avoided at all costs because once the mischief was done it would be impossible to remedy." He had made his temporary headquarters at St. Louis in 1817 to avoid this danger. In 1826 he saw it threatening the diocese again and returned to France.

His was not a desertion for the sake of self. Writing to Peter Caprano, the Secretary of Propaganda, on March 10, 1826, still smarting at the Alabama-Florida vicariate humiliation, DuBourg said, "Even though the bonds uniting me to this church are to be severed, yet I shall never cease to wish it well, and promote its increase by all the means in my power."[33] As subsequent chapters will suggest, he was as good as his word. In 1825-1826 DuBourg was quite correct in his evaluation of the situation in the Diocese of Louisiana, soon to be the Dioceses of St. Louis and New Orleans. The subsequent history of these two sees would attest to that. The men who had served under DuBourg and became his successors—Joseph Rosati, Leo De Neckere, and Antoine Blanc—made worthy bishops and enjoyed both respect and the fruits of their predecessor's labors.

DuBourg, naturally, could not see into the future. In 1826 he was determined to arrange his affairs as efficaciously as possible so that, in the event Rome accepted his resignation, the institutions begun in the Mississippi Valley need not suffer. He told Rome on January 30 that his departure from New Orleans would take place immediately after Easter Sunday.[34] He hoped to leave St. Louis in early May. It did not allow much time to clear titles to property, pay last visits, and scrape up enough money to pay for his voyage.

He had never been one to allow despondency to govern his activities, and DuBourg's last months in his diocese were as active as any previous. In January he had Rosati pass on to Madam Duchesne the papers relevant to the land he had given the Religious of the Sacred Heart.[35] On January 8 in St. Louis Cathedral, he delivered before the governor and legislature of the state of Louisiana an address on the anniversary of the Battle of New Orleans. His sense of occasion, coupled with his own vivid memory of the events of 1815, produced a rousing address of the genre so appreciated on great occasions combining patriotism and an acknowledgment of deity. It was the last address of its kind that he ever gave in English, and it displays the rhetoric of which he was capable in that tongue as he recalled the feat of Jackson against Pakenham and his men who had defeated Napoleon but fell in New Orleans:

> What a day, Gentlemen, for all of us who witnessed the awful event! Methinks it still sounds in my ears, that dreadful and continued fire and thundering, which in the space of two hours whilst it enveloped our City in lightning and smoke, and convulsed all its habitations, leveled down to dust the most gallant Commander and the flower of the British Army. Veterans who had encountered in Europe the first Captain that ever adorned the page of Military records, who had stood unmoved on the brow of the fiercest battles, were mowed like grass by the scythe of our rude peasantry . . . whilst hardly a hair fell from the heads of those over whom the hand of the Almighty was extended.
>
> Surely the finger of God was there—and no wonder—is He not the friend and protector of Justice? Were not His holy altars, during the whole continuance of danger surrounded by fervent votaries, who reminded Him of His ancient Mercies? Yes, the finger of God was there. And the glorious commander of the day, the Man of His Providence, fitted by

His own hand to be the tutelary angel of his country in its days of need and distress—the heroic Jackson, honored himself much more by that humble and pious acknowledgment than by all the deeds of fame which it was given him to achieve.[36]

Later that month he took pen in hand for quite another purpose: to reply to pressing inquiries from Sister Margaret George in behalf of a woman who had inherited "immense claims in the Island of S. Domingo" and whose claims needed to be validated by a missing will. Reminded of the DuBourg family claims still not indemnified, the bishop may have grimaced. After advising his Maryland friend, who was in Frederick where another house of the Sisters of Charity now existed, DuBourg was carried back in memory to other days and he confessed, "If anything could console me, my dear Margaret, for the barrenness of my efforts here, it would be the benedictions which it has pleased almighty God to give my first undertakings, and particularly the courage and prosperity of yr. dear Society. Seven branches already! God be forever blessed."[37] When he left Maryland in 1812 there was only one house, St. Joseph in Emmitsburg; at Mother Seton's death there had been three. Now in 1826 there were seven: Baltimore, Washington, Lancaster and Frederick, all having been added in less than five years. His had been a very small part in that saga, but God made use of even the poorest straw.

He never thought of Emmitsburg without thinking of Bruté. There was a man who really had trials. The affairs of the Mount had gone from bad to worse for Bruté and Dubois since DuBourg had last seen them there. In 1824 while in Paris, Bruté had done his best to persuade the Sulpicians to refrain from suppressing Mount St. Mary's, but he returned from France on November 24 with the news that the Gentlemen of Paris were adamant in their refusal to continue both the Emmitsburg schools as Sulpician institutions. In Bruté's absence a fire had destroyed some of the Emmitsburg property, but happily it had been quickly rebuilt. When DuBourg learned of Bruté's return, he wrote jovially:

I congratulate you, my very dear friend, but I felicitate even more our dear brother Mr. Dubois and Maryland for your happy return. I knew of the miraculous restoration of the college which burned. It must certainly have surprised you; it is quite a work. God preserve this good confrere for putting this latest hand to a work so important to Religion and the assurance of its perpetuity. I ask Him for this quite sincerely, I assure you, as I pray Him to preserve you yourself for an establishment to which you will still be very necessary for a long time.[38]

DuBourg had not yet realized how determined Maréchal was to separate Emmitsburg from any Sulpician connection. The October following DuBourg's sanguine remarks about the Mount's future to Bruté, the Archbishop of Baltimore told the Sulpician superior, "Mr. Dubois is no more a Sulpician than Mr. DuBourg. This spirit will never yield to the rules of St. Sulp. By far the wisest thing would be to inform him he no longer belongs to the Society. That done, I will take charge of the rest."[39] On January 8, 1826, both the college and the seminary at Emmitsburg were stricken from the Sulpician list. Dubois and Bruté were no longer considered Gentlemen, and Bruté was writing his heart-wrenching letters to Paris crying, "Here I am separated from Saint-Sulpice after 23 years."[40]

In January DuBourg had not yet heard this last news. Instead, he was giving advice to a fellow bishop of the West, Edward Fenwick of Cincinnati. It was inexcusably tardy, for Fenwick's question had been posed in September, and DuBourg began ingratiatingly, "*Late* is better, as they say, than *never,* and as my conscience is clear of either remissness or oblivion, I hope you will not be more severe than she is. . . ." As a Dominican friar with a vow of poverty, Bishop Fenwick had scruples about having disposed of some property in favor of the Dominicans of Ohio, scruples that DuBourg quickly dispelled. Fenwick further wished to know how DuBourg was treating the Jesuits in Missouri so that Fenwick could follow the same plan.

The Bishop of Louisiana, who was glad just then to be consulted at all, replied:

> I have attributed to the Fathers a certain number of Parishes, as is done in Maryland, which they are to furnish with subjects of my satisfaction. Should they fail to [do] it, I must try to supply the deficiency; well understood that the Bp. always preserves the right of visitation and an entire jurisdiction on the parochial churches, so that no one can officiate in them without his approbation, and in case he had reasons to desire the removal of one, the Superior at his desire must withdraw him and send another in his place.

This was, DuBourg believed, the general system of the Catholic Church wherever religious orders had parishes to serve.[41] He said nothing of the withdrawal of satisfactory subjects by religious superiors. Perhaps the memory of his misunderstanding with Rosati over the Vincentians still made him uncomfortable.

As February began, DuBourg learned from the Ursulines that a fire had destroyed the kitchen of the Lorettine Sisters of Bethlehem near the Barrens. At Rosati's request the Ursulines were sending some supplies to the Missouri women. The fire had wiped out the wooden cabin which the sisters used not only as kitchen but also as refectory and a weaving room where they made cloth for the orphans in their charge and for the men of the Barrens seminary. Gone up in the flames were their poor furnishings for cooking and eating and in, addition, the looms by which they earned the food the seminary farm supplied.[42] It was a dreadful loss, and DuBourg was a trifle peevish that Rosati had not informed him directly of the disaster. Rosati retorted reasonably enough, "Knowing your finances I did not wish to write of the misfortune suffered by our Religious." DuBourg meanwhile sent upriver a bale of cotton as well as six bolts of "good cotton cloth," a barrel of sugar and more than a third of a barrel of rice.[43]

On February 4, 1826, DuBourg announced to Rosati his intention of going to Europe. Everything in the diocese was suffering, everything was languishing. He elaborated his thoughts for Rosati:

> In a few more years, there will remain for us not more than ten priests in Louisiana; and perhaps your Congregn. will

764

perish in Upper Louisiana for lack of sustenance. This prospect saddens and discourages me. I seek a remedy for it, and I believe I have found it; at least I have a project which has occupied me for two months, and seems to me the only one offering a chance to consolidate here the religious establishment. This project is a trip to Europe (France and Italy, above all Rome). I have at heart primarily the deferment of the division of the diocese, which given the state of things, would be a mortal blow. I want to represent strongly to your Congn. the indispensable necessity of establishing a house in Lower Louisiana. . . . Finally I believe it necessary to go in person in order to enlist the zeal of the association for the propn. of the Faith, and assure us of its continued aid.[44]

None of these goals could be effectively attained by letter, and without such a trip he could foresee only more series of afflictions. He had told *no one,* he said. Immediately after Easter he would come up to the Barrens with Hercule Brassac, who wished to see again the places so dear to him before going to France on leave to visit his old father.

In this February letter DuBourg added one more bit of news: Louis Sibourd, his faithful old vicar general, was returning to France permanently and wished to give Rosati his furniture and Mass stipends for 500 Masses. He was also putting DuBourg in his will for $1,000, which DuBourg intended to give to the Congregation of the Mission.

With his intention of making the trip announced, DuBourg turned more energetically to putting affairs in order. He had already in January written to Caprano for an authentic copy of the bull erecting the Diocese of Louisiana with the Church of St. Louis designated as the cathedral of the diocese. Sedella and the *marguilliers* had always denied that it was the bishop's cathedral in DuBourg's time, but the bishop wanted to ensure that his successors had no such difficulties. Only recently in the troubles over the convent and Segura there was talk of even removing the episcopal throne from the church. DuBourg told Caprano, "I read in the hands of the Most Rev. Archb. Maréchal a copy of the Bull of this erection, in which the Parish-church of St. Louis is explicitly designated as the Cathedral of New Orleans, until another could be assigned. I beg you, therefore, to forward me at your earliest convenience this most precious document. . . ."[45]

On April 1 at the Ursuline Convent, in the presence of the twelve nuns who had made their perpetual vows, the Bishop of Louisiana signed a declaration that "by special commission of Our Holy Father the Pope, I accept for myself and my successors the donation above mentioned and conditions under which it was made."[46] DuBourg himself had enjoyed very few moments of peace of mind in the only episcopal residence worthy of the name during his years as bishop in the United States, but he hoped his successor would enjoy such an *évêché* from the start. He headed for Donaldsonville with a lighter heart. It was the last time he was to see his relatives at Post Office Bringier, but no one could be certain of that in April 1826. It may have been under Aglaé's roof that he wrote his touching farewell to the Ursulines, devoting a paragraph to each member of the community from Mother St. Joseph down to the youngest novice.[47]

On March 8 DuBourg had notified Rosati, "I am day by day confirming my grand project and consequently I will embrace you toward the end of April,"[48] and true to his word he arrived at the Barrens on Thursday, April 20, carrying letters for his coadjutor from Philip Borgna, Michael Portier, and Mother St. Joseph Laclotte in New Orleans, and from Joseph Tichitoli at Donaldsonville. His departure was already in process.

DuBourg's manner of leaving his diocese has been open to criticism. It has been implied on occasion that he deliberately deceived his friends and co-workers by withholding his intention to resign. From this view it appeared particularly unjust that DuBourg's friend and coadjutor bishop should have been kept in the dark, since he was the man left with the responsibility for the diocese. Rosati was not certain of DuBourg's resignation until five months after DuBourg's departure for France.

The fact is that DuBourg, usually a talkative and confiding man, on those rare occasions when he had grave doubts about the outcome of a decision, could become non-communicative. He had no assurance that his resignation would be accepted in 1826; it had been refused before. Should he be refused again it would not enhance his reputation among his enemies, nor would it make resuming his position in New Orleans pleasant. His requests for secrecy suggest his uneasiness.[49]

That he considered the possibility of being refused is evident from the bill of sale for his Negroes Anthony and Rachel to Aglaé's husband with the reservation that Du-Bourg could have them back if he repaid the money he was borrowing for his trip.[50] Further, as the decennial of his consecration approached DuBourg requested the renewal of his faculties as Bishop of Louisiana.[51]

After Rosati noted in his diary on April 20, 1826, "The Bishop talked to me at great length about the journey which he thinks of making to Europe for the good of the Diocese,"[52] he wrote a letter DuBourg could carry to Baccari in Rome in which he summarized their talk. DuBourg's purpose in going was to assure the continuation of the good already done; he was desirous of making another Vincentian establishment in Louisiana, although Rosati could not consent to it on account of their lack of subjects and means. "You may remedy the first," he suggested, "by sending us Frs. Tornatore and Boccardo; we trust in Providence to remedy the other."[53] To the superior of the Vincentian College at Piacenza, Rosati said further, in introducing the Bishop of Louisiana, "The purpose of his journey is to consolidate our establishment in his vast Diocese. We need subjects. If anyone among the pupils of the College should feel an inclination for the Mission and to join our Congregation the Bp. will obtain for him from Rome the necessary dispensation."[54]

These were things DuBourg intended to do, whether he remained in Europe or returned to Louisiana. He had sincerely said *fiat* to Rosati, agreeing that a new seminary was premature, but he was still convinced that it must come to Louisiana, no matter who was bishop there. (His later letters from France bear this out.) He expected to go to Rome;

he anticipated visiting Lyon to seek more money; he planned on either sending or bringing new recruits. There was no deception in talking of these matters. He had written exactly the same thoughts to Louis in Bordeaux as the year began, saying that in concert with Rosati he was planning a trip to Europe after Easter. "With whatever strength remains to me, it could not be put to better use than in consolidating what has been begun," he ended.[55] His one reservation was his hope that this time his request to resign would be granted and that he could accomplish good for his former diocese from afar.

DuBourg spent four days at the Barrens, visiting the Lorettines, preaching at the high Mass on Sunday at the seminary, and renewing old acquaintance with the faculty and students there. At eight o'clock on Monday morning, the two bishops started for Ste. Genevieve, where Rosati stayed overnight before bidding DuBourg good-bye. During their trip from the Barrens to the river, DuBourg had persuaded his coadjutor that he ought to descend to Lower Louisiana in May and, as was so natural to DuBourg, Rosati was scarcely gone before DuBourg figured out when the steamboat *General Brown* would reach Ste. Genevieve from St. Louis, urging his coadjutor, "I beg you to come here Monday, May 15, in order not to miss the steamboat."[56] The Bishop of Louisiana had planned itineraries for his sons in religion too long to break the habit even now.

Later that week he arrived in Florissant to visit Madame Duchesne's school and St. Regis Seminary of the Jesuits. At the former he was given a little reception by the children of the boarding school and at the latter he baptized six Indian lads. Throughout the parish of St. Ferdinand he confirmed sixty people.[57] While in Florissant he cleared the titles to the properties of the Jesuits and the Religious of the Sacred Heart.[58] Then he sat resting at the convent, while Madame Duchesne hastily wrote letters for him to carry to Paris. She suspected it was their last meeting. She had written to Paris on December 27, 1825, "Mother Xavier Murphy thinks the Monseigneur DuBourg is planning to return to France. It is astonishing how this country discourages people."[59] Yet she said nothing, nor did the prelate in the next room. He was thinking of the first time he had sat in that parlor; and now it well might be his last, but he could not bear farewells any better in 1826 than in 1823, and still counted on his old friend to put the best interpretation on his silence as of yore.

He had hoped to make a quick trip to St. Charles with Father Van Quickenborne but reported to Rosati in some disappointment, "Bad weather kept me from crossing the Missouri but I am told all goes well at St. Charles." Old Father Savine who had done such yeoman service at Cahokia in Illinois now wished to be transferred to a post where he could be tranquil in his old age, and DuBourg wanted him made pastor at St. Charles, advising Rosati, "He will tell you what instructions I have given him."[60]

Bishop DuBourg arrived in St. Louis on the eve of Ascension Day, May 3. Saulnier had told him earlier that the people truly wished to see the bishop, but DuBourg had not been sure that it was not wishful thinking on the pastor's part. To his surprise and delight, the crowds came out to meet him, music sounded, cannon roared; it was an old-fashioned welcome, French-style, enough to warm any prelate's heart. When he wrote to Rosati on May 11, he said, "I forgot to tell you all the population here came to visit me with tender and respectful haste. I received 21 bursts of the cannon, but what gave me greater pleasure was almost a hundred communions and Confirmations in St. Louis."[61]

Originally DuBourg had intended to embark immediately after his sermon on May 4,[62] but when he learned that some property destined for a college in St. Louis was in jeopardy, he remained in the city another week to straighten out that business. It was property he wanted for the Jesuits. Almost from the day of their arrival in Missouri a Jesuit school had been discussed. Rosati had mentioned it to Louis DuBourg three years earlier, saying that besides educating Indians the Jesuits would "perhaps even be a means by which to procure the youth of these regions a solid and Christian education."[63] DuBourg in writing to the Jesuit superior in Maryland that same autumn had said, "I would also feel disposed to give your Society two beautiful squares of ground in the city of St. Louis and help in the creation of a house for an academy as a preparation for a college if you thought you could spare a couple or three of yr. Maryland brethren even scholastics to command the establishment; in which case I will shut up the one that is now kept by some of my priests. . . ."[64] Maryland had been unable to furnish Jesuits for the school at that time, but DuBourg's intentions had not changed, and he confided to Louis in 1824 that the Indians did not provide an adequate income for the Jesuits and prophesied, "They will take the college of St. Louis, a means of assuring stability."[65]

Francis Niel's trip to Europe had done nothing to save his school from further decline. Saulnier believed the college would have to be closed. The president, Dr. C. G. Brun, was a pious man, but otherwise amounted to nothing. Mr. Shepard, the Protestant, in Saulnier's opinion was out of place. At the beginning of 1826 Saulnier himself was trying to head the school.[66] When DuBourg inspected the situation in May he told Rosati, "I believe I have at last obtained the suppression of this bad school, so ridiculously called *College* . . . The lay Professors are quitting with pleasure. There is only Mr. Brun who still seems held by certain considerations; but he will find himself forced to quit by the impossibility of procuring Masters; and this amalgam dishonoring the Church will disappear. I do not believe anyone in the city disapproves this measure, dictated by necessity as well as by expediency."[67] The way was almost cleared for a Jesuit school in St. Louis, although he admitted, "There is still some difficulty over the Connor lands. But I believe the principal ones are removed. I have given my procuration to P. Van Quickenborne who understands business very well and will do his best in the matter."[68]

The difficulty over the Connor land, however, proved more complicated than he had anticipated. In 1820 Jeremiah Connor had donated two squares of land lying respectively north and south of Washington Avenue between Ninth and Tenth Streets. Unfortunately, Connor's bond of conveyance had not been recorded until July 22, 1825, after Connor had died. DuBourg discovered to his dismay that during his residence in New Orleans one of the squares had been sold to meet a judgment against the property, and that title to the other lot was in jeopardy that spring. He hastily consulted the Honorable Luke E. Lawless, a distinguished member of the St. Louis bar, who advised him to have the remaining lot sold by order of the court. Lawless would get a judgment against the Connor estate for $100 which would enable the Jesuits to buy the property in their own name for that nominal sum. It was expected that there would be no bidders against them because of the danger of lengthy legal entanglements.

There had been no time that May to go down to Florissant to explain all this to Father Van Quickenborne; but he wrote to the Jesuit on May 10 advising:

> Don't fail to see Col. Lawless from time to time. He is a man to handle affairs and whom you can easily make a useful friend to your establishment, and to our Ladies of the Sacred Heart. He and his wife, and her mother have expressed to me a desire to go and visit these two missions. Show them everything. The Colonel can serve you in Washington and on many other occasions.[69]

It was DuBourg's customary way of departing on any important journey, trying to tend to a thousand things at once. On January 15 Leo XII had extended the Papal Jubilee from Rome to the whole world, and the news just reached DuBourg in St. Louis as he was finally boarding a steamboat for the East. He promised Rosati, "I am sending you copies and a translation in French and English of the bull *ad universos Christifideles*. I will not have time to regulate the method of gaining the benefits. You handle it, and issue a small *mandement* which should be printed, with or without the bull, to send to all the priests in the Diocese." His letter had to be finished on board the *Lawrence*. He meant to do the translating en route to Ste. Genevieve but, as it turned out, when he left the letter there for Rosati he had added a postscript, "I am obliged to send you the bull as it is in the original."

As his steamboat left the Mississippi to breast the current of the Ohio, DuBourg felt that at last he was leaving St. Louis behind him. He was content. He believed that Saulnier was doing satisfactorily in the parish, and without the college would do even better. Providence had permitted the bishop to come to St. Louis for many reasons, the most important being to witness the new resurgence the city and the whole of Missouri were making. It was an omen, he was certain, of the most extraordinary development for the future and it vindicated the ideas he and Rosati had nourished—until then rather vague, to be sure—of the importance of their foundations for the future of religion in this country.[70]

Although Hercule Brassac, who had accompanied the bishop from Donaldsonville to the Barrens, had gone ahead to visit Bardstown once again, DuBourg was content to send a letter to Flaget. Flaget told Rosati on May 26:

> Last week I received a letter from your venerable prelate, who was on his way to New York, and from there to Europe. He had not been able, he told us, to resist those pressing solicitations of his charge that invited him to make this long and painful journey for the good of his diocese; and, although he felt his strength weakening and knew that he certainly would find difficulties on this passage, he could not refrain from giving this mark of his perfect devotion for the good of the immense number of people that Providence had confided to his care. He finished by recommending himself to our prayers for the happy success of his enterprise.

Flaget added that since DuBourg had said nothing about the object of his enterprise, he and David were left to their own reflections. He admitted he had written to Rosati's superior and, now that he knew DuBourg was on his way to Rome, was beginning to have some compunctions. But he said stoutly, "Be that as it may, having done and said all that, in conscience, I believed ought to be done and said for the good of religion, I submit myself voluntarily to all the consequences that could follow."[71] Why DuBourg bypassed Bardstown on this journey is not certain. On reaching New York he reported to Rosati only that he did not know what had become of Brassac. "On my arrival at Louisville they told me that he had gone to Bardstown to celebrate the feast of Pentecost there, but that he was expected back the day after. Not being able to detour from my route in order to visit Bardstown, and desiring to see the Bishop of Cincinnati in passing, I begged a friend to tell Mr. Brassac that he would find me in Cincinnati."[72]

Brassac never caught up with his bishop either in Cincinnati or New York, and while DuBourg remained in the former place he discovered that he might have to reroute his own journey. The Ohio River was so low that month that steamboats seemed unlikely to reach Wheeling, to say nothing of Pittsburgh. "I go by land, to Lake Erie," he informed his Little Brother Bruté in Emmitsburg on May 18, "and then by this lake and the great canal to New York. . . ." He might see the Erie Canal for the first and last time. He assured Bruté that if he could be of use to him, to Dubois, or to "our Sisters," he could be reached through his brother Louis at 7, rue de l'Eglise St. Seurin, Bordeaux. He closed, "Pray for me with new fervor and commend me to our friends, especially those celestial inhabitants of the Valley, and rest assured that nothing will ever efface you from the heart of your best friend."[73] It seems likely that the Ohio rose sufficiently while DuBourg was in Cincinnati and that he never saw the waterway that attracted so much attention in the *Gazette de la Louisiane,* for he stopped in Philadelphia en route to New York.

On May 31, from New York, DuBourg told Rosati, "Here I am at the port of embarkation, all ready to set sail tomorrow for Le Havre, in the company of Messers Martial and Abel, who, as you can imagine, have been very surprised at my arrival and my project."[74] Although DuBourg had tried to keep his own trip a secret, Bertrand Martial's had been announced for some time. The previous autumn Flaget had mentioned it to d'Aviau saying, "I hope that he will leave in the spring to carry some important dispatches to the court of Rome and gather some honey on the way in order to consolidate our establishments already made and raise up some others."[75] Flaget's coadjutor had likewise spread the news of Martial's intended journey, telling Tessier in Baltimore, "He goes there in the capacity of vicar general," instructed among other things to find out what he could about the Society of Liautard to which Evremond Harrissart had belonged.[76] Martial himself had offered to carry to Rome any business of Rosati's, and DuBourg's coadjutor had replied courteously, "Thank you for offering to do my business in Italy. If you need letters of recommendation I will give them; but those of the holy Bishop who sends you are sufficient."[77]

The real surprise was that DuBourg and Martial should have chosen the same ship on which to sail. Martial had originally meant to tend to some business in New Orleans and sail from that port.[78] Now here he was in New York with Robert Abell, the giant Kentuckian who was rapidly earning a reputation for frontier wit and preaching style and who, Flaget hoped, might acquire a little polish from a European tour.[79]

None of this concerned the Bishop of Louisiana. He had long since on December 20, 1825, told Pope Leo XII his strong motives for wishing to retire and on the same day requested Peter Caprano of Propaganda to support him in his determination to resign, stating clearly that he would come to Rome if necessary to achieve this goal.[80] He was going home to France to stay, if God willed it. It was almost a decade since he had experienced an ocean voyage, and he intended to enjoy it. He trusted Louis could pay for the balance of its costs, for as usual Monseigneur DuBourg had no money.

CHAPTER XXXIV

A FOURTH TRANSPLANTING

Late in the spring of 1826, John Tessier in Baltimore opened a letter whose handwriting was so scrawling he thought at first the author must be ill, but he recognized it, nevertheless, as that of William DuBourg. The calligraphy was soon explained. "I write from a steamboat in motion, as you can easily perceive," announced the Bishop of Louisiana. "I hope you can read this!"

From his noisy and throbbing conveyance laboriously ascending the Ohio near Wheeling, DuBourg informed the Sulpician superior:

> I am en route to Europe by way of New York, where I am going in all haste in order not to miss the packet of June 1. . . . I am going straight to Rome on business of highest importance. If I can be useful to you in any way . . . be assured of the zeal I will apply to your commissions. Please say as much to the Archbishop. . . . I earnestly recommend myself to the prayers of all my pious friends who honored me with their friendship.[1]

Neither Tessier nor Archbishop Maréchal to whom he relayed the news noticed any oddity in the past tense of "honored me," for the latter wrote sourly to his Sulpician confreres in Paris, after reporting DuBourg's leaving "precipitously" from New Orleans, "What are his motives? I know of none. Some say he goes to solicit the dignity of archbishop. Others think that through his schemes he is on the verge of making a pile of ruins in New Orleans as he did in St. Louis." Perhaps DuBourg intended to make a general search for funds in Europe?[2]

Maréchal had already speedily notified Propaganda Fide of DuBourg's "secret" departure, warning Rome against the seductive trappings DuBourg liked to give his plans and expressing Baltimore's firm opposition to any notion of making New Orleans a metropolitan see with DuBourg as archbishop.[3] Clearly the Archbishop of Baltimore did not guess at his episcopal colleague's real intentions as expressed in DuBourg's own letters to Rome.

Maréchal's apprehensions this time were not solely fixed upon DuBourg's activities. Having learned that Bertrand Martial of Kentucky was also going abroad he alerted both Rome and Paris, warning that Martial should be watched. To Garnier in Paris he wrote plaintively, "Mgr. Flaget, who is very rich, has expedited M. Martial who is to join M. Badin and others to amass alms."[4] The allegedly wealthy Bishop of Bardstown, meanwhile, equally ignorant of DuBourg's intentions, was writing fretfully to Rosati, "He said he had undertaken the trip at the instance of his clergy for the good of his diocese; but did not state the purpose of that trip. We are afraid he may have once more obtained your consent for a postponement of that division [of his diocese]."[5]

The Bishop of Louisiana, the unwitting subject of these random speculations, arrived in Le Havre on July 3 and wrote at once to Propaganda:

> After a most happy voyage of thirty days, I have just joyfully landed in France and shall shortly start for Rome. . . . I am more than ever resolved to resign, and I trust I can easily demonstrate that not only the peace of my soul, but above all the interests of religion, demand that my resignation so often tendered be at last accepted. This persuasion is shared by all

those of my friends whom prudence permitted me to consult, who all agreed that I should withdraw as soon as
possible, and thought any delay to be detrimental.[6]

His expression "my friends whom prudence permitted me
to consult" might well have misled the Secretary of Propaganda since DuBourg had certainly *not* consulted Maréchal
and his fellow bishops, least of all his coadjutor Rosati. One
can only suppose he either meant members of his immediate family, perhaps his brothers, Pierre-François in New
Orleans and Louis in Bordeaux, or Louis Sibourd and Hercule Brassac who were likewise leaving for France that
summer. But before receiving this letter, Rome had already
decided to accept DuBourg's resignation. In fact, the very
day after DuBourg sailed from New York, Propaganda had
recommended to Leo XII that the Bishop of Louisiana be
permitted to step down, to which the pope agreed a month
later.[7] On July 8 Giulio Cardinal della Somaglia, the Prefect
of Propaganda, unaware of DuBourg's arrival in France,
addressed to New Orleans the following notification:

> His Holiness Leo XII has read the letters you addressed to
> him November 20, 1825, and January 14, 1826, and since
> you so justly begged it, our Holy Father has accepted the
> resignation from the See of New Orleans you offer. He
> wishes you to know he accepts completely.
>
> You will be happy to learn that you are discharged of so
> heavy a burden which you again ask to lay down. . . . I pray
> God will long protect you in health and happiness.[8]

On his arrival DuBourg was unaware that his repeated
requests had on that very day been granted; but while he
was still en route to Paris, the news reached him, and from
Rouen he wrote to Antoine Garnier, now Director of Saint-
Sulpice in the capital:

> You may have learned already by public means . . . the
> subject of this letter. The principal aim of my projected
> journey to Rome was to pursue the business of my resigna-
> tion, which I had solicited for a long time. I have just been
> informed by the Reverend Mr. Niel, recently arrived from

Rome, that he had the commission in case he met me in France to inform me that the Pope, struck by the force of my reasons, had deigned to sanction my retirement.

He confessed that now he was free of the burden of his American diocese he was tempted to seek asylum in the Séminaire Saint-Sulpice, except that it might be wiser to settle far from the capital. There was his brother Louis in Bordeaux who, since the death of their "unique and incomparable" sister the previous December, was living in painful isolation at an age when he most needed support and consolation. But he added quickly:

> I do not think, however, of spending the rest of my days in idleness. While my energies remain, they belong to the Church, no matter what kind of service she may demand. I confess, however, that my inclination draws me toward devoting myself to pastoral retreats, a genre of occupation which it seems to me could be useful to religion and most suited to resuscitating and supporting in me the ecclesiastical spirit. I would receive with gratitude your ideas and advice.[9]

For the moment he was assessing his situation sensibly enough. Certainly his talents for preaching were undeniable, and his desire to preserve in himself a fervent spiritual life was Emery's never forgotten lesson. With both Emery and Nagot gone, it was natural for him to seek Garnier's advice. Nevertheless, his mind was in turmoil, as were his feelings.

To a man of his temperament—impetuous, overly sensitive, craving appreciation, accustomed to making "profound impressions," swift to ignore his past miscalculations—his present situation was excruciatingly painful. He had, as he acknowledged to Garnier, repeatedly asked to be relieved of the dreadful *fardeau* of his diocese, but he had not visualized what would follow this demission. It was the old flaw Emery had repeatedly warned against, of not foreseeing difficulties.

His mood on landing at Le Havre was all buoyancy after passing a "most happy voyage" and "joyfully" landing in France. His first letter to Secretary Peter Caprano revealed his eagerness to get to Rome and report as an American prelate on the needs of "nearly all the Dioceses of that country," which he had recently seen with his own eyes. In his usual fashion he had not hesitated to recommend Anthony Kohlmann for the vacant see of New York, or to denounce again the appointment of Michael Portier to the Vicariate Apostolic of Florida and Alabama. He had concluded that letter with the words, "I earnestly long to fly to the feet of His Holiness and pay to Your Grace by word of mouth the tribute of my consideration and respect," signing himself the Bishop of New Orleans.[10] He was thinking of the way things had been a decade ago when Cardinal Litta had welcomed his views and Pius VII his petitions.

It was something of a shock to receive almost immediately thereafter the news that he was no longer Bishop of New Orleans, especially when the news came by way of a mere vicar general of Missouri, one of the very recruits not yet in minor orders whom DuBourg had brought with him from Europe in 1817. When Francis Niel reported to Rome that he had notified DuBourg of his altered status, he added cryptically, "He seemed to be satisfied."[11] Certainly DuBourg's second letter to Caprano was in a more muted tone. He was now hastening to Bordeaux, "to attend to his own sanctification." Even though he was "somewhat broken in health, and needed rest above everything else," he would, he offered, undertake the trip to Rome if Caprano thought his presence there might be of use to the interests of the Church in America. "There are indeed many things I had proposed to mention to Your Grace in conversation," he insinuated, "that could hardly be explained by letter. . . ."[12] This time he signed himself the *former* Bishop of New Orleans.

Something of his confusion and chagrin shows through these letters to Garnier and Caprano of July 11 written in Rouen. While traveling from Rouen to Paris, he had more time to realize what he had done. It was one thing to smart under his repeated failures to win over the hostile elements in his former see city; it was quite another to confront the future of a man sixty years old, divested of authority and deprived of any arena in which to give free rein to his talents and visions of splendid new institutions to glorify Holy Mother Church. He was still wincing from the sudden change in his situation on his arrival in the capital, and when *l'Ami de la religion et du Roi* on July 15 referred to his resignation with the comment, "One believes that the state of the health of the prelate has been one of the motives for this measure," it struck an already quivering nerve.[13]

The letter he addressed to *l'Ami* stated loftily:

> The motives of my resignation are of a higher order; and they were presented to the Holy See, to which they appeared so just that His Holiness the Pope did not hesitate a moment, when they were submitted to him, to dissolve the sacred ties that bound me to that important but laborious mission. But in ceasing to be head of it, I have not ceased to feel the most tender solicitude for it. . . . It is that solicitude which forced me to leave it, inasmuch that on the one hand it was evident my presence there would be more prejudicial than useful, and on the other hand, I flatter myself I would be able from Europe to render that mission more important services.[14]

None of these explanations to others, however, could banish the galling, recurring reminders that he was now a man without a country, a shepherd without a flock. There was little point in rejoining Louis until he was at peace with himself, and with that intention he entered the Trappist monastery near Laval. It was from there that he addressed to Denis Frayssinous, the king's Minister of Ecclesiastical Affairs, a lengthy analysis of his situation as he tried to put it into proper perspective.

He began by saying frankly that he knew all sorts of conjectures about his resignation were going around. "I ought to expect it," he conceded, "and accept with good grace the resulting humiliation." His task was to rise above it and refer himself to God's judgment—which he believed would be favorable. Yet, he did owe people some explanation of his conduct, and he was now "from the depth of this holy retreat," where he had come for repose after the long voyage and subsequent agitation, ready to open himself without reserve to Frayssinous. "Your kindnesses to me make me presume that this will not abuse your indulgence," he explained. "The majority of the details into which I must enter with you are of their nature to be communicated only to you under the seal of intimate confidence."[15]

He was baring his inmost thoughts to a man most likely to be sympathetic and trusted with these confidences. Whether DuBourg knew it or not, earlier that year Frayssinous, the Bishop of Hermopolis, in an impassioned speech in the French Chamber of Deputies defending the work of the Society for the Propagation of the Faith, and its contributions to overseas missionary activities in places like Louisiana, had paused to interject, "which has for its Bishop a Frenchman, Monseigneur Dubourg, a man of very rare spirit and capacity."[16]

DuBourg began his letter with his first arrival in New Orleans in 1812, the ecclesiastical anarchy he found there, the deplorable scandals of a clergy living in concubinage amid their progeny, the laity who wished no more from these priests than that they baptize, marry, and bury, but otherwise sanction their flagrant vices. The arrival of an apostolic administrator determined to preach the word of God became the signal for an atrocious persecution. He was accused by slaveholders on the one hand of preaching revolt to their slaves, while on the other to the slaves he was pictured as the enemy of their race. Because of his undeviating attachment to the Bourbon dynasty he was presented as a murderous fanatic. Two different times plots against his life resulted in violence within his very cathedral, and he escaped only because of the "visible protection of Providence." His brother's family—who had been settled in New Orleans for a long time—became objects of this furious hatred; and what horrified him most was the fact that his nephew felt obliged to draw his sword in defense of his uncle's honor. It was at this juncture that, in spite of his reluctance, he had been consecrated bishop in Rome. He reminded Frayssinous, "Your Excellency knows all that I did in Europe ten years ago, to prepare to execute that design."

He then recounted the course of his episcopacy—the years at St. Louis, the privations of the Missouri frontier, the foundations made by the Vincentians, the Religious of the Sacred Heart, and the Jesuits in the Mississippi Valley. From this northern center of his diocese he had sent his most prudent, wisest co-workers to fill posts in Lower Louisiana, where they were favorably received and succeeded in reforming many parishes. Changes even in New Orleans filled him with hope and finally, after five years in Missouri, he had ventured to return to that former theatre of so many of his woes.

But it was no use. As he described those last years in New Orleans to the Minister of Ecclesiastical Affairs:

> The fire was only hidden under the ashes and was not long in manifesting itself through a thousand openings. But I believed I had to hold firm at least until I had consummated the important work of establishing an episcopal seat, for until then there had existed neither a residence nor any revenues for a bishop.

The removal of the Ursulines to their new home and their gift of the former convent as a bishop's residence in the center of the city had assured him of this last aim. It was this small triumph that had resulted in a furious flaring up of the conflagration once more.

This time, however, there were more innocent victims involved. Three of his nieces had married; three nephews were thus added to an already numerous family. His brother's business affairs were more extensively at issue. Everything made him fear that the next attacks would be worse than those in 1814, that things would never improve in New Orleans so long as he remained on the scene. The diocese had a perfect coadjutor against whom there was no opposition; there was a modest property sufficient to his needs, a good library, furniture, and a chapel. Rosati could live like a bishop in peace, and being a Vincentian himself could undoubtedly get new recruits for the mission from Europe. However partially DuBourg may have phrased it, it was all quite true. He was evaluating the situation fairly enough when he concluded:

> I do not think that you will find a reasonable man who, after having weighed all these motives, would have hesitated to give me the advice I have taken for myself. . . . In fact, all that I could have done of benefit to that poor country, and which perhaps could never have been done by another, is already done or on the way to completion. . . . My presence could only hinder or harm. My successor, on the contrary, has in his hands all the elements needed to accomplish great good without having to struggle against personal opposition.

DuBourg was correct in concluding that his presence in New Orleans was a hindrance. Philip Borgna, C. M., expressed the same conviction in his letter to Propaganda after DuBourg's departure saying, "In this city, this sewer of all vice and refuse of all that is worst on earth, the prejudice against him is so strong that in spite of all his sacrifices and all his exalted ability, he could not have effected any good here. The very name of Dubourg has an irritating sound in the ears of . . . this new Babylon. You cannot imagine all the abominations which fill the newspapers." [17]

There were others who had appreciated the difficulties DuBourg had encountered. The Ursuline superior in New Orleans said of his departure:

> Our holy and respected Bishop, who is another St. Francis de Sales by his wisdom, his virtue, his kindness and his goodness, has gone to Europe for the affairs of his diocese. Many people believe that he will not return again to this country, but I need to have confidence that he will not abandon us and that he will return again to the post where Providence places him, where, indeed, he finds a field very difficult to cultivate. . . . It would be a terrible blow for us if we should lose our good, worthy, and respected father. This thought is too sad to contemplate. [18]

Madame Duchesne on reading a Paris newspaper announcing DuBourg's resignation said sadly, "That means a great loss for this ungrateful diocese that made him suffer so severely,"[19] while one of the Seghers of New Orleans, confirming the news of the bishop's departure to his former college, St. Mary's of Baltimore, said, "Very decidedly Mgr. Dubourg has left us. The last arrivals from Europe have brought the news. I am not astonished that he has sought a more tranquil place to finish his days. He experienced so much dislike in New Orleans."[20]

He had ever been adept at marshaling his defenses when his conduct was at stake. It would be consoling if Frayssinous could view his "naive exposé" as evidence that in resigning his see DuBourg had followed the will of God clearly indicated; but, whatever the outcome, in the process of presenting his case to the king's minister, DuBourg discovered he had at last assuaged his own uneasiness. He *had* done the right thing. "I do not know what His adorable designs are for the future," he said simply. "I will go and await a manifestation of them at Bordeaux, abandoning myself without anxiety to His paternal care and the kindness of Your Excellency."[21]

He was at peace once more.

It was merely interesting some days later to receive from Rome Cardinal Somaglia's letter addressed to Bordeaux containing a copy of the July 8 letter sent to New Orleans with the Holy Father's acceptance of his resignation, and the additional news that Louisiana was now divided into two sees, one at New Orleans, the other at St. Louis, with Rosati administrator of both for the time being. Caprano, the cardinal's secretary, had added, "I pray God to preserve your Lordship happy and well."[22]

The designs of Providence for the former Bishop of Louisiana were not long in emerging. As DuBourg in Rouen was composing his letters to Paris and Rome, in Bordeaux a great man lay dying. Charles-François d'Aviau du Bois de Sanzay, the archbishop of that city so bound up in the destinies of the royal family, did not live out the day of July 11, 1826. *Le Moniteur* in noting his passing five days later ventured the opinion that he would be a most difficult man to replace; it was a sentiment rather universally shared.[23] Even amid his present personal doubts and uncertainties

Guillaume DuBourg could recall those days in Baltimore sixteen years before, when the priests of St. Mary's Seminary and the Archbishop of Baltimore had struggled over d'Aviau's cramped script as they tried to read his analysis of the *Théologie de Lyon*—before Nagot made a more legible copy. Although in 1810 Baltimore's Saint-Sulpice was remote from European seminaries the Gentlemen had always tried to keep abreast of the trends abroad and d'Aviau had been their channel. D'Aviau had befriended Flaget when as bishop-elect of Kentucky Flaget had gone to France to seek recruits. Nor was DuBourg likely to forget d'Aviau's generosity toward himself and his own new recruits scarcely ten years ago as they waited in Bordeaux for their ships for the United States. He had been a man very easy to love.

The Archdiocese of Bordeaux was not long left vacant. On July 31 at his chateau Saint-Cloud, Charles X signed an ordinance naming the Bishop of Montauban, Jean Lefebvre de Cheverus—one-time Bishop of Boston—to the Archdiocese of Bordeaux.[24] On August 2 when *l'Ami* announced the news of Cheverus's nomination, it hinted broadly, "As to the choice of a successor to M. de Cheverus, at Montauban, we have reason to believe it will be very suited to appease the regrets which the news of his promotion is going to cause throughout the diocese."[25] Stephen Theodore Badin of Kentucky, who was in Paris at the time, wrote that same day to Edward Fenwick in Cincinnati that he was going to Bordeaux to see DuBourg and added, "Bishop Cheverus has just been nominated Archbishop of Bordeaux and DuBourg will succeed him at Montauban."[26] Badin was reporting only rumor, but it was rumor believed in other circles as well. From Montauban on August 4, Cheverus told Frayssinous:

> The noise of my nomination has spread here. I am tormented by everyone and I cannot reassure them. It seems to me very important that if His Majesty absolutely wishes me translated to Bordeaux, my successor be named immediately. If this is to be Mgr. Dubourg, I believe that if he spent some time with me I could manage to have him appreciated and wanted upon my leaving.[27]

Whether DuBourg himself had heard the rumor prior to Badin's visit to Bordeaux is not certain, but his note to Vicar General Pierre Barrès on his own arrival on August 2 showed him to be in fine fettle with all his old ebullience returned. "I arrive, *Monsieur l'abbé*," he announced, "and while waiting until I can go to greet you in person, which will be at the first free moment, I hasten to reconnoiter your jurisdiction and ask you, in case of need, for the powers needed to exercise my functions in this diocese."[28] Certainly his spirits were not dampened to learn from Canon Gignoux of the Saint-André Cathedral that the young man serving as Bordeaux's Roman agent, on learning of DuBourg's return to France, had inquired:

> Please tell me something of this respected and unfortunate prelate who has been inundated with great hardships in the terrible mission he filled in America. My father was a pupil of his, and his whole life he never stopped telling us his memory of the virtuous and wise practices his former preceptor had inspired in him. . . . If he is at Bordeaux and you see him, assure him that in spite of the death of my father his family feel the highest veneration for this bishop.[29]

Emery had always said, "Your students can not forget you." How long ago were those days at Issy!

On August 13, 1826, the rumor became official news when the king signed an ordinance naming Louis-Guillaume DuBourg to the Diocese of Montauban.[30] In reporting the event *l'Ami* first summarized his career and then speculated:

> The King, in hastening to attach him to the French hierarchy, doubtlessly not only has regard for his merit and episcopal virtues; it is probable that His Majesty is also thinking that M. Dubourg, accustomed to living in a country peopled by Protestants, would be most suited to governing a diocese which includes a great number of them, and would make the loss of so beloved a bishop [as Cheverus] more easily forgotten.

The rest of the article was devoted to Cheverus, how beloved he was, the touching letters from his flocks begging the king to let him stay in Montauban, even the grief of his American flock at his departure from Boston three years earlier. *L'Ami* concluded, "Such farewells are the most flattering eulogy a bishop can collect."[31]

If it rankled at all that in the press DuBourg always played second fiddle to Cheverus, to whom he had once gratuitously imputed ambition as a motive for leaving Boston, DuBourg never gave any sign of it. To Cheverus he said:

> For the love of your diocesans who will become mine, prepare the way for me, my dear Excellency. Yes, you can indeed promise them that I will love them tenderly without distinction. They have all won my heart by the regrets they show for your departure. I hope to win theirs in trying to follow myself in the footsteps of the good shepherd taken away from them.[32]

He knew how to say the appropriate and ingratiating thing, and somehow a letter he wrote to New Orleans found its way into the pages of the local paper where *les Montalbanais* could read:

> I feel very vividly the extent of the task imposed on me by my saintly and learned predecessor. . . . I pray without ceasing that Providence may supply what is lacking in me that I may be able to console the flock for the loss of so worthy a shepherd, and keep up the great good he has done. . . . The consummate wisdom, the gift of persuasion which enchains souls, the fine talent for words, and the profound wisdom of Bishop Cheverus leave such a void that they can not hope to see it filled by his successor.[33]

Cheverus in turn did what he could to prepare the way for DuBourg, urging his flock to receive cordially the prelate he had known for so long in America—a man endowed with a superior talent for preaching, an exemplary zeal in exercising his episcopal functions, a truly edifying piety, and not least of all a spirit of love and tolerance which made him regretted in his former diocese by both Catholics and Christians of other communities.[34] A reunion in person, however, of these two French prelates, who had had so much to do with setting the feet of Elizabeth Ann Seton on the path to sanctity, was not possible for some weeks to come. When DuBourg went up to Paris the first week in September to receive his *informations* (briefing) on taking over Montauban, he found that Cheverus had been excused from the same formality for Bordeaux. The latter was engaged in preaching the Jubilee in various parts of his diocese and giving retreats to both the military and his clergy while the doyen of the cathedral in Montauban, Jean de Trélissac, acted as his proxy in Paris.[35]

In the interim DuBourg had plenty to occupy his time and thoughts. There was querulous old Louis in Bordeaux, eternally preoccupied with the legalities of regaining, through governmental indemnification, some remnant of the family investments in Saint-Domingue. After the bishop had left New Orleans, Pierre-François had mailed to Le Havre a large package of his own and Guillaume's reclamations. (Arnould, as usual, insisted on acting independently and refused to unite his claims to theirs.)[36] The papers from Louisiana had still not arrived in late August, and Louis fretted at length in his letters to Guillaume and their attorney, even though the latter assured him the prospects of eventual settlement appeared good.[37] The bishop's share of any settlement that might be achieved would be less than half of Louis's and only one-sixth of the whole; but any share would be welcome, heaven knew. He wished Louis luck. The business of facts, figures, and forms had always been his brother's *metier,* and in his own way Louis at least was happy.

It was quite another story in the case of Pierre Babad, the bishop's old schoolmate and confrere of their Baltimore days. From the Society of Saint-Sulpice in Paris, DuBourg learned with some distress that Babad had never been content since his return to France over five years ago. After a brief stay in Issy, he had gone to Reims to direct a seminary, but he was restless and unhappy there. Only that April he had asked Propaganda if, together with some others, he might return to Baltimore, or perhaps go to the Antilles.[38] Tessier had discouraged his return to Maryland,[39] and now in September Babad was announcing his retirement because of age and infirmity. He would live out his days near his brother in the Archdiocese of Lyon where he had been born. On September 27, 1826, the Society voted him a pension.[40] By contrast with Babad, the Bishop-elect of Montauban felt himself filled with vigor and quite ready to embark on a new phase of episcopal service.

Already on September 16 he had officiated at a Mass in the Chapel of Saint-Denis to commemorate the death of Louis XVIII. He had been assisted by four canons of the Royal Chapter of Saint-Denis in the presence of the Dauphin, the duc d'Orleans, and the Duc de Chartres among other dignitaries.[41] On the Saturday of the September Ember Days he had ordained twenty-three clerics in the chapel of the Daughters of Charity at rue du Bac. Almost half the ordinands were Irish while the others were from the seminary directed by the Lazarists; none was destined particularly for Paris.[42] The combination of those three elements—Daughters of Charity, Irish, and Lazarists could not help but remind him of his American past. By odd coincidence, only four days later he was reintegrated in his quality and rights as a French citizen.[43]

Louis, who followed his brother's pursuits with interest and pride, wrote from Bordeaux, "I see with pleasure, but nevertheless with some concern for your health, the grand affairs to which you are devoting yourself," but he recommended that they come to an end with the Ember Day ordinations.[44] Guillaume was not, however, likely to be dissuaded from his prospective journey to Soissons set for Monday, September 29. It had been a long time coming, but his comrade of the old Issy days, Jules de Simony, was himself a bishop now, having been consecrated for Soissons on April 24, 1825.[45]

Although the king's nomination of DuBourg for Montauban arrived in Rome on September 7, it had to go through proper channels.[46] It was not until October 2 that a secret consistory at the papal palace named prelates to the French vacancies: Cheverus to Bordeaux, DuBourg to Montauban, and Simon Garnier to Vannes.[47] When

Cheverus relayed the news of his own appointment to his friend Vernou Bonneuil in Guadeloupe he added, "The former Bishop of Louisiana and head of the college of Baltimore is named my successor at Montauban. We are both awaiting our bulls from Rome."[48] Under its "Montauban News" the *Journal de Tarn-et-Garonne,* however, on October 21 could be no more definite than to say:

> It appears certain that Mgr. Dubourg, named to the Diocese of Montauban, will not be long in receiving the bull of canonical institution and in taking the oath between the hands of the King which must precede his installation. The time of the arrival of this prelate is not positively known; but it is permitted to hope that as he has announced in a letter written to the first magistrate of the *département* he will come soon. . . .[49]

As November was ushered in, Parisians of non-ecclesiastical circles were much more excited about the anticipated arrival of the celebrated English author, Sir Walter Scott. He was coming to France, one read, to imbibe information for his history of Napoleon. Reporting on the felicitations the king had received from his family on November 4, the Fête de Saint-Charles Borromée and the king's feast day, the press elaborated:

> The same day the celebrated Sir Walter Scott, accompanied by his daughter and Mme Mirbel, found themselves in *la galerie vitrée* at the moment the King passed through on his way to Mass. His Majesty deigned to address a few words to Scott to which the illustrious writer replied with an expression of lively sensibility.[50]

History does not record whether Charles X shared the views of Frayssinous who had publicly denounced Romanticism and Romantic writers for being concerned only with things "false, bizarre, and nebulous"—but certainly in intellectual circles the arrival of Scott brightened the grey days of the season of umbrellas in 1826.[51] His influence could be perceived in Augustin Thierry's *Histoire de la conquête de l'Angleterre par les Normands,* published the year before, and in the operas of Daniel-François Auber and François-

Adrien Boieldieu.[52] The latter's *La Dame Blanche*, which popularized the old Scottish song "Robin Adair," was as much a favorite in New Orleans as in Paris. The erstwhile bishop of the former city, while eschewing theatres and opera houses as one of the causes for loose living in that cauldron of vice, could well remember the avidity with which Louisiana readers awaited the announcements in the *Gazette* or *Courier* of Scott's latest Waverly novel. Sir Walter was generally, throughout the South, the favorite European writer.

But the bishop had other things on his mind in early November. For one thing he was preparing to officiate at the Church of Saint-Roch, where the paternal association of the Chevaliers de Saint Louis were offering a Mass in honor of the feast of Saint Charles.[53] For another, he must reply to Madame Duchesne's July letter in which she taxed him with her suspicions that he had returned to France to stay. He defended himself as best he could:

> You were not deceived in your presentiments about my voyage. I knew it at the time when I bade you adieu, but what is the use of agreeing? It was necessary to let time inform you. I do not need to tell you that I had imperative reasons for acting as I did. The Pope has judged them such, as well as all the serious authorities I have consulted. Neither [need I tell you] that my heart bleeds for my separation from so many dear persons, so many precious establishments. My body is here; my spirit and my heart are always in Louisiana, and it was not in vain that I had graven above the door of your Church: "My heart shall be here always." My consolation in this sorrow, and it is one to which I attach great importance, is the hope that here I will be more useful to my first spouse than I could be by remaining near her. Her interests keep me incessantly busy. Father Van Qui'n will be able to tell you and you will soon have personal proof in the valuable reinforcement that I have at last obtained for your houses from your excellent mother. I had to beg, but I have obtained all.[54]

St. Michael's at La Fourche would have a new recruit named de la Croix, a name revered both there and in Florissant.

Grand Coteau was getting a subject especially capable of aiding Madame Xavier Murphy with the French language. Both St. Ferdinand and St. Charles likewise would receive reinforcement. Whether near or far away, he could always be in Louisiana and especially "with you, my dear Mother, and your dear daughters whose Father I shall always consider myself to be."

In a postscript he added, "I count on being in Montauban on the 21, no longer being held here for my oath of fidelity, which I hope will be administered on the 13." It was a hope soon to be realized. At last, on November 10 at Fontainebleau the king signed the ordinance providing for the publication of the bulls officially confirming Cheverus, DuBourg, and Garnier for the sees they were to fill.[55] Frayssinous took advantage of that occasion to present the matter of the subsidies for the expenses of taking possession of the three sees, which perforce followed the publication of the bulls in Latin and French. According to custom and a royal ordinance of September 4, 1820, an archbishop received 15,000 francs and a bishop 10,000 for this formality. Cheverus, having already had 10,000 on entering Montauban was now entitled to only an additional 5,000; but DuBourg and Garnier, not having held French sees before, were each entitled to 10,000. Charles automatically affixed his signature then and there.[56]

There was one more matter delaying the oath-taking at the king's hands. Simon Garnier had never been consecrated a bishop. Like both Cheverus and DuBourg, he had fled France in the early years of the Revolution; but unlike them he had returned from his years of exile in Switzerland and Russia in 1802 after the concordat arranged by Napoleon seemed to herald a happier day for the Church in France. It had proved to be a period of suppression of episcopal sees, and former nonjuring clergy were not given preferential treatment. Now, in November 1826, Garnier was to be consecrated at the Church of Saint-Germain-des-Prés with Guillaume DuBourg assisting.[57] On Monday, November 13, Frayssinous presented the three prelates to

Charles X to take their oaths of loyalty between his hands.[58] The required official ceremonies were over at last.

DuBourg had hoped to leave Paris on Wednesday, and Louis's legal adviser was counting on this "occasion" to send to Bordeaux information about the declarations they needed to make to the Commission of Liquidation before further steps could be taken in the affair of their properties.[59] DuBourg was delayed, however, because the king graciously granted him and Cheverus a special audience on Thursday, a mark of courtesy neither could, nor would, wish to forego.[60]

After the rebuffs, insults, and public humiliations of his last years in Louisiana, the ceremonies and civilities of the Bourbon court and capital were balm to his wounded sensibilities. His sixty years for the moment lay lightly on his patrician shoulders as he savored the prospect of new ventures in a new vineyard where laborers would not be so few. He could scarcely wait to get to Montauban. Once again Providence had permitted good to come from evil for Louis-Guillaume-Valentin DuBourg.

CHAPTER XXXV

LOUIS-GUILLAUME DE MONTAUBAN

The see city to which DuBourg was going presented sharp contrasts to those he had known in the American Midwest, especially as to things aesthetic. While Paris was enlivened by the visit of a distinguished English author during the first week in November, the city of Montauban on November 3 was even more excited by the prospect of the return of a native son. A member of the Beaux-Arts class of the Royal Institute, Chevalier of the Legion of Honor, and one of the most distinguished painters of France, Jean-Auguste-Dominique Ingres after an absence of nearly thirty years was coming to preside over the installation of his "Vow of Louis XIII" in the Cathedral of the Assumption.[1] Actually, Ingres himself did not arrive until the following week, and it was November 19 before *les Montalbanais* got their first glimpse of the canvas which was to become his most famous work.[2]

While relatives and special friends of the artist vied for the pleasure of offering him smaller fêtes, the civic dignitaries wanted a grander occasion to show public gratitude for the "monument" with which he was enriching their city.

Powerfully supported by the mayor, Monsieur le vicomte de Gironde, who possessed a "most refined taste for beaux-arts united with the desire to do all that could be useful and honorable for his constituents," there was no difficulty in starting a subscription for such a testimonial.

The occasion began with a banquet limited to eighty in the great hall of the Hôtel de Ville. At the moment the guests were assembled in an adjoining room, the painting was revealed, Ingres was presented to his compatriots, and the mayor gave a discourse which produced a show of "the most lively emotions" and tastefully expressed the sentiments of the city. The guests then processed into the dining hall blazing with tapers and magnificently adorned. The *Journal de Tarn-et-Garonne* regretted that it could not give space to every detail but did include the tidbit that two of the clergy delighted the honored guest with their verses both "animated and *spirituel.*" Following the dinner a larger group was admitted to be regaled with vocal and instrumental music which did honor to the tastes and talents of the performers both amateur and "artistic," and when all these diversions were exhausted, with one voice the guests demanded dancing, whereupon a ball, "one of the most beautiful the country had ever seen, lasted until three o'clock in the morning." As the *Journal's* reporter put it: "French gallantry could scarcely fail to offer the ladies, whose youth and beauty were the principal ornament of this numerous society, any amusement which would prolong so delicious a soirée."[3]

After being displayed in the city hall for two days, the "Vow of Louis XIII" was taken to its final destination in the cathedral, where its arrival on November 21 was celebrated in the presence of a huge gathering by a religious ceremony, during which a choir of musicians and singers chosen especially for the occasion performed Cherubini's Mass. Amid the excitement of Ingres' sojourn, the civic and religious celebrations, and the crowds milling around trying to get a glimpse of the great man and his painting, the importance of the work itself was momentarily obscured. It was only after his departure when one could stand alone before the "Vow"—regretting, perhaps, that it had been hung too high,

or was poorly lighted—that those who savored art could feel
both a rush of gratitude toward the king, who had commis-
sioned the work and given it to the cathedral, and a profound pride in the genius of the artist who had conceived it.
As one such viewer recorded his musings:

> We no longer hesitate to believe that this picture is one of
> those that does most honor to the French school, and that
> the beauties with which it is filled are beauties of the first
> rank. We are no longer astonished that the journals of Paris
> signalled the contrast offered at the last exposition between
> this work . . . and the odd productions of the new school
> called Romantic. . . .[4]

The new Bishop of Montauban, in whose cathedral the
Ingres masterpiece now hung, did not participate in any of
those November festivities welcoming the artist and his
work. DuBourg was still in Paris until November 20, winding up some matters relating to his diocese which could be
handled more effectively in the capital.[5] For one thing, his
old friend and trusted vicar general in Louisiana, Louis
Sibourd, was now returned to France and DuBourg wanted
him at Montauban. It required the king's signature on an
ordinance to assure Sibourd the first vacancy to occur in the
cathedral chapter, with a place in the choir and a voice in
the deliberations of the canons.[6] Another devoted co-
worker in Louisiana, Hercule Brassac, was also in France
just then on a leave of absence DuBourg himself had
granted a year ago. Brassac's father had lost in swift succession his wife and ten children, and his remaining son had
begged leave to embrace his aged parent once more. Du-
Bourg explained to the Papal Nuncio to France, "I could
not deny such a favor to a father more than three score years
and ten, so cruelly tried in his most tender affections."
There would have been no difficulty if he still had jurisdiction over Brassac, who was prepared to return to Louisiana
whenever his superiors manifested God's will. Would the
nuncio intercede with Propaganda to permit Brassac's remaining in France a little longer as the only prop of his
father's last years?[7]

A third matter more immediately urgent to the Diocese of Montauban was that of a new vicar general. Cheverus in leaving for Bordeaux was taking with him two of his most trusted subordinates from Montauban, Jean de Trélissac and Antoine Carles, to become his vicars general in Bordeaux.[8] Vicar General Turcq could not go on for long in Montauban without assistance. On November 15, the king solved this situation by naming Abbé Pouget as second vicar general for Montauban.[9] Meanwhile, after taking his own oath of loyalty to Charles X, DuBourg had already empowered Turcq to take possession of the episcopal see in the presence of the pastor of the cathedral parish on Sunday, November 19, the day of the banquet honoring Ingres.[10] At last it was time for DuBourg to depart for Montauban.

The American traveler today who wishes to visit Montauban for historic or artistic purposes tends to think of the city as a convenient stopover between Toulouse and Bordeaux, with excellent trains running regularly and swiftly between those larger cities. It takes a very real effort of the imagination to envision the modes of travel in the 1820s. One historian of the Bourbon Restoration has commented perceptively that if France was, in fact, much smaller in the early nineteenth century, yet she was much larger, if one counts distances by the time it took to travel them.[11] The speediest method of overland travel was the mail coach, a rugged, four-wheeled, leather-topped vehicle drawn by four horses which were changed every six or twelve miles. These express coaches carried a maximum of four passengers, and seats were naturally at a premium. Even with all the improvements made by the end of the reign of Charles X, in 1830 the trip from Paris to Bordeaux still took forty-five hours at best.

Wealthy travelers, using their own equipages or those hired for a particular journey, proceeded at a more leisurely pace and were apt to make more frequent stopovers, all of which added enormously to the cost of moving from place to place. The average Frenchman could not even consider this kind of jaunt.

The most popular and practical means of passenger

service in the period of DuBourg's episcopacy was the great *diligence*. This heavy—alas, too often topheavy—conveyance could carry from sixteen to twenty passengers as well as the driver and postilions. Travel was much slower with many rest-stops along the way where rooms, meals, and tips added to the cost. A trip from Paris to Bordeaux by diligence might take five days, with another day or two added for the trip to Montauban. Going directly from Paris to Montauban in July—the best season for road conditions—Jean de Cheverus in 1824 had needed six days just to reach the limits of his diocese at Lamagistère. Small wonder that a contemporary of DuBourg's remarked, "Next to a famine what Parisians fear most are journeys. For them a foreign land begins a few furlongs beyond their city's tollgates."[12]

Quite apart from the time and expenses involved in going from Paris to Montauban was the inescapable discomfort, if not almost unbearable hardship, of such a journey. The roads of Restoration France undeniably underwent many improvements, especially in the decade after DuBourg's return to his native land. Certainly the king's highways were superior to the corduroy roads of the American frontier. And the visitations to Florida and Natchitoches the previous year had traversed no roads at all. Yet, in more recent years the Bishop of Louisiana had traveled the length of his diocese by waterways where steam-driven craft were improving rapidly, and service during the greater portion of the year was becoming regularized. But comparisons such as these blur the physical realities November travel presented to a man approaching his sixty-first birthday.

If the centers of roads were paved—and only a third of the royal roads were—the paved part was so narrow and steeply sloped above the unpaved shoulders that carriages could not leave or return to the paved center without risk of overturning; passing an oncoming vehicle demanded dangerous maneuvering. Potholes often forced the diligences off into fields where their wheels sank into muck above the axles. "It was not unusual for horses to die on the road, and their half-decomposed bodies sprawled perilously across the most heavily travelled routes."[13] And those were the major highways!

Roads maintained by the departments, or smaller communities, depended entirely upon the energies of the prefects and mayors and the support of the local citizenry. The notorious disrepair of secondary roads remained one of the major obstacles to agricultural progress in France for years to come.

None of this deterred the Bishop of Montauban as he jounced and swayed behind the lathered and straining horses pulling him southward. Old habits were too strong to be broken; and he had ever been an impatient man. He had already persuaded his brother Louis to go on ahead of him to Montauban to pave the way.[14] How impenetrable were the ways of Divine Providence. Louis and he were the only ones left on French soil of that proud patriarchy, the Du-Bourgs of Rochemont. Victoire had always cared so much about the achievements of *Monsieur l'abbé,* believed so staunchly in his prowess, remained so devoted to his interests. If only she might have lived to join them in the bishop's residence in Montauban. Instead, the first anniversary of her death, only a few days away, would be celebrated at an altar she had never known and he had yet to see on his own arrival.[15]

With the departure of Ingres from Montauban plans for DuBourg's arrival went rapidly ahead. It was generally known he had requested that the formalities be dispensed with; but, while his modesty was applauded, the city after having had no bishop for thirty-four years had no intention of foregoing the solemnities only recently revived for the entry of Cheverus two years ago.[16] Granted, an entry in late November was not so easy to arrange as one in July; it was difficult to build grandstands beyond the city on the Promenade du Cours at that season. But in order to give more éclat to the reception, the prefect and the duc de la Force who commanded the military of Tarn-et-Garonne would go out with an escort of gendarmerie to meet Monseigneur. The prelate would then pause at the Hôtel de la Prefecture where the civil authorities and clergy would be waiting to compliment him. After being robed in all his episcopal regalia, he would go in procession up the street where double rows of troops from the garrison formed a brightly colored aisle in his honor. Vicar General Turcq would then hand over the keys to the cathedral at the central door of its impressive façade, and the crowds would surge in behind the dignitaries to listen to the voice of their new shepherd. It was expected that DuBourg would arrive in Caussade on Saturday night, spend Sunday there, and then early on Monday morning set out for his see city and the *entrée*.[17]

But Montauban, like Louisiana earlier, was to learn that their bishop fixed his own timetables. For the second time that year he had kept virtually everyone in the dark as to his intentions. Although the French press was more guardedly polite in its allusions to his November arrival than Maréchal had been toward his departure in June, there was equal astonishment on both occasions at the behavior of this Franco-American missionary prelate.

Instead of stopping in Caussade and spending a leisurely Sunday there, DuBourg had pushed on to Montauban Saturday night. Arriving on the outskirts of the city, he had ordered his postilion to see to it that his carriage must not be noticed as it approached his palace, where at eight o'clock at night he descended without fanfare to the complete astonishment of most of its residents. The Paris press reported this arrival as quite *à l'improviste* or *sans être aucunement attendu*.[18]

Announcing this premature arrival, the *Journal de Tarn-et-Garonne* began on a somewhat disgruntled note, commenting that "Mgr. Dubourg . . . had deprived himself of the honors prepared to receive him. Instead of arriving in this city on the 27th of this month, the day fixed for his solemn entry, this prelate arrived there unheralded the evening of the 25th." By the time the *Journal* concluded its report, however, it had succumbed to the DuBourg spell and acknowledged graciously:

> If people were charmed by his words in the Cathedral they
> were no less charmed by the responses he gave to the

authorities who came to call. We cite especially as a model of grace, urbanity, and discretion the one he addressed to M. Marzials, the President of the [Protestant] Consistory, and which is a most certain gauge of the continuance of the unity existing between the Christians of the two communions.

The *Journal* particularly regretted not having a copy of that speech to report to its readers.[19]

The *Mémorial du Midi* in its account was ecstatic from beginning to end. After describing the Saturday arrival and the astonishment of those living in the episcopal residence the *Mémorial* went on:

> The next day only a few people had learned of the good fortune which had happened when the noise of the cannon announced that Monseigneur, accompanied by his clergy, was going to the Cathedral. In an instant, that vast basilica, the Square and all the nearby streets were filled with people avid for the first smile, the first blessing of this prelate-consoler. His majestic height, his venerable face, the tenderness lighting up his glances, the emotion so easy to read in his expressions, the brilliance of his virtues, the thought of his apostolic works, for the moment won all hearts. But when he mounted the pulpit and opened his soul to the flock confided to his care, when in altered voice . . . the name of Cheverus came from his lips the feeling of his listeners reached a climax. From then on, each one of them vowed to keep this shepherd who knew how to elicit such tears in recalling the eminent virtues of his predecessor, in charging the clergy to abandon him if he ever strayed from the path of such a model.

On everyone's lips, it seemed, rose the exclamation, "What a man! What a bishop! We have a new Monseigneur de Cheverus; we have a father."[20]

If the Catholics of Montauban could not help contrasting the abbreviated form of this November entry with the grander one two years earlier when Cheverus arrived, their new bishop was more aware of other contrasts. The cathedral in New Orleans had never really been his, least of all had he been welcomed to it on his arrival in 1812 as apostolic administrator. In 1817 when he returned from Europe as bishop it had not even been safe to return to the city, to say nothing of the cathedral. Even now in the city of St. Louis the jerrybuilt red brick "cathedral," which the trustees had made of his dream of another St. Mary's of Baltimore, was a sadly curtailed facsimile still unpaid for, and rain and cold weather had so weakened the walls (which had never been meant for an exterior frame) that Rosati had taken to referring to it as "a sort of hay barn" of an "unfinished rustic appearance."[21]

The Cathedral of the Assumption, whose keys Du-Bourg now held in his hand, had been the dream of Jean-Baptist-Michel de Colbert, the Bishop of Montauban from 1674 to 1687. Raising money to implement this dream was authorized by the Council of State on August 7, 1685; but it was not until the reign of his successor, Henry de Nesmond, that the foundation stone was laid on April 10, 1692. The building of the church had taken forty-seven years before services were actually held there.[22] Although interior adornments were still being added, as in the case of the "Vow of Louis XIII," a royal ordinance of September 16, 1738, had finally permitted the chanting of the Office in the choir, and the following April sacred relics had been acquired for the main altar. At last, on November 1, 1739, the cathedral was first taken possession of in ceremonies just repeated by DuBourg that morning eighty-seven years later.

In the days before the Revolution, the Cathedral of the Assumption was one of the most magnificent churches of its province. Built in the form of a Greek cross, seventeen great interior arcades surmounted by large windows gave entrance to the nave which was bordered by the smaller chapels within each arcade. The great altar which stood between the nave and choir was directly under the dome where the four branches of the cross converged. Originally there had been very beautiful iron grillwork enclosing this area, but the desecrations of the Revolution had removed it and it was never restored.

The noble façade presented to the Place d'Armes was still virtually intact with its twin campaniles topped successively by clocks, then gilded domes, and finally by crosses, its great central door between two lesser ones; these in turn were flanked by niches for the statues, which no longer exist today. Above the central door stood the Four Evangels, ten feet high, which had been executed by the celebrated sculptor Marc Arcis of Toulouse.[23] The symmetry of that facade in 1826 delighted the taste of the man who had once in concert with Godefroy and Latrobe achieved that architectural gem which is St. Mary's Chapel in Baltimore. He could cease regretting the church in New Orleans, whose clock-and-bell tower Latrobe had not lived to complete, whose interior walls were only now being decorated by the Italian painter chosen for the task.[24] At last DuBourg had a cathedral worthy of the name, and one in which he could banish forever the dread of assassination.[25]

The city DuBourg had scarcely glimpsed in the darkness of Saturday night's arrival and the press of Sunday's welcoming formalities was one of proud lineage. Situated on the major route from Toulouse to Cahors, it graced the hill on the right bank of the Tarn River where it is joined by the Tescou. "Peopled by the Celts, cleared for habitation by the Greeks, civilized by the Romans, and conquered by the Goths," it had existed as *Mons Aureolus* or *Mont Doré* before modern French history even began.[26] The "new city" was born on October 6, 1144, when Alphonse, le comte de Toulouse and his son Raymond de Saint-Gilles, ceded land they called Montauban for the purpose of founding a city in return for such onerous feudal obligations as shoeing the count's horses on his passages through the city. Alphonse built three castles to defend his creation, infuriating in the process some monks on whose properties he had encroached. Thus, from its very birth Montauban seemed destined for a long history of religious struggle.[27]

In more recent times, together with Toulouse and Albi, the city was more apt to be thought of as one of the "three roses," because of the lovely color of the brick which characterized the finest architecture of those municipalities. In fact it resembled a miniature French Budapest because of the topographical contrasts connected by the bridge across the Tarn. There was the upper city, with the magnificent Old Regime episcopal palace whose occupants had been princes in every sense of the word—a palace that today houses the Ingres Museum. Rising above that was the single rosy spire of Saint-Jacques, where in earlier days the cathedral chapter had sung the Office of the day. Up the Rue des Bains and Rue Lacaze one emerged into the Place d'Armes and confronted the Cathedral of the Assumption whose stone walls and pillars were so noticeable in a city almost entirely built of brick. Across the bridge on the left bank of the river, the streets leveled out and disappeared among the houses which made Saint-Orens Parish in Villebourbon.

The bridge itself, the Great Porte du Pont, was one of Montauban's most splendid monuments. Dating from the early fourteenth century, it was built to withstand both the ravages of the river and the projectiles of the enemy in a day when the city had been an outpost of royal power. In 1701 the towers guarding the entrance to the bridge had been converted into an enormous *porte,* or arch of triumph, in memory of the Peace of Ryswick, and until the Revolution it had always been guarded by the king's men. At the middle of the bridge, there was on one side a chapel dedicated to Sainte-Catherine; on the other, a cage for enclosing blasphemers or plunging erring women into the water far below. Both the arch of triumph and the chapel were still very much in evidence as DuBourg surveyed the more visible portions of his ecclesiastical domain in 1826.[28]

The Department of Tarn-et-Garonne, of which Montauban was the *chef-lieu,* numbered in 1826 some 238,000 people, with the city itself accounting for one tenth.[29] Although the two sub-prefects resided at Castel-Sarrasin and Moissac, the prefect, his secretary-general, and councilors had their headquarters in Montauban as did the garrison under the duc de la Force. The French system of departments centralized all ultimate political authority in Paris under the monarchy; the union of church and state centralized all ecclesiastical regulation there as well. Being the Bishop of Montauban would be a radical change for the former Bishop of Louisiana, whose experience in a missionary country, in a region only politically organized into states during his own episcopacy, and in a nation committed to a republican form of government and a separation of church and state, had not prepared him for the restraints he would now have to accept. Gone were the days when he wrote freely to Rome advising Propaganda on vacant sees, divisions of dioceses, or appointments of coadjutors. Socially, too, he would find—as Cheverus had before him—that the upper classes of French society were firmly rooted in traditions, making life in Montauban quite different from that of Boston, St. Louis, or New Orleans. Cheverus had complained mildly, "I am bound by a certain etiquette and no longer enjoy the sweet and unceremonious freedom which was so pleasing."[30] There would be times when the less tractable, more impatient DuBourg would find the red tape and protocol hard to bear. In spite of all the hardships of the Mississippi Valley, jurisdiction there had been an exhilarating freedom, which had suited his nature.

In their limited time together in Paris, Cheverus had been able to suggest to his successor only the dim outlines of the Montauban situation. It was now DuBourg's turn to discover for himself how his next years were to be spent. Happily the first days, at least, were made easier by the presence of Antoine Carles, who stayed on in Montauban through mid-December.[31] A dozen years older than the new bishop, Carles was a humble, sweet-tempered man who not only knew Montauban but had had many years in the American mission field as well. Like DuBourg he had been influenced by John Carroll, the founder of the American hierarchy, under whom they both had served.

Carles spent his first years in the Diocese of Baltimore as a member of the Asylum Colony of Pennsylvania. In December 1803 he had gone to Savannah, Georgia, where there were French Catholics from Saint-Domingue. Aside from a two-year interim in France from 1805 to 1807, he had remained in the stormy Georgia mission for some fifteen years. After his permanent return to France he had joined Cheverus at Montauban. Although Carles had known best the eastern coastal region of the United States while Du-

Bourg had divided his American years between Baltimore and the Mississippi Valley, they had much in common, and having Carles in Montauban during those first weeks eased the transition for DuBourg.[32]

A second cause for satisfaction during those first days was the news from Paris that on December 2 Louis Sibourd had been granted the canonicat left vacant by Carles's transfer to Bordeaux.[33] After all the years he and Sibourd had supported each other's labors in New York and New Orleans, there was no priest with whom DuBourg felt more at home than his former vicar general. To have him as a canon in the Montauban cathedral, and that so promptly, was ample cause for elation. Advent was more than ever a season of promise and joy in 1826. With every confidence in the future, the bishop took quill in hand to pen his first *Circulaire* as Louis-Guillaume de Montauban.

Words were his delight, and when he chose to use them to his own advantage they did his bidding. His "Circular to the Gentlemen of the Clergy of the Diocese of Montauban" dated December 8, 1826, shows something of his skill. Even the date was propitious, the Feast of the Immaculate Conception. What better time to address his confreres than on a feast day of the Lady to whom their diocese and cathedral were dedicated?[34] He began ingratiatingly, "In bequeathing to me his tender affection for you, my illustrious friend, your last Bishop, also bequeathed to me that lively solicitude which was the mark of every moment of his episcopate. One of the aims which never ceased to occupy his thoughts during his short stay among you was to reestablish in this Diocese uniformity of Rites and religious practices." He was sure everyone of the clergy desired uniformity of liturgy, the canonical Office, sacred rites, ceremonies, elementary instruction, and those fees for functions of the ministry which involved offerings. Already, he said, many of his coworkers had spoken to him on the subject in such a way as to persuade him that they spoke for all. "It is pleasant for me, in fulfilling a sacred duty, to have confidence that I am only following the wishes of those to whom I am speaking."

He knew they would be pleased to learn at the outset that the measures to be taken did not *have* to be binding until the end of the coming year—a year he hoped would be one of graces and good fortune for all of them. Already, under Cheverus's direction, the Breviary had come from the press; and the Missal and Catechism were presently being printed. He would himself attend speedily to the remaining formularies necessary. He hoped the first three would be universally adopted as soon as possible; but he was ordaining or decreeing that they must be in use by the end of 1827 by all priests of the diocese. In this way, he trusted, there would disappear those anomalies which so strongly resembled disorders emanating from arbitrariness; and there would reappear through unity of practices those bonds of charity which unite all hearts in Jesus Christ.[35]

DuBourg had, of course, as was his wont, quite ignored the advice given by Carroll so long ago—that in dealing with an unknown people in a new place one should proceed with "one bushel of zeal to nine bushels of prudence." Time would tell whether in his rush to take command he had read his clergy aright.

As December 23 approached DuBourg prepared for the conferring of Holy Orders in his new diocese. The Saturday of the December Ember Days, or *Quatre-Temps*, in the Church's liturgy was traditionally a most solemn one, being the day in Rome when priests were ordained in the great basilica of St. Peter. In days gone by it had been the only time of ordinations.[36] Now, in 1826, it marked for DuBourg the first time he would pontificate in his cathedral church in ceremonies that for a bishop were most poignant, presenting as they did the image of John the Baptist, the precursor who prepares souls for the coming of the Messiah, the recollection of his own ordination so many years ago with its high hopes and fervent resolves, and the piercing knowledge of the trials ahead for the earnest young candidates so piously affirming their desire to be tonsured, or ordained as doorkeepers, readers, exorcists, acolytes, subdeacons, deacons, or priests. The *Journal de Tarn-et-Garonne* was pleased to announce that the number of ordinations that December Saturday was large and that "the imposing ceremony attracted a large concourse of the faithful."[37]

And then it was Christmas Eve. How often in the past this Feast of the Nativity had been celebrated in the midst of uncertainty about the future! There was that first Mass in the New World after his arrival from Spain with no knowledge of the English language spoken all around him; the Christmas Day in Georgetown in 1798 when his resignation as president took effect; that harsh time in 1817 when, struggling to arrive in St. Louis in time for Christmas, he and Flaget were marooned by ice at the mouth of the Ohio River and were prevented from offering any Masses at all, having to be content with three meditations instead. And how could he forget the Christmases in New Orleans—that one in 1814 when it seemed the British were certain to capture the city; the joyous one in 1820 when Sibourd and Martial had been his deacons of honor at the throne, and a temporarily reconciled Sedella celebrated the midnight Mass; and then the one only a year ago when, having written to Rome of his wish to resign, he was in such acute turmoil over the future of his diocese, his family, his flock, and the wisdom of his decision.

Christmas was likely to be a time of memories, yet so rarely was memory consoling. One did better to face the future. Here in this city, in this splended cathedral, with the ineffable repose of Ingres' Virgin a reminder of the meaning of the feast, the Bishop of Montauban could survey the crowded nave, the large numbers of the faithful receiving Communion, and be at peace. He had no intention of saying his *"Nunc dimittis"* just yet; but it was agreeable to believe that his Christmases hereafter were all to be spent like this in a diocese where "the cathedral, the other churches, and the Protestant temple could scarcely contain the crowds which attended in moods perfectly attuned to the ceremonies of the feast."[38] He wondered how his old friend John Dubois, now Bishop of New York,[39] was facing a new year in surroundings as strangely remote from Mount St. Mary's in Emmitsburg as DuBourg's were in France. At their ages it was an odd time to be making new beginnings.

CHAPTER XXXVI

TAKING COMMAND

When Philip Borgna, C. M. told Propaganda in October 1826 that everyone who knew DuBourg rejoiced at his
resignation from New Orleans, that it was about time his
sufferings should cease, that it was simple justice that toward the end of his life he might enjoy a little peace and
rest,[1] Borgna was only echoing what Billaud, the *Garde des
Archives* of the French Embassy in Rome, had expressed
the month before when he wrote to Bordeaux, "It must be
said it is high time that venerable pastor should have a rest
from the rigorous labor he has had for so long."[2] Neither of
these younger admirers knew the heart of their hero very
well. DuBourg may have welcomed peace as the new year
began, but rest was farthest from his mind. So long as his
erratic health would support him he was determined to
pursue as indefatigably as before the objectives of the good
shepherd whose sheep must be fed, watered, and defended
from the ravening wolves of impiety and vice.

Before the first week of the new year ended, he had
already announced to his clergy a reorganization of the
diocese, which very carefully defined a hierarchy of responsibilities and the lines of communication between the lowest
assistant priest and the Bishop of Montauban. His *Circulaire* of January 5, 1827, explained at the outset that his plan

for *doyens ruraux,* or rural deans, was nothing novel, having existed for some centuries before being suppressed by the French Revolution. In reestablishing what in some places were formerly called *vicaires forains,* or traveling vicars, he was merely following the example of the majority of his colleagues in the episcopate.

For greater regularity of administration the diocese was being divided into three archdiaconates corresponding to the three political districts of the Department of Tarn-et-Garonne: Montauban, Moissac, and Castel-Sarrasin. Each of these three divisions would have its own vicar general to whom rural deans, parish pastors, and assistants would all address themselves on any administrative matters. The rural deans, who were directly below the vicar general in the chain of command, varied in number according to the importance of the district; Montauban had seven, while Moissac and Castel-Sarrasin had three and four respectively. The functions of the rural deans—which were numerous—were intended to relieve both the bishop and his vicars general of the minutiae of running efficiently and with some degree of uniformity a diocese as extensive and diverse as this suffragan see of Toulouse. The deans were to keep informed of the conditions within the cantons assigned to them, even to the point of visiting them on occasion. It was the dean's responsibility to see that divine services were observed with decency, that the word of God was regularly preached, that altars, linens, ornaments and sacred vessels were properly cared for, and most particularly that the Blessed Sacrament, holy oils, and baptismal waters be accorded the respect due to these sources of grace. Deans were further to insure that church records were kept precisely. Finally, they were to report to their archdeacons or vicars general the situation regarding schools, hospitals, pious establishments, sodalities, and other organizations within their areas. The archdeacons, of course, reported all this information to the bishop himself.

DuBourg explained that he thought of the rural deans as the "eyes of the bishop" and the guarantee of the discipline and honor of the priesthood. They were to be sharers in episcopal authority, and as need arose he would grant them other of his faculties which could properly be shared without detriment to the bishop's prime authority. The system would not, he assured them, prejudice their natural right to seek recourse to the bishop directly, and he would always be happy to respond to the confidences of his worthy brothers. Certainly, in his desire for regularity and uniformity, he would not refuse to make exceptions. Already he had learned that in some of the more distant country parishes the poor would find the imposition of the new catechism a hardship. "I will always be ready to receive such observations," he said, "and do what is right according to the localities."[3] He had thought of everything—even down to naming all fourteen of the new rural deans! Less than a week later, in spite of the rigors of the January weather, he began his visitations of the diocese to confer the sacrament of confirmation at Moissac, Caussade and Finham.[4]

The diocese which DuBourg was now beginning to survey had some 353 priests, and 100 students of philosophy and theology in the *grand séminaire* and another 105 doing their preparatory studies. As in all the dioceses of France, there were many religious institutions. Sisters of Charity ran four hospitals; Sisters of Nevers administered three others; Ursulines and Sisters of Mercy between them five academies and schools for the poor; the Christian Brothers had a school educating four hundred boys, and the Carmelites had two monasteries.[5] At first glance it would seem to have been an ideal situation presenting few problems to a prelate of a dozen years' experience. Yet the more DuBourg learned of his spiritual domain the more he perceived its complexities.

The Diocese of Montauban had not had a typical history in recent decades. The Revolution of 1789 had barely begun when the diocese was suppressed and the city of Montauban, owing to the division of France into eighty-three *départements,* in spite of its commercial importance became simply the *chef-lieu* of a district of Lot. The diocese as an entity remained suppressed for eighteen years, partitioned among the bishops of Toulouse, Cahors, and Agen.[6]

Then, only a few months before he was forced to flee from Rome, Pius VII had reerected the Diocese of Montauban on February 17, 1808.

When Napoleon and his Empress Josephine visited Montauban in July that year, the Catholics of the city received the imperial couple with double joy, believing the emperor was responsible for resurrecting their see city. Certainly his official approval was given by his decree of November 21 creating the Department of Tarn-et-Garonne and the Diocese of Montauban to take effect simultaneously on January 1, 1809. As re-created, Montauban comprised 23 cantons, 270 parishes, and 68 *succursales,* or auxiliary chapels, all under the Cathedral of Our Lady of the Assumption. But no bishop was named and the see remained vacant for the rest of the First Empire. It was not until the restoration of the Bourbon dynasty after the fall of Napoleon that any real hope for a bishop revived in Montauban. In the meantime the see was administered by a vicar general, the same Jean-Armand Chaudru de Trélissac whom Cheverus had so recently taken with him to Bordeaux.

It was fascinating to think the pope had passed through this very city on his way back to Rome only the year before making DuBourg a bishop. Freed from the prison of Fontainebleau on January 23, 1814, Pius VII had taken the road home by way of the cities of the Midi. True, in the dreadful weather of midwinter, with the papal carriage stopping on the outskirts only long enough to change horses, the clergy and crowds turning out to greet the Holy Father had only time enough to erupt in transports of joy, to admire his "heavenly appearance," to receive the pontifical benedictions amid shouts of "Long live the Pope," and marveling asides, "See, how he resembles Jesus Christ!"

When some days later the cardinals, who had been the pontiff's companions during the months of duress at Fontainebleau, took the same route home, they found their most ardent welcome in Montauban. Their Eminences Somaglia, Pacca, and Brancadero had arrived on a Saturday night and on Sunday at the Church of Saint-Jacques were given all the honors due their dignity amid the brilliance of lights and adornments reserved for the most solemn feast days in France. From that moment the royalist sympathies, which the Revolution had suppressed in the city, reawakened with noisy enthusiasm.[7]

For all that, the Diocese of Montauban had remained fatherless another ten years. A new concordat arranged in 1817 between Pius VII and the restored Bourbon monarch Louis XVIII confirmed all the dioceses created by Napoleon's Concordat of 1801, and a specific papal bull reerected Montauban as a suffragan see of Toulouse under the title: *Montis-Albani sub Invocatione Mariae Virginis.* The king, certainly, had tried to give the diocese a bishop immediately. But the scarcity of available candidates and a delay in carrying out the Concordat of 1817 until 1822 circumvented him. Even the nomination of Cheverus on January 13, 1823, had encountered technicalities which kept the see vacant another year and a half, and it was July 28, 1824, before the first bishop in thirty-four years took up residence in the city on the Tarn.[8]

The very brief reign of Cheverus had worked wonders in "raising the church from ruins," as he had expressed it. He had reconstituted the cathedral chapter which was now composed of the rector of the cathedral, two vicars general, and nine canons; he had reestablished a major seminary; he had maintained gently courteous relations with the city's Protestants. Although the elegant pre-Revolutionary episcopal palace was never restored to a Bishop of Montauban, an excellent house was acquired the year before DuBourg's arrival and was now a suitable residence for a bishop. Liturgical dignities were revived, regular episcopal visitations resumed, Holy Orders conferred—in short, all the regularity and discipline that could be accomplished within a brief period of two years was a legacy DuBourg could only marvel at and enjoy.[9] It was, nevertheless, only a beginning as DuBourg's first letter to the clergy so clearly indicated.

Cheverus had not had time to carry out the work of restoring uniformity of practices throughout the diocese, or, more importantly from DuBourg's view, of clearly centralizing authority in the hands of the bishop. In that first circular

DuBourg had diplomatically used the phrase "anomalies which resemble so strongly the disorders emanating from arbitrariness," but he was in fact serving notice; his experience in another see left vacant for many years had only too painfully convinced him that bishops should play the role of bishops from the very start. He himself would set a good example by demonstrating his own spirit of cooperativeness with authority both civil and ecclesiastical. With that in mind, he barely paused in Montauban on his return from Finham before setting out again on Tuesday, January 23, for Toulouse.

The metropolitan See of Toulouse in 1827 was presided over by Anne-Antoine-Jules Cardinal de Clermont-Tonnerre, the *doyen,* or dean, of the French hierarchy, being then seventy-eight years old, and conscious of his years. He came from an illustrious family of Dauphine, which had furnished France with many a military leader and prelate in the past. At the moment, the Marquis of Clermont-Tonnerre was Minister of War in the king's cabinet. The Cardinal Archbishop of Toulouse had been Bishop of Chalons for a decade before the Civil Constitution of the Clergy compelled so many priests and bishops to emigrate from France. Exiled in Germany for his loyalty to the Bourbon dynasty and to the papacy, he was now in his sunset years enjoying the rewards for that devotion. With the Restoration in 1814 he was made Peer of France, then Archbishop of Toulouse, and finally in 1822 a cardinal. He was, to many, "the French representative of the spirit of ultramontaine intransigence," but his correspondence shows him to have been as devoted to the French monarchy and Church as any prelate.[10]

Clermont-Tonnerre had been on the best of terms with DuBourg's predecessor. Shortly after Cheverus's arrival, the old prelate had come to Montauban to welcome his new suffragan and invite him to preach at the dedication of some new Stations of the Cross erected by the Recollect fathers in Toulouse. Clermont-Tonnerre had been quite moved by the meditations Cheverus gave at each of the fourteen stations, and at the conclusion asked his suffragan to give them all his blessing. When Cheverus protested, "it is not my place to bless your people in your Eminence's presence," the cardinal's finesse was equal to his suffragan's humility. He gave the kneeling Cheverus a blessing, which he insisted must be passed on to the others. It had all been very graceful and gracious. It became the cardinal's custom to stop for a visit in Montauban on his trips to and from Normandy.[11] DuBourg hoped, as he started out that January with Vicar General Pouget, to have the same cordial relations with his metropolitan.

As it turned out, these hopes were not dashed. DuBourg had always enjoyed exchanging *bons mots* and more solid ideas with men of breeding, first-rate education, and deeply ingrained piety. Not since his days in Baltimore and his exchanges with Archbishop Carroll had a prospect of such pleasure stretched ahead. Meanwhile, DuBourg and Pouget enjoyed their stay in other ways as well. They made a pilgrimage to the Basilica of Saint-Sernin, where people could not help noticing how long the Bishop of Montauban knelt in prayer before the relics of the Toulousain Saint Exupère. And, of course, DuBourg was elated to find that his views on the reparations and decorations of the church were deemed very judicious and were even to be put to use.

But the most emotional moment came when the headmistress of the royal boarding school for girls invited him to visit her institution. Among her charges was a young girl only recently arrived from New Orleans, the pupil chosen to give the students' welcome to the visiting dignitary. When her eyes were lifted to DuBourg's face and she recognized her former bishop, she was so overcome with emotion she could scarcely speak through her tears. DuBourg, for his part, was likewise deeply moved. It is one thing to accept with the reason, the intellect, the deprivation of people and places one has loved. "Time heals all wounds." But to come suddenly without warning upon the face, the intonation of voice—or even the name—of some connection with that past can fleetingly revive old heartaches and the sense of loss. His concern was more for the child and her homesickness. He called her to his side and chatted with her about her own family and those he himself had left behind in New Orleans—his brother Pierre-François, his nieces, and their mutual friends.[12] For a brief moment the chill of the Toulouse *pension* was dissipated in the languorous warmth of Louisiana-remembered, and French accents of the Midi were drowned out in the cadences of Creole voices an ocean's journey away. He recalled that on his return to Montauban he would be preaching in an Ursuline chapel once more. He and Pouget arrived back in time Saturday to make their preparations for Sunday's liturgies, if not rested, at least refreshed.

The Monday after the return from Toulouse was the feast day of Saint Francis de Sales, and the bishop was scheduled to preach at the parish Church of Saint-Joseph. Taking as text for his panegyric, "Blessed are the meek, for they shall inherit the earth," DuBourg was as effective as if he had been resting for days. His audience, which was as select as it was numerous—including the personnel of the Royal College—was visibly impressed by the authority and beauty of the expressions that were part of the secret of his art and persuasiveness as a homilist. They found particularly appropriate his peroration, in which he exclaimed, "And we, too, have brothers who have strayed. O Saint Francis, remove this wall which separates us so that they may come into our embraces!"[13]

Everyone understood the allusion to the Calvinists whose forebears had penetrated Montauban in the mid-sixteenth century, and founded the only existing Protestant seminary in the whole of France, an institution which, since an imperial decree of September 17, 1808, had been educating a Protestant clergy. Cheverus, who had remained on friendly terms with its directors, found its principles rather like those of the Andover theological seminary he had known near Boston.[14] Montauban's 11,000 Calvinists contrasted sharply with the 60,000 Saint Francis was reputed to have brought back in seventeenth-century Chablais and Geneva; one did not expect nineteenth-century straying brethren to be led so docilely back to the fold, and Catholic shepherds were prudent to encourage living in brotherly love in the meantime.

Bishops did well, in addition, to be sure their own seminarians were being properly trained. Amid his other activities that first January in Montauban, DuBourg presided at the session of his *sabbatines,* those first-year philosophy students who at the end of their courses were defending their modest theses. He wanted to judge for himself the excellence to be found in the *grand séminaire* of his diocese. As February began he visited the minor seminary on the feast of the Purification, and addressed the students on the mysteries of that solemnity. While he was there he organized a *Congrégation,* or sodality, with a view to recruiting for the major seminary the boys whose virtues and talents stood out.[15] Nagot had always believed that it was in the minor seminaries that permanent vocations were nurtured.

Preparatory ecclesiastical education in Restoration Montauban owed its origins to the era during which the see had been partitioned among Toulouse, Cahors, and Agen. The impulse came from two places, the cities of Montauban and Moissac. The abundance of vocations in the calm following Napoleon's Concordat of 1801 led Trélissac, who was then administering the parishes of the former diocese, to believe Montauban might supply some of the preparatory training expected from minor seminaries. Supported by the pastors of Saint-Jacques and Saint-Joseph, he had opened on April 20, 1806, a boarding school which was one of the nuclei of the future *petit séminaire,* and indirectly the germ of the *grand séminaire.* This experiment began in a most modest way, with one priest serving as both rector and *économe,* and another as sole professor! Nevertheless, on opening day ten students presented themselves, and three days later that number had doubled.[16]

After the restoration of the Diocese of Montauban in 1808–9, Trélissac entrusted the Lazarists, or priests of the Congregation of the Mission, with conducting the boarding school which to all intents and purposes *was* a preparatory seminary. Headmaster Jacques Perboyre, C. M., and his chief associate, Antoine Gratacap, bought a former Carmelite convent in the parish of Saint-Etienne where in 1811 they were authorized to open a chapel for their students. When Louis XVIII was restored to the throne he officially recognized the school as a seminary and, beginning in 1818, Holy Orders were once again conferred in the Diocese of Montauban.[17]

A second nucleus of preparatory seminary education emerged in Moissac as the result of the extraordinary generosity of a family named Gouges, whose head was a prosperous merchant of that city. A son who was the pastor of Saint-Jacques of Moissac and his widowed sister, who became the foundress of the Sisters of Mercy, started a second school for boys on the site of the celebrated Abbey of Moissac. Confided first to the care of a distinguished and wealthy layman, it was later run by priests appointed by the bishop. Madame Genyer, or as she was better known later, Mother Mary of Jesus, was determined to get the school recognized as an ecclesiastical seminary and she succeeded on April 2, 1823, the same year Cheverus returned to France to head the diocese.[18]

Preparatory education was thus well established by the time the Diocese of Montauban received a resident bishop. But the final training for the priesthood was quite another matter, and one which Cheverus could only begin to resolve. He had devoted his very first pastoral to the subject, saying he did not doubt that the government would aid the diocese in securing a site and buildings for a major seminary; but the responsibility of recruiting students and supporting them was a task all must share. "This labor alone can perpetuate religion among us," he urged. Within a few months donations, pledges, and legacies began coming in. The owner of a former Capuchin monastery, Pierre Garrison, offered his property for sale as a seminary site, and after all the red tape was removed in August 1825, Cheverus fixed the opening of the *grand séminaire* for All Saints' Day.

Cheverus had wanted, as his first choice, to have members of the Society of Saint-Sulpice as directors of the seminary, but he was unable to secure them. He then turned to the Lazarists, who were already in Montauban.[19] He was more successful in getting *bourses* (scholarships) for his seminarians. By the time he was transferred to Bordeaux he had secured from the king five additional scholarships, and the report on *bourses* issued in May of the year of Du-Bourg's arrival showed that of 675 scholarships in France, Montauban had 14—as many as any other diocese, and two more than Paris![20]

The groundwork, then, had all been laid before Du-Bourg's coming. Vocations and students were numerous by American standards he had known. But from his view—that of an unchastened dreamer of dreams and schemer of schemes—things could not go on as they were. When on June 12, 1827, the will of Madame Genyer bequeathed to the Bishop of Montauban land for a seminary, land situated in Piac in the commune of Saint-Paul d'Espis, his thoughts whirled with excitement. Under French Church-State routines, before he could include the legacy in his plans he must wait for a royal ordinance authorizing him to accept the legacy, but weeks before that formality was forthcoming, he had already composed an impassioned letter to his clergy on the subject of the seminaries.[21] He had always been an educator at heart, and in his later years seminaries were his constant, his dearest preoccupation. His quill flew over the pages he was preparing for Philippe Crosilhes, Printer to His Excellency the Bishop of Montauban.

He depicted in harrowing phrases the dire conditions existing both from the view of the buildings then in use, and the lack of adequate financial support. True, Montauban and Moissac had both been witnesses to the "prodigies of devotion and generosity" of a worthy son of Saint Vincent de Paul and a venerable widow deserving of being ranked among the great female saints—he was referring, of course, to Jacques Perboyre in Montauban and Madame Genyer in Moissac—but unless the work of recruiting and educating a diocesan clergy was aided by the charity of *everyone,* he feared for the future.

He was now inviting every priest to impose voluntarily on himself an annual sum of twenty francs, which would be reimbursed to his parish in the form of half-scholarships and quarter-scholarships to be used for students presented by the parish with fair assurances of priestly vocations. He was asking them to invest in the future of their own profession, to provide, as it were, a patrimony for their spiritual sons.

In the buoyancy of mood produced by his satisfaction with what he sensed was one of his better pastorals, and by the soaring hopes he now entertained for the future of his *pépinières,* he celebrated the next day at the cathedral with more than customary panache the feast day of the king; and after the *Te Deum* was concluded he had the pleasure of baptizing with considerable éclat a new bell for his cathedral in the presence of its godparents, M. le comte de Vandeuvre, the Prefect of Tarn-et-Garonne, and Mme. la Duchesse de Polignac. Perhaps he found it appropriate that, on the first anniversary of his arrival in Montauban, King Charles chose to authorize the Bishop of Montauban's acceptance of Mme Genyer's legacy of land for a more spacious seminary in the future.

Meanwhile, his passion for expansion could be vented in another direction. On his return from his visitations of the parishes for confirmations in 1827, he had the joy of blessing and inaugurating a chapel in the new home of Notre Dame du Refuge. This worthy institution had been founded by a priest very concerned about the rehabilitation of women who had fallen into sin and whom society tended to reject.[22] The House of Refuge was run by women whose only bond of union in the beginning was that of love for their less fortunate sisters. Their small house had existed for months in a suburb of Villebourbon virtually unnoticed on the left bank of the Tarn. But the numbers of applicants for admission arriving almost daily led DuBourg to take action. He liked nothing better than projects demanding more space and new buildings. Through the benefactions of several families headed by Baron Jacques-Antoine Delbreil of Scorbiac, he soon found sufficient means to proceed. He was, of course, delighted to preside at the opening of the enlarged facilities and to address to the generous patronesses of the House of Refuge a homily which warmed all hearts including his own. Providence seemed to favor the community as time went by. In 1832 expansion again was necessary, this time moving the establishment to a much more extensive site on the upper side of the river in the suburb of Sapiac where, in 1836, its direction was turned over to the Daughters of Our Lady of Charity who were already famous for their work in the House of Refuge in Toulouse. The women who had been the pioneers in the Montauban house then joined the religious order from Toulouse under whose aegis the work continued to expand.[23]

It seemed the year had scarcely started when Lent began. Disregarding his fatigue and the erosion of his health since his return to France, DuBourg felt compelled to outdo himself this penitential season, taking on the preaching at alternate services at Saint-Jacques and the cathedral. At the cathedral on Mardi Gras he gave a sermon on sin; at Saint-Jacques on the First Sunday in Lent he treated temptation. When on the Second Sunday in Lent he took the theme of the Transfiguration as an introduction to the place of prayer in their lives, his listeners remembered it as "the most beautiful sermon he ever preached at Montauban," one which held them enthralled for a whole hour. In addition to the Sundays, twice a week he drew crowds to the foot of the pulpit to hear his meditations on the Mass of the day. Years ago he had said to John Carroll, about another Lenten season of zealous preaching, "I will see better at Easter what dependence is to be placed on these early demonstrations."[24] Certainly if Paschal Communions were a reliable gauge, his efforts this Lent had been well worth the strain he had placed upon his diminishing forces.[25]

A man plunges energetically into new responsibilities for a variety of reasons. His own personality and character may impel him to rush forward to meet all challenges with zestful impetuosity. The ethics of his profession may have instilled the habit of making a clean break when moving from assignment to assignment. He may have imbibed in his youth the biblical injunction: "No man, having put his hand to the plough, and looking back, is fit for the Kingdom of God." In DuBourg's case something of all these motives was involved in his taking up the reins in Montauban, in immersing himself so swiftly in the ebb and flow of life in the Department of Tarn-et-Garonne. Yet, no man of any depth, of any genuine concern for those whom he has served, of any capacity for loving his neighbor with Christ-like love, can divorce himself completely from his past. Certainly this was true of Louis-Guillaume de Montauban. When he told Frayssinous the previous summer, "I am no longer the pastor in name; but I will be to the end the father and purveyor of Louisiana," he was stating a simple truth. Part of his indignation at *l'Ami* that same summer had been at what he took to be an implication that he was placing his own welfare above that of his flock. In returning to Europe he had had every intention of continuing to serve the interests of that mission so long as it remained within his power.

The letter he had written to Rosati, his former coadjutor, from Paris in September 1826 was full of concern for things still undone at the time of his leaving Louisiana. Although he was now appointed to Montauban, he told Rosati, "My heart will remain with my former flock." He assured his successor that he would do his utmost to help him in founding a seminary for Louisiana. He had already secured four more ladies of the Sacred Heart for Madame Duchesne's work, and they would soon be on their way to the Mississippi Valley. He urged Rosati to write often to the Society for the Propagation of the Faith in Lyon, since letters published in their *Annales* were so effective in securing assistance for the American missions. DuBourg himself, together with his brother Louis and sister Victoire, had made use of this kind of publicity ever since the Society began its publications, and Louisiana had benefited enormously from the French generosity thus aroused. DuBourg wished Father Van Quickenborne would do the same thing for the Jesuit interests in Missouri and among the Indians.[26]

Rosati, on his part, had every intention of keeping DuBourg informed of developments in the United States. He was an inveterate letter writer who crammed his pages with details. Although he had been almost the last to learn of DuBourg's resignation, he was not a man to hold a grudge. He *had* been shocked, he said plainly, at the unexpected news of DuBourg's resignation and appointment in France; but he accepted DuBourg's explanation that what might have appeared as dissimulation was in reality discretion. "I could not do otherwise," DuBourg said. Rosati knew the New Orleans situation well enough to imagine the furor if DuBourg's resignation had been rejected in Rome and he had been compelled to return to a city where his enemies were celebrating his defeat.

Rosati was also moved by his former superior's expression of attachment to his Louisiana diocese and to its new bishop. He knew DuBourg could and would be useful to them. Especially he wished DuBourg would use his influence with Rome to permit Rosati to stay at St. Louis instead of New Orleans. The Diocese of Louisiana was now divided; neither Rosati nor DuBourg could alter that.[27] Rosati for the time being was to administer both; but he preferred to do it as Bishop of St. Louis. He had the best of reasons for his choice, and asserted positively that he would never consent to accept New Orleans.[28]

DuBourg quite agreed with Rosati and did not hesitate to express his views to the Cardinal Prefect of Propaganda. "In view of my sentiments toward a Church which was and shall ever be the first object of my solicitude," he began, "Bishop Rosati, my successor in Louisiana, begs me insistently to write to your Eminence to support the petition he recently directed to the Sacred Congregation of Propaganda." While not agreeing at all with Rosati's claim that his talents were inadequate to the demands of New Orleans, he was in perfect accord with his other arguments. It was quite true that the climate of New Orleans did not suit everyone's constitution; Rosati's in particular could not endure the scorching heat which prevailed there half the year. In proposing Leo De Neckere, C. M., as his coadjutor, Rosati was suggesting for New Orleans a man admirably suited to Lower Louisiana. *His* health had been undermined by the cold, dry climate of Upper Louisiana. In fact, he was then on sick leave with his family in Belgium. De Neckere's constitution would benefit from the damp heat of New Orleans.

Both men were members of the Congregation of the Mission, both were priests of exceptional knowledge and virtue; both were universally respected by their fellow priests and by the people. The one drawback to De Neckere was his youth; he was not yet twenty-seven years old. But, as DuBourg saw it, "His gravity and wisdom are that of a man of forty." For the time being—"to reconcile all interests"—the Bishop of Montauban recommended leaving Rosati as administrator of both dioceses, but with his headquarters in St. Louis, and giving him an assistant for the Dioscese of New Orleans. "It is not so much eloquence as solid knowledge, profound wisdom, and virtue above suspicion which are demanded. The first of these qualities," he said wryly, thinking of his own case, "would perhaps only invite censure; the others have already won for him the affection and respect of all."[29] In his letter to Rosati written the Sunday after Easter, DuBourg had been more frank on the subject of De Neckere:

> You must have a coadjutor, and Mr. de N. would certainly be the man, if . . . if . . . But that indecision of character, that imaginary sickness, that depression, that hypochondria, all that makes me fear. And then this good young man, besides so full of precious and rare qualities, has so little knowledge of men, of the world. However, I know that he redeems all these by so many virtues, so much eloquence, so much knowledge, that I believe if he is named he could perhaps decide to accept, that the grace of ordination will make him capable of all, and that the firmness of your hand will have its effect.[30]

He was counting on Rosati to guide De Neckere.

Within the same month Rome replied to DuBourg that

Rosati's request to be left in St. Louis was granted and that he was free to name De Neckere as his vicar general in New Orleans—an outcome that gave satisfaction on both sides of the Atlantic.[31] Once Rome was satisfied that De Neckere's youth was not an insuperable handicap, the spiritually mature Flemish priest was named Bishop of New Orleans on August 4, 1829. There was equal satisfaction in both quarters when that same month of May found Madame Duchesne at long last living within the city of St. Louis. Generous John Mullamphy had donated a house to the Religious of the Sacred Heart, and they had taken up residence there on May 2. By the end of the month an academy was begun in this *Maison de Ville*.[32]

During Easter Week a long letter from Rosati arrived in Montauban. Having only learned definitely of DuBourg's new assignment the first week in November 1826, Rosati had been thunderstruck by the news and was definitely unhappy at being left alone, without a word of warning, in charge of the whole Diocese of Louisiana. His first letter had been reproachful. This second one, written on December 29, was much more to DuBourg's liking and the Bishop of Montauban replied happily, "I don't know how to express to you the good this letter has done me. . . . I see with inexpressible pleasure that the first impressions of surprise and grief, which my unexpected retreat caused you, are beginning to disappear and your thoughts are settling down." It was so good to be able to be on former terms again with the man now holding the fate of his old diocese in his hands.

Rosati had mentioned asking the Duchess of Berry to become a benefactor of his jurisdiction and DuBourg replied, "I heartily approve. . . . I will have your letter passed on with one of mine by the channel of the excellent Duke of Rivière, Governor to the young and amiable *Duke of Bordeaux,* to whom I have already spoken of our Savages, and who has promised me his interest. A good letter from you to this excellent and pious lord . . . will do a great deal of good."

DuBourg asked Rosati to deal with his creditors in

New Orleans, saying, "On *that condition* I will cede to you all I have left there, Negroes, Library, furniture, pictures, chapel, linens, silver, etc. etc." He was sending Rosati his pretty little chalice of vermeil to use on his missions, also his *pyxide* and case of holy oils likewise of vermeil. Then he gave news of Brassac and Sibourd. Brassac was full of fervor and a desire to return to Ascension, and DuBourg for his part hoped he would. "I wish him to return to Louisiana," he assured Rosati, "but the matter is delicate for his family." They had written to Rome, hoping to have him settle in France. As for Sibourd, he was in Montauban, very happy and very well. "I urge you to write to him," DuBourg added. Sibourd was fond of Rosati and very interested in his labors; he could still do something for the American missions.

Happy in his present place, the Bishop of Montauban explained with his habitual optimism:

> I will say only one word to you about my position. God has treated me like a spoiled child. I only fear not being grateful enough. Universally loved by my new family, pursued by their zeal, I have the satisfaction of presiding over a clergy obedient, affectionate and generally virtuous. The people of these regions are naturally religious and attached to their pastors. However there is evil as everywhere. I am working to have good missions given in my principal cities, and to form a band of diocesan missionaries, for which they have just given me a house with a little revenue.[33]

At the start he could never keep from seeing things as he hoped they might be.

In Montauban the month of May had its darker side. Melting snows higher up on the mountains together with torrential rains late that spring caused the Tarn and one of its tributaries, the Aveyron, to flood the countryside simultaneously. Two years earlier, in the winter of 1825–26, Cheverus had experienced the same kind of catastrophe, only one more harsh on the flood victims because of the cruel weather. This time the inundations surpassed even those of 1825 in the ravages to property. The flooding began in the night of May 20 and at daybreak DuBourg went to Sapiac, the most exposed part of Montauban, to offer Mass and lead the prayers of rogation for turning back floodwaters. As he finished praying, the Tarn stopped rising, and by 10:00 that morning the waters began receding. But the damage was frightful. In the interval between the cresting of the river and the beginning of its recession, the bishop went through both Sapiac and Villebourbon, distributing tickets for lodgings in his episcopal residence while the pastors of these two suburbs gathered information on the most urgent needs of their parishioners and listened compassionately to the litany of misfortunes. The following day DuBourg went to the other two chief cities of the diocese, Moissac and Castel-Sarrasin, and visited all the other riverbank parishes in between. Returning to Montauban by Sunday, he found the skies ominously threatening another deluge and once again, like the prophets of old, he stormed heaven to turn away its wrath from his flock.[34] Not since Pakenham's British veterans stormed the cotton-baled defenses of New Orleans had he prayed with quite such fervor and urgency, or felt so fiercely paternal toward his people.

The feast of Corpus Christi that year was really a family affair. After the disasters they had experienced, or narrowly escaped, everyone wanted to demonstrate his faith and gratitude. On the day itself the bishop pontificated in the general ceremonies of the city parishes; then on the Sunday following he crossed the Tarn to the Church of Saint Orens in Villebourbon where he presided over the procession, celebrated a pontifical high Mass, and preached at Vespers.[35] There were times when deep feelings called for high ceremonies and taxing one's resources beyond the limits of common sense.

That summer fixed a pattern that was to become rather routine as the years went by: visitations of the diocese interspersed with visits from friends and episcopal colleagues. Clermont-Tonnerre returned DuBourg's January visit and Charles Brault, the eminent Archbishop of Albi, spent a week at the bishop's residence on Rue des Bains. "These agreeable distractions," says the historian of the diocese, "did not prevent our bishop from being actively occupied." In July he toured the southwest portion of his domain, beginning with Beaumont and continuing through the canton of Lavit; in September he went eastward to Nègrepelisse and the hill country.

On the occasion of the seventh birthday of the duke of Bordeaux, the Bishop of Montauban took pleasure in presenting to this "miracle child" a costume of an American Indian chief complete with quiver, arrows, and other Indian weapons. The lad, born on September 29, 1820, more than seven months after the assassination of his father, the duke of Berry, was viewed in pious royalist circles as an omen that Providence favored a Bourbon succession to the throne presently occupied by his grandfather, Charles X.[36] DuBourg's gift was taken as a charming gesture.

American Indians were much in the news in late summer and early fall that year. Visits from American Indians were not unknown to France. Some Osage tribesmen had arrived there in 1725 and had been presented to Louis XV. More recently in 1826 Jean-Baptiste Fauvel had conducted a group of Iroquois to Rome. Nevertheless, the summer of 1827 was for Parisian curiosity seekers one to remember. "After having received, at the end of June, the first giraffe ever brought to France the capital witnessed the arrival in mid-August of a group of Indians of the Osage tribe, whose popularity was to present a redoubtable competition with that of *la belle africaine.*"[37]

A dozen Osages early in 1827 had started down the Missouri River with enough fur pelts to pay their passage to Europe accompanied by Paul Loise, the son of a Frenchman and his Osage wife, as their interpreter. As they were approaching St. Louis their raft sank and with it their riches. At this point a David Delaunay, hoping to profit from it, offered to arrange their voyage and accompany them. Six of the Indians accepted his offer and went with him to New Orleans to embark on the American sailing vessel *New England.* They disembarked at Le Havre on July 27, 1827, creating a furor among the people crowding the quais, hanging in clusters over the sides of ships, or peering down from rooftops. Aristide Anduze, who had met them in the Diocese of Louisiana, had arrived only a few days earlier on the *Bayard,* and he introduced the party to the officials of the seaport. The complexions and costumes of the Osages entranced the French of Le Havre as much as they had the young French missionaries in St. Louis some five years earlier, and the Indians were escorted to a hotel where a representative of the mayor greeted them and the Indian chief declared he had come to France to present his homage to Charles X.

On August 7 Delaunay took the Indians on board the steamboat *La Duchesse d'Angoulême* heading for Rouen where according to *le Moniteur* of August 12:

> The six Indians made a furor at Rouen. The crowds continually besieged the hotel they occupied, encumbered the streets and the places where they appeared. . . . On August 8 in an open carriage they went in the costume of their country to the theatre. They were seated in the loge of the governor. . . . After the first act, the prince rose and said to them in his language many very agreeable things no doubt, but which they understood not at all.

On August 18 the Osages resumed their journey to Paris by *velocifere.* In the capital *l'Ami* reported:

> The Osages, who were invited on the 18th to a fine meal at the home of Baron de Damas, Minister of Foreign Affairs, have been presented to the King in their full dress after Mass on the 21st. The savage chief addressed His Majesty in a speech translated on the spot, recalling that his tribe still preserved the memory of the kind reception Louis XIV had once accorded one of their ancestors, and his advice that the Osages should cultivate the friendship of the kings of France.[38]

The dinner for forty given by the baron of Damas was only the start of gustatory delights. After the reception by the king, the Osages were regaled by the duke of Luxembourg, the captain of the guards. Delaunay, who somewhere along the way had added the title of "colonel" to his name, now made the Indians the prey of the Parisian public. He inserted in the journals notices giving the exact address where tickets could be purchased to get in to see his troupe. Everyone was soon trying to capitalize on the Indians; places of amusement had only to announce their presence in advance; the seats would all be taken.

For a few weeks the vogue was all-encompassing. In cafés one drank *punch aux Osages,* milliners favored Osage brown for their chapeaux, *haute couture* launched creations *osagiennes* or *missouriennes.* Music was enriched by the *Chant national des Osages;* lithographs in brilliant color sold for ten francs; theatrical spectacles outdid themselves for the moment.

Then, as swiftly as it had appeared, the vogue vanished. On September 11 *le Figaro* remarked, "The Osages are becoming as amusing as sonatas," and by October's end the press had ceased to mention them.

Abandoned by their guide Delaunay, who during the winter had been discovered to be a swindler and was imprisoned, the Indians wandered to Liège, Fribourg-en-Brisgau, Germany, Switzerland, and finally into Italy. On June 30, 1829, a "Reverend Julian Delaunay," who described himself as a "conductor of the Osages," petitioned the pope for financial aid for his party: the chief of the tribe, his wife, and another member of the tribe. This letter was forwarded by the French chargé d'affaires who said that Delaunay was a French citizen.[39] In a general congregation on August 17, 1829, Propaganda decided that Delaunay was to be arrested and that the Indians were to be set free from exploitation by him.[40] In mid-November 1829 these three Indians who were now separated from the others came to Montauban asking for DuBourg. Chief Kaikechinka had insisted on seeing once more this revered *Grand Père des Blancs,* and was filled with joy at finding in the bishop's study the ivory crucifix and other objects the bishop had used in the course of his missions among them in Missouri.[41]

The Osage chief had come for more than the pleasure of a reunion with his old friend; he needed DuBourg's help and advice in regard to returning home. The bishop received them with his usual hearty hospitality and gave them shelter for the eight days they remained, days during which he solicited from his more wealthy diocesans enough funds to set them on their way once more.[42] By the beginning of December the Osages were safely in Paris where the American consul arranged their passage home.[43]

The ending of the Osage affair in 1829, of course, was not anticipated in 1827, when the Bishop of Montauban was trying to take command of his new charge. In November of the latter year DuBourg was complaining mildly to Rosati:

> I no longer hear talk of the nomination of Mr. de Neckere. Propaganda does not seem to wish to discuss it with me. Besides that excellent young man has been for some time between life and death from vomiting blood. I have no fresh news of him. They tell me he is at Amiens, still full of the desire to return to the mission. I wish it were the same with Mr. de la Croix, who is recovered, and seems, however, decided to settle in Flanders. I am to write to him to try to get him to return with some recruits.[44]

And then it was Advent again. After sixty the years seemed to gallop by. He had had a good first year, all in all. The one major disappointment had been felt more keenly by Louis, whose letters from Filleau in Paris were still hopeful, but demanding more and more documentation and reporting increasing counterclaims from all sorts of distant connections. A family genealogy would help, Filleau suggested. But the best their attorney could truthfully tell them was that there was general agreement that the debts to the DuBourgs *ought* to be paid, "public faith and the sacred rights of property" demanded it. But the fact was that Haiti was unable to pay 120 million francs in four years. There was still no solution to the question of how to arrange the discharging of the debt.[45]

The DuBourg family seemed destined to go through life plagued by debts—either those they contracted in their zeal for God's house, or those owed them and unlikely to be satisfied while Louis and the bishop survived. If only the generosity of one's impulses could shrink in ratio to one's income as time and circumstance so often eroded the latter. Perhaps *next* year Filleau could manage something. Meanwhile the DuBourgs would do better to attune themselves once more to the spirit of the season and in the words of the liturgy invoke God's mercy "that we may with becoming honor prepare for the approaching solemnities of our redemption."[46]

CHAPTER XXXVII

PROGRESS AT HOME
AND ABROAD

As the decade of the 1820s moved toward its close, innovation was in the air. In Montauban the Pont Vieux with its arch of triumph and its chapel dedicated to Saint Catherine no longer seemed wide enough for the increased traffic between the upper and lower city. Although no one was yet ready to sacrifice the arch of triumph at the Ville-Bourbon end of the bridge, the chapel in the middle of the span fell victim to the times.[1] In Toulouse editors were planning a new journal to replace the *Echo du Midi* and the cardinal archbishop was sending his colleagues in the hierarchy in that region a prospectus of the new paper to be established in his see city, with the request that they promote this good work by getting as many subscriptions as possible. Cheverus in Bordeaux as well as DuBourg in Montauban received his package of harbingers of things to come.[2]

The title of the new venture was more typical of its sponsors than of the time. *Le Mémorial de Toulouse, Journal Politique, Littéraire, Commercial et Administratif, dédié à tous les amis de la Religion et de la Monarchie,* quickly abbreviated to the *Mémorial de Toulouse,* began with the issue of January 20, 1829, to appear thereafter every Tuesday, Thursday, and Saturday. It was still "devoted to the sacred causes of religion and the monarchy," as the *Echo* had been; but in addition to news of the Church and throne, the *Mémorial* was concerned with a wider range of interests. It promised its subscribers:

> The particular position of Toulouse at the gates to the Peninsula and between the two seas which bathe the Midi of France, permits us to be promptly informed of events in Portugal and Spain, and to receive directly news from our own seaports. Correspondence established with Paris assures us of the means to give, even before the papers of the capital, an analysis of the sessions of the legislature. . . . We will offer our readers . . . a general glance at the theatres and dramatic productions which exercise so much influence on the customs and mind of the public.[3]

It was the view of the editors that "in an epoch when reading newspapers had become a sort of necessity for everyone it was imperative that the friends of order should have their gazettes as more turbulent spirits had theirs."[4] Lamennais's *l'Avenir* was still a year and a half off, but already acute observers sensed the coming importance of what twentieth-century jargon would term "the media."

In the United States, Bishop John England's *United States Catholic Miscellany,* which had been compelled to suspend publication during DuBourg's last days in America, in its resurrected form after July 1826 was gaining momentum as the organ which created an informed Catholic opinion by frankly discussing the problems the Church faced in an age of reform. Benedict Fenwick, the Jesuit successor of Cheverus in Boston, in September 1829 founded the Catholic weekly, which under its eventual name, *The Pilot,* continued an unbroken record of publication thereafter.[5]

DuBourg, while not involved in launching journalistic enterprises, was aware of the efficacy of the printed word, and in 1828 he began his Lenten message with the words:

In our impotence to speak to each one of you directly we feel pressed—as much by the sentiment of the heart as by the authority of duty—to substitute for the first time a short allocution, which when repeated on the same day from all the pulpits of our diocese may remind you of the tender solicitude with which we are filled for your true interests.[6]

The printer to his excellency the bishop, was kept busy over in Place Royale that February.

The bishops of France were much more deeply involved in the changes dictated by the government's increasing preoccupation with education. At the beginning of 1828, Cheverus of Bordeaux, who was still a member of the Chamber of Peers, had been ordered to present at its next session "an important work on Catholic primary schools." Pastors were to report to their superiors the age, reputation, religious principles, loyalty to the throne, conduct, teaching methods, and assiduity in service of every teacher in the parish primary schools. The urgency in Paris was reflected in Cheverus's own letter to his *curés* which ended, "Please don't lose a minute in making these reports."[7] The outcome of these surveys presented to the national legislature was a royal ordinance dated April 21, 1828, which involved every member of the hierarchy in a major revision of education within his jurisdiction. The general effect of the ordinance was to take away from the bishops some of the power over primary education which they had enjoyed since 1824. In the future, supervision would rest with a nine-member committee of which the bishop's men constituted only one-third, with the rest representing the departmental administration and the non-religious schools.

The Minister of Public Instruction, Antoine-François Lefebvre de Vatimesnil, explained the implications of the ordinance in forwarding it to the hierarchy in May, emphasizing that its several parts were all aimed at assuring the youth of the realm the benefit of religious education, and bishops were expected to concur with its execution since the supervision of religious instruction was their responsibility. Candidates for teaching positions were to be examined by a delegate chosen either by the bishop or the pastor of the parish. Bishops or their delegates were also expected to visit the schools regularly. To soften the effect of the new nine-member committee, Vatimesnil said, "The composition of these committees is of the gravest importance; please give to your choice all the attention it deserves."[8] Close on the heels of this circular came an equally urgent one from the Minister of Ecclesiastical Affairs ordering the bishops to name as soon as possible the president and two other ecclesiastical members of this committee; and to inform the headmasters of the schools involved what the new qualifications for instructors were to be.[9]

These peremptory directives from Paris came at a most inconvenient moment for DuBourg. For some time he had been planning a mission for Montauban which he hoped would cause a notable rejuvenation of religious fervor.[10] In other parishes of the diocese the mission had already begun on April 27 and was scheduled to open in the city of Montauban on May 27. In addition to the usual notifications to his clergy he had announcements affixed to church doors warmly inviting all the inhabitants of the city to attend the services beginning the last Sunday in May. When the day arrived, high Mass was followed by a procession through the city streets. After it returned to the Place d'Armes in front of the cathedral, DuBourg preached, as he knew so well how to do, on the spiritual advantages of a mission and blessed all those who would be preaching during its sessions, conferring on them "all his powers." Then the director of the preaching band, the celebrated Father Claude Guyon, S. J., gave an ardent talk and summoned all to Vespers, when the mission itself would begin.[11]

The mission of 1828 was everything DuBourg had hoped for. *L'Ami* reported that the Montauban ceremonies were performed with more than usual fervor and that both Pentecost Sunday and Corpus Christi had three general communions. The closing on June 3 was accompanied with splendors seldom seen by the eyes of those reporting the event. But the excitement was still not over. To perpetuate the event for history, a gigantic Mission Cross was to be erected in the middle of the Place d'Armes on June 15 and on the eve of the ceremony there arrived not only the Cardinal Archbishop of Toulouse but also Bishop François de Latour-Landorthe of Pamiers, Bishop Joseph-Jules de Saint Romme-Gualy of Carcassonne, and Bishop Etienne M. B. d'Arbou of Verdun.[12] "Their presence," *l'Ami* suggested, "gave a new éclat to the ceremony."

> The procession began at 3:30 in the afternoon. The number of priests, the concourse of the faithful, the presence of the authorities, the preparations which had been made, the songs of the choir made the solemnities very imposing. Fifteen thousand people encircled the Place. As the Cross was raised on high the cannon roared and the whole crowd burst into cheers. M. Guyon gave a moving talk after which the Cardinal gave his benediction. Inscriptions placed on the faces of the pedestal of the Cross commemorated this grand day and the prelates who assembled for the occasion.[13]

For Louis-Guillaume DuBourg it marked the summit of his career. He loved panoply and oratory; he particularly loved reaching crowds with the Christian message. In order to perpetuate the memory of the mission, he addressed to his clergy a circular authorizing parish processions to the Mission Cross for the purpose of securing indulgences.[14] He was realist enough to know the indescribable enthusiasm of that Sunday in June could not last. Yet the Mission Cross could stand as a lasting proof that there once had been such a moment, such fervor, such good will.

The very day after the planting of the Mission Cross, the king signed additional ordinances affecting education, this time the minor seminaries. It was becoming obvious that the ministry in Paris was determined to remove public education from clerical control, particularly that of the Jesuits. The investigation in which Cheverus had participated in January had been only the tip of the iceberg. The April ordinance revising the supervision of primary education revealed more of the overall intentions, as did the removal of public instruction from the Minister of Ecclesiastical Affairs. The full import of the new order came with the ordinances signed by the king on June 16, which gave the French liberals the victory they had been seeking for years, the removal of the Jesuits from secondary education.[15] When his ministers proposed these two ordinances, Charles X at first hesitated. Denis Frayssinous, had declared himself adamantly opposed to them unless extreme necessity demanded them; he preferred to resign rather than be a party to the measures. His portfolio was offered to Cheverus, and when the Archbishop of Bordeaux refused it, it devolved upon the Bishop of Beauvais, Jean-François-Hyacinthe Feutrier.[16]

Charles X, caught between his true attachment to the Church and the crisis in his government, appointed a commission to examine the question as moral theologians: supposing reasons of state demanded concessions to the liberals within the ministry, could the king in conscience accede? While the commission went on record that the advantages promised by the ordinances could never compensate for the ill consequences, the principle of *salus populi suprema lex* justified the king's signing them. The vote was unanimous.[17]

The ordinances signed by Charles X on June 16 put the eight colleges directed by Jesuits under the control of the University of France and demanded of all those engaged in teaching a written assurance that they were not members of an "unauthorized religious community." They further placed minor seminaries under government control to ensure that they were not camouflaged secondary schools. The number of students was limited to a total of 20,000; ecclesiastical schools could accept only resident students; and after their second year seminarians were to wear clerical garb.

The bishops of France, generally, were outraged. Led by Archbishop de Quelen of Paris, seventy signed a protest concluding with the assertion, "Like the Apostles of old we say *non possumus*." The king, however, was vindicated when Pope Leo XII held that the June ordinances did not violate episcopal rights. Eventually most of the seventy rebellious bishops gave in. A few refused, among them

Clermont-Tonnerre who announced haughtily, "The motto of my family, given to it by Callistus II in 1120, is this: *Etiamsi omnes, ego non,* even if everyone else does, I will not."[18]

Existing evidence does not indicate where his suffragan DuBourg stood in the anti-Jesuit crisis. Unlike Cheverus in Bordeaux, the Bishop of Montauban had no Jesuit secondary schools or *petits séminaires* to lose.[19] The secondary school in Montauban conducted by Perboyre was in essence a Lazarist house and since the death of Gratacap was legally the property of Perboyre alone. Perboyre now turned it into a boarding school, which he eventually sold to Father Marc Gratacap, the nephew of his late confrere. DuBourg moved his minor seminarians to a site adjoining the major seminary and placed their direction under his diocesan clergy. A year later, through an amicable agreement with the Lazarists, Montauban's preparatory *collège* was also placed under the diocesan priests.[20]

Although the decrees on secondary education did not noticeably complicate DuBourg's summer, it was, nevertheless, a busy one. As he told his clergy on July 14, "You have hardly finished the memorable Mission exercises, which produced such admirable fruits of grace, when I come announcing a benefaction of the same sort for the clergy." The Abbé Pierre-Denis Boyer, known throughout France for his erudition and zeal, had consented to give a pastoral retreat of eight days beginning on August 5. DuBourg trusted his priests would not show themselves less eager for the "things of salvation" than the simple laity had proved during the seven weeks of the mission.[21] If anyone could renew their zeal, it was Boyer. A Sulpician of DuBourg's own time, after the overthrow of Napoleon he had devoted himself entirely to the ministry of ecclesiastical retreats and writing. Scarcely a diocese in France had not heard him, and most had invited him back three of four times.[22]

Unhappily, not everyone could take part in this retreat since some priests must remain in each canton to care for the sick; those who had missed the last retreat for that reason now had first right to attend this one. The most recently ordained should give place to the older men. But they could arrange these matters among themselves. The care of the sick was the only thing that need keep them away; Sunday services the week of the retreat could be satisfied by announcing the retreat on the previous Sunday and urging the parishioners to come to their churches to pray for the clergy of France in general and for their own priests in particular. "It will give me pleasure to be reunited with my brothers," he ended, signing himself "Your very affectionate servant."

It truly did please him to share the spiritual exercises of the retreat; but it did not restore him physically, as he had hoped. At sixty-two he did not expect to feel like a boy, of course, but it was disheartening to have to push so hard just to accomplish the ordinary duties of his office. The reorganization of the diocesan educational system, the long mission weeks, the regular summer pastoral visits, all left his energies more than usually depleted.[23] He felt compelled to go southward to Ax-Les-Thermes where the waters of that spa might work their restorative powers. The duchess of Berry was making a "progress" or tour of France that summer and the bishops had been alerted regarding the cities through which she might pass or favor with a longer stay. Montauban, a center of royalist devotion, was on her route. DuBourg would prefer to feel more like himself in making her passage through his diocese all it might be.

As it turned out, neither Cheverus nor DuBourg had the pleasure of welcoming the royal lady to their sees. Cheverus had to remain in Paris for a session of the Chamber of Peers and missed her four-day stay in Bordeaux.[24] DuBourg, from exhaustion, was in Ax while she paid her respects to Montauban. It was from this health resort on September 4 that he despatched an ordinance announcing the prospective visit of the duchess, prescribing prayers and exposition of the Blessed Sacrament throughout his diocese for Sunday, September 27.[25] He still had not given up all hope of seeing her. Clermont-Tonnerre of Toulouse, in spite of having been banned from court for his insolence in rejecting the June ordinances, was also on the Berry itinerary.

L'Ami reported that he had invited his suffragan bishops from Montauban, Pamiers, and Carcassonne to come to Toulouse for the occasion of her visit. They were expected to arrive on Saturday, September 19, the eve of her own coming. But subsequently all that journal mentioned of the Toulouse visit was to say, "On the 24 Madame went at eight o'clock to the metropolitan church where she was received by the cardinal archbishop accompanied by the Bishop of Pamiers and the vicars general." Nor did *l'Ami* allude to DuBourg in reporting "the most brilliant reception" the duchess enjoyed in Montauban on September 24.[26] The historian of the diocese says only, "The reception given the royal traveler proved how well the bishop had been understood."[27]

Certainly the bishop was back in Montauban by the end of the month, for on September 29 he was again devoting his attention to the minor seminaries, "daily becoming more precious for the good they had produced in the year which had just passed." Through the alacrity with which the clergy had responded to DuBourg's first appeals for contributions, Montauban had been able to give financial aid to fifty students. A circular now begged the clergy to impose on themselves voluntarily another levy of either twenty francs or twenty Masses in the interest of those "dear heirs called to continue in your parishes the tradition of your good works."[28]

During the days of reorganization and recuperation, French concerns were not his only interest. The year had begun with the death of Ambroise Maréchal in Baltimore[29] and his succession by James Whitfield. DuBourg and Maréchal had never been *en sympathie*, but they were both French and Sulpicians and for a few brief years had labored at the same time in Baltimore.[30] As American bishops, neither man had remained impervious to the fact that the immigrants pouring into the United States, digging the canals and the coal mines, manning the steamboats, and toiling in the factories of the mushrooming cities were more and more dissatisfied with French priests and bishops. The new Archbishop of Baltimore seemed to be another sign of the times. DuBourg's old friend Flaget, who consecrated him on May 25, 1829, was the last of the bishops in the United States consecrated by John Carroll. James Whitfield, who had been born in England and spoke English as a native son, almost immediately decided to call for a provincial council of the nine American dioceses—a move Maréchal had resisted to the end of his days. Perhaps in America the day of the preeminence of the French clergy in the Church was over.

For the moment, however, the American missionaries visiting France and calling on the Bishop of Montauban confirmed that French money and recruits were still very much in demand. When Stephen Theodore Badin, Flaget's vicar general, left France the month after Whitfield's consecration, he had from DuBourg 500 francs for his voyage and another 500 francs for the Jesuits of Missouri.[31] Aristide Anduze, who had accompanied DuBourg's last extensive pastoral visit of the Diocese of Louisiana, had been in France since 1827 and most recently had given both Cheverus and DuBourg up-to-date knowledge of the needs of the American missions before going on to Madrid.[32] Bishop Michael Portier, who headed part of DuBourg's former diocese, Florida and Alabama, was in Europe almost as a last desperate measure, having told Rosati, "If I do not succeed . . . . I do not believe I shall return to America. I shall either hand in my resignation or ask for a change to the missions in China."[33]

Portier arrived in France in the summer of 1828, and DuBourg and Sibourd both received letters postmarked Le Havre, which Portier had carried with him from St. Louis and New Orleans;[34] but Portier himself was delayed by quarantine at Le Havre, by visits to his relatives in Montbrison, and by official business in Lyon and Rome. It was not until the following summer that he finally reached Montauban,[35] where Portier and DuBourg had a warm reunion and animated exchanges on topics both French and American. While waiting for Portier's arrival, the Bishop of Montauban prepared subjects for Portier's diocese.[36] Nothing remained of the umbrage taken when DuBourg's young protégé had been removed from his college to be made bishop without DuBourg's being consulted. The two veterans of service in New Orleans found they agreed heartily on the man for that diocese. As DuBourg told Rosati:

> Mgr. P. thinks that Mr. Blanc is the bp. who suits N. O. I share his conviction. It is he who is the *pious, prudent, humble, chaste* man of your beautiful Roman hymn, and he has in my opinion the talent and knowledge necessary to that place. His knowledge of the localities, the customs of the country, the confidence he enjoys, are a very great point which should make him preferable to a man who would be superior to him but would not have these advantages.[37]

Since Rosati was going to be at the Baltimore Provincial Council, DuBourg added, "Doubtless you will discuss this matter."

It was interesting to learn from Portier that his jurisdiction was now the Diocese of Mobile and suffragan to Baltimore. *L'Ami,* commenting on this after Portier's departure for New Orleans, said:

> The present Pope erected this diocese last May 15, and named M. Portier to the new diocese. . . . The city has about 10,000 souls, of whom one-third are Catholic. . . . M. Portier was of the group of young ecclesiastics who left a dozen years ago for Louisiana with M. Dubourg; he was molded by this prelate and used by him either in the ministry or in directing a college established in New Orleans.[38]

Rome had given Portier 20,000 *scudi* for his diocese, a very large sum by most standards,[39] but DuBourg, who knew Portier's jurisdiction well, could understand how much more was needed. He gave Portier a warm introduction to Frayssinous—now the king's Grand Aumônier, or First Almoner—which read:

> Your penetration will discover with a glance of the eye, beneath those youthful features, that force of soul, that maturity, and that breadth of vision which distinguish this young prelate and merited for him in Rome a most satisfying reception; and the zeal with which your Excellency is ani-

mated for the propagation of the faith will lead you to assist him . . . with all the influence your virtues and dignities give you before the King and his august family. Please, Monseigneur, introduce him and manage for him a part of the royal munificence.[40]

Embarked on assisting Portier and recalling how he once meant Portier to come under Bruté's influence, the Bishop of Montauban decided that his two recruits destined for Mobile should go to Bruté at Mount St. Mary's to learn their English. Since Portier was going to the council in Baltimore, it would be easy to arrange. DuBourg notified Bruté:

> More happy than I, my very dear confrere, the *abbés* Lapoujade and Massip, bearers of this letter, have the advantage not only of seeing you in passing, but of living under your sweet laws and being formed by your school. They are the two gifts I am making Mgr. Portier, who I hope will be useful to him, when they have acquired near you, in addition to the knowledge of English, the science of saints as well. . . . It is important for our dear missions that these first fruits of the Diocese of Montauban correspond to the hopes which they give me. Their example can then attract others; and I will have the consolation of serving until the end of my life *and beyond* a country to which I have devoted my existence.[41]

DuBourg supposed that Bruté would also be present at the Baltimore council. In a way, he envied those attending this "first and solemn reunion of ten bishops in a country which in 1790 still had only one" and—the way things were going—would count fifteen in another ten years. He had always believed the episcopacy should be as one and still argued that it was "urgent to remedy the inconveniences which resulted in isolating the different churches, to fix upon a method of presenting [candidates] for vacant sees, and decreeing the principal points of general discipline necessary to establish uniformity."[42] He sent his regards to all who would be there, especially Bishops Flaget and Dubois. By André La Poujade and Jules Massip, his *Montalbanais* deacon and subdeacon, DuBourg sent Bruté some lithographs of himself with the direction, "Distribute them among my better friends, especially not forgetting the haven of St. Joseph where I desire to live, long after I am dead, in the memory of its holy inhabitants as you and they do in that of your old friend."

Even more than these visits from Franco-American travelers, DuBourg's correspondents kept his thoughts constantly returning to the scenes of his former labors in the United States. Only that summer Henri Elèves, a French priest, had inquired if DuBourg could tell him anything of the connection Samuel Sutherland Cooper had once had with establishing the Daughters of Charity in the United States. It was a question reopening the door to a past not entirely flattering to the Bishop of Montauban, and that may explain why in answering Elèves he referred to himself in the third person—"a priest much occupied with religious establishments," or Mrs. Seton's "director."[43] He recalled only too vividly how Cooper's offer to give $10,000 had led to the foundation in Emmitsburg in 1809. Cooper's later idiosyncrasies, erratic behavior, and regrets for having placed funds in Sulpician hands in no way detracted from the importance of his generosity and providential support of Elizabeth Seton's desire to found an American religious community. Indeed, Rosati's recent letter announced:

> You will learn with pleasure that we will have an establishment of the Sisters of Emmitsburg at St. Louis. It is to be a hospital. Mr. Mullamphy has given me a fine lot in the city and also another which furnishes an income of 600 piastres annually; the first will serve for the hospital, the second for the support of the Sisters. He has further given to pay for their trip and furnish their house. We will probably see them before winter. This establishment can not fail to prosper.[44]

Although DuBourg did not enjoy admitting to himself that he had not precisely suited his lady-foundress's preferences, nor enjoyed uniformly serene relations with Mother Seton, time was proving that at least he had not insuperably hampered the progress of the Sisters of Charity.

The Jesuits reported that the Religious of the Sacred

845

Heart at St. Charles were soon to settle in a house spacious enough to serve as a presbytery, to which they were joining a little building to serve as a school from which they hoped "much good will" might come.[45] Mother Duchesne herself wrote to him that October in terms calculated to soothe all his sensitivities. "I am not the only one to complain of your silence," she said. "Whenever I ask for news of you they tell me you do not write." Was he already forgetting the land watered by his sweat and tears? The people who had always looked to him as the one to whom they owed everything— "this people could rebel against the voice of their shepherd," she confessed ruefully, "but they are not ingrates. Your name is never pronounced among them without veneration."[46]

Women knew how to interject those little details which made the past come more instantly alive, as if something of themselves had entered the room with their letters. Du-Bourg found himself almost imperceptibly buoyed up by Philippine Duchesne's account from St. Louis:

> On October 12, the feast you fixed for honoring our holy Angels, I assisted for the first time in my life at the consecration of a church. It was that at St. Charles built by the Jesuits. . . . This church whose façade overlooks the Missouri, is built on the land that was your former garden, the very place where you helped with your episcopal hands to uproot a little tree. It is entirely made of stone. Mgr. Rosati, who presided over the ceremony, was assisted by all the Jesuits, two Lazarists, and several young seminarians. Father De Theux and Mr. Dussaussoy preached, one in English, the other in French, to a crowd in front of the door of the church. No one had ever seen such a great celebration. Your beautiful dalmatics shared in it.[47]

The Sacred Heart nuns now had six establishments in the former Diocese of Louisiana. The last was still quite unfinished—without window panes—and because of the cold the shutters had to be kept closed during the meal they gave Bishop Rosati. In the gloom Philippine put a copious amount of salt in the bishop's coffee, mistaking it for Louisiana sugar! But other houses were less primitive; St.

Michael's had eight boarders, Opelousas had forty, and La Fourche within two months would have thirty. In addition to boarding schools, free Catholic education was beginning to expand in the Mississippi Valley for both girls and boys; the Jesuits at St. Charles had a free school, and most of the eighty externes at Madame Duchesne's most recent experiment in St. Louis were received free of charge.[48]

The ladies were not the only ones reporting progress to their former episcopal patron. Father Charles Van Quickenborne, S. J., wrote from St. Ferdinand that in addition to the Catholic parish expanding around the newly consecrated Church of St. Charles, the Jesuits there served five new congregations begun since DuBourg had departed two years earlier. At first Protestants in those regions had come to see if Jesuits had horns on their heads; but later some became Catholics. Already at St. Charles, Protestants were sending children to the Jesuit school.[49]

The Jesuit work among the Osages, too, was going forward. Major John Francis Hamtramck, the Indian Agent, had recently increased the number of Indian pupils to twenty-five, although the federal government's subsidy had not changed. Van Quickenborne was having second thoughts, however, about the best way to achieve the civilizing and Christianizing of the Indians. He told DuBourg:

> The plan proposed by your Excellency according to which children educated in our seminary would return to their nation accompanied by two missionaries is very good. But in place of two children from each nation, as we have done until now, I think it would be more advantageous to take all the children we could from one or two nations at a time . . . that is 30 or 40 children from the most distinguished families. From these . . . only 12 or 15 would be returned at a time because they would not all be ready to return at precisely the same time. With the first . . . two missionaries would go and settle in the nation. Soon they would be joined by another 12 or 15 the next year. . . . These well educated young men, being sons of chiefs or the most brave, would necessarily have an influence over the others. I like to believe one could thus make a permanent establishment within the nation

which could not fail to convert, if not the whole tribe, at least a great part of it.[50]

It touched DuBourg deeply that Van Quickenborne had taken time to write such a lengthy letter, had believed Du-Bourg still cared about all the minutiae of his first diocese, had wanted to confide in him, "Monseigneur, you know the country, the United States and its government. There is no law which restrains us in the exercise of our ministry. The government is interested in the civilizing of its Indians, and the glory of the task belongs by right to our Holy Church." It was the way DuBourg had felt in 1823 when he approached Calhoun; it was the way he would always feel.

It gave the former Bishop of Louisiana satisfaction to still serve, in the small ways available to him, the needs of the Church in his first jurisdiction: the books on spirituality shipped by way of South Carolina, the missionaries from Montauban destined for Alabama, and the linens sent to Florissant for St. Ferdinand's.[51] At Rosati's request he forwarded a letter to the duchess of Berry trying to enlist aid for his jurisdiction. It had not brought results and DuBourg confessed, "I sent your letter to *Madame* which she received with kindness, but you can expect nothing; her alms in France absorb all the surplus her rank allows her." Du-Bourg recommended instead assiduous attention to the Society for the Propagation of the Faith. "Don't let their interest in Louisiana grow cold; it was the first object of the association." Their aid had been more than doubled since 1822. "For the year just past they assigned you 25,000 francs," he reminded Rosati. Another important avenue to pursue was the assistance of the new *Procureur* of the Congregation of the Mission of Paris, who could plead Rosati's case with the king's *grande aumônerie* which presided over the division of the society's funds among the mission countries.[52]

DuBourg kept Rosati *au courant,* as much as he could, on Francis Niel who had now been in Europe four years without materially benefiting Missouri. On August 28, 1828, the most he could say was, "Mr. Niel is always on the prowl, always sick and unable to do any work."[53] The following

January he only confirmed what Rosati already knew: "I believe that he sent you, or spent for the mission all he received. He paid the passage for three priests and sent the 2,000 piastres which were lost by Mr. Angelo Boccardi."[54] After Portier departed, Niel showed up at Montauban. He talked of going to Belgium in 1830 and DuBourg assured Rosati, "I will give him a letter with which there is reason to hope for something from that quarter."[55]

When Rosati, by now quite of DuBourg's mind about a religious order of men for Lower Louisiana, talked of getting Jesuits for Opelousas, DuBourg made a trip to Bordeaux to talk with the Jesuits there before their departure for St. Sebastien. He also approached their Father Provincial of Paris. He had success with neither and told Rosati, "It is proof that the project is not ripe, not that it is bad. God has his moments for everything, as he has never ceased proving to us. Let us wait. If we are not destined to do this good, it will be done by others."[56] Writing to Rosati made the past flash so vividly before him that the Bishop of Montauban found himself resorting to the phrases that came so naturally in the days when they were trying to build everything from nothing.

In August even Rome served to remind DuBourg of his American days, for Cardinal Capellari had written to ask what had been done about feasts and fasts in the Diocese of Louisiana in DuBourg's time. DuBourg explained in reply:

> The Diocesan Synod I called did nothing in regard to them except to publish in that Synod the pronouncement signed by our Holy Father Pius VII's own hand (which, at my departure, I left in the Episcopal Archives of New Orleans) whereby the sovereign Pontiff granted: 1st that we should follow in my Diocese the custom already introduced in that of Baltimore in regard to the reduction of feasts and vigils; 2nd that nothing should be changed in another custom introduced into Louisiana by the Spaniards, to eat meat on Saturdays during the year.[57]

On leaving Rome in January 1816, DuBourg had gone to Pius VII with a list of petitions, only one of which involved feasts and fasts, and the pope had written at the bottom of that list: *pro gratia, ad judicium Episcopi.* The original list was left in New Orleans in 1826. "No wonder," DuBourg told Capellari, "that nothing about it should be found in the records of the Sacred Congregation."[58]

All that seemed a long time ago, and now another Pius was on the papal throne. After a short reign of only six years Leo XII, who had accepted DuBourg's resignation from Louisiana and had named him to Montauban so soon afterward, died in his sixty-ninth year. DuBourg had issued on February 24, 1829, a circular announcing his death to the clergy of Montauban and prescribing the procedures to be followed: a low Mass of Requiem celebrated at once, daily prayers for the election of a new pope, a solemn memorial service in each church, to which the political authorities residing in the parish should be invited. Pastors should take advantage of all these occasions to instruct the faithful on the authority and prerogatives of the Holy See as well as the love and docility owed to it. "In these days of mourning and alarm for the Church," he urged, "we can not do too much to reform our ranks, reinforce the ties which bind us to the Chair of Saint Peter."[59]

Men of his generation were not likely to forget an earlier time when religion in France had been the target of hatred and political attack. "Who knows," he reflected, "if we are not destined to see reborn those evil days of forty years ago which brought desolation to this beautiful Church in France, and caused such defection in our ranks?" The Holy See, even though popes had been captives, had been the only rallying point then; it might be again the solitary support of the clergy and the faithful in days to come. DuBourg had never been particularly politically minded; but neither was he tone-deaf to the nuances echoing from Paris and reechoing from the prefecture of Tarn-et-Garonne. It was the Church of Rome upon which the faithful must constantly rely as the anchor of salvation, and that church was for the moment left fatherless. He added a postscript to his circular to the clergy: "I don't need to recommend that you read this from the pulpit."[60]

The conclave, which opened as DuBourg was composing his circular, had only thirty-seven cardinals present, and until the French members Clermont-Tonnerre and the Prince de Croij arrived on March 23, Frenchmen like Chateaubriand regarded the conclave's deliberations as "purely formal." On March 31 French agents in Rome reported, "The cannon of Chateau Saint-Ange announce the election of the new Pontiff. Cardinal Castiglione has been proclaimed this morning. He has taken the name Pius VIII."[61]

Francesco-Xavier Castiglione was an eminent jurist, possessed of a cultivated mind and taste, and had been a cardinal since 1821. He proved to be a pope of wisdom and moderation. DuBourg's *mandement* celebrating his election exuded the general relief and rejoicing normal to the faithful after a period of doubts and uncertainties. After praising Pius VIII for his recognized accomplishments as head of the several learned congregations, which had enlightened and supported the Holy See, and for his distinguished response to the French king's ambassador-extraordinary to the conclave, which had already delighted France, the Bishop of Montauban added:

> But few people in the Catholic world know that this choice, written in Heaven, was long ago announced to him by Pius VII of happy memory. It was ten years ago, my very dear Brothers, that we learned this prediction from the mouth of worthy witnesses of complete credibility; and we like to attest here to our intimate friends that we have frequently thought of it before the event, until the day of its accomplishment permitted us to proclaim it to the Church, both as a striking testimony to the sanctity of the Prophet-Pontiff as well as to his later successor, and as a new proof of the constant care of our God over the Roman church, our mistress and mother in the Faith.[62]

In France as in the United States, the election of a new pope was for DuBourg an occasion for reasserting the primacy of Peter's Chair and the loyalty of Catholics everywhere to the bishop who occupied it—and never more so than in 1829. "In what period," he demanded, "has this assistance of God in the election of the supreme Heads of his Church shone more brilliantly than in this mortal combat for more than a century with modern unbelief?" The present election presented compelling motives for reverence and submission to this august chair, whose perpetuation— visible to every eye—was no less an enduring miracle of divine power. "After the tempest He restores the calm; after the sadness and tears, He again diffuses joy. May your name, O God of Israel, be blessed forever!"

The Diocese of Montauban would celebrate the accession of Pius VIII first on Easter Sunday in the cathedral with a *Te Deum* to which all the clergy and civil authorities were invited. The rest of the diocese would offer their *Te Deums* the Sunday following. For fifteen days all priests would recite at Mass the prayer for the reigning pope; all the faithful were urged to go to Communion during the following month.[63]

On June 18 the papal secretary notified the hierarchy of the Jubilee accorded in celebration of the pope's accession. In Rome it would begin on June 28 and last for two weeks; elsewhere a two-week period would be fixed by bishops, pastors, and religious superiors. But the same regulations applied universally: that two visits should be made to the designated churches for devout prayer; fasting was to be observed on Wednesday, Friday, and Saturday of the Jubilee weeks; confession and communion must be devoutly received, and alms should be given to the poor in return for a plenary indulgence.[64]

DuBourg set the opening of the Jubilee in Montauban for the first Sunday in Advent. On the Saturday evening before the opening, all the bells would ring at six o'clock; all Masses after that would add prayers for both the pope and the king. All parish churches were designated stations for Jubilee visits, and cloistered religious, invalids, prisoners, and others legitimately unable to go out could fulfill the obligation in their houses. Travelers absent during those two weeks in Advent could satisfy the requirements on their return.[65] Whenever he could anticipate impediments DuBourg tried to eliminate them; he wanted all his flock to enjoy the benefits of the Jubilee. Up in Bordeaux Cheverus had set his Jubilee for the same two weeks in Advent; on the eve of the opening, all the bells of Saint-André were also to ring. Cheverus was even planning to have a special preacher for the occasion.[66]

Perhaps men trained in the American missions were more sensible of the graces emanating from the visible head of Christendom. Perhaps, having labored so long as solitary soldiers, or second lieutenants in charge of only token forces in barely charted theatres of operations, they were more keenly aware of the value of a commander-in-chief and of *esprit de corps* in preserving morale in the front lines? Certainly the episcopal recommendations of these two Franco-American prelates of Restoration France never lapsed into the merely perfunctory. Their *mandements* and *circulaires* still seem to pulse with a fervor and zeal for souls sensible across a century and a half. DuBourg's pleas that November still have relevance to the human condition:

> This is not the first time, my dearly beloved brethren, you have been invited to receive the grace of a Jubilee. Scarcely three years have passed since you enjoyed that of the Holy Year. Did you profit from it? . . . And among those who fulfilled their duty at that time, or that of the mission, how many since then have proved, by the ease with which they slipped back into their former habits, how little disposition they had for reform?

> What are we thinking of? That the eternal salvation of our souls is something to play with? While we procrastinate life is slipping away; and this new grace may be for us the last token of a bounty offered to remove our resistance. . . . At this very moment prepare your hearts; hasten to the tribunals of penitence—even before the opening of the Jubilee, lest the crowd which will surround them during these holy days prove for you an obstacle to the grace of absolution.[67]

"Life is slipping away" was a constant refrain running through DuBourg's mind that year; and so much remained to be accomplished. Up in Paris the Society of Saint-Sulpice recorded on March 15, 1829, "Monseigneur the Bishop of Montauban requests with the greatest urgency that we take his seminary; we can not accept." This cryptic entry in the minutes of the *Assemblée des Consultations* represented a dreadful disappointment for DuBourg. The establishment of a major seminary which could mold priests according to the standards he most admired was his most cherished project; and the older he got the more certain he became that only the Sulpicians would satisfy him. Toward the end of June he wrote at length of his dilemma to Antoine Garnier, who was now Superior General in Paris.

The Congregation of the Mission were going to cease directing the seminary of Montauban. "The matter is settled with the Superior General," DuBourg explained, "as it is with my whole diocese." Among his secular clergy he had two good professors who had already given proof of their capacities. But the real difficulty was in getting a superior who could command respect and confidence. He still wanted a Sulpician. "If you have one to recommend to me, or better yet to send me," he persisted, "you will render me a great service." Otherwise, DuBourg himself would take on the task until able to do better. As he put it humorously:

> That is to say that I will pass most of my time in the Seminary in order to animate all by my presence. That will do no harm, do you think? It is high time that I became regular and fervent as a good Sulpician should be. I imagine then you would feel less pain in preserving my name on our sacred *dyptiques*.[68]

The lightly jesting tone belied his deep feelings. He had loved Emery and Nagot with that undeviating respect and loyalty that so often goes unperceived in men of mercurial disposition and impulsive behavior. He had felt the "slings and arrows" of Maréchal's unrelenting disapprobation and complaints to Rome; to a lesser degree he had winced under Emery's gentler suggestions that DuBourg was too quixotic to be a true member of the Society of Saint-Sulpice, had too much of *l'esprit de Toboso* for the restrictions of the Society. He now said earnestly to Garnier:

> You know very well that it is the rule and method of Saint-Sulpice that I want to establish. Without bias I believe them the best. . . . In order to succeed in implanting them in my Seminary I have thought of using two of the young subjects

who have had the good fortune to make their studies at Saint-Sulpice in Paris. I have cast my eyes on Messers Couzy, Tieys, or Tuffeau. The last seems to me preferable to the second because I believe him to be more calm and more wise, although I do not think he has as much talent. He has enough for teaching philosophy, which would be the task I plan for him.

Tuffeau could also serve as *économe,* an administrative job for which he had shown capacities in Paris. In self-mockery DuBourg added, "You know that in this latter capacity I would not have much to teach him!" In Paris as in Baltimore his old reputation for leaving a trail of debts behind him would never fade, as the Bishop of Montauban very well knew.

As future director of the seminary, DuBourg planned to groom Couzy, who could also teach sacred liturgy. What did Garnier think? Did he agree that Tuffeau was to be preferred to Tieys? The latter could be used in the minor seminary which was now contiguous to the major, and thus be of service to both. If Garnier agreed with the bishop's thinking, would he give these young men the rules of Saint Sulpice and all the instructions needed to run a seminary? The two destined for the major seminary should be informed that they should return to Montauban in August to prepare for ordination to the priesthood and hold themselves in readiness for October 15, the day fixed for the opening of the seminary.[69]

In spite of his humorous tone, DuBourg had been quite serious when he told Garnier he would live in the seminary himself if necessary, and that is precisely what he did for a while. For entire months he fixed his residence in the major seminary, following the exercises of that community almost as if he were back in Paris in the 1780s. He visited classes, sitting at the foot of the lectern listening to both professors and students perform. Sometimes he would take a thesis or passage of Scripture under discussion and develop its ramifications with surprising precision. "Endowed with a prodigious memory, he possessed a sort of Bible he could recite almost in its entirety."[70]

Feeling himself in need of spiritual rejuvenation before the harsh winter set in, DuBourg decided to accept his archbishop's invitation to join the ecclesiastical retreat in the Toulouse seminary that autumn. Clermont-Tonnerre, in spite of his infirmities, was determined to make the retreat with his priests and both DuBourg and the former Bishop of Verdun, Etienne d'Arbou, accepted the old cardinal's invitation. *L'Ami* reported that the assiduity of these elderly prelates had edified the younger clergy as together they assembled twice a day to listen to the stirring conferences of Nicholas Mac-Carthy, S.J., and marched through the streets of Toulouse on the closing day of the retreat.[71]

DuBourg emerged from the retreat determined to do something to alleviate the hardships persisting in his rural parishes. Sundays were the only days most of the pastors could get the people together for religious instruction and confessions, and when the pastor was responsible for both a parish church and an outlying annex or chapel, sometimes far distant, this double service was dreadfully fatiguing. The annexes or auxiliary chapels were located in *arrondissements* where the aged, the infirm, and the very young were unable to come every week to the parish church; thus, consolidating or closing these adjuncts was out of the question.

To relieve some of the pressures of this situation, the bishop believed a few immediate changes must be made. Henceforth, priests who had annexes to serve need celebrate Mass, Vespers, and Benediction there only once a month. One parish weekday Mass should be offered, confessions heard, and instruction given to old or young. This should be on a fixed day, preferably a Monday. Pastors might also on the days which were no longer feast days celebrate funerals in the annexes, and if circumstances seemed favorable hold processions there on the Sunday of the octave of Corpus Christi.[72]

Years ago, when he was faced with the administration of a diocese in the New World as a younger, inexperienced man, he had confessed to Archbishop Carroll of Baltimore, "I am perpetually wavering between extremes of laxity and excesses of severity, of suspicions and indiscreet freedom," in regard to the flock confided to his care. Age and experience had modified the poles of this pendulum; they were now less easy to define. Where did love for the Church and her laws end and a father's compassion for his prodigal children begin? He knew something of the physical hardships of life; more recently he understood relentless fatigue. When he saw the drudgery of the small farms in the rural areas beyond his see city, the worn faces of his old priests trying to serve two altars remote from each other, when he thought of the vacancies to be filled—only recently another canon had had to be replaced[73]—his heart ached. If in this latest *ordonnance* he had been guilty of laxity, he hoped God would forgive him.

There was always more than one way of judging things, he knew. He was reminded of the death of Antonio de Sedella in January 1829 and the difference of opinion that event elicited. Flaget on hearing the news had commented:

> Up to that time we had only to admire the enthusiasm of all the province for a man who, for 50 years of his ministry, never announced the Word of God, has left no monument of piety and of self-sacrifice for the public, and never failed to maintain his authority. . . . Alas! What a black record, I say![74]

In New Orleans, on the other hand, the death of Père Antoine had been regarded as the passing of a saint. Three thousand wax candles blazed in St. Louis Cathedral where he lay, public buildings were draped in black, flags of even foreign ships in the harbor hung at half-mast. The *Courrier* on January 21 announced: "In respect to the memory of the Rev. Père Antoine de Sedilla, [*sic*]and in order to give those in our employ an opportunity of attending the obsequies, the *Courrier* will not appear again until Friday, January 23." Edward Livingston, that least orthodox of men, rose in the First District Court to move its adjournment for the purpose of attending the funeral, and in the course of his motion declaimed:

> His holiness and virtues would have entitled him to canonization; and if his title to that distinction were to be tried, as it is said in Rome, the advocate of the evil one would burn

857

his brief, and despair of showing one reason why he should not be received as a Saint in heaven who led the life of one on earth.[75]

The funeral on January 22 was unique in the city's history. All the public officials attended. Masons of "all rites and degrees" had been urged to remember that "Father Antoine never refused to accompany to their last abode the mortal remains of our Brethren," and they turned out in full force. In truth, since all theatres, warehouses, courts, and newspapers were shut down it could be said that the entire city paid homage to the fallen Capuchin, with the members of the City Council pledged to wear their crepe for thirty days thereafter.[76] An eloquent sermon was preached to the throng by Father Louis Moni, who it was rumored had been designated by Père Antoine as his successor.[77]

Moni had been DuBourg's appointee at the cathedral parish, serving as second in command for many a year. Père Antoine, who had become very appreciative of Moni, doubtless looked upon him as a natural successor, as did the public. The importance for the Church, however, was that Moni was a priest of obvious virtue and his docility to episcopal authority was evident from the beginning of his tenure. When Bishop Rosati reported the death of Sedella to Propaganda on April 3, 1829, he also reported that the *marguilliers* had peacefully transferred the cathedral.[78] For DuBourg the news could only be consoling.

Trusteeism was not scotched in his former see, to be sure. His successor would discover that for himself. As Flaget still viewed the *marguilliers* in 1829, they were the same trustees "who from time immemorial have controlled the revenues of the church according to their own good and unique pleasure, who comported themselves toward Mgr. DuBourg, not as equal, but as very high and very powerful lords with their vassal."[79] Yet violence had been avoided in 1829, and a new spirit could now prevail. As he liked to remind Rosati, "The Lord has his moments." Even trusteeism might some day vanish.

CHAPTER XXXVIII

THE JULY REVOLUTION

The new year of 1830 arrived with frigid foreboding. In Paris the streets were vast glaciers. In Toulouse temperatures plummeted six and a half degrees below zero Celsius. For the first time in over ten years the Garonne River was completely frozen over. Although the Mayor of Bordeaux announced that beginning on January 2 all indigent men over the age of sixteen would be admitted to the ateliers of charity, to receive pay of a franc a day, elsewhere in the Gironde the rigors of the cold led to disorders. A crowd of 600 unfortunates armed with axes began cutting down trees for fuel on the great domains and even the intervention of the gendarmerie could not prevent the disastrous loss of thousands of trees. While the cold brought the worse suffering to the industrial cities of Bordeaux, Lyon, Perigueux and Bayonne, in the mountainous regions it was cruel to the agricultural workers as well. People died along country roads, or while trying to work out of doors.[1]

The bishops of France hastened to mitigate Lenten penances in the face of their flock's sufferings, and DuBourg in Montauban in his circular of February 17 followed suit, saying:

After the disastrous winter which has destroyed the principal foods permitted during days of abstinence and, naturally, has greatly increased the price of others, our solicitude for the urgent general needs leads us to mitigate as much as possible the laws of abstinence during the holy season approaching.[2]

Relaxations of quite another sort were received by the bishops themselves from Martial, comte de Guernon-Ranville, the Minister of Public Instruction in Paris. The ordinances of 1828 regulating primary education had not pleased the hierarchy, and some archbishops like Cheverus in Bordeaux had not hesitated to seek further clarification. On February 9 Guernon-Ranville stated that girls' schools did not fall under Article 21 of the 1828 decrees but continued to come under ecclesiastical supervision. Five days later a royal ordinance urged the communes to act speedily to create additonal primary schools where they were needed and ordered the departments to create model schools for teacher training. The national budget would include appropriations to aid poorer communes. When Guernon-Ranville forwarded the new ordinance to Montauban he commented, "I am confident that you will do all you can to promote the king's wishes. The circumstances which made some bishops hesitate to carry out the Ordinance of April 21, 1828, no longer exist. Let not the clergy themselves surrender the rights which this ordinance gives them."[3]

This new sign of the king's solicitude for Christian education was reassuring to DuBourg, and he decided to go himself to Paris to plead for assistance in repairing his seminary.[4] The Archbishop of Paris, Hyacinthe de Quelen, on March 15 had announced his intention of translating the remains of the body of Saint Vincent de Paul to the new chapel of the Lazarists, or Vincentians, which he had blessed in 1827. On April 6 he invited all the faithful to participate in the ceremonies at Notre Dame and in the ensuing solemn procession between the cathedral and the chapel in rue de Sèvres. With all the reasons DuBourg had to revere the saint and his spiritual sons, who were accomplishing so much in his former American diocese, it was an occasion he yearned to attend. Heralding the ceremonies on April 5, *l'Ami* recalled that in 1817, when the container of the saint's bones was opened, "a bone had been given to M. Dubourg, then Bishop of Louisiana"; the newspaper was soon reporting that the Bishop of Montauban was expected to come "from a great distance to attend a ceremony offering so many attractions to piety."[5] If he could finish up his diocesan duties in time, he meant to reach Paris by April 24 when the public rites were to begin.

There were two things particularly pressing that he must complete by mid-April: his plans for expanding the Society for the Propagation of the Faith in Montauban, and the organization of ecclesiastical conferences and retreats for his clergy. Since DuBourg was not one to leave the press in ignorance of his current projects, the May 19 issue of *l'Ami* could later be discursive on the subject of the first of these, the extension of the Society for the Propagation of the Faith:

> M. Dubourg, the Bishop of Montauban, who had already established the association . . . in his episcopal city, has just extended it throughout his entire diocese. On last April 10 the prelate published a *mandement* in which he made known the importance of this work, recalling the progress of religion in the United States, the foundation of sees, of seminaries, and other establishments which can only consolidate and spread this progress. . . .
>
> The Bishop of Montauban, who was himself a missionary in the New World, . . . announces that he envisions a *commissaire* who will establish the association in every city and town in his diocese. . . . Father Fourgez, the vicar of Saint-Jacques, who established the association in Montauban, is named to do likewise in the rest of the diocese. In his *mandement* the bishop particularly cites the esteem for the association which the bishops of the United States expressed in the Council of Baltimore. . . .[6]

The newspaper account was an accurate summary of Du-Bourg's *mandement,* except for its omission of the text of Flaget's letter adopted by the Provincial Council of Baltimore in 1829. DuBourg told Bruté, "I have followed with rapture the workings of the council; how happy you must be there to hold these saintly meetings!"[7] Only the bishop knew how much pleasure it gave him to publish in Montauban a letter written by Benedict Flaget of Kentucky,[8] his old comrade-in-arms on the American frontier, who like DuBourg had many reasons to appreciate the inestimable aid supplied by the Lyon association and its branches in other French cities.

On the same date as that of his *mandement* on propagating the faith in foreign lands, DuBourg issued a circular which had required a great deal more thought and organization: his outline for the ways by which his priests were to be kept spiritually alive and refreshed throughout the year. He had already secured Nicolas Mac-Carthy for their retreat to begin on August 25.[9] The famous Jesuit had just given a fine series of sermons that January for Cheverus in Bordeaux and DuBourg found it "singularly agreeable to be able to announce" that the celebrated preacher was coming to Montauban. He had already fixed, as well, the dates for the annual examinations of the clergy, which in 1830 would be held on November 9 through 12.

The most detailed part of his circular described the clerical conferences to be held each month from May through October. This *Règlement Pour Les Conférences* shows DuBourg at his best as an administrator. He anticipated every exigency that might arise, every variation which might be preferred; he even recommended frugality in meals and gravity of deportment as they passed to and from their meeting places! It appears that in Montauban ecclesiastical conferences were not to degenerate into clerical galas or Roman feasts in the absence of their bishop. It was this circular of April 10 which informed his flock that he was leaving for Paris in the interest of the diocese and begged their prayers for the success of his undertaking. In his absence the diocese would be administered by his vicars general in whom he had every confidence.[10]

The transferring of the relics of Saint Vincent de Paul was a project particularly dear to the Archbishop of Paris.[11]

The remains of the saint had escaped dispersion during the Revolution when they had been kept safe, first in the church of the Lazarists and later in the main house of the Daughters of Charity. Through the generosity of Charles X, the chapel in honor of Vincent de Paul was now completed and once the relics were inspected, authenticated, and enclosed in a new precious reliquary they were to find a permanent home in rue de Sèvres.

On April 6, 1830, Quelen in the presence of witnesses both ecclesiastical and political had authenticated the relics which had been brought to his episcopal residence. By mutual agreement between the archbisop and the superior of the Lazarists some bones were withheld to be given to the churches and chapels most intimately connected with the saint's life.[12] The rest of the relics were then placed on April 23 in the new *châsse,* or reliquary, which was sealed in the presence of most of the witnesses present at the authentication.

The actual ceremonies of the translation began at noon on Saturday, April 24, when the reliquary was carried in cortege from the archiepiscopal palace to Notre Dame Cathedral. After Vespers that evening Vicar General Jacques-Marie-Adrien Mathieu delivered a panegyric. (Neither Mathieu who preached that Saturday nor DuBourg who took part in all the ceremonies of Sunday could foresee that each in his turn would become Archbishop of Besançon within so few years.) April 24, as *l'Ami* took pains to point out, was the saint's birthday.[13]

The next day, the second Sunday after Easter, a pontifical Mass was celebrated at ten o'clock in the cathedral by the Archbishop of Genoa, Luigi Lambruschini, then Apostolic Delegate to France, in the presence of a huge throng of civil and religious dignitaries. At two that afternoon the magnificent procession began, crossing the parvis of Notre Dame and Petit-Pont, moving along the quays of Saint-Michel, the Augustins, and Monnaie, up the street of Saints-Pères, past the crossroads of Croix-Rouge, and arriving at last at the entrance to the new chapel in rue de Sèvres where Archbishop Quelen addressed the Superior-General of the Lazarists and received his response. Entering the chapel the crowd offered prayers in honor of the saint and in favor of the king—who as a souvenir of the translation had given metal for 30,000 medals showing the Blessed Virgin on one side and Saint Vincent on the other; they prayed for his family and all the citizens of Paris. The day ended with a pontifical benediction. From Paris DuBourg described the event for his "Little Brother" of Mount St. Mary's in Emmitsburg:

> We had here a gathering of 18 bishops for the solemn translation of the body of saint Vincent de Paul. . . . The saint clothed, couched in a magnificent silver *châsse,* surrounded by more than 500 Sisters of Charity, priests of his congregation, accompanied by a cortege of bishops, a huge body of the clergy, principal authorities, protected by a numerous guard, crossed Paris through a population of 300 thousand souls in the midst of the universal blessings of the Sunday of the Good Shepherd. May this beautiful triumph of faith and charity draw down his protection upon this capital and upon this flourishing kingdom, where everything indicates a great decline in faith. *Je porte Paris sur mes épaules.*[14]

Afterward many commented on the remarkable peacefulness, the lack of violence, which prevailed during the translation and the novena which followed—when crowds jammed the Vincentian chapel from four o'clock in the morning to nine at night. When the king himself came with the dauphine and duchess of Berry at five o'clock one afternoon, the royal family received the acclamations of the faithful who were there. But the *mandement* Quelen issued at the close of the novena ended on a note of uneasiness when he expressed the hope that a "solid and lasting peace" would be reaffirmed under Charles X, a peace which "true Frenchmen" would never allow to be altered.

The truth was that even as unpolitical a prelate as DuBourg could sense the undercurrent of unrest, which less than three months later erupted in the July Revolution. While he enjoyed preaching in Paris, as he did on Monday,

May 3, at the church of the Foreign Missions honoring the eighth anniversary of the Association [Society] for the Propagation of the Faith, and again on Tuesday, May 4, at St. Roch during the octave of the Finding of the Holy Cross,[15] the plans he had come to Paris to forward were inopportune and received scant attention amid the government's anxiety over the elections coming in June and the outbreak of war in Africa.

Having missed the duchess of Berry in Montauban, he did take advantage of his stay in Paris to present a second letter from Rosati, but was compelled to tell Rosati on May 19:

> Madame received me with perfect courtesy, and spoke to me of you and your work with great interest. I asked her to take the Mission of St. Louis under her august protection, reminding her that her aunt the Duchess of Orleans had done so for Kentucky. She smiled at this proposal, observing that the Mission of St. Louis was much larger; and being asked the nature of the aid to send, whether money or useful objects, I replied that money was preferable, and that Madame could send a succession of donations according to her convenience. "Good," she told me, "I will send you something from time to time." At this I observed that it would be better to give to M. le Supr. Général de St. Lazare what seemed to him most appropriate.

DuBourg felt sure the duchess would soon send something and urged Rosati to write to her, thanking her for accepting the title Protectress of the St. Louis Mission, and then giving an account every now and then of what seemed most suited to engaging her benevolence. "She is an excellent Princess," he assured Rosati, "full of soul and spirit, and gifted with an affability which should put you entirely at your ease."[16] Aside from this rather nebulous promise of support for Missouri, the Bishop of Montauban had achieved very little, from his point of view.

While DuBourg remained in Paris, the king from Saint-Cloud addressed his bishops with the words:

> At the moment that the French flag goes to punish the insult of a barbarian power we like to recall to you the pious

examples of the Kings our Ancestors, who always placed their military undertakings under Divine protections. . . . Our intention is, therefore, that you ordain public prayers in all the churches of your diocese to ask that the God of armies always may protect the banner of the lilies, that He give the victory which already seems promised by the justice of our cause and the valor of our soldiers.[17]

DuBourg's vicars general Turcq and Pouget speedily relayed the king's request to the clergy of Montauban with orders that every priest of the diocese was to include in the Mass of the next three Sundays the collect, secret, and post-communion prayers in the missal *pro tempore belli*. In the see city prayers for the success of the king's armies would also be recited for nine days at Vespers.[18]

Whether it was the justice of the cause, the valor of the soldiers, or the fervor of the prayers, the French expedition to Algeria speedily succeeded, and on July 10 Charles X again addressed his prelates from Saint-Cloud saying, "Heaven has blessed our armies; justice, religion, and humanity have triumphed. Algiers has fallen. . . . The first need of our heart is to carry to the foot of the holy altars, amid acclamations of public joy, the solemn expression of our gratitude."[19] Montauban hastened on July 13 to make the monarch's wishes known.[20]

While the African war was going well, the political situation at home was rapidly deteriorating. In May the king had dissolved a hostile legislature and called for new elections to be held on June 23 and July 3. The French clergy were expected to support the throne and were told so. As the outcome of the elections grew more doubtful, Charles X himself actively intervened by a proclamation of June 14 exhorting the voters to hurry to their voting places. "May you all rally around the same flag!" he said. "It is your King who asks you to do this; it is your father who calls upon you. Do your duty and I will do mine."[21] The next day Guernon-Ranville forwarded this proclamation to the hierarchy with a pointed rebuke:

I thought that by the organ of the cooperators of your zeal the august words from the throne would be understood sooner and with more effect among the faithful population of our countryside. I pray you therefore, Monseigneur, to transmit *immediately* a copy of the royal proclamation to each pastor and *desservant* of your diocese, giving them an instruction needed to make understood by all his subjects the noble language of our beloved monarch.[22]

Bishops were expected to be at their posts, and loyal ones sent out pastoral letters recommending the government's candidates.[23]

In spite of all the pressure exerted prior to the election days, the results showed a "sweeping and unequivocal defeat" not only for the ministry but for the king himself.[24] On July 6 the defeated ministers proposed to dissolve the legislature just elected, secure another one by a new electoral system, and suspend freedom of the press. The denouement was rapid and categorical. The ordinances of July 25 were merely the last straw. On Tuesday, July 27, the gendarmerie charged into the crowds around the Palais-Royal and the first insurgent was killed, but only two barricades were raised there. On Wednesday the "Three Glorious Days" of street fighting in Paris really began to take shape at dawn and by 8:00 A.M. a message to the king announced, "This is no longer a riot, it is a revolution." By Thursday 6,000 barricades had appeared, and the evening papers were rejoicing at the victory of the people, while mail coaches flying the tricolor set out for the provinces. On July 30, sixty deputies assembled at noon in the Palais-Bourbon and after a long discussion decided to invite the duke of Orleans to come to Paris to act as lieutenant-general of the realm. On July 31 the Parisians accepted the duke of Orleans as their new monarch believing, as Lafayette put it, "What the people need today is a popular throne, surrounded by republican institutions." Three days later the duke of Orleans announced to the national legislature the abdication of Charles X and his own acceptance of the Crown. Thus it was that the restored Bourbon dynasty came to an end in the summer of 1830.[25]

The accession of the duke of Orleans to the French throne as Louis-Philippe, the "Citizen King" of the French people, meant for the French bishops the end of an era. As one historian phrased it, "In the July days, the Church seemed to have been defeated *au même titre* as the old dynasty, irreligion equally victorious as liberalism."[26] The cruel times of the Revolution of the 1790s seemed to have returned. To arouse the people's anger, the same old accusations were dug up again—caches of arms in episcopal palaces, in seminaries and religious houses, the clergy guilty of plotting Saint Bartholomew Massacres against the heroes of the July Days.[27]

Everywhere it was a time of confusion and uncertainty for the clergy; some were in very real danger. Archbishop de Quelen had to go into hiding and other prelates like Rohan-Chabot of Besançon, Forbin-Janson of Nancy, Tharin of Strasbourg, and Latil of Reims went into exile.[28] The destruction of property, especially in the capital, was horrifying:

> At the same time that the people of Paris seized the Tuileries they devastated a first time the archiepiscopal palace, profaned the sacristies of Notre Dame with a thousand gross sacrileges, sacked the house of the Missionaries in rue d'Enfer and that of the Jesuits at Montrouge, and destroyed the Calvaire of Mont Valérien.[29]

News of the vicious vandalism at Mont Valérien was particularly painful to DuBourg. He had preached the Stations of the Cross there in the spring of 1817 when his episcopal career had scarcely begun and his dreams of the future had been irrepressible. Now in the late summer of 1830, who dared predict what the future held for the Church? In Toulouse, to which archdiocese DuBourg was suffragan, there were impieties almost as devastating as those in Paris. Since the new king tolerated these excesses, he seemed to approve them. Certainly, in the first months of his reign the conviction took root that the July Monarchy was "systematically hostile" to Catholicism.[30]

Although Montauban was remote from Paris and the lesser centers of anticlerical violence, DuBourg could not escape the immediate effects of the revolution. As the historian of *L'église de Montauban* explains:

He was never free from cares of all sorts. It was a time when difficulties with the civil power became more and more aggravated. Now it was a question whether to suppress, or ordain, or modify prayers for the king and country, processions on Corpus Christi and the Assumption; in some cases the clergy might reach a compromise with the civil authorities, in others the laws had to be obeyed in all their rigors; in still others the intent could be ignored in spite of orders from Paris or their bishop.[31]

The most immediate question facing DuBourg as a bishop was that of his obligations to a government that had not yet been officially recognized by the Holy See. Especially perplexing and urgent was the uncertainty over the oath of allegiance to the new king and constitution, the insertion of the name Louis-Philippe in the liturgy at the *Domine salvum fac regem,* and the replacing of the Bourbon banners, which flew over episcopal palaces with the tricolor flags of the July Revolution.

In August several of the hierarchy wrote individually to Rome expressing their uncertainty over these matters.[32] Archbishop de Quelen was particularly concerned about the oath since he was still a Peer of France as well as metropolitan of the capital. Quelen relayed his reply, which he received only in mid-November, to the other bishops with the words, "The delay probably renders it useless to many persons."[33]

One can only guess when DuBourg learned officially that Pope Pius VIII had found little difficulty: in recognizing Louis-Philippe as worthy of the title "Most Christian King" (one formerly reserved to the Bourbons), in finding the oath of allegiance nothing new (being the same as that used in 1817 for Louis XVIII), and in authorizing the inclusion of *regem nostrum Ludovicum Philippum* in the *Domine salvum fac regem.*[34] There is, however, ample evidence that in the first weeks after the "Three Glorious Days" bishops who wished to lead their flocks in loyal submission to both Church and State remained in most uncomfortable confusion. In the interim prior to the reception of either the papal briefs or governmental decrees, local civil authorities rushed ahead demanding immediate compliance with oath-taking, praying for the king by name, and lowering the flag of the lilies. In Marseilles a member of the bishop's staff inquired querulously of the mayor, "What was the reason behind this eagerness to anticipate the desires of the government, as well as the recognition of that government by our Holy Father the Pope?"[35]

DuBourg in Montauban on August 19 issued a circular ordering the clergy in his diocese to delay inserting the name of Louis-Philippe in their public prayers until the royal government demanded it.[36] This action did him no harm in Paris, apparently, because his request for a canonicate for one of his priests was processed without delay.[37] After Achille-Victor, duc de Broglie, the new Minister of Cults, notified the bishops on October 12 of the government's directives in regard to public prayer and flying the tricolor, DuBourg quickly complied, prescribing the insertion of the king's name in the liturgy and the blessing of new flags.[38] But he still had lingering compunctions.

Although he had consulted his clergy before issuing the circular of October 18, he suspected there were hard-core legitimists among the older men who would not gracefully comply with the order to substitute the name Louis-Philippe for Charles. When this resentment surfaced in a protest meeting he formally notified the clergy of Montauban on October 30 that "the bishop who gave them his orders, under pain of canon law, that they conform to the Ministry's decisions, engages them not to address a petition to him on the subject, particularly since they had been consulted on the resolutions taken."[39] While the eventual news of the pope's decisions in these matters eased his own mind, he was beginning to realize that in some quarters of his diocese there were those who did not intend to be reconciled to either the king's name or his person.[40]

These political technicalities of adjusting to the revolution—which may seem picayune to the twentieth-century mind—required prudence and patience, qualities which DuBourg had schooled himself to improve over the years. But it was quite another matter where encroachments threatened things of religion involving traditional practices or deep convictions. In many places crosses were publicly, it almost appeared officially, knocked down. To save the cross on the top of his church's spire, one pastor in a village near Paris confronted a rabble armed with ladders and hammers, sternly demanding,

"What are you doing? You wish to pull down this cross? I know others much easier to remove with which you ought to start."

"Where are they?" yelled the mob.

"Follow me," the priest ordered. And leading them to the cemetery of the parish he pointed to the crosses on the graves of their relatives and friends.

The effect was remarkable. The unhappy villagers slunk off with lowered heads in silence.[41]

For DuBourg, the safety of public crosses, especially his mission cross erected with such ceremony and pride only two years earlier, demanded something more than patience or guile. At the very first rumor that orders had been given to remove outdoor crosses, DuBourg approached the prefect of the Department of Tarn-et-Garonne requesting the truth. DuBourg was a formidable figure when aroused and the prefect lost no time in getting an answer for him:

> Monseigneur, I hasten to inform you that I have received from the Minister a letter in which he formally denies the removal of mission crosses. The government enjoins me to calm all uneasy spirits in this regard by guaranteeing them in his name tolerance and protection, and by assuring them that nothing shall disturb the confidence and security of the inhabitants of this department. May I hope, Monseigneur, that you will cooperate with me in giving this declaration the greatest publicity? It will succeed in reassuring the people and contribute to the maintenance of peace.[42]

DuBourg had this letter read in every church in the diocese and published in journals which were eventually copied in the Paris press.

It was not the end of the affair, nevertheless. The mayor of the city, caught between the sympathies of the rival political factions, subsequently tried to persuade DuBourg privately to take the mission cross inside the cathedral. In no time the public got wind of the mayor's request and there was a fierce outcry. On February 26, 1831, the bishop addressed the mayor formally:

> I had promised you secrecy on the object of the visit with which you honored me yesterday, and on my part it has been scrupulously guarded, even in regard to my council, until, informed of the publicity given your actions, and the anxiety they cause this population, I am freed from my promise and am forced to manifest my sentiments, which ought never to be problematical for anyone.

The cross was the property of the *Montalbanais* who had paid for it, property guaranteed by law, and, since the change in government, by "august promises and reassuring words" on the part of the new regime. Why should a feeble minority dictate to an entire population? This was not freedom of religion or respect for public opinion. He would never consent to such an "arbitrary" displacement. Even if the mayor produced a petition requesting it, the Bishop of Montauban would never be a witness to such an act of impiety. "That act," he said with finality, "will signal my resignation."[43]

Other men might use what methods they chose in handling the mission cross matter. In Bordeaux Cheverus directed his clergy, "In parishes where it is deemed necessary to remove mission crosses the pastors will let the civil authorities act, as we did in Bordeaux, to use their influence to prevent this action from becoming an occasion for trouble."[44] Outside his cathedral the gigantic cross in Place Pey-Berland was removed[45] but in Montauban the mission cross was still standing in the Place d'Armes when DuBourg left to become Archbishop of Besançon, and it still stands there today.[46]

It is doubtful that DuBourg took much delight in this first minor triumph over the forces of irreligion, for his private life was falling at his feet in ruins as 1830 came to a close. Early that year Filleau, who handled the family's financial affairs, had written optimistically from Paris, "I hope to have a happy ending in two or three months."[47] That had been in February. On July 9 things still looked hopeful, when Filleau notified Louis DuBourg that he had received a total of 838,342 francs for Louis and his brother the bishop. Debts and costs would have to be deducted, of course, but while waiting, Filleau said, "I am ready to forward some funds if you desire it."[48] With a brief note of his own, the bishop sent this letter on to Louis who happened to be in Bordeaux at the time. Before the month was out Filleau was all gloom again. Louis, who was back in Montauban, learned that his version of one of the important claims against the government was now being seriously disputed by other parties to these claims. Everything was once again up in air. DuBourg de Sainte-Colombe of New Orleans could no longer be consulted, for the father of so many daughters had died on January 29.[49] His heirs, nevertheless, must be considered and counterclaims must be prepared.[50]

For Louis, it meant a return to Bordeaux, where so many of the controversial depositions originated. He was seventy-eight years old and it was beginning to appear that while he was in Bordeaux he would have to undergo surgery. Filleau wrote reassuringly that "the progress in that art" had removed all danger;[51] but the operation was not a success and Louis DuBourg, the head of the DuBourgs of Rochemont, died in rue de l'Eglise Saint-Seurin not long afterward under the ministrations of a distant relative to whom the bishop wrote on November 15:

> The tender cares you lavished, Mademoiselle, on our dear Louis, in the last days of his existence are not one of the least consolations I find in this dolorous loss. They contributed no little to easing him toward this separation. . . . He has bequeathed to us all splendid examples. May he obtain for us the grace of following him and being reunited with him in the bosom of God!
>
> P. S. Please add to all your other kindnesses that of informing the family in Jamaica of the loss we have just suffered. I have instructed the family in New Orleans.[52]

It was the formal letter of a bereaved brother to a family connection he scarcely knew. It revealed nothing of the force of such a blow striking at such a time. He and Louis had lived together in adult life longer than most brothers are privileged to do. It had been Louis who had eased his first days in Baltimore as an *émigré* in the 1790s. It was Louis who had acted as *économe* of his college in those days when both Victoire and Louis lived on St. Mary's grounds. Since 1826 Louis had shared his episcopal palace in Montauban. Added to the cruel loss of an accustomed companion was the appalling realization that now all the responsibility for assisting Filleau in his efforts to salvage something of the family's remaining rights to financial restitution rested on the bishop's shoulders. And this at the very moment when a new monarch, a new constitution, and a new situation for the Church made every aspect of his life uncertain.

God knew Filleau would do the best he could. He had received the news of Louis's death in bewilderment, writing on November 27, "I learned with most painful surprise by your letter of the 17th that you had lost your brother. I believed that he had undergone the operation without danger."[53] He then went on to outline the state of their affairs at the moment. He had paid Louis's personal debts, and explained that if and when the family Dominican estate was completely settled the share due Louis's estate would be more than double the bishop's share because Louis had inherited all or part of the shares of his two sisters Marie and Victoire at their deaths. The rest would go to the heirs of Pierre-François in Louisiana and to the three children of Joseph-Patrice. The remainder of Filleau's letter, describing the continuing appeals which still had to be made, was discouraging, and the bishop wondered morosely if any of his father's children would live to benefit from the DuBourg patrimony.

Sorrow did not dilute his concern for his old Louisiana diocese. On October 27, 1830, he told Rosati that four good priests were going to reinforce Leo De Neckere, the Bishop of New Orleans. To these were joined four Jesuits for Flaget's college at Bardstown "to make him tranquil about the future of his beautiful establishments. . . ." He consoled Rosati, "I am busy forming another company for Père Van Quickenborne, with whom I believe he & you will have cause to be content. You can talk to him about it." As for his own diocese he said guardedly:

> I will say nothing to you of the last events in France, for which it is truly difficult to predict the outcome. We are however here, and everywhere in general, except in Paris, rather tranquil. The new government seems to want to control Religion, for which it will need to consolidate itself, I believe. God protect us, as well as it, against the blows of anarchy![54]

DuBourg had been gone from Lower Louisiana more than four years, yet he still was thinking of the right man for the jobs as he recalled them. He told Rosati that one of the priests going for New Orleans would make a good replacement for Benedict Richard and devote himself to Madame Duchesne. The others for Lower Louisiana would make good preachers in the cathedral or in other parishes.[55] When he sent Rosati a man recommended by a "respectable lady of Lille" in November he assured the Bishop of St. Louis that M. de Bruyn would make an excellent addition to the Congregation of the Mission.[56]

On the heels of the bad news in Filleau's letter came the news that Pope Pius VIII had died at nine o'clock the night of November 30 of "a malady of the chest." The pontiff's death came at a time when French influence in Rome was most precarious. The conclave to elect a new pontiff opened on December 14 with only one of the four French cardinals actually present in his diocese and in a position to relay whatever instructions the government of the Citizen King might decide upon.[57] Something of Du-Bourg's temporary frame of mind may be deduced from his *mandement* on the occasion of the death of Pius VIII. Whereas the death of Leo XII in 1829 and the election of his successor had evoked from his facile pen three separate documents brimming over with DuBourg's devotion to the papacy and his confidence in its future, the *mandement* he issued on December 17, 1830, ran less than two perfunctory pages, half of whose space was shared with rules for celebrating the election of Pius's successor. Perhaps the most heartfelt words were those he could have meant for his brother, as well: "We cry, but we do not let ourselves be prostrated by grief. For him, no one doubts that death was a gain. Engaged from his youth in the combats of the Faith, it was time he exchanged a diadem of dolors for the crown of justice."[58]

The conclave which opened that December did not succeed in electing a pope until February 2, 1831, when Mauro Capellari emerged as Gregory XVI; his coronation took place four days later. It was even later before the clergy of France received official notification. New brooms in Paris, it seemed, were not sweeping as clean as they ought. On February 18, 1831, the Minister of Cults felt compelled to notify the Minister of Foreign Affairs that although the news of the election of the new pope had already appeared in the public press, the archbishops and bishops of France had not been formally notified. It was *customary* to give them this official notification. The Minister of Cults would be obliged if he could be given an official communication in that regard to pass on to the hierarchy.[59]

Eventually, of course, the bishops were informed; but by then the sins of commission of the new regime had begun to overshadow those of omission and, as the following chapter will suggest, local events in France took precedence over those in Rome. As for the year just past, in retrospect it seemed as though the only thing of any lasting value to have come out of the Diocese of Montauban in 1830 might prove to be the *Concordance of the Four Gospels* which the bishop had forwarded to his fellow prelates for their approval on his return from Paris in early summer.[60]

As another year began, the Bishop of Montauban wrote to Edmond Saulnier in St. Louis:

You have had, by this time, the news of the events of July; and certainly they could not have surprised you more than us, who were scarcely expecting them. What surprises me further is to be still tranquil at my post. How long will it last? It is difficult to say; but what we well know is that *Capillus de capite nostro non peribit sine patre nostro.*

It was even possible that the clergy might be once again forced to flee from France. He ended his letter with the speculation, "Am I destined to terminate my career among those who remember me in St. Louis? That would certainly be for me a very sweet consolation, God knows; for my heart is always fixed on the first theatre of my episcopal care."[61]

CHAPTER XXXIX

CHANGING TIMES

The complexities first perceived in the issue of the mission crosses multiplied as the months passed. In Paris, when anniversary services were held for the late duke of Berry in the presence of Bourbon sympathizers, the outcome was reminiscent of the storming of the Bastille in 1789. On February 14 rioters sacked the rectory of Saint-Germain l'Auxerrois and knocked down the great cross in front of the church, while the intervention of the National Guard served only to postpone until the next day the invasion of the church itself, where the mob profaned everything they could get their hands on. The only thing saving the building was that the crowd preferred to vent the brunt of its wrath on Archbishop de Quelen and his quarters. After wrecking the archiepiscopal palace in Paris they rushed to his country house in Conflans and destroyed that, even sinking so low as to defile the tomb of Quelen's aunt.[1] As news of the days of February 14 and 15 spread throughout France, so did the pillaging of other churches. In many a diocese the pastors, terrified and disheartened, would have fled their parishes if their bishops had been less courageous in dissuading them.[2]

The press had a large part in exacerbating the impact of these events, using any pretext to whip up irrational suspicions and outright hatred of the clergy. Brochures and caricatures abounded in calumnies. The theatre was equally guilty. "Each one had to add to its store of costumes and accessories a complete assortment of cardinal's robes, surplices, cassocks, crosses and church banners" in order to satirize and degrade the clergy. Saints, angels, virtues, and beliefs were all held up to ridicule as leading actors lent their talents to hideous detractions. "Nothing was more rare than a man of the world acknowledging himself to be a Christian."[3] Bishops had to steer a perilous course between valorous acts which might only serve to inflame passions the more and those humiliating compliances which might appear to surrender the Church's claims even though preserving public order.

For DuBourg it meant dealing with each challenge as it appeared, as a separate issue. He was not a Jean Cheverus, who gently bent with the winds of change, striving always for the role of peacemaker in Bordeaux. Nor was he a Bishop Charles-Joseph-Eugene de Mazenod, who belligerently delayed as long as he could complying with directives from Paris, and within his diocese continually bickered with the Mayor of Marseilles and the Prefect of Bouches de Rhône.[4] In his early days on the American frontier, DuBourg had seldom been restrained by consistency, that "hobgoblin of little minds."[5] With a rapidity which startled, if not dismayed, his contemporaries he could change his mind over his nominees for coadjutors, the locations of religious houses, the nature of Jesuit Indian missions, or a score of lesser matters. Now in his mid-sixties that impulsiveness was tempered by experience. The caution with which he reached decisions in the years following the fall of Charles X displayed acuity in distinguishing between major and minor issues, a perspicacity accompanied by an unwavering resolve to protect his flock at all costs.

On February 28, 1832, the Minister of Public Instruction and Cults issued to the prefects of France a directive which read:

The *fleur de lys* could recall to Frenchmen memories which would stir up agitation of spirit. The government must order that they disappear from all places and monuments where they are publicly shown. I invite you to cooperate with the ecclesiastical authorities in your department to have removed all *fleurs de lys* from monuments and objects sacred to religion.[6]

When DuBourg was notified of this directive, without hesitating he issued a circular to his clergy ordering them to act in concert with the local authorities in their areas to remove from religious monuments "without trouble or degradation" these symbols of the former dynasty.[7] The things of religion did not belong to the Bourbons and would doubtless survive the Orleanist monarchy as well.

Public processions presented a more perplexing question. As the feast of Corpus Christi neared, confidential reports coming to his palace led DuBourg to fear troubles on the occasion of the general procession which customarily left the cathedral and wound up and down the major streets of Montauban before returning the Blessed Sacrament to the sanctuary. He confided his apprehensions to the prefect, saying that he was resolved to keep the procession within the church unless the authorities could assure him of "efficacious protection."[8]

The prefect replied complacently that the bishop's fears were unfounded.

M. le Maréchal de Camp, who commanded the department's military, had ordered 100 men—more to lend éclat to the procession than to protect it, since protection was unnecessary; the most perfect calm reigned among all classes of the population, and no one would be imprudent enough to disturb it. Furthermore, all measures necessary to order had been taken by the civil and military authorities.

DuBourg was not convinced by these lofty reassurances. There was more beneath the surface of his see city than the prefect perceived. But he did not wish to offend the civil authorities or disappoint his flock who loved processions, and quelling his uneasiness he issued on May 30, 1831, a circular ordaining the celebrations of Corpus Christi throughout the diocese "as in the past."[9] He took in advance, however, all the precautions he could to prevent the least incident. On the eve of the Sunday procession, he advised all pastors to admit to the procession only those women who were dressed in blue or black, without colored sashes, with white veils on their heads. The semblance of a uniform should lend the dignity which commands respect.

Corpus Christi fell on June 2 that year and the procession took place the following Sunday. The events which ensued occupied *l'Ami*'s attention in two succeeding issues, the first of which reported sketchily:

> In Montauban some people chose to see in the procession some signs of royalism; they were dragged away, but calm was not restored. The noise of a firecracker threw terror into the women in the procession; they fled, and the procession changed its course and reentered the cathedral after having passed only a few streets. The people were angry with the national guard whom they accused of not respecting the procession. The tumult lasted well into the night. We will return to the circumstances of this event which has led to a judicial inquiry.[10]

A few days later *l'Ami* returned to the Montauban disorders, this time citing "several journals of the Midi" as its sources:

> At the moment that the procession passed in front of a café called Mille Colonnes a man seized the white banner which preceded a group of young girls and destroyed it while other fanatics screaming ugly insults struck the children who were singing hymns. The Catholics would not stand for this scandal and forced the troublemakers back into their den where even then one of them provoked the national guard to fire. Then they deprived the guard of their sabers and guns and the procession returned to the cathedral.[11]

DuBourg was furious. He said during the formal inquiry into the affair, "The authorities could not have been unaware—if their police were at all informed—that along the route there were one or two cafés where troublemakers habitually congregated. These points were left without any protection while troops were stationed in places remote from the actual line of march!" Small wonder things had gotten needlessly out of hand. Two or three thoughtless people came out of a café and threw panic into a choir of young girls. Their first cries of fright spread like wildfire, and in seconds women, small children, and clergy gave way to panic and this frightful confusion spread to the end of the procession three blocks away.

DuBourg, who was carrying the Blessed Sacrament at the end of the line, had no idea of the cause of the tumult and, fearing some horrible profanation of the Sacrament, entered a nearby house until the gendarmerie arrived to announce that it was safe to return it to the cathedral. In his deposition of the whole affair he reported that there was general indignation, with the air filled with cries of "Long live Religion! Let us die for our Faith!" People were sure that the authorities had connived with the enemies of religion to ruin their demonstration. If one wished to have the bishop's opinion, "The magistrates perhaps at this moment," he said coolly, "owe their safety to the unbelievable efforts I had to make to calm the public resentment." Certainly if he had followed his first impulse the general procession would never have left the church![12]

As for the processions usually held during the octave of Corpus Christi, he preferred not to exasperate his flock by suppressing them, but he refused to accept responsibility for new outbreaks. "Do what you wish in that regard," he told the prefect, "at your peril, at your own risk. Your orders will be obeyed." But he advised the department head to surround himself with people who could give him sounder advice, in order to know the inhabitants of the region better. There were times, DuBourg said quite candidly, when the prefect would do well even to resist orders from above if his own sources indicated public processions were imprudent. When on June 10 the prefect reported that the government still wished things done as in the past, DuBourg retorted, "You cannot doubt that is also my desire." But the next day he issued a pastoral letter to the faithful of Montauban which demonstrated the way he thought skillful administrators should handle these matters:

After the deplorable scenes which afflicted this peaceable city last Sunday, on the occasion of the general procession of the most holy Sacrament, the first thought to strike your pastors, as well as your magistrates, my very dear brothers, was that prudence dictates that, for this year, the particular processions of the octave should be suspended. Nevertheless, the religious fervor of your hearts soon changed our ideas.[13]

In collaboration with the prefect and the commanding general of Tarn-et-Garonne, plans had been agreed upon to "reconcile public tranquillity with this external manifestation" of piety. Only the opinion of the ministry had been lacking, and this arrived to support the earlier decision of the prefect. With all the effect his skillful pen could achieve, DuBourg continued, "It must be consoling for you, my very dear brothers, as it has been for ourselves, to see the government and the first authorities of this department equally assiduous in calming your apprehensions about the freedom of your religion." If his flock knew all the measures the prefect and commandant had taken to insure "the tranquillity and splendor of these holy solemnities" they would share their bishop's lively gratitude.

Then he got to the point:

But events of the last three days, events entirely beyond their control, in adding new misfortunes and profound afflictions to our commune, have determined me, in spite of my keen regrets, to return to my former position and, in opposition to your wishes, *to suspend for this year the emergence of the processions.* You know me well enough to be perfectly convinced that nothing less than the interests of religion and yourselves would move me to such a resolution.

He urged them to remain calm, to submit to the law, to refuse to engage in any act which might disturb the public order. "Don't give by the slightest imprudence," he begged, "an opportunity for an attack on your faith." God would be more honored in this way than by all the pomps of religion, by all the most striking demonstrations of their attachment; thus would they fulfill the wishes of their bishop and justify his confidence in their "docility and wisdom."

One by one, it seemed, the old and beloved customs were destined to disappear. The Feu de Saint Jean by which Frenchmen on the eve of June 23 had once ushered in the summer season was now replaced by the simple blessing of crosses above the doors of their homes. The procession on the feast of Saint Lazare so popular in Marseilles was discontinued in 1831; that in honor of Saint John vanished two years later. Even the very heart of a French Christmas, the midnight Mass, in general disappeared except in the chapels of religious communities where the laity did not ordinarily participate. The first December after the July Revolution DuBourg had decreed that in Montauban midnight Masses would be held, but only in parish churches.[14] In Bordeaux, however, when the mayor offered to take police measures if Cheverus wished to revive the custom, the archbishop refused, saying he would offer his Mass at five o'clock in the morning since there was little fear of danger from opening churches at that hour.[15]

It was like rubbing salt in open wounds when the government in Paris requested that special prayers be offered for the soldiers fallen during the July days of 1830. Quelen in Paris was particularly bitter and passed on the request to his clergy with the minimal words, "The king claims in their favor the commendations the Church accords all Christians who die in her bosom."[16] It was one thing to bear the destruction of his episcopal properties; it was quite another to be expected to honor with special distinction the men who had ushered in a government that permitted these atrocities. DuBourg's own circular on the subject no longer remains; its title merely reads: "Prescribing prayers for the 27th, for the intentions of the soldiers dead in Paris in the days of the 27th, 28th, and 29th of July, 1830."[17]

Privately, DuBourg told Rosati, "Here we are still sitting on a volcano, whose smoke thickens more and more. Pray to God for France: she is running on all fours toward anarchy. They say from chaos comes order, but many of those who see it are not destined to survive it and will certainly perish in travail."[18] Five days later DuBourg determined to go to Paris "for several important reasons, of which the principal one was to see at close range the state of our affairs and to follow the operations of the chambers." From Versailles at the end of July he reported to the Bishop of St. Louis:

> Our future is extremely obscure. The proximity more or less great of a crisis, which almost everyone regards as inevitable, depends upon the struggle the parties are going to engage in. I count on spending in this neighborhood a couple of months which I am trying to put to the profit of my Diocese's interest.[19]

The real jolt came on July 30 when the Minister of Cults issued a circular putting an end to the processions of August 15 which had taken place every year all over France on the feast of the Assumption of the Blessed Virgin for the accomplishment of the vow of Louis XIII. Parishioners were to be notified that they could have neither the procession nor the special prayers for the vow of Louis XIII.[20] The banning of processions that year might have been justified on the ground of preventing public disorder, but prohibiting references to a king who had dedicated the nation to the Virgin was surely mere vindictiveness against anything smacking of the fallen dynasty. The Bishop of Marseilles who refused to comply had cause to regret it.[21] He said afterward, "We had reason to hope that our rights as Catholics would be respected, that a cortege uniquely religious could advance peacefully in the streets of a city known for its Catholicism."[22] DuBourg, who had had his fill of street brawls, left it up to his vicars general to word the circular suppressing "by order" the procession of August 15, 1831.[23] By the time the next year rolled around passions had cooled considerably, and his circular of August 4, 1832, could safely grant permission for the procession of August 15, provided no public allusions were made to the vow of Louis XIII.[24] His eyes may have glinted as he wrote the restrictive clause. In his cathedral, where Ingres' masterpiece had hung since DuBourg's arrival, no one needed any reminder that a former king had once made a vow to the Mother of God who was the patroness of the nation.

To tell the truth, authorities on all sides—civil, military, and ecclesiastical—were coming to perceive that the hasty judgments reached in 1830 were too jejeune. To be sure, the old order had been swept away, in that Catholicism was no longer the official religion of the monarchy, and under the new constitution was merely recognized as the religion of the majority. The name of God disappeared from official discourses and the Chamber of Deputies was blatantly hostile to a Church which had been hand-in-glove with the deposed dynasty. Nevertheless, the surge of anti-clericalism which accompanied the accession of Louis-Philippe was secretly deplored by him. He did not take part in any overt act of aggression or persecution against religion. "If through weakness [the new monarchy] too often left the field free, or even bowed to impious passions, at least it was nothing like a later regime when the civil power gave the signal for a war against God."[25] The "King of the Barricades" was a realist. Knowing he was too weak to do otherwise, for the time being he would have to wait until he was in a position to initiate a religious policy more to his liking.[26]

Meanwhile in the Ministry of Public Instruction and Cults, men like the duke of Broglie and François Guizot tried to prevent the worst anticlerical excesses. Broglie by his prudent moderation averted several conflicts which could have proved both embarrassing and dangerous to the new government. When Guizot replied to Montauban's query about mission crosses he told the prefect, "Freedom of religion must be total, and the first condition is that no cult be insulted. We must not furnish our enemies any pretext for taxing us with indecency or tyranny. I will not suffer my administration to give room for such a reproach."[27]

Just as the notion of a government systematically hostile to Catholicism was an exaggeration so was the notion of Catholicism as the prime enemy of both the Orleanist regime and the French nation. While some prelates like the Archbishop of Paris and the Bishop of Le Mans found it difficult to bow, others like DuBourg and Cheverus became in the government's eyes valued supports.[28] The unitary nature of the nation's government made collaboration of prefect and prelate as essential, and in most cases as natural, as it had been under the Restoration. Together with the military commander of the local forces, these men constituted the authority of the department. The success and ultimate contentment of each benefited from a minimum of friction.

It pleased the new regime's liberals to regard the former Restoration prefects as senile country squires nostalgic for the abuses of the Old Regime. In fact they had been in large part former officers, magistrates, diplomats, with even a former priest on occasion. The career of prefect, informal in nature as it tended to be, had not suffered from this kind of experience. "With political patronage all-important, technical qualifications were inessential."[29] While the prefects after 1830 in some respects tended to be a new breed, the Orleanist government was mainly concerned to place in senior positions men it could trust, while representing more adequately the rising interests of commerce and industry. What distinguished the new prefect most from his predecessor was social rank. Three-fourths of the former prefectoral corps had been members of the nobility; the new men represented the victory of the bourgeoisie. Nevertheless, in France the wealthiest men were still landowners and aristocrats; their enormous economic and social power continued to persist in the rural areas.[30] Both prefects and prelates faced this reality.

It has been remarked that in societies in which group solidarity and exclusiveness were preserved in large measure by marriage and other social intermingling, in which kinship networks exerted influence, and personal contacts were of the essence, officials in the public eye to be effective had to be received in society and had to avoid giving offense to the relatively few people who mattered.[31] DuBourg was quite correct in advising the new Prefect of Tarn-et-Garonne that he would be wise to gather about himself men who knew the structure of Montauban society. However slowly the aristocrats and middle classes merged socially, in practice there was after 1830, as before, an essential unity of those groups possessing economic and political power.

In those places where legitimist sentiments remained stronger—as in Montauban and Marseilles—the settling down took a little longer. Hopes of a Bourbon rising under the duchess of Berry were slow in dying, and correspondence during the first months after the revolution indicates that Montauban was relied on to support such a rising. Reports to the duchess in November 1830 were confident that in Montauban enthusiasm was at its crest, that the militia was organized and prepared to occupy Lozère, Aveyron, Hérault, and Tarn. The civil organization was believed to be strongly legitimist as well.[32] While "lame duck" local officials remained in power, there seems little doubt that in and around Toulouse, Carcassonne, Béziers, Montpellier, and Montauban, legitimist magistrates under pressure from friends and relatives allowed comparative immunity to local partisans of the deposed dynasty.[33] Even as late as June 23, 1831, the duchess of Berry was assured that the Montauban legitimists numbering 4,000 were strongly organized and that when the signal was given the whole Department of Tarn-et-Garonne would rise.[34]

When, however, an attempt at a rising was made in Marseilles in April 1832, it proved such a fiasco that one contemporary sneered, "I still wonder whether those who dreamed up such a ridiculous plan should not have been put into an insane asylum rather than the prison where they are now confined."[35] The duchess, who disembarked at Marseilles in the dark of night with "a sword at her side and the white plume of Henry IV on her head," waited in vain for a signal from Saint-Martin's belfry. Not a sound floated down. After two days, of the 2,000 supporters anticipated, only sixty stragglers appeared. The attempt to take over the city by a mere 200 committed conspirators was an exercise in futile bravado. By midday the national guard of Marseilles had restored order. The rising was nothing more than a "firecracker that fell into the mud."[36] A last attempt at a rising, made a year later, ended in the duchess's betrayal and imprisonment at Blaye.[37] The Protectress of the St. Louis Mission was rendered impotent to play that role any longer, if she had ever assumed it.

Other than the pathetic episodes associated with the duchess of Berry, the Orleanist regime did not have to contend, "except in imagination," with legitimist-inspired insurrections. In Paris the government may have remained constantly concerned over the possibility of such plots, but in the countryside after 1831 the brawling, the shouts of *"Vive Charles X, à bas le drapeau tricolore, à bas Louis-Philippe!"* bursting from cafés in cities like Montauban gradually faded away.[38]

Beyond his see city DuBourg's flock were hard-working farmers much more concerned with their harvests and their health than Parisian politics. True, on February 7, 1832, he had issued "for reasons of prudence" a circular forbidding the celebration of requiem Masses on the thirteenth and fourteenth of February unless a corpse was present. He was remembering when attempts to celebrate Masses for the duke of Berry on those days the previous year had precipitated the atrocious attacks on Church properties in Paris. He wanted no provocations of that sort given in the city of Montauban.[39] For the most part, however, the Diocese of Montauban during the months that conspirators were completing plans for the landing in Marseilles was primarily concerned over the *Grande Peste,* cholera morbus, sweeping into western Europe from Russia.

Paris in March was already feeling its threat, and by April the deaths were so numerous it was impossible to give individual Christian burial to the plague's victims. Quelen granted permission to his priests to celebrate once or twice a week a Mass for all who had died of the cholera.[40] In Bordeaux fear and ignorance brought the people to the verge of hysterical resistance to the city's health measures.[41] While Montauban seemed out of the main path of the plague's devastation, DuBourg nevertheless issued a *mandement* on the subject on April 10, and knowing that many people might not be in churches to hear the reading of his decree he had it printed on large placards that could be posted in public places. The following day he issued a circular clarifying the applications of his regulations to their Lenten observances.[42] Easter was only ten days away but it was never too late to remind his people of his fatherly concern.

DuBourg's own private interests were set back by the cholera, unfortunately. His urgent request for money sent to Filleau on March 31 was not answered until the middle of May, and then only by a form letter explaining that the cholera epidemic in Paris had interrupted Filleau's work, particularly for clients with interests in Dominican indemnities.[43] As spring turned into summer, a prolonged drought took precedence over everything else and DuBourg's circular of July 23 authorized special prayers for rain throughout the diocese.[44] With the coming of the rain, and the harvests better than they had been in some years, tensions eased and life in Tarn-et-Garonne, in both town and country, resumed its normal routines.

What of the bishop's own relations with Paris and the new king? It has been suggested that William DuBourg and Louis-Philippe enjoyed more than the customary formalities between bishop and monarch. A French biographical essay by René Surugue asserts that DuBourg "was on excellent terms with Louis-Philippe who received him at his court and enjoyed asking his advice."[45] The reason sometimes given was that as duke of Orleans the king had known DuBourg in the United States.[46] At present there is scanty evidence to elaborate on this theme.

In the first place the occasions for their meetings in the United States could have occurred only in the brief period between Louis-Philippe's arrival and departure in the later 1790s. The future king of France at the beginning of December 1795 escaped from prison in Marseilles and made his way first to Hamburg, Germany, where there were other French émigrés and, as Talleyrand put it, the cockade was "very fashionable," and subsequently he arrived in Philadelphia on October 23, 1796.[47] He was joined there by his two brothers, the duke of Montpensier and the count of Beaujolais, in February 1797. He was last known to have been in Philadelphia in December of that same year.[48]

The only day-by-day account extant which alludes at all to DuBourg's goings and comings in those years when he

lived in Baltimore is the diary of one of his Sulpician confreres, John Tessier. In 1796 Tessier made only one reference to DuBourg's being in Philadelphia and that was in
July, some three months before the duke of Orleans arrived.
In fact, by the time Orleans had reached that city DuBourg
had been made president of Georgetown, after which
Tessier noted only his goings and comings between
Georgetown and Baltimore. Although evidence amply at-
tests that DuBourg went often to Philadelphia between 1796
and 1812 and knew many people there, no proof exists that
he was there during Louis-Philippe's sojourn.

The duke of Orleans did visit Baltimore and
Georgetown, the city of Washington, and Mount Vernon
sometime in 1797 and could have visited Georgetown College, but histories of the college do not record it.[49] A more
likely possibility seems to be Havana, Cuba. The duke and
his brothers sailed from New Orleans to Cuba, arriving on
March 31, 1798, and remaining there until May 21, 1799.
DuBourg sailed for Havana on January 22, 1799, and was
still there on April 16. Given the size of the island, and the
distaste the Spaniards exhibited for the French at the time,
French *émigrés* were apt to gravitate toward each other.
Flaget's biographer mentions Flaget's kindness to the duke
at Havana, and Flaget was DuBourg's companion there.
Again, no precise document places DuBourg and Orleans
together. Wherever it was, tradition supports a meeting
between the two men in the New World before the king-to-
be arrived back in Europe in 1800.

In regard to the assertion that DuBourg's advice was
valued by the Citizen King, the evidence is scarcely more
conclusive. Surugue holds that "it was on the advice of Mgr.
Dubourg that the King resolved to name to vacant sees only
subjects recommended by the episcopate."[50] Certainly the
July Revolution raised some questions regarding the nomination of bishops. In the spring of 1831 Dom Prosper
Guéranger published a treatise on the *Election and Nomination of Bishops,* a subject the noted Benedictine had
studied at length, from the point of view of both history and
law.

In his monograph Guéranger argued that Louis-Phi-lippe must renounce the right to name bishops, a right the Concordat of 1801 had conferred on French kings and the accord of 1817 had reaffirmed. His reasoning rested on the new, revised charter which no longer made Catholicism the state religion but recognized the freedom and equality of all cults.[51] Louis-Philippe's first choices for sees falling vacant after his accession had not been judicious, and critics like the followers of Félicité de Lamennais made both king and hierarchy fear the possibility of a movement to separate Church and State completely.

DuBourg's proposals for nominating French bishops were certainly known by the fall of 1831 for Hercule Brassac carried the news of them to the United States when he returned there in late November.[52] When Benedict Flaget learned of them in Kentucky he wrote to DuBourg, "I take a very lively interest in the mode of choosing bishops which you propose to submit and if it is possible you would give me great pleasure if you yourself would give me the details of the plan for I believe it could very well be applied to our country."[53] One part of DuBourg's plan as suggested to the king was the wisdom of keeping in readiness a list of four-teen names to propose, with the approval of the suffragan bishops, for the fourteen metropolitan sees of France.

On July 1, 1834, a circular marked "Very Confidential" was sent from Paris to the hierarchy on the subject of episcopal nomination. The Minister of Cults explained that the government was very solicitous that worthy subjects for the episcopacy be chosen. "The best means," he suggested, "would be to have the bishops themselves notify the Minis-ter of Cults of the ecclesiastics of their dioceses—or of any other—who seem to combine the highest degree of piety, education, spirit of wise tolerance, and the other eminent qualities which the episcopal dignity requires."[54] Whether this circular emanated from counsel given by DuBourg to the king, history does not make clear. DuBourg by that time was in his grave. From the knowledge one has of the bishop, however, it is fair to say that he always had ideas on the naming of bishops, whether in the New World or the Old, and it was never his wont to keep his opinions to himself.

What is more certain is that DuBourg weathered the storms of those first Orleanist years with grace and typical aplomb. The letter he sent to Flaget, written in the summer of 1831, had reported soberly, "The present in Europe offers nothing consoling, and the future is full of uncertainty and alarms."[55] But that was at the time of the suppression of traditional celebrations of the feast of the Assumption, and recollections of the Corpus Christi disorders were still vivid. Less than two years later he was assuring the Sulpicians in Baltimore, "Our gentlemen in Paris enjoy health and tranquility. They are very esteemed by the new government. In general, the *sage* clergy can only congratulate themselves."[56]

There remains in the archives of the Archdiocese of Bordeaux an interesting unsigned, undated report on the conditions confronting the French bishops in those first years after the revolution. It concludes with the judgment that although on one or two points accord with the government might prove more difficult, "If the bishops preserve silence for several months, I do not doubt that the ministry will consult some bishops on the modifications to be made in the law; and furthermore I do not doubt that an entente will be established on *almost* all points."[57] The unknown reporter proved something of a prophet.

There were things the clergy had to swallow. The Chamber of Deputies was never again quite so liberal in budgetary matters. For example, a royal ordinance decreed that vicars, canons, and pastors would no longer receive their salaries from the date of their nomination by the bishop but, instead, would be on the payroll only from the date of installation in their offices.[58] The ordinance also stipulated that absences from posts of duty could not exceed eight days, even in case of illness, without authorization from the Minister of Public Instruction and Cults. It meant new forms to be filled out, more red tape for the bishops, and some disgruntlement among the clergy at the implication that they were not devoted to their duties. Gone was the modest luxury bishops enjoyed under the Bourbons of the Restoration and DuBourg told Rosati, "I assure you if I could make any economies they would be consecrated to you with good heart. But the poor oppress me, and I am reduced, in order to have something to give them, to putting myself in the Seminary. For four years I have been on foot. That is to say that I am still an American bishop."[59]

Yet in areas closer to DuBourg's designs there were improvements. From the beginning of his incumbency Guizot had steadily worked to achieve a system of primary education more satisfactory to the church. The liberal bourgeoisie seemed unopposed to the influence of Christian education on the masses. As Tocqueville remarked, "All recognized the practical utility of religion."[60] DuBourg was a man least likely to find this odd. He had seen how the United States, a nation paying loud lip-service to the theory of a separation of Church and State, had not hesitated to support Catholic priests among the native Indians when it was a matter of "civilizing" them. Education was the universal panacea for the ills of nineteenth-century society—even when it remained Christian. A law of December 14, 1832, dealing particularly with the primary schools of Montauban, Bordeaux, Nîmes, Versailles, Strasbourg, Colmar, and Mende clearly preserved the influence of religion; and another law of June 28, 1833, restored to the clergy their positions on school committees.[61] As DuBourg had told Deluol, wise clergy had nothing to complain of from the new regime.

The Bishop of Montauban did have cause for deep sorrow, however, in 1832. On March 4 the vicar general who was his chief support died at the age of sixty-nine. In reporting the sad event *l'Ami* said:

> The diocese of Montauban has just lost one of its most distinguished priests, the Reverend Turcq, vicar general and *grand-penitencier*. M. Joseph Turq was originally from Rodez . . . Sent to Toulouse, he pursued successfully courses in philosophy and theology. . . . At the time of the Revolution he refused to take the prescribed oath and went to Spain. When Montauban was established as a see, in 1823, Mgr. de Cheverus, the new bishop, . . . named him vicar general and archdeacon. . . . Mgr. Dubourg was delighted to have such a co-worker. He put all his confidence in M. Turq

and especially gave him the responsibility of the supervision of studies.[62]

DuBourg had never felt a moment's uneasiness while away in Paris, Versailles, or Bordeaux, knowing Turcq was in command of the diocese. Scarcely two years older than the bishop, his vicar general was his alter ego, a one-time exile in Spain repatriated in later life, a lover of scholarship, and most of all devoted to the ideal of providing Montauban with the highest quality of seminary education. While the Chamber of Deputies did not balk at providing primary education, it was very critical of the institutions which trained the clergy. The state scholarships which under Charles X had exceeded a million francs were suppressed in 1831 and the ministry took no alternate measures in regard to seminary support.[63] To lose Turcq under such circumstances was particularly painful, and DuBourg's circular of March 23 ordering collections for the seminaries was half necessity and half *in memoriam*.

Another adjustment to change came at a higher level. The Archdiocese of Toulouse, of which Montauban was a suffragan see, lost its head, Cardinal Clermont-Tonnerre, in the year of the July Revolution, and the Bishop of Montauban had to accustom himself to the new archbishop, Paul-Thérèse-David d'Astros. D'Astros was a strong-willed and opinionated man determined to make his mark among the French hierarchy and in Rome. His first aggressive step in that direction filled DuBourg with mixed feelings, for the object of d'Astros' attack was Félicité de Lamennais.

From the very first days of his friendship with Simon Gabriel Bruté, DuBourg had known of the Lamennais brothers, Jean-Marie and Félicité. Bruté and Féli in those days corresponded as often as three times a week,[64] exchanging essays they had written and views Bruté shared with DuBourg as well. When DuBourg was in Paris following his consecration in Rome he had met Féli, who had given him a letter to carry to Bruté on which was written:

> The bearer of this letter will give it worth. It is no other than
> Mgr. the Bishop of New Orleans, a most lovable saint whom

the old world cedes to the new. There you have a man going far from this poor France, which he has edified for too short a time, but where he leaves memories which will not soon be erased. . . . I was only able to see him once, and even then for only a short time, but it was enough to know him.[65]

For DuBourg, too, the sense of rapport had been instantaneous, and although their paths had not crossed again he still vividly recalled that meeting in May 1817.

When Lamennais in the December following the accession of Louis-Philippe founded his General Agency for the Defense of Religious Liberty, DuBourg and his fellow bishops had found little to carp at in a prospectus which announced its principles to be: the redress of governmental infringements of religious liberty, the defense of Christian education, and the right of all French people to unite to pray, to study, and promote French civilization.[66] But in no time the agency took on an international flavor which annoyed the government, the hierarchy, and even the Vatican. England and Austria protested that their dissident minorities were being aroused by incendiary propaganda. French bishops grew increasingly irate at ferment provoked within their dioceses. Rome was disturbed by the complaints leveled against Lamennais and his associates and the direction Lamennais's ideas were taking.[67]

Lamennais provoked even more irritation by his journal, *l'Avenir,* founded two months prior to the General Agency.[68] He angered the king by criticizing his first episcopal nominations, while bishops took umbrage at theories judged inimical to their authority and conducive to schism. Bruté in Baltimore became very uneasy reading Lamennais's second part of *l'Essai sur l'indifférence,* and said so in a letter to Féli on September 2, 1831, in acknowledging which his friend retorted with light irony, "I am touched, as I ought to be, by the sentiments of friendship and Christian charity which it contained. At the same time it expressed fears about which I can say nothing direct to you, since I do not understand them. The impression I got was a little like that I could have had if you told me to be very careful not to become a Moslem."[69] But he could not shrug off so lightly the snowballing episcopal criticism in France. By the end of the year enough bishops individually attacking *l'Avenir* had forced the suspension of Lamennais's organ for want of subscriptions.

This first defeat of "Mennaisianism" did not satisfy the Archbishop of Toulouse. "The personal and, in fact, the political prejudices d'Astros injected into his list of what he called theological dangers and the impassioned stubbornness with which he hounded Félicité and his school" were not to be so easily subdued.[70] On February 29, 1832, he informed Cardinal de Gregorio, Prefect of the Sacred Penitentiary in Rome, of his intention to mobilize the French hierarchy in a formal censure of the novel and subversive doctrines he detested.[71] Believing he had Roman approval, after consulting three noted Sulpicians—Joseph Carrière, Benoît-Hippolyte Vieusse, and Pierre-Denis Boyer—he arrived at fifty-six censured propositions extracted from the writings of Lamennais and his disciples, which he presented to the bishops most likely to adhere. By April 23, 1832, he had a dozen prelates, chiefly from the south of France, willing to support his censure and he had it printed in both Latin and French to send to Rome.[72] DuBourg's name was fourth on the list of signers, partly for reasons of courtesy but more because he was, and always had been at heart, a Sulpician and in matters theological was in sympathy with the pronouncements of the great minds of the Gentlemen.

D'Astros forwarded this censure with its thirteen signatures to Rome on July 15 and immediately began pressuring the rest of the hierarchy to climb on the bandwagon "to halt the propagation of false doctrines which begin to divide the clergy . . . the singular opinions of M. l'abbé la Mennais." He assured the laggards that "the Holy Father is grateful for our zeal."[73] The replies to this appeal were guarded; only twenty-one adhered completely, three were still examining the doctrines at issue, and two were bluntly opposed to censure, according to his report of August 15.[74] Nevertheless, for the time being it appeared that the Archbishop of Toulouse was vindicated. On that very day in

Rome, Pope Gregory XVI issued his encyclical *Mirari vos* which, while not singling out Lamennais by name, condemned the doctrines at issue. In September Lamennais submitted to Rome's decisions and together with his associates announced their suppression of both *l'Avenir* and the General Agency.[75] On May 8, 1833, d'Astros received from Rome a papal brief praising the French hierarchy for its "pastoral zeal and fidelity to the Apostolic See" demonstrated by its recent interests in purity of doctrine.[76] As far as DuBourg was concerned the Lamennais affair appeared to be at an end, and Féli's friends on both sides of the Atlantic could rest easy that he was not lost to the Church.[77]

As 1832 came to an end, only one permanent reminder of the more turbulent times remained to pierce the bishop's heart. The graceful tops of the towers of his cathedral—those lovely elipsopyramidal domes lifting their twin crosses to the sky—were no more. Under the pretext that their decaying framework threatened danger to both the edifice and the populace below, the spires were replaced in 1831 by a heavy stone ledge heading which had no esthetic rapport with the style of the whole. "Thus the façade of the beautiful cathedral lost its harmony and elegance."[78] It was, perhaps, the most painful accommodation he made to the new order. For some men an offense against beauty is almost as abhorrent as an offense against God. With the government's appropriations for cults decreasing and the bishop's own finances in such desperate condition, he had no prospect of restoring in his own lifetime the *flêches* which had given such delight to his artistic sensibilities.

Yet he could be grateful that there still remained atop the cathedral, in the center of its façade, the fine statutes of Religion and Hope facing the remaining cross which still rose on high. Religion, hope, and the Cross—these were, one knew, the enduring treasure of bishops in this world.

CHAPTER XL

SUPER FLUMINA BABYLONIS

As the frictions of the post-revolutionary days faded into the background, events across the Atlantic reemerged on DuBourg's horizon with persistent demands for his attention. On August 6, 1831, *l'Ami de la Religion* presented a lengthy article on the state of religion in the Diocese of St. Louis in the United States,[1] which one suspects may have been furnished by its bishop. After tracing the history of the region from its French-Canadian origins through the reign of DuBourg, the article went on to list the twenty-one parishes within that diocese in 1831,[2] and to describe three new major religious institutions within the city itself: the Convent of the Sacred Heart, the Jesuit college, and the Mullamphy Hospital. Seeing in print the changes made since he had last been in St. Louis, DuBourg could marvel at the progress in this diocese, which had been only the northern part of his total jurisdiction in the old days.

Philippine Duchesne had always wanted to have a house in St. Louis and now, through John Mullamphy's generosity, she was there—"in a vast building of bricks, with twenty-five acres of land situated in the heart of the city." With twelve ladies of the Sacred Heart, Madame Duchesne was conducting a charity school for poor orphan girls and a boarding school for young ladies desiring an education *la plus soignée*. *L'Ami* reminded its readers that it was Bishop DuBourg who had brought the Sacred Heart nuns from France in 1818, and those five had increased to the sixty now directing six separate houses in the Mississippi Valley. In 1831 fifty of the nuns were Americans, born for the most part in Missouri or Louisiana.

Of the Jesuit school *l'Ami* reported:

> Saint-Louis College was opened November 2, 1829. M. Du-Bourg first had the idea for this establishment, and ceded the land on which it has been built. M. Rosati, his successor, sensed equally what an advantage this college would be for the country; he collected 15,000 francs among the most respectable citizens of St. Louis, and erected a brick building fifty by forty feet rising four stories. This institution is located in a most agreeable and healthy spot in the city. Six professors are now attached there under Father P. Verhaegen, S.J., and more than one hundred students attend.[3]

How he had connived to get that Jesuit contingent to Missouri in 1823, DuBourg reflected. Now Rosati was reaping the rewards. Even before the July Revolution reports from Missouri had brought the Bishop of Montauban deep satisfaction, which he had expressed to Rosati:

> I hope that in Belgium they are going to work efficaciously to aid your [Jesuit] Fathers of Missouri. That will always be conducive, and very powerfully, to the good of your diocese, where I regard them as the principal support for the immense part of it which devolves on them. I have learned with great pleasure that their Church and their Establishment at St. Charles are completed. That will be, without doubt, the center of considerable good. I rejoice no less to see them undertake the enterprise of the College of St. Louis, which can not fail to succeed; and which will bring to realization all our former projects in favor of the young people of that important city.[4]

In 1823 as Bishop of Louisiana, DuBourg had offered the Jesuits very little, God knew, except an opportunity to sacrifice. Yet they had risen magnificently to that challenge in less than a decade.

DuBourg had never regretted bringing the Jesuits to Missouri. Their Indian school near Florissant had been slow in developing, to be sure, but now according to *l'Ami* they had thirty pupils and were planning to move from Florissant to a place better suited to their purposes. Van Quickenborne was convinced that an institution of learning had better chances in St. Louis and would offer greater inducements to Indian boys. Back in 1828 he had told DuBourg:

> In my opinion an establishment at St. Louis is indispensably necessary to our Indian mission for it is there that all Indian affairs come to be treated; it is there where the tribal chiefs come from time to time; it is there the Superintendent of Indian Affairs and all the agents reside. It is therefore there where we need to be very often and where the future of our interests, our establishments, will be decided.[5]

The St. Louis house would further increase their chances of getting candidates for the Society of Jesus. Rosati had offered no objections; in fact, he had been "charmed with the news" of these Jesuit plans. Now, in 1831, besides conducting schools in the city, the Jesuits were also going beyond St. Louis's parishes, to visit two or three times a year some five hundred Catholics scattered along the Mississippi and Missouri Rivers. It was like the biblical tiny grain of mustard seed, that planting of the Society of Jesus in the American Midwest.

As for the Mullamphy Hospital, there was another dream come true. From the first days of his assignment as administrator apostolic of Louisiana, DuBourg had wanted Mother Seton's daughters in that territory.[6] Granted, his request then had been for teaching sisters; but in the decades since 1812 their work had expanded in many directions and, as *l'Ami* remarked, hospitals were establishments which "honor at the same time religion and humanity." The four Sisters of Charity who arrived at St. Louis on November 5, 1828, at Rosati's request were now directing a twenty-bed institution whose patients were received free of charge.[7] Again, it was Mullamphy who made it possible— land, houses, furnishings, all from his open purse.

In spite of that good man's reluctance to have it so, it was high time that something in St. Louis was named after him. The Bishop of Montauban, who could never be accused of ingratitude, determined to compose a tribute which he trusted Rosati would pass on:

> The good Mr. Mullamphy, after having amassed treasures on earth, has decided, as I see it, to make friends in heaven, who at the supreme moment will receive him into eternal tabernacles. The Church of St. Louis will recount his charities to future generations: all the poor orphans who owe to him their existence and their station; all the widows whose lot he will have softened; all the sick whom he will have snatched from the grave and preserved for their families, form a concert of blessings which will accompany him from century to century. I unite my feeble voice with theirs, and I wish that the accent of my fitting gratitude may reach his ear and gladden his heart. Happy is he who provides with so much wisdom for the needs of the indigent and the poor. God deliver him on the evil day. May God preserve him, grant him long life, and make him happy on earth, protect him from his enemies, sit by his bedside, and brush away for him his last sorrows. *Beatus qui intelligit super egenum.*[8]

It was a bit flowery, he admitted, but being DuBourg he was pleased with himself. Who knew what further benefactions might result for the diocese he had loved so well? Besides, he meant every word of it.

The first article on the Diocese of St. Louis brought *l'Ami* notices and notes correcting errors in the August report, and as a result a second installment appeared, this time including a description of the contributions of the Vincentian, or Lazarist, priests:

> At St. Mary-of-the-Barrens there is a seminary founded by M. Dubourg directed by the Lazarists. They have combined there the diocesan seminary, a college, and a Lazarist novitiate. The seminary has 25 students, the college 80 pupils, and the novitiate has 10 novices. The superior of the three estab-

lishments is an Italian Lazarist, M. Tornatore. Besides directing students the Lazarists still have the care of the parish which numbers 1,600 Catholics. . . . Several of them are employed in the missions among the savages.[9]

The numbers changed, DuBourg mused, but the pattern of life did not. After Rosati became Bishop of St. Louis, he had begged the Congregation of the Mission over and over for someone to relieve him of his office as superior of the American Vincentians. Only the year before *l'Ami*'s articles appeared, John Tornatore, C.M., arrived; and Rosati could write happily to Paris, "In Father Tornatore we have an excellent superior for the seminary, a good director of our novices, and a strong supporter of the observance of our rules."[10] But Tornatore, like most newcomers to the missions, was already burdened with four assignments instead of one. There were never enough workers, never enough hours in the day, for all the tasks crying to be done.

On May 19, 1831, DuBourg wrote to Rosati encouragingly:

> You must have received recently three good subjects from Lyon, who will contribute much to easing your situation. I would not be surprised if others arrive. The great difficulty is paying for the voyages, which decreases your pecuniary resources so much. But at last the epoch when the Seminary and the Novitiate of the Society will supply all your needs cannot be far away.

He praised Rosati's plan to send two of his subjects to be educated at the college of the Propaganda in Rome, saying that this would surely interest that congregation in the Diocese of St. Louis.[11]

The underlying theme of Rosati's reports to Montauban, of course, was the ever-present need for money. On the eve of the July Revolution, DuBourg had urged Rosati to come to Europe to solicit funds, as soon as the Diocese of New Orleans had its own bishop, saying, "I think you should make this trip as soon as possible." In the meantime, Louis Sibourd would turn over to Rosati the annual rent of seven hundred dollars from a property he owned in New

York. "It is a fine gift," DuBourg assured Rosati. "While Sibourd lives he will continue to give you this rent of $700 a year. You see we do not forget you."[12]

The next year DuBourg told Rosati that Louis Du-Bourg had left the bishop some *inscriptions de rente* worth over 20,000 francs which should be easily sold, in which case Rosati could borrow that money. Rosati's notion of going to Saint-Domingue did not find favor with DuBourg, who advised against it. "It is not the time to undertake it," he said. "You don't speak of one to Mexico. That could be profitable to your Cathedral."[13]

DuBourg was enormously interested in the prospect of a real cathedral to replace the ramshackle one he had left behind in St. Louis. He meant to do all he could for Rosati's new church, but he reminded his old friend that, as a result of the July Revolution, "Our salaries are almost cut in half." Advice, however, cost nothing and the Bishop of Montauban delighted in giving it, especially after he saw Rosati's plans.[14]

DuBourg was as concerned for the Diocese of New Orleans, but his efforts to do things for the good of that city only succeeded in wounding his feelings. When he tried to pay the passage of one priest by a draft on Philip Borgna, no one would honor his signature, and the draft was protested. Happily the protest required the French consul's legalization and faithful Guillemin stopped it, saving DuBourg from an affront he had not yet experienced. Describing this humiliation to Rosati, he complained:

> There are other things as singular as that. You remember that you wrote to me asking for a replacement for Mr. Richard in concert with the Ursuline ladies. It was not easy; I succeeded, however, because I find nothing impossible when it concerns you and the good of my old diocese. I announced this priest to the Ladies; I made my arrangements with him in their name. He left, and then found his place taken two months before by Mr. Martial.[15]

Something similar had happened in the case of the preacher Louis Moni had asked DuBourg to send. The recruit's departure had been announced and expected; he had arrived to find he had been supplanted by Aristide Anduze. "All this scarcely encourages doing things for others," DuBourg said. "A bishop more concerned with his job would not fall into errors like that and would prevent others from doing so."[16]

He could not stop trying to have a hand in the affairs of the dioceses he had once ruled; it was not his nature. A few months after this grumbling letter he was telling Rosati, "A respectable priest from the Diocese of Coutances, who is leaving for New Orleans, has spoken to me of one of his confreres, a young priest of high *virtue* and *remarkable erudition*, who has an *exeat* for your diocese." The Lyon Association would advance the costs of his voyage, but Rosati would have to reimburse the Association. "I am opposed to his departure until you consent," DuBourg said; but he was sure the priest would be a great acquisition for the Barrens seminary. He enclosed three hundred francs for Mr. De Theux, the new head of the Jesuits in Missouri, who was much less "stiff" than Van Quickenborne.[17]

If he were younger, DuBourg reflected, he might be tempted to join Hercule Brassac, who was returning to the United States that autumn.[18] As it was, he would at least write some letters Brassac could carry to the stalwart laborers in that far-off vineyard. Leaving DuBourg in good health in Paris, Brassac departed for New York on the same ship Bishop John Dubois of New York had chosen;[19] in Brassac's care were letters for Flaget in Bardstown, and for Rosati and Duchesne in St. Louis.

Afterward, the Bishop of Montauban may have wondered if he had been wise to thus open the floodgates of memory. He had, of course, been in regular correspondence with his successor since leaving the United States. He had owed it to him, after having left so many matters unfinished. Rosati, on his part, delighted in reporting to DuBourg. No one could appreciate better than DuBourg what Rosati had already accomplished, or more warmly applaud what he intended for the future. The letters carried by Hercule Brassac in 1831, were they perhaps a kind of self-indulgence, of entertaining sentiments which had no other validity save that of bittersweet recollection of time beyond recall?

He had sent messages to Flaget and Duchesne by others in the past. To Saulnier most recently he had written:

> When you see them . . . give my respectful compliments to the Ladies of the S. C. and to the good Sisters. I learn with acute distress of the severe illness of Mme Regis, and the state of Mme Octavie's suffering. Before this letter arrives these Ladies will have received a good reinforcement. I greatly rejoice over it, above all for that venerable Mother Duchesne, to whom I beg you to say for me the most affectionate things. Recommend me to her prayers. Recently I saw their Ladies in Paris. They still hold on, and I believe they will survive. At least the turn of things in the Chamber of Deputies makes me hope so. Mme Barat is at Chambery; Mme de Grammont is now head of the house in Paris.[20]

Through Bruté and Rosati he had often asked to be especially remembered to Flaget. Yet writing hastily, with no little emotion, and at length—to make use of the occasion of Brassac in late October—was quite another matter. In the end his impetuosity brought rich dividends.

Philippine Duchesne responded first, writing on January 29, 1832, with all the irrepressible warmheartedness of her nature:

> I have just had the inexpressible pleasure of receiving your letter from Versailles dated October 27; we all experience great joy when you mention us in your correspondence, but a direct souvenir really assures us of the loving concern of our first shepherd, father, and founder. Our sentiments are shared by all who have enlarged our family since it lost you.[21]

Then she rushed ahead with all that had happened since she had written last. Of their houses, St. Michael's had the greatest number, eighty in all, including six sisters of bishops and two of their nieces. They cared for some 120 boarders, a house of orphans, and a school for externes. La Fourche was beginning to get out of debt and through a subscription hoped to continue a much needed building. Grand Coteau was getting much help for an academy from the relatives of their students. One of these, a congressman who had formerly placed his daughters in a Georgetown *pension,* was heard to say haughtily that he preferred Grand Coteau and that he regarded it as the first in the Union. "You know, Monseigneur," Duchesne reminded him, "how much such praise in the mouth of a man of highest repute among Protestants can do to give confidence in this house."

Duchesne also relayed what news she had from the Diocese of New Orleans which might interest him. She enjoyed rambling on, she confessed, "not fearing to weary you while entertaining you!" The Ursulines were at the peak of prosperity; the Sisters of Charity of St. Joseph were all settled in the house founded for orphans, and were doing great good.

Again it was Rosati, DuBourg reflected, who succeeded in getting Mother Seton's daughters for New Orleans. This smaller band had left the valley in Emmitsburg just before Christmas in 1829, and had faced many difficulties in getting started.[22] Yet, if Madame Duchesne were as well informed as she usually was, this establishment, too, was destined for a fine future.

Coming back to the Diocese of St. Louis again, Duchesne said feelingly:

> If Mgr. Rosati now sees so many establishments—his college as well as the seminary—flourishing he cannot forget any more than you can that you made all the plans and bore up under all the first difficulties. Your name can never be forgotten; too many monuments recall it, too many hearts carry gratitude.

It meant a great deal, coming from her. If anyone had borne the hardships and disappointments of those other days it had been Philippine Duchesne, and her bishop on occasion had been the cause of some of those disappointments. But it was not her way to harbor old dissatisfactions. It was now many a year since his visit to rue des Postes in Paris, hoping to persuade Madame Barat to give him Duchesne for his diocese. How little any of them imagined what the decision reached that day portended for the Mississippi Valley.

Antoine Blanc, too, belonged to that era of recruiting workers for the vineyard. He had sailed with DuBourg aboard the *Caravane* and first glimpsed American life at the mansion of Charles Caroll in Annapolis, a sort of luxury he was not destined to enjoy in the stations he served in the West. Now, according to Duchesne, he was vicar general in the Diocese of New Orleans and likely to rise even higher.[23]

Privately, DuBourg had always favored Blanc for New Orleans. That see needed someone in robust vigor. Leo De Neckere, who was preferred in some quarters for his talents and linguistic ability, was always in poor health—or believed he was—when DuBourg knew him in Louisiana. The year after DuBourg's return to France, De Neckere had also returned, where reports of his vomiting blood soon reached Montauban. Nevertheless, in Rome on August 4, 1829, he had been named Bishop of New Orleans despite his protests. Back in the United States, he became ill again; but while DuBourg was in Paris in the spring of 1830, he heard that the consecration was to take place anyway. He commented glumly to Rosati on May 19, "I learned from your Supr. Gen'l that he had just received a letter from you of March, in which the forthcoming consecration of Mr. de Neckere was mentioned, which proved to me that the news Mr. Niel gave me 15 days ago touching on the recurrence of his vomiting blood was false. God's will be done."[24]

DuBourg's uneasiness over New Orleans increased when people wrote him that Bishop De Neckere rarely appeared in the city; and DuBourg told Rosati forcefully, "I think he is wrong. I will write to him; and you would do well to do as much." If De Neckere's health failed, he ought to be replaced by an intelligent, active man who was not a slave to his fears—a man like Blanc. But, in the meantime, DuBourg urged Rosati:

> Do not become a stranger to that so important part of our former Diocese. You owe him your care, if only because of

your promises to Mgr. de Neckere, who would not have been accepted without that, and who as a matter of fact will need your support and advice for a long time.[25]

When Blanc was made coadjutor to the ailing Bishop of New Orleans, DuBourg could not understand why Rosati advised him to refuse the post. Montauban wrote reprovingly to St. Louis:

I have received, my very dear Lord, a letter from Mr. Blanc informing me that having been named Coadjutor of N. Orl. he had, on your advice, sent back his bulls. I am replying making him lively reproaches; and permit me to address you to join me. I am convinced as you are that the Bp. was only asked for a Coadjutor to relieve himself of the burden; but I am astonished that you have not judged as I have that it would be a great good fortune for his Diocese, where everything suffers as a result of his indecisions and his pusillanimous character. I believe before God that you are obliged in conscience to write at once to Rome to repair an error so grave.[26]

Two weeks later DuBourg again importuned Rosati to get Blanc's bulls back and have him consecrated with as little delay as possible. "Without that," he said categorically, "nothing will be done at New Orl. All will continue to languish there, discouragement will engulf all hearts, and you will be principally to blame for it. Consider whether you wish to run such risks."[27] In the end, Blanc became Bishop of New Orleans, but by that time the Bishop of Montauban was in his grave.[28]

It was Flaget's letter from Kentucky which really wrenched DuBourg's heart. When Brassac reached Louisville he had found the Bishop of Bardstown suffering an attack of influenza, which had greatly depleted his forces. Flaget was overjoyed at receiving DuBourg's letter—his first since DuBourg's departure for France—and he replied in high emotion:

I at once kissed the paper your hands had touched, picturing in my old imagination the handsome man I had known in

1785 or 86, with whom I had formed a most intimate, a most sincere friendship in 1796, which will continue in all its force until my last sigh. What reflections present themselves to my mind of all those times gone by. O, my very dear Madame Fournier; O, my very good friend, M. Louis. What sweet moments I passed in your company. Alas, you are no longer in this world. But you dwell in that place for which I sigh and where I hope to rejoin you. You will pardon me this effusion which has poured from a heart you know so well.[29]

"What sweet moments!" DuBourg could echo Flaget's words as he, too, went back in memory to their seminary days at Saint-Sulpice in Paris (before the great Revolution put them to flight), their reunion in Baltimore, the months of teaching together there and in Georgetown, and the later years when they were brother bishops on the frontier. Theirs was surely a rare friendship.

Flaget excitedly expressed his joy at having in his diocese Jesuits of his own, particularly from France. He envisioned providing them with a fine plantation of three hundred acres and a college having sixty-six to eighty scholars and fifteen masters. Like the good husbandman pioneer bishops still had to be, he listed the farm tools, the horses and oxen for work, the pigs, the sheep, the cows—enough "to run a farm well and support a numerous family." He continued:

> Once the sons of St. Ignatius have taken root in the country, and especially in the college, I don't doubt that they will form several subjects fitted for their Company and that in a very few years the majority of subjects will be American and speak English naturally, which would fit them for taking over the college of Bardstown which is an English college where everything is translated into that language.[30]

Flaget's exuberant optimism filled DuBourg with an odd mixture of surprise and relief. It was so contrary to the story going the rounds in France about the Jesuits in Kentucky. Only recently DuBourg had relayed to St. Louis the Lyon version, received from Didier Petit. DuBourg had told Rosati:

Mr. Petit communicated to me what I have suspected for a long time, and what afflicts me profoundly, about the derangement of the finances of the St. Bp. of Bards T. They carry a deficit of 30,000 piastres, enormous for those regions, especially at a time when his college must have lost much of its vogue. Poor Bishop! In what a state of mind he must find himself. . . . If only he knew how I share his cruel embarrassments. They have resulted in the fact that Fathers *Chazel, Petit* and *Ladavière,* who departed 15 months ago to take charge of the College of Bardstown, have recoiled in the face of this enormous debt, and Mr. Petit, the brother of the second, asks my advice on what these Gentlemen should do in America.[31]

DuBourg had naturally recommended that these Jesuits offer themselves to the Diocese of New Orleans, where De Neckere could use them to start a college at Opelousas.

Now, with Flaget's letter in his hand, he was reminded that in the American missions, even with debts, things were never as bad as they might seem! Frontier bishops and missionaries in writing to the Association for the Propagation of the Faith in France always stressed their needs. Heaven knew he had done it often enough himself.

It took only Rosati's letter of that May, delivered in person by dear Auguste Jeanjean, to give DuBourg the sensation of having made an actual visitation of his old jurisdiction. Some problems in Missouri, it seemed, could never be satisfactorily solved. Among those persisting in 1832 was that of achieving some sort of equilibrium between the needs of the parish and the lure of the Indian missions. The latter was a recurring subject with Rosati. Soon after DuBourg's return to France, Father Joseph Anthony Lutz had arrived on the Missouri scene from Germany, "burning with a desire to consecrate himself" to the Indian missions. Lutz was one of the recruits whom Francis Niel had sent to St. Louis, and Rosati had hoped Lutz would augment the faculty of either the Barrens seminary or the college in St. Louis.

Like so many Europeans dreaming of the American missions, Lutz greatly preferred work among the Indians to the humdrum life of a parish priest; he went west to the Kansas tribe, where Rosati felt he must have a companion. The Indian Agent, General William Clark, had tried sending a Protestant minister to the Kansas, but the Indians rejected him. "The chief absolutely wants a priest," Rosati said.[32]

In the intervening years it had remained hard for the bishop to keep good assistants in his see. The Reverend Rondot, whom *l'Ami* had described as attracting such crowds to St. Louis by his preaching in French,[33] had already returned to France because of his health. The two other men who had come with Rondot from Lyon, "excellent subjects who do very well," Rosati assured DuBourg, were unfortunately disgusted with the city and wanted to go work among the Indians. "If you could procure for me a good preacher," Rosati pleaded, "who would want to stay with me in St. Louis . . . you would singularly oblige me." He could offer no inducements except that of sharing a bishop's lot, and DuBourg would need to explain what that meant in St. Louis.[34]

Replying to this request while Jeanjean remained in Montauban, DuBourg reported wryly: "You ask me for a French predicator who will be content with *victum et vextitum*. . . . The trouble is that the majority of good French priests who go to America dream only of the Indian missions; and it must be that they have the attraction, since Mr. Jeanjean himself thinks only of that. I have preached to him . . . but I fear I have preached to a deaf man."[35] Jeanjean, who by then had been in the Missisippi Valley even longer than DuBourg, was still hankering for a post among *les sauvages!*

Rosati, like Philippine Duchesne and Flaget, could not help noticing the changing population trends in the 1830s. "I will need some priests from Alsace or Lorraine," he explained, "who speak German. Already a great number of very good Catholics of that nation have arrived here and many others are expected. A good number of these families are established . . . in the vicinity of the new convent I've mentioned to you in other letters. Many are here at St. Louis, others in Illinois."

Rosati was proudest of the building going on in Missouri. Eight churches were in the process of being erected: three in stone (the Cathedral, the seminary chapel, and the new Church of Ste. Genevieve); two in brick (one at the English settlement, the other at Keachwood); and three in wood (Poste des Arkansas, New Madrid, and Salt River). The new wing of St. Louis College was already roofed. He hoped DuBourg would approve of another project he had undertaken, saying:

> I have changed our old college that you built into a church. It is a gem. I will bless it next Sunday and thereafter there will be a Mass every Sunday at 9:00 o'clock and instructions for people of color; every Sunday evening Rosary and instruction or catechism. . . .
>
> Apropos of the chapel, send me, I beg you, Mgr., some ornaments. Our church is very poor; those used every day are already so old it is almost indecent to use them. I have to give some to each priest who goes out to start a new mission. I had to furnish M. Pouilleson . . . at New Madrid everything to a pot to do his cooking in.[36]

A pot for cooking—this kind of poverty DuBourg understood only too well. He could remember his early days in St. Louis when Judge Pratte had been horrified at the crude pine bedstead which was the bishop's lot, and offered to give him a more elegant one, and DuBourg had retorted jocularly:

> My palace is too small and too poor to admit of any such luxury. You will therefore, dear friend, allow me to convert it into something which will be of more immediate utility. Bread is what my people lack, everything is exorbitantly expensive; and I dare not allow myself the least furnishings. Would you believe we are obliged to lend each other the writing table? But this does not detract from my good humor. On the contrary, I experience the truth of the proverb: An empty purse renders the heart light.[37]

It had seemed so easy, in those days, to joke about hardships. What a blessing it was that Rosati preserved a strong sense of humor. He could cheerfully sum up his day, which began at four o'clock in the morning, with the words: "I do not have a moment of free time; but also I have never enjoyed better health than at present. . . . Thus, instead of losing, work makes me gain."

Rosati's letter relayed little news of New Orleans, whose bishop wrote rarely, and, when he did, very briefly. Rosati commented:

> I think you know better than I what goes on in the Diocese of New Orleans. . . . I have not received from Louisiana one *liard* of help for the building of my church. You know the sacrifices I made for that diocese as I devoted to them all the help the Association [for the Propagation of the Faith] sent me, not giving anything to the Diocese of St. Louis which had at least as great need. They took it badly that I brought the library to St. Louis although they knew very well it belonged to me. . . .

Ah, that library! It had been the great pride of DuBourg's life as an educator. Those books had traveled more than most people. But Rosati was right to return them to St. Louis, where Catholic education seemed to have a brighter future. DuBourg had not been able to found a seminary in Lower Louisiana, and after Maréchal succeeded in getting Portier made a bishop, Portier's college in New Orleans had quickly closed.

The Bishop of Montauban steered his thoughts back to the letter from St. Louis. Yet its hurried close was an equally sharp reminder of other days. Rosati had been writing on in his usual leisurely fashion, saying he hoped that his letter might travel by Jeanjean, who was going to France. "I would be enchanted if, on his return, he wished to live with me. I think of making him my Vicar General. I will give him a copy of the decrees of the Council of Baltimore for you," Rosati meandered. Then, suddenly, the letter broke off— ending "May 7. Jeanjean is here. He will go to see you and give you all the details viva voce."[38] How often in the past had DuBourg himself been compelled to abruptly close a report to Europe, in order to take advantage of someone's trip abroad, thus saving the cost of postage!

Jeanjean not only brought the letter and the decrees; he brought as well a copy of the architect's drawings of the new cathedral, plans for which DuBourg had been clamoring for months. Rosati had from the start welcomed DuBourg's excited curiosity, but he needed money more. "Interest yourself in me," he begged. "You know I did not get myself into this predicament. Come to my assistance." The Bishop of Montauban knew he could read that both ways—that Rosati had never wanted to be a bishop, and that he had not created the financial complexities with which his administration had begun. "I count on your cooperation," Rosati insisted, as he forwarded the first drawing of the floor plan and the façade.[39]

On September 11, 1832, after nearly a year's work had been accomplished, Rosati wrote:

> The construction of my Cathedral causes me much uneasiness and embarrassment. I have already paid about $11,000 and every Saturday it is necessary to pay the contractors from three to five hundred dollars. Until now I have been able to meet all my debts, so that the Protestants, jealous of the erection of such a beautiful edifice and knowing that the subscription did not amount to $40,000, including the six hundred which I subscribed myself, are displeased that their calculations have failed. They believe that we will be obliged for lack of money to suspend operation; some among them still cling to this hope. We will not be able to finish the church without $18,000 more, because I figure it will cost about $30,000; but it will last for centuries.[40]

It was an exposition calculated to touch a harder heart than that of the Bishop of Montauban. Earlier, at Rosati's request, he had agreed to buy a city lot in St. Louis from the diocese.[41] But where properties were involved there were constant impediments to financial transactions taking place across the sea. DuBourg sent two drafts—one for 30,000 francs, and the other for 6,000—but when Rosati tried to cash the one for 6,000 at the Branch Bank of the United States at St. Louis he was informed that Dr. Chatard in Baltimore, on whom the draft was drawn, refused to accept it because the rents from a DuBourg property in Baltimore had not been paid to Chatard as stipulated, and there were no funds on hand.[42] DuBourg then arranged to have the Baltimore property sold, and wrote to the Sulpicians at St. Mary's Seminary:

> I am taking the liberty of sending you two drafts on Dr. Chatard, one for 6,000 francs the other for 2,000 with interest from this date until payment, dependant upon the sale of the Baconais house in Baltimore which the good doctor has been kind enough to take charge of. . . . The funds provided by these drafts are meant for Mgr. Rosati who has most urgent need of them. I desire for my own sake as much as for his that they soon be realized.[43]

When the sale of the Baltimore house was delayed, DuBourg wrote again to the Sulpicians, "The delay in payment for my draft on Dr. Chatard making it necessary for me to satisfy my commitments to Mgr. Rosati in another manner, I beg you to hold at my disposition the product of my drafts . . . when the funds are paid to you." He trusted in their kindness to notify him promptly when this occurred.[44] It was not pleasant to be thus engrossed in money matters just when a visitor from the States was in Montauban.

For DuBourg the pleasure of Jeanjean's visit was further diluted by the news of the death in New Orleans on July 31, 1832, of Bertrand Martial. *L'Ami* devoted most of its *notice* to Martial's life in France, adding only at the end: "*L'Abeille,* a New Orleans journal, has also paid tribute on August 2 to the memory of Father Martial. We have seen a letter from that country which speaks of the loss in most touching terms."[45] So few lines to commemorate a mission career in America which had lasted from 1818 to 1832! DuBourg could recall the months of uncertainty before Archbishop d'Aviau finally consented to give Martial his *exeat* from Bordeaux, and how at last the secular priest had found passage on the same vessel carrying Philippine Duchesne and her little group to Louisiana. Martial had been openly impatient in New Orleans while waiting for DuBourg to summon him to St. Louis. But DuBourg, noting how the influence of Martial seemed to be healing the schism in that strife-ridden city, had not hurried to reassign him. The Ursulines had come to love him, and the young boys whose catechetical instruction he organized flocked after him. By the end of 1819 Martial was reconciled to running a college in Louisiana.[46] No one there in 1822, when the frightful yellow fever epidemic swept over New Orleans, would forget how selflessly Martial had cared for the sick and the dying.

If DuBourg's involvement with Angelo Inglesi had disillusioned Martial,[47] it could have given the headmaster no more discomfort than his bishop suffered in the denouement of that sorry affair; when DuBourg had moved permanently to New Orleans, the relationship between the two men had become undeniably difficult. Martial's departure for Kentucky had been without DuBourg's blessing, and after Martial returned to New Orleans to take a position DuBourg had hoped Pouget would fill, DuBourg was only half jesting when he told Rosati, "That man seems to have been expressly created just to get in my way!"[48]

One always winced at the memory of having fallen in the esteem of those one most admired. The death which intervenes before a healing reconciliation can take place is more difficult to bear. Thank God, this had not been the case with Martial. DuBourg recalled that "most happy voyage" they had shared from New York to Le Havre in 1826.[49] Martial was indeed a great and good man. Onetime canon of Saint-André Cathedral in Bordeaux, vicar general—however briefly—to DuBourg and Flaget in turn, and most notably a contributor to Catholic education in both France and the United States, his loss was undeniable. It was bittersweet, now, to think of Martial's having spent his last days among the Ursulines whom DuBourg loved so well.

One regretted one's insufficiencies and errors where good friends were concerned. The memory of estrangements never quite vanished. DuBourg was reminded that he had been estranged from Flaget, too, for a while. Yet one was permitted to do God's work in spite of human frailty. DuBourg consoled himself rereading Flaget's recent praise:

> Very dear friend, be sure I am not seeking to pay compliments and that I speak with all the sincerity of my soul in assuring you that I have always admired the extent of your projects and the extraordinary good which was bound to result from them and which still results in great benefit and edification in all the United States. They tell me I become quite eloquent when I speak of the Sisters of Charity of Emmitsburg, the Ladies of the Sacred Heart, the Reverend Jesuit Fathers and the Lazarists of Missouri. When you have only good works like these to present to God on leaving this world, rest assured you could not be guaranteed a better passport to the kingdom of his most industrious and faithful servants.[50]

Once again his thoughts wandered back over the years to those beginnings in Maryland and the foundation of Elizabeth Seton's little community in the valley, John Dubois's college on the mountain; those months in Europe collecting Vincentians in Italy and the Ladies of the Sacred Heart in France; the wild wintry trip with Flaget to take possession of the diocese at St. Louis; the throbbing, noisy trips up and down the Mississippi; the negotiations with Calhoun and the Belgian Jesuits for educating Indian boys—what exhilarating times those had been!

And how he missed them! He was reminded of one of Bruté's favorite passages from the Psalms, "By the streams of Babylon we sat and wept when we remembered Sion."[51] Here in his episcopal palace high above the Tarn he felt like weeping for that American Sion which had given him so many sorrows and yet so many joys. But tears were idle, and no matter how much his heart clung to that other vineyard there was work still to be done in Montauban, and with the time and strength remaining to him the Bishop of Montauban would persevere.

CHAPTER XLI

INTIMATIONS OF MORTALITY

Sometimes a new year is ushered in on a somber note. For DuBourg, 1833 began with the king's confirmation of Charpentier de Cossigny for a vacancy in the Cathedral Chapter of Montauban.[1] There had been so many vacancies to fill since that summer in 1826 when the bishop had requested a canonicate for dear old Sibourd. Death, it seemed, was no respecter of canons, honorary or otherwise.

The affair of the relics of Saint Théodard was also a reminder of death, although at a time more remote. Théodard, according to *les Montalbanais* tradition, was the ancient city's patron whose bones had escaped pillage in the mid-sixteenth century and since then had been preserved in the church of Villebrumier. With the gift of a fine new reliquary by the bishop and chapter of Montauban in 1652, the bones of Saint Théodard had been placed in ten little white silk bags, authenticated by the bishop's seal, and placed in the new reliquary for safekeeping. Now, more than a century and a half later, Bishop DuBourg was to renew this authentication after extracting a relic for his cathedral in the city of Montauban.[2] With Lent beginning early this year, the Church's traditions, liturgy, and calendar all seemed bent on reminding Louis-Guillaume de Montauban that he was dust and unto dust was destined to return.

As he began his Lenten pastoral he seemed to be addressing himself more than ever before. His first phrase warning against concupiscence of the flesh, concupiscence of the eyes, and pride of life he hastily revised to read, "In other words, pride, greed, and sensual pleasures." Pride was always, alas, the first temptation on his list, and daily joustings did not develop any lasting skill against the veteran enemy's artfulness.

His flock nevertheless needed practical suggestions for the forty days' observances. What good were all the shepherd's oratory, *mots justs,* apt scriptural allusions and splendid perorations if no one was present to be moved? His pastoral turned to church attendance, and for thirteen pages exhorted his people to sanctify the Sundays and feast days, those sweet occasions which nourished and sustained amid the pains of this life and presaged, under diverse guises, the great feast of Eternity.

And then, as always, his concern circled back to the seminary. If only among their good works for Lent they would remember this primary necessity!

> The first pastors of a Diocese pass, and go to join their predecessors. "Again a little while," each one of them can say, "and you will see me no more, because I go to my father." But Religion does not pass with them. The generations which succeed you are *bone of your bone, flesh of your flesh.* It is for you and for them that we work, in forming these lasting establishments from which come, generation after generation, the fathers of each parish, the benefactors of every age, the *models of the flock* of Jesus Christ.

He had always been accused of too liberal spending, he knew. He would be in this present case. But he could not regret it; he could only justify it, saying:

> If you are tempted to accuse us of temerity for having undertaken a work which seems to you beyond our means, accuse us of solicitude for your good and that of your children, accuse us of having had too much confidence in your love for

them, for yourselves, and for Religion. Remember, besides, that avarice too often disguises itself as prudence. It costs less to call a work impossible than to give![3]

On the day that DuBourg signed his Lenten pastoral in Montauban there died in Besançon not far from the Swiss border a cardinal archbishop of the Church, Louis-François-Auguste, duc de Rohan-Chabot. *L'Ami,* in announcing his death at the age of forty-five on Friday, February 8, remarked that he had been Archbishop of Besançon only four years, two of which he had spent away from his see.[4] But the youth of the cardinal and his absence from his duties were only a small part of the exotic story of his career as gossip and fact suggested it.

Born in 1788, two years before DuBourg was ordained, as the sun was setting on the Old Regime, Rohan-Chabot entered the political arena as a chamberlain of Napoleon. In those days he had been a "pious correspondent" of Simon Bruté who, from his post in the seminary in Baltimore, acted as intermediary in passing on Rohan-Chabot's news from Europe to Carroll, DuBourg, and Cheverus. Carroll had written to the Jesuit John Grassi on October 14, 1814, that:

> Prince Rohan de Chabot, now Prince de Léon, who having been formerly one of the Chamberlains of Bonaparte contrived means to see sometimes at Fontainebleau, and gain his confidence, the Pope, and since had some commission to Italy, which gave him an opportunity of beholding his Holiness' solemn entrance into Rome, of which the letter to Bruté is said (for I have not seen it) a most splendid and edifying description. But the most interesting part to us . . . is, that being at Rome he had a private audience of three-quarters of an hour, in which the Pope assured him, that amongst other means of healing the wounds of the Church, one was the reestablishment of the Society [of Jesus], concerning which he was warmly occupied.[5]

That period of the young nobleman's life ended tragically in 1815 when his young wife, Armandine de Serent, burned to death in an accident. Four years later he entered the Seminary of Saint-Sulpice to study for the priesthood.

In rapid succession he passed from Holy Orders to Vicar General of Paris, Archbishop of Auch and, before he ever took possession of that see, Archbishop of Besançon. On July 5, 1830, he was made a cardinal of the Church.[6] A man who could rise from seminarian to cardinal in eight years obviously was in the good graces of the Bourbon dynasty, and it was not surprising that his consecration as archbishop on January 18, 1829, took place in the presence of Charles X while the Archbishop of Paris presided amid great pomp and circumstance. Nor was it surprising that the newly named cardinal in 1830 should remain devoted to that monarch after the latter's overthrow in July.

Having gone to Paris for the purpose of receiving his cardinals' *barette* from the hands of the king, Rohan-Chabot had barely arrived when the first violence of the July Revolution erupted, forcing him to take to the road again. Arrested at Vaugirard and maltreated by the anticlerical insurgents, the Cardinal Archbishop of Besançon escaped on July 29 only by disguising himself and fleeing to Belgium and thence to Switzerland where he took refuge with the Jesuits in Fribourg. His *barette* was belatedly conferred in Lucerne by the papal nuncio.[7]

Rohan-Chabot asked the pope to be allowed to spend his exile in Rome, but Pius VIII replied that a shepherd's place was in the midst of his flock and urged him to return to Besançon. This the cardinal archbishop was not prepared to do; his ties to the Bourbon dynasty made him view Louis-Philippe, who had replaced Charles X on the throne of France on August 9, 1830, as a usurper. Further, the first months of the new regime, as previously noted, displayed a hostility to the Church reminiscent of the worst days of the great Revolution of the 1790s, a hostility the "King of the Barricades" appeared to sanction. Certainly in Besançon the July Revolution provoked a "violent effervescence," which the new governmental officials aided and abetted by an extensive program of pillage and destruction directed against the archbishop's palace, the rectory of Sainte-Madeleine, old priests who had been nonjurors in 1791, diocesan missionaries, and especially the seminaries and other religious houses. The old canards—that the clergy had amassed huge stores of arms and powder together with sizeable funds destined for foreign powers to make war on France—were revived.[8] A prelate who was reputed to enjoy preaching "at dusk, in shadowy pulpits, before devout women, taking care to light his pale face in half-tones . . . with the help of two or three candles artistically placed," was not likely to rush eagerly to his station while statues were being overturned and mission crosses ripped up, and the lower clergy imprisoned by Prefect Chopin d'Arouville of Doubs.[9]

The absence of Rohan-Chabot unhappily encouraged the rift between the government and the Catholics of Besançon. Although the vicars general of the archdiocese prudently did all they could to promote a spirit of peace, concord, and charity, the activities of their superior elsewhere filled Paris with outrage at the shepherd and a smouldering resentment toward his flock. When Pius VIII died, Rohan-Chabot, with a livery whose "number and éclat of display would recall all the former grandeur of the houses of Rohan and Soubise," did not hesitate to go to Rome in December to participate in the consistory to elect the pope's successor, announcing that he desired to enter the conclave for the French nation, and would receive with pleasure all the instructions his government might send, "if they were not opposed to his character and conscience."[10] During the conclave he roomed next door to Cardinal Maurus Cappelari, with whom he was reported to have conversed lengthily the whole time. When Cappelari emerged from the conclave on February 1, 1831, as Gregory XVI and begged Rohan-Chabot, "Recommend me to our Lord," his tone seemed especially paternal.[11] Later in the year it was the Cardinal Archbishop of Besançon whom the pontiff delegated to present the three notable French pilgrims: Lamennais, Lacordaire, and Montalembert, when they reached Rome.[12] The coupling of Rohan-Chabot's name with that of Félicité de Lamennais could only incense Louis-Philippe further since Lamennais's fulminations in his journal *l'Avenir* had attacked the king's episcopal nominations.

When the French cardinal then proceeded to accompany the duchess of Berry on her peregrinations in Italy, he appeared to have put himself irrevocably beyond the pale.

The king's visit to Besançon in June 1831 already showed something of the royal displeasure. In spite of almost unceasing rain on the day of his arrival, he was greeted enthusiastically by the citizens and military of both Besançon and those who had come over from Dole by boat, disembarking at Quai Vauban on the Doubs River. The vicars general had naturally selected their *doyen,* or senior member, Jean-Joseph Loye, to do the honors of presenting the clergy who wished to offer His Majesty the homage of their "respect and submission which religion commands toward those entrusted with power." The phrase irked the king, who was already irritated by the absence of the archbishop, and persuaded that all the clergy shared their superior's sympathies, Louis-Philippe snapped, "I believe that something more is necessary than submission to the law; it is necessary to believe you entertain a spirit of obedience and affection for your government as well! Permit me to tell you that it is your duty and to your interest to recommend this spirit which was lacking in your discourse."

Poor old Loye, who had been ailing for some time, nearly collapsed and went home tottering at the vehemence of this reprimand, took to his bed, and did not live long afterwards. The next day Louis-Philippe, wishing to make some amends for his ill-temper on his arrival, invited to the royal banquet the pastor of Saint-Pierre, but when the Prefect of Doubs reminded him that this priest had been a favorite of the missing Rohan-Chabot, His Majesty arranged to have the pastor seated at the foot of the table between a lieutenant of the fire department and the chief of police.

Rohan-Chabot did eventually return to his see city. Gregory XVI, like his predecessor, urged him to return, and Father Felix-Antoine Dupanloup, who had some influence with the cardinal as well, persuaded him that especially when his people were threatened by a dreadful calamity he must be in their midst. Cholera morbus by March of 1832 had reached Paris, where Archbishop de Quelen was permitting mass-funerals twice a week for those having died from the plague.[13] Leaving Rome on April 29, Rohan-Chabot traveled day and night to reach Besançon, where he arrived on May 11.

By a most unfortunate coincidence, the duchess of Berry chose that precise time to attempt in Marseilles the same sort of rising which later also failed to materialize in Midi. The returning prelate was suspected of having favored this plan and he was received in Besançon with marked hostility. Less than two weeks after his arrival a furious mob rushed upon the archiepiscopal palace, breaking the glass in its windows and screaming filthy insults at the mother and family of the cardinal. After two days of violence the civil authorities with the aid of the military brought things under control, and by May 27 relative order again prevailed.

During these scenes of savagery, Rohan-Chabot remained quite calm and very much master of himself, attending the May devotions in the cathedral unperturbed. From the pulpit he accepted his own responsibility for having unchained these human passions, asked for prayers for the rioters and for himself, and earned in this way the good will of sincere Catholics. By the time of his death, brought on by his efforts to assist the victims of cholera, he was noted for his humility, his generosity, sincerity and Christian charity. His Lenten *Mandement* released posthumously by his vicars general touched the hardest hearts, and *l'Ami* found it worthy of publication.[14]

Today the statue in the Cathèdrale Saint-Jean showing the prelate as a slim and handsome man kneeling in quiet meditation is oddly moving to a twentieth-century visitor who knows something of the legend of the young nobleman whose excesses were those of loyalty in an age when more prudent men trimmed their sails to the winds of change. In 1833, however, the "Citizen King" was relieved at the opportunity Rohan-Chabot's death gave him to fill the vacant see with a prelate more to his liking.

Only a week after Rohan-Chabot's death, by royal ordinance dated February 15, Louis-Philippe named Louis-Guillaume-Valentin DuBourg to the metropolitan See of

Besançon.[15] This nomination did not mystify the politically-minded prophets.

> After the odious scenes hailing the return of Rohan-Chabot to Besançon, the nomination of Bishop Dubourg as his successor was very significant. The virtue of the two prelates was the same; nevertheless public opinion attributed tremendous differences between them when it came to character and sentiments. The government intended to oppose the simplicity of the missionary to the ostentation of the prince, to detach the clergy from the fallen monarchy— naturally dear to the older priests—by replacing a Rohan with a man without political antecedents and whose vicissitudes during his apostolic career in the New World had drawn him toward the duc d'Orleans, now become King of the French people. Mgr. DuBourg had been very well-received at the Tuileries; great hopes rested on his administration.[16]

When the Minister of the Interior, Apollinaire-Antoine-Maurice, comte d'Argout, forwarded the news of this nomination to Montauban on February 18, he added that it gave him pleasure to transmit this proof of the particular esteem with which the king honored DuBourg and requested that he reply promptly in order that the Minister of Foreign Affairs might experience no delay in settling matters with the Holy See.[17]

On receiving the news of his nomination, DuBourg replied at once:

> I have received my nomination to the Archdiocese of Besançon as a most flattering testimony of the King's goodness. I thank you, M. le Ministre, for the kind things you had to say. I wish to cause no delay in bringing this affair to a conclusion with the Holy See. I therefore have the honor to join to this despatch my canonical resignation from the See of Montauban. I enclose also a letter for the King which I pray Your Excellency will kindly forward to him.[18]

L'Ami, ever devoted to keeping its subscribers *au courant*, said on February 23, "We can announce as certain that M. DuBourg, Bishop of Montauban, has been named to the Archdiocese of Besançon."[19]

Given the time of year and distance between Paris and Montauban, the speed with which these first exchanges were made suggests more than the customary urgency in filling vacant sees. Something has been suggested to account for the king's impatience; but what of DuBourg? Was his letter of acceptance as matter-of-form as it appears? As further exchanges in March reveal, there were compunctions—not only in Montauban but in Bordeaux as well.

A year earlier, in February 1832, anticlerical French liberals under the pretext of reducing the budget proposed that the thirty sees created or restored in 1817 should be suppressed to return the number to that of Napoleon's Concordat of 1801. An amendment to this proposal recommended a gradual reduction by the simple expedient of not filling sees as they fell vacant through deaths or resignations. Particularly in jeopardy in 1832 were Beauvais, Langres, and Verdun; and when Louis-Philippe filled these sees with excellent nominees the danger seemed temporarily averted. But the clamor for reduced spending for religion was not permanently silenced, and when budgetary questions were debated in the spring of 1833 the proposals resurfaced.[20]

With DuBourg's prospective removal to Besançon, both DuBourg and Cheverus were now apprehensive about the fate of Montauban. In Paris it was presumed that DuBourg could be replaced by Trélissac who had administered Montauban from 1809 to 1824, and then served there as vicar general to Cheverus for another two years. In fact, Trélissac had been deemed suitable for Montauban more than two years earlier. At the time of the vacancy of the Archdiocese of Avignon, the Minister of the Interior had prepared for Louis-Philippe a report on both DuBourg and Trélissac, suggesting the former for Avignon and the latter for Montauban.

The report noted that during DuBourg's more than ten years as Bishop of Louisiana he had lived in the midst of people of diverse faiths and had demonstrated an enlightened character suited to becoming Cheverus's successor at Montauban, a region likewise mingling Catholics and non-Catholics. Since 1826 he had perfectly fulfilled the hopes placed in him. Especially in recent months one had nothing but praise for his enlightened prudence. He could be replaced at Montauban by Trélissac, a vicar general of Bordeaux, whose selection by Cheverus for that office in both cities was recommendation enough. DuBourg's age was given at that time as sixty-five, Trélissac's as "around sixty-six."[21]

Apparently Trélissac was selected for Montauban at the same time that DuBourg was chosen for Besançon in 1833, for Cheverus wrote to a friend on February 22, "Monseigneur Dubourg has just been named Archbishop of Besançon & the dear Abbé de Trélissac Bishop of Montauban." And then he added the clause which contained the cause for the uncertainty and delay which no one had anticipated: "but he refuses & is staying with me."[22] The official notification of the king's wishes in regard to Trélissac was forwarded to Bordeaux on March 5 and l'Ami reported the nomination as settled only to retract its error a few days later after learning that the *Journal de la Guienne* had already reported on March 7 that "M. l'abbé de Trélissac, vicar general of Bordeaux, reported to have been named to the Diocese of Montauban has modestly refused."[23]

Cheverus had mixed feelings, as his letter to the Minister of the Interior reveals:

> I have received the letter with which you honored me dated March 5, and that addressed to M. l'abbé de Trélissac, one of my vicars general. He will reply to you himself. I share his sentiments of gratitude to His Majesty and you, but I believe you will be convinced of the validity of the reasons which cause him to refuse the Diocese of Montauban. Please believe that in spite of the sorrow of being separated from a most tender & excellent friend whose sage counsels have often been useful to me, the lively interest which I take in the Diocese of Montauban & above all the wishes of His Majesty had led me to anticipate the acceptance of dear Abbé de Trélissac; but I believe like him that his forces & his health demand rest for him.[24]

If Cheverus felt chagrin that his willingness to sacrifice Trélissac to Montauban had come to naught, DuBourg was even more disturbed that his resignation of the diocese now left the danger of its suppression more acute. The *inter-nonce,* Antonio Garibaldi, told Rome on April 5 that Du-Bourg was now insisting that he would not leave a flock so dear to him in unworthy hands.[25] Parisians, who refused to believe any governmental news until it appeared in the *Moniteur,* could not understand why the king's ordinance of February 15 naming DuBourg to Besançon had still not appeared; but *l'Ami* had it on good authority that Besançon, although not personally acquainted with DuBourg, was joyously anticipating an archbishop so renowned for his zeal and labors on the American missions.[26]

From Versailles on April 27 DuBourg brought his old friend Rosati up to date on the situation as far as he knew it, saying:

> The public papers by now will have informed you of my nomination to the Archdiocese of Besançon. I have been here waiting for more than a month. I do not expect to receive my bulls before two or three more, which is a little annoying. This change in position for me will only be an increase in travel and responsibility, my new Diocese being double the one I am leaving. The advantage which it offers me is finding there a numerous clergy, educated and edifying and a population in general religious.

He and Rosati both had worked, so often in discouragement, in places where these two advantages were only wished for and never quite achieved. Certainly in the 1820s DuBourg had found neither advantage in St. Louis or New Orleans. Nor had there ever been enough money in those days. He experienced a pleasant satisfaction as he told Rosati of Besançon:

> My predecessor, His Eminence the Cardinal Duc de Rohan, had rendered the situation there most agreeable for his successors, by the enjoyment he leaves them of his furniture, his chapel, and his library; by the considerable gifts he has made to its Cathedral and Seminaries, and by the useful reforms he had begun there in the methods of teaching.

Imposing as it all was, he confessed to his old comrade, he would willingly change it for St. Louis. Yet, he added realistically, "For the few years, or days, which remain to me, what does the place I occupy matter? I will probably no longer be threatened with change; and I can find in the tomb of the archbishops the lesson of time."

As he thought again of all Rosati had accomplished since they parted in 1826—the fine new hospital, his college-university, his beautiful cathedral "ready to receive its crown," the enlarged establishments of Vincentians and Religious of the Sacred Heart—he found it almost astonishing, certainly most consoling. Steamboats now ascended the Missouri River eight hundred leagues from St. Charles. But he had in a vague way believed in all this progress and he reminded Rosati:

> Nothing of all this surprises me, unless it is the rapidity. A dozen years ago I foresaw the great destiny of St. Louis, but I did not believe it could be accomplished so soon. At the rate things are going, one can not measure the future of this fine country. What good fortune, or rather what Providence, that forced us to direct toward those climes a religious expedition, which seemed destined elsewhere! How well chosen that moment was![27]

Benedict Flaget had always believed in St. Louis's future, too. The latest news about Bardstown astonished DuBourg. Flaget had retired from his diocese and then resumed control again.[28] DuBourg in some amusement inquired of Rosati:

> What is this fantastic notion of Mgr. Flaget? Does he perhaps, like Charles V, want to see how things will go after he is gone? But these things, in his position, are always dangerous. You tell me that he has reassumed the administration: but how can that be, if his resignation has been accepted, and his successor put in possession of the see, with Mr. Chabrat as coadjutor?[29]

DuBourg thought making Chabrat a coadjutor was most unsuitable and would produce bad results. But that was Kentucky's business. He was delighted, however, that both Detroit and Vincennes were to be dioceses. He and Flaget had advocated that years ago. Perhaps, at last, Bruté would be made a bishop in spite of himself? Certainly both Rosati and Flaget had proposed him for Vincennes.[30] But Rome was as slow in making decisions for American dioceses as it was for those in France, where DuBourg was growing restive.

It was not until the last week in May that the question of Montauban was resolved. DuBourg wrote confidentially to Argout from Versailles on May 24:

> Your Excellency will doubtlessly permit me to express my joy at the news I receive of the forthcoming nomination of M. l'abbé de Trélissac to the See of Montauban. I know he still struggles against a distinction which without question demands a harsh sacrifice of him. . . . Nevertheless I was certain he would not resist a royal ordinance and I believe that in the interest of my diocese I owed it to you to advise ending as soon as possible the state of uncertainty so afflicting to my older priests and for the faithful of Montauban, and to me. For all of us who know this worthy ecclesiastic it will be a source of happiness for which we like to bless His Majesty's government.[31]

Two days after this confidential expression of satisfaction was composed, Louis-Philippe signed the ordinance naming Trélissac to Montauban.[32] If Ambroise Maréchal had been alive to read between the lines he would probably have accused DuBourg of intriguing once again in episcopal appointments! If such it was, at least in the summer of 1833 the diocese Trélissac, Cheverus, and DuBourg all loved was saved. It was one of history's ironies that Trélissac was destined to outlive both DuBourg and Cheverus, and his incumbency—either as administrator or bishop—was three times as long as their combined reigns at the city on the Tarn.

Writing to Baltimore from Versailles on May 28, DuBourg was in an optimistic mood, saying he counted on being moved to his new destination in two months' time. There were always the formalities, of course: the papal consistory approving the nominations, the despatch of the bulls from Rome, the publication of the bulls in France, the oath at the hands of the king, taking possession of the see and, at last, the *Grande Entrée*. But it was his nature to believe the future promised better days. He was pleased to assure the American Sulpicians, "Our Gentlemen in Paris enjoy health and tranquility. They are very esteemed by the new government." Health, tranquility, and esteem—the three prerequisites for happiness in this world from the view of a French ecclesiastic, surely. In general, prudent clergy could only congratulate themselves.

He was overjoyed that prospects in Maryland were equally rosy, and exclaimed to Deluol:

> What pleasure you gave me in telling me of the prosperity of your establishment, and above all that it is free from debts! I hope that Emmitsburg eventually will achieve the same result. . . . Please give me from time to time news of you and details such as those you were kind enough to give me in your last letter about our Gentlemen in Baltimore, your dear Daughters of Charity who are also those of my heart. I have no greater happiness than learning that all goes forward and prospers—*majorem non habeo gratiam, &, &*.[33]

Addressing a letter to Baltimore reminded him that in going over old papers in preparation for leaving Montauban he had come across a letter from Sister Margaret George in Frederick dated October 6, 1828. The details had become so "mouldy it would be now ridiculous to notice them"; but the custom of their friendship ought never to grow stale. She, more than anyone, had been his own entrant to the Sisters of Charity at Emmitsburg. He took up his pen again, this time writing to Frederick, Maryland, "One thing only I find in that letter, which old as it is, has I am sure, preserved all the freshness of youth; it is, my dear Margaret, your grateful affection for yr. first Father, which he is so happy to acknowledge." Gratitude was a lovely virtue, and particularly in someone who had had few opportunities to see her sponsor in so many years. In fact, there were few left who could even recall DuBourg's connection with St. Joseph's House. He was glad he had found Margaret's letter for the memories it evoked, and he told her quite earnestly:

> I admire more and more every day the attentions of Providence on our dear Sisterhood. Who could have foretold,

twenty years ago, its present usefulness! You do justice to my feelings in thinking that every mention I receive of it fills my heart with delight and gratitude. I am happy in the rememberance [sic] of my old relations with it, and in the hope that fervent prayers continue to be addressed to the Almighty in my behalf, not only from that sacred vale of St. Joseph, where I fostered the promising infant, yet in the cradle; but also from every quarter, where it has extended its gigantic strides. In that concert of prayers I lay the chief foundation of my hopes in the mercies of my God. Oh! how much I need them, my dear child![34]

He did not mention that ever since his journey to Bordeaux by steamboat a few months earlier—when he caught cold, contracting a vicious inflammation of the bronchi and larynx—he continued to suffer intermittent fever, and had still not recovered three-fourths of his voice.[35] When he returned to Paris he would see some good doctors and tend to his health. After all, at sixty-seven one could not expect to be as good as new. All his life his body had tried to deter him from the apostolic ministry, and had not won yet!

But the best doctors in Paris were unable to reverse the course of whatever the malady was which daily eroded his physical resources. And after the events of July 1 and 2 he was never again the man he had been. Around 11:00 P.M. on July 1, a fire broke out on the grounds of his *Grand Séminaire* in the area where all the lumber and other materials for enlarging the seminary had been stacked. Students, awakened by the flames, called for help, but the seminary was so far from the center of town it was already ravaged by the blaze before firefighters, troops, and other assistance could arrive. In spite of the heroism of everyone, the violence of the fire was such that to isolate and save the part still standing, the rest had to be sacrificed. The residence section that faced on the Quai Montmurat and the adjoining wing were completely destroyed. Some of the students were trapped by the flames and, unable to reach the stairways, leaped from the windows; some recovered from their injuries, others died.

It was fairly certain the origins of the fire were criminal. The report given in the Chamber of Deputies on July 20 said, "It is estimated the damage caused by the fire at the Montauban seminary was 60,000 francs. The cashbox of this establishment containing some 30,000 francs was stolen in the midst of the confusion caused by the event."[36] Searching through the ruins, people found large numbers of books and other objects belonging to the superior of the seminary and the professors torn up or mutilated in other ways. To the citizens of good will this viciousness, and in such circumstances, was inconceivable.[37]

To DuBourg, the seminary fire was a mortal blow. After the months of collecting the little driblets of offerings from his people of small means, and the rarer larger benefactions from the wealthy, after all his dreams of leaving, at least in Montauban, a fine school for the shaping of a holy clergy, the culmination of his life's work was this devastation on the river's edge. All the failures of his American ventures came rushing back.[38] Theft, pillage, and arson had dogged his footsteps wherever he strode. Mount St. Mary's, which he and Dubois had founded with such high hopes, had burned two years before he returned to France. Only last December a fire in the chapel at Natchez had consumed the little organ, which once belonged to Louis XVI and was given by his brother Louis XVIII to DuBourg for his mission church on the Mississippi River.[39] The profound melancholy that seemed to rise from the very marrow of his bones was something more than the periodic depressions one learns to accept in old age. "I am going to Besançon," he said somberly to a Paris confrere, "to dig my grave, and sooner perhaps than one thinks."[40] It was as if, deep within him, a spring had snapped. If he did not get to his new see city soon he might not arrive at all.

In mid-July he sent a note over to Argout in the Ministry of the Interior:

> Given the bad state of my health, the doctors order me to the waters of Luxeuil in Haute-Saône which takes me into my future diocese. I have, consequently, obtained from the King permission to take my oath of fidelity before my departure in order not to have to return to Paris. Would you be so kind as to indicate, after having received the King's orders, the day and hour of this ceremony.[41]

When Argout passed this request on to his chief of the Division of the Catholic Religion his subordinate pointed out a technicality: although it was immaterial whether a bishop took his oath before or after his consecration, it did matter whether it was taken before or after the arrival of his bulls from Rome and their verification by the Council of State. Since DuBourg wanted to go at once to Luxeuil, and no one could predict when Rome would forward his bulls, he could not take his oath in Paris at that time.[42] Argout was very apologetic when he relayed this information to Du-Bourg, and hoped the archbishop-elect understood the impossibility of setting a date for the oath-taking.[43]

DuBourg did understand; he had been back in France long enough to know regulations were regulations, laws were laws. But he also knew his own condition and sent an immediate reply the same day saying, "I am sorry the rules prevent my taking the oath. . . . My health makes the trip to the waters indispensable. You know how hard it would be for me to have to return to Paris for this formality. Therefore I request permission to take my oath in writing at the time desired. This favor has already been granted to others who had less reason than I to request it."[44] Argout saw no difficulty in this arrangement and suggested only that Du-Bourg let him know when he had his bulls and that he still wished to take the oath in writing.[45]

As July ended, *l'Ami* expressed the pious wish that all the information on the prelates nominated to fill the three French vacancies at Besançon, Montauban, and Albi might have arrived in Rome in time for the consistory soon to be held, and almost immediately thereafter announced that in the consistory of July 29 the pope had precognized Louis-Guillaume DuBourg for Besançon, the only French prelate on a list of fourteen, the information on the other two not having arrived in time.[46]

In mid-August from the mineral springs of Luxeuil-les-Bains, DuBourg wrote to Argout:

> The moment seems to have come for me to renew the request I made . . . at the time of my departure from Paris . . . to be permitted to take the oath to the King in writing or between the hands of a magistrate impowered to receive it.

Already arrived in my Diocese you can perceive that it would be for me a double and grave inconvenience to be obliged to traverse twice the distance separating me from Paris to satisfy a duty which the King regards as pure formality.

Although his health had benefited from the waters, it still required a great deal of care and rest; therefore DuBourg begged the minister to obtain the king's decision on this matter before the royal departure for the west.[47]

But again timetables were fixed by formalities. The Ministry of Foreign Affairs had first to inform Interior that it was sending over DuBourg's pallium and a letter addressed to him which Argout would kindly forward. Everyone by then knew the bulls had been drawn up on August 4 but they were not sent to the Council of State until August 31! With something of his old impatience DuBourg wrote directly to Argout's subordinate in the Division of Religions:

> Here it is a month since my bulls arrived in Paris and they have not yet been expedited. I can not understand the cause for the delay in registering them. We are now approaching the normal season of ordinations; the ecclesiastical retreats in Besançon, already delayed a month, are now beginning; a host of very important matters which can only be handled by me require prompt decision; thus I am compelled to go to my archiepiscopal city and will definitely be there in a few days.

He went on to say he had sometime ago asked his nephew in Paris to approach the chief in charge of religions in regard to this matter and had received no response. "I address you directly," he said pointedly, "and count on your kindness, which I know, to tell me: 1. the likely time my bulls will be sent; 2. if the Minister will agree to my oath in writing." The stark truth was that he could not survive a trip to Paris. His forces were quite spent. "If ever necessity made law," he said simply, "I have the right to invoke it in this circumstance." It would be embarrassing to enter Besançon without any legal right to act, but matters would not brook a long delay. He concluded, "I will establish residence in my seminary and await my bulls to enter the Archiepiscopal Palace. Therefore you should address the despatches concerning me to Besançon."[48]

The weeks at Luxeuil were not all mineral baths and frustrations over red tape, to be sure. He found time and generosity enough to pen a testimonial for an old widow, protesting her removal from the civil list of pensioners at the age of seventy-five.[49] A voluminous letter from Rosati reached him by way of Vesoul, congratulating him on his "happy promotion" and bringing DuBourg up to date on developments in the Mississippi Valley. Seven religious of the Georgetown Visitation Convent had arrived in Kaskaskia, where they were received "like goddesses," and already had a great number of students. The house destined to receive the Daughters of St. Vincent de Paul was already finished and their arrival was eagerly awaited. Rosati's cathedral was rapidly coming to completion and his dearest wish was for "three lovely bells" to enhance the majesty of Catholic worship. When people saw the processions advancing, heard the singing of hymns and canticles, Rosati wrote exuberantly, "We expect a great effect—particularly from the sound of the bells. If I could have good ones, . . . a fine sound being one thing unheard of in this country, it would produce a big impression and attract much of the world to our holy religion." He had heard of a man in Normandy who made fine bells, but he was a simple fellow and might think of America as existing only in fables—or so lost and far away it was scarcely reachable. "Would this man," demanded Rosati, "send me bells worth several thousand francs?" And then he got to the heart of his matter:

> The Archbishop of Besançon would easily lift this difficulty if he would write to the pastor of this foundryman to reassure him that he ran no risk in the matter of payment. When this good man saw that one of the prelates of France was involved he would work with entire confidence. If you have the goodness to render us this service people will continue to say with even more truth that there is nothing, however

great or small, of importance to religion in this country that Mgr. Dubourg has not had a large part in.[50]

DuBourg didn't know whether to laugh or cry. It was so like Rosati—the childlike faith in the efficacy of "lovely bells," the shrewdly ingratiating request for DuBourg's intervention, and the businesslike way in which he enclosed the exact name and address of the foundryman's pastor down to the village, canton, district and department! It was almost as if his rotund Italian successor were here in Luxeuil taking the waters with him. It was a letter DuBourg needed just then, the proof that in spite of his mistakes and deficiencies he had laid a foundation on which others might build. Perhaps there was still time to serve God's purposes in this new vineyard.

Back in Paris the mills of the gods were grinding slowly, but as the old adage had it, "exceeding fine." On September 18 the king signed the ordinance authorizing the publication of DuBourg's bulls. On September 22 a report was made to the king regarding the indemnity due newly installed archbishops.[51] On September 23 Argout prodded the Council of State for the return of the bulls so that they could be forwarded to Besançon. At last, on September 26, 1833, the Minister of the Interior reported all of this to DuBourg, saying he was enclosing the bulls, the ordinances authorizing their publication, the pallium, the correct form for a written oath to be returned to Paris, and the notice of the 2,000-franc indemnity. Even then, Argout left one of the documents out![52]

DuBourg, who by now had left Luxeuil for the seminary in Besançon, hastened to copy the prescribed form of the oath: "I swear fidelity to the King of the French, obedience to the constitutional Charter, and to the laws of the realm," and returned it to Argout with the comment:

> I did not find in the dossier the royal ordinance concerning the publication of the bulls although it was mentioned. I will conform to the prescription made me not to take possession of my see until after being notified of the reception of my oath of fidelity; as always I ask Your Excellency to hasten

938

this response because the long time which has elapsed between my precognition in Rome and the publication of my bulls has brought criticisms of the Government and has been very odious to me. Thus, for this motive and for others I want to see a prompt end to this business.[53]

At last *l'Ami* could say that the Archbishop of Besançon had received his bulls, had taken his oath in writing, and that the day of his installation was set for October 10. And then, with the *non sequitur* of a city paper repeating local news from the provinces, added that M. DuBourg had subscribed 1,000 francs toward the monument to be erected in honor of his predecessor Cardinal Rohan-Chabot.[54]

A few days later Argout forwarded the missing royal ordinance and notified DuBourg that his written oath had safely arrived and had been "placed under the eyes of the King."[55] The *prise de possession* of the see took place at once on the Feast of the Holy Rosary, Sunday, October 6, 1833. As was customary, the ceremony took place after the parish Mass in the presence of the canons of the cathedral chapter, assembled in the sanctuary to solemnly witness the event. Presiding was Vicar General Antoine-François de Bouligny, now the *doyen,* or senior vicar general, since the demise of old Loye, who never recovered from his humiliation at the king's hands; Bouligny was assisted by Jean-François Cart and Thomas-Marie-Joseph Gousset. The secretary of the chapter read aloud the official documents from Paris as well as DuBourg's procuration authorizing Bouligny to act in his name. "The taking possession was done solemnly according to custom and in the traditional forms," and the nine canons affixed their signatures to the *Procès-verbal* to be forwarded to Paris by the Prefect of Doubs.[56]

DuBourg's installation in the Archdiocese of Besançon four days later was to be quite different from the one seven years earlier in Montauban. For one thing, he had been living within his archdiocese more than three weeks before the formal entrance on October 10; and since his residence had been at the *Grand Séminaire* he was already acquainted with many of his clergy and seminarians. For another thing, an ecclesiastical retreat was beginning the very day of the entrance and consequently there were more than two hundred priests present to escort him to his episcopal palace and then conduct him processionally to his cathedral. Great preparations had been made for this long-awaited day, and this time DuBourg did not deprive himself or the people of the splendors of the occasion.

God knew it would have been easy to do so. The waters of Luxeuil had not really restored him. He now had to rest for long periods of time between every effort. He could never climb to the heights of the mountain behind his cathedral where the marvelously enduring fortifications of Vauban's *Citadelle* still merited the money spent in erecting this "monumental ensemble" which cost as much as if "the walls of Besançon were made of gold."[57] Surely, viewed from below in early October, the vast panorama of tile and stone gave an illusion of golden splendor as the brilliant sun of midafternoon lay upon the Tour du Roi and almost matching Tour de la Reine. There came a time in every man's life when he knew there were far horizons he would never see again, and others he would never see at all.

He knew as well that he had not the strength nor voice for the kind of oration he should like to give on the occasion of his forthcoming first appearance before his flock. He had so much he wished to say, so little time to say it. He would have to content himself with a *mandement* which could be read by one of his vicars general to those present on the occasion, and read later by all those he had once tried to serve. If his old body had turned traitor this past year, at least his wits had not. If only the written word could express the impetuous élan of the heart—his only part which had not lost its vigor! How was he to depict for this new flock the mixed emotions which now pressed upon him—sentiments so acute, so disparate yet so interlaced he could not himself untangle them? Still, he must try:

> O, Church of *Louisiana* and *Montauban*! Dissolved is the saintly alliance which in succession identified my existence

with yours! But the ties of paternity will never be severed; it will always be true that I was your spouse and your children still mine. Always your welfare and theirs will be the object of my most ardent wishes, and for my heart a source of never-failing joy. *Louisiana, Montauban*—cherished names—I can not separate you in this effusion because you were never separated in my tenderness. In passing from one to the other I felt nothing changed in my first affections— only the sphere had been enlarged; and I understood how a father can retrieve all the same intensity of love for the children of his later life as that he held for his first-born.

He then turned to Besançon, with the incredible good fortune which gave him, from his first setting foot on the soil of his see, the unremitting generosity of his fellow bishops, vicars general, directors of his seminaries, and canons of his cathedral in doing his work for him when he was powerless to act. "What a source of sage counsels in this venerable senate associated with my labors to light my steps from my very entry into this new career! What consummate masters of sacred studies to interpret in my place! What eloquent tongues always ready to supplement the impotence of mine! No, I know of no other diocese in Christianity which could have offered me more abundant resources to relieve me of the most pressing portion of the pastoral burden."

And then, with that godly guile which seemed to come so easily to him but more often required careful research and skillful weaving into his text, he spoke of a former priest of Besançon whom many had forgotten and others had never known—a man once called "the Charles Borromeo of Franche-Comté." It was his example that had inspired so many worthy priests to devote themselves in saintly obscurity to lives of unremitting toil and prayer. "Honor and eternal gratitude to those veterans of this precious corps of reserves who, during the days of destruction, at the risk of a thousand perils, gathered up the debris of the sanctuary and who, since the dawn of religious peace, have worked with such steadfastness to rebuild it from the ruins."[58] In this same vein he praised at length the work of the Maison de

Beaupré, the center of diocesan missions, the establishment of Saint-Rémi where the Sons of Mary educated boys, the Christian Brothers, the other religious institutes of the diocese.

His last praise, that for his predecessor Cardinal Rohan-Chabot and especially for his devotion to the Holy Virgin, led him to his peroration in which he consecrated himself and his people anew to the Mother of God. Beseechingly he asked for her protection, especially for the young who had turned away through weakness or discouragement.

> Recall to them, O Blessed Virgin, the days of their innocence, reawaken in their hearts the confidence they should have in you, give a rebirth to that sweet hope which saves us. This youth avid for dangerous novelties, led astray by the passion of this age which wears itself out in vain desires, and who, cut loose without a compass in the midst of reefs, are at every moment exposed to perishing. Let shine in their eyes the luminous star which shows the way to port where, after so many agitations, they may at last find safety and repose.[59]

Afterward, it was generally agreed that the *mandement* of October 1833 was a *chef d'oeuvre* of its genre, a "magnificent monument to an elevated soul and feeling heart" of the father who in his supreme hour summons around him all his children dispersed in so diverse and distant lands. "It was the language of the Grand Siècle on the lips of an apostle."[60] Even though it had to be read by Jean-François Cart on the actual day of DuBourg's installation, its effect was so powerful that the attention of those present never flagged throughout a ceremony lasting almost three hours.

At four o'clock on the afternoon of October 10, 1833, the first booming of the cannon announced the start of the official entry of Louis-Guillaume, Archbishop of Besançon, into his jurisdiction and the thunder of the great guns continued every five minutes thereafter until the cortége reached the cathedral. The carriage bringing DuBourg to the archiepiscopal palace approached by way of the Porte Noire

or Black Gate, that time-darkened triumphal arch which
had been erected toward the end of the second century to
commemorate the exploits of Marcus Aurelius against the
Alemans and Scythians. It originally was the entrance to the
city by way of the Roman road leading from the *Citadelle*
into the lower city. In Christian times it marked one limit of
the archbishopric. In modern photographs it appears to be a
very part of the Cathèdrale Saint-Jean itself; but in historical flavor it more properly belongs to Place Castan on the
other side of the Porte with its eight surviving Roman-
Corinthian columns still marking the site of the *Nymphe* or
reservoir fed by the Arcier aqueduct of Roman times.

Descending from his carriage the archbishop was conducted to his palace where he robed for the cathedral ceremonies. Happily his residence was close by, and his meager
energies could be husbanded as much as possible for the
lengthy rituals ahead. As it was, the immense concourse of
the faithful, who had come out in the superb weather which
graced the *Grande Entrée*, pressed about him as the procession moved at snail's pace toward Saint-Jean. All the priests
who had come for their retreat joined the procession as the
beating drums rose in crescendo. Everyone wanted the first
blessing of those fragile, long-fingered hands, of the voice
scarcely audible at even such close proximity. As wasted
away as he was by the disease no doctors could retard, he
was still a majestic figure.

It seemed to DuBourg that they were entering the
cathedral by a side door and, once inside, he could see that
Saint-Jean was unlike any cathedral he had known in Europe or America. There was no main façade or great door!
Instead, there were two apses facing each other from opposite ends of the cathedral—like a great ship with two
prows. In the one sanctuary dating back to 1127–1161,
where he was to preside, the main altar had been built as
recently as 1829 by Cardinal de Rohan-Chabot. The candelabra and crucifix had been the gift of Charles X and bore
the royal monogram and coat of arms of France. On either
side of the altar were two adoring angels of sculptor Luc

Breton carved in 1769. The throne on which DuBourg was to sit was a gift of Napoleon I to Archbishop Lecoz and bore the imperial eagles.

The other apse, the one nearest the entrance, belonged to the part of Saint-Jean rebuilt in the eighteenth century and was called the *Abside du Saint-Suaire,* whose cult was inextricably entwined in the history of Franche-Comté. Midway between the two main altars arose a flamboyant fifteenth-century stone *chaire,* or pulpit, one of the very oldest in France, where in 1608 Saint François de Sales had preached after venerating Saint Suaire so long in tears. DuBourg, who was already almost fainting from pain and fatigue, told his doctor afterward, "The first thing that struck my mind on entering this venerable basilica is that it is a tomb where soon my ashes will repose at the side of my saintly predecessors and surrounded by the prayers of my children."[61] He knew he would never mount those winding stairs nor raise his voice to fill that majestic vessel nearly eighty meters long. Let young Cart ascend with the elastic step of youth. He was just the age DuBourg had been when he founded St. Mary's College in Baltimore and Emery so constantly cautioned him against his "spirit of Toboso" and against so rashly rushing forward to charge the windmills of uncalculated risks. In those days the future had stretched endlessly ahead, like the summers of one's childhood. In age, alas, dreams were tailored to the shrinking fabric of one's being and one had to measure more meticulously the garment to be worn lest it prove a shroud.

For a moment those around the archbishop thought he was going to be unable to endure the fatigues of so long a ceremony. When asked if he felt very tired he said, "It's a long time since I've done as much," then added, "but also never has so much been done for me."[62] But he quickly rallied and the fears of the faithful were dissipated in their joyful relief.[63] Unlike the great cathedrals of Beauvais, Chartres, Reims, or Bourges, the aura of Saint-Jean was not that of "immensity, airy lightness, profoundness or mystery but one of grandeur and serenity."[64] And in the serenity of this his last cathedral his energies seemed to spring to life once more. No one believed that late afternoon that Du-Bourg was so near the close of his ministry.[65] Not even the newly installed Archbishop of Besançon. His thoughts were on the next day when his committee on the future of the "mixed college" for the archdiocese was to meet. Later that month the *Petit Séminaire* chapel was to be blessed. Meanwhile, the second retreat for his clergy was beginning. There was no time for dying just yet.

CHAPTER XLII

THE SPIRIT OF TOBOSO
LAID TO REST

In his pastoral letter read in the cathedral the day he was installed the Archbishop of Besançon had eulogized his clergy, whom he had already gotten to know, saying, "In the presence of this holy militia I swear, my very dear brothers, I feel my forces reanimated, and my courage reborn. Erudition, devotion, discipline—what is lacking to inspire me with confidence!"[1] As was so often the case with his most graceful rhetorical public statements, he was speaking the simple truth. From the moment he had entered his jurisdiction at Luxeuil in August he had been overcome by the courtesy and caliber of the clergy holding positions of trust, and it seemed that he was going to be able, after all, to plunge into splendid designs for his new jurisdiction.

He had scarcely tested the waters of Luxeuil when the Bishop of Langres, Césaire Mathieu, hurried over to offer his episcopal services in any way he might be of use while DuBourg was still incapacitated. DuBourg was very touched by the sincerity of this collegial gesture, and in accepting it on August 22 wrote:

Your offers, Monseigneur, are so very obliging. Aren't you afraid I will abuse them? I confess they present this temptation. How could it be otherwise! To be overwhelmed with fatigue and at the same time to be given the happiness of finding a brother whom I love as much as I respect—truthfully, I cannot resist. My health improves very slowly. I will never be worth much as a bishop. What good fortune in my powerlessness to be able to present to God and to my flock such a supplement.[2]

With the September *Quatre-Temps* ordinations only weeks away and his bulls not yet arrived, DuBourg had been only too glad to have Mathieu to rely upon.

When *l'Ami* reported the Besançon ordinations of Saturday, September 21, the week after DuBourg's arrival in his see city, it implied that the archbishop himself had officiated at the ceremonies in the seminary chapel; but the Bishop of Langres actually took on that task, and subsequently offered to make the rounds of the archdiocese when confirmations were due. DuBourg, unwilling to impose on Mathieu incessantly, asked the government for an auxilliary bishop, but was refused.[3] At a time when one faction remained determined to reduce the number of existing episcopal places it was not politic to create a new one, even for a friend of the king.

With the ordinations out of the way, the retreats for the clergy began. While still in Luxeuil, DuBourg had envisioned these retreats as an excellent way to get to know his priests early in his administration. Because they involved some 350 pastors and assistants, two separate retreats were scheduled almost back-to-back: the first, beginning on September 24 and ending on October 2, had as its retreatmaster the celebrated Sulpician Abbé Pierre-Denis Boyer; the second, opening the day of DuBourg's installation, was led by the Jesuit Abbé Charles-Joseph Gloriot, whose knowledge and experience were known to all the dioceses of France.[4]

DuBourg had hoped to take an active part in the retreats when they were first planned, but by now was too weak even to offer Mass. His attacks of fever and racking pain were accelerating in frequency, and it was only during the brief respites that he could manage any physical duties. He did address the second retreat once, but otherwise attended only the closing exercises at which each priest renewed his vows between the hands of his archbishop. At least he had the opportunity of seeing something of the piety, fervor, and fine spirit which animated his co-workers.

The archbishop dearly loved retreats. In the last message he sent back to his clergy in Montauban just before he died, he said:

> There are three things toward which you know I constantly directed my efforts: the seminaries, the diocesan retreats, and the catechism instruction. Please express to the students of the sanctuary and the numerous children composing the catechism classes that I am satisfied with the past and send every wish and hope for the future.[5]

It was, in truth, a resumé of his episcopal career after his return to France.

In these last months of 1833, DuBourg resembled the American Revolutionary general, Nicholas Herkimer, who after being shot in battle so that he could no longer sit his horse, had himself propped on his saddle beneath a tree and continued to command his men from there, winning, some say, the strategic Battle of Oriskany. DuBourg was a mortally wounded commander. His doctor said later, "When he arrived among us his zeal and prodigious activity of spirit alone sustained a nature worn out and failing. One who recalls the feebleness of his voice, the collapsing of his forces, and the profound alteration of his features finds it easy to understand that nothing remained for him but to die."[6] But he died commanding, and while he was in command he had the support of remarkable subordinates.

Like the Bishop of Langres, his vicars general proved to be a joy. Gousset, the distinctly superior administrative talent of the three, had formerly headed the major seminary and together with François-Joseph Gaume, whom he had shaped to his own mold, had raised the seminary to a repute known and envied throughout France. Like DuBourg he had taken a position against Lamennais and supported Gregory XVI in his condemnation in 1832. Rohan-Chabot, whom Féli had ridiculed in *les Affaires de Rome,* had called Gousset from the seminary to become his vicar general in 1831 and, with the continued absence of the late Cardinal Archbishop of Besançon, Gousset had already had an opportunity to refine his administrative skills. Only the year before DuBourg's arrival, Gousset had distinguished himself as well by a learned *Justification de la doctrine morale du B. Alphonse de Liguori.*

Jean-François Cart, who like Gousset had been on the seminary faculty prior to his appointment as vicar general, was less renowned for doctrine but was a man of remarkable piety and gentleness. His personality was delightfully vivacious, and he had a flair for eloquent writing which drew him and his new archbishop toward each other immediately. During Rohan-Chabot's absence and the later vacancy of the see, it had been Cart who had "held the pen" which produced the *circulaires* and *mandements* of the archdiocese. Bouligny, who by reason of his age and seniority of appointment was the *doyen* of the vicars general, was less active than Gousset or Cart, but he was the priest who had organized the Association of the Propagation of the Faith in Besançon, and that alone would have endeared him to DuBourg who owed so much to that organization's generosity to his American diocese.[7]

These three men could be trusted to furnish reliably detailed *précis* of the assets and needs of the archdiocese. Even before he left Luxeuil in mid-September DuBourg was sufficiently informed about the educational establishments within his jurisdiction to perceive that there were too many, and resources in both men and money were spread too thin. He decided that the preparatory schools, or *petits séminaires,* should be reduced to two in order to facilitate both the apportioning of faculty and increasing the number of courses that could be properly offered on any one campus. The one for Haute-Saône would be located in Vesoul as soon as necessary renovations were made, with seminarians from there in the interim transferred to Luxeuil; the other, for the Département de Doubs, would be located in a complex of buildings known as Consolation, a former monastery which from all appearances was perfectly suited to a house of education.[8] DuBourg had reached this decision by very sound reasoning. The Consolation property, which in the aftermath of the Revolution of 1789 had been sold and defaced, had been repurchased by Rohan-Chabot in 1829, and more recently had been restored and enlarged by the efforts of Jean-François Goguillot, the *économe* of the seminary. It eventually could easily handle more than 200 students and by November 15 of the present year would accommodate 150. The lovely chapel of the monastery would be restored to its original purposes, and was already redecorated by order of the seminary's superior.[9] Gifts for the chapel had been pouring in from nearby communities delighted with the prospect of having divine services in their region once more.

The town of Ornans, east of the city of Besançon, would suffer, to be sure, from losing a *petit séminaire;* but it was not an ideal place for the education of young ecclesiastics. The buildings in which the preparatory school was then located belonged half to the city and half to the department, which used some of its space for the gendarmerie. The space used by the school was in dire need of some very expensive renovations. Perhaps Ornans might become later the site of the mixed college, which the archdiocese contemplated reviving. In any case, one *petit séminaire* in each *département* was sufficient. Since the death of his brother Louis three years ago, the archbishop's news from Filleau in Paris made it clear he would never benefit from any residue from his father's fortune.[10] The days of confident borrowing on the credit of anticipated inheritances were long since past, and he winced at the recollection that he was still being dunned by people duped by Inglesi's deceits a decade before.[11] The old faults of "liberality and schemes from a long custom of spending," for which Mother Seton had criticized him so long ago, must be subdued.

When DuBourg arrived in Besançon from Luxeuil on

September 14, to live in the seminary until his installation in October, he had a chance to learn at close hand something of the men who were *"comme la tête du clergé,"* the priests of the major seminary and of the missions. The superior of the seminary, Charles-François Cuenot, who had been elected only that year, had been there since 1816 and in some ways reminded DuBourg of Nagot, his own superior in those Baltimore days still so vivid in memory. Cuenot personified tradition. "His principal glory was to preserve the rule of the seminary as it had been established in 1670." Those who knew him best said he could have died a wealthy man, for he had been left a considerable legacy; but he used it all for good works known only to his archbishops. His favorite advice to newly arrived directors of the seminary was, "Come here, stay here, and you will learn what it is to live harshly but to die sweetly."[12] DuBourg may have raised an eyebrow at Cuenot's insistence that ecclesiastical dress conform to eighteenth-century models; but, of course, Franche-Comté was not the American missions!

By the side of the seminary there was l'Ecole-Beaupré, the house of the missionaries, whom DuBourg had praised in his *mandement* as the apostolic workers to whom, after 1816, Franche-Comté principally owed the survival of the faith and piety in its cities and countryside. "Their arrival in each parish was an event; their stay a public benefit." The mission house was headed by François-Joseph Gaume, a former director of the seminary. While at the seminary during Gousset's reign, Gaume had taught moral theology and shared his superior's liking for that of Liguori.[13] The two men worked together without friction, and now that Gousset was increasingly DuBourg's alter ego in administering the archdiocese, it was heartening to have such men ready and willing to carry to completion the changes DuBourg believed were necessary to make ecclesiastical education more effective in the Archdiocese of Besançon.

Before his death Cardinal Rohan-Chabot had been hoping to create a "mixed college," which would replace the kind of schools unfortunately suppressed by Charles X in 1828. DuBourg, who envisioned such an institution as combining all the best features of the Baltimore academy he had founded in 1799, meant to bring his predecessor's project to reality, and shortly after his arrival in Besançon, he named a committee to make recommendations on the location and curriculum for this *collège mixte*. The membership of this planning board reveals the keenness of his judgment and his administrative tact. It included his three vicars general, the superiors of the major and two minor seminaries, the pastor of the cathedral parish, the secretary of the cathedral chapter, the superior of the mission house, and a former director of the seminary.[14] The meeting of this committee the day following DuBourg's installation was primarily concerned with locating the college on one of two sites presenting certain advantages. Ornans, which had so recently lost its minor seminary, was offering to cede a site in perpetuity southeast of Besançon; Marnay almost equidistant to the northwest offered both the advantage of being at the juncture of four departments and having property already belonging to the seminary where an ecclesiastical school had formerly existed. Experience had shown that offers like that of Ornans too often proved hazardous since in time of revolution commitments were not kept. When the vote was taken, it was unanimously in favor of Marnay.[15]

It was not long after this decision was reached that DuBourg suffered a new attack that dismayed those who witnessed it. He had gone into the choir to hear Mass when he completely lost consciousness. The young priests around him believed he had died; no one seemed able to detect his pulse. But in a moment the raging fever returned, followed by copious perspiration, and that crisis was over.[16] In the remission which followed, he had a *circulaire* issued for the Jubilee that Pope Gregory XVI had announced on the occasion of his election to the pontifical throne.[17]

It was out of the question, however, for him to go to Consolation for the blessing of the chapel of the newly located minor seminary. That joy had to be delegated to Bouligny on October 22, and the senior vicar general, assisted by some fifty priests, presided over the ceremonies, which attracted a large crowd. Cuenot, from the major seminary, gave the homily and baptized the new bell for the chapel's steeple with unction sufficient to the pride of its godparents, Vicar General Bouligny and Madame de Maiche.[18] Next to the painful deprivation of offering his own Mass, the thing DuBourg minded most was being unable to share with his seminarians and their directors the inauguration of these changes from which he hoped new blessings might come to his people.

The archbishop had still not gone through the formal ceremony of the conferring of his pallium which had arrived in Paris in August. This simple white wool symbol of the pope's sharing of his pastoral powers with his archbishops meant a great deal to its recipient. He could recall the first time he had witnessed such a ceremony. He had just returned from Martinique in 1811 when John Carroll had received his pallium on August 18 and had taken *his* oath of loyalty to the Holy See, in the reign of Pius VII. The conferring of the pallium was uniquely suited to emphasizing the position of the papacy and the relation of Catholics everywhere to one spiritual head. DuBourg intended to have it a public ceremony, it if were humanly possible.

He chose All Saints Day, November 1, 1833, since it was a day his flock would be attending services anyway. It was a day, too, on which he would like to be once more in his cathedral. Those present may have been less struck by the significance of the occasion than by the awesome contrast between the youth and agility of the Bishop of Langres and the advanced age and gauntness of the Archbishop of Besançon. DuBourg insisted that Césaire Mathieu be the prelate to do the honors that day, Mathieu who had been his episcopal "right arm" with such unstinting generosity. It was Mathieu's vigorous voice which proclaimed the meaning of the lengthy ceremony; DuBourg's was scarcely audible as he took the oath:

> I, Louis-Guillaume, Archbishop of Besançon, from this hour will be faithful and obedient to Blessed Peter, to the Holy Roman Church, and to our Father, Pope Gregory XVI, and to all his legitimate successors. I will not plan nor consent nor act so that they may lose their lives, nor a member, nor

be deceived; their advice, directly or by messengers or messages, I shall reveal to no one to their harm. I shall sustain the Roman Papacy and the kingdom of Saint Peter against every man. I shall honor the legate of the Apostolic See on his arrival and departure, and I shall come to his assistance in his necessities. When called to a Synod, I shall come unless hindered by canonical impediment. I shall make the *ad limina apostolorum* visit every ten years, either personally or through my ambassador unless excused by papal permission. The possessions which pertain to my archiepiscopal estate, I shall not sell, I shall not give away, I shall not pawn, I shall not infeudate anew, nor in another way alienate without the consent of the Roman Pontiff; and I shall observe the Constitution concerning the prohibition of investitures, and of jurisdictional goods pertaining to lesser churches, published in the year of our Lord, 1625. So help me God and His Holy Gospels.

He suffered visibly during the rite and there were those, seeing him that day, who could not help thinking of another apposition of the pallium which takes place when an archbishop is being placed in his tomb.[19]

He still held some large gatherings in his palace. The civil and military authorities were constant in their attentions and devotion, from the lowest rank to the highest.[20] In the brief time he lived in Besançon he exerted a remarkable influence on the local interplay of Church and State. Prefect Amadée Thierry of the Department of Haute-Saône reported to the Minister of Interior on August 2, 1834, "The direction given to the clergy when it was solely administered by the Cathedral Chapter of Canons was bad. It improved in the last months of the administration of Mgr. de Rohan and above all since the advent of Mgr. Dubourg."[21] The Prefect of Doubs expressed even more emphatically the change in relationships due to DuBourg's presence in the archdiocese, when he reported to his general council:

It is with the keenest satisfaction that I announce that my relations with the diocesan authority leave nothing to be desired. To what do we attribute this happy harmony which can be the source of so much good? Gentlemen, this question awakens in me a very sad memory: that of the venerable prelate who appeared among us only long enough to cast a last, lively éclat among us and then exhale his beautiful soul. His touching goodness to me, the benevolent speed with which he seconded my projects, the instructions—so full of gentle unction and such heights of wisdom—which he gave his clergy leave me with no doubt of the influence his saintly memory still exerts today. We have lost this great prelate but his spirit still reigns in our midst.[22]

Prefect Derville-Malechord concluded his report with the prediction that if the diocese was destined to have as its head another prelate invested with the confidence and friendship of a DuBourg there was hope that in the future the clergy would contribute powerfully to the peace and prosperity of the country.

The man who may have known him most intimately during those last months of DuBourg's life, his physician, said of him:

> Mgr. Dubourg, who arrived at the highest ecclesiastical dignities through merit alone, combined with profound learning a high capacity for administration and vast experience. Of a character at the same time firm and full of kindness, of a conciliating spirit and sage tolerance, he could, according to need, act through persuasion or decide with authority.

It was clear to Dr. Joseph Auguste Gaspard Pécot that the archbishop hoped to be the occasion—as Louis-Philippe had hoped he might be—of many rapprochements. DuBourg would say, "Religious sentiment and the need for order must unite us all." No one in the given circumstances was more capable than he of achieving this goal, from Pécot's view:

> Endowed with perfect tact for judging men, great competency in exercising a salutary influence upon them, his long experience with life had enabled him to understand with rare perception the real position of the clergy in the midst of the contemporary social movement. The welfare of religion,

which he was called to defend, and his influence for maintaining order and public morality were the motivations of all his actions and the objectives of all his efforts.[23]

History does not suggest that prefects and doctors are endowed with infallible prescience; but in the case of Doubs and the Archdiocese of Besançon one prefect was something of a prophet. Césaire Mathieu, whom DuBourg had loved and respected from the moment they met, became Archbishop of Besançon and continued the reconciliation of clerical and civil sensibilities. Nor was Mathieu the only one of the clergy around DuBourg destined for episcopal rank or promotion. Biographers cannot prove that the example of one man causes things to happen in the lives of others; they are, however, permitted to notice how things turn out. It is a fact that the men closest to DuBourg in those last days of life—when the mortal frame diminishes and the immortal soul may be refined to virtual incandescence, when all of the latent capacities seem perfected— these men did get chosen. Thomas-Marie Gousset went on to become Bishop of Perigueux, then Archbishop of Reims, and finally cardinal; Jean-François Cart became Bishop of Nîmes. Jean-Jacques Guerin, who had first welcomed Du-Bourg to Luxeuil, was named to the See of Langres; Jean-Marie Doney, one of DuBourg's canons, succeeded Trélissac in Montauban; and Philippe Gerbet, the most literary man at the major seminary, became Bishop of Perpignan.

As November passed, the archbishop's pulse grew weaker every day. His face, yellowish straw-colored, changed more and more. As a last cause for anxiety his legs and feet began swelling unmercifully. The ultimate crisis came on Monday, December 2. His fever and agitations worsened and the least movement brought back the by now habitual fainting.[24] On December 7 all the churches of the city began Forty-Hours prayers for the archbishop. It was known that in the night of December 5–6 he had received Communion to celebrate the papal Jubilee and that on the eve of the Forty-Hours he had requested the last rites of the Church, Extreme Unction.[25]

Yet his intellectual faculties remained intact. He sensed that death was not going to come easily and said to Jean-François Cart with wry humor, "I do not know what God has in store for me, but with my athletic physique I should be able to sustain with Death a battle of giants!"[26] Like Elizabeth Seton, who had remembered him in her last hours, he believed that these last trials and temptations could be the worst of all.[27] The Devil, who had not been able to win while one's vigor and will were at their peaks, might stake all on the moment of passing. "It is the last moment of agony I fear most," he confessed. "My God, ease for me this terrible passage."[28]

He was constantly surrounded by devotion and deep affection. He had always had the gift of "instant friendship," or as Emery used to say, "making profound impressions" which endured; and now that he had become through age and anguish almost pure spirit, the impact of his gaiety, his tact, his learning, and above all his understanding heart won him unstinting care. He told Pécot in their presence, "The good young men care for me as they would care for their father." And added appreciatively, "And they *pray* for me!" He was always telling them with gentle raillery to suggest pious thoughts appropriate to a man in his position. If God were willing to receive him, he would pray for them hereafter. Meanwhile he put them to work writing letters for him to all the dear friends and associates to whom he wanted to bid farewell.[29]

With perfect composure he made all the arrangements for his funeral. He knew Pécot wanted an autopsy afterward and he himself had intended for a long time that his heart should be returned to his first diocese—"whose difficult and astonishing creation comprised the most laborious and most beautiful part of his life"—to repose in the chapel of the New Orleans Ursulines who had remained the one steady beacon shining through all the storm clouds threatening him in the first years of the American political jurisdiction and his own religious incumbency.[30] He ordered that he was to be buried without any pomp; the plain wooden coffin was not to be open, and would be on public view only twenty-four hours.[31] He had always loved liturgies of grandeur when they honored God and his Church; but he feared display and ostentation where he was concerned. He would be buried with only a small wood cross. The truth was that he had already sold his fine pectoral cross to have some money to distribute among the poor.[32]

On December 5, 1833, DuBourg drew up his will with the aid of his secretary, the honorary canon François-Aimé Querry, and in the presence of his vicar general Gousset; his doctor, Pécot; Frédéric de Marguerye, a titulary canon; Jean-Alexis Gaume, a professor of theology; François-Emmanuel Pidoux, a former merchant; and Victor Thiebaud, the assistant secretary at the episcopal residence.[33] It was with gentle resignation that the archbishop dictated:

> Of the seven branches of my family there is only one I believe to be in veritable need, that is my very dear niece Caroline DuBourg, the legitimate daughter of my brother Joseph Thomas Patrice, the widow of Monsieur de Sainte Marie. Not being able to give a reasonable share to each of my nephews and grand-nephews as I would desire if it were within my power, I believe I ought to name the said niece Caroline . . . my sole heir.

Caroline's older son Charles was enrolled at l'Ecole des Arts et Métiers at Châlons-sur-Marne, and DuBourg trusted Querry to pay his way there until Charles could be admitted to l'Ecole de Saumur "when the time comes." Perhaps Natalis de Wailly, the Archivist of France, would also continue his kindness to Charles; Wailly had been acting as a tutor to the boy and DuBourg hoped he would have the generosity to continue this supervision until Charles no longer needed it.

Contrasted with his predecessor's wealth, which was used so prodigally for the archdiocese both before and after his death, DuBourg's poverty was starkly apparent. As Césaire Mathieu's biographer remarked later, "The prelate who succeeded Rohan-Chabot brought to Besançon no other treasure than a great soul and the merits of a holy missionary."[34] His little parting gifts to those about him were pitifully—almost comically—modest: his spectacles, some small pictures of himself, a few snuffboxes.[35] The only thing of real value left after the sale of his cross was his episcopal ring, decorated with a precious stone having once belonged to Saint François de Sales, and this he gave to Cart, who reminded him with such a pang of the way *he* had been half a life ago.[36] When Querry reported the contents of DuBourg's will to the archbishop's niece the list of Du-Bourg's possessions consisted chiefly of a picture and cameo of Pius VII bequeathed to his successor at Besançon, the archbishop's clothes, a barrel of *vin ordinaire,* and some 500 bottles of wine (only the Bordeaux evaluated at very much). The total of these assets came to 6,729 francs; his legacies to his household servants and the funeral expenses came to 3,108 francs. Everything else, with one exception, was a claim on the unpaid Saint-Domingue indemnities through the wills of Louis and Victoire or in his own right. The exception was some property in St. Louis against which he had borrowed in the interests of a widow named Baconnet.[37]

On December 8, 1833, the archbishop's extremities became icy cold and in his continual agony he asked to be carried to an armchair which he never again left. By now the swelling in his legs had reached his waist. "On the evening of December 11 his pulse appeared to be no longer beating and death was in his extremities. But nature made a last effort. A violent trembling seized his frame, fever flashed for a moment, the pulse reappeared. Then calm. Death came like a profound sleep."[38] He was sixty-seven years and eleven months old, give or take a month or so depending on the birthday one accepts as accurate. On December 12 the Prefect of Doubs wrote to the Minister of the Interior in Paris, "I have the honor to inform you that the Archbishop of Besançon, whose health for several days left little hope, has succumbed today at 9:00 o'clock in the morning."[39] The announcement reached the Ministry of the Interior exactly ten months after the king's ordinance naming DuBourg to his last see.

The funeral was held two days later on a rainy Saturday

in Advent and Louis-Guillaume-Valentin DuBourg was "borne to the tomb accompanied by a numerous clergy, a vast concourse of people, and all the civil and military authorities."[40] The simple coffin was lowered into the *Caveau des Archevêques* underneath the elegant altar of Rohan-Chabot. Thus was *"l'esprit du Toboso,"* that once reckless, restless spirit, laid to rest.

When Filleau in Paris received Canon Querry's notification of DuBourg's death, he wrote at once to the late archbishop's secretary-executor:

> What dolorous news your letter of December 12 brought me! To appreciate my regret it would be necessary to know how attached I was to the venerable prelate you have just lost, and what affection he had for me. His four trips and fairly long sojourns here (the last ones in such critical circumstances) brought us into frequent and intimate communications, and I could read his heart as he read mine. This excellent friend consoled me after the loss of my beloved spouse. With all his generosity he sympathized in good times as well as bad. Those who knew him as we have, Monsieur, regret him profoundly.[41]

Filleau said he would give the sad news to Mme Guillemin who possessed a portrait of DuBourg showing him as he had looked when he was Bishop of New Orleans. Monsieur Guillemin, the French consul general at Havana, the mutual friend who had first introduced Filleau to "our saintly archbishop" eight years earlier, would share their grief. It was the same Guillemin who some thirty-five years ago had so yearned to follow DuBourg to America and led Emery to say, "The youth who have lived under your guidance can not forget you."[42]

In Lyon DuBourg was equally mourned. Didier Petit of the Association for the Propagation of the Faith, who more than anyone in France had reason to know the enormity of DuBourg's tasks in Louisiana, replied to Querry's news:

> You can judge my feelings for the venerable prelate you so justly mourn. . . . I am inconsolable at not having his last blessing, which I would have had if I had left as I first

intended on Tuesday by the mail coach from Paris to Besançon; but I was hoping instead to see the saintly archbishop later at greater length. No one more than I can comprehend the enormity of your loss; the more you knew Monseigneur Dubourg, the more you loved and appreciated him. Everyone here who knew him deplores this loss and asks how he can ever be replaced.[43]

The newspapers of France and the United States, of course, commented at length on DuBourg's passing. *L'Ami,* which had ever followed his career with such regularity, printed two obituary notices in swift succession; the *Annales* of the Association for the Propagation of the Faith summarized the French phases of his career and referred their readers to an earlier issue which had given a "précis of all the good this prelate had done in America." Stirring eulogies were delivered on special occasions in the cities where he had lived or worked; that in Besançon was delivered on January 28, 1834, by Canon Antoine-Joseph-Sebastian Domet, the Vicar Capitulary, in the Cathedral of Saint-Jean at the *service du Quarantal.* Perhaps the most perceptive and enduring estimation was that concluding a "Biographical Notice of the Most Rev. William Louis Valentine Dubourg, Late Archbishop of Besançon, in France, and formerly Bishop of New Orleans," which appeared in the *Laity's Directory* six years after his death and ended:

> In the name of heaven he set out "as a giant to run the way."
> . . . When we reflect that the jurisdiction of Archbishop Dubourg extended at one time over the vast territory which is now distributed into five episcopal districts; when we look back at the colleges, the religious institutions, the parishes that sprang into existence and flourished under his wise administration; the innumerable buildings he erected; the zealous and heroic clergymen whom he provided for the service of his people, the long and toilsome journeys he undertook for their welfare; when we consider the various positions in which he stood with legislatures, governments, kings and their ministers; his connection with religious communities and their heads, with boards of trustees, with literary and scientific men, with friends and adversaries; if we

follow the man, the priest, the bishop, through so many responsible and trying relations, we will not stop to examine the imperfections of frail humanity; they all vanish before this galaxy of brilliant and virtuous deeds, like spots in the firmament swallowed up in the gorgeous light of the mid-day sun. We will rather exclaim, as he did, in contemplating the astonishing progress of religion in the West: *a Domino factum est istud, et est mirabile in occulis nostris,* this is the Lord's doing, and it is wonderful in our eyes."[44]

ABBREVIATIONS

AAB	*Archives of the Archdiocese of Baltimore*
AABord	*Archives of the Archdiocese of Bordeaux*
AABost	*Archives of the Archdiocese of Boston*
AANO	*Archives of the Archdiocese of New Orleans*
AASL	*Archives of the Archdiocese of St. Louis*
AAQ	*Archives of the Archdiocese of Quebec*
ADB	*Archives Départemental de la Gironde, Bordeaux*
ADM	*Archives Départementales de Montauban*
AEM	*Archives de l'évêché de Montauban*
AMSJ	*Archives of Mount St. Joseph (Cincinnati)*
AMSM	*Archives of Mount St. Mary(Emmitsburg)*
AMSV	*Archives of Mount St. Vincent*
ASJPH	*Archives of St. Joseph's Provincial House*
AUC	*Archives of the Ursuline Convent in New Orleans*
AUND	*Archives of the University of Notre Dame*
BJC	*Boagni-Judice Collection*
CHR	*Catholic Historical Review*
CHSR	*Columbia Historical Society Records*
DFP	*DuBourg Family Papers*
GUA	*Georgetown University Archives*
MPA	*Maryland Province Archives*
NAP	*National Archives of Paris*
RASH	*Roman Archives of the Sacred Heart*
SAB	*Sulpician Archives in Baltimore*
SAP	*Sulpician Archives in Paris*
SLCHR	*St. Louis Catholic Historical Review*

NOTES

CHAPTER XXII: Harsh Beginnings

1. Perrin du Lac, *Voyages dans les deux Louisianes, et chez les nations sauvages du Missouri, par les Etats-Unis . . . en 1801, 1802, et 1803* (Paris, 1805), 188–89.

2. *SLCHR*, 5 (April–July 1923):149. Of the whites, two-thirds were French, one-third American; the blacks were estimated between 400 to 500. Irish pewholders in 1818 included Thomas McGuyre, Jeremiah Connor, Thomas Hanley, John Mullamphy, Thomas Brady, and John McKnight.

3. Rothensteiner, *History of the Archdiocese of St. Louis*, 1: 251, citing Flaget to Neale, June 26, 1816.

4. Gilbert J. Garraghan, *St. Ferdinand de Florissant* (Chicago, 1923), 98, citing Badin to Carroll, January 3, 1807.

5. *Annales de l'Association de la Foi* (Lyon, 1828) 2:338–39, citing DuBourg to Petit, January 8, 1818.

6. *SLCHR*, 5:155.

7. *Annales*, 2:338–39.

8. Paul C. Schulte, *The Catholic Heritage of St. Louis: A History of the Old Cathedral Parish* (St. Louis, 1934), 111.

9. Unless otherwise noted, the present account of DuBourg's cathedral relies upon Charles L. Souvay, "Around the St. Louis Cathedral with Bishop DuBourg, 1818–1820," *SLCHR*, 5 (April–July 1923): 155–59, on which most other accounts are based.

10. Schulte, *Catholic Heritage of St. Louis*, 110.

11. *Ibid.*, 105.

12. *Ibid.*, citing De Andreis.

13. DuBourg to Rosati, June 18, 1818, AASL.

14. The first was blessed on June 24, 1770, by Pierre Gibault; the second, which replaced it, was completed in 1776 while Bernard de Limpach was pastor. *See* Gregory M. Franzwa, *The Old Cathedral* (Gerald, Missouri, 1980), 22–25.

15. *Ibid.*, 60–61.

16. Frederick John Easterly, *Life of Rt. Rev. Joseph Rosati, C.M., First Bishop of St. Louis, 1789–1843* (Washington, D.C., 1942), 52–55. Unless otherwise noted, the story of DuBourg's seminary is based on Easterly's chapter "St. Mary's Seminary, the Barrens," 52–61.

17. The agreement is in the Roman Archives of the Congregation of the Mission.

18. DuBourg to Rosati, April 22, 1818, AASL. DuBourg wrote to Flaget on April 20, asking that de la Croix come with the Flemish workmen, whose number is given as either five (Easterly, *Rosati*, 55) or four (*SLCHR*, 3:307).

19. *Ibid.*

20. J. M. O'Malley, "The Centenary of the Foundations of the St. Louis Diocesan Seminary," *SLCHR*, 1 (October 1918):48, citing De Andreis to Rosati, April 20, 1818.

21. DuBourg to Rosati, August 2, 1818, AASL.

22. *Ibid.*

23. *Ibid.*

24. At 9:00 A.M. on May 16, 1818, Duchesne wrote to her superior in Paris, "A year ago today at this very hour we were receiving the last visit of the Bishop of Louisiana, and you gave your consent to a foundation in the New World."

25. Louise Callan, *Philippine Duchesne: Frontier Missionary of the Sacred Heart, 1769–1852* (Westminster, Maryland, 1957), 207. Four women actually accompanied Mme Duchesne; two were Mothers Octavie Berthold and Eugénie Audé and two were Sisters Catherine Lamarre and Marguerite Manteau.

26. *Ibid,* 217, Duchesne to Mme Barat.

27. Litta to Perreau, April 3, 1818; Fontana to Perreau, April 10, 1818, DFP.

28. Callan, *Philippine Duchesne,* 247, citing Duchesne to Abbé Barat, June 21, 1818.

29. *Ibid.,* February 18, 1818.

30. Letter 10, n.d., Roman Archives of the Sacred Heart, hereafter cited RASH.

31. Callan, *Philippine Duchesne,* 240, citing Duchesne to Mme Barat, June 7, 1818. The rich man John Mullamphy was on his way to Philadelphia and thence to France to place his daughters in school there after having their education begun by the Ursulines of New Orleans.

32. Letter 10, n.d., RASH.

33. *Ibid.*

34. Abbé Baunard, *Histoire de Mme Duchesne: Religieuse de la*

Societé du Sacre-Coeur de Jésus et fondatrice des premières maisons de cette societé en Amérique (Paris, 1882), 203.

35. Callan, *Philippine Duchesne,* 205, citing Duchesne to cousin, January 4, 1818.

36. *Ibid.,* 709, August 18, 1851.

37. *Ibid.,* 257, citing Duchesne to Mme Barat, August 22, 1818.

38. *Ibid.,* 261–62, citing Duchesne to Mme Barat, August 31, 1818.

39. Marjory Erskine, *Mother Philippine Duchesne* (New York, 1926), 175, citing Duchesne to Mme Barat, August 31, 1818. Callan omits these details in her rendition of this letter.

40. Hercule Brassac went to Prairie du Rocher; Pierre Desmoulins went to Kaskaskia.

41. Callan, *Philippine Duchesne,* 272.

42. Erskine, *Mother Philippine Duchesne,* 172, citing Duchesne to Abbé Barat, August 29, 1818.

43. *Ibid.,* 168, citing Duchesne to Mme Barat, August 22, 1818.

44. *Ibid.,* 173, citing Duchesne to Abbé Barat, August 29, 1818.

45. *Ibid.,* 181, citing Duchesne to Mme Barat, September 12, 1818.

46. *Ibid.,* 179.

47. Callan, *Philippine Duchesne,* 274, citing Duchesne to Mme Barat, September 12, 1818.

48. *Ibid.,* 273.

49. DuBourg to Duchesne, September 14, 1818, Letter 2, RASH.

50. Erskine, *Mother Philippine Duchesne,* 191–92, Duchesne to Paris Society of the Sacred Heart, November 20, 1818.

51. DuBourg to Duchesne, September 14, 1818, Letter 3, RASH.

52. DuBourg to Duchesne, September 22, 1818, Letter 4, RASH.

53. It has been traditional to place Portier's ordination in the old log church in St. Louis. (AASL, Memoranda and Catalogue, 22 and Oscar H. Lipscomb, "The Administration of Michael Portier, Vicar Apostolic of Alabama and the Floridas," Ph.D. diss., Catholic University of America, 1938, 48.) Since DuBourg's correspondence clearly places the bishop at the Barrens from September 27 to October 10, 1818, if the ordination took place on September 29, 1818, it was probably "the first ordination ever held in Perryville" as the *SLCHR,* 3:307, asserts.

54. Lipscomb, "Administration of Michael Portier," 47.

55. Mem. and Cat., 22, AASL.

56. Easterly, *Rosati,* 57, describes the house in detail.

57. DuBourg to Rosati, September 26, 27, 1818, AASL.

58. Rothensteiner, *Archdiocese of St. Louis;* 1:297.

59. DuBourg to Duchesne, October 10, 1818, Letter 5, RASH.

60. DuBourg to Duchesne, November 13, 1818, Letter 6, RASH.

61. Callan, *Philippine Duchesne,* 279.

62. *Ibid.,* 274, citing Duchesne to Mme Barat, September 12, 1818.

63. *CHR,* 21 (January 1936):433–34, July 14, 1818. Lalanne was one of the first Marianists trained by Père Chaminade, taking his vows on September 5, 1818. In later years John Henry Newman considered Lalanne a foremost French authority in educational problems.

64. This notice appeared in both English and French. For facsimiles, *see* Rita G. Adams et al., *St. Louis University: 150 Years* (St. Louis, 1968), 7. The ecclesiastics assisting Niel cannot be identified.

65. Adams et al., *St. Louis University,* 7.

66. William B. Faherty, *Better the Dream: Saint Louis University & Community, 1818–1968* (St. Louis, 1968), 9, citing the *Missouri Gazette,* March 10, 1819.

67. Rothensteiner, *Archdiocese of St. Louis,* 1:275–76.

68. *Missouri Gazette,* September 11, 1819.

69. DuBourg to Rosati, April 22, 1818, AASL.

70. *Ibid.*

71. Flaget to Chanut, April 15, 1818, SAP.

72. DuBourg to Rosati, December 4, 1818, AASL.

73. *Ibid.*

74. DuBourg to Rosati, December 24, 1818, AASL.

75. DuBourg to Duchesne, December 24, 1818, Letter 8, RASH.

76. Mde Ghyseghem to DuBourg, March 1 to May 30, 1818, D-88, DFP.

CHAPTER XXIII: Vast Pastures, Scattered Sheep

1. Kenneally, 1:206, *Ponenza* of December 11, 1815.

2. DuBourg to Rosati, March 15, 1819; July 27, 1820; February 23, 1820; March 10, 1820, AASL.

3. DuBourg to Rosati, May 31, 1826, AASL.

4. DuBourg to Rosati, October 18, 1819; February 23, 1820; July 27, 1820, AASL.

5. DuBourg to Rosati, February 29, 1820, AASL.

6. *L'Ami,* 24 (1820):281, citing a letter from Felix De Andreis dated September 23, 1819.

7. DuBourg to Rosati, October 18, 1819; February 23, 1820, AASL.

8. DuBourg to Rosati, September 14, 1820, AASL.

9. DuBourg to Rosati, October 30, 1822, AASL; Rosati, "Recollections of the Establishment of the Congregation of the Mission in the United States of America," *Vincentian Heritage,* 5 (1984): 117–18. Hereafter "Recollections."

10. DuBourg to Rosati, January 25, 1820; February 23, 1820; October 18, 1819; January 29, 1820, AASL.

11. Callan, *Philippine Duchesne,* 290.

12. DuBourg to Rosati, January 30, 1819, AASL.

13. Tessier to DuBourg, June 22, 1819, Letterbrook 1:28, SAB.

14. DuBourg to Propaganda, February 16, 1819, Kenneally, 1:339.

15. In September 1821, for example, James Cummings of St. Louis published DuBourg's *Officia Propria pro Diocesi Ludovicensi.* See William B. Faherty, *Dream By the River: Two Centuries of St. Louis Catholicism, 1766–1967* (St. Louis, 1973), 23, n. 37.

16. DuBourg to Rosati, January 4, 1819, AASL.

17. F. G. Holweck, "The Language Question in the Old Cathedral of St. Louis," *SLCHR,* 2 (January 1920):5–17.

18. Martial to Billaud, July 14, 1822, Kenneally, 1:795.

19. Callan, *Philippe Duchesne* 374, citing Duchesne to Barat, January 4, 1823.

20. The territories becoming states between 1812–1826, the period of DuBourg's incumbency as administrator and bishop, were Louisiana, 1812; Mississippi, 1817; Illinois, 1818; Alabama, 1819; Missouri, 1821.

21. DuBourg to Rosati, February 29, 1820, AASL.

22. Callan, *Philippine Duchesne,* 321. The capital for the first six years was in fact at St. Charles.

23. *Ibid.,* 328.

24. *Gazette de la Louisiane,* July 29, 1820.

25. *SLCHR,* 3 (October 1921):296.

26. *Gazette de la Louisiane,* January 9, 1821, quoting the city of Washington's *Gazette.*

27. *SLCHR,* 3 (October 1921):296.

28. DuBourg to Duchesne, January 29, 1819, Letter 11, RASH. The Prior was Joseph Dunand.

29. For precise details of these two properties, *see* Garraghan, *St. Ferdinand,* 129, 162–63.

30. Callan, *Philippine Duchesne,* 290–91, citing Duchesne's Journal, February 21, 1820.

31. *Ibid,* 298.

32. *Ibid.,* 301.

33. He may have been accompanied by A. Millet and Evremond Harrissart with whom he departed for New Orleans in October. *See* DuBourg to Rosati, October 8, 1819, AASL.

34. Little is known about the Baton Rouge experiment. On February 29, 1820, DuBourg told Rosati, "Martial has begun at Baton Rouge with 20 boarders"; *l'Ami* on May 3, 1820, in an item on Martial also alluded to his opening a school in Baton Rouge with 20 boys.

35. Callan, *Philippine Duchesne,* 305.

36. David to d'Aviau, February 15, 1819, SAP.

37. The Barrens seminary was finally occupied in October 1819, a year after the recuits arrived there.

38. DuBourg to Maréchal, 16-A-8, AAB.

39. DuBourg to Litta, May 12, 1819, Kenneally, 1:344.

40. *Ibid.*

41. *Ibid.*

42. Callan, *Philippine Duchesne,* 246. On June 21, 1818, Duchesne wrote to Père Barat, "Father Sibourd has just left for Philadelphia, where he is to have a very bad growth removed from his nose. He seems lost to the mission."

43. DuBourg to Rosati, November 14, 1818, AASL. The priest was Francisco Cellini; the clerks were Filippo Borgna and Antonio Potini; the name of the brother is given only as Bettelani.

44. The *Régistre* of Professions in the Ursuline Archives in New Orleans shows the attendance on May 4, 1819, of Louis Sibourd, vicar general; Louis Moni, first assistant, and Auguste Jeanjean, second assistant at the cathedral parish; and Bertrand Martial, "missionary priest."

45. DuBourg to Litta, Kenneally, 1:360; DuBourg to Propaganda, Kenneally 1:352. The co-worker at the cathedral was probably Louis Moni, Sedella's first assistant and DuBourg's vicar general in Sibourd's absence. The scandalous priest was Pedro Juan Koüne, whose name continued to appear in the parish baptismal records until his death in 1821.

46. Martial to Billaud, July 14, 1822, Kenneally 1:795.

47. DuBourg to Litta, June 7, 1819, Kenneally 1:360.

48. *Ibid.,* 352.

49. DuBourg to Litta, June 25, 1819, Kenneally 1:361. Again Du-

Bourg wrote more formally to Propaganda. *See* Dubourg to Litta, June 25, 1819, Kenneally 1:358.

50. Litta to Pedicini, September 23, 1819, Kenneally 1:359.

51. Fontana to DuBourg, October 2, 1819, Kenneally 3:1519.

52. Fontana to DuBourg, December 11, 1819, Kenneally 3:1522.

53. DuBourg to Fontana, March 4, 1820, Kenneally 1:390.

54. *Ibid.* Sibourd seems to have been sixty years old at the time. On one occasion DuBourg referred to him as "about sixty," and on another as "six years or so older" than himself. DuBourg was fifty-four in 1820.

55. Fontana to DuBourg, August 26, 1820, *SLCHR*, 2 (January 1920):51–52.

CHAPTER XXIV: New Orleans Revisited

1. Tessier's Epoques, August 27, 1820, SAB. The Sulpician superior recorded,"I had advised, and even more than advised him to do so, and that is what helped him to make up his mind."

2. Maréchal to Duclaux, February 16, 1819, SAP.

3. Tessier to DuBourg, June 22, 1819, Letterbook 1, SAB.

4. DuBourg to Bruté, July 22, 1820, AUND.

5. *Ibid.*

6. DuBourg to Rosati, October 7, 1820, AASL.

7. *SLCHR*, 5 (April–July, 1923): 137, citing letter of Pratte to [?], October 10, 1820.

8. DuBourg to Rosati, October 10, 1820, AASL.

9. DuBourg to Rosati, October 16, 1820, AASL.

10. DuBourg to Baccari, October 27, 1820, AASL.

11. DuBourg to Rosati, November 1, 1820, AASL.

12. Callan, *Philippine Duchesne,* 329, citing Duchesne to S. Barat, October 30, 1820.

13. *Ibid.,* 331.

14. *Mandement* dated November 15, 1820, AASL.

15. DuBourg to Rosati, November 12, 1820, AASL. Ferrari's first name appears as Angelo in Baudier, Anthony in Easterly, and Andrew in Callan. *L'Ami* gives it as André.

16. DuBourg to Rosati, November 24, 1820, AASL.

17. DuBourg's request was made on June 7, 1819 (Kenneally, 1: 352); and was granted by Propaganda on December 11, 1819 (Kenneally, 3:1522).

18. Roger Baudier, *The Catholic Church in Louisiana* (New Orleans, 1939), 279.

19. *Gazette de la Louisiane,* October 9, 1820. The property included two brick houses, pigeon houses, cotton gin, flour mill, brick kiln, 32 head of slaves, 60 head of sheep, 50 milch cows, oxen, breeding horses, draft and saddle horses, tools and farm implements, orchards, vegetable and flower gardens, and all kinds of out-buildings. The other executor was A. D. Tureaud.

20. *Ibid.,* January to December 1820. DuBourg & Baron listed such diverse items as coffee, cassia, tamarinds, a box of prayerbooks, and a house on Chartres Street occupied by Harrod & Ogden.

21. *Ibid.,* January 18, 1821.

22. *Ibid.,* November 25, 1820.

23. *Ibid.,* November 28, 1820.

24. *Ibid.,* November 29 to December 23, 1820.

25. *Notice sur l'état de la mission de la Louisiane à laquelle on a ajouté de nouveaux détails* (Turin, 1822), 58–61.

26. Actes de déliberations prises par la Communauté, Minutes 120–23, AUC.

27. *Ibid.*

28. Baudier, *Catholic Church in Louisiana,* 280.

29. DuBourg to Rosati, October 27, 1819, AASL.

30. DuBourg to Propaganda, February 24, 1821, *SLCHR,* 2 (April–July, 1920):235.

31. DuBourg to Propaganda, September 18, 1829, Kenneally, 1: 1242.

32. Rosati to Pastors, December 10, 1827, AASL; Rosati, "Recollections," *Vincentian Heritage,* 5 (1984):108.

33. In this case on May 4, 1821, Joseph Rosati had written to a friend in Naples a description of the mission which was published in l'*Encyclopédie ecclésiastique* of Naples, which was summarized in *l'Ami* on March 30, 1822.

34. *L'Ami,* 31 (1822): 212.

35. DuBourg to Duchesne, February 21, 1821, Letter 21, RASH.

36. *Ibid.*

37. DuBourg to Plessis, February 25, 1821, *Records,* 19 (1908): 189.

38. Baudier, *Catholic Church in Louisiana,* 292, 286. According to Plattenville Church Registers, this second Church of the Assumption had been blessed on December 21, 1819, by the pastor Bernard de Deva. DuBourg consecrated it on February 19, 1821.

39. *CHR,* 3 (January 1918): 396–97, DuBourg's entry in the parish records of St. Charles Borromeo, March 10, 1821.

40. *Ibid.,* 396, Gabriel Isabey's entry in the parish records, October 23, 1820.

41. DuBourg to Bruté, July 22, 1820, AUND. Mary Sentee Smith seems to have had some connection with St. Joseph House in Emmitsburg while she lived in Maryland.

42. For a more detailed version of the advantages DuBourg presented to Duchesne, *see* Callan, *Philippine Duchesne,* 344–45.

43. *SLCHR,* 3 (January to April 1921): 27.

44. DuBourg to Antoine Blanc, April [?], 1821, AANO.

45. Baudier, *Catholic Church in Louisiana,* 284.

46. DuBourg to Maréchal, November 12, 1818, 16-A-6, AAB.

47. DuBourg to Maréchal, April 27, 1819, 16-A-7, AAB.

48. Maenhaut's first recorded baptism was on June 24, 1820. He tried to resign on July 14, 1823, but DuBourg persuaded him to remain until January 1824. *See* R. O. Gerow, *Cradle Days of St. Mary's at Natchez* (Natchez, Mississippi, 1941), 19–22.

49. Annabelle M. Melville, *Elizabeth Bayley Seton, 1774–1821,* 3d ed. (New York, 1976), 295–96.

50. *Ibid.,* 269–70.

51. William Seton arrived safely home in June 1821.

52. Bruté to Maréchal, Maréchal Papers, 39, AAB. Bruté's letter to DuBourg is missing but it is safe to conclude that Bruté in this case, as in many others, revealed his distress to DuBourg.

53. Seton to Filicchi, April 18, 1820, Souvay-Filicchi Copies, 53, ASJPH.

54. DuBourg to Maréchal, June 11, 1821, 16-A-10, AAB.

CHAPTER XXV: O Absalom, My Son

1. DuBourg to Bruté, October 4, 1819, AUND.

2. F. G. Holweck, "Ein dunkles Blatt aus DuBourg's Episkopat," *Pastoral-Blatt,* 50 (February 1981): 17.

3. DuBourg to Rosati, October 8, 1819, AASL.

4. Holweck, "DuBourg's Episkopat," 17.

5. Book of Ordinations, 1816–1862, AASL.

6. DuBourg to Rosati, November 10, 1819, AASL. According to the Book of Ordinations Inglesi seems to have been given minor orders

on December 5 with a seminarian named Quin, and was made subdeacon on December 19, 1819, when Leo Deys was ordained priest. These first ordinations in the Diocese of St. Louis appear to have been filled in later. They were certainly not in DuBourg's hand.

7. DuBourg to Rosati, November 12, [1819], AASL.

8. Book of Ordinations, 1816–1862, AASL.

9. DuBourg to Rosati, March 22, [1820], AASL.

10. DuBourg to Rosati, January 29, 1820, AASL.

11. DuBourg to Rosati, March 22, [1820], AASL.

12. DuBourg, Letter of Introduction, March 26, 1820, *SLCHR*, 5 (January 1923): 28.

13. DuBourg to Inglesi, May 22, 1821, *SLCHR*, 5 (January 1923): 32.

14. Martial to Billaud, October 8, 1822, Kenneally, 1: 804.

15. Boagni-Judice Collection, hereafter BJC, Historic New Orleans Collection, 553 Royal Street, New Orleans. This daughter of Pierre-François DuBourg was known in the family as "Noémie."

16. DuBourg to Bruté, July 22, 1820, AUND.

17. DuBourg to Fontana, April 20, 1820, *SLCHR*, 3 (January 1921): 110.

18. Louis DuBourg to Maréchal, October 29, 1820, 16-A-17, AAB.

19. *L'Ami*, 26 (1820): 56.

20. René Rémond, *Les Etats-Unis devant l'opinion français, 1815–1852* (Paris, 1962), 136, citing Lamennais to Bruté, December 18, 1820; Félicité de Lamennais, *Correspondence Générale,* ed. Louis Le Guillou, 4 vols. (Paris, 1971), 2:184, citing Lamennais to Bruté, June 30, 1821.

21. December 28, 1820, D-123, DFP. A printed form acknowledged that M. l'abbé Angelo Inglesi of 28, rue Notre Dame des Camps, acting in the name of the missionaries of Louisiana agreed to acquire land for the investors, with the Louisiana mission having sole charge of cultivating the land, with revenues shared annually—one-fourth to investors, three-fourths to the mission—and after ten years the investors could buy the land outright from the mission. One suspects that Inglesi devised this method of raising large sums of money, and that DuBourg, who solicited outright gifts, knew nothing of it until later.

22. *L'Ami*, 26 (1821): 247, January 6, 1821. *L'Ami* on January 13, 1821, announced that the *Notice* published by Adr. LeCere at Paris would sell for two francs.

23. Joseph Burnichon, S. J., *La Compagnie de Jésus en France* (Paris, 1914), 1: 214–16. Mac-Carthy was forty-nine when he entered the Jesuit novitiate on February 7, 1818. For fifteen years he occupied the

greatest pulpits of France. His sermons were published in four volumes in 1834–1836.

24. *L'Ami,* 27 (1821): 41, February 21, 1821.

25. F. G. Holweck, "Contribution to the 'Inglesi Affair,' " *SLCHR,* 5 (January 1923): 29. Holweck mistakenly asserts that Inglesi left Laibach on August 18 and arrived in Rome on August 30, 1821. He may have intended April for August, for Inglesi was clearly in Rome by May when the *Diary of Rome* of May 12 alluded to his presence.

26. *Ibid.,* 33.

27. DuBourg to Fontana, April 20, 1820. *SLCHR,* 3 (January 1821): 110.

28. Fontana to DuBourg, July 21, 1821, AASL. Fontana replied that for breaking the law of November 4, 1694, bishops were suspended from conferring orders for one year, and the one ordained was suspended from the exercise of his ministry. Both DuBourg and Inglesi would come under this penalty; but because DuBourg was in good conscience and not in contempt, the pope absolved him of penalties.

29. DuBourg to Fontana, May 3, 1821, Kenneally, 1:701.

30. Holweck, "Contribution," 32–33.

31. Kenneally, 3:1582.

32. *Ibid.,* 1601. The general congregation met on July 9; the pope gave his sanction to their decision on July 15, 1821.

33. Fontana to DuBourg, July 21, 1821, AASL.

34. Holweck, "Contribution," 33, gives the amount of these contributions as 20,400 francs from the pope and an unknown amount from Consalvi.

35. Kenneally, 1:490.

36. Maréchal, who arrived in Rome on January 9, 1822, said later that Pierre-Casimir, the Duke de Blacas, particularly acted with such promptitude that the king of France was the first person in his realm to be informed of the scandal. *See* Maréchal to Harold, October 15, 1823, *Records,* 27 (March 1916): 80. The Austrian Ambassador Apponyi sent reports to Vienna on September 18, October 20, and December 6, 1821, on Inglesi. *See* Archives d'Etat de Vienne, Staats Kanzlei, Rom 25 (Bericht). This information from the Vienna archives was furnished by Guillaume de Bertier de Sauvigny of Paris.

37. Kenneally, 3:1611.

38. Consalvi to DuBourg, September 22, 1981, Kenneally 3:1608.

39. Martial to Billaud, October 20, 1822, Kenneally, 1: 804, quoting DuBourg's letter verbatim but giving no date.

40. "Letter of Signora Marianna Perret to Abbate Inglesi," Kenneally, 1: 548.

41. *SLCHR*, 2 (October 1820): 212–13, January 11, 1822.

42. Holweck, "Contribution," 34.

43. *Ibid.*

44. Kenneally, 1: 489, March 2, 1822.

45. Holweck, "Contribution," 34.

46. Kenneally, 3: 1822, April 22, 1822. An Abbé François Marc sent an inquiry to Rome about Inglesi, to which Propaganda replied guardedly that although his bishop spoke highly of him, Propaganda had reasons for being dissatisfied with him.

47. Edward J. Hickey, *The Society for the Propagation of the Faith: Its Foundation, Organization and Success, 1822–1922* (Washington, D.C., 1922), 8, citing *Annales*, 52:149.

48. *Ibid.*, 12.

49. For a treatment of religious activities of laymen during this period, *see* Guillaume de Bertier de Sauvigny, *The Bourbon Restoration*, tr. Lynn M. Case (Philadelphia, 1966), 313–17.

50. Hickey, *Society for the Propagation of the Faith*, 10–21.

51. *Ibid.*, 23.

52. *Annales*, 7:101.

53. Holweck, "Contribution," 29.

54. Consalvi to DuBourg, April 27, 1822, *SLCHR*, 2 (October 1920): 215.

55. Martial to Billaud, July 14, 1822, Kenneally, 1:795.

56. DuBourg to Rosati, April 7, 1822, AASL.

57. Martial to Billaud, July 14, 1822, Kenneally, 1:795.

58. *Ibid.*

59. *Ibid.*

60. DuBourg to Rosati, July 16, 1822, AASL.

61. DuBourg to George, July 6, 1822, AMSJ.

62. Martial to Billaud, October 20, 1822, Kenneally, 1: 804. Martial quotes DuBourg's letter verbatim but gives no date.

63. Charles L. Souvay, "Rummaging through Old Parish Records," *SLCHR*, 3 (October 1921): 256–57.

64. DuBourg to Rosati, August 7, 1821, AASL.

65. Souvay, "Rummaging," 256–57. John Baptist Blanc was the brother of Antoine Blanc, a future Bishop of New Orleans; John Mary Odin eventually became a bishop; the third Frenchman in the group was a deacon, Eugene Michaud. Lawrence Peyretti of Turin together with John Audizio and John Caretti of Orbrazzana in Piedmont made up the Italian complement.

66. DuBourg to Rosati, August 7, 1821, AASL.

67. DuBourg to Fontana, August 10, 1822, Kenneally, 5:1736.

68. Martial to Billaud, October 20, 1822, Kenneally 1:804.

69. Martial to Billaud, November 30, 1822, Kenneally, 1:550.

70. Martial to Plessis, November 13, 1822, Etats-Unis, 1:119, AAQ.

71. Martial to Plessis, November 24, 1822, Etats-Unis, 1:120, AAQ.

72. Plessis to Martial, March 5, 1823. Kenneally, 1:552. Plessis enclosed irrefutable proof that Angelo Inglesi, "Clerk, Bachelor, aged about twenty," on February 27, 1815, had married Marie Anne Morin in the presence of Alexander Spark, Minister, and that after failing to marry a second woman he had furtively left Quebec owing $424 back rent, which he never paid.

73. DuBourg to Association for the Propagation of the Faith, January 29, 1823, *Annales* 1: 61–63.

74. DuBourg to Petit, January 29, 1823, *ibid.*, 59–61.

75. Plessis to DuBourg, October 3, 1822, Régistre des Lettres, 11: 17–18, 211A, AAQ.

76. DuBourg to Louis DuBourg, February 6, 1823, Kenneally, 1: 822. In addition to Plessis's revelation, DuBourg may have also received disturbing letters from Louis DuBourg and F. A. Baccari, for in his letter to Philip Borgna of February 27, 1823, he asked Borgna to thank Baccari for his information, which Louis probably passed on from Bordeaux.

77. *Ibid.*

78. The letter of February 10 arrived by way of Le Havre on Easter, March 30; that of February 6 reached Bordeaux directly on April 1.

79. Louis DuBourg to F. A. Baccari, May 6, 1823, Kenneally, 1: 867.

80. *Ibid.*

81. *SLCHR,* (July 1922): 165, n. 4. In his "Recollections" Rosati does not mention Inglesi, but credits the Vincentian superior, F. A. Baccari, with sending Oliva, a Brother Sargiano, and Valerio Faina, a layman who hoped to become a brother. *See Vincentian Heritage,* (1984): 125–27.

82. Conwell to Plessis, October 13, 1823, *Records,* 27 (March 1916): 78. DuBourg may have received some of these items, for on November 22, 1823, he wrote to Rosati, "I will request Mr. Moni to reclaim the cases Mr. I. has imported. He has already written he was going to send them." *See* AASL for original letter.

83. Holweck, "Contribution," 35.

84. For an account, *see* Francis E. Tourscher, *Hogan Schism and Trustee Troubles in St. Mary's Church, Philadelphia, 1822–1829* (Philadelphia, 1930).

85. Inglesi to Propaganda, September 12, 1823, Kenneally, 1: 555.

86. Angelo Inglesi, *An Address to the Public of Philadelphia, Containing a Vindication of the Character and Conduct of the Reverend Mr. Inglesi* (Philadelphia, 1824), 33. This thirty-six page article was dated March 22, 1823.

87. Kenneally, 1:933, extract from R. W. Meade's *Address* on Inglesi.

88. Inglesi, *Address,* 32–33, citing his letter dated November 25, 1823.

89. *Ibid.,* 34–35, citing DuBourg's letter but giving no date.

90. Propaganda to Inglesi, December 27, 1823, Kenneally, 3: 1759.

91. Propaganda to Harold, January 3, 1824, Kenneally 3: 1765.

92. Meade to Maréchal, February 4, 1824, 16-A-15, AAB, with enclosure of DuBourg to Meade, December 19, 1823.

93. *Ibid.*

94. DuBourg to Borgna, February 27, 1823, *SLCHR,* 3 (April–July 1921): 123ff.

95. Kenneally, 1:568. There was no need to advise Archbishop Maréchal about Inglesi, since he had arrived in Rome shortly after Inglesi's misconduct was first known and told Vicar General Harold of Philadelphia on October 15, 1823, "It is a notorious fact that Cardinal Consalvi, secretary of state, has expelled l'Abbé Inglesi from the territory of the pontifical government. This fact has been repeatedly related to me by cardinals, prelates, and a number of clergymen and laymen of the first distinction in Rome." *See Records,* 27 (March 1916): 80.

CHAPTER XXVI: Seeding New Fields

1. DuBourg to Caprano, January 29, 1824, *SLCHR,* 3 (January–April 1921):144.

2. Petit to DuBourg, June 11, 1824, AANO.

3. Callan, *Philippine Duchesne,* 341.

4. *Ibid.,* 344.

5. *Ibid.,* 346.

6. *Ibid.,* 347. The first American postulant who joined the Religious of the Sacred Heart, Sister Mary Layton, accompanied Madame Audé.

7. DuBourg to Duchesne, August 13, 1821, Letter 22, RASH.

8. Callan, *Philippine Duchesne,* 349.

9. *SLCHR,* 3 (October 1921): 300. Perry County was organized on May 21, 1821.

10. Richard became the territorial delegate to Congress in 1822.

11. DuBourg to Duchesne, October 11, 1821, Letter 23, RASH.

12. *Ibid.*

13. September 29, 1821, AANO.

14. October 11, 1821, Letter 23, RASH.

15. For the laying of the cornerstone on February 19, 1821, *see* Garraghan, *St. Ferdinand,* 163–64.

16. *Ibid.,* 168–69, text of decrees. Other witnesses of the decrees were Francis Niel, Leo Deys, and Aristide Anduze, the clergy of the college.

17. Charles E. Nolan, *A Southern Catholic Heritage* (New Orleans, 1976), 1:67, Parish Register, November 6, 1821.

18. DuBourg to Duchesne, December 26, 1821, Letter 24, RASH.

19. Blessing of the Church of Vermillion, December 30, 1821, AASL. Vermillion was the older name of Lafayette.

20. Minutes, 118, AUC.

21. DuBourg to Plessis, July 17, 1821, *Records,* 19 (1908):191.

22. DuBourg to Plessis, February 4, 1822, *Records* 19 (1908): 193–94.

23. DuBourg to Duchesne, February 2, 1822, Letter 25, RASH.

24. "Remise des interêts et affaires de la communauté entre les mains de Mgr. DuBourg," April 2, 1822, AUC.

25. DuBourg to Plessis, May 30, 1822, *Records,* 19 (1908):202.

26. Baudier, *Catholic Church in Louisiana,* 287. The dedication took place on March 7, 1822, in the presence of Michael Portier, Charles Marliani and Philip Borgna, as well as a visiting Augustinian, the Reverend Dr. Emanuel Vidal. Modeste Mina assisted DuBourg.

27. Callan, *Philippine Duchesne,* 358.

28. DuBourg to Carroll, October 5, 1815, 8A–H6, AAB.

29. DuBourg to Neale, February 5, 1816, 12A–B1, AAB.

30. DuBourg to Petit, January 8, 1818, *Annales,* 1:20.

31. Joseph Rosati, *Sketches of the Life of the Very Reverend Felix De Andreis,* tr. James Burlando, C.M. (Baltimore, 1861), 157. Rosati wrote this life of De Andreis after his death in 1820, but it was not published in Rosati's lifetime. *See also* Easterly, *Rosati,* 196.

32. John Rothensteiner, "Early Missionary Efforts Among the Indians of the Diocese of St. Louis," *SLCHR*, 2 (April–July 1920): 64.

33. *L'Ami*, 24 (1820):280, citing a letter of De Andreis, dated September 23, 1819.

34. St. Louis University Library, Department of War Circular, September 3, 1819. A facsimile of this circular is found in Rita Adams, et al., *St. Louis University*, 10.

35. Callan, *Philippine Duchesne*, 327, citing Duchesne to S. Barat, August 29, 1820.

36. Eugene Michaud to the Vicar General of Chambery, n.d., but carried to France in the spring of 1823, *Annales*, 1 (1827): 53–54.

37. John M. Odin to Jean Cholleton, October 21, 1822, *SLCHR*, 2 (April–July 1920): 66.

38. Garraghan, *St. Ferdinand*, 173. St. Louis was founded by the Chouteau family.

39. Rothensteiner, "Early Missionary Efforts," 64.

40. DuBourg to Propaganda, February 24, 1821, Kenneally, 1: 694.

41. *Gazette de la Louisiane*, April 20, 1821.

42. Fontana to Fortris, June 15, 1821, Kenneally 1: 682.

43. Fontana to DuBourg, June 23, 1821, AASL.

44. Garraghan, *St. Ferdinand*, 175.

45. Callan, *Philippine Duchesne*, 358.

46. Michaud to the Vicar General of Chambery, n.d., *Annales*, 1 (1827): 53.

47. DuBourg to George, July 6, 1822, AMSJ. DuBourg mistakenly wrote "Baptists" instead of Presbyterians.

48. In 1818 Bruté was reproved by both Elizabeth Seton and John Cheverus for wanting to go off to China (Melville, *Seton*, 289–95); while Ambroise Maréchal told Antoine Garnier in 1822 that he did not want to lose Bruté to Botany Bay (March 24, 1822, SAP).

49. Garraghan, *St. Ferdinand*, 180, n. 33.

50. John Mary Odin to Jean Cholleton, October 21, 1822, SLCHR, 2 (April–July 1920): 65.

51. Garraghan, *St. Ferdinand*, 181, n. 36.

52. Note 50, *supra*.

53. Garraghan, *St. Ferdinand*, 182, citing La Croix to Rosati, November 4, 1822.

54. *Ibid*.

55. Callan, *Philippine Duchesne*, 377, citing Duchesne to S. Barat, January 16, 1823.

56. Tessier to DuBourg, August 13, 1822, Letterbook 1: 87, SAB.

57. Odin to Cholleton, October 21, 1822, *Annales,* 1 (1827): 50–51.

58. Godecker, *Bruté,* 103.

59. Bruté to Maréchal, June 23, 1819, 13-P-10, AAB.

60. SAB.

61. DuBourg to Bruté, July 22, 1820, AUND.

62. Anduze signed the compact of September 29, 1821.

63. DuBourg to Bruté, July 6, 1822, AUND.

64. DuBourg to Rosati, October 30, 1822, AASL.

65. *Ibid.*

66. DuBourg to Rosati, December 3, 1822, AASL.

67. Dubois's letter of February 25 ran to four large, closely written pages, 15-T-8, AAB.

68. Bruté to Deluol, May 25, 1818, SAP. Louis Regis Deluol arrived in Baltimore on October 24, 1817, where he rose rapidly, becoming president of the college in 1822, Superior of the Sisters of St. Joseph in Emmitsburg in 1826, and Superior of the Sulpicians in the United States in 1829. *See* Ruane, *Society of St. Sulpice,* 208.

69. DuBourg to Bruté, July 4, 1818, AUND.

70. DuBourg to Bruté, October 4, 1819, AUND.

71. Ruane, *Society of St. Sulpice,* 184. The Mount's struggle for survival as a Sulpician house is almost too copiously documented in the Paris Archives of the Sulpicians but to date no thorough monograph on the subject exists. Dubois's most recent biographer, Richard Shaw, makes only cursory allusions to the eight-year controversy which ended with Dubois and Bruté ceasing to be Sulpicians in January 1826. Sulpician historian Boisard says, "In Baltimore they regretted that Paris had followed the advice of Monseigneur Maréchal, and would have preferred to keep Emmitsburg." *See Trois Siècles d'Histoire.* 1: 319.

72. DuBourg to Bruté, December 8, 1822, AUND.

73. DuBourg to Rosati, December 3, 1822, AASL.

74. DuBourg to Bernabeu, April 11, 1823, Box 27, National Archives of Puerto Rico, Spanish governors, consuls, Cartagena-United States.

CHAPTER XXVII: Jesuits for Indian Missions

1. DuBourg to Louis DuBourg, March 17, 1823, *Annales,* 1 (1827): 37.

2. Rothensteiner, "Early Missionary Efforts," 69, Circular of the War Department, February 29, 1820.

3. *The Papers of John C. Calhoun,* ed. W. Edwin Hemphill, 7 (Columbia, South Carolina, 1973): 477.

4. *Ibid.,* 478–79, February 15, 1823.

5. *Ibid.,* 484–85.

6. *Ibid.,* 512, March 10, 1823.

7. *Ibid.,* 513, March 11, 1823.

8. J. A. Griffin, *Contribution of Belgium,* 88–91.

9. Garraghan, *St. Ferdinand,* 185.

10. For a treatment of this controversy, *see* Murtha, *Maréchal,* 248–92.

11. DuBourg to Tessier, December 23, 1822, SAB.

12. Tessier to DuBourg, December 31, 1822, Letterbrook 1: 91, SAB.

13. DuBourg to Maréchal, December 28, 1822, 16-A-11, AAB.

14. DuBourg to Maréchal, March 6, 1823, 16-A-12, AAB.

15. DuBourg to Louis DuBourg, March 17, 1823, *Annales,* 1 (1825): 462.

16. DuBourg to Calhoun, March 17, 1823, *Calhoun Papers,* 7 (1973): 526–27.

17. Maryland Province Archives (hereafter MPA), 30, Z-1 at Georgetown University (GUA). The place of the document's signing is uncertain. The document itself gives Georgetown, but a second document contingent upon it says it was signed at Port Tobacco. Given the age and physical condition of Charles Neale, who died soon afterward, it seems probable the document was drawn up in Georgetown and signed at Port Tobacco where Neale resided.

18. MPA 30, Z-2, Z-2A, GUA. DuBourg signed both versions, with Benedict Fenwick and Adam Marshall witnessing one and Benedict and Enoch Fenwick witnessing the other.

19. DuBourg to Maréchal, March 21, 1823, 16-A-13, AAB.

20. *Ibid.*

21. *Ibid.*

22. Maréchal to Garnier, March 25, 1823, SAP.

23. Murtha, *Maréchal* 152, citing letter of Fenwick to Fortris.

24. Calhoun to DuBourg, March 21, 1823, Calhoun Papers, 7:536–37; DuBourg to Calhoun, March 22, 1823, *ibid.,* 538–39.

25. Calhoun to DuBourg, March 23, 1823, *ibid.,* 539.

26. DuBourg to Menou, March 25, 1823, *ibid.,* 541.

27. DuBourg to Propaganda, March 29, 1823, Kenneally, 1: 829.

28. Francis Roloff, originally from Bavaria, entered St. Mary's Seminary in Baltimore in July 1804 and was ordained priest on June 11, 1808. He served the congregation at Conewago until Bishop Michael Egan called him to Philadelphia in 1812 to be pastor of Holy Trinity Church there. *See* Ruane, *Society of St. Sulpice,* 56–57.

29. AASL. Photocopies of the originals dated "Easter Sunday" but no location of the originals given.

30. Tessier Diary, SAB.

31. National Archives of Puerto Rico, Spanish governors, consuls: Cartagena-United States, Box 27. Bernabeu forwarded DuBourg's letter on May 1, 1823, attesting that "the signature and seal are those of DuBourg, Bishop of New Orleans; he uses them in all his writings and correspondence and they are well known to me."

32. Easterly, *Rosati,* 62, citing Rosati to Baccari, November 29, 1822.

33. DuBourg to Rosati, April 13, 1823, AASL.

34. Bishop Fenwick left Cincinnati on May 30, 1823.

35. M. Liliana Owens, "The Pioneer Days of the Lorettines in Missouri, 1823–1841," *Records,* 70 (1959): 70, Nerinckx to DuBourg, April 29, 1823. This letter names and evaluates each of the thirteen sisters going to Missouri in 1823.

36. *Ibid.,* 70–71.

37. Spalding, *Flaget,* 249.

38. Callan, *Philippine Duchesne,* 383. This visit occurred on May 8, 1823.

39. DuBourg to Rosati, May 10, 1823, AASL.

40. J. A. Griffin, *Contribution of Belgium,* 145. The other members of the group were Van Quickenborne's assistant, Peter J. Timmermans, a priest, and novices Judocus Van Assche, John A. Elet, Felix Verrydt, John B. Smedts, Francis De Maillet. The three lay brothers who went to Missouri were Peter De Mayer, Charles Strahan, and Henry Reisselman, the last-named having been a lay brother of the Trappists before Father Urban Guillet disbanded the Trappists at Monks' Mound in Missouri.

41. *Ibid.,* 151.

42. Garraghan, *St. Ferdinand,* 188.

43. Clark to Calhoun, June 2, 1823, *Calhoun Papers,* 8 (1975): 87.

44. Van Quickenborne to DuBourg, June 13, 1823, AANO.

45. Fenwick to DuBourg, September 11, 1823, AUND.

46. *Ibid.*

47. Van Quickenborne to Francis Neale, MPA, 30, Z-2, GUA.

48. Propaganda to DuBourg, July 26, 1823, Kenneally, 3:1729.

49. Maréchal to Fesch, February 18, 1824, Kenneally, 3: 1777. For Maréchal's letter to Fesch in draft *see* 21-A-05, September 16, 1823, AAB.

50. *Calhoun Papers,* 9 (1976): 528, January 28, 1825.

51. *Ibid.,* 556–57, February 12, 1825. McKenney replied to Du-Bourg on March 17, 1825.

52. *Ibid.,* 599. Senator Benton referred to the school as the "Indian seminary."

53. Garraghan, *St. Ferdinand,* 189.

54. DuBourg to Dzierozynski, July 10, 1825, MPA 30, Z-7, GUA.

55. For a history of St. Regis Seminary, *see* Gilbert J. Garraghan, "St. Regis Seminary, First Catholic Indian School, 1823–1831," *CHR,* 4 (January 1919): 452–78.

CHAPTER XXVIII: Episcopal Confreres

1. Bruté to Maréchal, October 29, 1820, SAB. indicates that Bruté composed an English-language *mandement* for this occasion which may have been the one Maréchal issued on May 10, 1821.

2. DuBourg to Maréchal, June 11, 1821, 16-A-10, AAB.

3. Litta to DuBourg, March 4, 1818, D-75, DFP.

4. Flaget to Plessis, January 22, 1818, *Records,* 18 (1907): 30–31. The Anglo-American border of Louisiana was fixed by the Convention of 1818 as the 49° north latitude from the Lake of the Woods west to the Rocky Mountains.

5. DuBourg to Plessis, March 13, 1818, *Records* 19 (1908): 186.

6. Laval Laurent, *Québec et l'Eglise aux Etats-Unis* (Washington, D. C., 1945), 201.

7. The correspondence with Plessis suddenly ended with Bishop Plessis's revelation of Inglesi's true character. Plessis told Maréchal two years later, "Monseigneur DuBourg has not written to me since I enlightened him concerning Inglesi, who grossly deceived him." DuBourg's sensitivity may have been at fault; yet it should be noted that after May 1823 DuBourg remained in New Orleans and Rosati conducted the correspondence between St. Louis and Quebec.

8. DuBourg to Maréchal, May 7, 1819, 16-A-8, AAB. Flaget's biographer says that by December of that year they also talked of one for Vincennes. *See* Spalding, *Flaget,* 248.

9. Murtha, *Maréchal,* 133, citing Flaget to Maréchal, March 7, March 16, 1820.

10. *Ibid.,* 134–35, citing letters of April 4, April 28, 1820.

11. *Ibid.,* 135.

12. Flaget to Chanute, June 19, 1820, SAP.

13. Schauinger, *Cathedrals,* 194.

14. Murtha, *Maréchal,* 138–39, citing Flaget to Maréchal, October 30, 1826. By this date DuBourg was no longer an American bishop.

15. Spalding, *Flaget,* 250, November 28, 1825.

16. Maréchal to Suffragans, March 24, 1826, 21-P-4, AAB.

17. Maréchal, March 24, 1826, 21A-P-4, AAB. This letter seems to have been written to Fesch.

18. Cheverus to Plessis, May 22, 1815, AAQ.

19. For a brief account of these troubles, *see* Melville, *Cheverus,* 239–43.

20. Cheverus to Maréchal, December 20, 1819, 14-J-33, AAB.

21. DuBourg to Plessis, August 26, 1820, *Records,* 19 (1908): 187–88. DuBourg uses the word coadjutor loosely, sometimes implying a simple auxiliary, sometimes a bishop with the right to succeed to the see.

22. Kenneally, 3:1856.

23. DuBourg to Propaganda, October 6, 1825, Kenneally, 1: 898. For New York Maréchal proposed Charles Nerinckx of Kentucky who had died on August 12, 1824. *See also* Kenneally, 7: 2285.

24. DuBourg had nominated Benedict Fenwick for Philadelphia, Cincinnati, Detroit and Boston. Fenwick was consecrated on November 1, 1825.

25. Cheverus to Maréchal, January 25, 1819, 14-J-28, AAB.

26. DuBourg to Propaganda, February 16, 1819, Kenneally, 1: 339.

27. DuBourg to Plessis, February 25, 1821, *Records,* 19 (1980): 190.

28. DuBourg to Maréchal, August 6, 1821, SAB.

29. Laurent, *Québec et l'Eglise,* 179, citing Plessis to DuBourg, May 10, 1822.

30. DuBourg to Plessis, March 19, 1822, *Records,* 19 (1908): 196.

31. Melville, *Cheverus,* 241.

32. DuBourg to Propaganda, May 10, 1824, Kenneally, 1:570.

33. Caprano to DuBourg, July 24, 1824, Kenneally, 3:1811. The Kenneally *Calendar* précis of these documents mentions the names of William Harold and J. Ryan but neither DuBourg nor Caprano mentioned these names in this first exchange on the subject.

34. James F. Connelly, ed., *History of the Archdiocese of Philadel-*

phia (Philadelphia, 1976), 112, n. 119, states that the Propaganda *Acta* noted that Maréchal, DuBourg, and Francis Patrick Kenrick all endorsed the transfer.

35. Peter Guilday, *The Life and Times of John England: First Bishop of Charleston, 1786–1842* (New York, 1927), 300–301. Guilday gives the text of the letter to Maréchal, the only one extant.

36. John England's diary in the archives of the Diocese of Charleston, entry for March 10, 1823, cited in Lipscomb, "Administration of Michael Portier," 86.

37. DuBourg to Propaganda, March 29, 1817, Kenneally, 1:248.

38. Antonio de Vargas to Propaganda, April 27, 1817, Kenneally 1: 252.

39. Lipscomb, "Administration of Michael Portier," 22.

40. DuBourg to Fontana, April 25, 1820, Kenneally, 5:1712.

41. DuBourg to Propaganda, October 1, 1822, Kenneally, 5:1740.

42. Maréchal to Gradwell, July 14 and August 1825, Kenneally 7: 2286, 2287.

43. John England, *The Works of the Right Reverend John England,* ed. Sebastian G. Messmer, et al. (Cleveland, 1908), 7 vols., 2:241–43.

44. England to Rosati, December 29, 1826, AASL.

45. England, *Works,* 4: 294, England to the Society for the Propagation of the Faith at Lyon, September 1836.

46. DuBourg to Maréchal, June 11, 1821, 16-A-10, AAB.

47. DuBourg to Somaglia, October 6, 1825, Kenneally, 1: 898.

48. For the story of Cheverus's return to France, *see* Annabelle M. Melville, "Some Aspects of Bishop Cheverus' Return to France in 1823," *Records and Studies* of the United States Catholic Historical Society, 45 (1957): 2–31.

49. Cheverus to Maréchal, September 1, 1820, 14-K-37, AAB.

50. Cheverus to Maréchal, December 20, 1819, 14-J-33, AAB.

51. DuBourg to Somaglia, June 14, 1824, Kenneally, 5:1799.

52. Robert H. Lord, et al., *History of the Archdiocese of Boston,* 3 vols. (New York, 1944), 2: 26.

53. Maréchal to Fesch, March 24, 1826, SAB.

54. Lord, *Archdiocese of Boston,* 26. Lord comments, "Bishop Flaget and DuBourg, who so often recommended him for the episcopate, had put him first on their lists. Archbishop Maréchal and Bishop England had preferred him if Father Taylor were to be passed over. Bishop Conwell recommended him, if only in fourth place."

55. *Ibid.,* 27.

56. *Ibid.*, citing Louis Regis Deluol to Samuel Eccleston, November 20, 1825. For a description of Fenwick's consecration, *see* Louis Deluol, "Consecration of Early American Bishops," *The Voice,* April 1941, 15.

57. Flaget to Maréchal, April 29, 1820, SAB.

58. Laurent, *Québec et l'Eglise,* 191, citing Plessis to Propaganda, November 23, 1821, and Plessis to Poynter, March 23 and June 10, 1821.

59. *Ibid,* 179.

60. Plessis to Maréchal, February 7, 1821, *Records,* 8 (1907): 439–40.

61. Maréchal to Plessis, March 11, 1823, *ibid.,* 450.

62. Murtha, *Maréchal,* 137, citing Flaget to Maréchal, December 30, 1822.

63. Kenneally, 7: 2309, 1822.

64. Murtha, *Maréchal,* 147.

65. Letters from Maréchal to Gradwell, Kenneally, 7: 2268, April 9, 1823; 7: 2270, April 20, 1823; 7: 2272, June 24, 1823.

66. Kenneally 1: 835, April 17, 1823; Murtha, *Maréchal,* 151.

67. DuBourg to Borgna, February 27, 1823, AASL. The letter alluded to: his horror at learning of Inglesi's true character, his desire to have the division of his diocese postponed for three years and have Rosati for his coadjutor meanwhile, his pleasure at having the promise of federal funds for the Indians, and a request to have the parishes contribute to the support of the bishop, who had no regular support except that of the Ursulines. For the full text of the letter, *see SLCHR,* 3 (January–April 1921): 123–28.

68. Maréchal to Gradwell, August 9, 1823, Kenneally, 7: 2268.

69. The first was to a see of St. Louis to be created in the distant future; the second was for coadjutor of the Diocese of Louisiana; the third was as second choice for the Vicariate of Alabama and the Floridas; and the fourth was for the Diocese of Boston. Bruté's biographer says, "Upon Bishop Cheverus' departure for France, Bishop DuBourg . . . wrote to Father Bruté to inform him that his name had been sent to Rome. . . . The humble priest immediately refused. . . . In response, Bishop DuBourg assured him that his name never reached Rome, or if it had, no appointment would take place." *See* Godecker, *Bruté,* 115, citing Bruté's journal, GUA.

70. DuBourg to Bruté, July 6, 1822, AUND.

71. DuBourg to Rosati, September 11, 1822, AASL.

72. Maréchal to Consalvi, September 7, 1823, Kenneally, 5: 1745.

73. Maréchal to Fesch, September 16, 1823, 21A-O-5, AAB. This

letter is unsigned and unaddressed and the recipient has been assigned by the author since Kenneally 3: 1777, February 18, 1824, attributes such a letter to Fesch as recipient.

74. *Ibid.*

75. DuBourg to Plessis, February 25, 1821, *Records,* 19 (1908): 190.

76. DuBourg to Caprano, March 10, 1826, with enclosure. Copy, AASL.

77. Flaget to DuBourg, January 18, 1826, Kenneally, 1: 949.

78. DuBourg to Propaganda, March 10, 1826. Copy, AASL.

79. Maréchal to Fesch, March 24, 1826, 21-A-P4, AAB. Maréchal apparently had read DuBourg's letters to Propaganda.

80. *Ibid.* On second thought Maréchal crossed out the words "of respectable authority."

81. Murtha, *Maréchal,* 153, citing Maréchal to Somaglia, June 4, 1826.

82. *Ibid.,* 153–54, citing Maréchal to Fesch, June 6, 1826.

83. *Ibid.,* 154.

84. John Tracy Ellis, "Selecting American Bishops," *Commonweal,* March 10, 1967, 643–49.

85. The first and second provincial councils met in 1829 and 1833.

CHAPTER XXIX: A Coadjutor at Last

1. Rosati, "Recollections," *Vincentian Heritage,* 5 (1984): 118. These "Recollections" are believed to have been written about 1839 and are not necessarily accurate in every detail.

2. Fontana to DuBourg, October 3, 1821, *SLCHR,* 2 (April–July 1920): 148.

3. DuBourg to Fontana, February 8, 1822, Kenneally, 1: 731.

4. DuBourg to Plessis, March 19, 1822, *Records,* 19 (1908): 197.

5. DuBourg to Propaganda, May 30, 1822, Kenneally, 5:1739.

6. DuBourg to Propaganda, October 1, 1822, *SLCHR,* 3 (January–April 1921): 117–18.

7. Lipscomb, "Administration of Michael Portier," 26, citing letter of October 28, 1822.

8. Easterly, *Rosati,* 65. The brief establishing the vicariate was dated July 13, 1822. *See* Lipscomb, "Administration of Michael Portier," p. 27, n. 67.

9. DuBourg to Rosati, December 3, 1822, AASL.

10. Lipscomb, "Administration of Michael Portier," 30, citing letter of January 7, 1823.

11. Flaget to Maréchal, January 20, 1823, 16-U-22, AAB.

12. Murtha, *Maréchal,* 138, n. 22.

13. DuBourg to Baccari, December 4, 1822, Kenneally, 5:1738.

14. DuBourg to Propaganda, December 6, 1822, Kenneally, 5: 1729,

15. DuBourg correctly referred to Fenwick as having been Carroll's vicar general and as presently serving as president of Georgetown. Enoch Fenwick was pastor of St. Peter's pro-cathedral in Baltimore for the last six years of Carroll's life and served as the archbishop's secretary as well. Daley, *Georgetown,* 250, mistakenly says that Benedict Fenwick replaced Enoch as president of Georgetown in September 1822; Benedict succeeded Enoch in January 1825. *See* Lord, *Archdiocese of Boston,* vol. 2: n. 54.

16. Charles L. Souvay, "Rosati's Election to the Coadjutorship of New Orleans," *CHR,* 3 (April–July 1917): 13, citing Rosati to Baccari, January 24, 1823. Easterly, *Rosati,* 65, gives November 1822 as the time of the letter's arrival in Perryville, based on Rosati's "Recollections" written in 1839.

17. Rosati to Baccari, January 24, 1823, CHR 3 (April–July 1917): 14.

18. Rosati to Nicola Rosati, February 24, 1823, CHR 3 (April–July 1917) 14–15.

19. Easterly, *Rosati,* 68–69, April 2, 1823. The note of April 3, 1823, which accompanied the returned documents is found in *SLCHR,* 3 (October 1921): 315, n. 13.

20. Propaganda to Flaget, David, March 8, 1823, Kenneally, 3: 1710.

21. Baccari to Rosati June 25, 1823, *Vincentian Heritage,* 5 (1984): 123.

22. DuBourg to Rosati, November 22, 1823, AASL.

23. Lipscomb, "Administration of Michael Portier," 27.

24. Souvay, "Rosati's Election," 13.

25. *Ibid.*

26. Lipscomb, "Administration of Michael Portier," 29.

27. Easterly, *Rosati,* 69; Souvay, "Rosati's Election," 14.

28. *Vincentian Heritage,* 5 (1984): 123.

29. Lipscomb, "Administration of Michael Portier," 29.

30. *Records,* 19 (1908): 207. DuBourg was alluding to the White-

marsh property, which the Jesuits refused to grant Maréchal, in spite of the papal judgment.

31. DuBourg to Rosati, February 6, 1823, AASL.

32. DuBourg to Maréchal, November 23, 1823, 16-A-14, AAB. An apostolic brief of July 14, 1823, revoked Rosati's nomination as vicar apostolic of Alabama and Mississippi and made him DuBourg's coadjutor. DuBourg was notified on July 15, 1823. *See* Kenneally, 6:1381–1382.

33. DuBourg to Plessis, March 19, 1822, *Records,* 19 (1908): 198. Although DuBourg did not learn the full story of Inglesi's deceit until February 1823, Propaganda had notified him early in 1822 of its rejection of Inglesi as a candidate.

34. *Ibid.*

35. DuBourg to Propaganda, May 3, 1822, Kenneally, 5:1739, Du-Bourg was replying to Propaganda's proposal to divide his diocese and suggested Rosati and Bruté for a future diocese of St. Louis.

36. DuBourg to Propaganda, October 1, 1822, Kenneally 5:1740.

37. DuBourg to Propaganda, December 6, 1822, Kenneally, 5:1729.

38. DuBourg to Bruté, December 8, 1822, AUND.

39. DuBourg to Rosati, December 29, 1823, AUND.

40. DuBourg to Rosati, January 1, 1824, AUND.

41. Charles L. Souvay found this pastoral no longer extant but points out that the gist of it is given in a letter of Rosati to Baccari of March 29, 1824. *See* Souvay, "Rosati's Election," 165.

42. Easterly, *Rosati,* 66.

43. *Social Justice Review,* October 1969, 207.

44. Benjamin Latrobe wrote of Sedella in 1820: "Father Anthony is a sensible and very benevolent man. . . . He lives in a miserable hut in the corner of the street opposite to the rear of the church. It has more of the air of a Polish hermitage than of a principal parsonage of New Orleans. . . . His benevolence is always active. He has an arrangement with a baker and butcher, on whom he distributes orders, in the shape of tickets, to the poor that apply to him." *See* Huber and Wilson, *Basilica on Jackson Square,* 18.

45. Unless otherwise noted, the details of the consecration are based on Rosati's diary published in *SLCHR,* 3 (October 1921): 318–21, covering March 4–25, 1824; and Souvay, "Rosati's Election," 165–68.

46. Rosati praised the sermon in a letter to Baccari on March 29, 1824, as did Tichitoli in a letter to Victoire Fournier on April 1, 1824. *See* *SLCHR,* 3 (1921): 320, n. 29.

47. DuBourg to Propaganda, April 5, 1820, *SLCHR*, 2 (January 1920): 5.

48. DuBourg to Propaganda, April 25, 1820, SLCHR, 2 (April–July 1920), 131–32.

49. DuBourg to Maréchal, August 6, 1821, SAB.

50. Fontana to DuBourg, June 23, 1821, *SLCHR*, 2 (January 1920): 143–44.

51. Fontana to DuBourg, October 3, 1821, Kenneally, 3:1613.

52. DuBourg to Propaganda, February 8, 1822, *SLCHR*, 2 (April–July 1920): 149.

53. Propaganda to DuBourg, January 22, 1822, AASL.

54. Propaganda to DuBourg, April 27, 1822, *SLCHR*, 2 (April to July 1920): 215.

55. Maréchal to Garnier, January 14, 1822, SAP.

56. Maréchal to Beausset, August 11, 1822, SAP.

57. Murtha, *Maréchal,* 147, citing 21A-O-3, AAB, "Responses to Questions Proposed by the Eminent Cardinal Consalvi. . . ," Rome, June 4, 1822.

58. DuBourg to Propaganda, September 5, 1822, Kenneally, 5: 1735.

59. DuBourg to Rosati, September 11, 1822, AASL.

60. Leo de Neckere was consecrated Bishop of New Orleans on June 24, 1830, and Joseph Rosati, who had administered both St. Louis and New Orleans for four years, continued as Bishop of St. Louis.

61. Spalding, *Flaget,* 251, citing DuBourg to Flaget, October 21, 1819.

62. David to Maréchal, July 25, 1820, 15-F-8, AAB; Flaget to Propaganda, November 5, 1820, cited in Murtha, *Maréchal,* 136.

63. DuBourg to Propaganda, April 25, 1820, *SLCHR*, 2 (April–July 1920): 131–32.

64. Murtha, *Maréchal,* 135, citing a letter to Propaganda of May 23, 1820.

65. DuBourg to Maréchal, May 5, 1820, 16-A-9, AAB.

66. Maréchal to Propaganda, June 28, 1820, Kenneally, 5:1577.

67. DuBourg to Consalvi, February 8, 1822, *SLCHR*, 2 (April–July 1920): 149.

68. Consalvi to DuBourg, September 28, 1822, SLCHR 2 (April–July 1920): 149.

CHAPTER XXX: An Episcopal Residence in New Orleans

1. Callan, *Philippine Duchesne,* 382–83, citing Duchesne to Barat, May 20, 1823.

2. Letter 26, July 12, 1823, RASH.

3. *Ibid.*

4. Letter 27, August 24, 1823, RASH.

5. Sister Jane Francis Heaney, "A Century of Pioneering: A History of the Ursuline Nuns in New Orleans, 1727–1827," Ph.D. diss., St. Louis, University, 1949, 481, states, "When the contractors were ready to begin construction in May 1823, more than a hundred forty thousand bricks were ready."

6. DuBourg to Rosati, July 29, 1823, AASL.

7. The papal briefs to Rosati and DuBourg on the coadjutorship were dated July 14, 15, 1823; the papal audience of July 25, 1823, permitted the Ursulines to cede their convent to DuBourg.

8. DuBourg to Rosati, July 29, 1823, AASL.

9. *Gazette de la Louisiane,* Friday, July 4, 1823.

10. *Ibid.,* July 7, 1823.

11. *Ibid.,* October 20, 1823; November 14, 1823.

12. *Ibid.,* August 5, 1823. The protest cited the precedent of Congress in the case of General Simon Bernard.

13. *Ibid.,* October 14, 1823.

14. *Ibid.,* July through August 12, 1823.

15. *Ibid.,* October 29, 1823.

16. Seghers to F. X. Xaupi, October 6, 1823, AMSM.

17. *Ibid.*

18. *Gazette de la Louisiane,* August 4, 1823.

19. *Ibid.,* December 11, 1823. The figures given for the last two years of this study were estimates based on growth in previous years.

20. Callan, *Philippine Duchesne,* 384, citing Duchesne to S. Barat.

21. Maréchel to Plessis, November 6, 1823, *Records,* 18 (1907): 451.

22. *Ibid.,* 452. Although Plessis replied with alacrity that he would take fifteen nuns from Georgetown, by May 1824, Maréchal reported that their affairs were improving and they would remain in the United States.

23. *Gazette de la Louisiane,* August 16, 1823.

24. *Ibid.,* December 9, 15, 1823.

25. *Ibid.,* August 8, 12, 1823.

26. DuBourg to Louis DuBourg, August 6, 1823, *Annales,* 1 (1827): 42–43.

27. DuBourg to Rosati, July 29, 1823, AASL.

28. *Gazette de la Louisiane,* September 14, 1823.

29. DuBourg to Rosati, October 3, 1823, AASL.

30. DuBourg to Rosati, November 9, 1823, AASL.

31. *Ibid.*

32. *Gazette de la Louisiane,* October 29, 1823.

33. DuBourg to Rosati, July 29, 1823, AASL.

34. At his death in Besançon in 1833, DuBourg's will left the portrait and the cameo Pius VII had given him to DuBourg's successors, the Archbishops of Besançon.

35. A copy of this *mandement* dated November 25, 1823, is preserved at AUND. Charles de la Croix was made pastor of St. Michael, an offshoot of St. James Parish, in December 1823. See Baudier, *Catholic Church in Louisiana, 293.*

36. DuBourg to Rosati, November 22, 1823, AASL.

37. For the text of Rosati's circular letter, see *SLCHR,* 3 (October 1921): 316.

38. DuBourg to Rosati, October 3, 1823, AASL.

39. Callan, *Philippine Duchesne,* 374-75, citing Duchesne to S. Barat, January 4, 1823.

40. F. G. Holweck, "Father Edmond Saulnier," *SLCHR,* 4 (October 1922): 191–92. The lottery attempts were made in St. Louis and St. Charles.

41. Schulte, *Catholic Heritage of St. Louis,* 123–25.

42. Faherty, *Better the Dream,* 12–16.

43. Easterly, *Rosati,* 61.

44. Callan, Philippine Duchesne, 379.

45. DuBourg to Church Trustees, April 24, 1824, AASL.

46. *Ibid.* The pictures to be left at St. Louis were the "Saint Louis" at the altar, the "Marriage of the Virgin and Saint Joseph," a "Virgin and Child" facing the pulpit, "Saint Bartholomew," and a large "Crucifixion."

47. *SLCHR,* 4 (October 1922): 192.

48. *Ibid.,* 3 (January–April 1921): 328, n. 68.

49. *Ibid.,* 353, n. 152.

50. DuBourg to Rosati, September 24, 1824, AASL. Fenwick was allotted 17,600 francs by the Society for the Propagation of the Faith as

compared with DuBourg's 15,400 and Flaget's 13,200 for the year May 1, 1825 to May 1, 1826.

51. *Ibid.*

52. Niel to Rosati, November 25, 1824, AASL.

53. *SLCHR,* 3 (October 1921), Rosati Diary.

54. DuBourg to Rosati, December 28, 1824, AASL.

55. Saulnier was ordained on September 22, 1822, before Bishop DuBourg left for Baltimore. For a biographical essay, *see* F. G. Holweck, "Father Edmond Saulnier," *SLCHR,* 4 (October 1922): 189–205.

56. Saulnier to Rosati, November 24, 1824, AASL.

57. DuBourg to Saulnier, July 3, 1825, AASL.

58. *Ibid.*

59. Niel to Propaganda, March 10, 1826, Kenneally 5:1898.

60. Rosati to Niel, February 17, 1826, AASL.

61. Rosati to Niel, July 1, 1826, *SLCHR,* 4 (October 1922): 258.

62. Rosati to Niel, December 29, 1826, *SLCHR,* 4 (October 1922): 258.

63. Callan, *Philippine Duchesne,* 420, citing Duchesne to S. Barat, June 8, 1825.

64. Undated fragment addressed to Rector of Florissant, GUA. De la Croix left New Orleans on June 8, 1827. On his return he brought 10,000 francs, a new library, and three Religious of the Sacred Heart. *See* J. Griffin, *Contribution of Belgium,* 136–37.

65. Daley, *Georgetown University: Origin and Early Years* (Washington, D.C., 1957), 253, citing Bescher to Dzierozynski, September 24, 1824, and Diary of Thomas C. Levins, October 14, 1824.

66. *Researches,* 7 (January 1890): 12, citing extracts from "Travel Through North America During the Years 1825 and 1826 by His Highness Bernhard Duke of Saxe Weimar Eisenach." The quotations used appear in Volume 2: 16, 64. The duke also visited Father Constantine Maenhaut in Pensacola, Florida.

67. Bruté had left for France on March 1, 1824, and returned to New York on November 13, 1824. For the details of his stay in France, *see* Mary Selesia Godecker, *Simon Bruté de Remur, First Bishop of Vincennes* (St. Meinrad, Indiana, 1931), 116–23.

68. DuBourg to Bruté, February 1825, AUND.

69. *Ibid.*

CHAPTER XXXI: *Lilium Inter Spinas*

1. DuBourg to Rosati, October 3, 1823, AASL.

2. DuBourg to Rosati, December 23, 1823, AASL.

3. DuBourg to Rosati, October 3, 1823, AASL.

4. Flaget to Rosati, December 10, 1823, AASL.

5. Schauinger, *Cathedrals,* 225.

6. DuBourg to Rosati, May 24, 1825, AASL.

7. Flaget to Chanut, May 25, 1825, SAP.

8. Flaget to d'Aviau, October 10, 1825, a copy, SAB.

9. David to Tessier, January 17, 1826, SAB.

10. Flaget to DuBourg, January 18, 1826, Kenneally, 1: 949.

11. Schauinger, *Cathedrals,* 239–240.

12. J. Herman Schauinger, *Stephen T. Badin: Priest in the Wilderness* (Milwaukee, 1956), 214. Martial sailed from Le Havre on June 8, 1828, with Stephen Theodore Badin and arrived in New York on July 23, 1828.

13. *Régistre,* 124, February 16, 1832, AUC, shows Martial signing himself "Supr."

14. DuBourg to Rosati, December 24, 1818, AASL.

15. Kenneally, 1:352; 3:1522. The request was made on June 7, 1819, and granted on December 11, 1819.

16. DuBourg to Rosati, January 29, 1820, AASL.

17. Rosati to Baccari, May 24, 1821, *SLCHR,* 4 (October 1922): 207. In this letter Rosati said Cellini went three or four times a year to New Madrid, but since Cellini went for the first time in March 1821 a letter written two months later could only speculate on Cellini's intentions about future trips taking four to five weeks to accomplish.

18. DuBourg to Rosati, July 16, 1822, AASL.

19. *Ibid.*

20. DuBourg to Rosati, August 7, 1822, AASL.

21. *Ibid.*

22. DuBourg to Sibourd, September 19, 1822, AASL.

23. *SLCHR,* 3 (October 1921): 322, n. 38. The detailed story of Cellini and Grand Coteau was painstakingly constructed from original documents by Charles L. Souvay, C. M., and is found in the extensive footnotes to Rosati's Diary appearing in volumes 3 and 4 of the *SLCHR.*

24. *Ibid.* Souvay states that no rectory was in existence at that time, yet Charles Smith before his death made provisions for both a church and presbytery and on March 10, 1821, DuBourg himself within this presbytery left a record of Smith's beneficence. *See CHR,* 3 (January 1918): 396–97. Mrs. Smith's residence was about a mile west of the convent and a mile and a quarter northwest of St. Charles Borromeo Church.

25. Cellini to Rosati, January 27, 1823, *SLCHR,* 3 (October 1921): 322, n. 38.

26. *Ibid.,* May 7, 1823.

27. Callan, *Philippine Duchesne,* 379, citing Duchesne to Rosati, February 17, 1823.

28. DuBourg to Rosati, July 29, 1823, AASL.

29. Cellini to Rosati, September 3, 1823, AASL.

30. DuBourg to Rosati, November 14, 1823, AASL.

31. *Ibid.,*

32. *SLCHR,* 3 (October 1921): 323.

33. DuBourg to Rosati, August 22, 1824, AASL.

34. *Ibid.*

35. De Neckere to Rosati, *SLCHR,* 3 (October 1921): 363.

36. Rosati to Baccari, *SLCHR,* 4 (October 1922): 267.

37. DuBourg to Rosati, January 9, 1825, AASL.

38. Cellini to Rosati, May 1, 1825, AASL, copying DuBourg to Smith, n.d.

39. DuBourg to Rosati, October 8, 1824, AASL.

40. *Ibid.*

41. De Neckere to Rosati, November 8, 1824, *SLCHR,* 4 (January–April 1922): 78.

42. DuBourg to Rosati, December 28, 1824, AASL.

43. *Ibid.*

44. Rosati Diary, November 30, 1824, *SLCHR,* 3 (October 1921): 366.

45. DuBourg to Rosati, March 8, 1825, AASL.

46. DuBourg to Rosati, April 12, 1825, AASL.

47. Propaganda to DuBourg, October 16, 1825, Kenneally, 3: 1910.

48. DuBourg to Propaganda, January 26, 1826, Kenneally 1: 948.

49. Flaget to Rosati, May 26, 1826, *Social Justice Review* (December 1969): 278–79.

50. Cellini to Rosati, June 14, 1826, AASL.

51. Rosati to Cellini, July 22, 1826, *SLCHR,* 4 (October 1922): 262, n. 142.

52. Rosati to Flaget, July 22, 1826, SLCHR, 4 (October 1922): 262, n. 141.

53. Rome in July 1826 accepted DuBourg's resignation, divided the diocese into the diocese of St. Louis and the Diocese of New Orleans, and named Rosati administrator of both.

54. Rosati to Baccari, August 9, 1826, *SLCHR,* 4 (October 1922): 267.

55. John Rothensteiner, *St. Michael's Church, Fredericktown, Missouri,* (St. Louis, 1917), 26.

CHAPTER XXXII: Year of Decision

1. DuBourg to Propaganda, October 1, 1822, *SLCHR,* 3 (January–April 1921): 117.

2. DuBourg to Rosati, December 3, 1822, AASL.

3. DuBourg to Borgna, February 27, 1823, SLCHR, 3 (January–April 1921): 123.

4. DuBourg to Propaganda, March 8, 1824, Kenneally, 1:568.

5. Propaganda to DuBourg, May 29, 1824, *Ibid.,* 3:1795.

6. Didier Petit to DuBourg, September 26, 1824, AANO.

7. Widow Petit to DuBourg, June 11, 1824, AANO.

8. DuBourg To Propaganda, January 29, 1825, *SLCHR,* 3 (January–April, 1921): 149–50.

9. DuBourg to Pope Leo XII, February 1, 1825, *SLCHR,* 5 (January 1923): 17.

10. *Ibid.*

11. Inglesi to DuBourg, February 25, 1825, Kenneally, 1: 574.

12. DuBourg to Caprano, April 16, 1825, Kenneally, 7: 185. Propaganda acknowledged receipt of this letter on July 9, 1825. *See* Kenneally, 3:1870.

13. DuBourg to Propaganda, December 20, 1825, Kenneally, 5: 1902.

14. Rosati to Baccari, November 17, 1826, *SLCHR,* 5 (January 1923): 75. Rosati wrote, "Fr. Inglesi died, quite some time ago, of the yellow fever shortly after landing in Hayti."

15. Bouillier to ? , March 1, 1828, *Annales,* 3, c. 18. John Bouillier (also spelled Bouille) was a Vincentian priest who came to Louisiana during DuBourg's New Orleans residency.

16. DuBourg to Duchesne, January 22, 1825, Letter 28, RASH.

17. DuBourg to Duchesne, January 26, 1825, Letter 29, RASH. The name also appears as Dessaussoi.

18. After DuBourg returned to France, Rosati transferred Dussaussoy to St. Louis as assistant to Saulnier, but the Missouri climate was too harsh for him and on April 11, 1829, Dussaussoy left St. Louis to return to France.

19. DuBourg to Rosati, May 24, 1825, AASL.

20. *SLCHR,* 4 (January–April 1922): 103. Sister Johanna Miles went as superior, Sister Regina Cloney as teacher, and Sister Rose Elder as general assistant.

21. *SLCHR,* 3 (October 1921): 307. The work was completed on Saturday, March 26, while Easter fell on April 3, 1825.

22. Easterly, *Rosati,* 78.

23. Rosati Letters, 31, September 28, 1824, RASH.

24. Easterly, *Rosati,* 78–79, citing Rosati to Caprano, November 1, 1825.

25. Lipscomb, *Administration of Michael Portier,* 86–87.

26. *Ibid.,* 85, citing Portier to Propaganda, December 29, 1828.

27. DuBourg to Rosati, May 24, 1825, AASL. Antoine Ganilh had previously served in Kentucky and Ohio.

28. *Annales,* 3 (September, 1829): 501–9. Unless otherwise noted the account given is based on Anduze's letter to an unidentified friend in France.

29. These letters were written on October 4–6, 1825.

30. Erskine, *Mother Philippine Duchesne,* 283–4.

31. DuBourg to Duchesne, n.d., Letter 35, RASH.

32. Callan, *Philippine Duchesne,* 419, citing letter of May 10, 1825.

33. DuBourg to Van Quickenborne, November 9, 1825, AASL.

34. Rosati to Duchesne, November 19, 1825, Letter 2, RASH.

35. Francis Cellini on January 27, 1823, severely criticized an existing plan to establish Vincentians at La Fourche. *See SLCHR,* 3 (October 1921): 322.

36. *Annales,* 1 (1827): 75.

37. DuBourg to Rosati, November 9, 1823, AASL.

38. DuBourg to Rosati, December 23, 1823, AASL.

39. DuBourg to Rosati, January 10, 1824, AASL.

40. DuBourg to Rosati, December 28, 1824, AASL.

41. DuBourg to Rosati, April 12, 1825, AASL.

42. DuBourg to Rosati, May 24, 1825, AASL.

43. *SLCHR,* 4 (January–April 1922): 94–95.

44. The council consisted of Leo De Neckere, John Mary Odin, Bernard Permoli, and Francis Xavier Dahmen.

45. Easterly, *Rosati,* 84–85. Easterly treats this subject extensively.

46. Rosati to Baccari, January 17, 1826, AASL.

47. Rosati to David, February 1, 1826, AASL.

48. Flaget to Baccari, February 7, 1826. Kenneally, 5:1903. Souvay suggests in "Rosati's Election," 179–80, that this action of Flaget's was a major cause for DuBourg's resignation and departure.

49. DuBourg to Rosati, December 9, 1825, AASL.

50. DuBourg to Tessier, February 5, 1826, SAB.

51. *SLCHR,* 5 (January 1923): 17, February 1, 1825.

52. De Neckere to Rosati, September 22, 1824, AASL. De Neckere told Rosati he believed the Italian clergy in Louisiana, at least Father Bigeschi, were shocked by the way Cellini was treated by DuBourg, "but they are ill-informed."

53. DuBourg to Rosati, October 3, 1823, AASL.

54. DuBourg to Rosati, December 29, 1823, AASL. Acquaroni sailed for Europe on June 27, 1824.

55. DuBourg to Rosati, February 4, 1826, AASL.

56. DuBourg to Rosati, March 8, 1825, AASL. The priests were Louis Dussaussoy, Bertrand Permoli; and the younger men were John Bouillier, a subdeacon from Lyon, and Gabriel Chalon, a cousin of Michael Portier, who directed DuBourg's college in New Orleans.

57. Segher to Xaupi, March 18, 1825, Segher Letters, AMSM.

58. *SLCHR,* 4 (July 1922): 183, n. 75, citing entry in the Parish Register of Funerals.

59. DuBourg to Tessier, February 5, 1826, SAB.

CHAPTER XXXIII: The Return to France

1. *Gazette de la Louisiane,* August 23, 1823, showed Arnould DuBourg, the bishop's nephew, to be a justice of the peace for the "5th section of the city of New Orleans." Before his death on April 28, 1829, he also served as a judge in Plaquemine Parish, Louisiana.

2. DuBourg to Propaganda, December 20, 1825; January 6, 1826; January 10, 1826; February 17, 1826, Kenneally 5: 1896, 1901, 1900, 956.

3. Heaney, "A Century of Pioneering," 492, n. 42.

4. DuBourg to Louis DuBourg, March 20, 1824, *Annales,* 1 (1827): 46–47.

5. Baudier, *Catholic Church in Louisiana,* 302. Baudier combines the charges made by a variety of newspapers and pamphlets.

6. DuBourg to Caprano, February 17, 1826, *SLCHR,* 3 (July 1921): 204.

7. Sister Marie Trouard was the first to make her vows there, on June 21, 1825.

8. DuBourg to Saulnier, July 3, 1825, AASL.

9. DuBourg to Caprano, July 9, 1825, Kenneally, 3:1870.

10. Baudier, *Catholic Church in Louisiana,* 301–2. Baudier emphasizes the clear support Antonio de Sedella gave DuBourg in this crisis, which in turn was used against the bishop: that DuBourg had warped the views of this great sage. Père Antoine could be forgiven this lapse because of his years of service, but for DuBourg there must be no mercy.

11. DuBourg to Caprano, January 10, 1826, Kenneally, 5:1900.

12. DuBourg to l'Espinasse, n.d., *Annales,* 2: 407.

13. Lipscomb, *Administration of Michael Portier,* 37–38. Unless otherwise noted, the present treatment is based on Lipscomb, 36–41.

14. August 26, 1825, Kenneally, 7: 1385, 1382.

15. *Ibid,* 1384.

16. Lipscomb, *"Administration of Michael Portier,"* 40.

17. Kenneally, 1: 926, Pastoral of October 4, 1825. This letter is also included in DuBourg to Propaganda, March 10, 1826, Kenneally 1: 961.

18. DuBourg to Propaganda, December 20, 1825, Kenneally 5: 1896.

19. DuBourg to Propaganda, February 17, 1826, Kenneally 5: 956.

20. Lipscomb, "Administration of Michael Portier," 42 ff.

21. Murtha, *Maréchal* 140–41.

22. DuBourg to Caprano, February 27, 1826, *SLCHR,* 3 (July 1921):206–7.

23. Portier to Rosati, November 1, 1819, AASL. Portier may have occasionally assisted at the cathedral, but Sedella's first and second regular assistants were Louis Moni and Auguste Jeanjean; until 1821 Koüne and Thomas were likewise administering the sacraments.

24. Portier to Rosati, April 26, 1819, AASL.

25. Portier to Rosati, November 1, 1819, AASL.

26. DuBourg to Propaganda, March 10, 1826, Kenneally, 1: 961.

27. Commiskey to Elder, May 29, 1826, SAB.

28. Lipscomb, "Administration of Michael Portier," 41.

29. Maréchal to Propaganda, June 5, 1826, Letters, 1814–1826, AAB.

30. DuBourg to Frayssinous, July 20, 1826, SAP.

31. *Dictionnaire d'Histoire et de Géographie ecclésiastique,* 10: 813–14.

32. DuBourg to Dugnani, June 24, 1816, Kenneally, 1: 221.

33. DuBourg to Caprano, March 10, 1826, Kenneally 1: 961.

34. DuBourg to Propaganda, January 30, 1826, Kenneally 5: 1899.

35. Rosati to Duchesne, January 2, 1826, AASL.

36. *Missouri Advocate and St. Louis Inquirer,* April 8, 1826. The text of the address is also found in *SLCHR,* 1 (April 1919): 181–83.

37. DuBourg to Sister George, January 17, 1826, AMSJ.

38. DuBourg to Bruté, February 16, 1825, AUND.

39. Maréchal to Duclaux, October 19, 1825, SAP.

40. Bruté to Garnier, April 2, 1826, SAP.

41. DuBourg to Fenwick, January 10, 1826, AASL.

42. Easterly, *Rosati* 88.

43. DuBourg to Rosati, February 4, 1826, AASL.

44. *Ibid.*

45. *SLCHR,* 3 (July 1921): 200.

46. *Régistre,* 122, AUC. For the four conditions attending the donation, *see* Heaney, "A Century of Pioneering," 490. Heaney points out that it was not until 1920 that the Ursulines surrendered the titles to this property to the "Roman Catholic Church of the Diocese of New Orleans."

47. Semple, *Ursulines in New Orleans,* 88.

48. DuBourg to Rosati, March 8, 1826, AASL.

49. DuBourg requested that Leo XII address him at Pierre-Francois's consulate (January 14, 1826, Kenneally, 5: 1897). He asked Secretary Caprano to keep his plea to resign, a secret (January 30, 1826, Kenneally, 5: 1899). He told Rosati to say nothing of his plan to go to Europe until they met face-to-face prior to his departure (February 4, 1826, AASL).

50. March 11, 1826, D-110, DFP.

51. Kenneally, 1: 913, July 26, 1825. Rome renewed his ordinary and extraordinary faculties on July 3, 1825 (Kenneally 6: 286).

52. *SLCHR,* 4 (October 1922): 248.

53. *Ibid.,* n. 89.

54. *Ibid.,* n. 92.

55. *Annales,* 2 c. 12, 396, January 30, 1826.

56. DuBourg to Rosati, April 26, 1826, AASL.

57. Callan, *Philippine Duchesne,* 431.

58. For the complete text and account of this transfer of the church property to Van Quickenborne on May 1, 1826, *see* Garraghan, *St.*

Ferdinand, 162–63. The original deed is in the archives of St. Louis University.

59. Callan, *Philippine Duchesne,* 430, 432.

60. DuBourg to Rosati, May 11, 1826, AASL.

61. *Ibid.*

62. Souvay, "Rosati's Election," 171, incorrectly states that on May 4, 1826, DuBourg preached and immediately after Mass went to the steamboat.

63. Rosati to Louis DuBourg, May 24, 1823, *Annales,* 1: 48–49.

64. DuBourg to Neale, November 27, 1823, MPA 30:24, GUA.

65. DuBourg to Louis DuBourg, June 24, 1824, *Annales,* 1 (1827): 48.

66. Holweck, "Saulnier," 193–94.

67. DuBourg to Rosati, May 11, 1826, AASL.

68. *Ibid.*

69. DuBourg to Van Quickenborne, May 10, 1826, AASL.

70. DuBourg to Rosati, May 11, 1826, AASL.

71. Flaget to Rosati, May 26, 1826, AASL.

72. DuBourg to Rosati, May 31, 1826, AASL.

73. DuBourg to Bruté, May 18, 1826, AUND.

74. DuBourg to Rosati, May 31, 1826, AASL.

75. Flaget to d'Aviau, October 10, 1825.

76. David to Tessier, January 17, March 11, April 15, 1826, SAB.

77. Rosati to Martial, January 18, 1826, AASL.

77. David to Tessier, January 17, 1826, SAB.

79. Schauinger, *Cathedrals,* 243–44.

80. DuBourg to Leo XII, Kenneally, 5: 1896; DuBourg to Caprano, Kenneally, 5: 1902.

CHAPTER XXXIV: A Fourth Transplanting

1. DuBourg to Tessier, May 23, 1826, RG 1-11, SAB.

2. Maréchal to Garnier, June 20, 1826, SAP.

3. Maréchal to Propaganda Fide, June 4, 1826, Kenneally, 1: 972.

4. Maréchal to Gradwell, May 16, 1826, Kenneally, 7: 2292. Maréchal to Garnier, June 20, 1826, SAP.

5. Flaget to Rosati, May 26, 1826, AASL. This letter in English translation appears in the *Social Justice Review,* December 1969, pp. 278–79.

6. DuBourg to Caprano, July 3, 1826, Kenneally, 1: 983.

7. Baudier, *Catholic Church in Louisiana,* 304. The pope's consent was given on July 3, 1826.

8. D-78, DFP. Neither the Souvay translation in the *St. Louis Historical Review* nor the Kenneally *Calendar* indicates letters from DuBourg to Propaganda dated November 20, 1825, although both compilations include resignation letters dated February 17 and 27, 1826. Kenneally, 5: 938, does cite one dated *December* 20, 1825.

9. DuBourg to Garnier, July 11, 1826, SAP.

10. DuBourg to Caprano, July 3, 1826, Kenneally 1: 983.

11. Niel to Somaglia, July 18, 1826, Kenneally 1: 984.

12. DuBourg to Caprano, July 11, 1826, Kenneally 1: 982.

13. *l'Ami,* 48 (1826): 295.

14. *Truth Teller* (September 16, 1826): 294; *Catholic Almanach* (1839): 63; Clark, *Deceased Bishops,* 235; l'Ami, 48 (1826): 336.

15. DuBourg to Frayssinous, July 20, 1826, SAP.

16. *Le Moniteur Universel,* no. 148, May 28, 1826. The speech was given on May 25, and news of it could not have reached the United States prior to DuBourg's departure on June 1. It was not until October 23 that Maréchal wrote tongue-in-cheek to Garnier, "One has been a little surprised here at the reference made to Mgr. Dubourg by Mgr. de Hermopolis in his discourse addressed to the Chamber of Deputies." *See* Maréchal Letters, SAP.

17. Borgna to Propaganda, October 17, 1826 Kenneally, 1: 997; Baudier, *Catholic Church in Louisiana,* 305.

18. Heaney, "A Century of Pioneering," 504, citing Mother St. Joseph Laclotte to Mother St. Henry, July 8, 1826.

19. Callan, *Philippine Duchesne,* 438.

20. Seghers to Joubert, November 18, 1826, SAB.

21. DuBourg to Frayssinous, July 20, 1826, SAB.

22. Somaglia to DuBourg, July 29, 1826, D-79, DFP.

23. Melville, *Cheverus,* 306.

24. Ordinance du Roi, July 31, 1826, Archives Nationales (hereafter NAP), F19-683-3586.

25. *L'Ami,* 48 (1826): 374, August 2, 1826.

26. Badin to Fenwick, August 2, 1826, Badin Letters, AUND.

27. NAP, F19-5688.

28. DuBourg to Barrès, August 2, 1826, SAP. During the vacancy of the see, the Archdiocese of Bordeaux was administered by three vicars general. The other two were Philippe-Louis Marginier and Barthelmy Maurel (sometimes spelled Morel).

29. Billaud to Gignoux, July 27, 1826, Archives of the Archdiocese of Bordeaux (hereafter AABord.). Young Billaud was employed in Rome at the Gardes des Archives de l'Ambassade de France.

30. NAP, F19-683-3617; F19-282-922. The nomination was registered on August 21, 1826. Cf. F19-282-3617.

31. *L'Ami*, 48 (1826): 41, August 19, 1826.

32. *Journal de Tarn-et-Garonne*, August 23, 1826, citing DuBourg to Cheverus, August 20, 1826.

33. *Ibid.*, September 20, 1826; Daux, *Histoire de l'église de Montauban* (Paris, 1886), vol. 2, sec. 9, pp. 2–3. The letter was addressed to a Mr. Mialert-Becknell of New Orleans.

34. *Journal de Tarn-et-Garonne*, August 26, 1826.

35. *L'Ami*, 49 (1826): 119, September 6, 1826. Trélissac had administered the vacant see between its re-erection by Napoleon and the arrival of Cheverus in 1824. *See* Melville, *Cheverus*, 286.

36. P. F. DuBourg to Louis DuBourg, June 23, 1826, D-12, DFP.

37. Filleau to Louis DuBourg, August 24, 1826, D-17, DFP.

38. Babad to Propaganda, April 2, 1826, Kenneally, 1: 964. In Reims Babad was assigned to the Sulpician seminary only recently restored to the Society. *See* Ruane, *The Beginnings of the Society of St.-Sulpice in the United States, 1791–1829* (Washington, D.C., 1935), 156.

39. Tessier to Garnier, May 4, 1826, Letterbrook 1, SAB. Alcoholism among clerics gave more scandal in the early nineteenth century than at present when it is regarded more often as a disease than as a vice.

40. *Régistre des Assemblées des Consulteurs*, September 27, 1826, SAP; Celestin Moreau, Les prêtres français emigrés aux Etats-Unis (Paris, 1856), 191–92. As it turned out, Babad lived on another twenty years, dying on January 13, 1846.

41. *Journal de Tarn-et-Garonne*, September 27, 1826.

42. *L'Ami*, 49 (1826): 215, September 27, 1826. The ordinations took place on September 23 and included 12 priests, 4 deacons, 5 subdeacons, and 2 for minor orders.

43. NAP, F19*-685-4040, November 10, 1826.

44. Louis DuBourg to Bishop DuBourg, September ? , 1826, D-18, DFP.

45. *Séries Episcoporum, Ecclésiae Catholicae* (Ratisbon, 1873), 634.

46. Billaud to Gignoux, September 7, 1826, AABord.

47. Billaud to M. l'abbé ? , October 3, 1826, AABord.

48. Cheverus to Bonneuil, October 12, 1826, *Records*, 15 (1904): 235.

49. The Prefect of Tarn-et-Garonne in 1826 was M. de Limairac. *See Almanach Royal et National,* 397. DuBourg's letter to Limairac is not extant in archives of Montauban.

50. *Journal de Tarn-et-Garonne,* November 4, November 11, 1826.

51. Frayssinous had used the words at the main commencement of the Sorbonne in August 1824.

52. Guillaume de Bertier de Sauvigny, *The Bourbon Restoration,* tr. Lynn M. Case (Philadelphia, 1966), 340, 361. Hereafter cited Bertier-Case, *Bourbon Restoration.*

53. *Journal de Tarn-et-Garonne,* November 11, 1826.

54. DuBourg to Duchesne, November 6, 1826, Letter 40, RASH.

55. NAP, F19*-685-4040, F19-282-1235, 1236; Melville, *Cheverus,* 310–11. The bulls were registered on November 13, 1826.

56. NAP, F19*-685-4039, November 10, 1826.

57. *L'Ami,* 50 (1826): 7. The consecration took place on Sunday, November 12, 1826. The Bishop of Aire presided; also assisting was the Bishop of Imeria.

58. The *Journal de Tarn-et-Garonne* of November 22, 1826, and Daux, *L'église de Montauban,* vol. 2, sec. 9, p. 7, give the date as November 14, but the Arch. Dept. Bord., 2, vg-222, contains a declaration of the Prince de Croij that the oath was taken on November 13; *l'Ami,* 50: 7, also gives November 13.

59. Filleau to Louis DuBourg, November 9, 1826, D-16, DFP.

60. *Journal de Tarn-et-Garonne,* November 22, 1826.

CHAPTER XXXV: Louis-Guillaume de Montauban

1. *Journal de Tarn-et-Garonne,* October 31, 1826.

2. *Ibid.,* November 15, 1826.

3. *Ibid.,* November 22, 1826. The poet-priests were Sylvestre de Molières and a M. l'abbé Aillaud; the verses of Molières were subsequently printed and offered for sale at 25 centimes.

4. *Ibid.,* December 6, 1826. This quotation from a lengthy review is by an unidentified critic. Ingres left Montauban on November 22, 1826.

5. *Ibid.,* November 18, 1826.

6. Ordonnance royale, November 15, 1826, NAP, F19*685-4087.

7. DuBourg to the Nuncio, November 15, 1826, Kenneally, 1: 1006; *SLCHR* 3 (July 1921): 216–17.

8. Melville, *Cheverus,* 308. A royal ordinance of November 15, 1826, named Trélissac and Carles vicars general of Bordeaux. *See* NAP

F19*-685-4082. Cheverus deprived Montauban of a third priest, Guilleux, whom he brought with him from Mayenne in 1824.

9. *La Chapelle to Limairac, November 18, 1826, Packet 2-V-1,* Archives Départementales de Montauban (hereafter ADM); *Journal de Tarn-et-Garonne,* November 25, 1826.

10. Frayssinous to Langloix, December 7, 1826, F19-1758, NAP; Daux, *L'église de Montauban,* vol. 2, sec. 9, p. 7; *Journal de Tarn-et-Garonne,* November 22, 1826. The pastor was a M. l'abbé Fondomie.

11. Bertier-Case, *Bourbon Restoration,* 201. Unless otherwise noted, the treatment of travel in this chapter is based on Bertier-Case 201–210.

12. *Ibid.,* 207.

13. *Ibid.,* 202.

14. Louis DuBourg to Filleau, December 14, 1826, D-19, DFP. This letter fixes the time of the bishop's arrival as "the evening of November 25." The *Mémorial du Midi,* 1: 369, gives the hour (8:00 P.M.) as well as the manner of arrival. If DuBourg left Paris on November 20 and arrived in Montauban on November 25 he did not linger en route nor place his own comfort above other considerations.

15. Victoire DuBourg Fournier's will was deposited with the firm of Darieux-Fils on December 16, 1825.

16. For a description of Cheverus's entry in July 1824, *see* Melville, *Cheverus,* 285–88. The *Journal de Tarn-et-Garonne,* November 22, 1826, alludes to DuBourg's request to forego formalities.

17. *Journal de Tarn-et-Garonne,* November 22 and 25, 1826. Caussade is some twenty kilometers northeast of Montauban.

18. *Moniteur Universel,* 339, 1628–29, December 5, 1826; *l'Ami,* 50 (1826): 104.

19. *Journal de Tarn-et-Garonne,* November 29, 1826.

20. Daux, *L'église de Montauban,* vol. 2, sec. 9, p. 8.

21. Easterly, *Rosati,* 128.

22. Daux, *L'église de Montauban,* vol. 2, sec. 4, pp. 73–74. The spelling of "Henry" is Daux's.

23. *Ibid.,* sec. 5: 45–48.

24. Huber and Wilson, *Basilica on Jackson Square,* 21–22. Francisco Zapari was hired at a fee of $1,855 to decorate the interior of the church and its altars.

25. [Mary Teresa A. Carroll], *A Catholic History of Alabama and the Floridas* (New York, 1980), 1: 253. The author of this work, a Mercy nun who knew descendants of DuBourg's relatives in Louisiana, says the bishop lived in constant fear of assassination when in New Orleans.

26. Z. Le Bret, Gabriel Ruck, et Marcellin Ruch, *Histoire de Montauban* (Montauban, 1841), ii, 6.

27. Mary-Lafon, *Histoire d'une ville Protestante* (Paris, 1862), 1–10.

28. Melville, *Cheverus,* 285, 294.

29. *Almanach Royal et National* (1826), 397, 905. The precise figures given are 238,143 and 25,300.

30. Melville, *Cheverus,* 291.

31. Cheverus to Bonneuil, December 19, 1826, *Records,* 15 (1904): 237. The name is also spelled "Carle."

32. For Carles's American career, *see* Martin I. J. Griffin, "A Colony of French Catholics in Bradford County, Pa., 1794–1800," *Records,* 18 (1907): 245–61; 421–33; "Correspondence," *Records,* 22 (1911): 199–200. For Dominican refugees in Georgia, *see* Joseph D. Mitchell's list in the Catholic Laymen's Association of Georgia's *Bulletin,* 2 (1921): 6; *Carroll Papers,* 3: 11, 20.

33. La Chapelle to Limairac, December 27, 1826, Packet 2-V-1, ADM.

34. Although the dogma of the Immaculate Conception of the Virgin Mary was not proclaimed by Pius IX until December 8, 1854, the feast day had been observed on December 8 in western Europe for several centuries.

35. Archives de l'évêché de Montauban (hereafter AEM). Of the fifty-one circulars or *mandements* of DuBourg extant in 1882 only twenty-one remain in the Montauban archives today. Daux, *L'église de Montauban,* vol. 2, sec. 9, p. 28, suggests there may have been more than fifty-one originally. His list given in 1882 offers valuable clues to the purposes of the now missing documents.

36. The Ember Days, or as the French appropriately called them "Quatre-Temps," came four times a year in connection with Christmas, Lent, Pentecost, and September or harvest time, and consisted of the Wednesdays, Fridays and Saturdays of the Ember Weeks. Ember Saturdays were occasions of ordinations to major and minor orders. Present liturgical practices no longer note the Ember Days.

37. *Journal de Tarn-et-Garonne,* December 27, 1826.

38. *Ibid.*

39. John Dubois was consecrated Bishop of New York on October 29, 1826, by Archbishop Ambroise Maréchal in the Baltimore Cathedral.

CHAPTER XXXVI: Taking Command

1. Borgna to Propaganda, October 17, 1826, Kenneally, 1: 997.

2. Billaud to Gignoux, September 7, 1826, AABord.

3. *Circulaire of January 5, 1827,* Archives of the Diocese of Montauban (hereafter ADM). The three vicars general or archdeacons were Turcq for Montauban, Pouget for Moissac, and Gasc for Castel-Sarrasin. On January 10 that same year an ordinance of the king (NAP, F19* 686-11) decreed that Ferdinand Gasc was to be given the first canonicate vacant in Bordeaux. Existing evidence does not indicate whether Gasc's transfer had any connection with DuBourg's reorganization plan, or whether Cheverus had requested the transfer earlier.

4. Daux, *L'église de Montauban,* vol. 2, sec. 9, p. 10.

5. *Laity's Directory,* 1839, "Biographical Notice of the Most Rev. William Louis Valentine Dubourg," 64. The sisters of Nevers were *les Dames de la Charité et Instruction Chrétienne de Nevers.*

6. Daux, *L'église de Montauban,* vol. 2, sec. 7, pp. 22–23. Unless otherwise noted the history of the Diocese of Montauban is entirely based upon Daux.

7. *Ibid.,* sec. 8: 3–8; 13–14.

8. The king first tried to name Nicholas Mac-Carthy to Montauban, but Mac-Carthy refused to accept; then Louis XVIII named Jean-Brumauld de Beauregard, but before Rome confirmed this nomination the See of Orleans became vacant and Beauregard was named to the latter see without ever having gone to Montauban. Although Jean Lefebvre de Cheverus was named to Montauban by the king on January 13, 1823, it was not until July 1824 that he took possession of the vacant See of Montauban. For a more extensive treatment of this question, *see* Annabelle M. Melville, "Some Aspects of the Return of Bishop Cheverus to France in 1823," *Records and Studies,* 45 (1957): 7–20.

9. Melville, *Cheverus,* 271–84.

10. R. Limouzin-Lamothe, *Monseigneur de Quelen, Archevêque de Paris* (Paris, 1955), 1: 258; François-René de Chateaubriand, *Mémoires d'Outre-Tombe,* édition du Centenaire par Maurice Levaillant (Paris, 1949), vol. 1, 2me partie, 84.

11. Melville, *Cheverus,* 296, 300.

12. Daux, *L'église de Montauban,* vol. 2, sec. 9, p. 11. The headmistress was a Madame Calais.

13. *Ibid.*

14. Melville, *Cheverus,* 290. The city of Montauban had almost half of the Protestants living in the Department of Tarn-et-Garonne or the Diocese of Montauban. In general, the nobility, merchants, and manufacturers remained loyal to the old faith; Calvinism made its inroads among the clothmakers, traders in grain, and working people.

15. Daux, *L'église de Montauban,* vol. 2, sec. 9, p. 11.

16. *Ibid.*, sec. 8:25. The rector-*économe* was a M. Cazes; the professor was a M. Rey.

17. *Ibid.*, 26. Owing to the vacancy of the see, Bishop Cousin de Grainville of Cahors conferred these orders.

18. *Ibid.*, 19–21.

19. Melville, *Cheverus*, 289–90. The purchase was made on November 22, 1824; the Prefect confirmed it on February 24, 1825, and the circular announcing the completion of the transaction was dated August 11, 1825.

20. Report of May 9, 1826, F19-683, ff. 3014, NAP.

21. The royal ordinance was dated November 25, 1827; DuBourg's *Circulaire* was dated November 3. This circular no longer exists but is well summarized in Daux, vol. 2, sec. 9, p. 15.

22. The priest was a M. Arnac.

23. Daux, *L'église de Montauban,* vol. 2, sec. 9, pp. 12–13. DuBourg was dead by the time the religious from Toulouse took charge of the Montauban Refuge.

24. DuBourg to Carroll, February [?], 1813, 3-E-7, AAB.

25. Daux, *L'église de Montauban,* vol. 2, sec. 9, pp. 13–14.

26. DuBourg to Rosati, September 19, 1826, AASL.

27. The division of the diocese was made by a papal brief dated July 18, 1826, and forwarded to Rosati on July 22, 1826. *See* Kenneally, 3: 1943. DuBourg learned of it by a letter from Somaglia dated July 29, 1826, and addressed to Bordeaux. *See also* D-79, DFP; Kenneally, 3: 1944.

28. Rosati to DuBourg, December 29, 1826, AASL.

29. DuBourg to Propaganda, May 1, 1827, Kenneally, 1: 1063.

30. DuBourg to Rosati, April 22, 1827, AASL.

31. Propaganda to DuBourg, May 26, 1827, Kenneally, 3: 2006.

32. Easterly, *Rosati,* 148. This house did not flourish at first and Duchesne returned to Florissant in October 1834, leaving the direction of the *Maison de Ville* in St. Louis to Mme Thiefry.

33. DuBourg to Rosati, April 22, 1827, AASL.

34. Daux, *L'église de Montauban,* vol. 2, sec. 9, p. 14.

35. *Ibid.*, 15.

36. Bertier-Case, *Bourbon Restoration,* 172–73. Daux says DuBourg brought the Indian costume with him from New Orleans but the circumstances of DuBourg's departure in 1826 raise some question regarding this detail.

37. Guillaume de Bertier de Sauvigny, "Les 'Bon Sauvages' à Paris

en 1827," *La Croix,* July 12, 1954. Unless otherwise noted the description of the Osage visit relies on this account.

38. *L'Ami,* 53 (1827): 58–59.

39. Kenneally, 6:504.

40. *Ibid.,* 503.

41. M. Michaud, *Biographie Universelle Ancienne et Moderne,* Nouvelle edition (Paris, 1852), 11: 371. The Osages arrived in Montauban on November 17, 1829.

42. Daux, *L'église de Montauban,* vol. 2, sec. 9, p. 20.

43. *Moniteur,* June 2, 1830.

44. DuBourg to Rosati, November 29, 1827, AASL.

45. Filleau to Louis DuBourg, August 3, 1827, D-21, DFP.

46. Postcommunion prayer of the First Sunday in Advent.

CHAPTER XXXVII: Progress at Home and Abroad

1. *Le Tarn-et-Garonne* (Montauban, 1902), 175. The arch of triumph was eventually demolished in 1871.

2. Clermont-Tonnerre to Cheverus, January 19, 1829, AABord.

3. *Prospectus* (Toulouse, 1829): 2, AABord.

4. *Ibid.,* 3.

5. The *Miscellany* ceased publication at the outbreak of the Civil War in 1861; the *Pilot* celebrated its centennial in 1979 in a variety of ways, including a special edition, *The Pilot, America's Oldest Catholic Newspaper,* and a banquet on September 12 at which the distinguished Church historian John Tracy Ellis gave the main address.

6. *Mandement pour la Carême,* February 8, 1828, AEM.

7. Melville, *Cheverus,* 329.

8. Vatimesnil to Bishops, May 27, 1828, 2 Vg. 22, AABord.

9. Bishop of Beauvais to Bishops, May 27, 1828, *ibid.*

10. Bertier-Case, *Bourbon Restoration,* 320–21 describe what missions were like in the 1820s.

11. The story of the mission by M. l'abbé Moncet appeared in the *Stenographe Montalbanais ou relation de la Mission. See* Daux, *L'église de Montauban,* vol. 2, sec. 9, pp. 16–17.

12. *L'Ami,* 56 (1828): 231–32.

13. *Ibid.* The Mission Cross was restored in 1951 through the generosity of the Catholics of Montauban and was still standing in 1980, when this chapter was written.

14. Circulaire aux curés, June 21, 1828, Daux, *L'église de Montauban*, vol. 2, sec. 9, pp. 17–18; 29. This circular no longer exists.

15. Bertier-Case, *Bourbon Restoration*, 410–11.

16. Melville, *Cheverus*, 332.

17. *Ibid.*, 332–33. The commission was composed of Frayssinous, Cheverus, Quelen, and Quelen's vicar general Desjardins. Quelen later retracted, but the others stuck to their guns. As Frayssinous put it, "We were consulted as moral theologians. As a matter of conscience we did not have a right to impose our political views on the King."

18. Bertier-Case, *Bourbon Restoration*, 412–13.

19. For an account of the impact of the June ordinances on the Archdiocese of Bordeaux *see*, Melville, *Cheverus*, 335, 344–46.

20. Daux, *L'église de Montauban*, vol. 2, sec. 9, pp. 18–19. DuBourg explained to Rosati, "I have deprived the Lazarists of my seminary. I had to; the Cong. will never be in France what it is in Italy." *See* letter, September 25, 1829, AASL.

21. *Circulaire*, July 14, 1828, AEM.

22. E. Levesque, "Boyer," *Dictionnaire d'histoire et de géographie ecclésiastique*, 10, cols. 312–13. After Boyer's death his *Discours pour les retraites ecclésiastiques* were published in 1843. DuBourg seems to have admired him particularly, for in his correspondence with Saint-Sulpice he usually sent regards to him.

23. DuBourg seems to have taken the April ordinance quite seriously. He not only gave his priests very precise directions for supervising religious education in the primary schools; he himself exercised great care in assuring that the conduct and capacity of the teachers suited the standards of the new regulations. He took pleasure in distributing prizes to masters and students who proved most meritorious. *See* Daux, *L'église de Montauban*, vol. 2, sec. 9, p. 18.

24. For the activities of the duchess of Berry in Bordeaux, July 15–18, 1828, *see* Melville, *Cheverus*, 342–43.

25. Daux, *L'église de Montauban*, vol. 2, sec. 9, pp. 18, 28. This circular no longer exists.

26. *L'Ami*, 57 (1828): 201, 220, 234.

27. Daux, *L'église de Montauban*, vol. 2, sec. 9, p. 18.

28. *Circulaire*, September 29, 1928, AEM. In this circular DuBourg refers to his seminaries in the plural. The June ordinance regulating secondary ecclesiastical schools had limited the number to one in each diocese; but in October a royal ordinance applying especially to Albi, Autun, Belley, Vannes, and Montauban eliminated the difficulties involved for these dioceses. The bishops were notified on October 8; the ordinance was dated October 12, 1828.

29. A biographical *notice* of Maréchal appeared in *l'Ami*, 61 (1829): 141–43.

30. Since Maréchal was in charge of Bohemia from 1793–1799 and returned to France in July 1803, he and DuBourg were together in the Baltimore Sulpician establishment only from 1799 to 1803. By the time Maréchal returned from France in 1812, DuBourg was destined for New Orleans as apostolic administrator.

31. Schauinger, *Badin,* 214. The gift was not without strings since 100 Masses were expected in return. W. S. Reilly in "An Historical Sketch of Archbishop DuBourg," *The Voice,* 20 (October 1942): 24, states that DuBourg sent the Jesuits $1,000 and promised them $100 a year thereafter.

32. Anduze to Rosati, November 1, 1828, *CHR,* 3 (January 1918): 466.

33. Lipscomb, "Administration of Michael Portier," 104, citing Portier to Rosati, November 16, 1827.

34. DuBourg to Rosati, August 15, 1828, AASL.

35. DuBourg began expecting Portier in January 1829 but the death of Leo XII on February 10, 1829, delayed Portier's affairs in Rome.

36. Portier told Propaganda on August 20, 1829, that DuBourg received him warmly and hospitably, presenting him with "three excellent subjects which he prepared for my diocese." *See* Lipscomb, "Administration of Michael Portier," 114–115. DuBourg's correspondence with Bruté and Rosati names only two.

37. DuBourg to Rosati, September 25, 1829, AASL.

38. *L'Ami,* 61 (1829): 377–78.

39. DuBourg to Rosati, October 11, 1829, AASL.

40. DuBourg to the Bishop of Hermopolis, August 31, 1829, SAP.

41. DuBourg to Bruté, October 10, 1829, AUND. Lapoujade and Massip never reached the Mount. Portier went directly south without stopping in Baltimore.

42. *Ibid.*

43. DuBourg to Elèves, July 15, 1828, Annals of the Community, 1882, 2:71, ASJPH.

44. Rosati to DuBourg, September 14, 1828, D-11, DFP.

45. Van Quickenborne to DuBourg, September 21, 1828, LG-VD-4, DFP.

46. Duchesne to DuBourg, October 21, 1828, *Annales,* 3 (September 1829): 571–73.

47. *Ibid.*

48. *Ibid.*

49. [Van Quickenborne] to DuBourg, September 21, 1828, LG-VD-4, DFP. The five new congregations were at: Jefferson on the Missouri River; Boonville, Louisiana on the Mississippi; New London and Palmyra on Salt River, all within a radius of some ninety miles from St. Charles.

50. *Ibid.*

51. DuBourg to Mlle Elizabeth Bruslé, January 27, 1829, unnumbered, DFP; DuBourg to Bruté, October 10, 1829, AUND; DuBourg to Rosati, January 28, 1829, AASL.

52. DuBourg to Rosati, January 28, 1829, AASL.

53. DuBourg to Rosati, August 28, 1828, AASL.

54. DuBourg to Rosati, January 28, 1829, AASL.

55. DuBourg to Rosati, October 11, 1829, AASL.

56. DuBourg to Rosati, January 28, 1829, AASL.

57. DuBourg to the Prefect of Propaganda, September 18, 1829, *SLCHR,* 3 (July 1921): 222. DuBourg's reply to Capellari's request dated August 29, 1829.

58. *Ibid.* This list, along with other archival materials of the DuBourg episcopacy in the United States, may have been destroyed during the Civil War.

59. *Circulaire,* February 24, 1829, AEM.

60. *Ibid.*

61. Billaud to Cheverus, March 31, 1829, AABord.

62. *Circulaire,* April 13, 1829, AEM.

63. *Ibid.*

64. Universal Jubilee Proclamation, June 18, 1829, AEM. Cardinal Albani was the papal secretary.

65. *Mandement* for the Jubilee, November 12, 1829, AEM.

66. Melville, *Cheverus,* 348–49. The preacher at Bordeaux was Nicholas Mac-Carthy, S. J.

67. *Mandement,* November 12, 1829, AEM.

68. DuBourg to Garnier, June 27, 1829, SAP. The decision to remove the Lazarists from the seminary was taken June 15, 1829. *See* Daux, *L'église de Montauban,* vol. 2, sec. 9, p. 19, n. 2, citing an extract from the Congregation of the Mission's *délibérations du conseil,* 47. The agreement was signed by their Superior General Salhorne, Secretary Etienne, and council members Le Go, Boullangier, Baccaré, and Richenel.

69. DuBourg to Garnier, June 27, 1829, SAP.

70. Daux, *L'église de Montauban,* vol. 2, sec. 9, p. 20.

71. *L'Ami,* 60 (1829): 375–76. The retreat was held October 13–20, 1829.

72. Ordonnance, October 30, 1829, AEM.

73. Secretary of State of Ecclesiastical Affairs to Prefect of Tarn-et-Garonne, June 24, 1829, ADM. L'abbé Bandol was the new canon.

74. Flaget to Rosati, February 20, 1829, AASL.

75. [Carroll] *Alabama and the Floridas:,* 1:279–83.

76. *Ibid.,* 276.

77. Flaget to Rosati, February 20, 1829, AASL.

78. Rosati to Propaganda, April 3, 1829, Kenneally, 1: 1214.

79. Flaget to Rosati, February 20, 1829, AASL.

CHAPTER XXXVIII: The July Revolution

1. *Mémorial Bordelais,* 7143, January 1, 1830, 3–4; *l'Ami,* 62 (1830): 283, 331.

2. *Circulaire,* February 17, 1830, 1–2, AEM.

3. Melville, *Cheverus,* 358. The ordinance was forwarded from Paris on March 6, 1830.

4. Daux, *L'église de Montauban,* vol. 2, sec. 9, p. 21.

5. *L'Ami,* 63 (1830): 261, 311.

6. *Ibid.,* 64 (1830): 38. American usage refers to this organization as "Society" instead of the French "Association."

7. DuBourg to Bruté, May 5, 1830, AUND.

8. Schauinger, *Cathedrals,* 250.

9. *Circulaire,* April 10, 1830, p. 2, AEM.

10. *Ibid.*

11. R. Limouzin-Lamothe, *Monseigneur de Quelen, Archevêque de Paris* (Paris, 1955), 1:304. Unless otherwise noted the following account of the translation is based on this work, 304–9. An even more detailed account is preserved in the issues of *l'Ami* of April 28 and May 26, 1830. See 63 (1830): 341–44; 64ʼ(1830): 65–69.

12. These included Notre Dame de Paris, the parishes of Saint Vincent de Paul and Clichy, the motherhouse of the Daughters of Charity, the Hospice of Pity, the Hôtel de Dieu, and the cathedral of Versailles.

13. *L'Ami,* 64 (1830): 67.

14. DuBourg to Bruté, May 5, 1830, AUND. "I am disturbed by conditions in Paris."

15. *L'Ami,* 63 (1830): 343, 361.

16. DuBourg to Rosati, May 19, 1830, AASL.

17. Melville, *Cheverus,* 360.

18. *Circulaire* published by the bishop's printer in 1830, n.d., AEM.

19. Melville, *Cheverus,* 361.

20. Daux, *L'église de Montauban,* vol. 2, sec. 19, p. 29. Mandement sur prières d'actions de graces pour l'expédition d'Afrique, July 13, 1830. This document is no longer extant.

21. Bertier-Case, *Bourbon Restoration,* 429–31.

22. Melville, *Cheverus,* 362.

23. There is no evidence remaining that DuBourg wrote such a pastoral; but on the basis of what is known of his actions taken in regard to other royal wishes it may be speculated that he wrote as persuasive a pastoral as any other prelate.

24. Bertier-Case, *Bourbon Restoration,* 431.

25. *Ibid.,* 440. For the precise chronology of the overthrow of Charles X in July 1830, see 441–54.

26. Paul Thureau-Dangin, *Histoire de la Monarchie de Juillet,* 3d ed. (Paris, 1897), 1:247.

27. Jean Leflon, *Eugene de Mazenod,* tr. Francis D. Flanagan, O.M.I. (New York, 1966), 2:344.

28. Forbin-Janson eventually reached the United States; Latil went to England, while Rohan-Chabot and Tharin fled to Fribourg, Switzerland.

29. Thureau-Dangin, *Monarchie de Juillet,* 1:247.

30. Leflon, *Mazenod,* 2:344.

31. Daux, *L'église de Montauban,* vol. 2, sec. 9, pp. 21–22.

32. Melville, *Cheverus,* 374–75. The archbishop of Tours wrote on August 15, the bishop of Saint-Claude on August 18, Quelen and the bishop of Agen on August 19, and the bishop of Marseilles on September 6, 1830.

33. *Ibid.,* 375–76.

34. Jacques-Paul Martin, *La Nonciature de Paris . . . sous le règne de Louis-Philippe, 1830–1848* (Paris, 1945), 39–48.

35. Leflon, *Mazenod,* 2:354.

36. Daux, *L'église de Montauban,* vol. 2, sec. 9, p. 29. This circular is no longer extant.

37. Secretary of State for Public Instruction to the Prefect of Tarn-et-Garonne, October 14, 1830, Packet 2-V-1, ADM. The priest was an Abbé Certer.

38. Leflon, *Mazenod*, 2: 354; Daux, *L'église de Montauban*, vol. 2, sec. 9, p. 29. This circular of October 18, 1830, is no longer extant.

39. Daux, *L'église de Montauban*, vol. 2, sec. 9, p. 22, n. 1.

40. Roger Price, "Legitimist Opposition to the Revolution of 1830 in the French Provinces," *The Historical Journal* 17 (Cambridge, 1974): 762. Price suggests that at Montauban "the existence of Protestants and a long tradition of conflict helped to preserve among the masses an emotional attachment to the old order."

41. Thureau-Dangin, *Monarchie de Juillet*, 1:247, n. 2.

42. *L'Ami*, 66 (1830): 181, reporting a letter published in the *Mémorial de Toulouse*, November 20, 1830.

43. *Ibid.*, 67 (1831): 328–29. Daux, *L'église de Montauban*, vol. 2, sec. 9, p. 22, dates this letter February 25, 1831; *l'Ami* dates it February 26 and reproduces the entire letter.

44. Cheverus to Pastors, February 25, 1831, AABord.

45. Melville, *Cheverus*, 378.

46. The square which the cathedral faces is today named Place Roosevelt.

47. Filleau to Louis DuBourg, February 22, 1830, D-48, DFP.

48. Filleau to Louis DuBourg, July 9, 1830, D-50, DFP.

49. Charest de Lauzon records, January 29, 1830, BJC.

50. Filleau to Louis DuBourg, July 24, 1830, B-4, DFP.

51. Filleau to Louis DuBourg, October 14, 1830, D-53, DFP.

52. DuBourg to Mlle. E. Bruslé, November 15, 1830, unnumbered, DFP. The exact relationship of Miss Bruslé to the DuBourgs is not clear. The bishop's brother, Joseph-Patrice, married a Charlotte Bruslé in 1787; Miss Bruslé may have been a descendant of that sister-in-law's family.

53. Filleau to DuBourg, November 27, 1830, D-54, DFP.

54. DuBourg to Rosati, October 27, 1830, AASL. DuBourg, who had originally intended this priest, a M. Pouget of Montpellier, to serve the Ursulines, learned before Pouget sailed that Bertrand Martial, who was already back in New Orleans, had been appointed chaplain to that convent.

55. De Neckere to Rosati, November 22, 1830, AASL.

56. DuBourg to Rosati, November 23, 1830, AASL.

57. He was Joachim, duc d'Isoard, the Archbishop of Auch. The other three were Gustave Maximilien, Prince de Croij, Archbishop of Rouen; Jean-Baptiste, duc de Latil, Archbishop of Rheims; and Louis-François, Prince de Rohan-Chabot, Archbishop of Besançon. For this conclave, *see* Jean Leflon, *La Crise révolutionnaire, 1789–1846: Tome 20*

de l'Histoire de l'église depuis les origines jusqu 'a nos jours de Fliche et Martin (Paris, 1949), 426–28.

58. *Mandement à l'occasion de la mort du soverain pontife Pie VIII,* AEM. The three documents, two of which remain in Montauban today, relating to the previous change in popes were those of February 24, April 9, and April 13, 1829. There is no record of DuBourg's issuing any further decrees relating to either Pius VIII or his successor. The *mandement* for the latter's Jubilee was issued by the vicars general of Montauban after DuBourg departed for Besançon in 1833.

59. Minister of Cults to Minister of Foreign Affairs, February 18, 1831, F19-1930, NAP.

60. DuBourg to Cheverus, July 10, 1830, AABord. This appears to be a form letter recommending a *Concordance des Quatre Evangiles* compiled by his *grand vicaire.*

61. DuBourg to Saulnier, February 1, 1831, AASL.

CHAPTER XXXIX: Changing Times

1. Limousin-Lamothe, *Quelen,* 2:46–49; Bertier de Sauvigny, "Mgr. de Quelen et les incidents de Saint-Germain l'Auxerrois en février 1831," *Revue d'Histoire de l'Eglise de France,* 32 (January–June 1946): 110–120.

2. Thureau-Dangin, *Monarchie de Juillet,* 249, cites as notable the pastoral letter of the bishop of Orleans in this regard.

3. *Ibid.,* 252.

4. For Cheverus's actions *see* Melville, *Cheverus,* 368–73; for Mazenod *see* Leflon, *Mazenod,* 2:352–89.

5. Ralph Waldo Emerson in his essay on "Self-Reliance."

6. Directive of February 28, 1831, 2, Vg. 222, AABord.

7. Daux, *L'église de Montauban,* vol. 2, sec. 9, p. 29, circular, February 28, 1831.

8. In the absence of the original documents the account of the Corpus Christi disorders relies upon the report in Daux, loc. cit., 22–24, and his rendering of these documents.

9. Daux, *L'église de Montauban,* vol. 2, sec. 9, p. 29.

10. *L'Ami,* 68 (1831): 309.

11. *Ibid.,* 345.

12. Daux, *L'église de Montauban,* vol. 2, sec. 9, pp. 23–24.

13. *L'Ami,* 68 (1831): 345–46, pastoral letter of June 11, 1831. This pastoral was not listed by Daux. The complete text is in *l'Ami.*

14. Daux, *L'église de Montauban,* vol. 2, sec. 9, p. 29.

15. Melville, *Cheverus,* 380.

16. Limouzin-Lamothe, *Quelen* 2:94.

17. Daux, *L'église de Montauban,* vol. 2, sec. 9, p. 29, July 15, 1831.

18. DuBourg to Rosati, July 10, 1831, AASL.

19. DuBourg to Rosati, July 30, 1831, AASL.

20. *Ordinances et Mandements,* 2:554–55, AABord.

21. For the details of the uproar in Marseilles, *see* Leflon, *Mazenod,* 2:384–85.

22. Charles-Fortune de Mazenod to his pastors, August 26, 1831, 2, V-10, ADB.

23. Daux, *L'église de Montauban,* vol. 2, sec. 9, p. 29, circular of August 5, 1831. DuBourg was in Paris at the time.

24. *Ibid.,* 30, circular of August 4, 1832.

25. Thureau-Dangin, *Monarchie de Juillet,* 1: 253.

26. Leflon, *Mazenod,* 2: 344.

27. Thureau-Dangin, *Monarchie de Juillet,* 1: 253.

28. For prefects' evaluations of Cheverus and DuBourg, *see* Melville, *Cheverus,* 369–71; *infra,* pp.

29. Nicholas Richardson, *The French Prefectoral Corps, 1814–1830* (Cambridge, 1966), 14–15.

30. Price, "Legitimist Opposition" 17: 759.

31. *Ibid.*

32. Guillaume de Bertier de Sauvigny, *La conspiration des légitimistes et de la duchesse de Berry contre Louis-Philippe (1830–1832),* passim; idem, *Correspondence et documents inédits* (Paris, 1950), 18, 28, 48.

33. Price, "Legitimist Opposition," 17: 759.

34. Bertier de Sauvigny, *Conspiration,* 100.

35. Leflon, *Mazenod,* 2:391. The speaker was Eugene de Mazenod who later founded the Oblates of Mary Immaculate.

36. *Ibid. See also,* Guillaume Bertier de Sauvigny, *Le Comte Ferdinand de Bertier . . . et l'enigme de la Congrégation* (Paris, 1948) 519–20.

37. For an account of the imprisonment at Blaye, *see* Melville, *Cheverus,* 382–87.

38. Price, "Legitimist Opposition," 17: 763–73.

39. Daux, L'église de Montauban, vol. 2, sec. 9, p. 30.

40. Quelen to pastors, April 11, 1832, 2, V-10, 221, ADB.

41. Melville, *Cheverus*, 388–90.

42. Daux, *L'église de Montauban*, vol. 2, sec. 9, p. 30, circular of April 11, 1832. Easter fell on April 22 that year.

43. Form letter dated April 26, 1832, with Filleau to DuBourg, May 14, 1832, attached, D-60, DFP.

44. Daux, *L'église de Montauban*, vol. 2, sec. 9, p. 30.

45. René Surugue, *Les Archevêques de Besançon* (Besançon, 1930), 461.

46. Abbé Etienne Gaussens, "Eloge de Mgr. L.-G. Valentin Du-Bourg," in *Eloges, oraisons funèbres, et discours académiques*, 2d ed. (Bordeaux, 1878), 1:131.

47. Méderic-Louis-Elie Moreau de Saint-Méry, *Moreau de St. Méry's American Journey, 1793–1798*, tr. Kenneth and Anna M. Roberts (New York, 1947), 224.

48. *Ibid.*, 243.

49. George N. Wright, *Life and Times of Louis-Philippe* (London, 1842), 296, and T. Wood Clarke, *Emigrés in the Wilderness*, 79; both say the duke's party left Philadelphia "in the spring of 1797." Washington's *Diaries*, 4:263, show the duke at dinner on October 30, 1797, at Mount Vernon, returning to Alexandria afterward.

50. Surugue, *Les Archevêques de Besançon*, 461.

51. Limouzin-Lamothe, *Quelen*, 2: 93.

52. Brassac to Rosati, November 18, 1831, *CHR* 3 (January 1918), 453.

53. Flaget to DuBourg, March 1, 1832, LGVD-9, DFP.

54. Martin, *La Nonciature de Paris*, 147–48, gives the full text of this circular.

55. Flaget to DuBourg, March 1, 1832, quoting DuBourg, LGVD-9, DFP.

56. DuBourg to Deluol, May 28, 1833, RG-24, Box 8, SAB.

57. The identity of the author remains unknown.

58. Ordinance sur traitement, March 13, 1832, 2, V-10, ADB.

59. DuBourg to Rosati, December 30, 1831, AASL.

60. Alexis de Toqueville, *Correspondence inédit*, (Paris, 1860), 3 vols., 2: 48.

61. Melville, *Cheverus*, 393.

62. *L'Ami*, 71 (1832): 521–522.

63. Melville, *Cheverus*, 394.

64. For the Bruté-Lamennais friendship and correspondence, *see* Charles Lemarie, *Monseigneur Bruté de Rémur* (Paris, 1974), 40–43; 53–62; 96–114.

65. Lamennais, *Correspondence Générale,* 1:343–44, citing Lamennais to Bruté, May 15, 1817.

66. Montalembert to Cheverus, January 1, 1831, AABord. The founding members did not include Lamennais.

67. Melville, *Cheverus,* 401.

68. *L'Avenir* was launched on October 16 while l'Agence Générale was begun on December 18, 1830.

69. Lemarie, *Bruté,* 113, citing Lamennais to Bruté, October 9, 1831.

70. Leflon, *Mazenod,* 2: 414.

71. *Ibid.*

72. Besides Toulouse, the other twelve signers were the bishops of Albi, Montpellier, Montauban, Nîmes, Perigueux, Bayonne, Perpignan, Carcassonne, Limoges, Aire, Cahors, and Rodez.

73. Archbishop of Toulouse to the Bishops, July 17, 1832, AABord.

74. Archbishop of Toulouse to Cheverus, August 15, 1832, AABord.

75. Melville, *Cheverus,* 402.

76. Limouzin-Lamothe, *Quelen,* 2:105.

77. The Lamennais dissent, however, was not over. The spring following DuBourg's death *Les Paroles d'un Croyant* appeared, and on June 24 the pope solemnly condemned this work, classifying its author as a heretic. When Bruté, as Bishop of Vincennes, was in Europe in 1835 he tried to reconcile Lamennais to the Church without success.

78. Daux, *L'église de Montauban,* vol. 2, sec. 5, p. 49. In 1840 there was an attempt to raise 20,000 francs to restore the spires, but political events and Protestant influence prevented the realization of this hope.

CHAPTER XL: *Super Flumina Babylonis*

1. *L'Ami,* 69 (1831): 33–37.

2. The parishes named were Saint Louis (residence of the bishop), Carondelet or Videpoche, Saint Ferdinand or Florissant, Saint Charles, Dardenne, Cote-sans-Dessein, Portage Des Sioux, Vieillemine and Mine-à-Breton, Mine-à-la-Motte, Saint Geneviève, Saint Mary of the Barrens, New Madrid, all in Missouri; Mines-de-la Rivière-aux Fièvres,

Sangamo, Cahokia, Prairie du Rocher, Kaskaskia, Chura and the neighboring English settlements in Illinois; and one parish in Arkansas called Poste des Arkansas.

3. *L'Ami,* 69 (1831): 36.

4. DuBourg to Rosati, January 28, 1829, AASL.

5. Van Quickenborne to DuBourg, September 21, 1828, LGVD-4, DFP.

6. DuBourg to Bruté, July 22, no year given, AUND.

7. Easterly, *Rosati,* 114. The four Sisters were Francis Xavier Love, Martina Butcher, Rebecca Dellone, and Francis Regis. They left Emmitsburg on October 15, 1828.

8. DuBourg to Rosati, November 6, 1832, AASL.

9. *L'Ami,* 70 (1831): 247.

10. Easterly, *Rosati,* 126.

11. DuBourg to Rosati, May 19, 1831, AASL. The two seminarians, Hilary Tucker and George Hamilton, left for Rome in April 1832. *See also* Rosati to DuBourg, May 1, 1832, LGVD-8, DFP.

12. DuBourg to Rosati, May 11, 1830, AASL.

13. DuBourg to Rosati, June 13, 1831, AASL.

14. DuBourg to Rosati, September 28, 1831, AASL.

15. DuBourg to Rosati, May 19, 1831, AASL.

16. *Ibid.*

17. DuBourg to Rosati, September 28, 1831, AASL.

18. When Brassac followed DuBourg to France in 1826, he believed he was returning to be with his father in his last hours. But in 1831 the old man showed no signs of dying, and Brassac, who disliked the greatly altered conditions of the Church in France following the July Revolution, returned to the American mission.

19. Brassac to Rosati, November 18, 1831, *CHR,* 3 (January 1918): 453.

20. DuBourg to Saulnier, August 13, 1831, AASL.

21. Duchesne to DuBourg, January 29, 1832, RASH.

22. Easterly, *Rosati,* 121.

23. Blanc was consecrated Bishop of New Orleans in December 1835, two years after DuBourg's death.

24. DuBourg to Rosati, May 19, 1830, AASL.

25. DuBourg to Rosati, May 19, 1831, AASL.

26. DuBourg to Rosati, October 23, 1832, AASL.

27. DuBourg to Rosati, November 6, 1832, AASL.

28. Propaganda filled the vacant see at New Orleans on January 27, 1834.

29. Flaget to DuBourg, March 1, 1832, LGVD-9, DFP.

30. For the coming of the Jesuits to the Diocese of Bardstown, *see* J. Herman Schauinger, *Cathedrals in the Wilderness* (Milwaukee, 1952), 265–67.

31. DuBourg to Rosati, February 12, 1832, AASL.

32. Rosati to DuBourg, September 14, 1828, D-111, DFP.

333. *L'Ami,* 69 (1831): 247.

34. Rosati to DuBourg, May 1, 1832, LGVD-8, DFP.

35. DuBourg to Rosati, November 6, 1832, AASL.

36. Rosati to DuBourg, May 1, 1832, LGVD-8, DFP.

37. Erskine, *Duchesne,* 164, citing DuBourg to Pratte.

38. Rosati to DuBourg, May 1, 1832, LGVD-8, DFP.

39. Rosati to DuBourg, February 17, 1832, D-1, DFP.

40. *Annales,* 7 (1833): 108–112.

41. Title to *une rente,* November 3, 1831, SL-1, DFP. The lot was numbered 59 and was purchased from Rosati, Marie-Philippe Le Duc, Michael Rourke, James Lynch, René Paul, and Hugh O'Neil. The income from this lot was to be paid to DuBourg's heirs until 1930.

42. Rosati to DuBourg, May 20, 1832, D-113, DFP.

43. DuBourg to Deluol and Chanche, July 16, 1832, SAB.

44. DuBourg to Deluol and Chanche, December 9, 1832, SAB.

45. *L'Ami,* 74 (1832): 103–104.

46. Baudier, *Catholic Church in Louisiana,* 278–79.

47. *Ibid.,* 297–98; Schauinger, *Cathedrals,* 224–25. Both Baudier and Schauinger hold that Martial's leaving New Orleans was provoked by the Inglesi affair.

48. DuBourg to Rosati, May 19, 1831, AASL.

49. DuBourg to Caprano, July 3, 1826, Kenneally, 1: 983.

50. Flaget to DuBourg, March 1, 1832, LGVD-9, DFP.

51. Melville, *Seton,* 235. Bruté's words were: "Sometimes I could almost weep on a sudden with what only one of the most harmonious, tender, sorrowful words does to me—this Latin version, my old friend these twenty years past. O Flumina Babylonis, O Sion, O Eternity"! The English translation used here is from the Confraternity of Christian Doctrine Bible, Psalm 136 (137).

CHAPTER XLI: Intimations of Mortality

1. Ministère de l'Interieur et des Cultes au Préfet de Tarn-et-

Garonne, January 15, 1832, 2-V-1, ADM. The royal ordinance was dated December 31, 1832.

2. Daux, *L'église de Montauban,* vol. 2, sec. 3, p. 37.

3. *Mandement pour le Carême,* February 8, 1833, AEM.

4. *L'Ami,* 75 (1833): 68.

5. *Carroll Papers,* 3:298–29.

6. Bertier-Case, *Restoration,* 306.

7. Surugue, *Les Archevêques de Besançon,* 451.

8. *Ibid.*

9. The derogatory description was Chateaubriand's and is cited in Bertier-Case, *Restoration,* 306.

10. *Mémorial Bordelais,* December 30, 1830.

11. Charrier to Gignoux, February 5, 1831, AABord.

12. Surugue, *Les Archevêques de Besançon,* 451. Unless otherwise noted, the treatment of Rohan-Chabot is based on Surugue.

13. Melville, *Cheverus,* 388. A copy of Quelen's *mandement* of April 11, 1833, is preserved in the Departmental Archives of Bordeaux.

14. *L'Ami,* 75 (1833): 225–31. The *mandement* of February 19, 1833, was published by vicars general Bouligny, Cart, and Gousset.

15. F19-2504-A, NAP. The ordinance was registered in the Ministry of the Interior on February 16, 1833.

16. M. Besson, *Vie de son éminence Monseigneur le Cardinal Mathieu, archevêque de Besançon* (Paris, 1882), 1:168.

17. Argout to DuBourg, February 18, 1833, F19-2504-A, NAP.

18. DuBourg to Argout, February 21, 1833, F19-2504-A, NAP.

19. *L'Ami,* 75 (1833): 145.

20. Limousin-Lamothe, *Quelen,* 2:130; Leflon, *Mazenod,* 2: 432, 443.

21. Rapport au Roi, March 22, 1831, F19-2538, NAP. This folder also contains a very strong recommendation for Trélissac made by the Prefect of Tarn-et-Garonne to Interior dated November 19, 1830.

22. Cheverus to Bonneuil, February 22, 1833, *Records,* 16 (1905): 467.

23. *L'Ami,* 75 (1833): 263, 276.

24. Cheverus to Argout, March 9, 1833, F19-2538, NAP. Daux, *L'église de Montauban,* vol. 2, sec. 9, p. 36, says that Cheverus had strongly recommended that the king nominate Trélissac to Montauban, and implies that Argout's letter of March 5, 1833, was the direct result of this recommendation, but the chronology of existing correspondence does not clearly support this.

25. Jacques Paul Martin, *La Nonciature de Paris et les affaires ecclésiastiques de France sous le règne de Louis-Philippe, 1830–1848* (Paris, 1949), 152.

26. *L'Ami,* 75 (1833): 339.

27. DuBourg to Rosati, April 27, 1833, AASL. The suffragan sees of Besançon were Bellay, Nancy, Metz, and Verdun.

28. For the details of this odd situation, *see* Schauinger, *Cathedrals,* 260–62.

29. DuBourg to Rosati, April 27, 1833, AASL.

30. Godecker, *Bruté,* 198–99. It was not until May 6, 1834, that Simon Gabriel Bruté de Rémur was named first Bishop of Vincennes.

31. DuBourg to the Minister of the Interior, May 24, 1833, F19-2538, NAP.

32. Ordonnance royale, May 26, 1833, F19-2538, NAP.

33. DuBourg to Deluol, May 28, 1833, SAB.

34. DuBourg to George, [May 28], 1833, AMSJ.

35. M. le docteur [Joseph Auguste Gaspard] Pécot, "Notice sur la maladie et les derniers moments de Mgr. Dubourg, Archevêque de Besançon," *Académie des Sciences, Belles-Lettres et Arts de Besançon,* Séance publique de 28 Janvier, 1834 (Besançon, 1834), 62.

36. *L'Ami,* 76 (1833): 557.

37. *Ibid.,* 566.

38. Daux, *L'église de Montauban,* vol. 2, sec. 9, p. 21.

39. R. O. Gerow, *Cradle Days of St. Mary's at Natchez* (Natchez, 1941), 32. The chapel burned on December 28, 1832.

40. Daux, *L'église de Montauban,* vol. 2, sec. 9, p. 26. No identification of this colleague is given other than "a venerable prelate."

41. DuBourg to Argout, July 15, 1833, F19-2504-A, NAP.

42. Schmitt to Argout, July 17, 1833, F19-2504-A, NAP.

43. Argout to DuBourg, July 18, 1833, F19-2504-A, NAP.

44. DuBourg to Argout, July 18, 1833, F19-2504-A, NAP.

45. Argout to DuBourg, July 21, 1833, F19-2504-A, NAP.

46. *L'Ami,* 76 (1833): 613; 77 (1833): 85, 100.

47. DuBourg to Argout, August 14, 1833, F19-2504-A, NAP.

48. DuBourg to Schmitt, September 11, 1833, F19-2504-A, NAP.

49. Testimonial dated August 13, 1833, unnumbered, DFP. The widow was a Mme de Martigny née Le Mercier d'Equeville born in Taverney on April 8, 1758.

50. Rosati to DuBourg, July 15, 1833, LGVD-10, DFP.

51. This indemnity was used principally for the purchases composed of what was called *la Chapelle de l'évêque* and those necessities not otherwise provided for or furnished by the state—salary, table linen, carriage, etc. The old law of 1802 by which archbishops got 15,000 francs and bishops 10,000 had been in effect when DuBourg entered Montauban; but the new law of 1830 reduced the indemnities to 10,000 for archbishops and 8,000 for bishops. When a bishop moved to a metropolitan see he received only the difference, or 2,000 francs. Thus DuBourg in 1833 was already receiving an archbishop's indemnity and would get nothing toward the costs of his installation unless some exception were made. The report cited the case of the bishop of Dijon being made archbishop of Aix in 1832 and given 2,000 francs. The report proposed that DuBourg likewise be given 2,000 francs which should be included in the 1833 budget for religions. The king approved the report the same day, September 22, 1833.

52. F19-2504-A, NAP. All of this interbureau correspondence and documentation is contained in the same folder. Although Argout prepared his letter to DuBourg on September 26, the Council of State did not return the original bulls until the day afterward and the packet was despatched on September 27.

53. DuBourg to Argout, September 28, 1833, F19-2504-A, NAP.

54. *L'Ami*, 77 (1833): 470. *L'Ami* gave September 29 as the date the bulls reached DuBourg.

55. Argout to DuBourg, October 3, 1833, F19-2504-A, NAP.

56. *Procès verbal*, October 5, 1833, F19-2504-A, NAP. The church's report was forwarded by Bouligny; the civil authority's was forwarded to Paris by J. G. de Marguerye.

57. The remark is attributed to Louis XIV who sanctioned Vauban's work. The *Citadelle de Besançon*, "the acropolis of the city," dates back to the Gallo-Roman period. Its defenses were first renewed in the Middle Ages, and again in the seventeenth century. In 1674 Louvois set Vauban to extending the fortification, a project only terminated in 1711. It remains one of the most impressive of all Vauban's achievements.

58. The priest was a M. l'abbé Barnedet of whom *La Gazette de Franche-Comté* commented, "It took M. Dubourg to rescue this generous ecclesiastic from oblivion." See *L'Ami*, 77 (1833): 599.

59. A complete text of this *mandement* is preserved in AUND. The most extensive quotations from it appeared on October 19 in *L'Ami*, 77 (1833), 545–49. There is disagreement as to when it was written and when it was issued, most sources dating it October 6 and associating it with the *prise de possession* of that date. It was actually read in the cathedral at the *installation* of DuBourg on October 10. Internal evidence suggests it could not have been sent from Montauban, as Daux and Besson suggest,

since DuBourg left Montauban in March 1833, six months before the dates October 6 and 10 could have been fixed.

60. *Almanach du Clergé de France pour l'année 1835–1836* (Paris, 1836), 4; Besson, *Mathieu,* 144; Gaussens, *Eloges,* 1:149.

61. Pécot, "Notice sur la maladie," 61.

62. *Ibid.,* 64.

63. *L'Ami,* 77 (1833): 550.

64. Marcel Ferry et Bernard de Bregille, *Cathédrale Saint-Jean de Besançon* (Lyon, 1976), 3.

65. Besson, *Mathieu,* 144.

CHAPTER XLII: The Spirit of Toboso Laid to Rest

1. *L'Ami,* 77 (1833): 547.

2. Besson, *Mathieu,* 1:143. Mathieu, who was thirty years younger than DuBourg, was baptized Jacques-Marie-Adrien but when he was consecrated took the name of Césaire. Unless otherwise noted, the details of the Church in Besançon during DuBourg's tenure are based upon this source.

3. *L'Ami,* 77 (1833): 436–37; 78 (1833): 324.

4. *Ibid.,* 77 (1833): 549–50. According to the *Bibliothèque de la Compagnie de Jésus: Bibliographie,* 3: 1501, Gloriot entered the Society of Jesus on September 11, 1814. During the Restoration he preached at Paris and Lyon, and collaborated with the reestablishment of the seminaries of Besançon and Soissons. He died at the Jesuit novitiate of Avignon on February 18, 1844.

5. Daux, *L'église de Montauban,* vol. 2, sec. 9, pp. 26–27.

6. Pécot, "Notice," 61.

7. Besson, *Mathieu,* 1:165–70.

8. *L'Ami,* 67 (1833): 326. At that time Luxeuil had a minor seminary in which DuBourg was living.

9. *Ibid.,* 327; Surugue, *Les Archevêques de Besançon,* 461.

10. Filleau Letters, DFP. Letters to DuBourg from January 21, 1831, to November 21, 1833, indicate an increase in the number of claimants to DuBourg indemnities from the government, and a refusal on the bishop's part to go to law to recover sums awarded but not paid to the DuBourg family account.

11. Petit to Querry, December 17, 1833, D-122, DFP. This reply to DuBourg's executor indicates that debt claims against the bishop still

existed in noble French families like those of the Montmorency and Rochefoucauld ladies.

12. Besson, *Mathieu,* 1:198.

13. *Ibid.,* 198, 166.

14. *L'Ami,* 67 (1833): 631. In addition to Gousset, Cart, and Bouligny, vicars general; Cuenot and Gaume, respectively heads of the Seminary and the Mission, DuBourg named Jean-Jacques Guerin and Claude-Louis Girardet, the heads of the minor seminaries; canons J. G. Marguery and Jean-François Itteny, the former the Secretary of the Chapter and the latter Rector of Saint-Jean; and Antoine Courtois, a former director of the major seminary.

15. *Ibid.*

16. Pécot, "Notice," 65.

17. Besson, *Mathieu,* 1:144. Daux, vol. 2, sec. 9, p. 30, lists a circular dated October 28, 1833, under DuBourg's *mandements.* Neither Montauban nor Besançon has such a *mandement* today.

18. *L'Ami,* 78 (1833): 70.

19. Besson, *Mathieu,* 1: 144; Pécot, *Notice,* 66; Melville, *Carroll,* 228. The *Carroll Papers,* 3: 153–54, has the oath taken by Archbishop Carroll.

20. *L'Ami,* 77 (1833): 550; Pécot, *Notice,* 66.

21. Thierry to Interior, August 2, 1834, F19-2504-A, NAP.

22. *Ibid.* An extract of Derville-Malechord's report to the Conseil Général du Doubs was sent to the Minister of the Interior on July 24; the report was given at the session of the Doubs council opening July 12.

23. Pécot, "Notice," 71–72.

24. *Ibid.,* 67.

25. *L'Ami,* 78 (1833): 295.

26. Pécot, "Notice," 68.

27. Melville, *Seton,* 82, 296.

28. Pécot, "Notice," 68.

29. *Ibid.,* 67–68.

30. *Ibid.,* 70. Above the archbishop's throne in the sanctuary of the "new" Ursuline Convent chapel—which had been consecrated on May 17, 1830—a marble slab with a Latin inscription recorded that the hearts of both DuBourg and Leo De Neckere reposed there. Above the repository hung a fine painting of the Sacred Heart painted in Rome, which may have been a gift of DuBourg since he had sent the Ursulines a portrait of himself from Rome after his consecration in 1815. Semple, *Ursuline in New Orleans,* 83, 88, 91. Today DuBourg's heart is concealed

in the wall of the mortuary chapel on the grounds of the Ursuline Acadmey at 2635 State Street, New Orleans, Louisiana 70118. A commemorative plaque marks the location.

31. *Almanach du Clergé*, 503. This coffin of ordinary wood deteriorated and had to be placed in another of heavy oak at the time of the obsequies of Bishop Gauthy, August 1, 1918. Surugue, *Les Archevêques de Besançon*, 461.

32. Daux, *L'église de Montauban*, vol 2, sec. 9, p. 26; Surugue, *Les Archevêques de Besançon*, 461.

33. A copy of the will is preserved in AASL. The will was registered at Besançon on December 17, 1833.

34. Besson, *Mathieu*, 162.

35. *Almanach du Clergé*, 503.

36. *Surugue, Les Archevêques de Besançon, 461.*

37. Executor's statement made to Mme Caroline Sainte-Marie née DuBourg, LGVD, DFP. Bacconet was also spelled Baconais. The household servants' legacies were: valet, 673; cook, 400; porter, 100; and footman, 750 francs.

38. Pécot, "Notice," 69.

39. The letter reached Paris on December 15, 1833, F19-2504-A, NAP.

40. *Laity's Directory, 1839*, 66.

41. Filleau to Querry, December 15, 1833, D-62, DFP.

42. Emery to DuBourg, undated but addressed to DuBourg during his years as President of Georgetown, 1796–1799, SAP.

43. Petit to Querry, December 17, 1833, D-122, DFP. Petit furnished the addresses of Mme la Duchesse de Montmorency née de Luyne, who lived at Rue de Grenelle, and Mme la Comtesse de la Rochefoucauld of Rue de Varenes, both in St. Germain, and both apparently claiming to be owed money by DuBourg, since his vicar general Inglesi had gotten it under false pretenses of investing it in American land.

44. "Notice," *Laity's Directory, 1839*, 68.

BIBLIOGRAPHY

I ARCHIVAL SOURCES

A. American Archives

    Archdiocese of Baltimore, Maryland
    Archdiocese of New Orleans, Louisiana
    Archdiocese of Quebec, Canada
    Archdiocese of St. Louis, Missouri
    Georgetown University, Washington, D.C.
    Maryland Hall of Records, Annapolis, Maryland
    Maryland Historical Society, Baltimore, Maryland
    National Archives, Washington, D.C.
    Old New Orleans Historical Collection, New Orleans, Louisiana
    Mount Saint Mary's College, Emmitsburg, Maryland
    Saint Louis University, St. Louis, Missouri
    Saint Joseph Provincial House, Emmitsburg, Maryland
    Sisters of Charity of Mount Saint Joseph, Cincinnati, Ohio
    Sisters of Charity of Mount Saint Vincent, New York
    Sulpician Archives, Baltimore, Maryland
    University of Notre Dame, Notre Dame, Indiana
    Ursulines of New Orleans, Louisiana

B. European Archives

    Archdiocese of Besançon, France
    Archdiocese of Bordeaux, France
    Archdiocese of Montauban, France
    Archives of the Department of the Gironde, Bordeaux, France
    Archives of the Municipality, Bordeaux, France
    Archives privées of M. Georges de Sainte-Marie, Levallois-Perret, France
    Archives of the Municipality, Montauban, France
    Archives of Tarn-et-Garonne, Montauban, France
    Bibliothèques Nationale, Paris, France
    National Archives, Paris, France
    National Historical Archives, Madrid, Spain
    Sulpician Archives, Paris, France
    Propaganda Fide, the Vatican, Italy
    Religious of the Sacred Heart, Rome, Italy

II PRINTED SOURCES

Almanach Royale. Paris, 1823–1833.

Ami de la Religion et du Roi. Paris, 1814–1833.

Annales critique de littérature et de morale. Cahier 9. Paris, 1806.

Annales de l'Association de la Propagation de la Foi, Lyon, 1827–1834.

Bertier de Sauvigny, Guillaume de. *Documents inédits sur la conspiration légitimiste de 1830–1833*. Paris, 1951.

Calhoun, John C. *The Papers of John C. Calhoun*. Edited by W. Edwin Hemphill. Columbia, South Carolina, 1973–1976.

Carroll, John. *The Carroll Papers*. Edited by Thomas O. Hanley. 3 vols. Notre Dame, Indiana, 1976.

Code, Joseph B. *Letters of Mother Seton to Julia Scott*. Emmitsburg, Maryland, 1935.

"Correspondence between the Most Reverend Joseph Octavius Plessis, Archbishop of Quebec, Canada, and the Sees of Baltimore, Bardstown, New Orleans and St. Louis." *Records* of the American Catholic Historical Society of Philadelphia, 18 (1907): 12–43, 287–295, 436–495; 19 (1908): 185–211.

Dilhet, Jean. *Etat de l'Eglise Catholique en Diocèses des Etats-Unis de l'Amérique septentrionale*. Translated and annotated by Patrick W. Browne. Washington, 1922.

"Documents from Our Archives." *St. Louis Catholic Historical Review*. 5 vols. 1918–1922.

DuBourg, Louis-Guillaume-Valentin. *Circulaires et Mandements*. Montauban, 1826–1833.

———. *Missel Montalbanais de Mgr. DuBourg*. Montauban, 1830.

———. *Officia Propria pro Diocesi Ludovicensi*. St. Louis, 1821.

———. *Notice sur l'état de la mission de la Louisiane a laquelle on a ajoute de nouveaux details*. Turin, 1822.

———. *Sons of St. Dominick: a Dialogue between a Protestant and a Catholic, on the occasion of the late Defence of the Pastoral Letter of the Presbytery against the Vindication of St. Mary's Seminary, and Catholics at large, etc*. Baltimore, 1812.

———. *St. Mary's Seminary and Catholics at large vindicated, against the Pastoral letters of the ministers, bishops, etc. of the Presbytery of Baltimore*. Baltimore, 1811.

England, John. *Works of the Right Reverend John England*. Edited by Sebastian G. Messmer. 7 vols. Cleveland, 1908.

Inglesi, Angelo. *An Address to the Public of Philadelphia Containing a*

Vindication of the Character and Conduct of the Reverend Mr. Inglesi. Philadelphia, 1824.

Kent, James. "A New Yorker in Maryland: 1793–1821." *Maryland Historical Magazine,* 47 (June 1952): 135–145.

Laity's Directory, 1839.

Lamennais, Félicité de. *Correspondence Générale.* Edited by Louis Le Guillou. 4 vols. Paris, 1971.

Latrobe, Benjamin H. *The Journals of Benjamin Henry Latrobe. 1799–1820.* Edited by Edward C. Carter, II, John C. Van Horne, and Lee W. Formwalt. New Haven, 1980.

"Letters Concerning Some Missions of the Mississippi Valley." *Records of the American Catholic Historical Society of Philadelphia,* 14 (1903): 141–205.

"Letters from Bishop Benedict Joseph Flaget to Bishop Joseph Rosati, St. Louis, Mo." Translated by Sister Edward Barnes. *Social Justice Review,* September, 1969; July–August, 1970.

Mondésir, Edouard de. *Souvenirs sur Saint-Sulpice pendant la Révolution; la Fondation du Séminaire de Baltimore, la vie au Canada et aux Etats-Unis, et le voyage de Chateaubriand en Amerique.*

Moreau de Saint-Méry, Médéric-Louis-Elie. *American Journey.* Translated and edited by Kenneth and Anna Roberts. New York, 1947.

Perrin du Lac. *Voyages dans les deux Louisianes, et chez les nations sauvages du Missouri par les Etats-Unis . . . en 1801, 1802 et 1803.* Paris, 1805.

Richard, Gabriel. "Deux Lettres." *Bulletin de l'Institut Français de Washington,* 7 (December 1934):1–6.

Rosati, Joseph. "Recollections of the Establishment of the Congregation of the Mission in the United States." Translated by R. Stafford Poole. *Vincentian Heritage,* I (1980): 67–95; 2(1981): 33–55; 3(1982): 131–260; 5(1984): 108, 117–18.

Strictures on the Establishment of Colleges: Particularly that of St. Mary, in the Precincts of Baltimore: as formerly Published in the Evening Post and Telegraphe, by Different Writers. Baltimore, 1806.

Thornton, Mrs. William. "Diary, 1800." *Records of the Columbia Historical Society,* 10(1907): 90–224.

Travels in the Old South. Edited by Eugene L. Schwaab. Lexington, Kentucky, 1974.

Washington, George. *Diaries.* Edited by John C. Fitzpatrick. Volume 4: 1789–1798. New York, 1925.

———. *Letters and Recollections of George Washington.* New York, 1906.

III BIOGRAPHICAL WORKS

A. DuBourg *Notices* and Eulogies

Almanach du Clergé de France pour l'année 1835–1836 publié sur les documents du ministère des cultes. . . . Paris, 1835.

Bertrand, Louis. "M. DuBourg, Archevêque de Besançon, 1766–1833," *Bibliothèque Sulpicienne.* . . , 3:206–14. Paris, 1900.

"Biographical Notice of the Most Rev. William Louis Valentine DuBourg," *The Metropolitan Catholic Almanac and Laity's Directory,* 50–68. Baltimore, 1839.

Code, Joseph B. *Dictionary of the American Hierarchy.* New York, 1964.

Chambon, Célestin M. "Dubourg, Louis-Guillaume-Valentin," *The Catholic Encyclopedia,* 5:178–79. New York, 1909.

Clarke, Richard H. "Most Rev. William Louis Dubourg, DD.," *Lives of the Deceased Bishops of the Catholic Church in the United States,* 1:203–38. New York, 1872.

Domet, Antoine-Joseph-Sebastien. *Oraison Funèbre de Monseigneur L. G. V. Dubourg, Archevêque de Besançon prononcé en église metropolitaine au service du quarental, le 28 janvier, 1834.* Besançon, 1834.

Episcopat français depuis le concordat jusqu'à la séparation, 1802–1905, 364–65. Paris, 1907.

Feret, Edouard. "Dubourg," *Statistique générale . . . et biographique du Département de la Gironde,* 3:201–2. Paris, 1889.

Gaussens, Etienne. "Eloge de Mgr. L.-G.-Valentin DuBourg," *Eloges, Oraisons Funèbres et Discours Académiques,* 1:109–31. Bordeaux, 1854.

Kunkel, F. W. "Life and Times of the Most Rev. William Dubourg, S.S.," *The Voice,* 28 (March 1951): 14, 30; (June 1951): 8–9, 31–32.

Memorial Sketch of Bishop William Louis DuBourg and What his Coming Meant to St. Louis. St. Louis, 1918.

Michaud, M. *Biographie Universelle Ancienne et Moderne,* 11:370–71. Paris, 1852.

Morembert, Tribout de. *"Dictionnaire d'Histoire et de Géographie Ecclésiastiques,"* 14:947–48. Paris, 1960.

Rahill, Peter J. "Dubourg, Louis William Valentine," *New Catholic Encyclopedia,* 4:1081. Washington, D.C., 1967.

Reuss, Francis Xavier. *Biographical Cyclopaedia of the Catholic Hierarchy of the United States, 1784–1898.* Milwaukee, 1898.

Reilly, W. S. "An Historical Sketch of Archbishop DuBourg," *The Voice,* 20 (October 1942): 5–7, 24.

Ruskowski, Leo F. *French Emigré Priests in the United States, 1791–1815.* Washington, D.C., 1940.

Shea, John D. Gilmary. *The Hierarchy of the Catholic Church in the United States*. New York, 1886.

Surugue, Rene. *Les Archevêques de Besançon*. Besançon, 1930.

Trin, A. "Louis-Valentin-Guillaume Dubourg," *Dictionnaire de Biographie Française*, 11:1045–46. Paris, 1967.

B. Other biographical works

Baunard, M. l'abbé. *Histoire de Mme. Duchesne*, 2d ed. Paris, 1882.

Bausset, Louis-François, Cardinal de, *Notice Historique sur M. l'abbé Légris-Duval*, Preface to the first volume of *Sermons de M. l'abbé Légris-Duval*. Paris, 1820.

Besson, Mgr. de. *Vie de son eminence Monseigneur le Cardinal Mathieu, archevêque de Besançon*. Paris, 1882.

Callan, Louise. *Philippine Duchesne: Frontier Missionary of Sacred Heart, 1769–1852*. Westminster, Maryland, 1957.

––––––. "Rose Philippine Duchesne." Vol. 1, *Notable American Women*. Cambridge, Mass., 1971.

Castillo, Antonio de. *La Luisiana Española y El padre Sedella*. San Juan, 1929.

Easterly, Frederick John. *Life of Rt. Rev. Joseph Rosati, C. M., First Bishop of St. Louis, 1789–1843*. Washington, D.C., 1942.

Erskine, Marjory. *Mother Philippine Duchesne*. New York, 1926.

Fox, Sister Columba. *Life of the Right Reverend John Baptist Mary David, 1761–1841*. New York, 1925.

Gaussens, Etienne. "Jean-Baptiste Rauzan," *Eloges, Oraisons, Funèbres et Discours Académiques*, 1:151–75.

Godecker, Sister Mary Salesia. *Simon Bruté de Rémur, First Bishop of Vincennes*. St. Meinrad, Indiana, 1931.

Gosselin, M. l'abbé J. *Vie de M. Emery, neuvième supérieur du séminaire et de la compagnie de Saint-Sulpice*. Paris, 1861.

Guilday, Peter. *The Life and Times of John Carroll, Archbishop of Baltimore, 1735–1815*. 2 vols. New York, 1922.

––––––. *The Life and Times of John England, 1786–1842*. 2 vols. New York, 1927.

Hamlin, Talbot. *Benjamin Henry Latrobe*. New York, 1955.

Krebs, A. "Pierre Dubourg," *Dictionnaire de Biographie Française*, 11:1049.

Leflon, Jean. *Eugene de Mazenod: Bishop of Marseilles, Founder of the Oblates of Mary Immaculate*. Translated by Francis D. Flanagan. 4 vols. New York, 1961–1970.

––––––. *La Crise révolutionnaire, 1789–1846*. Tome XX de *l'Histoire de l'église depuis les origines jusqu'à nos jours de Fliche et Martin*. Paris, 1949.

––––––. *Monsieur Emery: L'église d'ancien régime et la Révolution*. Paris, 1944.

——. *Monsieur Emery: l'église concordataire et impériale.* Paris, 1946.

Lemarie, Charles. *Monseigneur Bruté de Rémur, Premier Evêque de Vincennes aux Etats-Unis, 1834–1839.* Paris, 1974.

Maes, C. P. *The Life of Rev. Charles Nerinckx.* Cincinnati, 1880.

Melville, Annabelle M. *Elizabeth Bayley Seton, 1774–1821.* 3d ed. New York, 1976.

——. *Jean Lefebvre de Cheverus, 1768–1836.* Milwaukee, 1958.

——. *John Carroll of Baltimore.* New York, 1955.

O'Daniel, Victor F. *The Right Rev. Edward Dominic Fenwick, O.P., Founder of the Dominicans in the United States.* New York, 1920.

Peronne, J. M. *Vie de Monseigneur de Simony.* Paris, 1861.

Rosati, Joseph. *Sketches of the Life of the Very Reverend Felix De Andreis,* tr. James Burlando. Baltimore, 1861.

Schauinger, J. Herman. *Cathedrals in the Wilderness.* Milwaukee, 1952.

——. *Stephen T. Badin: Priest in the Wilderness.* Milwaukee, 1956.

——. *William Gaston: Carolinian.* Milwaukee, 1949.

Shaw, Rev. Richard. *John Dubois: Founding Father.* New York, 1983.

Smet, J. J. de. "Broglie, Maurice-Jean-Madeleine, prince de, evêque de Gand," *Biographie Nationale de Belgique,* 3:83–87.

Spalding, M. J. *Sketches of the Life, Times, and Character of the Rt. Rev. Benedict Joseph Flaget, First Bishop of Louisville.* Louisville, Kentucky, 1852.

White, Charles I. *Life of Mrs. Eliza A. Seton, Foundress and First Superior of the Sisters of Charity in the United States of America.* Baltimore, 1853.

Wright, George N. *Life and Times of Louis-Philippe.* London, 1842.

IV NEWSPAPERS

L'Ami de la religion et du Roi

Baltimore Companion and Weekly Miscellany

Baltimore Evening Post

Baltimore Telegraphe

Centinel of Liberty and Georgetown and Washington Advertiser

Cincinnati Catholic Telegraph

Gazette de la Louisiane

Journal de Tarn-et-Garonne

Mémorial Bordelais
Moniteur Universel (Paris)
New Orleans Moniteur
New Orleans Telegraphe
New York Truth Teller
United States Catholic Miscellany

V SECONDARY WORKS

Adams, Rita G., William C. Einspanier, and B. T. Lukaszewski. *Saint Louis University, 150 Years.* St. Louis, 1968.

Alexander, Robert L., *The Architecture of Maximilian Godefroy*, Baltimore, 1974.

Allison, John M. S. *Church and State Under Louis-Phillippe, 1830–1848.* Princeton, 1916.

Bailey, James H. *A History of the Diocese of Richmond: The Formative Years.* Richmond, 1956.

Barbé-Marbois, François. *The History of Louisiana: Particularly of the Cession of that Colony to the United States of America.* Baton Rouge, 1977.

Baudier, Roger. *The Catholic Church in Louisiana.* New Orleans, 1939.

———. *Through the Portals of the Past: The Story of the Old Ursuline Convent of New Orleans.* New Orleans, 1955.

Bertier de Sauvigny, Guillaume de. *The Bourbon Restoration.* Translated by Lynn M. Case. Philadelphia, 1967.

———. *Nouvelle Histoire de Paris: La Restauration, 1815–1830.* Paris, 1977.

Bevan, Thomas R. *A History of the Catholic Community of Frederick Valley.* Frederick, Maryland. 1977.

Bibliographie Générale des travaux historiques et archéologiques publiés par les societés savantes de la France. Volume 1. Paris, 1888.

Brun, l'abbé Pierre. *La Cathédrale Saint-André de Bordeaux.* Bordeaux, 1952.

Bruns, J. Edgar. *Archbishop Antoine Blanc Memorial.* New Orleans, 1981.

Burnichon, Joseph. *La Compagnie de Jésus en France.* Paris, 1914.

[Carroll, Mary Teresa.] *A Catholic History of Alabama and the Floridas.* Volume 1. New York, 1908.

Childs, Frances S. *French Refugee Life in the United States, 1790–1800.* Baltimore, 1940.

Clarke, T. Wood. *Emigrés in the Wilderness.* New York, 1941.

Connelly, James F., ed. *The History of the Archdiocese of Philadelphia.* Philadelphia, 1976.

Contrasty, M. l'abbé Jean. *Le clergé français exilé en Espagne, 1792–1802.* Toulouse, 1910.

Cruchet, René. *France et Louisiane.* Baton-Rouge, 1939.

Daley, John M. *Georgetown University: Origin and Early Years.* Washington, D.C., 1957.

Dansette, Adrien. *Histoire religieuse de la France contemporaine de la Révolution à la Troisième République.* Paris, 1948.

Dargo, George. *Jefferson's Louisiana: Politics and the Clash of Legal Traditions.* Cambridge, Massachusetts, 1975.

Daux, Camille, *Histoire de l'église de Montauban.* Volume 2. Paris, 1882.

Degert, l'abbé A. *Histoire des Séminaires Français jusqu'à la Révolution.* 2d ed. Volume 2. Paris, 1912.

Droulers, Paul. *Action Pastorale et Problèmes Sociaux sous la Monarchie de Juillet chez Mgr D'Astros, Archevêque de Toulouse, Censeur de La Mennais.* Paris, 1954.

DuBourg, Henri. *Recherches sur la Maison du Bourg.* Toulouse, 1881.

Dudon, Paul. *Lamennais et le Saint-Siège (1820–1834) d'après des documents inédits et les Archives du Vatican.* Paris, 1911.

Dumege, Andre, et al. *Biographie Toulousaine, ou dictionnaire historique des personnages—rendus célèbres dans la ville de Toulouse.* Volume 2. Paris, 1938.

Durkin, Joseph T. *Georgetown University: First in the Nation's Capital.* Garden City, 1964.

Fabre, Marc-André. *La Duchesse de Berry, la Marie Stuart Vendéenne.* Paris, 1938.

Faherty, William B. *Better the Dream: Saint Louis University & Community, 1818–1968.* Saint Louis, 1968.

———. *Dream by the River: Two Centuries of Saint Louis Catholicism, 1766–1967.* Saint Louis, 1973.

———. "The Personality and Influence of Louis William Valentine Du Bourg: Bishop of 'Louisiana and the Floridas' (1776–1833)." *Frenchmen and French Ways in the Mississippi Valley.* Edited by John Francis McDermott. Urbana, Illinois, 1969.

Forestie, Em., neveu. *Notes historiques ou éphémerides montalbanais et du Tarn-et-Garonne.* Montauban, 1882.

Fourneron, Henri. *Histoire générale des émigrés pendant la Révolution française.* Volume 1. Paris, 1884.

Franzwa, Gregory M. *The Old Cathedral.* Gerald, Missouri, 1980.

Garraghan, Gilbert J. *The Jesuits of the Middle United States.* 3 vols. New York, 1938.

――――. *Saint Ferdinand de Florissant.* Chicago, 1923.

Gaullier, Ernest. *Histoire du Collège de Guyenne.* Paris, 1874.

Genevray, Pierre. *L'Administration et vie ecclésiastique dans la grand diocèse de Toulouse pendant les dernières années de l'Empire et sous la Restauration.* Paris, 1941.

Gerow, R. O. *Cradle Days of St. Mary's at Natchez.* Natchez, 1941.

Griffin, Joseph A. *The Contribution of Belgium to the Catholic Church in America, 1523–1857.* Washington, D.C., 1932.

Guenard, Alexandre. *Besançon: Description historique des monuments et établissements publics de cette ville.* Besançon, 1860.

Herbermann, Charles G. *The Sulpicians in the United States.* New York, 1916.

Hickey, Edward John. *The Society for the Propagation of the Faith: Its Foundation, Organization and Success, 1822–1922.* Washington, D.C.,1922.

Huber, Leonard V. and Samuel Wilson, Jr. *The Basilica on Jackson Square.* New Orleans, 1966.

Hughes, Thomas. *The History of the Society of Jesus in North America, Colonial and Federal:* Documents. Vol. 1, Part 2 (1605–1838). New York, 1910.

James, Marquis. *The Life of Andrew Jackson.* 2 vols. New York, 1938.

Kenneally, Finbar. *United States Documents in the Propaganda Fide Archives: A Calendar.* First series, 7 vols. Washington, D.C., 1966–1977.

Kenny, Lawrence J. "The Jesuits: The Missouri Province." Vol. 1 in *The Catholic Church in the United States of America.* New York, 1912.

Koester, Sister Mary Camilla. *Into This Land: A Centennial History of the Cleveland Poor Clare Monastery of the Blessed Sacrament.* Cleveland, 1980.

Laurent, Laval. *Québec et l'église aux Etats-Unis.* Washington, D.C., 1945.

Lavisse, Ernest. *Histoire de France contemporaine depuis la Révolution jusqu'à la Paix de 1919. Tome 1, La Révolution, 1789–1792. Tome 5, La Monarchie de Juillet, 1830–1848.* Paris, 1920–1921.

Leflon, Jean. *La crise révolutionnaire, 1789–1846.* Paris, 1949.

Levesque, Eugene. *Les bienheureux Martyrs du Séminaire Saint-Sulpice, 2 Septembre, 1792.* Paris, 1928.

Lord, Robert H., John E. Sexton, Edward T. Harrington. *History of the Archdiocese of Boston.* 3 vols. New York, 1944.

Mackall, S. Somervell. *Early Days of Washington.* Washington, D.C., 1934.

Martin, Jacques-Paul. *La Nonciature de Paris. . . sous la règne de Louis-Philippe, 1830–1848.* Paris, 1945.

Meline, Mary M., and McSweeny, Edward F. S. *The Story of the Mountain.* Vol. 1. Emmitsburg, 1911.

Mentque, Vicomte Robert de. *Le Vieux Montauban: six promenades à travers ses rues.* Montauban, 1944.

Merton, Thomas. *The Waters of Siloe.* New York, 1949.

Moreau de Saint-Méry, Médéric-Louis-Elie. *Description Topographique, physique, civile, politique et historique de la partie française de l'isle Saint-Domingue.* Philadelphia, 1787–1798.

Nolan, Charles E. *A Southern Catholic Heritage.* Vol. 1. New Orleans, 1976.

O'Brien, Michael J. *George Washington's Associations with the Irish.* New York, 1937.

Owens, Hamilton. *Baltimore on the Chesapeake.* Garden City, 1941.

Owens, Sister M. Lilliana. *The History of the Sisters of Loretto in the Trans-Mississippi West.* University Microfilms. Ann Arbor, Michigan, 1959. Ph.D. diss., St. Louis University, 1935.

Pastor, Ludwig. *The History of the Popes.* Vol. 40. St. Louis, 1953.

Rader, D. L. *The Journalists and the July Revolution in France: The Role of the political press in the overthrow of the Bourbon Restoration, 1827–1830.* The Hague, 1973.

Remond, René. *Les Etats-Unis devant l'opinion française, 1815–1852.* Vol. 1. Paris, 1962.

Richard, M. *Histoire des Diocèses de Besançon et de Saint-Claude.* Vol. 2. Besançon, 1851.

Richardson, Nicholas. *The French Prefectoral Corps, 1814–1830.* Cambridge, 1966.

Rosengarten, Joseph George. *French Colonists and Exiles in the United States.* Philadelphia, 1907.

Rothensteiner, Rev. John. *History of the Archdiocese of St. Louis, 1673–1928.* St. Louis, 1928. Volume 1.

———. *St. Michael's Church, Frederick Town, Missouri.* St. Louis, 1917.

Ruane, Joseph W. *The Beginnings of the Society of St. Sulpice in the United States, 1791–1829.* Washington, D.C., 1935.

Scharf, Thomas J. *Chronicles of Baltimore*. Baltimore, 1874.

———. *History of Maryland*. Vols. 2 and 3. Baltimore, 1879.

Schulte, Paul C. *The Catholic Heritage of Saint Louis: A History of the Old Cathedral Parish of St. Louis, Mo.* St. Louis, 1934.

Shea, John Gilmary. *History of the Catholic Church in the United States, 1763–1815*. Vol. 2. New York, 1888.

———. *Memorial of the Centenary of Georgetown College, D.C.: Comprising a History of Georgetown University*. Washington, D.C., 1891.

Sicard, l'abbé Augustin. *L'Ancien Clergé de France*. Tome 3. *Les Evêques pendant la Révolution de l'Exil au Concordat*. Paris, 1903.

Sioussat, Annie Leakin. *Old Baltimore*. New York, 1931.

Sorel, Alexandre. *Le couvent des Carmes et le Séminaire de Saint-Sulpice pendant la Terreur*. Paris, 1863.

Tarn-et-Garonne, le. Montauban, 1902.

Thureau-Dangin, Paul. *Histoire de la Monarchie de Juillet*. 2 vols. Paris, 1897.

Tourscher, Francis E. *The Hogan Schism and Trustee Troubles in St. Mary's Church, Philadelphia, 1820–1829*. Philadelphia, 1930.

Trollope, Frances. *Domestic Manners of Americans*, 2 vols. London, 1832.

Vidler, Alec R. *Prophecy and Papacy. A Study of Lamennais, the Church and the Revolution*. New York, 1954.

[Wolfe, Mother Therese]. *The Ursulines in Louisiana, 1727–1824*. New Orleans, 1886.

VI PERIODICALS

Alauzier, comte de. "Les noms des rues de Montauban." *Bulletin Archéologique, historique et artistique de la societé archéologique de Tarn-et-Garonne* 79 (1952).

Arnett, Earl. "Baltimore Has No French Quarter . . . ," *Baltimore Sun*. September 7, 1973.

Baisnée, Rev. Jules A. "The Early Years of Gabriel Richard, 1767–1790." *Records* of the American Catholic Historical Society of Philadelphia, 63 (1952): 233–52.

Barringer, George M. "They Came to G.U.: The French Sulpicians." *Georgetown Day*, (July 1977): 7–9.

Bernhard, Duke of Saxe-Weimar. "Extracts from his Travels Through North America During the Years 1825–1826." *American Catholic Historical Researches*, 7 (January 1890): 10–13.

Bertier de Sauvigny, Guillaume de. "Les 'Bon Sauvages' à Paris en 1827." *La Croix*, July 12, 1954.

———. Monseigneur de Quelen et les incidents de Saint-Germain l'Auxerrois en février 1831." *Revue d'Histoire de l'Eglise de France*, 32 (January–June 1946): 110–20.

Bispham, Clarence W. "Fray Antonio de Sedella." *Louisiana Historical Quarterly*. 2 (January–October 1919): 24–37; 369–92.

Boutruche, Robert. "Bordeaux et le commerce des Antilles Françaises au XVIIIme siècle," Extrait de *Nos Antilles*. (Orleans, 1935) 83–124.

Boyer, Arsenius. "Poor Clares in America." *Voice* 13 (May 1936): 7–10, 33–34.

Campbell, Bernard U. "Memoir of Rev. John Francis Moranville, late Pastor of St. Patrick's Church, Baltimore," *Religious Cabinet* 1 (August 1842): 434–43.

Chalumeau, l'abbé R. "La Cathédrale de Montauban," *Bulletin de Société Tarn-et-Garonne* 71 (1943): 21–39.

Debien, Gabriel. "Les colons de Saint-Domingue refugiés à Cuba, 1793–1815," *Revista de Indias* 14 (January–June, 1954): 559–605, 11–36.

———. "Refugiés de Saint-Domingue aux Etats-Unis," *Notes a'histoire coloniale* 17 (1950) 1–74.

Deluol, Louis Regis. "Consecration of Early American Bishops." *The Voice* (April 1941) 15.

Downing, Margaret B. "James and Joanna Gould Barry," *Historical Records and Studies* of the United States Historical Society of New York 15 (March 1921): 45–54.

Ellis, John Tracy. "Selecting American Bishops," *Commonweal* (March 10, 1967) 643–49.

Faherty, William B. "St. Louis Mosaic: Cultures from Many Lands," *The Heritage of St. Louis* (July 1982): 35–39, 134–41.

Flick, Ella M. E. "The Rev. Samuel Southerland Cooper," *Records* of the American Catholic Historical Society of Philadelphia 33 (December 1922): 300–16.

Flick, Lawrence F. "Matthias O'Conway, Philologist, Lexicographer and Interpreter of Language, 1766–1842," *Records* of the American Catholic Historical Society of Philadelphia 10 (1892): 257–99; 384–422.

Garraghan, Gilbert J. "St. Regis Seminary—First Catholic Indian School, 1823–1831," *Catholic Historical Review* 4 (January 1919): 452–78.

Goff, Frederick R. "The Federal City in 1793." *Library of Congress Quarterly Journal of Current Acquisitions* 9 (1951–1952): 3–8.

Gray, Ralph D. and Hartdagen, Gerald E. "A Glimpse of Baltimore Society in 1827: Letters by Henry D. Gilpin." *Maryland Historical Magazine,* 69 (Fall 1974): 256–71.

Griffin, Clifford S. "Converting the Catholics: The American Benevolent Society and the Ante-Bellum Crusade Against the Church." *Catholic Historical Review* 47 (October 1961): 325–41.

Griffin, Martin I. J. "A Biblical Distribution Among the Catholics of Louisiana." *American Catholic Historical Researches* 20 (April 1903): 123–25.

———. "Life of Bishop Conwell." *Records* of the American Catholic Historical Society of Philadelphia 26 (September 1915): 242–49; 27 (March, 1916): 74–87.

Hartridge, Walter C. "The Refugees from the Island of St. Domingo in Maryland," *Maryland Historical Magazine,* 38 (January 1943): 103–23.

Holt, Glen E. "The Heritage of Transportation," *Heritage of St. Louis,* (July 1982), 47–52.

Holweck, F. G. "Contribution to the Inglesi Affair," *St. Louis Catholic Historical Review,* 5 (January 1923): 14–39.

———. "Father Edmond Saulnier," *St. Louis Catholic Historical Review,* 4 (October 1922): 189–205.

———. "The Language Question in the Old Cathedral of St. Louis," *St. Louis Catholic Historical Review,* 2 (January 1920): 5–17.

———. "Origin of the Creoles of German Descent (Côte des Allemagnes, Louisiana)," *St. Louis Catholic Historical Review,* 2 (April–July 1920): 114–22.

———. "Ein dunkles Blatt aus DuBourg's Episkopat," *Pastoral Blatt,* 50 (February 1918): 17–20.

Jenkins, M. C. "The Most Reverend Leonard Neale, Second Metropolitan of the Catholic Church in the United States," *United States Catholic Magazine,* 3 (1844): 505–12.

———. "Notice of the Most Rev. Ambrose Maréchal," *United States Catholic Magazine,* 3 (1844): 32–37.

Kenny, Lawrence. "The Mullamphys of St. Louis," *Records and Studies* of the United States Catholic Historical Society of New York, 14 (May 1920): 70–112.

Ledeur, Chanoine E. "Cent vingt ans de vie catholique dans le diocèse de Besançon (1834–1954)," *Revue d'Histoire de l'Eglise de France,* 53 (janvier-juin 1967): 37–93.

Leflon, Jean. "Les Petits Séminaires au XIXe Siècle," *Revue d'Histoire de l'Eglise de France,* 61 (janvier-juin 1975): 25–37.

Lenhart, John M. "German Catholics in Colonial Louisiana, 1721–1803." *Central-Blatt and Social Justice,* 25 (1922): 17–19, 53–55, 89–91, 127–29.

McGarrity, John E. "Reverend Samuel Sutherland Cooper, 1769–1843," *Records* of the American Catholic Historical Society of Philadelphia, 37 (1926): 305–40.

Melville, Annabelle M. "John Carroll and Louisiana." *Catholic Historical Review,* 64 (July 1978): 398–440.

Messmer, Sebastian G. "The Rev. Hercule Brassac, European Vicar General of the American Bishops, 1839–1861." *Catholic Historical Review,* 3 (January 1918): 392–416.

Moreau de Saint-Méry. "Baltimore as Seen by Moreau de Saint-Méry in 1794." *Maryland Historical Magazine,* 35 (September 1940): 225–30.

Naughten, Gabriel J. "The Poor Clares in Georgetown." *Franciscan Studies,* 24 (March 1943): 63–72.

O'Malley, Rev. M. J. "The Centenary of the Foundation of St. Louis Diocesan Seminary." *St. Louis Catholic Historical Review,* 1 (October 1918): 40–80.

Owens, Sister M. Lilliana. "The Pioneer Days of the Lorettines, in Missouri, 1823–1841." *Records of the American Catholic Historical Society of Philadelphia,* 70 (1959): 67–87.

Pécot, Dr. [Joseph-August-Gaspard]. "Notice sur la maladie et les derniers moments du Mgr. Dubourg, archevêque de Besançon, 1766–1833." *Académie des Sciences . . . de Besançon,* Séance publique du 28 janvier, 1834.

Price, Roger. "Legitimist Opposition to the Revolution of 1830 in the French Provinces." *The Historical Journal,* 17 (1974): 755–78.

Quynn, Dorothy M. "Dangers of Subversion in an American Education," *Catholic Historical Review,* 39 (April 1953): 28–33.

Rahill, Peter J. "The St. Louis Episcopacy of L. William DuBourg." *Records of the American Catholic Historical Society of Philadelphia,* 77 (June 1966): 67–98.

Reilly, W. S. "Memoire of Edouard Mondésir." *The Voice,* 9 (October, November, December, 1931; January, 1932).

Rothensteiner, John. "Early Missionary Efforts Among the Indians in the Diocese of St. Louis." *St. Louis Catholic Historical Review,* 2 (April–July 1920): 57–96.

Schaaf, Ida M. "Henri Pratte, Missouri's First Native Born Priest." *St. Louis Catholic Historical Review,* 5 (April–July 1923): 129.

Smith, Sarah Trainer. "Philadelphia's First Nun." *Records of the Amer-*

BIBLIOGRAPHY

ican *Catholic Historical Society of Philadelphia,* 5 (1894): 417–522.

Souvay, Charles L. "Around the St. Louis Cathedral with Bishop Du-Bourg, 1818–1820." *St. Louis Catholic Historical Review,* 5 (April–July 1923): 149–59.

———. "A Centennial of the Church in St. Louis," *Catholic Historical Review,* 4 (April 1918): 52–75.

———. "DuBourg and the Biblical Society (New Orleans, 1813)." *St. Louis Catholic Historical Review,* 2 (January 1920): 18–25.

———. "Rosati's Election to the Coadjutorship of New Orleans." *Catholic Historical Review,* 3 (April 1917): 3–21; (July 1917): 165–186.

———. "Rummaging Through Old Parish Records." *St. Louis Catholic Historical Review,* 5 (October 1921): 256–57.

Sturges, Walter Knight. "A Bishop and His Architect." *Liturgical Arts,* 17 (February 1949): 53–64.

Tragle, Joseph G., Jr. "Andrew Jackson and the Continuing Battle of New Orleans." *Journal of the Early Republic,* 1 (Winter 1981): 373–93.

VII UNPUBLISHED WORKS

Boisard, M. "La Compagnie de Saint Sulpice: Trois Siècles d'Histoire." 2 vols. Privately typed and duplicated by the superior general in Paris, 1959.

Crumlish, Sister John Mary. "The History of St. Joseph's Academy, Emmitsburg, Maryland, 1809–1902." Master's thesis, Catholic University of America, 1945.

Faillon, Etienne-Marcel. "Histoire du Séminaire de Saint-Sulpice de Baltimore." Manuscript in the Archives of St. Mary's Seminary at the Sulpician Archives of Baltimore.

Gorka, Ronald. "Establishing Catholic Collegiate Education in America, 1784–1832." Ph.D. diss., Harvard University, 1964.

Heaney, Sister Jane Francis. "A Century of Pioneering: A History of the Ursuline Nuns in New Orleans, 1727–1827." Ph.D. diss., St. Louis University, 1949.

Kortendick, James Joseph. "History of St. Mary's College, Baltimore, 1799–1852." Master's thesis, Catholic University of America, 1942.

Lipscomb, Oscar H. "The Administration of Michael Portier, Vicar Apostolic of Alabama and the Floridas." Ph.D. diss., Catholic University of America, 1969.

Maloney, Mary Xavier. "The Catholic Church in the District of Columbia (Earlier Period: 1790–1866)," Master's thesis, Catholic University of America, 1938.

Murtha, Ronin John. "The Life of the Most Reverend Ambrose Maréchal, Third Archbishop of Baltimore, 1768–1828." Ph.D. diss., Catholic University of America, 1965.

Tessier, John Mary. "Epoques." Unpublished translation appended to Kortendick's thesis cited above.

INDEX

Abell (Abel), Robert, 773, 774
Acquaroni, John Baptist, 523, 545, 556, 557, 606, 664, 745–46
Adams, John, 44–45, 57, 71–72, 542
Alabama, concerning diocese of, 667, 669–70, 671–73, 674–76; see also Florida and Alabama, vicariate of
Alien and Sedition Acts, 71
Almonester y Roxas, Don Andres, 288–89
Alvarez, Mrs. Eugene, 530
l'Ami de la Religion et du Roi, 344, 352, 394, 399, 402, 576–77, 610, 780, 786–87, 822, 829, 836–37, 841, 843, 856, 861, 863, 881, 899, 900, 901, 902–3, 916, 925, 926–27, 935, 939, 961
Anderson, Eliza Crawford, 127, 128
Andrei, Giovanni, 143
Anduze, Aristide (also Matthieu Bernard Anduze), 605, 606, 615, 617, 631–32, 635, 680–81, 829, 842, 905; traveling with DuBourg, 734–38
Angela Merici, St., *see* Ursulines
Anges, Sister Marie des, *see* Rochefoucauld, Celeste Leblond de la
Angoulème, Duchess d', 577
anti-Catholicism (U.S.), 246–52
anticlerical French liberals, 927
anti-Jesuit crisis, in France, 837–39
Apalache Indians, 736
Arbou, Etienne M. B. d', Bishop of Verdun, 837, 856
Arcis, Marc, 803
Argout, Apollinaire-Antoine-Maurice, comte, d', 926, 931, 934–35, 935–36, 938–39
Arkansas, mission to, 732–33
Arnaud, Amadée, d', 272,
Arnaud, Jean, d', 272
Arouville, Chopin d', 923
Ashton, John, 48–49
Association for the Propagation of the Faith, *see* Society for the Propagation of the Faith

Astros, Paul-Thérèse-David d', Archbishop of Toulouse, 895, 897–98
Attakapas, Les, 307, 561, 567
Audé, Eugénie, 525–26, 604, 605, 691, 723, 738
Audizio, John, 636
l'Avenir, 834, 896, 897, 923
Aviau, du Bois de Sanzay, Archbishop Charles-François de, 17, 330, 332, 333, 381, 383, 404, 405, 416, 417, 517, 585, 589, 712, 773; death of, 784–85, 916
Avoyelles, mission of, 736
Ax-Les-Thermes, 840

Babad, Pierre: 20–21, 97, 98, 107; background of, 189–90; character of, 125, 192; critic of DuBourg, 124–25, 190–92, 275; in Cuba, 32, 65, 75–76, 78–81, 86, 190; at Paca Street school, 192–94; return to France, 554, 788–89; St. Mary's College and Seminary, Baltimore, 111, 123–25, 142, 178, 191, 220; Seton, Mother, and Sisters of Charity, 192–98, 206; in Spain, 29, 31, 32
Baccari, F. A., 594, 595, 596, 597, 670, 673, 725
Badin, Stephen Theodore, 256, 307, 425, 426, 508, 785, 847
Baltimore, Maryland: Cathedral of, 136–39, 644; description of, 39–40, 389–90; Diocese of, 805; Fell's Point, 409; Fourth of July, 182–83; refugees, 37–39, 42; St. Patrick's Church, Fell's Point, 42, 135, 141–42, 156, 223, 388; St. Peter's pro-Cathedral, 135, 388; War of 1812, 254, 310
Baltimore Companion, 127
Baltimore Evening Post, 127–30
Baltimore Federal Republican, 254
Baltimore Sun, 145, 251
Bankhead, James, 77
Barat, Mme Madeleine-Sophie, 397,